SOFTWARE DESIGN
AND DEVELOPMENT

SOFTWARE DESIGN
AND DEVELOPMENT

Philip Gilbert

California State University, Northridge

S R A ® SCIENCE RESEARCH ASSOCIATES, INC.
Chicago, Henley-on-Thames, Sydney, Toronto
A Subsidiary of IBM

The SRA Computer Science Series

William A. Barrett and John D. Couch, *Compiler Construction: Theory and Practice*
Marilyn Bohl and Arline Walter, *Introduction to PL/1 Programming and PL/C*
Mark Elson, *Concepts of Programming Languages*
Mark Elson, *Data Structures*
Peter Freeman, *Software Systems Principles: A Survey*
C. W. Gear, *Introduction to Computer Science: Short Edition*
Philip Gilbert, *Software Design and Development*
A. N. Habermann, *Introduction to Operating System Design*
Harry Katzan, Jr., *Computer Systems Organization and Programming*
Henry Ledgard and Michael Marcotty, *The Programming Language
    Landscape*
James L. Parker and Marilyn Bohl, *FORTRAN Programming and WATFIV*
Stephen M. Pizer, *Numerical Computing and Mathematical Analysis*
Harold S. Stone, *Discrete Mathematical Structures and Their Applications*
Harold S. Stone, *Introduction to Computer Architecture, Second Edition*

Acquisition Editor	Alan W. Lowe
Project Editor	James C. Budd
Editor	Betty Berenson
Production	Bookman Productions
Compositor	Lehmann Graphics
Illustrator	Reese Thornton
Designer	Judith Olson

Library of Congress Cataloging in Publication Data

Gilbert, Philip, 1933–
    Software design and development.

    (SRA computer science series)
    Bibliography: p.
    Includes index.
    1. Electronic digital computers—Programming.
2. System design.   I. Title.   II. Series.
QA76.6.G553 1983   001.64'25   82-16817
ISBN 0-574-21430-5

73 153

Copyright © Science Research Associates, Inc. 1983.
All rights reserved.

Printed in the United States of America.

10   9   8   7   6   5   4   3

To Dara and Josh

Contents

Preface

This book presents methods for developing small- to medium-scale software systems, with emphasis on the:

· Necessity of understanding the problem
· Importance of planning and design
· Integration of documentation into the development process
· Use of techniques to improve the quality of designs and programs

The increasing use of microcomputers will soon result in the widespread development of small- to medium-scale software systems. My intention is to prescribe the development of such a system in a way that is understandable to—and usable by—students whose previous experience in programming may be limited to one or two programming courses. The presentation is directed to the sophomore and junior undergraduate levels and presumes a knowledge of a structured programming language. Example programs are shown in PASCAL code or pseudocode and should be easily understandable by students who know a structured programming language.

The book is suitable for a second course in computing, or it can be used at a more advanced level. It covers the material of the undergraduate course in software engineering recently proposed as part of a model undergraduate electrical engineering curriculum by the Educational Activities Board of the Institute of Electrical and Electronic Engineers (IEEE). Such a course is also an appropriate elective for computer science students. At California State University, Northridge, all computer science majors take a junior design course, for which this text was developed. Successive versions of this text have been used in this class over the last five years.

Last but not least, the text is suitable for an Information Systems Curriculum, in a course on Systems Analysis and Design. It brings together many pertinent topics, including requirements analysis based on structured systems analysis techniques, data dictionaries, process specifications using decision tables, specification-based testing, and specification and evaluation of desired system qualities—as well as quality assurance and other project management techniques. Also presented are the data structure-based design method of Jackson and Warnier, and Jackson's technique for system design via process simulation. This text covers almost all of the material in the IS8 Systems Design Process Course contained in the Information Systems Curriculum Recommendations just made (Communications of the ACM, November 1982) by the ACM Curriculum Committee on Information Systems. About half of the material in the IS5 Information Analysis Course in that curriculum is also covered.

System development involves topics such as module organization, testing strategies, and project management. On the other hand, the limited experience of expected readers has dictated careful discussions of program structuring (using top-down design), implementation techniques, and testing methods. The presentation is balanced between larger-scale system topics and smaller-scale program topics.

Each phase is treated in a unified manner. Where several different methods exist, the discussion shows the relation of each method to the others and integrates them into a coherent whole. The concern is not to survey or contrast different methods but instead to show how they may be used in concert.

Concept and application are equally stressed. The techniques presented, while strongly based in concept, work for real-life problems. Concepts are clearly stated, and problems that sharpen understanding of the concepts are included. Wherever possible, a procedure for applying the concepts is also given—as a comprehensive sequence of steps, as a checklist, or as a project outline. Problems in the appendixes serve as a focus for student projects based on the project outlines.

A course in software design is not complete without the experience of projects. To provide such experience, problems in design (Appendix D), in evaluation (Appendix E), and in system formulation (Appendix C) are furnished. Almost every chapter has a project outline and sets of problems, and thus a project pertaining to each chapter can be applied to problems in the appendixes.

We emphasize design. For each phase of design, the underlying problems, solution possibilities, and principles are discussed, and a comprehensive approach (usually in the form of a sequence of steps or procedures) is given to guide the application of the technique to real problems. Design projects and problems are included.

The relation between design and evaluation/testing is also emphasized. Critical evaluation of program specifications and of design solutions is stressed. Testing is included in the project outlines of Chapters 2 and 3 to help foster the student's ability to evaluate designs objectively. Problems in Appendix E deal with the evaluation and analysis of previously written programs.

USE AT ELEMENTARY AND ADVANCED LEVELS

The topics in this book have varying levels of difficulty. Most of the book presents techniques for getting the job done right—the basic idea in design and development. These topics vary from simple code evaluation (Section 8.4) and charting methods (Section 4.1) through structured programming (Section 7.1) to more complex design topics. (A sequence of topics for inexperienced students is suggested later in this preface.)

A second layer of topics is concerned with overview of software development: documenting, ensuring that high quality is attained, guiding the system evolution (via testing, development, and delivery strategies), and managing the project. For advanced students, the materials on documentation, guidance, management, and quality can be strongly emphasized, by the use of extensive projects and papers. The problems in Appendix C are suitable for this approach.

The combination of basic and advanced information may be suitable for graduate students whose undergraduate work is in other disciplines. For these students, a spiral approach might be used, in which the basic techniques are discussed and then the development cycle is reconsidered from an advanced viewpoint.

PLAN OF THE BOOK

Part One, "Introduction," consisting of Chapter 1, gives an overview of the software development process, motivates the study of design and stresses the need for quality assurance and documentation in the development process. In accordance with this view, almost every chapter in the rest of the book has a section discussing appropriate documentation and one that presents techniques for assuring quality.

The next three parts present software development steps, in the order that would occur in development of a medium-scale system. Part Two, "Initial Design Steps," consists of Chapter 2, "Discovering the Problem," and Chapter 3, "The Design Concept." Chapter 2 discusses requirements analysis, program specifications, and quality specificatios. Data flow diagrams (called requirements diagrams in Chapter 2) are presented to annotate a network of activities, and to show the data flows between activities. The use of decision tables to define or analyze an activity specification (equivalently, a program specification) is shown. The student's attention is directed to understanding user needs and the possibilities for variations in the problem. The quality specification, which precisely states desired characteristics of a software system, is introduced. Methods of defining and measuring qualities are discussed.

Chapter 3 discusses the overall design approach. The use of data flow techniques is shown for a simple problem and for a design problem involving complex data transformations. Design using simulation models is discussed, and a documenting technique that aids development is described. Evaluation of the initial design with respect to the quality specification is also discussed.

Part Three considers system design and development. Chapter 4 introduces organizations of modules. Since undergraduate students are usually not familiar with the annotation of organizations of modules or the complexities and possibilities of such systems, these points are systematically introduced. Section 4.1 introduces the organization diagram to annotate organizations of modules. Section 4.2 develops all possible organizations for a simple program (thereby giving practice with organization diagrams), gives details of the more complex organizations, and compares the organizations. Chapter 5 discusses strategies for deriving program organization, for testing, and for implementation. A principle technique in Chapter 5 is the derivation of program organization from a data flow diagram, by partitioning the diagram.

Part Four deals with module design and development. Chapter 6 presents several techniques for module design. The necessity for analyzing problem situations and algorithms is stressed, and hints about analysis are given. The finite state model, data-structure-based design, and table-directed design techniques are discussed. Then Chapter 7 discusses module implementation using the top-down design technique of stepwise refinement.

Chapter 8 deals with problems of program construction. The features of popular programming languages, points of programming style, and the use of measurement or estimation techniques to achieve greater program execution speed are some of the topics presented. Chapter 9 considers test methods. The discussions of Section 9.2 parallel those of Section 2.3, and the example of Section 9.2 clearly illustrates the concepts of Section 2.3.

Finally, Chapter 10, which comprises Part Five, is concerned with management issues. The topics discussed are key points in managing software projects, organizing and scheduling techniques, resource estimation, peer reviews, and constraints on software development.

SEQUENCE OF TOPICS

Chapters 2 through 9 carry the student through the production steps of a medium-scale program system, with system design presented in Chapters 4 and 5. As is appropriate for a medium-scale system, large-scale problems such as module organization and testing strategies are considered before small-scale problems of module design and development.

The chapters have been written to allow easy variation of the sequence of topics. Single-program or small-scale development can be treated first, and medium-scale development can be treated later, by using Chapters 3, 6, and 7 in sequence. For example, the material in Section 6.1 relates back to discussions in Chapter 3. Module design material in the rest of Chapter 6 can be immediately treated or can be skipped initially and reconsidered later. Discussions in Chapter 7 relate back to Section 6.1 and also to Chapter 3.

Section 2.3, program specifications, and Section 9.2, on specification-based testing, are strongly related; the example test in Section 9.2 illustrates the concepts and techniques of Section 2.3. Accordingly, it may be desirable to discuss Chapter 2 and then Section 9.2 before proceeding to Chapter 3, to reinforce the notion of designing to specifications. Another possibility is to begin with a partial treatment of Chapter 9, to immediately introduce the notion of critical evaluation and test of designs, and then continue with Chapter 2. For this variation, an introductory project might involve writing a program for a simple problem (Problem 1 in Appendix D is a good choice) first, then writing a test to evaluate the solutions of other students, and finally cross-evaluating student solutions with student tests.

For students with very little programming experience, it may be useful to begin the course with documentation and evaluation, applying the techniques of Sections 4.1 and 8.4 to projects in Appendix E, in order to foster programming familiarity and to introduce immediately useful evaluation and documentation techniques. Structured programming and stepwise refinement (Sections 7.1 and 7.2) could then be presented, followed by simple applications of data flow concepts (Section 3.2). The course presentation might end in discussion of documentation and evaluation at a higher level.

ACKNOWLEDGMENTS

I am greatly indebted to the work of others. I have been much influenced by the works of Dijkstra, Parnas, Yourdon, and Kernighan and Plauger, to mention but a few. I am grateful to Robert Persig's *Zen and the Art of Motorcycle Maintenance* for suggesting the notion of quality and also ways to achieve it.

I would also like to thank the following for their help in reviewing the text: William W. Agresti, the University of Michigan—Dearborn; Dr. Anna Mae Walsh Burke, Director, Center for Science and Engineering, Nova University; John D. Gannon, Univerity of Maryland; Dr. A. F. Norcio, U.S. Naval Academy; Gruia-Catalin Roman, Washington University in Saint Louis; and David C. Rine, Computer Science Division, Western Illinois University.

It was Gary Hordemann who pushed me into working full-scale on this book; Jack Alanen read through a draft and pointed out errors of fact, style, and explication. Steven Stepanek and Elaine La Delfa examined and corrected all of the programs in the book (more precisely, all that I remembered to show them). Wendie Diane Edie provided word processing for many drafts.

Alan Lowe guided me through the publication process with great skill. And my wife Hadassa continually encouraged me through it all.

I must thank the many past students in my program design classes at California State University, Northridge. They suffered through the development of this manuscript, unerringly finding the inadequacies of each version.

Part One
INTRODUCTION

A cautionary tale about myth and reality . . . the basic development cycle . . . the right attitude . . . communication and documentation . . . the need for quality

chapter one
The Software
Development Process

1.1 A CAUTIONARY TALE

The phone rang. Before I knew it, the voice on the other end was reeling out a tale of woe. The software never worked properly, he said, and they'd been patching it for over a year. "We really need the system; what can we do? We're desperate for help!"

"Hmm," I said, deciding against the tweed jacket because it was a warm night, "I can be over there in 20 minutes. Of course, you know my fee—payable in advance."

"We've got it in cash."

"Twenty minutes, then." On with the silk instead. I picked up my personal computer and was out the door.

It would be a tricky one, but I knew I could pull it off. . . .

Perhaps the next pulp novel superhero will be the dashing computer consultant armed with trusty personal computer, who rushes off into the night and saves the faltering software system. Because coding is the most visible activity in software development, and because programmers do rush about fixing the errors in their programs, it is easy to fall prey to the myth of the superprogrammer who can instantly fix all of the problems of an ailing program. Unfortunately, the real story almost always has a different last line.

I didn't tell him that it was already too late. . . .

It would be wonderful if the original story was usually true. About two-thirds of the overall cost of software is spent in software maintenance [Boe 79b], and the situation of the story—that errors continue to be found after the software development has supposedly been finished—is a sad but common one. Obviously, program maintenance is by far the most costly software activity. Successful maintenance is greatly desired, but all the important decisions that affect maintenance have been made long before maintenance begins [War 78].

Two important factors that could cause our hero's efforts to fail are program scale and complexity. Large scale, in and of itself, changes the nature of a

3

problem or program. For example, a program to find a name in a telephone directory of 100 names could be written in any desired manner, and the names could be stored in the directory in any desired order. But now consider the problem of finding a name in the Los Angeles telephone directory! Although only the size of the directory has changed, a successful solution now depends on a careful ordering of the directory as well as a carefully defined strategy of using the directory. In other words, careful planning is necessary to overcome the effect of large scale.

Compared to the programs seen by novices, programs in industry have immense scale, typically from 10,000 to 100,000 high-level language instructions. And there are even programs on the order of millions of machine language instructions.

Programs (even small ones) may also be intricate, or they may deal with a great variety of conditions. Beyond a certain level of scale or complexity, a program becomes too large to be accomplished by one person, and it may even be beyond the intellectual grasp of a single person [Bela 77]. Such programs must be implemented by teams of programmers, designers, testers, managers, and so on, and thus advance planning and preparation are mandatory.

As an example, consider the development of an online airline reservation system using a central computer and 100 to 200 inquiry terminals, for an airline that schedules 100 flights a week. Such a system must keep track of reservations for hundreds of different flights; some are months in the future and others are minutes away. Each flight may have as many as 300 different seats in different price groups (first class, tourist, economy, and so on). Passengers may have reservations or may be wait-listed for seats. The system may include seat assignments and special diets. In addition to all this, the system must also manage communication between the central computer and the terminals. Such a system is both large scale and complex; it could not be mastered by one person, and it would have to be carefully planned before coding could be done.

Also, as users gain experience with any system, they begin to use it in new and different ways, and to insist that it be modified and enhanced to accommodate the new uses. As more economical hardware is developed, users want the system modified to take advantage of these economies. Thus a system in use undergoes continuing change until it is replaced by a new system [Bela 77].

In the original story, our hero might have been rushing out to deal with a never-before-tried usage of the program, or a brand new hardware configuration, or even a new error caused by the repair of an older error.

As a system is changed, it tends to lose its original structure, unless work is done to preserve that structure. The phenomenon of programs growing unstructured is familiar to programmers in industry. Tales are often heard of programs that have been patched so many times, by so many different people, that nobody knows exactly what they do, or how. Such programs are not maintained; instead, they are run every time in exactly the same way, in the hope that they will make it through just once more. It is worth repeating that planning *must* be done before maintenance begins, to prepare for repair of a program in such a way that its structure is preserved.

In sum, maintenance of a system can be effective only if adequate preparations are made during the development of the system.

> *Wait a minute—maybe we can save this story! Okay, so he can't do this bit of magic after the system has been maintained for a year. Okay, so it's got to be during development. I've got it! The program's just gone into testing, and he's going to help them meet this tight schedule . . . and he has to compete with another consultant who's also been called to help. . . .*

Many software developers are incurable optimists. Time after time, they believe that testing will be quick and easy! After working on their programs for a while, they decide that the programs are obviously correct, or perhaps have just a few minor errors that can easily be corrected.

Unfortunately, experience shows otherwise. Testing is the single biggest development cost—both in money and in time. On the average, testing accounts for 40–50 percent of development costs and also eats up 40–50 percent of the time schedule [Boe 73b, Bro 74].

The problems encountered in testing are similar to those found in maintenance. Changes in hardware and desired shifts in system usage must be dealt with. Of course, as the system grows bigger and more complex, there are more subprograms (possibly coded by many different programmers) that have to be made to work together, and there are more test cases that have to be tried, to ensure correct operation. There is not much chance of a "quick fix" in testing.

Effective testing is possible only if adequate preparations have been made beforehand. Such preparations are not always made.

> Surprisingly often, software testing and reliability activities are not usually considered until the code has been run the first time and found not to work . . . [there is] lack of an advance test plan to efficiently guide testing activities [Boe 79b, p. 58].

In other words, it is important to arrange the system to make testing easy, and to have a plan of testing so that the sequence of tests is well organized—and thus (we hope) less expensive and less time-consuming.

> *You're telling me that testing is usually long, involved, and expensive? It takes half the cost and HALF THE TIME of the whole job? You're a hard person to deal with. I'll have to do some surgery on this. . . .*

> *So here's another scenario. Let's have a beautiful, brainy geologist running a small oil research company. She's got a contract from a large oil company for a system to help find new oil, but she needs a prototype in three weeks.*
>
> *The system is developed and her whole team is flying over Wyoming where the plane crashes—nothing left! NOW comes the phone call to our hero.*
>
> *How's that for realism? No maintenance tricks, no testing— only a straightforward, snappy coding job to create the system from scratch in three weeks. . . .*

The vision of a coder creatively "building" a program to master the mighty computer is a compelling one. Not surprisingly, outsiders usually think that coding is the most important activity in software development.

But coding is only a small part of the total task. In addition to testing (which requires 40–50 percent of the total development effort and 40–50 percent of total time), it is necessary to prepare for coding by analyzing problem requirements, developing program specifications, and creating a preliminary design. Experience has shown that, for best results, the design effort should comprise about 30–40 percent of the total effort [Boe 73b, Bro 74]. Thus the relative effort and time expended for each development step should be:

Step	Effort, %	Time, %
Specification and design	30–40	30–40
Coding	14–20	14–20
Testing	40–50	40–50

Obviously, the coding step is the least important in terms of effort and time expended. Gilb [Gilb 77a] and others have even suggested that coding should always be done twice in different languages so that the two versions can be used to cross-check each other.

The design effort is needed so that the suitability of a proposed program can be assessed and potential problems or defects can be remedied before coding is begun. A design can be evaluated and critiqued in the same way as an architect's plan, and it can be evaluated with respect to specific properties, such as portability, or objectives such as ease of testing. More important, the design can divide a large or complex problem into independent subproblems, each of which can be handled separately by a different person.

Software design thus allows (1) evaluation of potential solutions before coding commences; (2) deliberate incorporation of reliability, ease of use, and efficiency; (3) provision in advance for possible changes and modifications; and (4) planning for multiperson development to overcome effects of large scale and complexity.

Proper design can reduce maintenance costs and thereby achieve lower overall software cost, but skimping on design to avoid development costs can incur higher maintenance cost and thus eventually higher total cost.

Design errors are more critical than coding errors. There are more of them (the ratio of design errors to coding errors usually exceeds 60:40 [Boe 79b]), they are harder to detect, and they are harder to fix. As a result, design errors consume over 80 percent of the cost required to fix errors. On the other hand, of all software development activities, design provides the greatest leverage for reducing costs [Boe 79b]. One analyst suggests that "a dollar more spent on design would have saved 5 dollars spent on testing and maintenance" [Alb 76].

When all is said and done, specification and design are more important activities than coding, and they take more time. Our hero could go and "code up a storm," but without time to discover what the problem is and carefully formulate a solution, he can't hope to get the job done.

You realists drive me crazy. Will you please tell me how we're ever gonna make a movie out of this?!

REFERENCES

[Alb 76] Alberts, D. S. "The Economics of Software Quality Assurance," *Proceedings of National Computer Conference*, New York, 1976. (Also in [Mil 78].)*

[Bela 77] Belady, L. A., and Lehman, M. M. *The Characteristics of Large Systems*. IBM Report RC6785, 1977. (Also in [Ram 78] and [Weg 79].)*

[Boe 73b] Boehm, B. W. "Software and Its Impact: A Quantitative Assessment," *Datamation*, May 1973. (Also in [Fre 80b].)*

[Boe 79b] ———. "Software Engineering: R&D Trends and Defense Needs," in P. Wegner (ed.), *Research Directions in Software Technology*. Cambridge, MA: M.I.T. Press, 1979.

[Bro 74] Brooks, F. P. "The Mythical Man-Month," *Datamation*, 1974. (Also in [Fre 80b].)*

[Bro 75] ———. *The Mythical Man-Month: Essays in Software Engineering*. Reading, MA: Addison-Wesley, 1975.

[Dij 72b] Dijkstra, E. W. "Notes on Structured Programming," in O.-J. Dahl, E. W. Dijkstra, and Hoare (eds.), *Structured Programming*. New York: Academic Press, 1972.

[Gilb 77a] Gilb, T. *Software Metrics*. Cambridge, MA: Winthrop, 1977.

[Pat 80] Patrick, R. L. *Application Design Handbook for Distributed Systems*. Boston: CBI, 1980.

*See Appendix B: Bibliography.

[Sho 75] Shooman, M. L., and Bolsky, M. I. "Types, Distribution, and Test and Correction Times for Programming Errors," *Proceedings of the International Conference on Reliable Software*, Los Angeles, CA, 1975.

[War 78] Warnier, J. D. *Program Modification*. Leiden and London: Martinus Nijhoff, 1978.

PROBLEMS

1. A file of 1000 customer records is kept in random order on a magnetic tape. When the record for a particular customer is requested, the customer names in the first, second, third, . . . , last records are compared to the requested name. Obtaining a desired record in this way takes an average of 0.020 second. How long does the search take on average if there are 10,000 customers? 100,000 customers? 1,000,000 customers?

2. Find out how many people worked on development, how many years were spent on development, and how many lines of text there are in:
   (a) The operating system of your favorite large computer.
   (b) The transaction processing system of your bank.
   (c) The reservation system of a particular airline.

3. Chat with some experienced programmers. Find out:
   (a) How much time is devoted to maintenance at their job and how many people are devoted to maintenance. Are there ever serious maintenance problems?
   (b) How much time do they personally allow for testing? Why? Do they plan for testing, and, if so, how? Are their programs always done on time?

4. Some employers believe that coding is the hardest and most important part of software development. What is your opinion? Can you think of any analogies, perhaps in the building of houses, which would tend to prove or disprove this notion? Would it be wise to work for such an employer? Why or why not?

1.2 THE BASIC DEVELOPMENT CYCLE

1.2.1 Steps in the Cycle

Our sad tale suggested that trouble could arise during software development from inadequate preparation for maintenance, testing, and coding. These are the major causes of difficulties in software development and maintenance. In large software projects, inadequate preparation is usually due to management's lack of insistence on preparation or to management's emphasizing "code it quickly." Accordingly, *poor management* is often said to be a major cause of software development difficulties.

To provide adequate preparation, a software system should be developed in a careful sequence of seven major steps (*the basic development cycle*):

1. *Requirements analysis* is careful formulation of the user's requirements so that the intent of the desired system, the properties it must possess, and the constraints on it are well understood by both the user and the system developer.
2. *Program specification* is formulating precise specifications of the software system to meet the requirements obtained in step 1.
3. *Design* includes analyzing the specification; planning of the system data flows and important algorithms, and organizing the system into modules.
4. *Coding of individual modules*.
5. *Testing of individual modules*.
6. *Integration of individual modules* into a cohesive system.
7. *Validation of system performance* is usually done by testing the system.

Steps 5, 6, and 7 may be combined in various ways.

The reasons for these steps can be best understood through an example. Suppose that the president of the university has asked us to develop an online system for class registration, to be used by students in registering for classes at the beginning of the term. Some universities already have such systems. How shall we proceed?

1.2.2 Requirements Analysis and Program Specification

First of all, in order to know exactly what to develop, we have to understand exactly what the problem is. To do this, we must ask a whole bunch of questions about the intent of the system, its use, and possible modifications. Some questions that come immediately to mind are:

· Roughly, how many students will need to use the system?
· What response time is acceptable?
· Will students use the system themselves, or will there be clerks who do the data entry?
· Should the system prompt the user, or can it depend on a trained user?
· What kinds of outputs should the system give?
· Will the system have to run on existing equipment, or can the equipment be chosen?
· Will the system later have to be moved to new equipment?

- What are the rules for use of the system?
   Will all students use it? Or just graduates, or just upper-class students?
   Will extension students be allowed to use it?
   Will it be possible for a student to use it, change his or her mind and use it again? How many times?
   If a chosen class is full, will it be possible for a student to be wait-listed for it and then check back later?
- What experience and what problems have other universities had with such systems?

Such questions may deal with any aspect of the desired system—speed and capacity, mode of use, internal rules, and so on. The asking and answering of these questions to elicit the user's intent for each aspect of the desired system, constitutes the requirements analysis step. Requirements analysis is critically important since it provides a clear understanding of what is to be done. (Errors due to misunderstanding the problem tend to persist until late in the development, and they tend to be expensive to correct.)

After the user requirements are formulated, attention is paid to the experience of other users so that requirements that lead to problems can be avoided. For example, the registration system at one university does not allow students to be wait-listed for currently filled classes, but it does allow students to drop classes in which they were previously registered. As a result, a student may find it impossible to register for Computer Science 100, while five seconds later another student is allowed to register for that class because someone else has dropped out during the five-second interval. Students complain that the system "isn't fair."

Some requirements impose system characteristics such as speed and capacity of the system or the necessity to later move the system to a new computer. Such requirements are important—I remember a system which had to be redone three times before it met the user's speed requirement.

Requirements analysis questions may also deal with the context, history, and future of the intended system:

- What is the present system? What are its desirable features and shortcomings? What other systems does it interact with? How?
- Should the program automate the present manual method or should a new method be devised?
- What properties are desired for the intended system? How will the system be used?
- Why has the company requested a computerized system?

These questions seek to place the desired program into the context of the university's overall operations.

The result of failing to do requirements analysis was clearly seen in the development of many of the first management information systems. Such systems were desired by top managers so that, by using all of the company's data gathered into one data base, a manager could get immediate answers to spur-of-the-moment questions such as:

- "How many salespeople in each state sold more than a million dollars worth of goods in the last six months?"
- "What percentage of the value of our inventory is due to the widget inventory?"
- "Show for each salesperson: total sales, total salary, and the ratio of total sales to total salary."

Application programs, such as inventory, payroll, accounting, sales projections, are part of the system and must work with the items in the data base.

Different application programs require different collections of data. For example, sales analysis programs may require sales personnel names and customer names but no other information about the salesperson or customer; payroll programs require the salesperson's tax information and possibly commission information; billing programs need to know customer discount terms, whether the customer has been delinquent in payments, and so on. The system must arrange for each application program to receive exactly the data it needs, and it must properly store the results of the program back into the data base. There must be a subsystem that interprets the manager's question and then gathers data and does computations to provide the answer. The system may also manage communications with terminals.

During the development of many early management information systems, top managers decided that they were too busy to formulate system requirements and left that job to the system developers. Systems developed in this way were almost unusable by top management.

Many system developers prefer to summarize the user requirements in a *requirements document*. After this is done, the next step is to formulate a precise specification for the desired software system, in terms that are understandable to designers, coders, and testers. The *program specification* obtained in this way is an interpretation, in software development terms, of the requirements document. The most careful practice, to be sure that no misinterpretations have occurred, is to cross-check the specification with the requirements document, thus ensuring that every part of the specification is properly derived from the requirements and, conversely, that every requirement is reflected in the specification.

1.2.3 Design

The designer can now begin to form a solution. First, the specification is analyzed to provide a precise breakdown of the functions desired. This procedure is intended to uncover any inconsistencies in the specification and, at the same time, to prepare for the development of test cases.

Also examined are ways to improve the specification by providing for modification and "growth" of the required system and for good communication facilities between program and user. The designer's goal is to make the intended system easy to use, helpful to the user, and easy to modify and extend. In this way, the design can minimize future modification costs, often with minimum development cost. For large systems, a detailed final program specification may be developed as a result of these steps. Some questions that might be asked at this stage are:

· What is the minimal system that will perform a usable function? Can the required system be built so as to be easily expandable from this minimal system?
· How might the required system be generalized or expanded? What is the maximal system that might be required in the future? Could this maximal system be built by easily expanding the required system?

Next, the overall design is blocked out, including determination of major data entities and major subprograms, determination of data flow through the system, and development of all important algorithms. Large systems, or systems expected to undergo extensive modification, need to be carefully organized into modules (i.e., subprograms).

At the same time, it is necessary to determine if the desired program is feasible; for example, whether the desired speed and capacity are achievable using present or planned equipment. Also, various economic questions must be considered. For example, the possible introduction of new equipment raises the decision of designing for the new equipment versus designing for the old equipment and then changing over to the new equipment.

1.2.4 Coding, Testing, Integration and Validation

Coding of individual modules can now begin. As the modules are completed, they need to be tested and integrated into a cohesive system, which then must be tested. Experience has shown that system integration requires a long time because of errors that arise in the transfer of information between modules. (Actually, these errors are often due to misunderstandings among the developers of different modules.) To overcome this time problem, most developers use the strategy of top-down integration and testing, in which "topmost" modules (those highest in the system organization) are completed first, each module is integrated into the system as soon as it is completed, and is tested in place in the system.

Many developers also use the strategy of incremental development and delivery, in which the sequence of completion of modules is arranged so that, at the earliest possible stage of completion, the partially complete system already delivers some small but usable portion of the desired function, and modules are completed in a sequence that continually enhances the function delivered.

The steps in the development cycle can be elaborated at great length. For example, in one handbook for design and development of distributed systems [Pat 80], over 150 different steps are discussed.

A software development effort must also deal with economic, management and communication problems. Figure 1.1 shows that software development involves the roles of user, designer, analyst/programmer, tester/evaluator, and manager, each of which has its own perspective. A common problem is misunderstanding or lack of communication between the user and the designer, between the designer and the analyst/programmer, between members of the designer team, and/or between members of the analyst/programmer team. There are some inherent conflicts among the different roles. For example, the user may desire a very broadly stated specification, while the designer may desire a very sharply defined one. The analyst/programmer may desire to have the program approved, while the tester/evaluator may desire to find every error and discrepancy. The manager's goal of minimizing costs often conflict with the other members' goals. And last but not least, the user and the end user may be different people. A user who is a junior system analyst and an end user who is a senior manager may have conflicting goals and requirements.

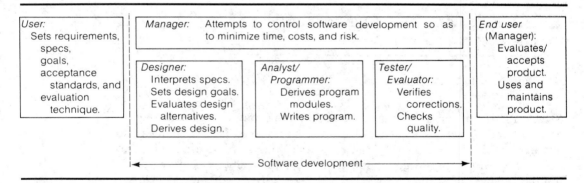

Figure 1.1   Different perspectives on software development.

REFERENCES

[Pat 80] Patrick, R. L. *Application Design Handbook for Distributed Systems*. Boston: CBI, 1980.

PROBLEMS

1. An architect was commissioned to design an art museum, and was told that she would have a free hand to design anything she liked. She began by taking a few months off to think about the objectives of a museum and then traveled around the world visiting famous museums. Do you think these were useful actions? If so, in what ways do you think they could benefit the final design? Do they correspond to any steps in the software development cycle?

2. In the discussion of an online class-registration system for students, some questions are given.
   (a) Can you think of any further questions?
   (b) Into what categories do these questions fall?
   (c) Is it important to answer such questions before beginning work on the system? Why or why not?

3. A programming management book suggests that no programming job should be undertaken without a written contract, including a program specification, delivery dates, and amount of money to be paid. Why do you think this suggestion is made? Is it overly cautious? What would happen if there were no contract and you and the customer later disagreed on what was supposed to be done?

1.3 THE RIGHT ATTITUDE

1.3.1 Forethought

Successful design and development do not require genius, but they do require concentrated thought—sustained over a period of time. The techniques and strategies of this book are *guides* toward good solutions, rather than rules that can be appled by rote to give good results automatically. A healthy mix of forethought and curiosity is an important asset for the software developer. Some aspects of forethought are:

- *Provision for the real environment:* A computer in an automobile, for example, is designed to provide for a stated problem—and also for maintenance and for faults in the environment caused by other components. Analogously, the software designer must make sure that assumed restrictions and limitations are realistic, that the solution is general enough to cope with its intended environment, and that error processing is provided for important classes of probable errors.

- *Caution:* Anticipating the ways in which solutions might go awry. Engineers, who have institutionalized such caution, speak of Murphy's Law: "Anything that *can* go wrong *will* go wrong."
- *Analysis* of the problem situation: To formulate a theory on which a solution can be based.
- Imaginative *speculation* about possible improvements or generalizations of a proposed program: To achieve a design that anticipates changes in required processing.
- Formulation of further *design objectives*, such as portability (the ability of a program to be executed at different installations with little or no change).
- *Anticipation of faults* in the program implementation and designing to allow easy recovery from such faults.
- *Evaluation* or *testing* of every analysis or solution: Using an *acceptance test* to try to make the solution fail. In other words, the designer first imagines a proposed solution. Then, he or she plays "devil's advocate" and tries to invalidate it. This procedure can reveal defects in the proposed solution, and the cycle is repeated each time defects are uncovered. If properly carried out, this approach leads to a valid design. It also leads to a set of inputs that comprise an acceptance test for the finished program.

1.3.2 Curiosity

Curiosity is a willingness to ask questions that define the problem and a solution. Pertinent questions about the problem are:

- *What* is the problem to be solved?
    What are the aspects or dimensions of the problem?
    What are the important requirements?
    Why are the requirements important?
    How can they be met?
- *Why* has this problem or requirement been posed?
    What is the underlying intent?
    Why is this intent present?
    How does the intent show itself in the specification?
- *How* is the scope of the problem restricted?
    What constraints are imposed on the solutions (e.g., with what other systems must the desired system mesh?)?
    Why are these constraints appropriate (e.g., how do other systems constrain this one?)?
    How can these restrictions be incorporated into the solution?

Such questions allow the designer to separate the problem into its component requirements and to justify each requirement. Any requirement that cannot be justified may be inappropriate.

Other questions consider the intent of the program specifications, the reasons why the user has this intent, and how the intent is reflected in the requirements. Failure to consider these questions may result in a common error—constructing a solution to an unnecessarily restricted problem. Good practice demands careful thought about each restriction and choice of the most general assumption in each case—unless the problem statement specifically suggests a restriction.

Other questions can determine a solution and then help ensure that it works in all cases. Some questions about solutions are:

- *What* is the solution?
  What are the processes and their sequence?
  Why were these processes and sequence chosen?
  How could they be better arranged?
- *Why* should the solution work?
  What is the theory underlying the solution?
  Why is this theory appropriate and correct?
  What could go wrong?
- *How* can the solution be implemented?
  What data blocks and processes are required?
  Why are these appropriate?
  How do they interact?

In sum, the designer questions and challenges every assumption and every solution, trying to arrive at assumptions and solutions that are rationally justified. Of all the questions the designer might ask, the most important one is "Why?" Orr [Orr 77] suggests three questions that can clarify problems and solutions:

Where am I going?

How will I know when I get there?

and a different appearing but equivalent question:

How would I recognize a successful product (or system) if someone gave it to me?

1.3.3 Effort

Concentrated thought means *effort*—a lot of perspiration. Guidelines or mottos that at first seem trivial or obvious may be hard to apply until you have personally struggled with problem situations. Insight will come only after the investment of such effort.

You might infer from reading about some of these techniques or guidelines that they could be rationally and mechanically applied just once to achieve a good design every time. In practice, as every designer knows, analyses or designs may have to be repeated many times, each time with more understanding of the problem and its pitfalls, until finally a solution without apparent defects is found.

Many works have been written about the process of design. One guide to the design process, which also lists many further references, is Koberg and Bagnall's *The Universal Traveler* [Kob 74].

REFERENCES

[Alex 64] Alexander, C. *Notes on the Synthesis of Form*. Cambridge, MA: Harvard University Press, 1964.

[Fre 80a] Freeman, P. "The Nature of Design," in P. Freeman and A. I. Wasserman (eds.), *Tutorial on Software Design Techniques*, 3rd ed. (IEEE Catalog No. EHO 161-0.) New York: IEEE Computer Society, 1980.

[Fre 80b] Freeman, P., and Wasserman, A. I. (eds.). *Tutorial on Software Design Techniques*, 3rd ed. (IEEE Catalog No. EHO 161-0.) New York: IEEE Computer Society, 1980.

[Kob 74] Koberg, D., and Bagnall, J. *The Universal Traveler*. New York: Harmony Books, 1974.

[Orr 77] Orr, K. T. *Structured Systems Development*. New York: Yourdon, 1977.

PROBLEMS

1. Thomas Edison once said "Genius is 1 percent inspiration and 99 percent perspiration." Is this statement valid? How does it pertain to software development?

2. Section 1.3.1 suggests that after inventing a solution, a designer should play the "devil's advocate" and try to destroy it. Is this a sensible suggestion? Could you do it?

3. Is it useful to ask the kinds of questions mentioned in Section 1.3.2? Why or why not?

1.4 COMMUNICATION DURING SOFTWARE DEVELOPMENT

1.4.1 The Need for Communication

Each phase of software development—determining specifications, design, coding, testing, and, finally, use and maintenance—has a particular view of the job to be done. In dealing with specifications, the focus is on the intent and consistency of what is to be done; overall design focuses on the broad outline of a solution; and so on. The results of each phase provide the basis for the work of the next phase.

Information flows from phase to phase, as people in each phase communicate their results to those in the next phase. This information should be conveyed by written documents.

Written documentation is necessary even if all phases are performed by the same people, since it is very easy for people to forget what they have previously agreed upon. In a small software project involving students [Kat 71], it was found that written records of specifications and overall design tended to prevent arguments among the participants. Working with written documents also helped in the critiques of specifications or design, and in clarifying goals and solutions.

1.4.2 Summary of Software Documents

The written documents are important products of the development process. The major result of detailed specification is the *specification document*, used by designers, and the major results of design are *design documents*, used by coders. At completion of the software development, *manuals* and *users' guides* are necessary to guide the users in the operation of the program, and a *program maintenance document* is needed for the person who will maintain the program. Table 1.1 summarizes the different kinds of information produced and the documents in which the information appears.

For example, the overall design document is based on the specifications document, and is sometimes called a "conceptual description" [Goos 73]. Detailed design documents are produced for each module and contain information for the particular module. The program maintenance document also includes, for each module: a statement of the module's function, module specifications, module interfaces, data and control flow, data definitions and file layouts, specific algorithms, the meaning of error messages, and test procedures. The document may include features to aid debugging and planned extensions. The program itself may be considered part of the document.

Table 1.1 Information requirements of software documents

Documents	Information											
	Objectives	Restrictions and limitations	Specifications	Data and control flow	Module division, organization and interfaces	Current status	Data definitions	Algorithms in each module	Test plan	How to use the program	Meaning of error messages	Sample execution
Requirements	●									●	○	
Proposal	●	○	○	○						●	○	
Specifications	●	●	●								○	
Overall design		●		●	●							
Detailed design				●			●	●	●			
Test plan									●			
Program maintenance				●	●		●	●	●		●	●
User's guide	●	●								●	●	●

● = final; ○ = preliminary

The program maintenance document is especially important. Maintenance programmers rely heavily on it when they are called upon to fix a program with which they are unfamiliar. It has been said that programmers do not like to document (and do not do it very well), but that those who most resist producing documentation also most demand it when they do maintenance.

1.4.3 Effectiveness of Documents

To effectively communicate information, documentation must include all relevant items of information. Documentation standards prescribing the information required in each document can ensure that the documents do contain all relevant items (see [Wals 69 and Har 73] for example standards). When documents follow a standard format, the reader knows in advance what items of information to expect and can quickly gain familiarity with the document.

For most manuals, it is desirable that questions about details should be answerable using a very small amount of time and the answers should be complete. The answers should also reference related details the reader may not know about. For this reason, Goos [Goos 73] suggests that a tree-structure organization allowing easy extraction of information should be required by the documentation standard.

To be effective, documentation must be up to date; relevant information has to be in the document, rather than in someone's head or on a piece of scrap paper. Maintenance programmers are constantly on guard for out-of-date program documentation because they are taught to be alert to the possibility that it won't match the program. Maintainers are also taught to check the listing of the source program to ensure that it is the latest version and matches the version that is to be maintained. Thus designers and coders must make sure that any change in specifications, design, or program is reflected in all documentation and that every change in documentation is dated. However, in some large projects, a specification or design document is frozen when it is accepted, and thereafter it may be changed only with the approval of high management. This procedure, which stabilizes the document, is called configuration control, or "baselining."

1.4.4 The User's Guide

Every user needs a guide that allows full use of the program without any additional knowledge about the program or reference to other documentation. The user's guide is a major end product of the development process—from the user's point of view, the ultimate results of the requirements are a software system and a guide telling how that system can be used.

The user of a program needs to know what the program does, the form and meaning of required inputs, what outputs are given, how to control the program, and the limitations and unusual conditions of the program. However, because a system may have several kinds of users, with different degrees of sophistication, a user's guide ideally consists of two (or possibly three) manuals: an *introductory manual*, a *user's reference manual*, and an *operator's manual* (if the program requires an operator).

The introductory manual and the user's reference manual describe system use from different points of view. The reference manual is intended for the sophisticated user who is familiar with the system and who may wish to exercise unusual features of the system. In contrast, the introductory manual is intended for every user, and especially for the naive user.

The introductory manual usually has three parts. An informal overview is given of the system, the problems served by the system, and system limitations. Next, all information needed for ordinary use of the program is summarized. Items summarized might include:

- Rules for punching or typing special characters
- Examples of a few most common options
- Job control cards or program parameters for the most common options
- Explanations of the most common error messages

A sample run is also included. For batch systems, a breakdown of the input deck structure is given, showing the required sequence of control cards and input data. The correlation between the sample run and the deck structure is shown. System restrictions are not mentioned.

These are details every user needs to know, and this part of the manual acts as an "instant reference" manual. If there are many users or if the system is complex, this information may be published alone as an "instant" manual [Hay 78].

Finally, the possible applications of the system are discussed informally and in common terms. No previous experience with the system is assumed, and programming experience is not assumed unless absolutely necessary. Background information is given, and suggestions are made for the most efficient use of the program.

The user's reference manual is a complete and detailed description of system use. All system options are described, and complete instructions are given for the use of each option. Input formats, the meaning of inputs, control parameters, output formats, and error messages are all completely described. Time and space estimates are given if possible. Instructions for installing the program (required hardware configuration, etc.) and planned changes or extensions may also be included.

The operator's manual should contain

- Program inputs (job control cards, data, tape files, disk files)
- Outputs produced (printer output, tape and disk files, etc.)
- Errors that might occur
- Procedures to be followed in case of error

If this information is supplied, the operator is able to run the program without additional knowledge about the program, and without reference to other documentation.

REFERENCES

[Goos 73] Goos, G. "Chapter 4.B Documentation," in F. L. Bauer (ed.), *Advanced Course in Software Engineering*. (Lecture Notes in Economics and Mathematical Systems No. 81.) New York: Springer-Verlag, 1973.

[Har 73] Harper, W. L. *Data Processing Documentation: Standards, Procedures and Applications*. Englewood Cliffs, NJ: Prentice-Hall, 1973.

[Hay 78] Hayes, J. A. "User-Accessible Publications: Help Your RSTS/E User Help Himself," *Proceedings of Digital Equipment Computer Users Society (DECUS) Symposium*, Spring 1978.

[Hay 79] ———. "Program Maintenance: A Commonsense Approach," *Proceedings of Digital Equipment Computer Users Society (DECUS) Symposium*, December 1979.

[Kat 71] Katznelson, J. "Documentation and the Management of a Software Project—A Case Study," *Software—Practice and Experience*, April–June 1971.

[Nau 76] Naur, P.; Randell, B.; and Buxton, J. N. (eds.). *Software Engineering. Concepts and Techniques, Proceedings of the NATO Conferences*, New York: Petrocelli/Charter, 1976.

[Pat 80] Patrick, R. L. *Application Design Handbook for Distributed Systems*. Boston: CBI, 1980.

[Wals 69] Walsh, D. *A Guide for Software Documentation*. Boston: Inter-Act, 1969.

PROBLEMS

1. Find and read the user's guide for a popular microcomputer program. Does it clearly show how to use the program? Does it show all the options of the program? Why or why not?

2. Read an article presenting a program and its text in one of the computer magazines. Is the program text well documented, so that you understand what is done by each portion of the program? Are the design, algorithms, and critical points clearly stated? Do you think you could maintain the program if trouble arose?

1.5 THE NEED FOR QUALITY

1.5.1 What Is Software Quality?

We all hope that our programs work correctly and efficiently. Unfortunately, even a correct and efficient program, delivered on time and within budget, may be unsatisfactory if it is:

- Poorly documented
- Hard to use, or easy to misuse, or requires excessive training
- Difficult to modify
- Unnecessarily machine dependent
- Hard to integrate with other programs

· Unreliable
· Not well suited to the user's needs
· Too expensive
· Not an improvement over the previous system

Software is said to have *quality* if it avoids these errors and is well documented, easy to use, hard to misuse, well suited to the user's needs, not too expensive, improves on previous systems, and so on. Obviously, quality is important.

Quality is even more important in software intended for users of personal microcomputers. Such software is distributed widely to the public rather than to a small, carefully controlled professional audience. As a result, each mistake is magnified 10,000 to 50,000 times. Documentation must be oriented toward naive users, who do not understand computers and wish to learn only one or two simple procedures to accomplish the entire job. User manuals for some personal software systems even cover weak points in hardware documentation, telling the user how to hook up the computer, how to hold a disk, and so on. Ease of use, good interaction between user and program, and good graphics capabilities are critical for such programs. The companies that market mass software agree that personal software systems should be portable (so as not to be tied to specific hardware) and that standards are needed.

Quality has many aspects; for example [Good 79]:

· *Correctness:* The extent to which a program produces required output for planned inputs.
· *Robustness:* The extent to which a program minimizes the unacceptable consequences of inputs by responding easily to arbitrary erroneous inputs and by foreseeing and indicating undesirable effects of an input. For example, a robust system might ask for confirmation of an order that would result in the destruction of a file.
· *Performance:* The extent to which a program meets prespecified requirements for response time, space usage, and so on.
· *Utility:* The extent to which a program meets user needs at a reasonable cost.
· *Reliability:* The extent to which a program works without failures an the extent to which the failures that do occur are not critical.

The class registration system of Section 1.1.2 suggests some other aspects:

· *Ease of use*
· *Work capacity:* The amount of work the system can do per unit of time
· *Response time:* The time required for the system to respond to a user
· *Portability:* The ease with which the system can be transferred to a new environment

We may easily think of other aspects, such as user friendliness, generality, and flexibility. Gilb [Gilb 77a, pp. 140–218] discusses many of these.

Some of these are related to others. For example, work capacity, response time, and space usage all contribute to performance, while performance, robustness, correctness, reliability, suitability, and price all contribute to utility.

1.5.2 Obtaining Quality

It is obvious that quality does not just accidentally happen—it must be "built in" through a conscious process of specification of quality, design for quality, and—last but not least—assurance of quality by means such as the use of standards, inspection, and cross-checking against those standards.

Quality specifications can be given for all products of the development (maintenance, user and training manuals) as well as for programs. The various manuals are important end products of development, and they contribute strongly to overall quality. For each manual or program, we must understand what aspects of quality we want, how the different aspects of quality are related, and how much each is to be emphasized.

The way aspects relate and their comparative emphasis are particularly important for the program since every application emphasizes a particular combination of aspects. For example, one application may emphasize minimum execution time while another may emphasize high reliability.

Designing for quality involves finding acceptable compromises among conflicting aspects of quality. For example, the designer may have to balance efficiency against portability and adaptability or may have to balance portability against accuracy, which must be obtained by dependence on word size.

Assurance of quality involves checking each end product against its quality specifications to see if the desired quality has been attained. Then, each desired aspect of quality is assessed, preferably by some formal measure, but, if necessary, by a rough or informal measure. If standards are used, the product can be checked against the appropriate standards. For example, programs can be checked against programming style standards, and documentation can be checked against documentation format and style standards.

To best assess the quality of each end product, we need to learn how to measure—or at least quantify—aspects of quality. For instance, portability is often specified as a quality goal—but no unit of measure is given with which the amount of portability can be determined. Gilb [Gilb 77a] suggests that the portability of a program is roughly inversely proportional to the effort it takes to convert the system from one installation to another. For example, a system is 90 percent portable if its developer guarantees to convert it for no more than 10 percent of the original development cost; it is 95 percent portable if the developer guarantees to convert it for no more than 5 percent of the original development cost, and so on.

An aspect of quality might be measured either directly or indirectly. Whenever possible, the software's performance should be measured directly to determine the extent to which the program possesses that aspect of quality. For example, program speed (in seconds, milliseconds or microseconds as appropriate) can be measured directly for certain inputs.

Unfortunately, some aspects (for example portability) cannot be directly measured. In this case it may be possible to find factors on which that aspect depends, and to estimate the extent of the aspect by measuring the factors and combining these values.

Checks of quality should be made before development is ended. Experience has shown that, in the development of large software systems, most errors occur in the specification and design stages [Boe 79b]. Also, the relative cost to fix an error rises exponentially with time. Figure 1.2 shows how the relative cost of fixing an error varies with the phase in which the error is detected [Boe 79b].

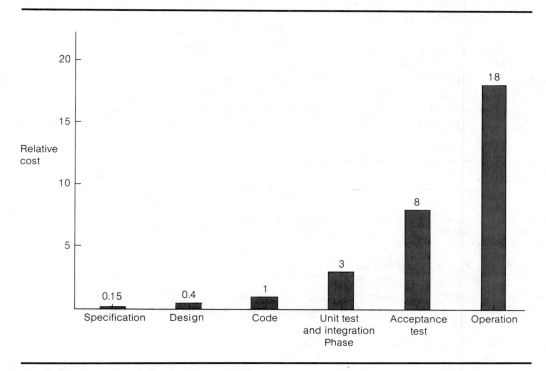

Figure 1.2 Relative cost to fix a typical error.

The sooner an error is found, the lower the cost of fixing it. Because early checking yields such strong economic benefits, many developers now check all intermediate products—the requirements document, the specifications document, the design document, and so on—for correctness. These intermediate products of development should also be checked for other aspects of quality.

Other intermediate products, such as test plans and drafts of user manuals, can also be profitably checked. Although the user guide cannot be finished until after the program is done, it is good practice to begin work on the guide early in a project. A preliminary draft of the introduction and overview, including program objectives, can be written after specifications are set and before design is started [Goos 73] and presented to the user for review. The reviewed (and reworked if necessary) objectives confirm the developer's understanding of specifications and can be used by the designers.

Next, preliminary versions of all user and operator manuals should be drafted after preliminary design is completed [Pat 80] and presented to the user for review. The user can correct any design errors or misconceptions reflected in these preliminary versions and can suggest changes. If pertinent assumptions are stated in the front of each document, they are sure to be reviewed by all readers, and any mistaken or controversial assumptions will be noticed immediately [Pat 80].

Such user review gives the designers tentative confirmation about many aspects of the system design, such as handling of errors, system throughput, and handling of transactions. Inadequacies can be corrected and modifications introduced at an early stage of the design. Another useful effect is that designers are sensitized to user-machine factors, so that a more user-oriented product is achieved. And, of course, the preliminary manuals provide assurance to the user that progress is being made on the problem.

REFERENCES

[Boe 79b] Boehm, B. W. "Software Engineering: R&D Trends and Defense Needs," in P. Wegner (ed.), *Research Directions in Software Technology*. Cambridge, MA: M.I.T. Press, 1979.

[Fagan 76] Fagan, M. E. "Design and Code Inspections to Reduce Errors in Program Development," *IBM System Journal*, Vol. 15, No. 3, 1976. (Also in [Mil 78].)*

[Fre 80a] Freeman, P. "The Nature of Design," in P. Freeman and A. I. Wasserman (eds.), *Software Design Techniques*, 3rd ed. (IEEE Catalog No. EHO 161-0). Long Beach, CA: IEEE Computer Society, 1980.

[Gilb 77a] Gilb, T. *Software Metrics*. Cambridge, MA: Winthrop, 1977.

---

*See Appendix B: Bibliography.

[Good 79] Goodenough, J. B. "A Survey of Program Testing Issues," in P. Wegner (ed.), *Research Directions in Software Technology*. Cambridge, MA: M.I.T. Press, 1979.

[Goos 73] Goos, G. "Chapter 4.B Documentation," in F. L. Bauer (ed.), *Advanced Course in Software Engineering*. (Lecture Notes in Economics and Mathematical Systems No. 81.) New York: Springer-Verlag, 1973.

[Pat 80] Patrick, R. L. *Application Design Handbook for Distributed Systems*. Boston: CBI, 1980.

PROBLEMS

1. Read through an issue of a popular computing magazine, paying attention to the advertisements for software packages.

    (a) What aspects of quality are commonly mentioned in these advertisements? Do these qualities make you confident that you could easily use the programs? Why or why not?

    (b) Compare several advertisements for a particular kind of program, such as a word processor or an operating system. Are there some qualities claimed for all of the competitors? If the programs have differing qualities, make a list of those claimed for each competitor. Which would you buy and why?

1.6 PREVIEW OF ATTRACTIONS AND USEFUL REFERENCES

The chapters in this book are based on the basic development cycle. Chapter 2 considers the tasks of requirements analysis and specifications analysis, which together constitute discovery of the problem to be solved.

Chapters 3, 4, and 5 discuss design phases. Chapter 3 deals with basic concepts, while Chapters 4 and 5 discuss methods of deriving module organization for larger systems.

Chapters 6, 7, and 8 consider the design and coding of individual modules. Chapter 9 presents testing methods. (Integration and testing strategies of larger systems are discussed in Chapter 5.)

As the last two sections have indicated, documentation of results and striving for quality are central concerns in software development. Accordingly, almost every chapter has a section discussing appropriate documentation and a section presenting techniques for assuring quality.

Chapter 10 presents a management perspective on software development. Section 10.1 summarizes all the bits of management advice scattered throughout the first nine chapters. Section 10.2 describes techniques for organizing and scheduling the activities of a software project, while Section 10.3 presents methods for estimating time and personnel required. Review procedures are detailed in Section 10.4. Finally, Section 10.5 discusses constraints on software development.

Ensuring adequate documentation and quality are basically management problems. Unfortunately, documenting and reviewing for quality are not perceived to be as exciting and challenging as developing the software itself. But if management does not insist on adequate documentation, it doesn't happen. If management doesn't insist on standards (for design, for programs, for documentation) and review to ensure that those standards are met, then they won't be met. Nevertheless, experience has shown that use of the review procedures of Section 10.4 results in less expenditure of effort and speedier completion of projects.

Listed below, according to category, are the sources that have been most useful in writing this text. They would form an excellent nucleus for any designer's library.

Software Design
[Berg 79] Bergland, G. D., and Gordon, R. D. *Tutorial: Software Design Strategies*. (IEEE Catalog No. EHO 149-5). New York: IEEE Computer Society, 1979. Contains papers on software development. Most important are the papers that survey and compare the major software design methodologies. This is an up-to-date look at aspects of software design that have a direct impact on the structure of the program.

[Fre 80b] Freeman, P., and Wasserman, A. I. (eds.) *Tutorial on Software Design Techniques*, 3rd. ed. (IEEE Catalog No. EHO 161-0.) New York: IEEE Computer Society, 1980. A collection of key papers with overview articles by the editors. The breadth of the tutorial and the excellent choice of papers make this possibly the best single reference for a beginning designer.

[Ram 78] Ramamoorthy, C. V., and Yeh, R. T. (eds.). *Tutorial on Software Methodology*. (IEEE Catalog No. EHO 142-0). New York: IEEE Computer Society, 1978. Papers on requirements formulation (including an extensive survey paper), design, implementation, and verification.

Programming Style
[Ker 74] Kernighan, B. W., and Plauger, P. J. *The Elements of Programming Style*. New York: McGraw-Hill, 1974. Elegant lessons showing how to (and how *not* to) achieve good programs.

[Ker 76] ———, and Plauger, P. J. *Software Tools*. Reading, MA: Addison-Wesley, 1976. Discussion of a set of text manipulation programs, showing how an experimental program system can be developed in an incremental way and giving informal design and programming hints throughout.

Testing
[Mil 78] Miller, E. F., and Howden, W. E. (eds.). *Tutorial: Software Testing and Validation Techniques*. (IEEE Catalog No. EHO 138-8.) New York: IEEE Computer

Society, 1978. Papers on theoretical foundations, testing methods, testing strategies, and management questions. Contains many of Howden's important papers.

[Mye 79] Myers, G. J. *The Art of Software Testing*. New York: Wiley, 1979. A short survey of most aspects of testing, which asks pointed questions and gives cogent hints. If you want to begin learning about testing, this is the place to start.

Quality Assurance

[Gilb 77a] Gilb, T. *Software Metrics*. Cambridge, MA: Winthrop, 1977. A book devoted to the idea that software quality and software performance can be objectively defined and that the quality and performance of software products and designs can be measured.

Management

[Bro 75] Brooks, F. P. *The Mythical Man-Month: Essays in Software Engineering*. Reading, MA: Addison-Wesley, 1975. The story of Mr. Brooks' experience as a software manager, pointing out lessons sadly learned and hints for the future.

[Horo 75] Horowitz, E. (ed.). *Practical Strategies for Developing Large Software Systems*. Reading, MA: Addison-Wesley, 1975. Papers surveying all phases of large system construction.

Advanced Topics and Research Questions

[Int 75] *Proceedings of International Conference on Reliable Software*, Los Angeles, CA. (IEEE Catalog No. 75CH0940-7CSR.) New York: IEEE Computer Society, 1975. Papers on all aspects of software development.

[Weg 79] Wegner, P. (ed.). *Research Directions in Software Technology*. Cambridge, MA: M.I.T. Press, 1979. An enormous (869 pages) overview of software technology, its problems, and the research directions that could be taken to overcome the problems. Also contains discussion papers that take contrasting viewpoints on the issues.

Periodicals

Communications of the Association for Computing Machinery. Monthly. Semi-theoretical and practical articles. Also contains a list of publications by special interest groups of the association.

Computer (published by the IEEE Computer Society, a special interest group of the Institute of Electrical and Electronic Engineers). Monthly. Articles of general interest in computing. Each issue contains a group of articles on a specific theme (e.g., testing) chosen for that issue.

Computing Reviews (published by the Association for Computing Machinery). Quarterly. Reviews of articles on computing.

Computing Surveys (published by the Association for Computing Machinery). Quarterly. Comprehensive survey and tutorial articles on selected topics, with extensive bibliographies.

IEEE Transactions on Software Engineering (published by the IEEE Computer Society). Bimonthly. Articles on all aspects of software engineering.

Journal of the Association for Computing Machinery. Quarterly. Theoretical articles in computer science.

SIGPLAN Notices (published by the Special Interest Group on Programming Languages). Monthly.

Software Engineering Notes (published by the Special Interest Group on Software Engineering). Quarterly newsletter.

Software—Practice and Experience (published by Wiley, Sussex, England). Quarterly. Practical articles on important programming techniques and applications.

Series

Infotech State of the Art Reports (published by Infotech, Ltd., Maidenhead, England). A series of reports based on conferences sponsored by Infotech, Ltd. At each conference, invited papers are given on a selected programming topic such as structured programming or real-time systems.

Science Citation Index (published by the Institute for Scientific Information, Philadelphia, PA). Yearly. An index of published papers, which also gives, for each paper, a list of papers published later that cite that paper. Having a paper on a subject of interest, one can then find further papers on that subject by using the index.

Microcomputer Magazines

Magazines for the hobbyist who owns a microcomputer can be found in computer stores everywhere. Some of these are:

Creative Computing (published by Ahl Computing, Inc.). Monthly. Introductory articles on software design and construction, discussions of software applications, and news about the latest equipment and software packages.

Dr. Dobb's Journal of Computer Calisthenics and Orthodontia. Articles describing inventive and exploratory software packages.

Silicon Gulch Gazette (published by the West Coast Computer Faire). Erratic publications schedule. News about equipment and software.

Part Two
INITIAL DESIGN STEPS

Discovering and understanding the problem: the specification document . . . requirements diagrams . . . program specifications . . . quality specifications

The design concept: principles of design . . . design using data flow concepts . . . design using simulation models . . . documenting the design . . . evaluating the design

chapter two
Discovering
the Problem

Go wrong at the beginning and nothing afterwards will go right.
C. Northcote Parkinson

2.1 INTRODUCTION TO USER REQUIREMENTS AND PROGRAM SPECIFICATIONS

2.1.1 Steps in Discovering the Problem

A program system can be responsive to a given problem only if the problem is properly understood. Errors in understanding must lead to design errors and to an inappropriate solution. Thus clarification and analysis of the given problem are the developer's first (and perhaps most important) step.

In fact, experience has shown that most programming errors are actually errors in design, due to improper understanding of the program specification or to imperfections in the specification. That is, they are errors in understanding *what ought to be programmed*, rather than errors in the execution of coding [Boe 79b].

Unfortunately, the user and the developer view the desired system from different perspectives. The user has in mind a broad picture of the desired system—its intent and its context. This picture includes required performance, costs, and benefits; how the system meshes with other systems; how it affects the organizational structure; and what future processing needs might be. In contrast, the developer has at hand the single task of building the required system, which must be precisely understood before it is built.

In addition, the customer often does not clearly articulate his or her needs, or may not really understand them, or may ask for a less general program than is possible, or may demand a particular technique because it is currently in style. To ensure customer satisfaction with the final program, the developer must help the customer to arrive at an appropriate and mutually agreeable specification for the desired system.

The developer's first task is to consider the problem from the user's viewpoint. This task, called *requirements analysis*, is usually done by a designer or system analyst having both data processing and managerial training. The designer or analyst typically interviews all the various users/customers, discusses the underlying intent of the proposed system, elicits their understanding of its intended detailed workings, coordinates the different information and viewpoints, and finally comes to an agreement with them concerning these requirements. This agreement may be formally stated in a *user requirements document*.

When the program is intended to replace an existing manual system, the designer or analyst first determines exactly what the existing system does and how it operates. The requirements analysis for the new system is done only after this grasp of the existing system is confirmed with the users.

Once the user requirements have been agreed upon, a *program specification* document is written indicating *precisely*, in data processing terms, the functions of the desired program. The program specification is the basis for the entire program development and, ideally, the user and the designer should understand it equally well. The specification should completely and unambiguously state *what* the software must do (and the constraints it must meet, such as meshing with other systems) but not *how* the software will do its job. The "how"—the overall design and specific algorithms and techniques—should be the province of the designer, whose freedom should be unconstrained [Bro 75, Boe 79b].

A program specification should not have omissions or contradictions and should provide default and error conditions wherever necessary. This point is crucial for large systems since detailed program specifications for large systems commonly contain many errors, ambiguous terms, and undefined terms [Bell 76, Boe 79b].

A precise specification greatly aids effective management control of a project. According to Boehm [Boe 79]:

· It allows clear communication with the ultimate user (who then has a good idea of what is actually being produced)
· It provides a solid definition for validating the design and for testing the final product so that a cohesive test plan can be drawn up
· It provides a clear way to estimate the project's progress

Needless to say, production of such a document is difficult, and some authors have used the term *requirements engineering* to emphasize that the specification document must be carefully produced.

After a specification is written, it must be analyzed to ensure that it is clear, complete, and consistent. This is especially important when, as often happens, the developer has been given a specification previously written by the user/customer. Care must also be taken to ensure that broad system requirements (such as response time, ease of use or portability) are expressed in a way that is testable, so that it can be objectively determined that they have been met.

2.1.2 Understanding the User's Present and Future Needs

Our objective in discovering the problem is to understand what the user *really needs*—now and in the future—and to reflect this understanding in the specifications. We need to visualize how the program will be used and how the specifications will relate to that use, and why this particular program is desired, what its purpose is, and how to enhance its usefulness.

Whenever a new system is desired, it is because the existing system (whether manual or program) is unsatisfactory in some ways. Discussions with the user about the existing system and its costs, delays, and frustrations can reveal which parts are unnecessary or not cost effective, why a new or improved system is wanted, and what objectives the user is trying to satisfy. These discussions can also reveal what constraints are imposed on the system, such as the use of specific accounting procedures or the use of specific hardware.

Other questions can be asked about the use of the desired system and the reasons for that use. For example, what is the best way for the user to conduct business, and what features of the system would help to do that conveniently and easily? Can the system provide a better way than is possible with manual methods? For this application, what is the relative importance of response time, transaction capacity, ease of use? What will the desired system cost, and what will its benefits be? How important are such qualities as portability, generality, and flexibility? How will the proposed hardware environment benefit or constrain the system?

Understanding the user's true needs is important when a specification does not correctly reflect the intended processing since such a defect is not detectable in any formal way.

It is necessary to anticipate and provide for growth and change in program specifications. Every software designer knows that requirements change continually, both during and after the development. One software installation found that, on average, a 25 percent change in requirements occurs during software development [Boe 79b]. Sometimes (especially with real-time systems) a final specification can be determined only after the user has had some experience with a partially complete system [Inf 73].

Change continues after the program has been developed. A good program, no matter how small or trivial, will be used by many people. These users will discover the program's weak points and ask for corrections, and they will also ask for additional features.

Future changes in requirements, and ways in which processing might be more general or more complex, can be anticipated through asking such questions as: How might users extend or enlarge the required function? How might this program evolve? The answers will suggest improvements in the program's ease of use and flexibility and anticipate future extensions in processing. Designing to this more general requirement provides in advance for anticipated changes, and thus later additions become easier.

2.1.3 Contents of This Chapter

The goal of problem discovery is a program specification document that:

· Is clearly understandable both to the developer and to the user
· Is mutually agreeable to the developer and to the user
· Precisely states constraints on the desired software system
· Precisely states all functions of the desired software
· Provides default and error conditions whenever necessary
· Provides testable criteria for acceptance of the system
· Indicates desired system qualities, their relative importance, and how they will be measured

This chapter presents techniques for obtaining such a document.

A desired system may be indicated to a developer by a written program specification or by a description of an existing activity that is to be replaced. Or sometimes a customer may informally outline the desired system and require the developer to determine the details by interviewing personnel and examining documents. The techniques of this chapter can be applied in any of these situations to yield a precise, understandable program specification.

Section 2.2 presents the *requirements diagram*, used for diagramming communication and data flows between parts of a system, and also between a system and its context (i.e., surrounding systems and manual procedures). Requirements diagrams can equally well describe systems of automated processes, systems of manual processes, or mixed systems containing both manual and automated processes. Thus system activities and interactions with surrounding systems (either automated, manual, or mixed) can be captured in the same diagram.

Section 2.2 also annotates how a given system or activity is composed of a network of simpler subactivities and also annotates the data flow between subactivities. The composition of each subactivity is determined, if necessary, so that a network of simple activities is determined.

Each simple activity must also be precisely defined. Section 2.3 provides methods for analyzing the statements that define such activities. The statements are put into a precise form, and missing cases and contradictions are discovered. Section 2.3 also discusses techniques for clarifying and enhancing the specification document.

Section 2.4 shows methods for refining and quantifying broad system requirements and desired system qualities, and it also presents a format for describing the requirements in quantified and measurable form. This format, called a *quality specification*, allows the user and developer to have a precise and testable understanding about system requirements and qualities.

REFERENCES

[Bell 76] Bell, T. E., and Thayer, T. A. "Software Requirements: Are They a Problem?" *Proceedings of IEEE/ACM Second International Conference on Software Engineering*, October 1976.

[Boe 74] Boehm, B. W. "Some Steps toward Formal and Automated Aids to Software Requirements Analysis and Design," *Proceedings of IFIP Congress 74*, 1974.

[Boe 79b] ———. "Software Engineering: R&D Trends and Defense Needs," in P. Wegner (ed.), *Research Directions in Software Technology*. Cambridge, MA: M.I.T. Press, 1979.

[Bro 75] Brooks, F. P., *The Mythical Man-Month: Essays in Software Engineering*. Reading, MA: Addison-Wesley, 1975.

[Fre 79] Freeman, P. "A Perspective on Requirements Analysis and Specification," *Proceedings of IBM Design '79 Symposium*, 1979. (Also in [Fre 80b].)*

[Het 78] Hetzel, B. "A Perspective on Software Development," *Proceedings of 3rd International Conference on Software Engineering*. (IEEE Catalog No. 78CH1317-7C.) New York: IEEE Computer Society, 1978.

[Inf 73] Infotech. *Infotech State of the Art Report on Real-Time Systems*. Maidenhead, England: Infotech, 1973.

[Orr 77] Orr, K. T. *Structured Systems Development*. New York: Yourdon, 1977.

2.2 REQUIREMENTS DIAGRAMS

2.2.1 Basic Concepts

2.2.1.1 Notation

Any system, whether manual or automated, can be described in terms of the activities comprising the system and the flow of data among these activities. Indeed, such a description conveys vital information, including the interactions between the system of interest and its context. Such a description is especially useful when a software system is intended to replace an existing manual system, or when the interaction between the desired system and other manual or automated systems needs to be considered. Since business systems usually involve these conditions, business data processing system analysts pay close attention to data flow.

---

*See Appendix B: Bibliography.

This section describes the *requirements diagram*[1] [DeMa 79, Gan 79], which annotates the data flow between parts of a system or between a system and its context. A requirements diagram can annotate an existing system or a logical model of a system. It can equally well describe systems of automated processes, systems of manual processes, or mixed systems containing both manual and automated processes. In Chapter 3, we will see that a variation of the requirements diagram can be used in software design.

Figure 2.1 shows the elements a requirements diagram may contain. The rectangle in (*a*) denotes an activity (or process or organization) that sends, receives, and processes data. A data flow from one activity to another is drawn as in (*b*), namely as an arrow from the sending activity to the receiving activity, and is labeled with the name of the data. The open-ended rectangle in (*c*) denotes a data store or data file. A data file holds data, and data can be put into or taken from a data file. Finally, the rectangle with bars in (*d*) denotes a source or destination of data, that is, a process, activity, or organization not included in the system of interest but which originates data for the system or ultimately receives data from the system.

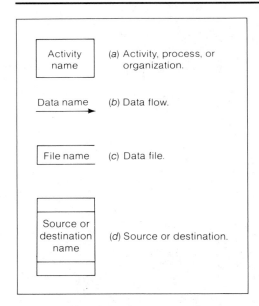

Figure 2.1 Requirements diagram notations.

[1]The collection of tools described in DeMarco [DeMa 79], and Gane and Sarson [Gan 79] formalize existing system analysis techniques and can lead almost directly from a diagram of an existing system to a diagram of a new system design. Our diagram notations are closest to DeMarco's [DeMa 79].

2.2.1.2 An Example

Let us consider how a system for determining student grades can be diagrammed. Suppose that the grading is for a computer science course and that the students submit test answers and programs to the grading activity. The graded tests and programs are returned to the students by the activity, which also sends final course grades to the registrar.

We will discuss further details of this system in a moment. However, even without knowing any further details, an overview of the student grading system can be diagrammed as in Figure 2.2.

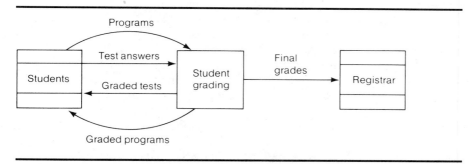

Figure 2.2 Overview of student grading system.

Figure 2.2 indicates exactly the facts known thus far: that programs and test answers are sent from students to the grading activity, which returns the graded programs and tests to the registrar. Students are a source of data for the grading activity but are not part of that activity, and, similarly, the registrar is a destination for the final grades but is not part of the grading activity. Sources and destinations are included in requirements diagrams to show the environment of the system of interest, but their inclusion is not required.

The diagram of the grading activity shows, as do all requirements diagrams, activities and the flows of data between these activities. An activity is best visualized as a place or an office; a data flow is best visualized as a type of message sent from one office to another. However, a requirements diagram does not suggest or indicate the sequence in which these data transfers occur. For example, Figure 2.2 shows that students send test answers to the grading activity, but it does not indicate when the tests are sent. Some possibilities are that the tests are sent at regular time intervals, when quizzes are given; that they are sent at times determined by the student, as in self-paced courses; and that they are sent at times dictated by the grading activity. The diagram of Figure 2.2 suffices for any of these variations.

The diagram also does not imply the sequence of grading. Depending on the grader, a variety of grading sequences is possible: each test is graded when received; a particular type of test is graded when tests have been received from all students or when the grader has accumulated more than a certain number of tests; or all tests are graded at the end of the term. (We have all heard of—though hopefully not experienced—the instructor or grader who waits until the end of the term to grade all tests!) The grader might even give out example graded tests at the beginning of the term, before any tests have been taken.

Figure 2.2 also does not suggest when grades are sent to the registrar. Our experience suggests that grades are usually sent at regular intervals (the end of the term) but they may also be sent at other times.

Finally, the diagram does not even suggest that a student's final grade can be sent only after receipt of all student tests. Indeed, we know from experience that if all of a student's tests have not been received at the end of a term, a final grade of Incomplete is sent to the registrar.

We may now draw a diagram of the activities inside the student grading activity. Figure 2.3 shows that student grading is actually accomplished by four subactivities using two files. Student programs are graded by a grade programs activity, which places the program grades in a class roster and grade file. Student tests are graded by a grade tests activity using an answer file. Essay and multiple-choice tests are handled differently. Each multiple-choice test grade is placed directly in the class roster and grade file by the grade tests activity, which also returns the graded test to the student. Essay tests and grades are sent from the grade tests activity to the review grades activity, which reviews and adjusts the essay grades, returns the essays and adjusted grades to the grade tests activity for return to the student, and places the adjusted grades in the class roster and grade file. The contents of the class roster and grade file are used by the compute final grades activity to calculate the final grades and send them to the registrar.

A diagram such as Figure 2.3, which shows the subactivities and data flows that comprise a "parent" activity, is called a *refinement diagram*. The data flows to and from a refinement diagram must be the same as the data flows to and from the "parent" diagram. Every refinement diagram should be checked to see whether its input and output data flows are the same as the flows to and from the parent diagram. If the flows are not the same, one of the diagrams is incorrect. Sources and destinations of the parent diagram may appear on the refinement diagram or may be omitted.

The activities in Figure 2.3 are numbered to help in drawing further refinement diagrams. For example, a refinement of activity 1 would contain subactivities 1.1, 1.2, and so on; while a refinement of activity 2 would contain subactivities 2.1, 2.2, and so on. The refinement process could continue to further levels, activity 2.2, say, being refined into subactivities 2.2.1, 2.2.2, and so on.

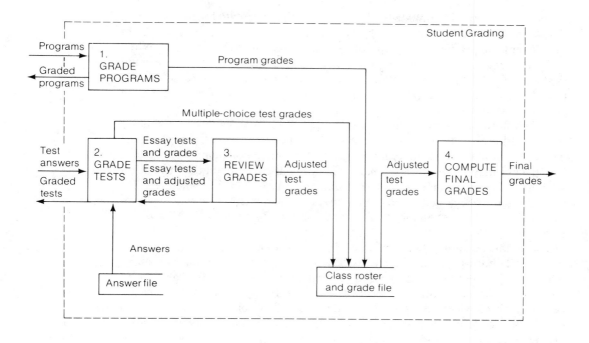

Figure 2.3   Refinement of student grading activity.

Systems typically have many activities; a system with hundreds of activities is not unusual. The best way to diagram such a large system is to partition its activities into a small number of major subsystems (say, 12 or fewer). The main diagram of the system then shows just the major subsystems, and refinement diagrams are drawn for each subsystem, subsubsystem, and so on.

If this procedure is followed, the requirements diagram of a system consists of a "top level" diagram showing the major activities, and, if necessary, a set of "second level" diagrams, each one a refinement diagram of a major activity. Each "second level" activity may in turn be refined in a "third level" diagram. The refinement process may be carried to as many levels as necessary to precisely describe the system activities. The "bottom level" activities (i.e., those for which no refinement diagrams are given) are the basic activities of the system. In conjunction with the requirements diagram, an activity specification must be given for each basic activity in the system. The decision table format of Section 2.3 is used for this purpose.

2.2.1.3 Some Points about Data Flow

A *source* is an activity outside the system that originates data for the system; a *destination* is an activity outside the system that ultimately receives data from the system. The same activity can be both a source and a destination. (When constructing a diagram, it is sometimes necessary to first guess the source and destination activities and then later to revise the guesses as more details are added.) An activity that performs part of the system's process cannot be a source or a destination.

A data flow should be thought of as a pipeline that carries packets of information of known composition. The packet of information may consist of one element or it may be a collection of information such as an entire tax return. The packet may have repeating parts, or optional parts, or both. In concept such a packet is a cohesive unit. For example, a customer payment always consisting of a check and a copy of the invoice is a cohesive unit and is shown as a single data flow, even though the receiving activity might split the information.

There can be more than one data flow from one activity to another. In Figure 2.2, both programs and tests flow from students to student grading, while both graded tests and graded programs flow from student grading to students. Because a data flow is always defined from one sender to one receiver, a data flow line is never drawn that starts from one sender, splits, and goes to two or more receivers. Similarly, data flow lines from several senders are never drawn so as to join and go to one receiver.

Data flow can occur from any activity to any file or other activity, or from any file to any activity. Activities can communicate with each other through use of a file, as in Figure 2.3.

It is important to remember that a requirements diagram is not a flowchart. Since the sequence of events is not portrayed, there is never any implication of "looping." Decisions between alternatives are not portrayed. For instance, we do not care how a student decides to send a program or a test to student grading, we just know that one or the other is sent. The student does not know, and does not care, that these two inputs go to different activities; we may assume that the student just drops the test or program into an "in" box.

Each particular type of input data may be thought of as a pipeline of a particular color that activates certain paths in the diagram. For example, in Figure 2.3, essay tests activate paths through activities 2, 3, and 4, while multiple-choice tests activate paths through activities 2 and 4 only.

It is important that each data flow be given a descriptive name suggesting what the data is and the facts known about it. For example, a customer accounts number could be labeled account-number, and a validated account number (one that has been checked for input errors) could be labeled valid-account-number. It is best to first name the data flows of a requirements diagram, and then as much as possible to name processes in terms of their inputs and outputs.

The crucial question in naming a data flow is: *What pieces of information are being transmitted?* If a data flow cannot be named, or can be given only a vague name such as input or output or data, it is because the question above has not been answered and it is not known what information the data flow should carry.

When it is difficult to name a data flow, it is also possible that the thing being named is not really a data flow. Remember that *data flow is the flow of packets of information*. Data flow is very different from the flow of control of a program—it does not convey program sequence control information of any sort, and it is not an activity.

Figure 2.4 shows two improper data flows that might have erroneously appeared in Figure 2.3. The improper data flow get-next-essay-test in (*a*) conveys program sequence control (which is wrong) and is also an activity, as shown by the verb *get*. The improper data flow end-of-semester in (*b*) might, in fact, correspond to a notice from the registrar, sent at the end of each semester to prompt the grade calculation. However, data flows whose only purpose is to control the sequence of activities are not shown in requirements diagrams.

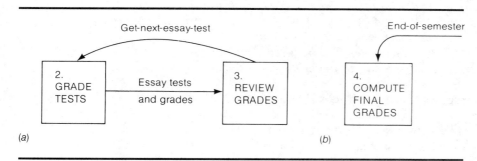

(*a*)   (*b*)

Figure 2.4   Improper data flow.

PROBLEMS

1. Provide requirements diagrams for the following situations:
   (a) The activity prepare patient's bill sends the patient's bill to accounting.
   (b) The receptionist looks up the customer's name in the customer file.
   (c) The accounts clerk gets the patient's account from the account file, credits the patient with the amount of payment, and then returns the patient's account to the account file.
   (d) The new student mails his proposed program to the registrar, a tuition payment to the cashier, and a housing application to student housing.

(e) When the employment office receives an application from a student, it sends back a request for a college transcript and one reference. The student writes a letter to the reference, who then sends a reference letter to the employment office. The student also sends a request to the registrar, who sends the transcript to the employment office.

(f) When a student wishes to determine what courses she needs for graduation, she files a request for confirmation at the registrar's office. She then requests a graduation check from her department advisor. The department advisor sends a signed requirements form to the registrar. After reviewing this form and the student's transcript (kept in the student file), the registrar sends the student a statement of required courses.

(g) When a new customer opens an account at a bank, the new accounts clerk enters the customer's name, address, and account number into a customer file. He gives the customer an initial set of checks, fills out an order slip for more checks, and also makes out a deposit slip for the customer's initial deposit. He gives the customer one copy of the deposit slip, sends the other copy to the bookkeeper, and mails the order slip to Super Check Printers, which prints the checks and mails them to the customer. The bookkeeper creates an account for the customer in the amount of the initial deposit, debits the account for the checks ordered, and puts the account in the accounts file.

Whenever a customer calls the bookkeeper for account information, the bookkeeper checks the customer's name, address, and account in the customer file.

(h) A special student mails his proposed program to the registrar, a tuition payment to the cashier, and an application and payment to the student housing office. The registrar determines which classes the student may enroll in, sends the student a confirmation notice for those classes, and sends the cashier a debit memo for the tuition of these classes. Housing for special students is allocated by lottery. Accordingly, the student housing office puts the application and payment in a lottery file. After the deadline for application has passed, the student housing office chooses the successful applicants from the lottery file. Each successful applicant is sent a housing confirmation notice, and each unsuccessful applicant receives back his or her application and payment. The student housing office sends the payments to the cashier. After a suitable time, the cashier sends each student a refund check or a request for further payment.

(i) Some European banks protect against robbery by using a special system for handling money. To change money from one currency to another, a customer hands the money to be changed to the bank teller, who fills out a currency exchange form. The teller puts the money and the form into a special cylindrical container and drops the container into a metal tube that runs from the teller's desk to the cashier's desk, which is in another room. The container and its contents travel through the tube, popping out on the cashier's desk. The cashier changes the money into the desired currency, signs the form, puts the new money and form back into the container, and sends them through an adjacent tube back to the teller's desk. The customer takes the money and signs the form.

2. Which of the following diagrams are correct requirements diagrams? Which are incorrect? Why?

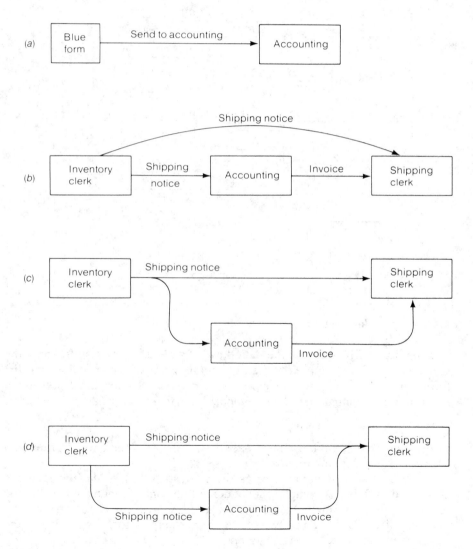

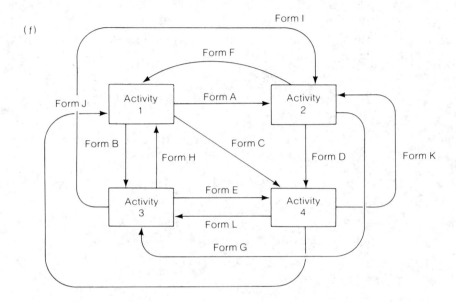

2.2.2 Composition of Data Flow

2.2.2.1 Data Flow Definitions

It is important when tracing the data flows of an existing system to know the composition of each data flow (i.e., the components of the data flow and the format in which these components are combined). Section 2.2.2 presents a notation for defining a data flow composition using the format

 data flow name=expression

where *data flow name* is a named data flow in the requirements diagram, and *expression* is a defining expression.

 The use of such definitions helps the analyst to understand the relations between data flows. A complete set of definitions, one for each data flow in the requirements diagram, is called a *data dictionary*. A data dictionary summarizes all of the data in the system, in a standard form, and shows the relations between the various data flows.

Defining expressions can be constructed with only a few notations. For a data flow consisting of a sequence of elements, we write the elements in that sequence, using the operation · to mean "followed by." For example, by using the name digit to mean a numeric digit (and assuming we know what a numeric digit is), an area code can be defined as

area-code=digit · digit · digit

As another example, if a customer transaction in a bank consists of an account number together with transaction details, we may write

customer-transaction=account-number · transaction-details

Although the operator · is not really necessary (since elements occur in the same order both in the data flow and in the defining expression), it is used to provide explicit punctuation between elements.

Also, in data flow definitions and in requirements diagrams, each data flow name consists of a single identifier which may be hyphenated as in the two examples above.

A data flow may also consist of alternative elements. For example, the data flow transaction-details may be either a deposit or a withdrawal. Using the operator | to separate the alternatives, we may write

transaction-details=deposit|withdrawal

It is understood that one, and only one, of the alternatives can occur. Likewise the definition

A=B|C|D

is read as "A consists of one (and only one) of the alternatives B, C, or D." The use of alternatives also allows the definition of digit:

digit=0|1|2|3|4|5|6|7|8|9

Sequence expressions and alternation expressions can be combined to define complex data flows. For example, the customer transaction above consists of an account number followed by a deposit transaction or a withdrawal transaction. By introducing a flow element transaction-details, we can express this structure with two definitions:

customer-transaction=account-number · transaction-details
   transaction-details=deposit|withdrawal

The first definition expresses the overall sequence, and the second expresses the alternatives for transaction-details. This process can be continued to express the composition of deposit and withdrawal:

deposit   ='D' · amount
withdrawal='W' · amount

and so on. Here we are annotating the use of a transaction code D to signify a deposit, and a transaction code W to signify a withdrawal. The single quotes enclosing D and W signify that these are literal constants.

It is convenient to write defining expressions that contain both sequence and alternation in order to reduce the number of required intermediate elements. For this purpose, two conventions are required. First, an expression enclosed in parentheses () is understood as a single entity with respect to the rest of the expression. Thus either of the expressions

$(E \cdot F \cdot G)$
$(H | J)$

would be understood as a single entity in the context of a larger expression, even though this entity has further internal structure.

Second, we assume that $\cdot$ always operates before $|$, in the same way that multiplication is understood to operate before addition. By this convention, a definition

$U = W \cdot X | Y \cdot Z$

is always understood to mean

$U = (W \cdot X) | (Y \cdot Z)$

In other words, U consists either of the sequence $W \cdot X$ or the sequence $Y \cdot Z$.

If we wish to designate a sequence where one element has alternatives, say, P consists of a Q, followed by either R or S, followed by T, we may write

$P = Q \cdot (R | S) \cdot T$

We may now define customer transactions by using the definitions

customer-transaction=account-number $\cdot$ (deposit|withdrawal)
deposit=‘D’ $\cdot$ amount
withdrawal=‘W’ $\cdot$ amount

If neither of the terms deposit or withdrawal is used elsewhere, we may wish to condense these three definitions into one:

customer-transaction=account-number $\cdot$ (‘D’ $\cdot$ amount|‘W’ $\cdot$ amount)

Note that

‘D’ $\cdot$ amount|‘W’ $\cdot$ amount

is understood to mean

(‘D’ $\cdot$ amount)|(‘W’ $\cdot$ amount)

in accordance with our second convention.

Two further notations are used. It often happens that an element or subexpression is optional; that is, it may be given or omitted. Optional expressions are enclosed in square brackets [ ]. For example, suppose that in the customer transaction, a D code must be given for a deposit, but a W code is optional for a withdrawal. This means that whenever a transaction code is not given, the transaction is assumed to be a withdrawal. Using square brackets, a withdrawal may now be defined as

withdrawal=[‘W’]·amount

We could have written

withdrawal=amount|‘W’·amount

but it would not be as convenient.

An element or expression may be repeated an indefinite number of times. For example, a telephone bill has a line for each telephone call made by the customer, and a customer file has a record for each customer. Braces { } are used to enclose a repeating expression. Thus the expression

{local-call-detail}

signifies that the data flow element local-call-detail, containing all information for one local call, is repeated some indefinite number of times.

Sometimes it is known that the number of repetitions will not be less than a given lower limit or will not exceed a given upper limit. If a lower limit is given, it is written as a subscript just to the right of the expression. For example, the definition

integer=$\{$digit$\}_1$

states that an integer is a sequence of one or more digits. If no lower limit is stated, the lower limit is understood to be 0 (i.e., the expression may not occur at all).

If an upper limit is given, it is written as a superscript just to the right of the expression. For example, the definition

label=$\{$digit$\}_1^5$

states that a label consists of from one to five digits. The definition

area-code=$\{$digit$\}_3^3$

states that an area code consists of a sequence of exactly three digits.

Remember that these definitions express the components of a data flow and the format in which these components are combined. The definitions do not express the significance or use of a data flow. In a system where many data flows have the same composition, it may be necessary to find other means to distinguish among the different data flows.

As an example, suppose that a system has a temporary magnetic tape file and a master magnetic tape file and that the records in the two files have identical formats. Furthermore, suppose that records are added to the temporary file, the temporary file is sorted according to some key, and then the temporary and permanent files are merged. All of the data flows have the same composition but different significance.

The differences in significance can be shown either by additional comments or by data flow names such as

temporary-record
sorted-temporary-record
master-record

where the data flow name itself conveys the significance of the data flow.

2.2.2.2 An Example

Let's use these notations in a simple example. Suppose that a program is desired to print invoices to the customers of an auto parts firm from an input file consisting of groups of records, one group for each invoice. The first record in each group is an identifier record containing the invoice number, the character I, and then the customer's name and address, and a discount percentage. Each succeeding record in the group contains the invoice number, the character P, and a part name, quantity, and price.

Each invoice begins with the invoice number and the customer's name and address. For each part record in the input, an invoice line is printed containing the part name, quantity, price, and total value, where total value=quantity× price.

The last few lines of the invoice depend on the discount percentage. For customers whose discount percentage is zero, a total amount, equal to the sum of the total values of the parts, is printed with the words FINAL AMOUNT. For customers with a nonzero discount percentage, the last three lines of the invoice are

the phrase TOTAL AMOUNT followed by a total amount;
the phrase LESS DISCOUNT followed by a discount amount;
the phrase FINAL AMOUNT followed by a final amount

where discount=total amount×percentage discount, and final amount=total amount−discount amount.

The input to the desired program is a file of records; use the name records to denote this data flow. The fact that the file consists of groups of records can be reflected by the definition

records={group}

where group stands for a group of records. Each group consists of an identifier record followed by an indefinite sequence of part records. Accordingly, we write

group=identifier · {part}

where identifier is an identifier record and part is a part record.

Since an identifier record contains an invoice number, the character I, and a name, address, and percentage, we write

identifier=number · 'I' · name · address · percent

A simple sequence of steps is used in defining a data flow, namely:

1. Assign a name to the (highest level) data flow (e.g., records).
2. Following the problem narrative, define the highest level data flow in terms of the next-highest-level data flows (e.g., identifier, part), assigning names to these next-highest-level data flows as necessary.
3. Continue the process of step 2, defining each data flow in terms of still lower-level data flows, according to the problem narrative.

This procedure was used to obtain the four definitions above. If done correctly, the procedure obtains a meaning for each term as well as a defining expression.

The output data flow is easily defined using the same sequence of steps. Begin by denoting the output as invoice-report. Since output is a sequence of invoices, we write

invoice-report = {invoice}

where invoice is a customer invoice. By reading the problem statement carefully, we find that an invoice contains three major parts. We write

invoice = customer · {part-line} · totals

where customer is the customer information, part-line gives the information for one part, and totals is the ending portion of the invoice. The problem statement immediately gives us

customer = number · name · address
part-line = partname · quantity · price · total-value

The totals portion of the invoice is either one line (which we denote as lastline) or a sequence of lines (which we denote as final-lines). Accordingly, we write

totals = lastline | final-lines

Final-lines is a sequence of three lines, and we write

final-lines = total-line · discount-line · end-line

The composition of each of these lines is given by

lastline = 'FINAL AMOUNT' · total-amount
total-line = 'TOTAL AMOUNT' · total-amount
discount-line = 'LESS DISCOUNT' · discount
end-line = 'FINAL AMOUNT' · final-amount

Table 2.1 summarizes the information for this example. The data flow components with definitions have been listed separately from those without. The data flows without definitions are the primitives from which all data flows are built. Depending on the desired application and processing method, primitives at this level can be used, or the data flows can be broken down still further.

Table 2.1 Data dictionary for example

Name and Composition	Meaning
customer=number · name · address	Customer information on invoice
discount-line=`LESS DISCOUNT` · discount	Line on invoice giving amount of discount
end-line=`FINAL AMOUNT` · final-amount	Line on invoice giving final amount with discount deducted
final-lines=total-line · discount-line · end-line	Invoice line used when customer has nonzero discount
group=identifier · {part}	Group of input records for one invoice
identifier=number · `I` · name · address · percent	Identifier record giving customer information
invoice=customer · {part-line} · totals	An invoice
invoice-report={invoice}	The output file
lastline=`FINAL AMOUNT` · total-amount	Last line on invoice when discount=0
part=number · `P` · part name · quantity · price	Part record giving part information and quantity sold
part-line=partname · quantity · price · total-value	Line on invoice for a part
records={group}	The input file
total-line=`TOTAL AMOUNT` · total-amount	Line on invoice indicating total amount of parts sold
totals=lastline | final-lines	Ending portion of an invoice
address	Customer address
discount	Dollar amount of discount to customer
final-amount	Total amount due from customer when discount is more than 0
name	Customer name
number	Invoice number
quantity	Quantity sold
partname	Name of a part
percent	Discount percentage
price	Price of a part
total-amount	Total amount sold = sum of total values
total-value	Total value of a particular part = quantity×price

PROBLEMS

1. At the end of the year, ABC Corporation gives some (but not all) of its employees bonuses. The president of the corporation receives a report containing each employee's name in one column and the amount of bonus in a second column. For employees not receiving a bonus, the second column is left blank. Annotate the composition of this report.

2. Each month your dentist has a report produced showing which patients owe money and which are paid forward. The report begins with a title line. Each line corresponding to a patient contains the patient's account number, name, and balance. Two columns are used for the balance. If the patient owes money (has a debit balance), the amount is shown in the leftmost column; if the patient owes nothing or is paid forward (has a credit balance), the amount is shown in the rightmost column. Two sample lines are shown on the next page.

Account Number	Name	Debit Balance	Credit Balance
1234	Smith	$50	
2345	Jones		$100

The final line is a totals line showing the total of all debit balances in that column and the total of all credit balances in that column. Annotate the composition of this report.

3. Each week, XYZ Supercorporation prints a report showing all salaries paid that week, by subsidiary corporation and division. The report has the following format.

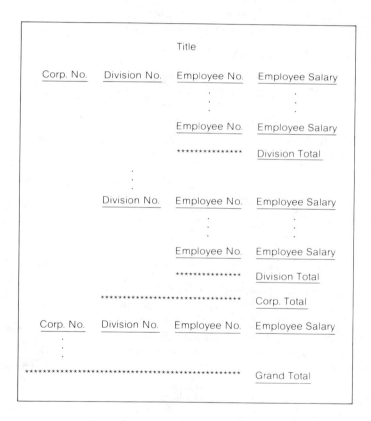

Annotate the composition of this report.

4. Use the notation of this section to annotate the composition of
   (a) a telephone bill.
   (b) a student registration card.
   (c) a telephone directory.
   (d) a bank statement.
   (e) Appendix B of this text.

5. Real Rock Records, a wholesale record dealer, uses a file of punched cards to keep track of the inventory of record titles. When a new title is put into inventory, a punched card with the word STOCK; the record's number, title, artist, and company; and the quantity of records placed in stock is put into the file, in order by record number. During each month, every time records are sent out, a punched card with the word OUT; the record number, title, artist, and company; and the quantity of records removed is added to the file as the last of the set of cards for that record. Every time replacement records come into inventory, a punched card with IN; the record number, title, artist, and company; and quantity replaced is added to the file as the last of the set of cards for that record. At the beginning of each month, the inventory punched card file is processed to produce a new file reflecting the changes in inventory. All of the cards produced for the new file begin with the word STOCK.

Annotate the composition of
   (a) the punched card file output by the program.
   (b) the punched card file used as input to the updating program.

6. Annotate the composition of
   (a) the input of Problem 2 of Appendix D.
   (b) the input of Problem 4 of Appendix D.
   (c) the outputs of Problem 11 of Appendix D.

2.2.3 USING REQUIREMENTS DIAGRAMS

2.2.3.1 Steps in Using the Diagrams

A desired system may be indicated in a written program specification or as a description of an existing system to be replaced. Sometimes a customer may just outline the existing system and require the analyst to determine existing procedures and details by interviewing personnel and examining documents. Requirements diagramming techniques allow us to convert any of these descriptions to a standard format consisting of

· Diagrams that divide the system into simpler activities and show the data flow between activities
· A data dictionary that summarizes and defines all of the system's data
· Activity specifications for each lowest level activity (derived by the methods of Section 2.3)

Refinement diagrams allow a complex system to be systematically decomposed into smaller, simpler subsystems, and each subsystem can be decomposed in the same way. Thus a set of diagrams, refined to as many levels as necessary, is obtained for a complex system. The diagrams can be checked for consistency since the data flows to and from a refinement diagram must be exactly the same as the data flows to and from the parent activity.

The first step in analyzing requirements, especially when an existing manual system is to be replaced, is a complete and careful study of the existing system and its environment, to discover all details of procedures, activities, and information flow. This step, which usually requires about 30 percent of the total analysis phase effort [DeMa 79], is crucial to the success of the analysis effort. One end result of this step is a *physical* requirements diagram, that is, a requirements diagram that describes a manual system in terms of specific organizations (e.g., Treasurer's Office), specific people (e.g., Henry, the bankteller), and specific documents (e.g., Form 2283). The other end result is a set of precise definitions of the lowest level activities. During the study, the analyst builds a rapport with the users and can ask them to check (and perhaps to formally approve) the diagrams as they are developed.

Since a physical requirements diagram describes a system in terms familiar to users, and since users are often familiar with the concept of data flow, many users can easily read the diagram.

The work done in understanding the existing system must inevitably be done sometime during the course of system development. If it is done carefully as a first step, the benefits of understanding the existing system are available to the rest of the project. Delay in performing this work may result in design without proper understanding—and perhaps the need to redesign.

After determining the data flows and activities of the existing system and its environment, the designer can analyze the time and money costs of each part of the system. The cost effectiveness of each part of the system can be assessed, for example, in cost per transaction for a transaction processing system. The error rates and time delays of each part of the system can also be determined.

The characteristics of the existing system provide a standard against which proposed systems can be evaluated. Figure 2.5 shows two alternative systems, system A and system B, which might be implemented. By using estimated total costs, capacities, and transaction rates for each system, these costs, capacities, and rates can be estimated for the entire system (consisting of all five activities) in each case. Thus the effectiveness of the existing system, the system resulting if alternative A is built, and the result with alternative B can be compared. Such comparisons might indicate that some existing activities are as effective as any proposed alternative and thus could remain as they are.

Reviewing the characteristics of the existing system with users can clarify their objectives for the desired system and also clarify important constraints such as required use of specific accounting procedures or hardware.

When beginning the analysis of an existing system, the designer may have only a rough idea of the boundaries of that system, and perhaps no idea at all which subsystems might profitably be altered. For this reason, surrounding activities and data flows (i.e., activities and data flows outside the tentatively chosen boundaries) are included in the physical diagram. It is then easy, after analysis, to include activities originally outside the boundaries if they can profitably be incorporated or to move activities outside the proposed system. For example, a system whose input data flow is incoming mail might have a major activity devoted to sorting the mail into different groups (e.g., new orders and repeat orders). The entire sort activity could be moved outside the system by using different post office box numbers for each type of order.

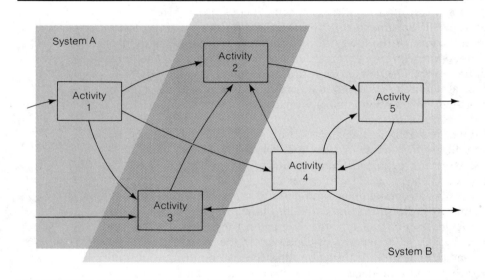

Figure 2.5 Alternatives in system implementation.

As an aid in clarifying objectives and proposed solutions, it may be useful to derive an abstract requirements diagram of the existing system, that is, to derive a diagram that describes the system as a set of logical operations and logical data files without reference to specific organizations, people, documents, or physical data files. Sections 2.2.3.3 and 2.2.3.4 describe methods for doing this step. A program system can sometimes be built directly from an abstract requirements diagram.

2.2.3.2 The Initial Diagram of an Existing System

In determining the requirements of a new system, first obtain a requirements diagram of the existing system. Then produce a physical diagram of the existing system, describing the system in terms of *specific* organizations, people, and documents. This requires some effort since manual systems tend to be poorly defined and documented and have somewhat complex communication with the surrounding procedures. As the diagrams of the existing system are developed, they can be discussed with the users so that the analyst can ensure that the existing system has been properly understood. Such discussions also convince users that the existing system is properly understood and gives them confidence in the developer.

Care should be taken, in diagramming the existing situation, to include as much as possible of the manual and automatic procedures that will surround the desired system. This will ensure that all data flows between the desired system and its surroundings are properly understood. It may be useful to diagram each of the surrounding procedures as well as the existing version of the desired system so that duplicated or redundant processes in different procedures can be spotted. Also, it often happens that alternative boundaries can be chosen for an automated system, with quite different costs and benefits. Inclusion of surrounding procedures allows you to investigate possible alternative system boundaries.

The existing situation should be diagrammed exactly "as it is" using organization names, people's names, and physical descriptions of documents as necessary. Parts of such a diagram may appear as in Figure 2.6. Although ultimately we wish to know the logic of the situation, it may be much easier to first describe the physical situation and then determine the logic after the diagramming has been done. At the same time, a data dictionary of the data flow entities in the system should be built.

Physical characteristics can help in the analysis of the existing system. For example, following existing company organizational boundaries may clarify required data flow. Discussion of existing procedures with a user in terms of people's names or existing forms may prompt the user to indicate the logical reasons.

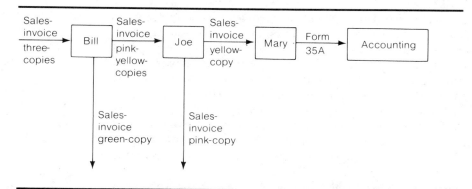

Figure 2.6 Sample existing system diagram.

The diagram of the existing system should be checked with users, to confirm that it is correct and that it takes all phases of the existing operation into account. Obviously, all subsequent analysis depends on a correct initial understanding.

2.2.3.3   Deriving an Abstract Diagram

When the initial diagram of the initial situation has been confirmed with users, an abstract diagram of the existing system is derived. The abstract diagram shows all of the activities of the existing system in an abstract form, without reference to specific organizations, individuals, physical devices, or specific documents.

Accordingly, each activity in the initial diagram is examined to determine *what* is done by the activity, in contrast to *who* (or which organization or device) does it. When the processing of an activity is understood, the information required by it, and produced by it, can be determined. In this way, the required information flow can be extracted from the physical document flow shown in the initial diagram.

An existing system typically is affected by politics, organizational procedures, historical accident, or the particular tools or devices being used. For example, the division of functions among departments may well be based on politics. These influences must be recognized and extracted from the diagram. In Figure 2.6, it is probable that Bill, Joe, and Mary each use only a small portion of the information on the sales invoice, but, procedurally, it is easier to pass a whole document. Also, there is no logical reason why Bill could not directly give Mary the yellow copy of the invoice; however, their desks may be arranged with Joe's desk in between Bill's and Mary's, so that, procedurally, it is convenient for Bill to give Joe two copies and for Joe to give Mary the yellow copy. Particular tools such as mail-routing systems or time-sharing systems are easy to spot since they appear explicitly. Details due just to history may be hard to spot, but if they have no other basis they will usually not make strong logical sense. Unfortunately, sometimes it is not possible to separate the logic of a system from the procedural or other physical aspects.

Political and tool-related aspects of the existing system tend to be reflected at the highest levels of the requirements diagram, where the existing system is partitioned into major activities. For example, a major activity at the highest level may be Controller's Office or time-sharing system. Fortunately, the requirement diagrams giving the details of such activities typically state the processing activity in functional terms rather than political or tool-related terms. Consequently, the entire model can be made more abstract by eliminating each political or tool-related high-level activity and replacing it in the high-level diagram by its refinement.

For example, suppose that, in the highest level diagram, step 4 is Controller's Office, and that the refinement diagram with steps 4.1, 4.2, and so on, states the activities of the Controller's Office in functional terms (i.e., the processes performed on the inputs to produce the outputs). Since the refinement diagram represents step 4 and has the same inputs and outputs, it can be plugged into the highest level diagram in place of step 4. This maneuver eliminates the political reference in the highest level diagram, which has now been made more abstract. In like manner, a political or tool-related reference at the nth level may be eliminated by substituting an (n+1)st level refinement diagram into the nth level diagram.

Another useful technique is analysis of the data flow. Determine the exact data components input to and output from each bottom-level activity. These components can now be inserted as inputs and outputs at the next higher level, and the process can be repeated until all diagrams reflect the data actually used in the processes instead of the manual forms used. Revise the data dictionary to reflect only this required data.

Extraneous data paths, such as the data transmission from Bill to Joe to Mary in Figure 2.6, will be revealed by a bottom-level activity transmit copy. In such cases, the extra transmit copy activity can simply be eliminated and the data routed to its ultimate destination (e.g., from Bill to Mary).

2.2.3.4 Deriving Abstract Data Files

2.2.3.4.1 Analysis of File Accesses   The final step in obtaining the abstract diagram is to derive abstract equivalents of the physical files by examining the patterns of data usage in the existing files. Note that the existing arrangement of data in the various physical files may be due to previous political, procedural, or historical decisions. In order that such previous decisions not influence the abstract diagram, the entire set of data in the system should be considered as a totality. In other words, the union of all data elements in all files should be considered as a "superfile" which is to be divided into component pieces.

For each reference to data in a file, list the activity involved, the type of access (i.e., read or write), the data flow entity, and the purpose of the access. If the file is accessed via a key such as the account number or Social Security number, list the file key also. Next, for each data read-out, examine the lower-level diagrams to determine the minimum data necessary in the reference, and replace the data flow found in the list by the minimum data. The data flow analysis of Section 2.2.3.3, reducing data flow elements to only those absolutely required by the processes, should make this job easier.

Now examine the lower-level diagrams for each data write. The data flows required for writes into files are determined by the data required to be read out; it is pointless to write something in a file that will never be read out.

Finally, decompose the superfile into private files, each private file serving the needs of one logical access. Think of each access as though it were the only one, and try to arrange a file structure ideally suited to that access alone. This step obtains private file 1, existing solely to serve logical access 1; private file 2, existing solely to serve logical access 2; and so on.

2.2.3.4.2 Normalizing and Decomposing Files   Each private file is now examined for the appearance of repeating data groups. As each repeating data group is found, it is split out from the file and set up in a separate file. The two new files now accomplish the same purpose as the one file did.

Splitting out of repeating data groups, called *normalization*, is repeated until all repeating data groups have been removed. The key for each new file is made up by concatenating the key of the "parent" file and the key of the repeating group. The file structures that emerge reflect the real needs of the data access.

The files of the previous step are now *decomposed* to obtain a set of single-purpose files. Assume the following definitions [DeMa 79]:

- The *object* of a file is whatever the file records information about.
- An *attribute* is an item of information recorded about an object.
- A *key attribute* is the principal identifier of an object.
- A *correlation* is an indication that one subject is associated with one or more other objects.

The files are now rearranged so that each resulting file either records the attributes of one and only one object or records a single correlation. This is done by separating attributes from correlation; associating attributes with the key attribute for the object they describe; and isolating correlations in pairs.

The resulting files are now fully normalized and decomposed.

2.2.3.4.3 Recombining Files   Finally, create a single file for each object, containing all the attributes for that object. As a result of the previous steps, there may be several different files, each having some of the attributes for that object. This may be the result of decomposition, or these files may have been derived through very different chains of accesses. Whatever their origin, the files are now combined so that there is one attribute file for each object.

There are now two kinds of files [DeMa 79]:

- *Attribute files*, referenced by a single key and containing all attributes that pertain to that key.
- *Correlative files*, allowing access among the files by correlating keys.

A diagram can be drawn showing each attribute file, its key, and the correlations as arrows.

The steps of Section 2.2.3.4 yield a logically simple file structure. On the other hand, the required processing is more complex. Processing complexity is not important when deriving requirements, and it can be traded against file complexity in the design of the new system. A further possible step in simplifying file structure at the expense of processing is to remove any stored data element that can be derived by reference to other stored elements.

REFERENCES

[Cou 74] Couger, J. D., and Knapp, R. W. (eds.). *System Analysis Techniques*. New York: Wiley, 1974.

[DeMa 79] DeMarco, T. *Structured Analysis and System Specification*. Englewood Cliffs, NJ: Prentice-Hall, 1979.

[Gan 79] Gane, C., and Sarson, T. *Structured Systems Analysis: Tools and Techniques*. Englewood Cliffs, NJ: Prentice-Hall, 1979.

[Luc 81] Lucas, H. C., and Gibson, C. F. *A Casebook for Management Information Systems*, 2nd ed. New York: McGraw-Hill, 1981.

[Orr 77] Orr, K. T. *Structured Systems Development*. New York: Yourdon, 1977.

PROBLEMS

The following narratives describe activities that companies wish to have automated. For each narrative provide the following responses:

a. List the major activities or organizations involved.

b. List each source of data to the system and each destination of data from the system.

c. List the inputs to the system (data flows from sources) and outputs from the system (data flows to destinations).

d. Draw a top-level requirements diagram showing sources, destinations, each major activity or organization, and data flows between these.

e. Draw a refinement diagram for each major activity or organization.

f. Draw one diagram showing all subactivities, data flows, sources, and destinations.

g. Provide a data dictionary listing all data flows and defining all data flows whose composition is stated.

Hints: In these examples, as in reality, it may be necessary to make assumptions in order to complete the diagrams. For example, the narrative may not clearly state which organization a given person is in, or which organization or person has responsibility for a stated activity. In each such case, make an assumption that seems harmonious with the narrative, and *state that assumption* in your answer.

Do not expect a first attempt at a diagram to look perfect or pretty; usually it takes several attempts to obtain a tidy diagram. Although each activity and each file is, in principle, at one specific place, it is permissible (if it allows the diagram to be made much tidier) to show the same file in two different places in the diagram. Whenever this is done, the file is marked with a vertical band as shown on the next page:

to indicate that it is shown more than once in the diagram.

For simpler activities, steps e and f can be developed together by drawing one diagram in which each major activity or organization is allocated to one section of the page and dashed-line boundaries indicate the boundaries of that activity or organization. When this diagram is done, each bounded section is one of the diagrams asked for in step e.

It may also be useful, when a person performs several logical duties, to allocate a bounded section of the page to that person.

1. Consolidated Computer Consultants does consulting work and also teaches seminars all over the United States. These seminars are profitable and have become a significant part of the company's work. The Seminar Office and the Accounting Office jointly handle all seminar matters, namely,

- Registrations for seminars
- Cancellations of registration
- Inquiries about seminar courses, schedules, and customers
- Payments
- Mailings to potential seminar customers

Registrations, cancellations, and inquiries may be received either by mail or by telephone; payments are received only by mail. When a registration is received, the company sends the customer back a confirmation letter and an invoice for the seminar fee. When a payment or cancellation is received, the company sends the customer a receipt or acknowledgement, as appropriate.

Mailings telling of future seminars are sent to all people who have ever attended seminars or who have ever inquired about them.

The receptionist handles all incoming mail as well as all telephone calls. Since Ms. Jones (the seminar coordinator) is responsible for dealing with registrations and cancellations, all of these are routed to her. Ms. Jones uses the enrollment form (either received by mail or just made up by her during the phone call) to update the enrollment in a seminar file and to add the new student's name to the customer file if necessary. She then fills out a small green enrollment slip, which she sends to the Accounting Office. Accounting produces an invoice from the green slip and sends the invoice to the receptionist, who types the customer's name and address on a form letter and sends the letter and invoice to the customer. Accounting also sends a copy of the invoice to Ms. Jones, who keeps it in an invoice file.

When Ms. Jones receives a cancellation, she changes the seminar enrollment in the seminar file. She fills out an orange cancellation slip (containing the customer's name and address) in two copies, clips these to the invoice copy that she pulls from the invoice file, and sends these to Accounting. Accounting uses the invoice and one copy of the cancellation slip to credit the customer's account and sends the other copy of the slip to the receptionist, who mails it back to the customers.

Ms. Jones shares her office with the seminar clerk, who handles all inquiries and all payments. The receptionist routes all of these to the clerk. The clerk uses the seminar file and the customer file to answer inquiries and adds the inquirer's name to the customer file if it is not already there. The clerk also clips each payment to the corresponding invoice, which is pulled from the invoice file, and sends these to Accounting. Accounting credits the customer's account and produces a white receipt slip with the customer's name and address on it. This slip is sent to the receptionist, who mails it to the customer.

2. Professional Book Distributors specializes in buying professional engineering books directly from publishers in large quantities and distributing them directly to individual engineers. The company has decided to automate its manual order-processing system and has written the following specification for the new system.

Orders may come in by mail or by telephone. For telephone orders, the new system must provide either a standard order form or a standard format entering the order into the system via a CRT terminal. Whether done manually or by the computer, each order must be checked for completeness. In other words, the order must contain all important information, the title and author must be correct, and the book must be still in print. Any order not meeting these criteria is to be sent to a supervisor for further checking.

Orders including payments must also be checked to ensure that the payment amount agrees with the order amount. If not, the process must generate, as appropriate, a credit or request for further payment, except if the difference in amount is less than 75 cents. If the order does not include payment, the customer file must be checked to see if the customer has a good credit status. Any customer not having a good credit status is sent a confirmation of the order and a request for prepayment. If the customer is new, the customer's name is added to the customer file.

Each order that includes payment or is from a customer with a good credit status is checked against the inventory to see if the order can be filled. If the order can be completely filled, then a combination shipping note and invoice (marked "paid" if prepayment was included in the order) is prepared and sent out with the books. When an order can only be partially filled, a combination shipping note and invoice is made up and sent with the partial order that can be filled, together with a confirmation and invoice for the unfilled portion of the order. (The invoice for the unfilled portion is also marked "paid" if payment was included in the order.) A copy of the invoice for the unfilled portion of the order is placed in a back-order file. Back orders should be filled and sent out to the customer as soon as the books ordered have been received from the publishers.

Sometimes these orders are for books not usually kept in inventory by Professional Book Distributors. Because publishers usually give a quantity discount on purchases above a certain dollar value, such orders are accumulated until the purchase from the publisher will earn the quantity discount.

Customers may also return books. These books are checked for damage and placed back in inventory, and a credit or refund is sent to the customer. If the returned book is not usually kept in inventory, and if the publisher's policy is to allow books to be sent back, then the book is sent back to the publisher.

Every shipment of books from a publisher is checked against the original purchase order to the publisher. The publisher's shipment might be a partial one, if the publisher is temporarily out of stock. If the publisher's shipping note, invoice, and order confirmation do not together agree with the original purchase order, a letter is sent to the publisher inquiring about each of the differences.

The publisher's shipment is then checked against the back-order file. Back-ordered books are placed on a special shelf, to be accumulated for each customer's back order. The rest of the books are put into inventory.

In this business it is important that proper inventory levels be maintained. Back orders are expensive to process, and if a customer tires of waiting, buys the book somewhere else, and cancels the order for the book, a credit or refund must be sent. On the other hand, books cost money; the cash invested in a large inventory might better be used (or might be needed) somewhere else, and the company may be paying interest on the funds invested in inventory. The management at PBD has decided that each book title should be reordered when the quantity on hand falls below a reorder level R, where

$R = F \times A \times D$
$F = 1.5$
$A = \frac{1}{4} \times$ total sales in the previous 4 weeks
$D =$ delivery time from the publisher in weeks

For example, a title that has sold 20 copies in the last 4 weeks and has a 4-week delivery time will have a reorder level $R = 1.5 \times (1/4) \times 20 \times 4 = 30$. The quantity F, which is a safety factor to ensure that there will be books in stock even if the delivery is delayed, may be increased for a book whose sales are rising and decreased for a book whose sales are falling. The quantity A includes back orders and orders received without payment, as well as books shipped.

When a book title is reordered, the quantity reordered depends on the factors A and D above, and also on the publisher's discount policy. Each publisher has a set of discount rates, depending on the quantity ordered.

For example, publisher X may offer a discount of 5 percent for 50 copies or more, 10 percent for 100 copies or more, and so on; while publisher Y offers 6 percent discount for 75 copies, 8 percent for 96 copies, and so on. To determine the reorder quantity, a nominal quantity $N = B \times A \times D$, where B is a "bulk factor" nominally ≤ 3, is calculated, and then N is rounded up to the publisher's next-highest-discount quantity, unless the rounding off increases the order by more than 25 percent. In the case above, $A = 5$ and $D = 4$, so that $N = 60$. If the title is being reordered from publisher X, the quantity will remain 60 copies. The bulk factor B may be varied by management.

Payments received from customers are checked against invoices. If the payment exactly matches one outstanding invoice, it is applied first to the oldest invoice; and so on until the payment is used up. When any invoice is more than 60 days overdue, a letter requesting payment is sent to the customer.

Invoices from publishers are put into an accounts payable file after they are checked against receipt of shipment records. If the publisher's prompt payment discount provides a rate of return greater than a return specified by management, then the new system should produce a payment check on the last day that the discount is available. When a publisher gives 3 percent for payment in 30 days, the rate of return is 36 percent per year, and thus (assuming that 36 percent is greater than the rate specified by management) a payment check should be produced on the twenty-ninth day.

The new system should regularly produce reports of invoices sent (by day, by week, and by month); reports of payments received (by day, by week, by month); reports of amounts overdue by 30, 60, and 90 days; and reports of back orders, books out of stock, and purchases from publishers. The system should be capable of producing analyses of sales by title, by publisher, and by subject on request, as well as lists of publisher delivery times. Reports on inventory status (quantity on hand, quantity on order, expected delivery date) and the capability to answer questions about particular orders would be very desirable.*

PROJECT OUTLINE: *Requirements Diagrams*
Consider a problem from Appendix C, or a case from a casebook such as Lucas and Gibson, *A Casebook for Management Information Systems* [Luc 81]. From the narrative:

1. (a) List each source and each destination.
   (b) Give a list of inputs (data flows from sources) and outputs (data flows to destinations).

---

*Chris Gane / Trish Sarson, *Structured Systems Analysis: Tools and Techniques*, © 1979, pp. 35–37. Adapted by permission of Prentice-Hall, Inc., Englewood Cliffs, N.J.

2. Draw a top-level requirements diagram showing sources and destinations, as well as the major activities and all data flows between these. Use a separate 8½ × 11 piece of paper for this diagram, and number the activities.

3. (a) Draw refinement diagrams for each of the major activities, showing the major subactivities and data flows for each. Use a separate 8½ × 11 piece of paper, and number each subactivity.

   (b) Complete the requirements diagram in as much detail as possible from the narrative, by drawing refinement diagrams to as many levels as necessary. Use a separate 8½ × 11 piece of paper for each diagram, and number each activity appropriately.

4. Provide a data dictionary including data definitions for all data flows whose composition is stated in the narrative. Data flows whose compositions are unstated should simply be listed without any data definition.

2.3 PROGRAM SPECIFICATIONS

2.3.1 Basic Concepts

2.3.1.1 Introduction to Specifications

A *program specification* (equivalently, an *activity specification*) describes the planned set of inputs, the desired processing, and the planned set of outputs of a program. Ideally a specification does not prescribe the particular algorithms or techniques the program should use. A specification of a program, or of an activity of a requirements diagram, may be given informally as a prose statement.

The intent of a specification is to define a function (in the mathematical sense) from input to output. However, in practice, a specification may contradict itself, or have ambiguities, or may leave processing unspecified for some case or condition of the input. In these cases the specification does not actually define a mathematical function. Sometimes there may be two or more entirely reasonable, yet conflicting, interpretations of the specification, and in this case a program cannot be written since the designer cannot know which processing is actually intended. The conflict must be resolved in consultation with the customer before the program is developed. The designer should also watch carefully for specifications that do not correctly convey the intended processing.

Section 2.3 presents methods for putting activity or program specifications into a standard format called a *decision table*. This form systematically delineates the processing of different input cases, so that the processing is precisely understood. The decision table serves as the basis for a test of the desired program and also reveals any unintended incompleteness, ambiguity, or contradiction.

A program deals with a class of inputs and yields a class of output values (one output value for each possible input). Figure 2.7 has an input class X and an output class Y, shown as geometric areas. Each individual element of X—say, x_1, x_2, or x_3—is visualized as a point[2] in the area X, and, similarly, individual elements y_1, y_2, y_3, etc., of Y are thought of as points in the area Y. The program function P is considered a path that leads from, say, x_3 in X to a unique corresponding point y_3 in Y according to an explicitly stated rule.

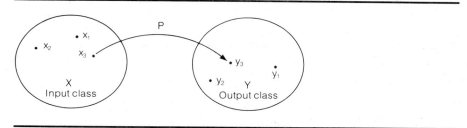

Figure 2.7 Input class, output class, and mapping P.

Figure 2.7 is concerned with *what* a program does, rather than with *how* the program does it (tests of conditions, searches, loops, etc.). The program function is viewed as instantaneously and effortlessly achieving the desired mapping—a program that executes instantaneously. From a mathematical standpoint, an equivalent view is that the program, for any conceivable input whatsoever, has already been executed, so that the path P merely leads to the predetermined result.

The class diagrams of Figure 2.7 can be used to show both some of the problems of specifications and a method for analyzing specifications. Suppose a program is desired to calculate, for all integers x in the range $-1000 \leqslant x \leqslant 1000$, the function ZIP(x) that yields an integer value defined as follows:

$$ZIP(x) = \begin{cases} x & \text{if } x > 2 \\ x^2 & \text{if } x < 2 \end{cases}$$

The planned input class for this program consists of the points $-1000, \ldots, -1, 0, 1, \ldots, 1000$. We may informally investigate the mappings given for

---

[2]In reality, each input x might be a collection of numbers, or even an entire program text when P is a compiler. Similarly, each output y might be a set of numbers or an object program.

several input values. As shown in Figure 2.8, ZIP(5)=5 while ZIP(−5)=25. However, ZIP(2) is undefined even though x=2 is certainly within the planned input class. Moreover, the apparent possibilities are ZIP(2)=2 and ZIP(2)=4, which are obviously unequal.

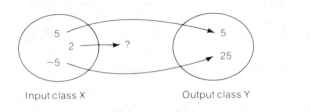

Input class X   Output class Y

Figure 2.8 ZIP(x) mappings for several input points.

Since the specification does not prescribe any output at all for the input 2, it is not complete.

On the other hand, suppose a program is desired to calculate, for all integers x in the range −1000≤x≤1000, the function ZAP(x) that yields an integer value defined as follows:

$$ZAP(x) = \begin{cases} x & \text{if } x \geq 2 \\ x^2 & \text{if } x \leq 2 \end{cases}$$

As shown in Figure 2.9, ZAP(5)=5 while ZAP(−5)=25. Now the output values 2 and 4 are both specifically prescribed for x=2. The specification is complete but contains a contradiction. These problems exemplify the imperfections found in the great majority of specifications.

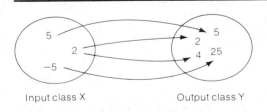

Input class X   Output class Y

Figure 2.9 ZAP(x) mappings for several input points.

Almost every specification contains conditions that inherently divide the input class into subclasses, each corresponding to a condition or combination of conditions and having its own subfunction. For example, as shown in Figure 2.10, the first problem defines a subclass X_1 containing all $x>2$, and each x in X_1 is assigned an output point $y=x$. The problem also defines a subclass X_2 containing all $x<2$, and each x in X_2 is assigned an output point $y=x^2$. The definition of ZIP(x) does not assign the point 2 to any class and also does not assign it an output value. However, because 2 is in the input class and not in X_1 or X_2, Figure 2.10 shows a subclass X_3 containing only the point 2.

The subclasses defined by the specification of ZIP(x) do not together include all input points, and thus there is a subclass for which no processing rule is assigned. This is the most common error found in specifications, and the "missed" points are most often the ones that lie on the boundaries between subclasses.

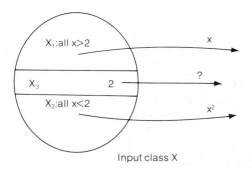

Figure 2.10 Division of X into subclasses by the conditions of the statement of ZIP(x).

The subclasses defined by the second problem are shown in Figure 2.11. Each point in the subclass X_4 containing all $x\geq2$ is assigned an output point $y=x$, while each point in the subclass X_5 containing all $x\leq2$ is assigned an output point $y=x^2$. However, the input point $x=2$ belongs both to X_4 and to X_5, so that for $x=2$, two different processing rules are now prescribed.

Specifications can be analyzed by first determining subclasses and their characteristic processing rules and then checking to see whether there are points that are left out or that are in conflicting subclasses.

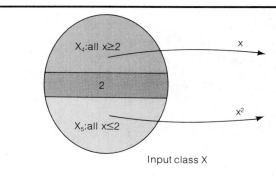

Figure 2.11 Division of X into subclasses by the conditions of
the statement of ZAP(x).

2.3.1.2 Points, Boundaries, and Classes

2.3.1.2.1 The Input Point Each time a program executes, it considers one input point and produces one output point. Remember that an input point may actually be a collection of elements. For example, for a "load and go" system that compiles a program P and then executes the object code on accompanying data D, an input point consists of both the source program P and the data D.

The following example will be used throughout the next few sections. A payroll program will have as input an employee file containing for each employee, an identifying number and an hourly salary rate (in dollars and cents) less than or equal to $50.00. Another input will be a sequence of punched cards containing, for each employee, an identifying number and the number of hours worked during a week (given in hours and tenths of hours). The program is to calculate each employee's weekly salary in dollars and cents, including time-and-a-half for overtime (hours above 40), and print the salary check. However, no salary check may have an amount over $500.00.

If we think of an input point as the smallest collection of data that the program considers independently of all other data, then for the example an input point consists of a punched card for a particular employee, in conjunction with the entire employee file. The employee file is required to be a part of each input point because information in the file is required to produce the output for each card.

We must be careful to choose input points so that they are independent. Note that an input point of a matrix inversion program must be the entire set of values constituting a matrix since all of these values are required in computing any element of the inverse matrix.

2.3.1.2.2 Boundaries of the Planned Input Class Problem statements may, either explicitly or implicitly, include restrictions on input points to precisely define the planned input class. For example, an input matrix may be required to have an equal number of rows and columns.

A boundary condition of an input class X is a condition that must be satisfied by every element of X. Examples of boundary conditions are:

C_1:each input matrix must have an equal number of rows and columns

and

C_2:all matrix elements must be integer

An error condition of X is a condition $\overline{C}$, which is the negation of a boundary condition C of X. The error conditions corresponding to the boundary conditions C_1, C_2 above are:

$\overline{C}_1$:number of rows of the input matrix not equal to number of columns
$\overline{C}_2$:some matrix elements not integers

Each pair of conditions $(C, \overline{C})$ defines a boundary of the class X. That is, for z a potential member of X,

z is in X only if z meets C
z is not in X if z meets $\overline{C}$

In determining the boundaries of X, we may ask:

· What boundary conditions must an input satisfy in order to be "correct" or "legal"?
· What error conditions will make an input "erroneous" or "illegal"?

Either formulation clarifies a boundary of the space.

In the payroll program example, we may infer the boundary conditions

Hours worked$\geqslant 0$	since a negative number of hours cannot be worked
Hours worked$\leqslant 168.0$	since there are 168 hours in a week
Salary rate$\geqslant 0$	since we assume there are no negative salary rates
Salary rate$\leqslant 50.00$	given in the specifications

The restrictions imposed by the boundary and error conditions strongly influence the analysis of the specification and also the form of the program design. The designer must take care that these restrictions are chosen to conform with real facts rather than for programming convenience. A great danger in program development is the introduction, at this step, of unnecessary bounds on inputs and the consequent development of a restricted (sometimes trivial) program that cannot process the inputs of the intended problem.

2.3.1.2.3 The Output Point   An output point of a program is the entire set of results yielded by the program for an input point.

For example, an output point of a "load and go" system may be the listing of the compiled program together with the results of the object program execution or may be a listing of the compiled program together with a diagnostic list of errors.

An output point of a matrix inversion program, for example, is the entire inverse matrix. For the payroll program example, an output point is a salary check. The specification might also have called for a print line stating the amount of the check, in which case an output point would be the salary check and the printout of the amount.

2.3.1.2.4 Output Boundaries   Problem statements may include restrictions on the outputs of a program, independent of restrictions on the program's inputs. In payroll programs, it is common to specify a maximum amount for salary checks the program may output. In the example here, a maximum salary check of $500.00 is allowed.

2.3.1.3 Conditions and Their Consequences

Every condition divides a set into (two or more) complementary subsets. For example, let $S = \{x\}$, and let C be a condition that, for each x in S, is either true or false. Then C divides S into subsets

$$S_1 = \{x \text{ in } S \mid C(x) = \text{true}\}$$
$$S_2 = \{x \text{ in } S \mid C(x) = \text{false}\}$$

such that

> Every x in S is either in S_1 or in S_2
> No x is in S_1 and also in S_2

In short, S_1 and S_2 together include all the points in S, but they have no points in common. S_1 might have no points at all, if $C(x) = $ false for all x in S, or, conversely, S_2 might have no points if $C(x) = $ true for all x in S.

A condition may have more than two values and thus may partition S into many disjoint complementary subsets. As an example, a transaction code c, where $0 \leq c \leq 10$, taken as a condition value, partitions S into 11 subsets. Characteristics such as size (e.g., small, medium, large) or color might be regarded as conditions.

The *numeric relation* is a condition based on numeric comparison of two values x and y. Since either $x > y$, or $x = y$, or $x < y$, a numeric relation C basically divides $S = \{x\}$ into three disjoint complementary subsets. We also commonly use combinations of these sets, corresponding to the relations $\{\leq, \neq, \geq\}$. When numeric relations are considered, it is important that each of the three possible relations is taken into account. The difficulties in Figures 2.9 and 2.10 arise from careless treatment of the condition $x = y$.

Although each condition of a specification directly implies two or more subclasses, in practice a specification usually does not explicitly state all subclasses. Instead, a condition value is stated that delineates one subclass, and the complementary subclass(es) must then be inferred.

For example, in the payroll program, the phrase "hours above 40" implies a condition "hours worked" that divides the input space X into two subclasses, say,

X_{H1}:input points such that hours worked ≤ 40
X_{H2}:input points such that hours worked > 40

However, the specification explicitly mentions only X_{H2}, leaving us to infer the complement subclass X_{H1}.

It is convenient to tabulate each condition, the subclasses it causes, and the result for each subclass, as in Table 2.2.

Table 2.2   Subclasses and results induced by a stated condition

Label	Condition Value	Result
X_{H1}	Hours worked≤ 40	Standard rate pay
X_{H2}	Hours worked> 40	Pay including overtime rate

PROBLEMS

1. A program is desired to calculate the function ABS(x) for all integers x in the range $-1000 \leq x \leq 1000$, where ABS(x) is given by

$$ABS(x) = \begin{cases} x & \text{if } x \geq 0 \\ -x & \text{if } x < 0 \end{cases}$$

    Describe the planned input class and the planned output class. Draw class diagrams showing some typical input points and the corresponding outputs, as in Figure 2.7. Does the problem statement appear to specify an output for every input? Does it appear to specify conflicting outputs for any input?

2. A program is desired to calculate the function ABS(x) defined above for all integers x. Describe the planned input class and the planned output class. Is this a legitimate input class? Draw class diagrams showing some typical input points and output points, as in Figure 2.7. Does the problem

statement appear to specify an output for every input? Does it appear to specify conflicting results for any input?

3. A program is desired that calculates, for all integers x in the range $-1000 \leqslant x \leqslant 1000$, the positive integer value y such that ABS(y)=x. The function ABS is defined in Problem 1. Describe the planned input class and the planned output class. Draw class diagrams showing some typical input points and corresponding output points, as in Figure 2.7. Does the problem statement appear to specify an output for every input? Does it appear to specify conflicting results for any input?

For each specification in Problems 4 to 9, describe: (a) a planned input point; (b) the boundaries of the planned input class; (c) an output point, and (d) the boundaries of the output class.

4. A program is desired that will be given a sequence of up to 10,000 integers and then will (1) print the given sequence and (2) sort the integers and print the sorted list (smallest integer first).

5. A subroutine P(a,b,c,T) is desired whose arguments are a table T and positive real numbers a,b,c. The subroutine P is to print the values

   n_a=number of elements of T>a
   n_b=number of elements of T=b
   n_c=number of elements of T<c

6. Write a program that, when given a sequence of alphabetic characters constituting a Roman numeral less than MMM (e.g., XII), calculates the equivalent decimal number. The correspondence of Roman and Arabic numerals is

I	V	X	L	C	D	M
1	5	10	50	100	500	1000

7. Write a program that, when given a positive integer less than 3000, calculates the equivalent Roman numeral.

8. Write a program that performs transformations from cartesian coordinates to polar coordinates. The program is to input a sequence of points (x,y), where $0.25 \leqslant x \leqslant 3$ and $-2 \leqslant y \leqslant 2$, and to output the sequence of points (r,θ) where r=f(x,y), θ=g(x,y), $1 \leqslant r \leqslant 10$, and $0.5 \leqslant \theta \leqslant 2.5$. The θ values are given in radians.

9. Write a program that will compile any PASCAL source program of less than 5000 lines. If the program has no errors, an object program should be produced; if it has only nonfatal errors, the object program and warning messages should be produced. If it has fatal errors, then only a set of error messages should be produced.

Each specification in Problems 10 to 14 contains one or more conditions that cause the processing function to vary. Identify these conditions and describe how they cause the variation in the processing function. Identify the subclasses created by these conditions and the result of each subclass.

10. Write a program that searches a table T for a value x and outputs YES if x is in T or else outputs NO.

11. A trucking company wants a program that calculates and prints the shipping charge of a package as the product of its length L, its width W, its height H, and the number of miles shipped, M. However, if the sum of the package length, width, and height exceed 150, the program is to print '___' because the company will not ship the package.

12. A program is desired that, when given a sequence of alphabetic characters, prints the equivalent decimal number if the sequence constitutes a legitimate Roman numeral or else prints 'IMPROPER INPUT.'

13. A program is desired that plays tic-tac-toe with a user at a terminal, and at the end of the game prints one of the messages: OK, YOU WIN; HOORAY! I WIN!; or DRAW—NO MORE MOVES POSSIBLE; as appropriate.

14. Write a program that is given three line segments in two-dimensional space. Each line segment is defined by its end points. The line segments must form a triangle. The program is to calculate whether the triangle is equilateral, isosceles, or scalene, and to output E (for equilateral), I (for isosceles), or S (for scalene). For an equilateral triangle, only E is output.
    The sample input consisting of

    Line 1 given by ((1,1),(2,2))
    Line 2 given by ((2,2),(2,1))
    Line 3 given by ((2,1),)(1,1))

    causes the output I.

2.3.2 Derivation of Decision Tables

2.3.2.1 Analysis of Problem Conditions

2.3.2.1.1 Steps in the Analysis Almost every specification contains conditions that cause variations in the processing given to different input points. That is, the processing of each input point depends on the conditions met by that point. And the conditions define different subclasses where each subclass meets a different combination of conditions and has its own characteristic processing function.

Section 2.3.2 shows how to analyze a specification to obtain a *decision table*, a format that precisely delineates each subclass and its results. The decision table is derived in a sequence of four steps:

1. Choose a planned input class and planned output class as a basis for the derivation. The input class chosen may be finite or infinite and may include erroneous inputs or not. Remember that the primary purpose of the decision table is to give a precise analysis of the specification for nonerroneous inputs.
2. Determine each condition that causes the processing rules to vary.
3. Determine for each condition found in step 2:
   a. the subclasses created by the condition and the ranges of values the condition has in each subclass;
   b. the result yielded by the processing rules for each subclass.
4. Determine the result yielded for every possible combination of conditions (formally, for every possible intersection of the subclasses found in step 3a).

Remember that analysis of the specification is concerned with *what* the intended program is to do and not with *how* it will be done. In other words, this analysis does not care how the intended program will test conditions or what searches or loops will be used.

The conditions that cause the processing of different input points to vary may be explicitly stated in the problem statement or may be implicit; they may be bounds on the input or the output class; or they may arise from interaction between components of an input point.

The payroll program example of the previous section explicitly varies the formula for pay according to a condition "hours worked," where

Either $0 \leq$ hours worked ≤ 40
Or $40 <$ hours worked ≤ 168

The sentence "No salary check will be issued for over $500" introduces a condition "salary check" that bounds the output class, where

Either $0 \leq$ salary check ≤ 500
Or $500 <$ salary check

Lastly, by considering the possible interactions between the employee file E and time card c, we discover an implied condition that the identifying number of c matches the identifying number in E; this condition is either true or false.

2.3.2.1.2 Conditions in the Payroll Problem   Table 2.3 summarizes the conditions, subclasses, and results obtained for the payroll program specification.

Table 2.3 Summary of conditions, subclasses, and results

Label	Condition Value	Result
X_{H1}	Hours worked ≤ 40	Compute s using standard rate only
X_{H2}	Hours worked >40	Compute s using standard and overtime rates
X_{S1}	Result will be $s \leq 500.00$	Output salary check s
X_{S2}	Result will be $s>500.00$	?*
X_{I1}	I_c found in E	Compute s according to other conditions
X_{I2}	I_c not found in E	?

*The notation ? signifies that the result is not defined.

The condition hours worked divides the input class into subclasses X_{H1}, X_{H2}. Table 2.3 shows the condition values and results for each of these subclasses.

Conditions or restrictions may be given for the output class, independently of any conditions on the input class. For instance, the payroll program specification states that no check may have an amount over $500.00, in order to prohibit program-controlled issuance of checks for large amounts.

Recall that for the payroll program example, an output point is a salary amount. Recall also that the hours worked are less than or equal to 168 and the salary rate per hour is less than or equal to 50. Therefore, in the absence of the $500.00 restriction, the bound on the salary amount is B, where B is the amount that would be earned by an employee working 168 hours at a rate of $50 per hour and being paid for 128 overtime hours. Although highly unlikely, B is the largest conceivable amount that could be paid to an employee according to the conditions of the problem.

Thus the bound of 500.00 divides the output class Y into subclasses Y_{S1} containing salary checks ≤ 500.00, and Y_{S2} containing salary checks >500.00. A check cannot be issued for the points in Y_{S2}.

This division into subclasses Y_{S1} and Y_{S2} influences the processing of inputs. Since outputs in the class Y_{S2} are prohibited, certain legal inputs (specifically, those that would result in salary amount >500.00) cannot be properly processed if the output bound is to be met. Thus the division of the output class induces a corresponding division of the input class into subclasses X_{S1} and X_{S2}:

X_{S1}=inputs resulting in salary amount ≤ 500.00
X_{S2}=inputs resulting in salary amount >500.00.

As in this case, output subclasses caused by bounds or restrictions on outputs must always be "reflected back" to determine the corresponding input subclasses since a condition on the output may cause certain legal inputs to be impossible to process. In the present example, Table 2.3 shows that correct inputs of subclass X_{S2} have no assigned mapping at all. The specification will not be complete until mappings are explicitly assigned for the points in X_{S2}.

Recall that for the payroll program example, an input point consists of an employee file E and an employee time card c. By considering the possible interactions between the employee file E and time card c, we discover an implied condition that the identifying number in c matches the identifying number in E. In other words, if an employee's identifying number does not match any identifying number in the employee file, then the salary cannot be calculated. This condition divides the input class into subclasses X_{I1} and X_{I2} and causes processing to vary as shown in Table 2.3.

2.3.2.2 Describing Combinations of Conditions with Decision Tables

Each condition C divides X into subclasses X_{C1}, and X_{C2}, and so on, each subclass having its own result. Suppose that a condition A divides X into X_{A1}, X_{A2}, and B divides X into X_{B1} and X_{B2}. In principle, A divides both X_{B1} and X_{B2}, and, conversely, B divides both X_{A1} and X_{A2}. Thus a subclass is formed for each combination of values of A and B. Each subclass thus formed may have a different processing rule. Subclasses having identical processing rules can be grouped into one subclass.

Whenever there are two or more conditions, the subclasses corresponding to all combinations of conditions must be determined, together with their results. The payroll program example has 3 conditions, namely, H=hours worked, S=salary amount, and I=identifier, each having 2 values so there are $8=2^3$ possible combinations of these values.

In step 4 of the analysis procedure, a result is determined for each of these combinations. The conditions, combinations, and results can be systematically presented in a format called a *decision table* [Mon 74, Met 77]. Every decision table is divided into quadrants as in Figure 2.12. Roughly speaking, the condition quadrant names the conditions (e.g., hours worked, salary amount), the condition value quadrant has combinations of values (e.g., hours≤40 and salary≤500.00), the result quadrant names results, and the result value quadrant has a result value for each combination of values in the condition value quadrant.

Table 2.4 shows two typical arrangements of a condition quadrant and a condition value quadrant.

One or more rows run through both quadrants. Each row contains the condition name in the condition quadrant and condition values in the condition value quadrant. A given row of either quadrant may have either the form of Table 2.4(a) or the true/false form of (b).

As stated, each column of the condition value quadrant contains a particular combination of condition values. Thus each column in (a) or (b) specifies a subclass formed by a particular combination of condition values. Both forms

Condition quadrant	Condition value quadrant
Result quadrant	Result value quadrant

Figure 2.12 Format of a decision table.

of the table are actually identical, even though in (*a*), generalized values (e.g., ≤500) have been used while in (*b*), the conditions have been restated to have only T or F values. These modes could be mixed, so that, say, the salary condition would be described using the set of values {≤500, >500}, while the hours condition would be described using hours worked >40 and the set of values {T,F}. The style of (*b*) is convenient for conditions with only two values, while the style of (*a*) is more appropriate for conditions with three or more values (e.g., a transaction code).

Table 2.4   Ways of tabulating combinations of conditions

Condition	Combinations of Condition Values							
H:hours worked	≤40	≤40	≤40	≤40	>40	>40	>40	>40
S:salary amount	≤500	≤500	>500	>500	≤500	≤500	>500	>500
I:identifier	Not Found	Found	Not Found	Found	Not Found	Found	Not Found	Found

(*a*) Condition and Condition Value Quadrants, with Tabulation of Combinations of Conditions.

Condition	Combinations of Condition Values							
Hours worked>40	F	F	F	F	T	T	T	T
Salary amount>500	F	F	T	T	F	F	T	T
Identifier found	F	T	F	T	F	T	F	T

(*b*) Condition and Condition Value Quadrants, with Tabulation of Combinations of Conditions Having Only T(True) and F(False) Values.

Parts (*a*) and (*b*) indicate identical results.

Decision tables may use either notation of Table 2.4, in conjunction with either notation of Table 2.5.

Table 2.5 Partial decision tables showing ways of indicating results for combinations of conditions

Hours worked>40		T	
Salary amount>500	. . .	F	. . .
Identifier found		T	
RESULT		Compute salary using standard and overtime rates; output salary checks	

(*a*) Partial Decision Table with Results Indicated Using Text in Each Column of Result Value Quadrant

Hours worked>40		T	
Salary amount>500	. . .	F	. . .
Identifier found		T	
Compute salary using standard rate only			
Compute salary using standard and overtime rates		X	
Output salary checks		X	
?			

(*b*) Partial Decision Table with Results Tabulated in Result Quadrant; Presence of a Result Indicated by an X in Result Value Quadrant

   Table 2.5 shows two partial decision tables, each illustrating a way in which the result quadrant and result value quadrant can be given. In either case, each column of the result value quadrant shows the result(s) corresponding to the combination of condition values in that column. The result quadrant may contain only the word RESULT, as in (*a*), in which case a statement indicating the appropriate result(s) is written in each column of the result value quadrant. Alternatively, the result quadrant can contain several rows, each naming a specific result as in (*b*). In this case, an X appears in each column of the result value quadrant for which that result occurs.

2.3.2.3 Deriving Decision Tables

The basic method of deriving a decision table is to tabulate all possible combinations of conditions, as in Table 2.4, and to determine a result for each column. This procedure ensures that every combination of conditions is explicitly considered. Columns that give the same results can be rearranged so that they cluster into groups (each group having the same set of results), or they can be combined.

The finished table preferably should be arranged so that each possible input satisfies the conditions of exactly one column of condition values. Alternatively, if any input satisfies the conditions of several columns, each of those columns must specify *identical* results for that input.

In deriving the table, we may observe that some conditions have precedence over others. For the payroll program, if the identifying number is not found, then the salary cannot be computed and a check cannot be output, no matter what the other conditions are. Table 2.6 gives the full tabulation of conditions and results for the payroll program. In Table 2.6, the notation - in the leftmost condition value column indicates "don't care," that is, the condition may take any of its values. The leftmost column indicates that when identifier found has the value F, that condition causes an undefined result regardless of the values of hours worked and salary amount. Thus the combination of values (-, -,F) groups into one case the four combinations

$$\begin{cases} (F,F,F) \\ (F,T,F) \\ (T,F,F) \\ (T,T,F) \end{cases}$$

so that a smaller table is obtained.

Table 2.6 Analysis of payroll program specification

Hours worked >40	-	F	T	F	T
Salary amount >500	-	F	F	T	T
Identifier found	F	T	T	T	T
Compute salary using standard rate only		X		X	
Compute salary using standard and overtime rates			X		X
Output salary checks		X	X		
?	X			X	X

Error conditions usually take precedence over other conditions. Accordingly, each of the first few leftmost columns usually delineates one specific error condition and the appropriate result. Throughout the rest of the table, the error condition is assumed false. For example, all the other columns in Table 2.6 have the value T for identifier found.

Cases can be grouped systematically throughout the table using the "don't care" value, so that a smaller number of columns is obtained. However, care must be taken to ensure that this practice does not introduce contradictions.

Note that the combination (T,T,-) includes both (T,T,F) and (T,T,T). A table has a contradiction if it contains the combination (-,-,F) and also (T,T,-), with different results shown in each of these columns, because two different results are then specified for the case (T,T,F).

In Table 2.6, each condition and each combination of conditions is accounted for. The sets of condition values include all possibilities (e.g., the values ≤40,>40 for hours worked include all possibilities). However, because the result is undefined for several combinations of conditions, the specification is not complete.

Manual performance of this technique may not be feasible for large specifications containing many conditions. However, programs may be written to mechanically generate combinations of given conditions, thereby aiding in the analysis of large specifications.

PROBLEMS

For each of the following problems, provide the following responses, in the order given:

(a) Describe a planned input point.

(b) Describe the boundaries of the planned input class.

(c) What errors might an input point have? Give a sample input point for each error.

Recall that every error condition is the converse of some boundary condition, and vice versa.

(d) Describe an output point.

The responses (a) through (d) define the planned input class and the output class that you must analyze. All of your further responses must assume the classes given by your responses to these. Remember also that the planned input space need not have erroneous points.

(e) Tabulate all input subclasses and the result for each input subclass.

Hint: Remember that you are to analyze the *intended* effect of a specification, in order to determine whether the specification truly defines a program. The method the required program will use is *not relevant* in this analysis.

1. A program is desired to aid a company in processing customer payments. The company bills its customers on the last day of each month. If payment is received within the first 10 days of the next month, the customer gets a bonus credit equal to 1 percent of the payment. If payment is received in the second 10 days of the month, the customer is credited with the exact amount of the payment. Otherwise, the customer is charged a penalty of 1½ percent on the unpaid balance, except that the minimum penalty is $1.50. (If

payment has not been received by the next billing date, then the billing program should add the 1½ percent or $1.50 penalty to the balance of the next bill.) Program inputs are the customer identification, the date and amount of payment, and a customer file containing last month's balance for each customer. The program should produce a transaction record containing the customer identification, date and amount of payment, and amount credited toward the bill.

2. A program is to be used to determine how much money a bank will loan each of its customers, by analyzing the customer's job, salary, and home value. The program will use certain tables to rate the customer's job title (on a scale of 0 to 5 inclusive), the customer's salary (on a scale of 0 to 7 inclusive), and the customer's house value (on a scale of 0 to 10 inclusive). The program will then use these ratings to determine the loan amounts. However, a customer with a job rating <2 may not be loaned any money, regardless of other ratings. For job ratings $\geqslant 2$, a customer may be loaned the following amounts:

$$\begin{cases} \$1000 \times (\text{job rating}) \times (\text{salary rating}) & \text{if house rating} \leqslant 5 \\ \$2000 \times (\text{job rating}) \times (\text{salary rating}) & \text{if } 9 \geqslant \text{house rating} > 5 \end{cases}$$

A customer with house rating=10 may be loaned $100,000 regardless of other ratings.

3. A program is desired to help in the firing of missiles at directly overhead targets. Assuming that both the missile and the target travel in straight lines, the diagram shows the paths to be traveled by the missile and target. In the diagram, a is the altitude of the target, V_T and V_M are the velocities of the target and missile, and t and m are the angles of travel of the target and missile with respect to the horizontal.

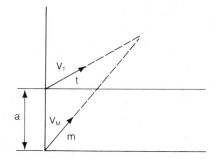

The program is given the values of $a, V_T, t,$ and V_M. According to the diagram, the required firing angle is

$$m = \cos^{-1}((V_T \cos t)/V_M)$$

However, if $(V_T \cos t)/V_M > 1$, the arc cosine does not exist, that is, the target is traveling too fast to be intercepted. Also, the missile controls only allow firing angles between 20° and 70°.

Finally, according to the diagram the time to intercept is given by

$$i = a/(V_M \sin m - V_T \sin t)$$

and if $i > 10$ sec, the missile will not have enough fuel. If the target can be intercepted, the program is to output FIRE followed by the angle in degrees; otherwise the program is to output DO NOT FIRE.

4. (*Project*): A certain university assigns letter grades of A, B, C, or D for passing coursework, and F for failing coursework. At the student's request, a grade of CR (signifying "passed with credit") or NC (signifying "no credit") is given in place of A, B, C, D, or F. For undergraduates, CR is given in place of A, B, or C, and NC is given in place of D or F; while for graduate students, CR is given in place of A or B, and NC is given in place of C, D, or F. Various other grades may also be given.

Each term, a term grade point average (term GPA) is calculated based on the number of units attempted for the grades of A, B, C, D, or F. Each letter grade is assigned a weight as shown in the table below.

Grade Symbol	Explanation	Weight
A	Outstanding	4
B	Very good	3
C	Average	2
D	Barely passing	1
F	Failure	0

A student taking N courses earns a number of grade points for these courses, namely,

$$G = \sum_{i=1}^{N} w_i u_i$$

where $\begin{cases} w_i \text{ is the weight of the grade obtained for the } i^{th} \text{ course} \\ u_i \text{ is the number of units of the } i^{th} \text{ course} \end{cases}$

The term GPA is then given by

$$GPA = G / \sum_{i=1}^{N} u_i$$

In other words, the GPA is the total number of grade points earned divided by the total number of units attempted for grades of A, B, C, D, or F.

At the same time that the term GPA is calculated, a university GPA averaging all course work at the university (attempted for grades of A, B, C, D, or F) is calculated. Finally, an overall GPA averaging all college work (including transferred coursework) is calculated.

On the basis of these three GPA values, the student's scholastic standings are calculated, according to the following rules:

a. Any student eligible to enroll in the university is said to be in *good standing*. Specifically, all undergraduate students who have at least a 2.0 university GPA and 2.0 overall GPA are in good standing, as are all undergraduate students on probation (see rule b). Also, all graduate students with a university GPA (based on graduate work only) of at least 3.0 are in good standing, as are graduate students on probation.

An undergraduate student may transfer to the university only with a GPA of at least 2.5, and upon transfer is in good standing. Similarly, a graduate student may transfer only with a GPA (based on graduate work) of at least 3.0, and upon transfer is in good standing.

A student who is disqualified is not in good standing (see rule c).

b. An undergraduate student is placed on *probation* if his or her university GPA or overall GPA is less than 2.0. An undergraduate student is continued on probation until both the university GPA and the overall GPA are at least 2.0, or until he or she is disqualified (see rule c).

A graduate student is placed on probation if his or her university GPA (based on graduate work only) is less than 3.0. A graduate student continues on probation until his or her university GPA is at least 3.0, or until he or she is disqualified.

c. An undergraduate student is *disqualified* if either:
   (1) while on probation, he or she fails to obtain a term GPA of at least 2.0; or
   (2) the student has a cumulative deficiency on either university GPA or overall GPA equal to or greater than the following:

Freshmen, sophomores (0–59 units completed)	15 grade points
Juniors (60–89 units completed)	9 grade points
Seniors (90 or more units completed)	6 grade points

In other words, the cumulative deficiency is equal to $(2.0 \times \text{total units attempted}) - (\text{GPA} \times \text{total units attempted})$.

A graduate student is disqualified if, while on probation, the student fails to obtain a term GPA of at least 3.0.

d. Finally, any student is given *dean's list* standing if his or her term GPA is equal to or greater than 3.5, and the number of units attempted (for grades of A through F) is at least 12 for undergraduates or 8 for graduates.

The Problem   After joining the university data processing center, you have been asked to write a procedure which is given

   Student status (freshman, sophomore, . . . , graduate)
   Term GPA for current term
   University GPA for current term
   Overall GPA for current term

and which produces the student's new scholastic standing(s).

1. Is the given input information sufficient to calculate the new scholastic standings? If not, what else is required?
2. Taking into account all necessary input information including the items you mentioned in answer to question 1, draw a decision table showing all input cases and the appropriate results.
3. State how you would develop an acceptance test for this program. How many input points would be required, and how would these be determined?

2.3.3 An Example

2.3.3.1 The Overall Sequence of Steps

Some obviously intended details are often omitted from a specification. In such situations, the designer routinely supplies such details in order to complete the input class. The designer may also find that the precise form of a required calculation has not been stated and that this calculation form can be left as an open question during analysis of the specification, to be resolved later. All such open questions must be noted, however. Analysis of real specifications usually begins by considering missing details and open questions.

   Realistic and reasonable boundaries should be set for the input class. If the input class is too severely restricted, the resulting program may solve an unrealistic problem. Facts bearing on the specification should be sought out to help in determining the boundaries.

   Analysis of a specification is done via the following sequence of steps:

1. Supply noncritical input details or other missing information. Determine open calculation questions.
2. Factor the problem into subproblems if desired.
3. Choose, for each subproblem, the input class and its boundaries. When in doubt, make the most general assumption.
4. Choose the output class and its boundaries.
5. For each input class,
   a. Identify parameters and conditions that affect the processing rules.

b. Determine subclasses based on conditions.

c. Determine all combinations of conditions and the result for each such combination.

2.3.3.2 Statement of the Example Specification

Rocky Raccoon Records is trying to improve record sales. For this purpose, the company has put together a list of names and addresses and has hired the Random Sampling Company to interview the people on this list every month. People on the list will be grouped into four categories, according to their age (age $\leqslant 20$ or age > 20) and sex (male or female), so that the company can examine the various groups that buy its records.

Each person on the list will be asked to state which records of the Top 40 he or she would rank first, second, third, . . . ninth, or tenth. This information, together with the interviewee's name and address, will be keyed into a file for input into a program.

A program is desired that will process the file and print out various lists:

· To find out which records are popular:

  1. A list of the Top 40 titles, in alphabetical order, with the number of times the title was mentioned

  2. A list of the 10 most popular titles, in order of their popularity

· To find out who are the best record customers:

  3. A list of all people who mentioned at least five of the titles in list 2

  4. Four separate lists (one for each of the four categories), each list naming all interviewees in the category who ranked first one of the three titles most popular with people in the category

This specification will be analyzed using the sequence of steps of Section 2.3.3.1.

2.3.3.3 First Steps in Analysis

The first step in the analysis is to look for missing input details. Although the problem requires that interviewees be categorized on the basis of age and sex, it does not explicitly provide for interviewee age and sex to be input.

These are noncritical details we must supply since the problem obviously intends that they be taken into account. We may choose to add age and sex to each interviewee record, or we may choose to pregroup the inputs according to age and sex, thus obtaining four separate sets of input. (The first solution is much preferable.)

Similarly, the problem does not provide for input of a Top 40 list of records. We might assume this list to be present in a table in the program, or (a better solution) we may provide for input of a Top 40 list.

Next, we look for open calculation questions. Note that the term "popular" is not defined. Does it mean the number of times a title is mentioned? If so, this might result in a title that was only mentioned 30 times as a tenth choice being more "popular" than another title that was mentioned 29 times as a first choice, a situation that is not reasonable. Thus the formula for calculating a "popularity function" must be defined by the customer. However, we may (having noted the necessity for defining the formula) proceed with our analysis without knowing the precise formula, just as we might develop the program leaving the popularity calculation as a subroutine to be done later.

For the purpose of analyzing the specification, each of the four subproblems can be dealt with separately. Each subproblem will have the same input but a different output.

What is an input point? Recall that an interviewee response is to have the interviewee's name, address, age, sex (we have added age and sex to the response), and 10 choices of records, $r_1, \ldots, r_{10}$. A response may be written as a sequence of components:

(name, address, age, sex, $r_1, \ldots, r_{10}$)

The Top 40 list T is a list of the Top 40 titles in some order, say, $T = (t_1, \ldots, t_{40})$. Thus an input point is the sequence of components

($\{$(name, address, age, sex, $r_1, \ldots, r_{10}$)$\}$, ($t_1, \ldots, t_{40}$))

that is, it is a set of interviewee responses in conjunction with a Top 40 list.

The following boundaries on the input class seem reasonable:

- The choices $r_1, \ldots, r_{10}$ of each interviewee must correspond to titles on the Top 40 list.
- Each interviewee response must contain at least one choice r_1. (This restriction allows an interviewee to make less than 10 choices. On the other hand, we may require:)
- *Alternate:* Each interviewee response must contain 10 choices.
- If the choices $r_1, \ldots, r_{10}$ are given as titles, these titles must be on the list. If $r_1, \ldots, r_{10}$ are given as integers (where $r_i = n$ signifies choice of the nth title), then we require $0 \leq r_i \leq 40$. ($r_i = 0$ signifies no choice, in case an interviewee response may contain less than 10 choices.)
- *Optional:* Interviewee name and address must correspond to a name and address on a Rocky Raccoon Records customer list. (This restriction assumes that a verified customer list exists, against which the interviewee name and address will be checked. Performing such a check requires input of the verified list.)

2.3.3.4 Analysis of First Subproblem

The first subproblem is the production of a list of all the Top 40 titles, in alphabetical order, with the number of times each title is mentioned.

A next step is to find parameters or conditions whose variations affect the processing rules. The titles of the records will vary, and the problem requires that these titles be sorted into alphabetical order. However, the process sort titles into alphabetical order does not appear to be sensitive to actual titles. How could titles vary and affect the sort function? More precisely, since the input to the sort function is a list of titles, how could variations in the list affect the sort function? Could some particular list cause the sort function to fail?

A variation that could conceivably cause difficulty is the presence of two identical titles. Two song titles could, in fact, be identical if there were renditions by two different performers. To permit this situation, we extend the definition of *title*:

· The term *title* includes the song title, the performer name, the record company, the arranger, and/or other distinguishing text.

It does not make sense that two titles (in this extended sense) could now be identical. We have also discovered an additional boundary condition:

· No two titles (in the extended sense) may be identical.

The sort function will now properly sort a list of titles that meets these boundary conditions.

The number of times that each title is mentioned may also vary. The process of counting these mentions does not appear to be sensitive to the actual counts. Assuming that the order of output of the titles has been decided on, the counting function is not conditional on any actual values or on relations between these values.

We conclude that, provided our boundary conditions are met, there are no variations, either of parameters or of conditions, which affect processing. Accordingly, there are no divisions of the input class. A decision table is not needed since there are no conditions and only one input class.

2.3.3.5 Analysis of Second Subproblem

An output point of the second subproblem is a list of the 10 most popular titles, in order of their popularity. Although the term "popularity" must be further defined, assume for the moment that the term "popularity of the title t" denotes a real number computed by a popularity function $p(t)$. Thus an output is a sequence of 10 titles

$$(t_1{}^*, \ldots, t_{10}{}^*)$$

where $p(t_1^*) > p(t_2^*) > \ldots > p(t_{10}^*)$. An important boundary of the output class is:

- An output list may contain only 10 of the 40 input titles.

This restriction might cause the processing to fail, just as in the payroll program.

Clearly, the number of mentions of each title as a first choice, second choice, and so on, will vary, causing variations in the values $p(t)$. The 10 titles are to be ranked in order of the popularities $p(t)$. This ranking might fail if there were two titles t_i, t_j such that $p(t_i) = p(t_j)$. In this case, neither $p(t_i) > p(t_j)$ nor $p(t_j) > p(t_i)$ is the situation, as the definition above requires. We may envisage three-way "ties," four-way "ties," and so on.

It appears that we have been too hasty in defining an output point. In using the condition $p(t_1^*) > p(t_2^*) > \ldots > p(t_{10}^*)$, we have implicitly adopted the boundary condition that no two popularity values can be equal. This is incorrect because two popularity values, being simply two real numbers, could, in fact, be equal.

The possibility of equal popularity values should not be ignored merely because it seems unlikely. It is conceivable that a customer would wish to consider two popularity values as equal, if they were within a few percent of each other.

To allow for the possibility of equal popularity values, an output can now be defined as a sequence of 10 titles $(t_1^*, \ldots, t_{10}^*)$, where $p(t_1^*) \geq p(t_2^*) \geq \ldots \geq p(t_{10}^*)$, and $p(t_{10}^*) > p(t')$ for all titles t' not in the output list.

The second condition, namely, $p(t_{10}^*) > p(t')$, is necessary if the output list is to stop at precisely 10 titles. But, again, there is a possibility of numeric equality when $p(t_1^*) > \ldots > p(t_9^*)$ and between the next two titles t_i, t_j, we have $p(t_i) = p(t_j)$. In this situation, we cannot list exactly 10 titles.

This situation defines the simple decision table of Table 2.7. When popularity values for the tenth and eleventh titles are equal, the output is not defined.

Table 2.7   Analysis of second subproblem

There are popularity values such that $p(t_{10}^*) > p(t')$ for all titles t' not in output list	True	False
RESULT	Output exactly 10 titles	?

There is no sensible boundary condition that can be imposed to avoid the problem of equal popularity values. The processing function could not simply be adjusted to avoid the problem. Students have proposed various remedies for the condition of equal popularity values, among which are:

- Ignore it.
- Rank the two titles according to their alphabetical order.
- Rank the two titles according to the order in which they were given in the input list T.
- Rank the two titles according to their total number of times mentioned.
- If there is a k-way "popularity tie" among titles for, say, rank n, list *all* k titles as having rank n.
- If there is a k-way tie for rank n, then assign (in any arbitrary order) the ranks n, n+1, . . . , n+k−1 to the titles, printing also an indication of the tie. If t_{10}* in the output list is part of a tie, then include further titles t_{11}*, and so on, as necessary until all titles in the tie are included.

These solutions would provide very different results for identical inputs. For this reason the required processing should be determined in consultation with the customer. It's easy to imagine, for instance, an instructor giving this problem to a class, having in mind one of the above remedies as the "obviously appropriate" response, and marking wrong all of the other remedies. A student would do well to resolve the imperfection in the problem statement before proceeding to a solution.

Analysis of the last two subproblems is left to you.

2.3.4 Clarification and Enhancement of the Specification

2.3.4.1 Completion of Conditions and Boundaries

Explicit statements can be added to a specification to complete the universe of possible values for each individual condition. Such statements clarify the conditions, thereby avoiding inconsistencies and providing for possible error conditions.

Suppose that a specification uses a condition C, stating that the procedure P_2 is used when C=2, and P_4 is used when C=4. We may ask:

- Are there values of the condition C that might arise by accident or by error (as, e.g., 1 or 3 or 5)?
- Are there nonerroneous values of the condition C that may occur, for which no procedures have been specified (as, e.g., 1 or 3 or 5)?—IF SO, THE SPECIFICATION IS NOT COMPLETE!
- How should further condition values be treated?

These questions are answered if the specification contains explicit statements providing for treatment of *all possible values* of C. If such statements are properly phrased, the specification will be consistent with respect to C, and it will also provide for processing of errors. The major variations of such statements are described below:

- *Default statement:* For all values of C not otherwise provided for, the procedure P_D is to be performed. (The values 1,3,5 are all defined as *default values*, and all receive the procedure P_D.)
- *Error statement:* All values not in the set 2,4 (alternatively, not otherwise described) are *error values*, for which the procedure P_E is to be performed. (The values 1,3,5 are all defined as error values, and all receive the procedure P_E.) Error statements and default statements may be given in conjunction, as, for example, in Figure 2.15.

- *Error statement combined with default statement:* For condition C, all values not in the range $2 \leq C \leq 4$ are error values for which P_E is performed. All values not otherwise provided for will receive the processing P_D. (The values 1,5 are defined as error values, receiving P_E, while the value 3 receives P_D.)

In all of these formulations, the input class is extended to include—whether as ordinary values, as error values, or as default values—all values in U_C.

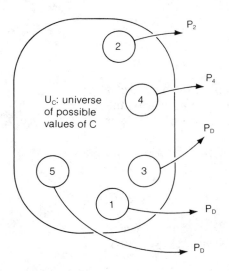

Figure 2.13 Default statement.

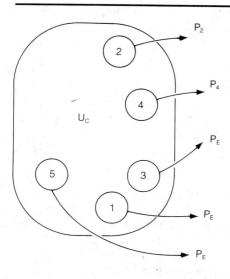

Figure 2.14   Error statement.

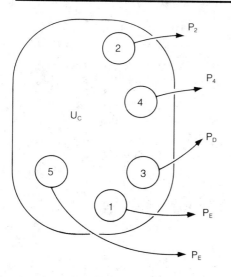

Figure 2.15   Error statement combined with default statement.

Thus provision is made for inputs that include an improper value for C, and for inputs in which a value for C is accidentally omitted. Some examples of default statements and error statements are given below.

2.3.4.2 Default Statements

An example of a default condition occurs in the use of a compiler. Usually a parameter may be given to the compiler, indicating whether or not the source program is to be listed. The parameter typically has the form

LIST   if the input is to be listed
NOLIST   if the input is NOT to be listed

However, if neither value of this parameter is given as input, then *the input is to be processed as if the value LIST had been given.*

In other words, if the input is not given in an expected way, then processing proceeds according to a convention (called the *default convention*) given in the specification. In the example, the default convention is: if neither of the values LIST,NOLIST is given, assume the value LIST. If a specification allows optional parameters but does not include corresponding default statements, the processing function may become undefined in the absence of some optional parameter. We suggest that a default statement be given for every optional parameter, and also for any complicated set of conditions. To allow programs to be easily used, defaults should be assigned to the more usual modes, that is, the modes with the highest percentage of use.

2.3.4.3 Error Statements

Input class boundaries may be given in a fuzzy manner or may not be quite complete. It is important to clarify these boundaries. With respect to a compiler, examples of clarifying questions are:

· Is there a maximum length for the name of a variable?
· If so, what is this maximum?
· Is there a maximum number of entries an array may have? Is there a maximum number of dimensions?

and so on. For each kind of input data, validity checks should be stated that carefully differentiate valid from invalid data.

2.3.4.4 Enhancement of the Specification

An improved specification can be derived to provide ease of use and flexibility and anticipate future extensions in processing. Designing to these more general requirements provides in advance for the anticipated changes, so that the changes can be made more easily.

The goal of such enhancements is to improve the input class or the processing function at low cost, balancing the benefits of each proposed extension against its costs. (Managers constantly speak of the cost/benefit ratio.) In contrast, program designs are commonly arranged for more convenient coding. Such designs usually cause an increased total cost of program use. When programmers impose restrictions on a program for convenience in coding, or "just to get the job done today," they often must recode for a more general situation.

For the example program of Section 2.3.3, possible enhancements are:

· More age categories
· Different age categories for each sex
· Definition of categories via input records, each record giving age bounds and sex for a category
· Categories based on interviewees' addresses
· Weighing of responses based on interviewees' purchases
· Variation in formula for computing popularity
· Choice of popularity formula via an input record
· Variation in the number of records in the Top list
· Calculation of top n records, where n is given on an input record

More enhancements could be suggested. To think of these enhancements, keep in mind the intent of the program, visualize how the program will be used, and then visualize how the user might want to improve it. Then, each enhancement either varies a problem aspect (such as the number of categories, the boundaries of categories, the popularity formula, the number of top records, etc.) or proposes that the aspect be defined via an input control card.

Allowing a problem aspect to be defined by user input is an important kind of enhancement, which forces a flexible program design. However, when definition by a parameter file or by the user at a terminal is allowed, the specification should also include a default statement. For the categories of the example in Section 2.3.3, the default categories could be

    male, age ≤ 20
    male, age > 20
    female, age ≤ 20
    female, age > 20

If the parameter file is incomplete or if the user does not choose categories, the program can print a message and use the default categories.

Some authors have suggested that outputs are the most likely candidates for change and that changes in outputs force changes throughout the rest of the system. Accordingly, provision should be made for enhancements to the required outputs.

2.3.4.5 Acceptance Tests

Specifications sometimes state how potential solutions are to be judged. It is useful to have, before beginning the program design, a criterion that determines whether a potential solution actually works. For this purpose, an acceptance test may be devised to precisely reflect the specification and for which any solution is required to process correctly. The acceptance test serves to clarify the designer's understanding of the specification and is also an instrument to measure the performance of the developed program.

A comprehensive acceptance test will have at least one input for each subclass disclosed by analysis of the specification. Test inputs should contain extreme values of the input range. For example, for an input variable x such that $99 \geqslant x \geqslant -99$, there should be one input with $x=99$ and another with $x=-99$. Test inputs should check special values (an example is 0), in case the input value might be used as a divisor. Finally, the test should try to anticipate incorrect program strategies and should provide inputs that will cause such strategies to fail.

Derivation of tests from decision tables is discussed in detail in Section 9.2.

2.3.4.6 Error Processing

Programs may receive many kinds of erroneous inputs, of varying severity. As an example, for an integer input parameter named year, representing the calendar year and intended to satisfy the bounds $1960 \leqslant year \leqslant 2000$, the following classes of errors may be input:

· A positive integer slightly out of bounds (year=1945 or year=2050)
· A positive integer way out of bounds (year=1305 or year=9999)
· A negative integer (year=−137)
· A decimal number (year=97.6)
· A nonnumeric sequence of alphanumeric characters (year=leap)
· A sequence of arbitrary codes

After the mappings from planned input class to planned output class have been determined, the processing of errors should be considered. The important questions are:

· What are the classes of erroneous inputs?
· Which of these classes will the program process?
· How will these inputs be processed?

These questions cannot be avoided: a program must react either by design or by default to every input, no matter how erroneous. One possible reaction is that the program halts, or aborts. Such a response is undesirable and to be avoided if at all possible.

A second possibility is that the program ignores the input, giving no indication to the outside world or to the program user that an error has occurred. This response is also undesirable.

Preferred responses to error inputs are

· Error messages
· Attempted partial processing (performing all processing that does not require the erroneous information)
· Attempted error correction (attempted discovery of the correct input embodying the intent of the erroneous input)
· Error forgiveness (acceptance of incorrect inputs as correct, if the error is one of format)

Details of the intended error processing should be reviewed with the customer to ensure that the error processing is adequate, and these details should be included in the specification document.

2.3.4.7 Some Final Suggestions

The programming process itself may introduce boundaries or error conditions. For example, restrictions, such as bounds on the number of entries in a table or bounds on the number of letters in a name, may be imposed due to lack of adequate memory space. Every such restriction defines a new error condition since an input that is correct in all other respects is now processed in an unexpected manner. We offer the following suggestions with regard to such restrictions.

1. When in doubt, assume that the most general condition is intended by the specification. For example, if no bound is given for a particular item, the presumption is that no bound is intended. If a "convenient" or "likely" or "usual" restriction is not given, the presumption is that no restriction is intended.

2. Programming-induced restrictions should be avoided if possible. Programmers sometimes introduce gratuitous restrictions for their own convenience ("It makes my program three steps shorter!"). AVOID THIS PRACTICE—it is likely to lead to an incorrect or unacceptable program.

3. Restrictions should be reviewed with the customer (i.e., the original provider of the specifications) since each restriction is essentially a modification of the specification.

4. Restrictions should be combined so that the total effect is as "loose" as possible.

5. Restrictions should be specifically stated (e.g., in a FORTRAN manual).

6. The program should incorporate error diagnostics, to inform the user that a restriction has been violated.

In other words, never introduce any restrictions if they can be avoided, and always document the restrictions you must introduce.

REFERENCES

[Lon 72] London, K. R. *Decision Tables*. Philadelphia: Auerbach, 1972.

[Met 77] Metzner, J. R., and Barnes, B. H. *Decision Table Languages and Systems*. New York: Academic Press, 1977.

[Mon 74] Montalbano, M. *Decision Tables*. Palo Alto, CA: Science Research Associates, 1974.

PROBLEMS

1. Consider one of the problems in Section 2.3.2 or in Appendix D.
   (a) Derive an acceptance test, consisting of *nonerroneous* input points and corresponding output points, via which the program's algorithm can be verified.
   (b) State three problem aspects that could be varied.
   (c) Give five ways in which the specification may be changed so that the desired input class or function or both are improved.

2. (*Project*): After each semester, each student receives a grade report including

   · His or her name and identification number
   · For each course taken in the semester: its course code (e.g., Comp 380), its name (e.g., Program Design), an identification number for the particular section taken, the number of units, and the grade awarded
   · Total units taken in the semester and semester GPA
   · Cumulative units taken and cumulative GPA
   · Scholastic status at the end of the semester (e.g., good standing, probationary, disqualified, or dean's list).

   A new programmer has been assigned to write the program to produce the grade reports. This programmer is from England and does not understand our system of courses, section identifying numbers, grades, units, GPAs, scholastic status, and so on.

   Write a specification describing precisely what the grade report program should do. Your specification should include at least
   (a) All definitions of terms.
   (b) A description of all data items required for the program.

(c) A precise description of the calculations performed by the program.

(d) A decision table showing all input cases and all output results.

(e) A set of test cases (showing input and corresponding output for each case) that will comprehensively test all nonerroneous situations. Use your college's catalog as your source of information.

PROJECT OUTLINE: Analysis of an Activity Specification Analyze a problem in Appendix D, responding in the following order. Supply missing details and note open questions as necessary.

1. Describe a planned input point.

2. Describe the boundaries of the planned input class. Are these boundaries realistic? If not, state why not and give realistic boundaries.

3. What errors might an input point have?

Recall that every error condition is the converse of some boundary condition and vice, versa.

4. Describe an output point.

5. Describe the boundaries of the planned output class.

Your responses to 1 through 5 define the planned input class and the output class you will analyze. Your further responses must refer to these classes.

Your planned input class should have input points for the erroneous inputs specifically mentioned in the problem statement. You may include more errors than the problem statement does, if you also provide appropriate error outputs for the additional errors.

6. List each open question, and assume that answers to all open questions will be given later. (If there are no open questions, just answer "none.") If necessary, assume an answer to each open question, and state the assumption. (For example, if a sort order is not specified, assume either an increasing or decreasing order of elements and construct the subclasses using the assumption.)

7. Derive a decision table showing each distinct combination of input subclasses (i.e., each distinct class of inputs) and the output result (i.e., each distinct class of outputs) for each such combination. If, in response to number 2, you gave realistic boundaries that are larger than the planned boundaries, give input subclasses and results for the additional input points. Discuss as necessary, noting especially any decision table columns for which the results are unknown or contradictory.

Your response to number 7 should constitute the basis for an acceptance test, through which the program's algorithm can be verified. Such a test is required even if the specification is incomplete or inconsistent or if there are open questions. Even under these conditions, the goal is to test as much as possible of the program's intended performance.

Remember also that you are analyzing the *intended* effect of the specification. The method to be used by the required program is *not relevant* in this analysis.

8. Show at least four *nonerroneous* input points and the corresponding output points derived from your answer to number 7, for testing the program's algorithm. Give complete data for each input and output.

9. (a) State three problem aspects that could be varied, in addition to those that already vary in the given specification.

   (b) Describe five ways in which the specification may be changed so that the desired program will be more easy to use, or more flexible to use, or able to accommodate a more general class of inputs.

2.4 QUALITY SPECIFICATIONS

2.4.1 Formal Quality Requirements

The request for a new program always begins with a user's analysis of some situation. The user may have in mind a specific task to be done, but more often she or he has in mind some economic goal (e.g., reduce the cost in billing customers) or some operational goal (e.g., produce a system clerks can use more easily). While perhaps not understanding exactly what the program will do, the user usually has already decided under what conditions the program will be considered successful and under what conditions it will be considered a failure.

In other words, the user has expectations of the program in addition to its performing a specified function. When these expectations are not precisely stated, the program may be unsuccessful or disputes may arise between user and developer. Thus it is important that the user's intent be formally and precisely stated.

A *quality specification* is a precise statement of a set of program characteristics, each characteristic being called a *quality*, or, equivalently, a *quality attribute*. For each quality, a minimum acceptable level, a maximum desired level, and an expected or planned level are specified. A priority ranking and weight are given to each quality attribute [Gilb 77a]. Table 2.8 shows a set of quality attributes, levels, and priorities chosen by Gilb for a portion of a business data processing program [Gilb 81].

Table 2.8   Quality specification for program to factor company accounts receivable (from [Gilb 81]). (Copyright 1981 by Tom Gilb. Reprinted by permission.)

Attribute Characteristics / Name of Attribute	Metric	Worst Case	Planned Level	Best Case	% Weight	More Important Than	Ref to
Reliability	Error rate to client	1/500	1/5000		15%	M	
Maintainability	Bug identification speed	90% in 30 min			15%	A	
Availability	Up % office day	95%	98%	100%	10%		
Cost, $	Per invoice	1.32	0.90	.65	15%	P	
Portability	To any supplier's BASIC	95%	97%		5%		
Security Breach	Customer to customer	1/yr	Never		5%		
Performance	Response under hi load	5 sec 90%	2 sec 95%		5%		
Learning Ease	For our office staff		1 day to solo use		15%	R	
Market Appeal	For external clients		Always judged better		15%	R	

Table 2.8 is intended to summarize on one page all important quality attributes and their characteristics. (The same format, consisting of the boxed-in leftmost column, boxed-in top demarcating columns, and dots indicating the "squares" formed by intersecting rows and columns, is used for all of Gilb's quality specification and review—see Section 3.6.)

The quality attributes are named in the leftmost column. The next column gives a metric (i.e., a unit measurement) to be used in determining the level of each quality. For example, cost is to be measured per invoice. The columns Worst Case, Planned Level, and Best Case are to be (if possible) numeric levels in terms of the stated metric. The Worst Case column designates the minimum acceptable level of the quality: a system not meeting the Worst Case level is unacceptable. For example, if the system cost per invoice is more than $1.32, the system is to be rejected as unacceptable. The Planned Level column designates the planned or target level of the quality, while the Best Case column indicates the highest level likely to be achieved.

The % Weight column gives a weight to be used in determining a single overall quality measure for the system; this technique is discussed in Section 2.4.5. Where two qualities have equal weight, the More Important Than column suggests which quality the designer should give preference to. In Table 2.8, Learning Ease and Market Appeal are both more important than Reliability, and Reliability is more important than Maintainability. Finally, the Ref to column is used to list titles of other documents.

Each system is different, and a quality specification should reflect both the qualities important in the desired system and the required level of each quality. For the system of Table 2.8, qualities such as learning ease and cost are important, processing speed is less important, and memory use is not important enough to be included in the specification. The priorities and weights together indicate precisely which qualities are most important in the system, which are least important, and which are in between. Such statements allow the suitability of different design choices or different design compromises to be gauged effectively. For example, the effect on quality of a simple, slow algorithm using very little memory can be compared to the effect of a more complex, faster algorithm using more memory.

The concept of *quality level* is an important one. It is easy to speak of "low cost" or "high performance," but such phrases do not help a software developer or a tester determine if a required quality has been achieved. Sometimes, of course, more precise descriptions cannot be obtained. Usually, however, a *metric* (i.e., a *unit of measurement*) may be given for a quality (e.g., cost per invoice, as in the table), and a quality level can be stated in terms of this measurement unit (e.g., $.90 cost per invoice). It is easy to determine whether a system meets a quality level stated in these terms.

A quality specification tells the designer which qualities are important in the desired system and what level of each quality is required, just as a precise function specification tells the designer which functions are required. The quality specification then becomes the agreement between user and developer as to the desired qualities and levels of quality in the software system. Without such a specification, there is no precise agreement between user and developer as to quality; there is no detailed information about quality requirements for the designer or later for the system tester; and, consequently, developing a system that meets user expectations will be difficult or impossible.

A related idea is developed by Hetzel [Het 78]. In discussing planning for software development within a corporation, he suggests that a first step in determining software should be formulating broad success and failure criteria that can be meaningfully measured. This step is similar to goal-setting corporate planning done at the start of any project activity, and would develop criteria defining project success and client expectations. Included would be performance measures, cost ranges, and functional specifications. The system would be developed and measured against these criteria. Clients would be urged to view the process as inherently iterative. Systems would not be defined totally in advance but, rather, effort would be spent in making systems flexible and simple in the expectation of change during use and maintenance.

2.4.2 Obtaining Quality Specifications

A quality specification can be obtained through the following three-step process:

1. Define the broad objectives of the system
2. Refine each broad objective into a set of detailed objectives
3. Quantify each detailed objective and desired system quality

Objectives can deal with any aspect of the system: its economic impact (reduction of cost or of time), its impact on personnel (ease of use or shifting of jobs in an organization) or its operational characteristics (response time, reliability, portability, etc.). A user typically has in mind some broad objectives and also some specific operational qualities.

The user should be encouraged to think of all the broad objectives the system should meet. This is important since the user may have conflicting objectives that should be discussed.

Each broad objective should then be refined into a set of detailed objectives. For example, the objective "improve the processing of client bills" might be refined as one or more of the following: reduce the cost of producing client bills; reduce the processing time in producing client bills; reduce the elapsed time (calendar time); process the bills with a reduced work force; and/or process an increased number of bills with a reduced work force.

The final step, quantification of each detailed objective, allows for measurement of the system with respect to the desired goal or quality. Table 2.9 shows qualitative and quantitative forms for several types of goals.

Table 2.9   Qualitative and quantitative goals

Qualitative Goals	Quantitative Goals
Reduce the cost of producing client bills	Reduce cost of producing client bills by at least 3%
Reduce cost of producing client bills	Reduce cost of producing client bills to no more than $5.00 per bill
Reduce processing time	Reduce time by 20%
Reduce processing time	Reduce time to no more than 1 hour
Reduce operator time necessary to enter information	Reduce operator time necessary to enter information to 20 seconds
Reduce elapsed time in a combined manual and program system	Reduce elapsed time to no more than 3 days
Process more transactions	Process 10% more transactions per minute
Process bills with reduced work force	Process the same number of bills per month with 10% fewer personnel
Process an increased number of bills with decreased work force	Process 10% more bills per month with 10% less people
System will be easy to use	After 1 day's instruction and 1 week's use of the system, the user will perform no slower than before the system was installed. After 1 month, the user will do work 20% faster [Meh 81].
System will be easy to use	(For systems whose use is voluntary) 70% of those with access to the system will choose to use it at least 20% of the time [Meh 81].

If the characteristics of the existing system have been analyzed, these detailed objectives can be translated into system qualities. For example, suppose the existing system processes 100 transactions per minute. The objective "process 10 percent more transactions per minute" then translates to the quality Transaction Rate, with the metric "per minute," and a planned level of 110. As a general rule the user should not be worse off with the new system than with the existing system; hence the Transaction Rate should have a worst case value of 100.

Likewise, the goal "reduce operator time necessary to enter information to 20 seconds" translates to the quality Operator Entry Time, with the metric "seconds," and a planned level of 20. If the existing system is known to take 30 seconds, then the worst case value for Operator Entry Time should be 30.

The refinement and quantification of objectives leads to a testable quality specification. In other words, we can objectively determine whether a system has met the specification. A related technique, which has been used to achieve testable and flexible specifications for small-to-medium systems, is the *requirements/properties matrix* [Boe 74]. A matrix is drawn in which each column is a requirement, and a row is assigned to each of the properties testability and modifiability, as in Table 2.10. Each broad system requirement is examined with respect to these properties, and the requirement is expanded as necessary to achieve them. Additional rows can be added for other properties, such as portability, maintainability, and so on.

Table 2.10   Requirements/properties matrix

Property \ Requirement	The system shall respond immediately to each user request.
Testability	When the number of users is ≤4, the system shall respond to each user request within 1 second; when the number of users is 5 to 8, the system shall respond in 3 seconds.
Modifiability	The user shall be able, by inserting the proper parameter, to designate no more than 2 user terminals that will always receive responses in 1 second.

Testability is achieved by refining and quantifying each broad system requirement, as in the formulation of a quality specification. Modifiability is achieved through use of an alternate parameterized (but still quantified) requirement.

Table 2.10 shows that the response requirement has been refined into two requirements: a response time for one to four users and a response time for five to eight users, each with a metric, "seconds." The information in the Testability row can immediately be placed in a quality specification such as Table 2.8, provided that it is further refined to indicate whether the measures of 1 second and 3 seconds are worst case measures or planned measures. The information in the Modifiability row (or other rows if used) can also be further refined and put into a quality specification format. In sum, the requirements/ properties matrix is a useful way of organizing the refinements of broad system requirements or desired qualities so that these requirements can be put into a quality specification.

2.4.3 Measurement of Quality Attributes

Quality attributes such as response time, input traffic capacity per unit time, memory requirements, and so on can be specified. In many instances, quality attributes not usually considered to be measurable can, in fact, be measured even though only crude measures (e.g., garbage in does not lead to garbage out) or specially invented measures may be necessary [Gilb 77a].[3] Indeed, the use of such measurements may be the only way that software development can be successfully managed [Het 78].

---

[3]Other discussions of measurement of quality of system performance can be found in [Lig 76 and Walt 79].

As an example, *maintainability* can be defined as the probability that, when maintenance action is begun under stated conditions, a failed system will be restored to operable condition within a specified time. In line with this definition, a possible performance specification is that 95 percent of all program bugs causing serious problems can be repaired within an hour. Assuming clarification of the phrase "serious problems," this specification has a clear interpretation, and the program's performance with respect to the specification can be measured. Table 2.8 has a similar maintainability measure: 90 percent of bugs are to be fixed within 30 minutes.

Let us assume that maintenance programmers file reports noting the time spent on each bug. After a suitable number of bugs (say, 100) have been dealt with, a graph can be drawn showing the number of repairs effected in 10 minutes or less, the number that required 10 to 20 minutes, and so on. From this graph it can be determined if 95 percent of the bugs fixed were repaired within 1 hour. If desired, the graph can be extrapolated to give a curve showing the probability of repair within 10 minutes, within 10 to 20 minutes, and so on.

A crude measure is obtained this way, since repair time varies depending on the programmer maintaining the system, the various delays (e.g., in bringing the maintainer to the scene, getting a run, etc.), and the time after installation (e.g., one week, three months) at which the measurements are begun. Nevertheless, adjustments can be made for these factors, and the definition does give some management control (analogous to the standard repair estimates commonly used for cars) instead of no control at all.

Well-written contracts for systems involving software have for many years used such measures [Gilb 77a]. In such contracts, if a computer is inoperable for any reason due to a vendor-supplied product, then the time interval between system failure and repair is noted in a log, and vendors who take too long to repair the software are subject to penalties. A book on software contracts [Bern 74] states:

> Error correction during the warranty period should always specify the "turnaround time" for repairs, i.e., the responsiveness required of the vendor in repairing user-detected errors, particularly errors which jeopardize the buyer's ability to perform the tasks for which he bought the software.

As another example, *portability*, the property that allows a system to be moved from one environment to another with relative ease, may be quantified by specifying the degree of necessary conversion. In other words, a system is 95 percent portable if the conversion for the new environment costs no more than 5 percent of the original programming and debugging costs (not counting system analysis and design), with the proviso that operational cost and reliability of the converted program not be degraded below the levels for 100 percent portable programs and files. The required conversion must include all programs, machine language subroutines, control cards, necessary software, job operational specifications, and physical and logical file data conversion. Table

2.8 specifies a 95 percent portability level to any BASIC system (presumably the desired system is to be coded in BASIC).

Robustness, another system property, is composed of three factors:

· The ease with which the specified output is produced for an input within the planned input class
· The extent to which unacceptable consequences are minimized for inputs within the planned input class
· The ease with which erroneous inputs are handled and the seriousness of the effects of those improperly handled

When we say a program is robust, we have in mind that it responds well, in the vast majority of cases, to the given inputs. Roughly speaking, robustness signifies the extent to which the system fulfills its functional specification, taking into account the actual input traffic (i.e., mix of input types). In contrast, a program is *correct* if and only if it produces the specified output for every input within the planned space. From a practical viewpoint, robustness is more important than correctness: "Even a formally incorrect program may be usable if its errors are minor in effect, and a correct program may be unusable if it does not satisfy robustness, utility or performance criteria" [Good 79].

Possible performance specifications are:

1. The system shall handle incorrectly no more than 0.01 percent of the transactions processed.
2. The system shall produce unacceptable consequences for no more than 0.01 percent of the transactions processed.
3. The system shall detect and treat for errors at least 99 percent of the erroneous inputs, and shall fail for no more than 0.01 percent of such inputs, and the downtime shall not exceed an average of 1 hour for each such failure.

Measures may be assigned to *reliability*, the probability that the system will perform with no malfunctions for at least a given time interval, under stated conditions. Note that the phrase "with no malfunctions" may be subjective, so that agreement between user and vendor is needed. Typically, reliability depends on actual operating time, downtime due to maintenance or repair time; and time spent in waiting for manuals, parts, or programmers. A possible performance specification is: the system shall have a probability of .91 of performing with no malfunctions during at least a 24-hour interval.

The definitions given here for maintainability, portability, robustness, and reliability are not necessarily most appropriate for all systems. It is only necessary that user and developer agree on the definitions used. Definitions of metrics for many attributes are given in Part II of Gilb's *Software Metrics* [Gilb 77a].

When an existing manual or automated system is being replaced, the quality levels of the existing system can be measured in accordance with the definitions adopted and can be noted on the attribute specification, using an Existing Levels column. This procedure can help the user and developer to understand the required changes in quality.

2.4.4 Use of Quality Levels in Tradeoffs

The quality levels collectively provide a quality specification against which the desired system can be judged. By designating the acceptable bounds of quality, this specification provides a *quality space* within which design tradeoffs can be made. Alternatively, the quality specification might be used to identify alternate potentially successful systems, each of different cost and quality, from which the user could choose.

Experience has shown that, especially for large systems, perfection of any quality attribute is impossible, and that the cost of attaining successive increments of quality increases as the system approaches perfection. For example, bringing a system from a reliability of .9999 to a reliability of .99995 might require doubling the testing cost. (This is an instance of the law of diminishing returns. To move a system closer and closer to some performance asymptote, successively larger amounts of effort are required for each successive smaller increment of performance.) Thus the quality specification could be used to find an optimal design specification giving a best balance between quality and cost.

2.4.5 A Single Quality Measure

It is useful to be able to give a single number as a measure of quality, so different systems or different variants of a system can be compared. Gilb [Gilb 77a] suggests giving points for each quality, ranging from 0 (barely acceptable) to 5 (average) to 10 (superterrific), and then weighting each measure. For example, in Table 2.8, the reliability points will be weighted 15 percent; the maintainability measure, 15 percent; the availability points, 10 percent; and so on. Thus a system rated at 7 for reliability, 4 for maintainability, and 8 for availability would receive

$$(7 \times 0.15) + (4 \times 0.15) + (8 \times 0.10) = 1.05 + 0.60 + 0.80 = 2.45$$

weighted points for reliability, maintainability, and availability combined. Since the weight given to a quality determines its influence on the final quality measure, assigning the weights is equivalent to saying which qualities are most important in the desired system.

A system evaluation technique called MECCA (for Multi-Element Component Comparison and Analysis) uses percentage weighting and also a hierarchy of attributes [Gilb 77a]. The attributes or objectives used in the evaluation are arranged into a hierarchical structure, and a percentage weight is assigned to each component attribute throughout the structure. Figure 2.16 shows a MECCA model used by the Swedish military to compare several data base management software packages.

The scheme specifies that in evaluating the Data Base Software Utility, the measure obtained for Fundamental Data Organization will count 35 percent, the measure obtained for Systematization will count 20 percent, and so on. In evaluating Fundamental Data Organization, the measure obtained for Data Structure will count 40 percent and the measure obtained for Accessibility will count 60 percent. Obviously, many more levels could be used, and evaluations of large systems may involve hundreds of elements.

A MECCA model is intended to show a strict hierarchy. The components of each attribute are assumed to be independent. If, however, attribute x is a component of both y and z, then it will appear twice in the structure. If two attributes actually overlap due to an unnamed common component, then the structure will unduly emphasize that component. For this reason, an attempt is made at each level to choose qualities that do not overlap.

The hierarchy shows the level of generality of each attribute and how attributes combine to form other attributes. Thus the diagram gives a framework for discussing either the evaluation of given systems or the relations between design choices.

The MECCA model systematizes the evaluation procedure by explicitly identifying every attribute and every component attribute to be considered and the relative importance to be attached to each attribute or component. The particular attributes and components chosen, and the relative importance attached to each, will depend strongly on the application and environment at hand. The practice of explicitly identifying everything allows the model itself to be varied and evaluated. For example, the relative weights could be varied and alternative evaluations corresponding to each set of weights could be obtained. Also, the validity and adequacy of the model can be examined. For example, the model of Figure 2.16 does not include such factors as costs, personnel resources, maintenance, and control of growth. Because the factors considered are explicitly stated, these inadequacies can easily be seen and corrected.

Gilb warns that just going through the exercise of model-making does not guarantee a good—or even adequate—model. For example, the model of Figure 2.16 lacks quality attributes which are vital for a military system, such as reliability, recovery, accuracy, performance, and portability to a backup system. Great care must always be taken to ensure that the system truly reflects user requirements. The model of Figure 2.16 would be much better if a general had written it (says Gilb), since it would then include the qualities vital for a military system.

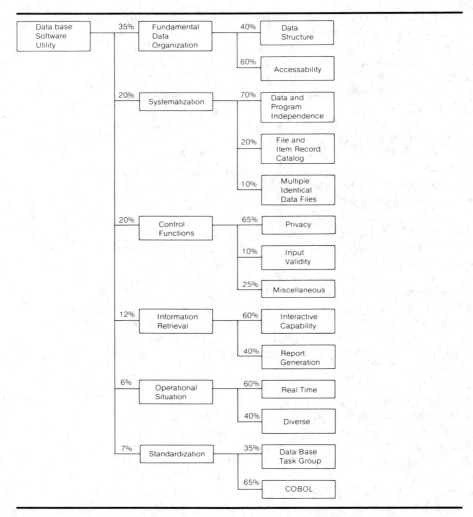

Figure 2.16   A MECCA model for system evaluation (from [Gilb 77a]). (Copyright 1977 by Tom Gilb. Reprinted by permission.)

Once the model has been developed, appropriate facts about the lowest level qualities are collected. These facts might include user experiences with the system; references to manuals, handbooks, or sales offers; references to contract clauses; or references to performance tests or measures of storage use. Then, based on these facts, a numeric measure is assigned for each lowest level quality, again using the range from 0 (barely acceptable) to 5 (average) to 10 (superterrific). Once the lowest level numeric measures have been assigned,

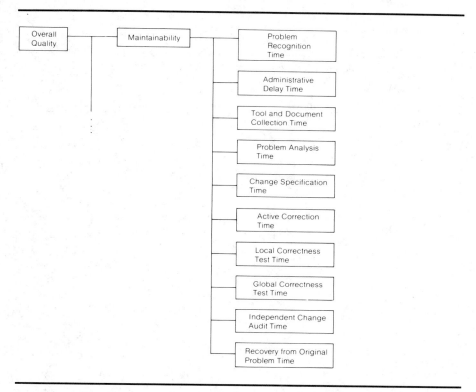

Figure 2.17 Subsidiary qualities in a quality evaluation model.

the evaluation is complete, and the points can simply be totaled up. As an example of this step, suppose that, in Figure 2.16, the quality Interactive Capability is assigned a measure of 7 and Report Generation is assigned a measure of 3. Then the quality Information Retrieval will be assigned the measure $(7 \times 0.6)+(3 \times 0.4)=4.2+1.2=5.4$. Later, when the measure of Data Base Software Utility is calculated, the contribution of Information Retrieval will be $5.4 \times 0.12 = 0.648$.

2.4.6 Specifying a Hierarchy of Attributes

A quality specification can be devised as a hierarchy of quality attributes, similar to the hierarchy of Figure 2.16. If it is appropriate, any quality may be regarded as being composed of subsidiary qualities, just as in Figure 2.16 Information Retrieval is regarded as being composed of Interactive Capability and Report Generation. Similarly, any of these subsidiary qualities may be "exploded" in the same way.

Table 2.11 Maintainability specification.

Goal Attribute / Subgoal	Measure	Worst Case	Planned Level	Best Case	Weight	More Important Than	Reference
Problem Recognition Time	(Clock time)	24 hr	60 min	1 min			
Administrative Delay Time		1 week	60 min	5 min			
Tool and Document Collection Time		1 hr	10 min	2 min			
Problem Analysis Time	90% solved in	50 min	5 to 10 min	30 sec			Artificial bug test
Change Specification Time		1 hr	5 min??	30 sec			
Active Correction Time		3X prob an. time	3 X prob. an. time?	30 sec			
Local Correctness Test Time		1 hr	5 min	5 min			
Global Correctness Test Time		1 day	100 X active correct	?			
Independent Change Audit Time		2 week (wait for)	Same day before use	Same hour			
Recovery from Original Problem Time		Same day	2 hr				

First published in the *Pergamon Infotech State of the Art Report on Structured Software Development*, Pergamon Infotech Ltd., 1979. Reprinted by permission of Tom Gilb.

For example, in discussing a definition of maintainability we noted that the time necessary to correct an error depends on the time required to get a maintenance programmer to the scene, the time required to make a correction run, and so on. These subsidiary factors can be brought explicitly into the quality evaluation model, as in Figure 2.17. Specific quality levels are then given only for the most subsidiary quality factors, as in Table 2.11. In this way, a more precise quality specification is obtained.

REFERENCES

[Bern 74] Bernacchi, R. L., and Larsen, G. H. *Data Processing Contracts and the Law*. Boston: Little, Brown, 1974.

[Boe 74] Boehm, B. W. "Some Steps toward Formal and Automated Aids to Software Requirements Analysis and Design," *Proceedings of IFIP Congress 74*, 1974.

[Boe 78] ———, et. al. *Characteristics of Software Quality*. Amsterdam: North Holland, 1978.

[Coop 79] Cooper, J. D., and Fisher, M. J. (eds.). *Software Quality Management*. New York: Petrocelli Charter, 1979.

[Gilb 77a] Gilb, T. *Software Metrics*. Cambridge, MA: Winthrop, 1977.

[Gilb 79] ———. "Structured Design Methods for Maintainability," *Infotech State of the Art Report on Structured Software Development*, Infotech, Maidenhead, England, 1979.

[Gilb 81] ———. "Design by Objectives: A Structured Systems Architecture Approach." Unpublished manuscript, 1981.

[Good 79] Goodenough, J. B. "A Survey of Program Testing Issues," in P. Wegner (ed.), *Research Directions in Software Technology*. Cambridge, MA: M.I.T. Press, 1979.

[Het 78] Hetzel, B. "A Perspective on Software Development," *Proceedings of 3rd International Conference on Software Engineering*. (IEEE Catalog No. 78CH1317-7C.) New York: IEEE Computer Society, 1978.

[Lig 76] Light, W. "Software Reliability/Quality Assurance Practices," *Proceedings from the Software Management Conference*. AIAA, 1976.

[McCal 77] McCall, J. A.; Richards, P.; and Walters, G. "Factors in Software Quality," 3 vols., AD-A049-014, 015, 055. NTIS, 1977.

[McCal 79] ———. "An Introduction to Software Quality Metrics," in J. D. Cooper and M. J. Fisher (eds.), *Software Quality Management*. New York: Petrocelli Charter, 1979.

[Meh 81] Mehlmann, M. *When People Use Computers*. Englewood Cliffs, NJ: Prentice-Hall, 1981.

[Walt 79] Walters, Gene F. "Application of Metrics to a Software Quality Management Program," in J. D. Cooper and M. J. Fisher (eds.), *Software Quality Management*. New York: Petrocelli Charter, 1979.

PROBLEMS

---

1. Derive a MECCA quality evaluation model, like Figure 2.16, which your English instructor can use in grading essay papers.

2. Derive a MECCA quality evaluation model that you would like your program design instructor to use in grading design proposals.

3. (a) Derive a MECCA quality evaluation model for evaluating new automobiles.
   (b) Evaluate three new automobiles with respect to this model.
   (c) Discuss the model. What are the reasons for the particular qualities and weights you chose?
   (d) What is the effect on the three evaluations of variations in the weights?

4. Derive a MECCA quality evaluation model for evaluating microcomputers, and evaluate three popular microcomputers with respect to this model. (Consult magazines such as *Creative Computing* and *Byte*.)

5. Derive a MECCA quality evaluation model for evaluating programs. Evaluate Problem C in Appendix E with respect to this model.

6. You have just been offered three different software jobs. Thy are in different parts of the country, in companies of small, middle, and large size; and have different salaries and deal with different areas of software. Derive a MECCA evaluation model you could use in deciding which job to take.

7. Derive a quality specification of the type of Table 2.8 for:
   (a) The student registration system described in Chapter 1.
   (b) An airlines reservation system.
   (c) A system to solve one of the problems in Appendix C.

PROJECT OUTLINE: Overall Problem Requirements

Introduction

This project summarizes all of the steps discussed in this chapter for reviewing problem requirements, understanding intent, and analyzing specifications. Each section of the project considers a specific aspect. Review of a requirement or specification following these steps should produce a comprehensive specification document that both the customer and the program developer can understand and that can constitute the agreement between them as to the desired program and desired qualities.

A. Requirements Diagrams

1. Derive a complete set of requirements diagrams for the given problem requirement or program specification, with as many levels of refinement diagrams as necessary. Use a consistent numbering scheme for activities (e.g., the subactivities of activity 3 are 3.1, 3.2, and so on). For hints on details and procedures, see the problems and project outline of Section 2.1.

2. Include a complete data dictionary and a list of all lowest level activities for which specifications are required.

3. If the diagrams developed in steps 1 and 2 are physical diagrams (i.e., stating requirements in terms of specific organizations, personnel, and physical data forms), derive a complete set of logical diagrams (i.e., state requirements in terms of abstract activities and logical data entities).

B. Analysis and Testing

Perform the steps of this section for each lowest level logical activity obtained in Section A. For hints on details and procedures, see the project outline of Section 2.3.

1. List all components of the planned input, give realistic boundaries for the planned input class, and indicate input errors that will be tested. List all components of the output.

2. Derive a decision table showing all input subclasses and the result for each input subclass, suitable for program testing. List all open questions, as well as assumptions made in constructing the table. Indicate all subclasses for which no output is provided, or for which conflicting outputs are specified. Suggest appropriate default conventions and error statements.

3. List any enhancements that could be provided at low cost for the input class or for the activity function.

C. Intent, Enhancements, and Quality

1. State briefly the intent of the overall program system, its mode of use, and its purpose. Indicate which functions and which qualities are most important for this system.

2. State how the desired intent, mode of use, purpose, important functions, and important properties might change in the future. Specifically, for the next 1-year, 2-year, and 5-year periods, consider the effects of:

· Growth or shrinkage of the company business
· Growth or shrinkage of the budget allocated to this system

In each of these periods, decide what are reasonable minimum and maximum expectations for the company business and the system budget.

3. Derive a requirements/properties matrix listing all overall system requirements, expanded as necessary so as to be testable and modifiable.

4. Provide default conventions and/or error statements for all important conditions and boundaries.

5. List the classes of errors that will be processed and the intended processing for each error class.

6. Derive a MECCA quality evaluation model and quality specification for the desired system.

chapter three
The Design Concept

3.1 THE DESIGN APPROACH

3.1.1 Overview

When the requirements of a desired system are understood,[1] a program can be designed to meet those requirements. Next to understanding the problem, design is the most important development step. The design lays the foundation for the coding, testing, and maintenance activities and also determines how well the end product will meet its requirements.

A design concept is a plan, or scheme of action, which outlines how a desired program will perform its intended function. It previews the characteristics of the intended program, just as an architect's blueprint previews the features of an intended building. This way the major details of a proposed solution can be determined before coding begins, so that that solution can be compared with alternative solutions and the intended program can be improved before commitments are made to specific programming details. Designing is thus planning in advance, which is quite different from coding. Planning and previewing can reduce costs; it has been said that "a dollar more spent in design would have saved 5 dollars spent on testing and maintenance" [Alb 76].

The design concept does not deal with small details, such as the exact format of an input record, but may give a detailed solution for a critical part of the problem. Analogously, an architect's blueprint of a house does not show every nail and usually indicates large portions of the proposed construction method by a footnote or two. However, critical construction points (e.g., the way that two large exposed beams are to be attached) are shown in great detail.

The broad yet precise presentation of a design concept shows the overall approach, omitting noncritical details but carefully detailing solutions to critical issues. As they gain experience, designers learn to think in just this way, keeping in mind the "big picture" while simultaneously zeroing in on critical issues and conditions that must be detailed.

---

[1]One should maintain a critical attitude toward specifications during design, since new difficulties with specifications may arise.

Either the overall design approach or the critical algorithms can be the key to a particular design, and sometimes both are required. In some situations, the entire design depends on a few critical algorithms. In other situations, there is a mass of detailed requirements, and achievement of a short, simple, and reliable program requires an overall design approach that provides general rules and abstractions covering the many cases with as few exceptions as possible. Section 3.1.4 presents some general design principles.

3.1.2 Contents of This Chapter

This chapter presents overall approaches based on data flow techniques. Section 3.2 introduces the data flow diagram, which annotates the important data blocks, data transformations, and movements of data of a design approach. The data flow diagram is very much like the requirements diagram of Chapter 2. As part of the introduction, Section 3.2 shows the development and improvement of a data flow diagram for a simple problem, including using the diagram in a low-level, mechanical way to determine which actions should be subroutines, and to improve the arrangement of data.

For small but complex systems, data flow concepts can be used systematically to determine an appropriate set of data blocks and processes. Section 3.3 presents design methods and shows the design for a small problem that inherently requires a chain of data transformations. These transformations can be blocked out in a straightforward way using data flow concepts, and a small (about 300 line) program can be derived directly from the data flow diagram. Nevertheless, without the use of a data flow diagram, students have found it difficult to understand the required program structure. Once the necessary data flows are seen, the program becomes straightforward.

Section 3.4, following Jackson [Jac 78], shows that one can first build a simulation model of the real-life system underlying the software and then incorporate desired software functions into the simulation model. The resulting design then corresponds closely to the underlying real-life system and can easily accommodate changes in requirements.

A design concept can be documented in a preliminary way or in an ongoing, detailed way leading to a final design description. Section 3.5 discusses both kinds of documentation. Section 3.5.1 discusses the design proposal, a preliminary writeup meant to convince readers that the proposed solution is feasible and appropriate. To be convincing, the proposal broadly outlines the proposed solution to show the overall approach, and it also considers and resolves critical issues.

Section 3.5.2 describes the working design manual [Ogd 78], a style of ongoing documentation that aids the design process. Information, problems, and decisions are noted in the working design manual informally and continually as events occur. The manual becomes an ongoing reference manual for project personnel, and later it can be a source of ideas for similar projects. This style of documentation can also be used in the requirements analysis, coding, and testing phases.

If quality objectives are to be met, it is important that the work be checked at every level. Section 3.6 describes methods and criteria to use in reviewing designs.

3.1.3 Relation to Other Chapters

A design concept can be detailed or it can be a global concept that just blocks out subsystems. A detailed approach is appropriate for small systems; for large systems, it is better to use a global blockout together with a detailed approach for each blocked-out subsystem.

Experience has shown that, for large systems, the crucial difficulties are organizational. That is, difficulties center around the organization of modules and the required schedules for module implementation and testing. Accordingly, for large systems, a data flow diagram can be used in a simple, straightforward way to block out subsystems. The required organization of program modules and the relations between these modules can be developed by the methods of Chapters 4 and 5.

A small complex system, such as the one in Section 3.3, might be organized as a collection of modules, or it might be implemented as a single module. Both alternatives are pursued for the diagram developed in Section 3.3. Section 5.3 shows how an organization of program modules can be developed from the system diagram developed in Section 3.3, while Section 7.2 shows the development of the structured text of a single module.

On the other hand, experience has shown that for small systems, the crucial difficulties center on critical problems. Accordingly, in a design concept for a small system, the components are first laid out in the overall approach and then are examined to identify critical problems. Such critical problems may be either important data transformations accidentally omitted from the design, or they may be nonobvious algorithms whose feasibility must be established. The design concept shows a solution for each critical problem.

Section 3.3 identifies a critical problem, which is discussed in Section 6.1. In general, Section 6.1 discusses the identification and handling of critical problems, as well as methods of obtaining greater efficiency. Section 6.1 also presents techniques to bound the calculations, heuristics that deal quickly with prevalent cases, and certain precalculations that can be added to the solution as refinements. Thus the discussion of Section 3.3 may be appropriately followed either by Chapters 4 and 5, which discuss module organizations, or by Chapter 6, which deals with the design of single modules.

3.1.4 General Design Principles

Below are some useful design principles. The discussion in Section 8.2.1.3 illustrates many of these points.

3.1.4.1 Conform to Requirements

Design techniques (whether presented here or elsewhere) provide only a guide for working through a design procedure. They cannot ensure the adequacy of a design. Only the designer can ensure that adequacy, by keeping in mind the larger issues as the design is worked through.

The most basic issue in design is conforming to the requirements—stated and implied, present and future. In addition to being correct, a system should be well suited to its users. Thus the designer must keep in the mind the substance, the circumstances, and the physical appearance (via printed pages, cathode ray tube screens, etc.) of messages from system to user and from user to system (via typewriter, magic pad, etc.). Communication with surrounding computer systems must also be kept in mind.

Requirements almost always change as a system is developed and used. They become broader and more complex or require that the system be used in new ways. Sometimes the requirements cannot be fixed until the user has worked with a prototype system, so that iterations in design are necessary during system development. A good designer anticipates such changes and provides in the design for each.

The goal of conforming to requirements has been built into the design maxims of many authors:

- *"Design to influence human behavior."* Lucas, Jr.
- *"Design for reliability and adaptability."* Warnier [Orr 77].
- *"Design for evolution and repair."* Corbató and Clingen [Cor 79].
- *"Design for ease of system expansion and contraction."* Parnas [Par 79].

Lucas's maxim concerns suitability to users, while the other three emphasize provision for robustness, change, and maintenance. Programs have to be developed carefully to provide for repair, but they later repay the effort.

Robustness is achieved by eliminating or relaxing restrictions on inputs whenever possible, by causing programs to react to inputs in a common-sense way, and by comprehensive treatment of bad as well as good data, including error processing and error recovery procedures [Jac 75].

Other maxims suggest ways to achieve adaptability: *"Design so that decisions are decoupled."* *"Design so as to separate concerns."* That is, the design should be arranged so that different design decisions do not affect each other or, in other words, so that different concerns are reflected in different portions of the design. Thus each design decision does not permeate the whole system but instead corresponds to a portion of the design—a "locality." The system should be arranged as a collection of independent subsystems, just as in a car the suspension system and the electrical system are independent.

Adaptability (the ability of a system to be easily maintained, modified, or enhanced) is, of course, a quality, and we might think of including adaptability in the quality specification. However, as can be seen from the maxims above, adaptability is mandatory in every design, except perhaps in the most extraordinary circumstances. We might almost say that it is better for a program to be easy to correct than to be actually correct but not modifiable.

3.1.4.2 Keep the Future in Mind

As the design is developed, it is important for the designer to keep in mind possible future enhancements and generalizations of the required processing. General actions or objects should be used to satisfy such future enhancements whenever the more general solution does not introduce too much complexity. Do not be afraid to consider a more general form of the problem; it often happens that the solution to a general problem is simpler and more effective than the solution to a restricted problem.

3.1.4.3 Problems of Scale

Successful programs are much used, and, as they are used, they are commonly required to handle more situations. Designers need to watch for variables or conditions that presently have only a few values but may potentially have many values. An example is the number of response categories in the example of Section 2.3.3. In such situations, it is best to use a general or structured approach that provides in advance for the potentially many values. Section 3.2.3 develops a design for the example of Section 2.3.3 and shows such an approach. See also the plotter control program in Section 8.2.1.3, in which a general solution provides for potential enhancements and also simplifies the design.

3.1.4.4 Divide and Conquer

Designers should separate a problem into independent subproblems. When each of the independent subproblems is solved separately, the group of solutions is the solution of the total problem. This is perhaps the most fundamental principle in design. It has been nicknamed "divide and conquer," and is part of the stepwise refinement technique of Chapter 7.

. Another way of stating this maxim is: separate a complex data transformation into a sequence of simpler independent transformations.

3.1.4.5 Evaluate for Improvement

Every completed plan should be evaluated for possible improvement. That is, designers should try to recognize subroutines, by looking for sets of identical actions performed on slightly varying objects; should try to combine actions using the same data; and should try to generalize the data, in order to reflect enhancements.

REFERENCES

[Alb 76] Alberts, D. S. "The Economics of Software Quality Assurance," *Proceedings of National Computer Conference*, New York, 1976. (Also in [Mil 78].)*

[Jac 78] Jackson, M. A. "Information Systems: Modelling, Sequencing and Transformations," *Proceedings of 3rd International Conference on Software Engineering*. (IEEE Catalog No. 78CH1317-7C.) New York: IEEE Computer Society, 1978. (Also in [Ram 78].)*

[Ogd 78] Ogdin, C. A. *Software Design for Microcomputers*. Englewood Cliffs, NJ: Prentice-Hall, 1978.

3.2 INTRODUCTION TO DATA FLOW

3.2.1 Overview

All software systems may be classified with respect to two properties. First, a system may be *embedded*, having inputs from another system, or outputs to another system, or both. Second, a system may be an *updating* system, holding data for its own reuse and updating the data at each execution (inventory control systems and accounts payable systems are examples of updating systems).

Of necessity, the design of embedded systems must carefully consider the format of communications between systems. The design of updating systems must be concerned with the structure of collections of data reused by the system or used by several systems.

Since businesses traditionally maintain many different types of ongoing records, most business data processing systems are updating systems, and

---

*See Appendix B: Bibliography.

many are also embedded systems. As a result, design of business data processing systems has long been concerned with input and output data formats, and with record, file, and data base design. In addition, business data processing has been concerned with input processing and editing methods that preserve the reliability of input data. These concerns have been found to be important in other kinds of systems, such as operating systems, systems executing on microcomputers, and extensible systems that modify their behavior by examining data held from one execution to another.

The design approach presented here, called the *data flow* approach, shares the concerns of business data processing.[2] Data-flow-based design methodologies have been proposed for business data processing systems [Jac 75] and for other kinds of systems [Ste 74, You 75b]. The approach has also been used to design operating systems [Phi 67, Phi 71].

Figure 3.1 diagrams the payroll program of Chapter 2 in terms of the processes and files required and the information flows to or from each file. This style of diagramming is common in business programming. A diagram of a program in terms of its data objects (such as files, arrays, or flags) and its processing actions, showing what data are used by each action and where each action places data, is called a *data flow diagram*.

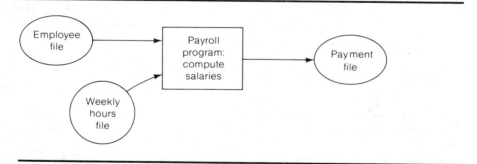

Figure 3.1 Data flow diagram of a payroll program.

[2]Business data processing has other special concerns. Business processing schedules normally fall into predictable calendar patterns. Thus, business system design is concerned with the actual time at which a result is produced, the timeliness of the result, and how a desired system fits into ongoing processing. Program structure may depend on the calendar time at which a program is run, the calendar frequency at which it is run, and the relation of these to the timing and frequency of systems which feed inputs or take outputs. The scheduling of certain events can be calendar-dependent; for example, a closed account might not be deleted from the system data until December 31, if it contains information which must be sent to the Internal Revenue Service.

·   See Orr [Orr 77] for discussion of many of these points, and Jackson [Jac 75] for discussions of file maintenance and process control.

The *data flow* of a program is the scheme for movement of data between the program's data objects and its processing actions. From the viewpoint of data flow, a design consists of objects and actions working together to form a solution. An example shown in Figure 3.2 is the use of a flag, initialized to false, which may be set to true by some other part of the program, and which is checked at the end of the program. These pieces of the program cooperate by sending data to each other, even though the initialization is at the beginning of the program, the checking of the flag is at the end of the program, and the action that sets the flag to true is in the middle of the program. By explicitly indicating this data flow, the notation of Figure 3.2 conveys the essence of the design.

A design, when created using data flow techniques, is built up piece by piece, in a series of iterations. At each iteration, one or more additional objects are determined, and these objects are linked to the rest of the diagram via appropriate actions. As we show later, a data flow diagram can be drawn at a system level and can be used as a basis for modularizing the design, or it can be used in the design of an individual module.

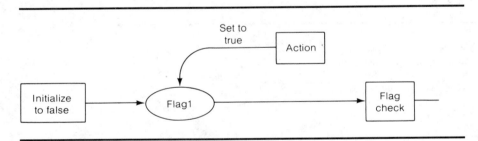

Figure 3.2   Data flow diagram of a scheme for setting and testing a flag.

3.2.2 Data Flow Notation

We wish to annotate how data is used throughout the program: what data is needed by each action and how each action moves data or modifies objects. Accordingly, in a data flow diagram, data objects are explicitly shown, transfer of information between data objects and actions is emphasized, and the sequence of actions is not considered.

In our discussions, the term *object* (equivalently, *data object*) means a major data entity of the program. Some examples are:

- Input objects such as files or cards
- Output objects such as printouts or cards
- Memory objects such as arrays, tables, variables, or flags

An object is pictured as a circle in Figure 3.3. It is both convenient and intuitively correct to regard every object as a "special hardware memory" that holds the appropriate data.

The term *action* means a process that moves data from one object to another, or transforms the data in an object. If correctly developed, such actions define the major subroutines of a program. Actions are pictured as rectangles in Figure 3.3. It is appropriate to regard each action as a "special hardware processor" that accomplishes the desired data movement or transformation.

In a data flow diagram, each object or action is shown once, and the transfer of data is shown by arrows. The data moves in the direction shown by the arrows. Figure 3.3(*a*) shows both data movement from an object to an action and movement from an action to an object. Figure 3.3(*b*) shows an invert array action that transforms the data in the array X. The invert array action both uses and sets the data of array X.

There is no limitation on the number of data transfers to or from any entity. Thus an action may use data from many objects or may set data in

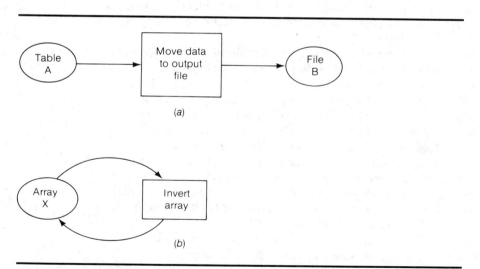

(a)

(b)

Figure 3.3 Data movement and data transformation in a data flow diagram. (*a*) The move data action moves data from table A to file B. (*b*) Data transformation: matrix inversion.

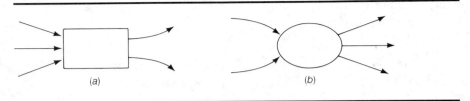

Figure 3.4   Actions (*a*) and objects (*b*) may have many data transfers.

many objects, as in Figure 3.4(*a*), while an object may be set by many actions or have its data used by many actions, as in Figure 3.4(*b*).

We previously suggested that every object can be regarded as a special hardware memory, while each action may be regarded as a special hardware processor. Similarly, each arrow may be regarded as a "signal line" carrying the required data from one entity to another. Continuing this analogy, special processors may be regarded as *active* devices that can initiate data transfers, while special memories are regarded as *passive* devices that can transfer data only in response to initiation from a special processor. With these conventions, a data flow diagram defines a hardware implementation of the desired program and shows exactly the data communications needed in a hardware version. That is, the design method and notation of this section can also be used for the design of hardware.

From a hardware viewpoint, a system is a collection of physical devices that communicate with each other via signal lines. Each device is self-contained and performs its function independently of the other devices. Also, each device contains all the logic necessary to determine exactly which function to perform and when to perform it. All information required by a device, such as condition values that help it choose which function to perform or signals that help it choose when to perform the function, are transmitted to it via signal lines from other devices. A hardware system diagram shows only the devices and the wires that connect them; in contrast to a program flow chart, it does not explicitly show the sequence in which processors perform, and it does not explicitly show the tests or conditions that determine which functions are performed.

Our notation is intended to capture the spirit of a hardware system diagram. Accordingly, a data flow diagram assumes that each object or action is self-contained and that each action is performed independently of other actions. We assume, moreover, that each action "knows exactly what to do": which function to perform and when to perform it. The notation does not provide any means for expressing information about the computation sequence; for many programs, this information is irrelevant to data flow, unimportant as compared to data flow, and confusing if added to a data flow diagram. For real-time systems, where sequence is important, "activation signal lines" can be added to the data flow diagram /Phi 67, Phi 71-.

In a data flow diagram, each object or action is thought of as a *place* (in contrast to a program flow chart, where an action is thought of as one of a sequence of *events*). An important consequence of this notion is that sequence of operation is not strictly implied in a data flow diagram. For example, Figure 3.5 shows the movement of data from A to B by the action MOVEAB and the movement of data from B to C by the action MOVEBC. This diagram does *not* imply that MOVEAB moves, say, one record from A to B, whereupon MOVEBC moves that record from B to C. Obviously, MOVEBC can take data from B only after MOVEAB has placed the data in B. However, B might be a buffer capable of containing many records; MOVEBC could operate at some undetermined time after MOVEAB or it might operate only after some number of records have accumulated in the buffer; or MOVEBC might be able to check the buffer, find it empty, proceed about other business, and check back later.

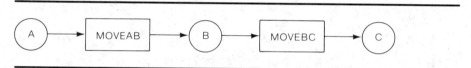

Figure 3.5   A plan for data movement.

A data flow diagram is very much like a requirements diagram of Chapter 2. An activity in a requirements diagram and an action in a data flow diagram are identical. Files are understood as data objects in both types of diagrams. However, the two kinds of diagrams differ in their assumptions about data flow. In the requirements diagram, it is assumed that data travels from one activity to another along the labeled arc, in the same way that a spoken message travels through the air from one person to another, or in the same way that an electrical signal travels from one computer to another.

In the data flow diagram, it is assumed that a sending action puts data into a data object (such as a buffer, a queue, an array) and that the receiving action takes the data from this object. This is the way that portions of a program really communicate. For example, a subroutine and the calling program communicate via parameter lists, common variables, and so on.[3]

---

[3]In Chapter 4 it will be seen that the ease with which the different subprograms of a system can cooperate depends greatly on where (i.e., in which subprogram) these data objects have been placed.

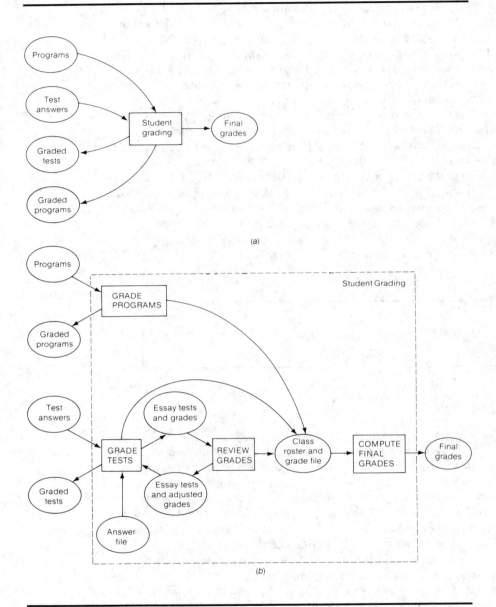

Figure 3.6   Data flow diagrams of student grading activity. (*a*) Overview of student grading system (source and destination not shown). (*b*) Refinement of student grading activity.

Thus the data flow analog of Figure 2.2 is the diagram of Figure 3.6(*a*), while the analog of Figure 2.3 is the diagram of Figure 3.6(*b*).

Figure 3.6(*b*) shows the refinement of the student grading activity, and other data flow diagrams may be drawn to show the further refinement of steps 1, 2, and 3 of Figure 3.6(*b*). In other words, a data flow diagram may be drawn at any level from a high (system) level to a low (detail) level. A process box may incorporate the data objects necessary for its processing, as in Figure 3.6(*a*).

Since a data flow diagram is intended to convey an overall approach, relatively unimportant conditions can be ignored. For example, suppose that an input record is held in a buffer, and, depending on a transaction code, this record is moved to one of three files using actions MOVE1, MOVE2, and MOVE3. Figure 3.7(*a*) assumes that one of MOVE1, MOVE2, or MOVE3 will operate as required, even though the finished program must test the transaction code. On the other hand, the dependence on the transaction code value can be explicitly shown as in Figure 3.7(*b*).

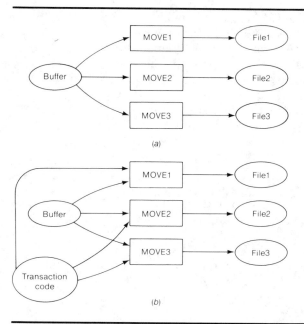

Figure 3.7 Expressing program conditions in a data flow diagram. (*a*) Unimportant conditions can be omitted. (*b*) Dependence on condition values can be explicitly shown.

3.2.3 Developing a Plan

3.2.3.1 Basic Method

A data flow diagram is developed by repeated consideration of two questions:

· What basic data objects are needed?
· What actions are performed on these objects?

The design is usually begun with the inputs and outputs. Then the objects to which the inputs are moved, or from which the outputs are produced, are determined; and then the actions that provide these data movements are determined. Thus the design is developed piece by piece, in a sequence of iterations. Objects and actions serve equally as the building blocks of the design. At each iteration, a piece of the design is developed, in the form of one or more objects, and then this piece is linked to the previously developed pieces by means of actions.

At each iteration, objects or actions are added to the solution in response to the developing requirements of the problem. The key question each time is, What data blocks (or actions) does the solution need now? Elements are added to the solution only as demanded by the answers to this question. Sometimes the design can be developed either "forward" from the inputs or "backward" from the outputs, as the designer wishes. At other times, the development is forced to proceed either completely forward or completely backward.

Along with development of the plan, a list of objects is developed, stating for each object

· What data is in the object
· The form of the object (e.g., table, array, number of dimensions)
· The method of access (e.g., how an element is subscripted)
· What information an element holds

A list of actions is also developed, stating for each action

· The exact form of the action
· What the arguments are if it is a procedure

3.2.3.2 A Simple Example: The Top 10

We now show how a simple data flow diagram can be developed and improved, using the problem of Section 2.3.3. We assume that the imperfection discovered in the specification has been resolved, though our discussion will not touch on this problem. We also assume that age and sex have been added to each interviewee record. The overall approach of the desired program is explicitly spelled out by the problem statement, namely:

1. Sort the titles into alphabetic order, count the total mentions for each title, and list each title and the number of times mentioned (LIST1).

2. Compute a popularity value for each title, and list the 10 most popular titles (as per the perfected specification) (LIST2).

3. List all interviewees who mentioned at least 5 of the 10 most popular titles (LIST3) based only on responses in the interviewee's category.

4. For each category, list all interviewees in the category whose first choice is one of the three titles most popular with interviewees in the category (LIST41, LIST42, LIST43, LIST44).

To produce LIST1, the responses and titles are read in, the titles are sorted, the mentions are counted, and the list of titles and numbers of mentions is output. For LIST2 (assuming that the responses and titles have already been read in), a popularity value is calculated for each title, the list of 10 most popular titles is calculated, and that list is output. In the production of LIST3, the previously calculated list of 10 most popular titles is compared to each interviewee response, and the interviewee's name is listed if he or she has chosen at least 5 of the titles on the list.

For each of LIST41, . . . , LIST44, a popularity value is calculated for each title using only responses from one category. The three most popular titles are determined. Each interviewee response in that category is compared against the list of the three most popular titles, and the interviewee's name is listed if he or she has given one of these as a first choice.

We first show how LIST1 is produced, beginning with an INPUT FILE object containing the list of Top 40 titles and the entire set of interviewee responses. Obviously, the INPUT FILE will be read into memory, so that objects are needed to contain the various kinds of data. Accordingly, we must assign data objects TITLE TABLE, CATEGORY 1 RESPONSES, CATEGORY 2 RESPONSES, and so on. These objects are linked with the input file via read statements as in Figure 3.8.

To sort the TITLE TABLE, we use an action SORT TITLES.

To accommodate the mentions for each title, we use an array MENTIONS initialized to 0, and add in the counts from each category later. The diagram that produces LIST1 is shown in Figure 3.8.

When further pieces are added to the plan for the production of LIST2 and LIST44, Figure 3.9 is obtained. POP ALL and POP 4 are arrays of popularity values. The array POP ALL LIST INDEXES is used in the production of LIST3.

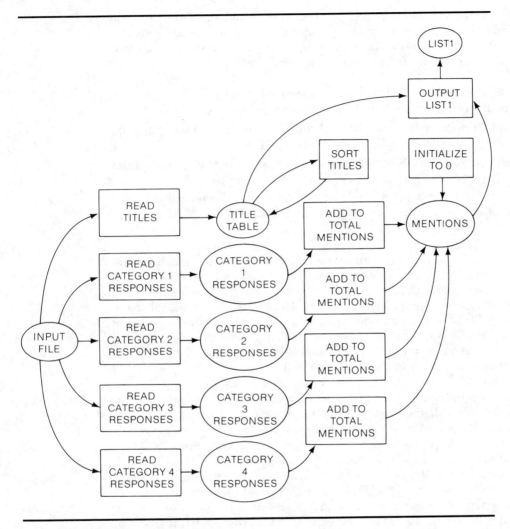

Figure 3.8 Plan for producing LIST1.

3.2.3.3 Improving a Plan

The plan will not be extended to produce the other outputs. Note that this plan was developed in a mechanical way: For each new storage requirement, a new object was created, and for each new processing requirement, a new action was created.

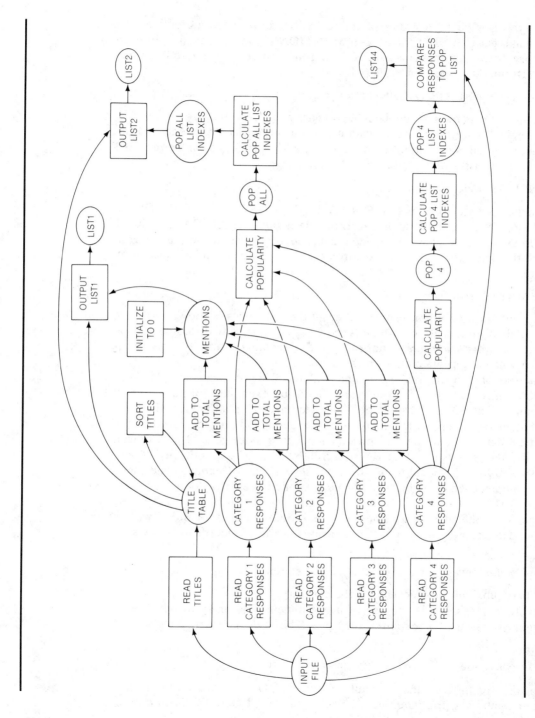

Figure 3.9 Production of LIST1, LIST2, and LIST44.

Can this plan be improved? Examining the plan for possible subroutines, we note that the action ADD TO TOTAL MENTIONS is an identical one for each category. If category-name is used as a subroutine argument, the four actions are performed by one subroutine,

ADD TO TOTAL MENTIONS(category-name).

In the full plan there would be five popularity functions p_1, p_2, p_3, p_4, and p_a (for "all"). If category-name is again used as a subroutine argument, and the special name all is permitted, then these popularity functions can be replaced by one popularity subroutine,

POPULARITY(category-name).

Finally, since the objects CATEGORY 1 RESPONSES, . . . , CATEGORY 4 RESPONSES all have identical form, the actions READ CATEGORY 1 RESPONSES, and so on, are all identical except for the name of the object in which the data is to be placed. Accordingly, these actions can be replaced by one read routine,

READ(category-name).

The data flow diagram resulting after all these changes is shown in Figure 3.10. In the figure, each subroutine is shown as a rectangle with double vertical lines, the word *subroutine* appears in the rectangle, and the argument category-name appears as part of the action name.

Each set of identical actions, or almost identical actions, can be replaced by a subroutine. Any data flow diagram should be examined for such sets of actions so that subroutines can be recognized and the plan improved.

Another improvement technique is consolidating data objects. Each set of identical data objects may be consolidated into a more general data object. Because the objects CATEGORY 1 RESPONSES, . . . , CATEGORY 4 RESPONSES have identical form, there are several ways to consolidate them. For example, each data object can be implemented as an array of records as in Figure 3.11.

The four data objects together require $4 \times$ max records. A quick way to consolidate them is to use a two-dimensional array of records as follows:

var
    response:array[1 . . 4, 1 . . max] of responseform.

The first subscript now designates the category.

Another possibility is the use of a one-dimensional array in which each category is assigned a section of the array. This is declared as

var
    response:array[1 . . max2] of responseform.

Typically, for this scheme, a small array BOUND of records is used, each record containing the quantities lower and upper. BOUND[I].lower is the

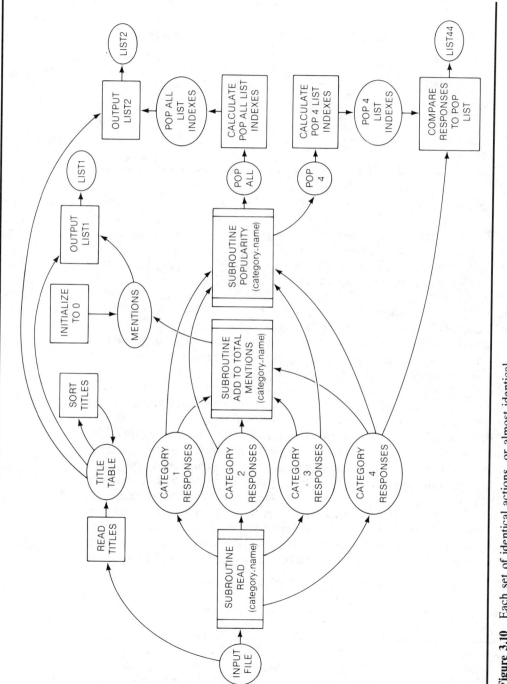

Figure 3.10 Each set of identical actions, or almost identical actions, can be replaced by a subroutine.

```
type
   sexcode=(M,F);
   responseform=record
                    name:array[1..30] of char;
                    address:array[1..50] of char;
                    age:integer;
                    sex:sexcode;
                    choice:array[1..10] of integer
                 end;
var
   cat1response, cat2response, cat3response,
      cat4response:array[1..max] of responseform;
```

Figure 3.11 Implementation of response data objects.

lowest index of the section of records assigned to the Ith category, and BOUND[I].upper is the highest index assigned to that category. Since BOUND specifies the upper and lower limits for each category, any action that references a response must initially interrogate BOUND. Figure 3.12 diagrams this scheme. The subroutine READ can set the elements of BOUND as the data is read in, and, of course, the subroutines ADD TO TOTAL MENTIONS and POPULARITY use elements of BOUND.

The scheme of Figure 3.12 is potentially more economical in its use of memory than the two-dimensional array, because it allows the number of elements in each category to be widely different.

When objects are consolidated, we should take into account possible future enhancement or generalization of the required processing. Since more categories might sometime be required, it is useful to generalize as well as consolidate the category response objects. This can be done by adding to the responseform record the field category of type integer, which can be set by the READ routine as the interviewee response is read in. Each interviewee record then explicitly indicates its category; the objects can be combined; and later the number of categories can be extended. Moreover, with this scheme, the responses can be stored in the array without regard to category. Note the use of an explicit data indicator to achieve generality, and the similarity of this technique to the use of a subroutine argument. The use of explicit data to achieve generality is an important technique, discussed in detail in Sections 6.4 and 8.2.1.

REFERENCES

[Berg 79] Bergland, G. D., and Gordon, R. D. *Tutorial: Software Design Strategies*. (IEEE Catalog No. EH0 149-5.) New York: IEEE Computer Society, 1979.

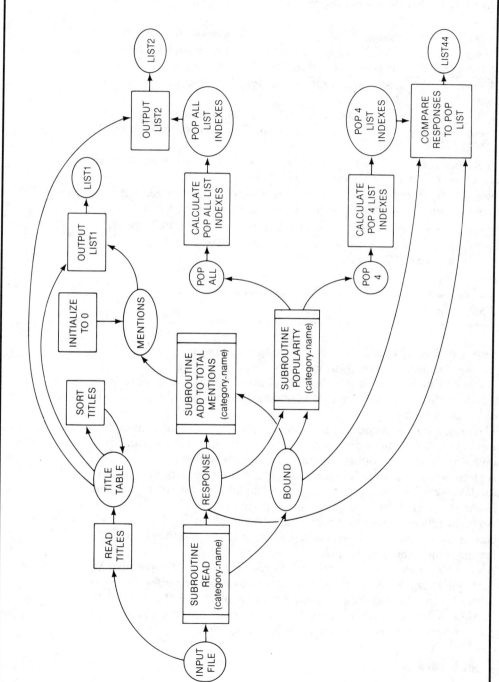

Figure 3.12   A scheme for consolidating category 1 responses,
. . . , category 4 responses into a single array.

[Jac 75] Jackson, M. A. *Principles of Program Design*. New York: Academic Press, 1975.

[Orr 77] Orr, K. T. *Structured Systems Development*. New York: Yourdon, 1977.

[Pet 77] Peters, L. J., and Tripp, L. L. "Comparing Software Design Methodologies," *Datamation*, November 1977. (Also in [Berg 79].)*

[Phi 67] Phillips, C. S. E. "Networks for Real Time Programming," *Computer Journal*, May 1967.

[Phi 71] ———. "Software Engineering, the Key to Expansion of Real Time Systems," in *Infotech State of the Art Report 3: Real Time*. Maidenhead, England: Infotech, 1971.

[Schn 76] Schneiderman, B. "A Review of Design Techniques for Programs and Data," *Software—Practice and Experience*, Vol. 6, 1976.

[Ste 74] Stevens, W. P.; Meyers, G. J.; and Constantine, L. L. "Structured Design," *IBM Systems Journal*, 1974. (Also in [Ram 78], [Berg 79], and [Fre 80b].)*

[Ste 75] ———, ———, and ———. *Structural Design*. New York: Yourdon, 1975.

[You 75b] Yourdon, E., and Constantine, L. L. *Structured Design*. New York: Yourdon, 1975. (Republished 1979 by Prentice-Hall.)

PROBLEMS

1. Develop data flow diagrams for the following situations:
   (a) An input program reads a file into a buffer.
   (b) A line of English text in a buffer is processed by the subroutine pack, which compresses each sequence of blank characters in the text to one blank character.
   (c) The program INV produces an updated stock inventory tape, using last week's stock inventory tape and a tape of inventory changes (stock into inventory and stock out of inventory) during this week.
   (d) A summary program processes a tape of customer orders filled during the last week, producing a weekly order summary and an error report listing those customer orders found to be in error.
   (e) An array-inversion program copies the array to be inverted into a duplicate array, computes the inversion in another array, and then moves the inversion into the original array.
   (f) A card file input contains transactions and also values for parameters par1, par2, and par3. The input is moved to a linear buffer and processed by proc1 using the value of par1. Then proc1 puts the buffer data into an array X which is transformed by proc2 using par2. Finally, proc3 prints a report from the array X, using par3.

*See Appendix B: Bibliography.

2. Processes A, B, C, and D might send messages (inputs) to each other via several different schemes. Draw a data flow diagram for each scheme.
   (a) Four buffers are used: from A to B, from B to C, from C to D, and from D to A. Each process sends messages by placing them in its output buffer. Each process takes messages one by one from its input buffer, examines them, and transfers them to its output buffer if they are meant for another process.
   (b) Each process has an input buffer from each of the other processes.
   (c) Each process has its own input buffer. The four processes share an output buffer, that is, A, B, C, or D may place messages from the common output buffer and transfer them to the appropriate input buffer.

3. Draw a data flow diagram showing inputs, outputs, and the program as a single action, for:
   (a) Problem 2 in Appendix D.
   (b) Problem 11 in Appendix D.
   (c) Problem 13 in Appendix D.

3.3 DESIGN USING DATA FLOW CONCEPTS

3.3.1 Data Flow Design Methods

3.3.1.1 The Sequence of Design Steps

Every design problem prescribes its own set of required—and inescapable—tasks. Regardless of the technique or methodology used, the designer must first understand what tasks are to be performed and must then prescribe a solution for each task. Each solution involves three decisions:

1. What information must be stored for the task?
2. What use will the program make of the stored information?
3. What data blocks must be used and what is their form?

Finally, the designer must connect these solutions together, forming a system.

In other words, a designer builds an overall design approach by deciding which particular kinds of information will be stored in data blocks and what use the program will make of each kind of information. These decisions suggest the form of the data blocks. Since many different kinds of information can be kept in a program, there are often many approaches to even the smallest program.

Thus any design must be concerned initially with the patterns of data storage and data flow throughout the system. The best designers have long understood this, and their overall design approaches are always couched in terms of data flow and storage. The data flow diagram formalizes this view of a system, allowing the designer to communicate the data flow and storage patterns and allowing the novice designer to visualize a system in these terms.

Design using data flow concepts is a way of thinking, equally suitable for blocking out a large system at a high level or for diagramming details of a complex algorithm. Section 3.3 shows a design for a small problem that inherently requires a chain of data transformations. With the application of data flow concepts, these transformations are blocked out in a straightforward way. Each transformation is simple (some can be accomplished in 1 line of code or even made implicit) and the entire program need be no larger than about 300 lines of FORTRAN or PASCAL. Nevertheless, without the use of a data flow diagram, students have found it very difficult to understand the required program structure.

The focus of the overall design approach is on objects. The designer seeks to pin a method on an object, which is then manipulated to give a solution to the problem. Rather than asking, Which actions will solve this problem?, the designer asks, What objects can be used to solve the problem? When objects are the focus of a method, actions are data moves or transformations. Consequently, the actions are well defined and easily programmed in a localized fashion, that is, as a small program block or as a procedure.

Every design requires answers to the following questions:

· What tasks must be performed?
· How can each task be done?
  (a) What kinds of information should be stored?
  (b) How will the program use the information?
· How can the various solutions be connected together to form a system?

Each of these questions involves the choice of data blocks. Finding an appropriate object is often the key to separating a problem into independent subproblems. One example is the plotter control program of Section 8.2.1.3, in which the problem of keeping track of the occurrence of card types is separated from the problem of checking whether specific combinations of types were used. This separation is made possible by the use of arrays COMBI and OCCURS.

Stepwise refinement and the choice of data objects often go hand in hand. In Section 7.2.3.2, a program is subdivided into independent subprograms by using an intermediate table.

Thus data objects can be chosen to achieve a best set of tasks. The solution of each task results in the choice of further data blocks. Finally, connecting the various solutions to form a system may require the introduction of more data blocks. Section 3.3.1.3 discusses the use of intermediate data objects to resolve incompatibility between a source data block and a target data block. The resolution also separates the source-to-target program into independent subprograms.

Elements should be added to the design only after analysis shows that the elements are needed. At each iteration, elements should be added only in response to the question, What further data or actions are needed now? Orr [Orr 77] suggests that one should strive for a minimal system, which does the absolute minimum to produce the desired outputs.

Thus designers should work backward from output to input. At each iteration of the diagram, the goal is to connect directly to the input via an obvious transformation. If this can be done, the diagram is then complete; if not, then intermediate data objects are necessary.

3.3.1.2 Typical Uses of Data Blocks

Figure 3.13 shows some typical uses of data blocks. For example, data blocks can be used to store relations between elements, to store combinations or groupings, or to store data. The information can pertain to input or background elements; it can be system information stored when the program is written and remaining constant for all executions, or it can be computed once at the beginning of each execution, or it can be constantly recomputed during a program.

Most of the situations in Figure 3.13 relate to Problem 6 of Appendix D, which concerns the capture of pawns by a knight. As indicated by situation 1 of the figure, groupings of chessboard squares can be stored as in solution 1a, or relations between chessboard squares can be stored as in solution 1b. Similar relations exist among input elements (the pawn positions), as seen in situation 3. The history of a pawn can be stored in several different ways (see situations 4 and 5), as can a knight's path (solutions 6a and 6b).

3.3.1.3 Resolution of Structure Clashes

Suppose that we desire to process data from a data object A to another data object B, via a program P_{AB}. There will be a *structure clash* between A and B if the two data objects have incompatible (i.e., dissimilar) structures, so that the desired program P_{AB} is a complex transformation.

A structure clash is resolved by introducing an intermediate data object and separating the complex transformation into a set of simpler transformations [Jac 75, Jac 76]. Specifically, the clash is resolved in three steps:

1. Decouple the clashing structures, that is, assume for the moment that data will *not* be processed from A to B.

Situation	Solution
1. Store for each square on a chessboard the set of squares reachable by a knight move. Assume squares numbered as follows: 	1	2	3	4	5	6	7	8
9	10	11	12	13	14	15	16
17	18	19	20	21	22	23	24
25	26	27	28	29	30	31	32
33	34	35	36	37	38	39	40
41	42	43	44	45	46	47	48
49	50	51	52	53	54	55	56
57	58	59	60	61	62	63	64		1a. Groupings of squares nextsquare:array[1..64,1..8] of integer 1 → 11, 18, 0 20 → 3, 5, 10, 14, 26, 30, 35, 37 ith row gives list of squares reachable from square i. --- 1b. Relations among squares knightmove:array[1..64,1..64] of integer $$knightmove[i,j]=\begin{cases}0 & \text{if no knight move from i to j}\\1 & \text{if knight move from i to j}\end{cases}$$
2. A set of pawn positions $p_1,...,p_N$ on a chessboard is input. Store these pawn positions.	2a. pawn:array[1..N] of integer pawn[i] contains number of square on which p_i sits --- 2b. board:array[1..8,1..8] of char $$board[i,j]=\begin{cases}\text{' '} & \text{if no pawn on square}\\\text{'P'} & \text{if pawn on square}\end{cases}$$
3. A set of pawn positions $p_1,...,p_N$ on a chessboard is input. Store, for each pawn position, the other pawn positions reachable by a knight move. (Relations among input elements.)	3. C:array[1..N,1..N] of integer $$C[i,j]=\begin{cases}1 & \text{if can get from } p_i \text{ to } p_j \text{ in a knight move}\\0 & \text{if cannot get from } p_i \text{ to } p_j \text{ in a knight move}\end{cases}$$ Note: Nonzero elements of C×C give paths of length 2, nonzero elements of C×C×C give paths of length 3, and so on.

Situation	Solution
4. Pawn capture status—continually compute.	4. capture:array[1..N] of boolean $$capture[i]= \begin{cases} \text{true if } P_i \text{ has been captured} \\ \text{false if } P_i \text{ has not been captured} \end{cases}$$
5. Pawn capture history—continually compute.	5. capture:array[1..N] of integer $$capture[i]= \begin{cases} 0 & \text{if } p_i \text{ not captured} \\ n>0 & \text{if } p_i \text{ captured on nth move} \end{cases}$$ Note: This also gives capture status.
6. Store a knight's path around on chessboard as the path is generated. (History.)	6a. Queue if the squares of the path are to be printed in the order traversed.
	6b. board:array[1..8,1..8]of integer $$board[i,j]= \begin{cases} \text{' '} & \text{if knight has not moved there} \\ n & \text{if knight moved there at nth move} \end{cases}$$ Notes: Can combine this with pawn positions. Also, may need a list for board[i,j] if knight moves there more than once.
7. Generate a tree of paths of knight around a chessboard.	7. Stack of pathsquare where pathsquare=record square:integer; index:integer end next square moved to is nextsquare[square,index]
8. Keep a record of whether elements $e_1,...,e_N$ have occurred in the input. (History.)	8. occur:array[1..N] of integer $$occur[i]= \begin{cases} 0 & \text{initially} \\ 1 & \text{if } e_i \text{ occurs} \end{cases}$$

Figure 3.13   Typical uses of data blocks.

2. Separate out from the desired program P_{AB} the following parts:
   (a) transformations that can be performed on the data in block A and
   (b) transformations that can be performed on the data in block B (assuming that, somehow, the appropriate data will be placed in block B).

   Note that the subprograms of part a are independent of those in part b, and vice versa.

3. Link the two structures by an intermediate object, that is, an object with a structure intermediate between the two incompatible objects. The rest of the desired program now consists of three parts:
   (a) a program P_{AC} that processes data from A to C,
   (b) transformations that can be performed on the object C, and
   (c) a program P_{CB} that processes data from C to B.

A flow diagram of this resolution is shown in Figure 3.14. Several intermediate blocks in series might be used to achieve the shift in structure from A to B via a series of smaller shifts.

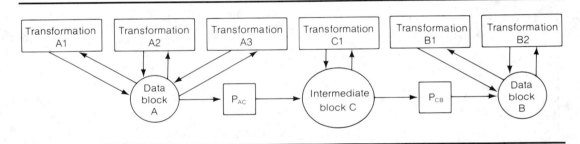

Figure 3.14   Resolution of a structure clash.

The concepts of structure clash and resolution are extremely important, and, accordingly, we present several illustrative examples. Suppose that in a company certain statistics have been compiled daily for a year and have been input to the computer on a biweekly basis. The data now resides in a biweekly file, which contains all the daily data for the year, blocked into 14-day subfiles. It is desired to print this daily data for the whole year in the company's annual report, except that for the report the data must be formatted on a monthly basis. Accordingly, before output, the data will be placed in a monthly file, containing all the daily data for the year, blocked into monthly subfiles.

However, the two files are incompatible since a biweekly format cannot be processed simply into a monthly format because the time periods overlap. A single program can, of course, be written to transform the data from one format to the other, but this program would have to deal with all of the intricacies that arise from the overlapping of 14-day periods and monthly periods.

The situation can be resolved by introducing an intermediate file, organized on a day-by-day basis, as in Figure 3.15. The format conversion is now separated into two independent subprograms, the BUILD FILE program, which converts from biweekly to daily, and the EDIT FILE program, which converts from daily to monthly. The day-by-day file is the interface between the other two.

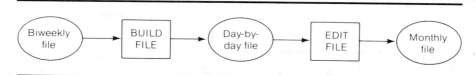

Figure 3.15   Resolution of a simple structure clash.

The second example is more difficult. Suppose that input cards are to be read until a completely blank card is read. The input cards contain words; successive words are separated by one or more blanks, and a word may be split onto two successive cards. The words are to be printed out, as many to an output line as possible, successive words separated by one blank, without splitting any word across two output lines.

We may regard the desired program P as processing data from a card file to an output line file. Because words may be split across successive input cards but not across output lines, and because presumably cards and output lines contain different numbers of characters, there is a structure clash between the card file and the output line file.

The desired program can be written in the form

```
while there is another card
    do process the card
```

or in the form

```
while more input
    do begin
        build next output line;
        write next output line
        end
```

However, because the input and output objects are not compatible, a program in one of these forms will be complex. The program will be forced to deal simultaneously with all of the differences between card file and output line file.

The structure clash can be resolved by the introduction of an intermediate object words, as in Figure 3.16. The desired program is now separated into P1, which processes the text words into words, and P2, which processes from words to the output line file. If words is allowed to be a file large enough to contain all of the input text words, then the desired program can be written in the form

```
begin
(*P1*) build words file;
(*P2*) process words file
end
```

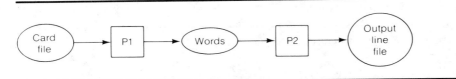

Figure 3.16   Resolution of card-to-output structure clash.

Alternatively, words could be a buffer capable of holding a small number of text words. P1 and P2 could be coroutines that concurrently fill and empty the buffer, or P1 and P2 could alternate to give a program of the form

```
while there is another word
    do begin
        (*P1*) fill buffer;
        (*P2*) empty buffer
    end
```

If words is capable of holding only one text word, the program could take the form

```
while there is another word
    do begin
        (*P1*) get next word;
        (*P2*) add next word to output
    end
```

In this last form, words has become a very small data block, P1 has become a one-line program, and P2 now contains almost all of the program text.

3.3.2 An Extended Example: Secret Sums

3.3.2.1 Formulation of the Plan

A secret sums puzzle is an arithmetic problem whose operands and results are letters, as in the example below:

```
  SEND
+ MORE
 MONEY
```

Such a puzzle is solved by finding a distinct numeric digit to correspond to each distinct letter (i.e., no two distinct letters are assigned the same digit) so that when these corresponding digits are substituted throughout the puzzle for their letters, the puzzle becomes a correct arithmetic addition problem.

We want to write a program that processes a sequence of cards in free format, each card containing a puzzle like the one above. Some possible puzzles are:

```
AA=AA
SEND+MORE=MONEY
ONE+TWO+FOUR=SEVEN
HE+CAN+NOT+STAND=NOISE
ADAM+AND+EVE+ON+A=RAFT
```

Each input card is to be printed out and then checked for errors; if an error exists, an error message is to be given. Otherwise, the program is to find every set of corresponding digits that solves the puzzle. For each set of corresponding digits that solves the puzzle, an output such as

```
CORRESPONDENCES ARE
LETTER   A   C
DIGIT    5   8
```

and so on is to be given. If no set of corresponding digits solves the puzzle, the output

```
NO SOLUTIONS EXIST
```

is to be given.

The design concept for this problem requires three steps. First, an overall approach is needed; next, critical problems must be found and then solved; and, finally, the solution is refined if necessary to enhance its execution speed. Section 3.3.2 develops and evaluates the overall approach and shows a basic form for solving a critical problem. Refinements of the critical algorithm are discussed throughout Section 6.1, especially in Sections 6.1.1 through 6.1.8. It is suggested that Section 6.1 be read in conjunction with this example.

For this example, the major tasks to be performed are

· Adding the digits for the addend words and comparing the sum to the digits for the sum word
· Assigning a digit to each distinct letter
· Cycling through all possible sequences of digit assignments

A data flow diagram will be developed from the outputs backward to the inputs, and each task will be discussed as the diagram is developed.

Table 3.1 Objects and associated actions for the secret sums example

Step	Object	Significance	Associated Actions
0	INPUT CARD	Holds contents of puzzle card	Input card to CARD BUFFER
0	SET OF CORRESPONDENCES	Printout of a solution consisting of letters and corresponding digits	Sum addends and compare
0	'NO SOLUTIONS EXIST'	Message indicating puzzle has no solution	Check flag at end
1	SOLUTION FLAG	Indicates whether a solution has been found	Initialize to false Sum addends and compare Check flag at end
2	NUMADD	Holds addend words in numeric form	Enter set of corresponding digits Sum addends and compare
2	NUMSUM	Holds sum word in numeric form	Enter set of corresponding digits Sum addends and compare
3	SYMADD	Holds addend words in symbolic form	Process addends into SYMADD Enter set of corresponding digits into NUMADD
3	SYMSUM	Holds sum word in symbolic form	Process sum word into SYMSUM Enter set of corresponding digits into NUMSUM
4	LETTER	Array of distinct letters (each letter in the puzzle appears exactly once in this array)	Process letters into LETTER Enter set of corresponding digits into NUMADD Enter set of corresponding digits into NUMSUM
4	DIGIT	Array of corresponding digits (DIGIT[I] is the value corresponding to LETTER[I])	Initialize Choose next legal set Enter set of corresponding digits into NUMADD Enter set of corresponding digits into NUMSUM
5	CARD BUFFER	Holds contents of puzzle card	Input card to CARD BUFFER Process addends into SYMADD Process sum word into SYMSUM Process letters into LETTER

The objects and actions of this example, together with the step at which each object is determined, are shown in Table 3.1. The data flow diagram begins as usual with the input object INPUT CARD and the output objects 'NO SOLUTIONS EXIST' and SET OF CORRESPONDENCES, as in the first three lines of Table 3.1.

Following the principle suggested by Orr [Orr 77], we will work backward from the outputs. The first key question is, How can the message 'NO SOLUTIONS EXIST' be produced? Recall that all possible correspondences of digits are to be tested and that this message is to be output only if none of these correspondences yields a solution to the puzzle. Thus the message can be output only at the end of processing a puzzle.

Let us use an object SOLUTION FLAG to indicate whether a solution has been found:

$$
\text{SOLUTION FLAG} = \begin{cases} \text{true} & \text{if at least one solution} \\ & \text{has been found for the} \\ & \text{present puzzle} \\ \text{false} & \text{if no solutions have been} \\ & \text{found} \end{cases}
$$

Accordingly, the flag should be initialized to false. An action CHECK FLAG AT END will be used to print out the message if the flag is false.

The plan for producing the message is shown in Figure 3.17. Since the action necessary to set the flag to true has not yet been determined, only a question mark and an arrow are shown.

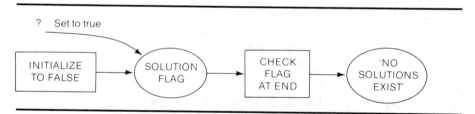

Figure 3.17   Plan to produce 'NO SOLUTIONS EXIST' message.

The next problem is how an output SET OF CORRESPONDENCES will be produced. A set of corresponding digits can be output only when there is an addition of numeric addends corresponding to, say, SEND+MORE, and a comparison of the addends to the numeric value corresponding to MONEY, and the comparison is successful. What objects should be compared? Let us choose a two-dimensional array called NUMADD (an abbreviation of numeric addends) to contain the numeric addends, and a one dimensional array NUMSUM (for numeric sum) to hold the digits corresponding to the sum word.

We intend that the first row of NUMADD will contain digits corresponding to the letters of the first addend (SEND in our example), and so on. Within each row, the last column will hold the digit corresponding to the last letter of the addend (e.g., the D in SEND), and so on. The last column of the NUMSUM array will hold the digit corresponding to the last letter of the sum word (e.g., the Y in MONEY), and so on. Figure 3.18 shows the appearance of the NUMADD and NUMSUM arrays when the correspondences

are being tested.

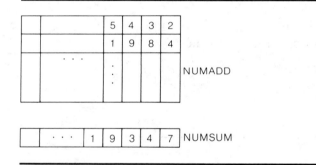

Figure 3.18   Sample contents of NUMADD and NUMSUM.

How large must NUMADD and NUMSUM be? Since each puzzle is contained on one 80-column card, the maximum number of addends is 39, for a card of the form

$$A+A+A+\cdots+A=B.$$

Since the sum word must have at least as many digits as an addend word, the maximum number of addend digits is 39, and the maximum number of sum digits is 39. Thus any conceivable puzzle can be accommodated by a 39-element NUMSUM array and a NUMADD array with 39 rows and 39 columns.

Figure 3.19 shows the plan thus far devised to produce the outputs. Clearly, the action that compares the sum of the addends in NUMADD with the

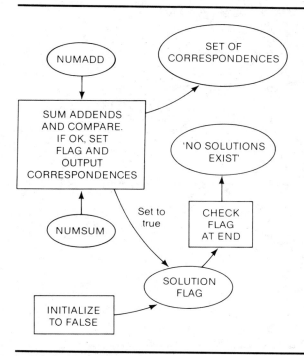

Figure 3.19 Plan to produce outputs.

contents of NUMSUM must also cause output of the set of correspondences and set the flag to true, if the comparison is successful.

The plan thus far contains the objects and actions shown in steps 0, 1, and 2 of Table 3.1.

To determine what further data objects are necessary, we ask, what else remains to be done? The plan thus far provides for reading in the puzzle card and for testing a particular set of corresponding digits. But now:

- How will digits be placed in NUMADD and NUMSUM?
- How will it be decided which digit goes where in NUMADD and NUM-SUM?
- How can one particular set of corresponding digits be assigned to the letters of the puzzle?
- How should the program cycle through all possible "legal" sets of corresponding digits?

Consider these questions in order. One way to determine where to place digits in NUMADD or NUMSUM is to use arrays containing the letters of the addends or sum word. We will use such arrays, calling them SYMADD (for symbolic addend) and SYMSUM (for symbolic sum). If a set of corresponding digits has already been assigned to the puzzle letters, then NUMADD is filled by placing the digit corresponding to SYMADD[I,J] in NUMADD[I,J].

Figure 3.20 shows the sample contents of SYMADD and SYMSUM. By adding these objects to the plan of Figure 3.19, together with the actions that enter corresponding digits into NUMADD and NUMSUM, we obtain Figure 3.21. Step 3 of Table 3.1 shows the additional objects and their associated actions.

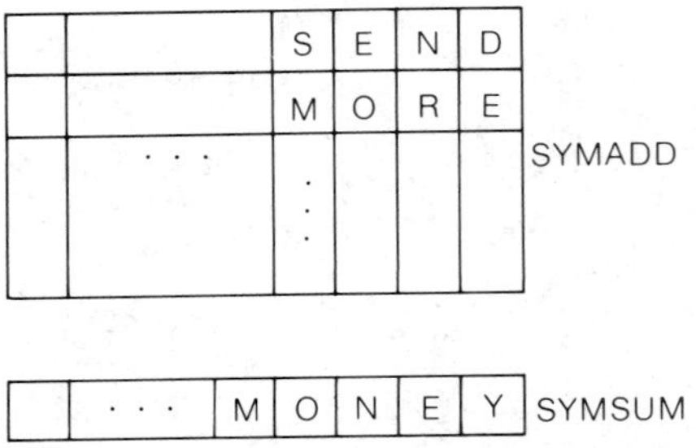

Figure 3.20 Sample contents of SYMADD and SYMSUM.

Each of the actions ENTER CORRESPONDING SET OF DIGITS in Figure 3.21 requires further information, namely, the digit value corresponding to the letter value obtained from SYMADD or SYMSUM. Again, we choose to satisfy this requirement by finding appropriate objects. A correspondence between letters and digits can be established by using two arrays:

· An array of distinct letters (one entry for each distinct letter in the puzzle) called LETTER
· An array DIGIT such that DIGIT[I] is the digit value corresponding to LETTER[I].

This formulation has been chosen primarily for discussion clarity. An equally appropriate alternative is using an array LETDIG of records such that LETDIG[I].letter is the Ith letter and LETDIG[I].digit is the digit value corresponding to the Ith letter.

The action enter a set of corresponding digits into NUMADD may now be defined as

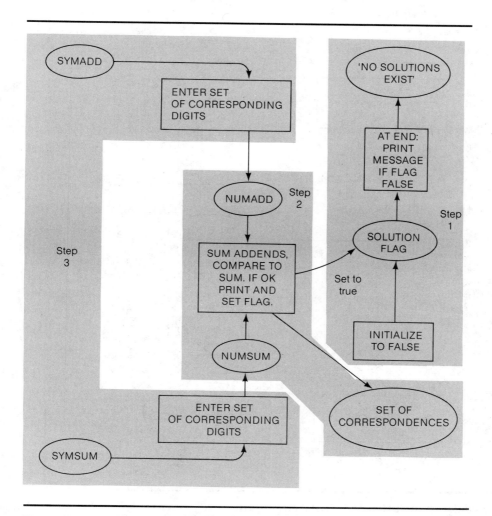

Figure 3.21 Addition of symbolic arrays to the plan.

For each SYMADD[I,J]≠"blank":
1. Find LETTER[K] such that LETTER[K]=SYMADD[I,J]
2. Set NUMADD[I,J]=DIGIT[K]

and the action that enters digits into NUMSUM may be similarly defined.
Figure 3.22 combines Figure 3.21 and the arrays LETTER and DIGIT.

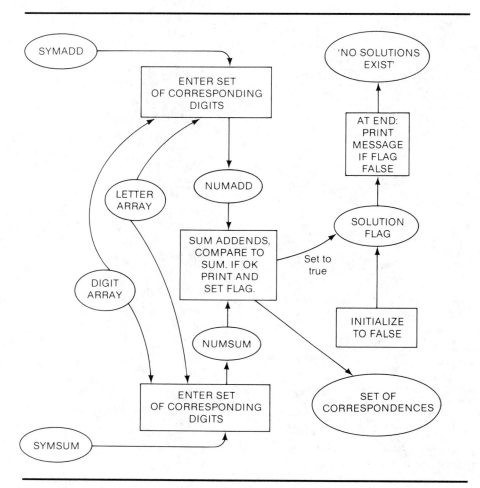

Figure 3.22   Addition of LETTER and DIGIT arrays to the plan.

What remains to be done? It is apparent from Figure 3.22 that

· The addends must be transferred to **SYMADD**
· The sum must be transferred to **SYMSUM**
· The letters must be processed into **LETTER**
· There must be a method for cycling through all possible "legal" sets of corresponding digits

To be cautious, let us add an object CARD BUFFER to hold the input card contents in memory and an action INPUT CARD TO BUFFER. The first two requirements are satisfied by an action that transfers the addends from the CARD BUFFER to SYMADD and an action that transfers the sum word from CARD BUFFER to SYMSUM.

The contents of the LETTER array may be obtained by processing the data in CARD BUFFER or, alternatively, by processing the words in SYMADD and SYMSUM. Recall that each distinct letter in the puzzle appears exactly once in the array LETTER so that each distinct letter corresponds to one digit value in DIGIT. Processing the letters from left to right in CARD BUFFER would yield, for the puzzle SEND+MORE=MONEY, the order of letters shown in Figure 3.23(*a*), while processing the letters column by column from SYMADD and SYMSUM (rightmost column first) would yield the order shown in (*b*).

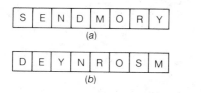

| S | E | N | D | M | O | R | Y |

(*a*)

| D | E | Y | N | R | O | S | M |

(*b*)

Figure 3.23   Different possible arrangements of letters in the LETTER array.

We choose to process the letters directly from CARD BUFFER. The final requirement is a method for cycling through all possible legal sets of corresponding digits. Recall that the digit corresponding to each letter is held in the DIGIT array. First, we add an action that initializes the DIGIT array to a legal set of correspondences, that is, a set of corresponding digits in which no two letters are assigned the same digit. We also add an action CHOOSE NEXT LEGAL SET, which transforms each legal set of digits in the DIGIT array to the next legal set of digits. The complete plan in shown in Figure 3.24.

3.3.2.2 Evaluation of the Plan

3.3.2.2.1 Preliminary Comments   Figure 3.24 shows the flow of information throughout the intended program and the data transferred between objects and actions, without regard to the sequence of execution. For example, the scheme for producing the message 'NO SOLUTIONS EXIST' involves the INITIALIZE action, which will be performed at the beginning of execution, and also the CHECK FLAG action, which will be performed at the end of execution.

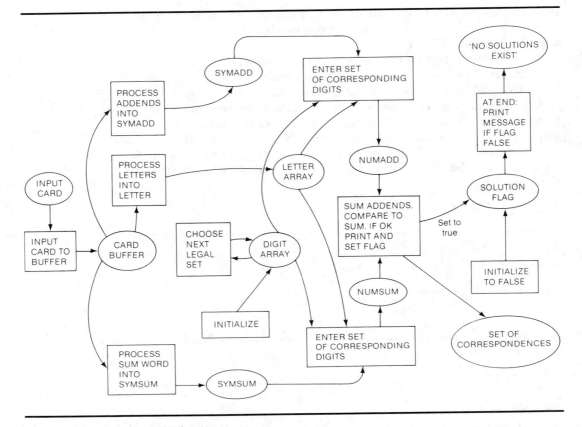

Figure 3.24 The complete plan.

This design concept can be coded in many different ways. For example, the action CHOOSE NEXT LEGAL SET might be coded as a block of text, or a subroutine, or as a set of subroutines. The plan does not prescribe any of these, and it does not preclude any of these. The actions that process data into the SYMADD, SYMSUM, and LETTER arrays might easily be combined in the implementation. The coding of SYMADD and NUMADD as 39×39 arrays would waste space, since at most only 160 elements would ever be used. More efficient implementations of these objects could easily be found.

Figure 3.24 also contains an action SUM ADDENDS and an action ENTER SET OF CORRESPONDING DIGITS that enters digits into NUMADD. In coding, the action SUM ADDENDS can be combined with the ENTER SET action so that each digit in NUMADD is obtained as it is needed. That is, each digit of NUMADD is obtained as needed by reference to SYMADD, then

LETTER, then DIGIT. Each digit of NUMSUM can be similarly obtained. In this case, the arrays NUMADD and NUMSUM need not actually appear in the code even though they are necessary in concept to show the required information flow. Section 6.1.8.3 discusses this point in detail.

It is important to remember that many alternative schemes could solve the problem equally well. For example, a somewhat different plan could be formulated using objects that are strings rather than arrays.

3.3.2.2.2 Feasibility   The correctness and workability of the solution hinge on the method used for the action CHOOSE NEXT LEGAL SET. This action is therefore a critical action. (Critical actions are discussed in Section 6.1.) We must determine an algorithm for this action and then ensure that the algorithm performs in the required fashion.

The CHOOSE NEXT LEGAL SET action is required to choose in succession all possible combinations of digit-for-letter substitutions, provided that no two letters are assigned the same digit. Assume that the puzzle contains K distinct letters. Regard the DIGIT array as a K-digit number, DIGIT[1] containing the highest order digit, DIGIT[2] containing the next-highest-order digit, and so on. For the sake of discussion, we will assume a radix of 10. We may define an action CHOOSE NEXT SET OF DIGITS, which obtains a next value of the DIGIT array by a two-step process:

1. Add 1 to the value in position K (respectively, position i) of DIGIT.
2. (a) Maintain the values in DIGIT as a number in base 10. If the value obtained in position K (respectively, position i) is 10, then set it to 0 and do these two steps for position $(K-1)$ (respectively, position $(i-1)$).
   (b) *Exception:* If the value in position i is 10 and i is the highest order position, there is no next set of digits. All sets of corresponding digits have already been considered.

If the DIGIT array is maintained by repetitions of this action, beginning, say, at 00 . . . 00, then further values 00 . . . 01, 00 . . . 02, . . . , 00 . . . 09, 00 . . . 10, . . . , 00 . . . 99, 00 . . . 100, . . . , 99 . . . 99, will be obtained. In this way, all possible numbers of radix 10—all conceivable assignments of digits to letters—will be cycled through. By adopting the action CHOOSE NEXT SET OF DIGITS, we will ensure that the program will test all possible assignments of digits to letters.

However, two distinct letters, such as, for example, S and E, should not have the same digit assigned to them, so that the values in the DIGIT array must be distinct from each other. The action CHOOSE NEXT LEGAL SET may be obtained as follows:

1. CHOOSE NEXT SET OF DIGITS.
2. If any two positions in the DIGIT array have the same value, repeat step 1.

Each successive use of the action CHOOSE NEXT LEGAL SET will produce the next number having all digits different. Because this action includes the action CHOOSE NEXT SET OF DIGITS, we have ensured that all possible legal sets of digits will be considered.

Also, the initial value of DIGIT can be 0123 . . . , and the final values can be 9876. . . .

3.3.2.2.3 An Alternate Form   We now consider an alternative formulation of the action CHOOSE NEXT LEGAL SET.

The concept of the action CHOOSE NEXT LEGAL SET is that successive sets of digits are chosen using both

· An object that holds a set of values, and
· An action that manipulates that set of values in a well-defined fashion

This concept has several advantages:

1. The action can be coded in a small number of consecutive lines (or as a procedure if desired).
2. After the action is completed, the object holds the new set of values, which can then be explicitly referred to by other program portions.
3. The action does not affect or constrict any other portion of the program.
4. Variation in the number of distinct letters in the puzzle is accommodated by varying the number of positions considered in the DIGIT array.

Alternatively, the action may be formulated without the use of a data object, by using a set of nested for statements. Assuming that up to 10 digits may appear in a puzzle, the alternate form commonly appears as in Figure 3.25.

```
for i1:=0 to 9 do
  for i2:=0 to 9 do
    for i3:=0 to 9 do
      for i4:=0 to 9 do
        for i5:=0 to 9 do
          for i6:=0 to 9 do
            for i7:=0 to 9 do
              for i8:=0 to 9 do
                for i9:=0 to 9 do
                  for i10:=0 to 9 do
                    begin
                    [Innermost loop
                    end
```

Figure 3.25   Basic formulation of CHOOSE NEXT LEGAL SET as nested for statements.

The for statement code of Figure 3.25 uses 10 lines of text in addition to the innermost loop, which contains the action SUM ADDENDS AND COMPARE. The code must also include explicit tests on the for statement indexes, as shown in Figure 3.26, to ensure that the digits are distinct. Within each for statement there will be a different set of explicit tests. Now there are 20 lines of text in addition to the innermost loop.

```
for i1:=0 to 9 do
  for i2:=0 to 9 do
    if i1<>i2 then
      for i3:=0 to 9 do
        if (i3<>i1) and (i3<>i2) then
          for i4:=0 to 9 do
            if (i4<>i1) and (i4<>i2) and (i4<>i3) then



              for i10:=0 to 9 do
                if (i10<>i9) and
                (i10<>i8) and (i10<>i7) and (i10<>i6)
                and (i10<>i5) and (i10<>i4) and
                (i10<>i3) and (i10<>i2) and (i10<>i1)
                then
                begin
              [Innermost loop
                end
```

Figure 3.26 Explicit texts are required to ensure that indexes are distinct.

How does this form accommodate the use of less than 10 digits? Since SUM ADDENDS AND COMPARE is in the innermost loop, tests based on the number of distinct letters actually used are needed, to allow the computation to drop into the innermost loops and later drop through the outermost loops. The tests for distinct digits are now more complex. Figure 3.27 shows the code required, where number is the number of distinct digits. Now there are more than 30 lines of complicated text in addition to the inner loop. Each execution of the i10 for statement requires the calculation of an enormous number of conditions. This is very inefficient since the i10 for statement is executed 10^{number} times. The i9 for statement, which is only slightly less complicated, is executed $10^{number-1}$ times.

Although the use of nested for statements at first appears obvious and efficient, it is neither simple nor straightforward. It is inefficient (not even counting the overhead required to maintain the for statements) and difficult to check out. The use of a data object (the array DIGIT) is more advantageous.

```
for i1:=0 to 9 do
  if (number=10) or (i1=0) then (*execute first time or if 10 digits*)
    for i2:=0 to 9 do
      if (number>=9) or (i2=0) then (*execute first time or if >=9 digits*)
        if (number=9) or (i2<>i1) then (*execute if i1 not used or if i2<>i1*)
          for i3:=0 to 9 do
            if (number>=8) or (i3=0) then
              if (number=8) or ((number=9) and (i3<>i2))
              or ((number=10) and (i3<>i2) and (i3<>i1)) then
                for i4:=0 to 9 do
                  if (number>=7) or (i4=0) then
                    if (number=7) or ((number=8) and (i4<>i3))
                    or ((number=9) and (i4<>i3) and (i4<>i2))
                      or ((number=10) and i4<>i3) and (i4<>i2) and i4<>i1)) then


                        for i10:=0 to 9 do
                        if (number=1) or ((number=2) and (i10<>i9))
                        or ((number=3) and (i10<>i9) and (i10<>i8))
                        or ((number=4) and (i10<>i9) and (i10<>i8) and (i10<>i7))
                        or ((number=5) and (i10<>i9) and (i10<>i8) and (i10<>i7) and (i10<>i6))
                        or ((number=6) and (i10<>i9) and (i10<>i8) and (i10<>i7) and (i10<>i6)
                          and (i10<>i5))
                        or ((number=7) and (i10<>i9) and (i10<>i8) and (i10<>i7) and (i10<>i6)
                          and (i10<>i5) and (i10<>i4))
                        or ((number=8) and (i10<>i9) and (i10<>i8) and (i10<>i7) and (i10<>i6)
                          and (i10<>i5) and (i10<>i4) and (i10<>i3))
                        or ((number=9) and (i10<>i9) and (i10<>i8) and (i10<>i7) and (i10<>i6)
                          and (i10<>i5) and (i10<>i4) and (i10<>i3) and (i10<>i2))
                        or ((number=10) and (i10<>i9) and (i10<>i8) and (i10<>i7) and (i10<>i6)
                          and (i10<>i5) and i10<>i4) and (i10<>i3) and (i10<>i2) and (i10<>i1)) then
                        begin
                        [Inner loop
                        end
```

Figure 3.27   For statement formulation with additions to allow variable number of digits.

REFERENCES

[Cor 79] Corbató, F. J, and Clingen, C. T. "A Managerial View of the Multics System Development," in P. Wegner (ed.), *Research Directions in Software Technology*. Cambridge, MA: M.I.T. Press, 1979.

[Jac 75] Jackson, M. A. *Principles of Program Design*. New York: Academic Press, 1975.

[Jac 76] ———. "Constructive Methods of Program Design, in K. Samuelson (ed.), *Proceedings of First Conference of the European Cooperation in Informatics*. (Lecture Notes in Computer Science, Vol. 44.) New York: Springer-Verlag, 1976. (Also in [Berg 79] and [Fre 80b].)*

[Orr 77] Orr, K. T. *Structured Systems Development*. New York: Yourdon, 1977.

[Par 79] Parnas, D. L. "Designing Software for Ease of Extension and Contraction," *IEEE Transactions on Software Engineering*, March 1979. (Also in [Ram 78] and [Fre 80b].)*

PROBLEMS

1. Draw a data flow diagram for the program of Section 8.2.1.3.

2. A 10×10 array has been punched on 10 cards, each card containing the values of a column of the array. In other words, the first card contains the values of the first column, and so on. A program CHANGE is desired, which will process these cards and produce a new set of cards, each card in the new set containing the values of a row of the array.
   (a) Derive a data flow diagram showing a solution for this problem.
   (b) Provide a program in PASCAL or FORTRAN 77, based on the data flow diagram.
   (c) Does CHANGE contain any internal data objects? Why or why not?

3. The texts of a group of telegrams have been stored in a sequence of 1000-character records on a magnetic tape. Each telegram is a sequence of words, in which consecutive words are separated by one or more blank characters. The sequence . . . (three periods) ends each telegram. Between the last word of the telegram and the terminating sequence, and between the terminating sequence and the first word of the next telegram, there are one or more blank characters. The words and terminating sequences may be split across the tape blocks.
   A program is desired to print a report showing, for each telegram, the number of words and the average number of characters per word.
   (a) Derive a data flow diagram showing a solution for this problem.
   (b) Provide a pseudocode version of the desired program, based on the data flow diagram.

4. Draw three different data flow diagrams for
   (a) Problem 1 of Appendix D
   (b) Problem 2 of Appendix D
   (c) Problem 6 of Appendix D

---

*See Appendix B: Bibliography.

Each data flow diagram should have different objects and therefore different actions that manipulate these objects.

5. A program is to have inputs of types 1,2,3, . . . , n. Define data blocks that can be used to
   (a) Store whether an input of each type has occurred.
   (b) Store how many inputs of each type have occurred.
   (c) Store when (e.g., as first input, second, third, etc.) inputs of each type have occurred.

6. A file has control records of types 1,2, . . . , n interspersed with other records. For such a file to be correct, no control record type can occur more than once, and the types must appear in a special sequence. Define a data block to store the sequence of control record types.

7. The inputs to a program contain names for which the program will substitute numeric codes. For output, the numeric codes will convert back to names. Define two types of code blocks that can be used for this purpose. Which is preferable if there are few names? Many names?

8. Sam's Sport Sedans specializes in putting sporty front suspensions on four-door sedans. Fortunately for Sam, the front suspension parts of many automobile makes fit the front ends of other makes. For example, a Cadillac front end can take the suspension parts of Pontiacs, Oldsmobiles, and even some foreign makes. Sam wants a program that will allow him to type in an auto make (e.g., Ford), a part type (e.g., front strut), and a classification (e.g., stock or firm or sport), and then get a list of all parts of that type (e.g., Ford J2795, Lincoln T578) that would fit. Define data blocks to store such data.

9. The computer science department is writing a program to detect conflicts in class schedules for each term. Two courses are *potentially conflicting* if the catalog lists both courses as required for the same year in a major. For example, if a major in computer science requires both Engineering 355 and Computer Science 310 in the junior year, then these courses are potentially conflicting. A *conflict* exists when the meeting times of sections of potentially conflicting courses overlap so that it is impossible for a student to simultaneously take all of the potentially conflicting courses in the same semester. If a conflict exists, the program is to print out the major, year, and set of conflicting courses.
   (a) Define two types of data blocks that can be used to store the class schedules.
   (b) Define two types of data blocks that can be used to indicate potential conflicts. Which is preferable if there are few courses? Many courses?

(c) Define a data block that can be used to indicate whether an actual conflict exists.

(d) What are the major tasks of this problem? What are the difficulties of each task?

10. A popular kind of microcomputer program is the *electronic spread sheet*, a program that maintains an array A of elements. In general, an element may contain either alphanumeric data or numeric values. For each element with numeric values, the user can define a formula giving the value of that element in terms of the values of other elements. For example, the user can define $A[1,6]=A[1,1]+A[1,2]+A[1,3]+A[1,4]+A[1,5]$. As the user enters data into an element, all of the elements whose formulas use that value are automatically changed.

(a) Assume that the formulas are stored as data. Define data blocks that allow the program, given the subscripts i,j of an element, to find the appropriate formula.

(b) Define data blocks that allow the program to find, for each element A[i,j], a list of elements affected by a change in the value of A[i,j].

PROJECT OUTLINE: Problem Tasks   Choose a problem in Appendix D or C.

1. List the major tasks required for the problem. State why each task is required. If you have a specific strategy or overall approach for the solution of the problem, state it.

2. List the major tasks whose solutions are not obvious. State why each of these tasks is difficult to implement.

3. Suggest a solution for each task listed in answer to question 2.

PROJECT OUTLINE: Design Miniproposal   Propose a design solution for a problem in Appendix D. Your solution should, as a minimum, include answers to the following questions. Your aim is to convince a technically competent reader that you understand the problem and that you have a correct solution. Keep your discussions clear and to the point.

Note: You may find it helpful to read the design proposal outline that appears at the end of Section 3.5.

1. Briefly discuss each major data block (object) in your solution, describing its form (array, table, etc.), number of dimensions, maximum size of each dimension, how an element is subscripted, and what information each element holds.

2. Briefly describe each major processing routine (action).

3. Provide a data flow diagram of your solution.

4. Provide an overall flowchart containing all the major processes of your solution. The processes in your data flow diagram should also appear in your flowchart.

5. Identify the critical actions of your solution, and propose a solution for each critical action that you identify.

3.4 DESIGN USING SIMULATION MODELS

3.4.1 Simulation Models: Purpose and Method

A *system* is a collection of interdependent elements (or components or entities) that act collectively. Business organizations, airline reservation networks, automobiles, and national economies are all systems.

We are often interested in predicting the behavior of a system. For example, it may be important to know the average response time of a proposed airline reservation system, or the way a car will ride with a new suspension, or the results of a rise in interest rates.

A common way of examining system behavior is to construct a *model*—an abstraction of the system that captures the system's essence for the particular purpose we are interested in.[4] A model may be formal or analytic (i.e., use only formal mathematics to state the system's properties, as for example, when a shock absorber is described by means of differential equations).

An analytic model may be useless or impossible when the formal operations are difficult, the system is complex, or the components do not interact in a precisely defined way. Then, we use a *simulation model*, that is, a model whose components represent the components of the system of interest on a one-for-one basis and in which each component's behavior mimics the behavior of the represented component. For example, a simulation model of a computer time-sharing algorithm will have a process representing the computer and a process representing each job (i.e., program being executed), together with mechanisms that provide execution sequence and allow interaction between the processes.

---

[4]Different purposes or viewpoints will suggest very different models. For example, a rise in interest rates might be examined by a speculator in gold, by a budget planner, by a historian of banking practices and their effects on small borrowers, or by a political forecaster. Examination of a shock absorber could focus on the stresses on the materials within the shock absorber, or on the forces at the linkage between absorber and car body, or on the dampening effect felt in the driver's seat.

The first step in simulation modeling is determining the components of the system. For example, suppose we wish to simulate order handling, customer credit and billing, parts inventory, and parts ordering for an automobile supply house. We can use the requirements diagramming technique to determine a set of activities, as in Figure 3.28, which can serve as the components of the system.

Each activity of Figure 3.28 can be a component of the system. The next step is to develop a *process description* or *scenario description* [Fra 77] for each component. A scenario description specifies the sequence of phases or steps taken for the component. For example, the order filling activity consists, for each order, of the following:

1. Receive the order.
2. Send credit request to Customer Credit for credit approval.
3. Wait for approved maximum amount of credit.
4. Receive approval of maximum credit amount.
5. Signal if maximum credit not sufficient.
6. Send order to parts inventory.
7. Wait for notices of parts available and parts unavailable.
8. Receive notices.
9. If parts are unavailable, prepare a back order.
10. Send partial or full order to Customer Billing.

Each phase of the order filling activity with respect to an individual order is specified, including the waiting phases in which no action is taken.

Likewise, scenarios are developed for the other activities of Figure 3.28. In the simulation, there will be a process for each entity in the system. Thus, while there will be only one order filling process, there will be many customer processes, one for each real customer. The customer processes will constitute a class of processes, each one following the same scenario. We assume that though each customer is, of course, different, each customer process incorporates a copy of the customer scenario.

From this viewpoint, each action (i.e., activity) of the requirements diagram is a process in the simulation. The behavior of the system is explicitly spelled out in terms of these actions. In contrast, the behavior of the system with respect to objects is indicated implicitly if at all.

The systems can be simulated equally well from the opposite viewpoint, in which each object (e.g., an order, a part, a bill) in the system is a process in the simulation. The scenario for an order process is roughly the following:

1. Order sent by customer to Order Filling.
2. Received by Order Filling.
3. Credit approval sent for.
4. Wait for credit approval.

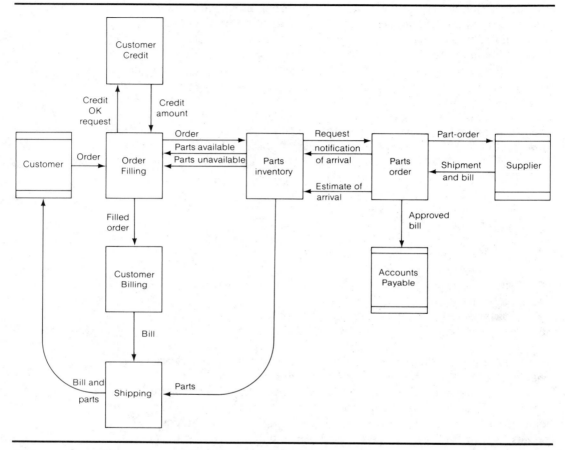

Figure 3.28 Customer and parts handling system.

5. Sent to Parts Inventory.
6. Received by Parts Inventory.
7. Wait for notices of availability.
8. Noticed received.
9. If parts unavailable, then back order initiated and filed.
10. Partial or full bill sent to Customer Billing.
11. Received by Customer Billing.
12. Bill sent to Shipping.
13. Bill received by Shipping.
14. Bill and parts sent to customer.

When the system is simulated from the *action* viewpoint, behavior with respect to objects is only implicitly stated. The flow of objects through the system is spread out among the action scenarios. When the system is simulated from the *object* viewpoint, behavior with respect to actions is implicitly stated, and the activity sequences are spread throughout the object scenarios.

3.4.2 Use of Models in Design

Jackson [Jac 78] notes that a system may be designed by using simulation modeling techniques. For a system like the one in Figure 3.28, the usual procedure would be:

1. Determine the requirements of the desired system.
2. Arrive at a specification of the program function.
3. Design a system to perform that function.

Jackson suggests that step 3 can be expanded into two steps:

3'. Develop a simulation model of the entire system.
4. Incorporate the program function into the simulation model.

The simulation model ensures that the entities of the software system explicitly correspond to the entities of the underlying real-world system. If the entitities of the software system mirror those of the real world, then (in Jackson's view) the program should be easy to understand and easy to maintain.

The correspondences between the model and the underlying reality should be apparent. Thus the model should provide the basis for understanding how and why the software system works, and it should also allow the program to be easily changed as requirements change.

Jackson [Jac 78] proposes that a system be modeled in a slightly unusual way. Each independently active entity in the real-world system is to be represented by a process. In other words, both the actions and the objects of the system are represented by processes. In addition to the processes Order Filling, Parts Inventory, and so on, the simulation model of Figure 3.28 has a process for each customer, for each order, for each supplier, and for each part. As suggested by the scenario descriptions of Section 3.4.1, each phase or state in the lifetime of the real-life entity is mirrored by a corresponding phase or state in the process representing that entity. (See Section 6.3 for related discussions of finite state models.)

As in all simulation models, each process is considered to be executing on a dedicated processor, so that questions of process scheduling or sharing of processors are not relevant. The processes are not synchronized in any way. Each process may have local variables that indicate attributes such as an address, or that summarize history (e.g., a customer's balance).

Jackson also proposes that processes communicate with each other via infinitely expansible queues that contain serial data streams. Each data stream consists of a sequence of records, each record written into the queue by the sending process and read by the receiving process. A process may have any number of input or output data streams. A receiving process is blocked when it attempts to read a record from an empty queue, but (since the queue is infinitely expansible) a sending process can always write another record into the queue. A process sends (writes) a record to another process when it takes an action that affects that other process; the record indicates the action taken or a result of that action; and the second process receives (reads) a record when it is ready to be affected by an action of the sending process.

We may visualize certain processes as initiating action by their own volition. For example, a customer process may be considered to initiate order transactions at will, just as a real-world customer orders parts at any time he or she desires. Alternatively, to give the model some properties of a software system, a process may be allowed to have special input queues, which carry messages from the real world directing the process to perform a certain action. For example, a customer process can have an input queue that directs the process to initiate an order transaction. Similarly, a process may be allowed to have a special output queue through which it sends reports or other outputs to the real world.

In general, each process will belong to a *process class*. For example, there will be a class of customer processes, a class of order processes, and so on. All of the processes in a class will be identical copies; we may visualize, say, a master-customer process, of which all of the customer processes are copies. A process may create a process of another class, may communicate with it by data streams, and may later terminate the created process by sending it a "terminate" message. For example, to simulate a customer initiating an order, a customer process creates an order process.

In any system, one process may perform an action that affects another process, or it may send a message to the other process. In the type of model proposed by Jackson, either of these activities results in the sending of a corresponding message through a data stream queue. In other words, both explicit interactions (i.e., messages) and implicit interactions between processes are formalized as messages.

3.4.3 A Static Simulation Model

Jackson's proposed model can be modified slightly to obtain a more static model. Since all customer processes are identical (except, of course, that at any instant each one is potentially in a different status), we may visualize just one slightly more general master-customer process that has a "status board" showing the total status (process number, state, messages to be sent, messages received, etc.) of each individual customer process. Likewise, we may visualize a master-order process that has a status board showing the status of each individual order. (See Section 6.4 for related discussions of table-directed processes.)

To signify a message from customer M to order N, the master-customer process simply prefixes (M,N) to the message and sends it to the master-order process. If customer M wishes to create order N, the message might be (M,*)create(N).

There is thus one master process for each process class, together with information for each individual instance of the class. The master process can change the status of an individual instance, or it can create or destroy individual instances. The static simulation model is closer to an implementable system.

To illustrate the static model, suppose that a lending library communicates with its customers by mail. A customer's message may request a book or return a book. If the book requested is available, the library sends it to the customer by return mail; otherwise, the library places the customer's name on a waiting list. The customer may have up to five books on loan at the same time.

If a program is desired to automate the processing, the first step is to create a model of the situation. The entity classes (process classes) of this situation are customer, library, book, and loan. According to Jackson's proposal, there is a process for each customer, a process for the library, a process for each book, and a process for each loan.

Also according to Jackson, there is a data stream from each customer to the library, carrying request and return messages, and a data stream from the library to each customer, carrying book sent or book wait-listed messages. There is a data stream from the library to each book, carrying customer requests, and a data stream from each book, carrying availability information. Finally, there is a data stream from the library to each loan, carrying loan information and perhaps queries, and a data stream from each loan to the library. (Remember that the library creates loans.)

In the static model there is a master-customer process, a library process, a master-book process, and a master-loan process, as shown in Figure 3.29.

The master-customer process reads request and return messages from the real-world customer and communicates these to the library process. The library process incorporates an algorithm that decides which customer is to receive the book when two or more customers have requested the same book. The master-book process incorporates a waiting list.

The system of Figure 3.29 clearly models the real world of the lending library problem. Each part of the real-world problem is specifically provided for, as are the interactions between these parts. How is this model affected by changes in the problem requirements? Any new problem requirements relating

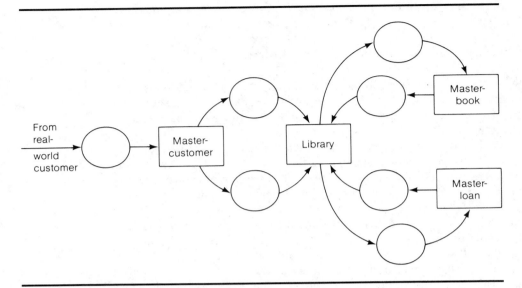

Figure 3.29 Model of the lending library.

to customers can be accommodated by changes *only* to the master-customer process. For example, the master-customer process might be extended to acknowledge requests from the real-world customer, to inform the customer when a book is not available and the request is wait-listed, to send reminders for overdue books, or to ask inactive customers whether they wish to retain their memberships. Likewise, new requirements relating to books can be accommodated by changes *only* to the master-book process. For example, the master-book process might be extended to estimate waiting times based on its wait list, to keep statistics on each book's popularity and usage, or to remind the library when books should be rebound. Finally, the master-loan process might be extended to calculate fines for overdue books, and so on.

3.4.4 Advantages of the Model

Two important observations can be made about the above example. First, because the system explicitly models each entity of the real-world situation, small requirements changes relating either to a specific entity or to some interactions between two entities are accommodated by localized changes in the model. If the final software system embodies this model, then small requirements changes will be accommodated by localized program changes.

Equally important, changes relating to *objects* of the real-world situation (as well as to actions) can be accommodated in localized program changes. (Recall the extensions that could be made to the master-book process.)

Other models do not provide explicitly for objects in the real world, and, consequently, systems derived using those models cannot reflect those objects. If an object is not mirrored by a localized portion of the system structure, then code pertaining to that object could appear anywhere in the program. Consequently, a small requirements change relating to that object could cause code changes throughout the program. This model avoids that possibility. The concerns and design decisions relating to each activity or each object are isolated within one process of the model.

REFERENCES

[Fra 77] Franta, W. R. *The Process View of Simulation*. Amsterdam: North-Holland Publishing Company, 1977.

[Jac 75] Jackson, M. A. *Principles of Program Design*. New York: Academic Press, 1975.

[Jac 76] ———. "Constructive Methods of Program Design," in K. Samuelson (ed.), *Proceedings of First Conference of the European Cooperation in Informatics: Lecture Notes in Computer Science*, Vol. 44. New York: Springer-Verlag, 1976. (Also in [Berg 79] and in [Fre 80b].)*

[Jac 78] ———. "Information Systems: Modelling, Sequencing and Transformations," *Proceedings of 3rd International Conference on Software Engineering*. (IEEE Catalog No. 78CH1317-7C.) New York: IEEE Computer Society, 1978. (Also in [Ram 78].)*

PROBLEMS

Questions 1 through 4 refer to the lending library system of Figure 3.29.

1. Write a scenario description for each master process.

2. (a) List the types of messages that would be sent

   - From the real-world customer to the master-customer process
   - From the master-customer process to the library process
   - From the library process to the master-customer process
   - From the library process to the master-book process

---

*See Appendix B: Bibliography.

- From the master-book process to the library process
- From the master-loan process to the library process

   (b) For each type of message given in part (a), list the information required in the message.

3. (a) List each possible status (or phase, or state) of each customer, each book, each loan, and of the library.

   (b) How would the sets of states and the sets of messages be extended to accommodate:

- Registration of new customers
- Suspension of borrowing privileges for customers with 2 or more books overdue
- Introduction of "special customers" allowed to borrow up to 10 books, and "probationary customers" allowed to borrow only 2 books
- Introduction of paperback books that have to be rebound after every 70 loans
- Reference book loans for 1 day only
- Introduction of special loans for current popular books, in which the customer pays 5 cents for every day the book is kept

4. Suppose that it is now desired to add a system of fines, keeping track of fines for all customers. Describe:
   (a) How the existing processes could be expanded to include the new fines system.
   (b) How a new fine process could be added and the other processes revised.

5. Describe the process classes, the scenarios of each process class, and the necessary messages that could constitute a model for:
   (a) The student grading system shown in Figure 2.3.
   (b) The seminar handling system described in Problem 1 of Section 2.2.3.
   (c) The system of Problem 11 in Appendix D.

3.5 DOCUMENTING THE DESIGN

3.5.1 The Design Proposal

3.5.1.1 Types of Documentation

In achieving a design, the designer makes assumptions about the scope of the problem and the characteristics of the inputs, develops an overall approach, and analyzes critical actions. The design is then evaluated, and after the evaluation it is transformed into code. In order to be evaluated or coded, the design must be *documented*, that is, written down in some standard fashion.

Inexperienced designers tend to believe that design documentation can be ignored for projects involving no more than a few people. However, it is easy for a person to forget assumptions and conclusions, and also easy for people to forget what they have previously agreed upon. In a small software project involving students [Kat 71], it was found that written records of specification and overall design tended to prevent arguments and also helped in critiques. A written record will allow a design to be easily continued after not being worked on for some time, and it will allow another person to continue if the original designer is unable to continue for some reason.

Section 3.5 discusses two types of documentation. Section 3.5.1 is concerned with a design proposal, in which a preliminary version of a design is proposed to a user, for evaluation. Section 3.5.2 discusses detailed ongoing documentation.

3.5.1.2 Overview of a Proposal

The purpose of any proposal, whether in the sciences, the arts, or in business, is to argue convincingly that a particular task ought to be done, or that it can be done, or both.

In particular, the purpose of a design proposal is to convince its reader that a proposed design is feasible and appropriate. The solution is outlined to show the overall approach, and the resolution of critical issues is discussed.

The elements of a design proposal are presented below, interspersed with hints that can be applied to the writing of any proposal. However, the most important hint of all is that a proposal *must be clearly written*.

The design proposal format of the project outline following this section contains four major sections:

1. *Scope of Solution:* This section discusses important assumptions and restrictions, and program design objectives.

2. *Overall Approach:* This section contains a broad outline of the solution, including:
   (a) Description of major data blocks
   (b) Description of major processing routines
   (c) Data flow diagram
   (d) Flowchart of major processes
   (e) Discussion of important data blocks and important mappings

3. *Discussion of Critical Actions:* This section discusses important conditions, algorithms of the actions, and efficiency questions.

4. *Evaluation of the Plan:* This section discusses major data blocks and a walkthrough of processing for a typical input and for a worst case input.

3.5.1.3 Motivation

In situations where the recipient of the proposal is not familiar with the proposed task or scheme, a proposal usually begins with the motivation for the proposed task. The discussion suggests why the project is being done, or why it should be done, and stresses the potential theoretical or practical benefits, for example, that the use of the proposed program would save employee time (a practical benefit), or that the successful development of the proposed program would show the theoretical possibility of some process (theoretical benefit). This "motivation" section of a proposal is usually entitled Introduction, and it also usually states the general objectives of the proposed task (e.g., "to develop a FORTRAN compiler").

3.5.1.4 Scope of Solution

This discussion precisely states the problem to be considered. Included are assumptions and restrictions about the problem, improvements and enhancements that the solution will provide, and important program design objectives.

Recall from Chapter 2 that restrictions and assumptions assign boundaries to the planned input class. Determining such boundaries is the first step in design. A review of known facts and known sources of data is usually necessary to ensure that the restrictions are sensible.

A programming task may be stated in general terms such as "to develop a FORTRAN compiler." This statement does not impose any restrictions on the input, and thus a program presented to this compiler might have an arbitrarily large number of statements, or might have arbitrarily many statement labels. Although a compiler could be written to accommodate arbitrarily long programs or arbitrarily many labels, most designs impose limits on the number of statements and on the number of labels.

Such restrictions should be stated since they delineate the actual capabilities being proposed (e.g., no more than 1000 labels) in contrast to the general objective (e.g., a FORTRAN compiler).

This point is important if the proposal is made in response to a request from a customer. The proposer, in stating an intended scope, is attempting to negotiate about the program specification in order to have a precise (and perhaps more manageable) statement about the proposed program. But, in attempting to shape the specification, the proposer takes the risk that the proposal—if its restrictions are too many or too sharp—will not be considered responsive to the request and thus be rejected. Conversely, a design that solves an enhanced form of the given problem may be preferred.

3.5.1.5 Design Approach

The proposal now discusses how it intends to solve the problem. This section may begin with a statement of design objectives and techniques, if it is important that the proposed program meet a specific performance specification.

Next, the task is briefly outlined, or (if the task can be sensibly broken down into smaller units) the important subtasks are suggested and outlined. In the program design, such subtasks should appear as major processing routines.

The overall design and techniques of the proposed program are now presented. First, a list of the major data blocks is given with a brief description of each block. The description states the form of the block (e.g., two-dimensional array) and indicates how a typical element is accessed.

Second, a list of major processing routines is given with a brief description of each routine. A data flow diagram is provided, and a discussion of the data flow diagram is included if appropriate.

Critical actions in the solution are identified and discussed. Important conditions are indicated, the difficulties caused by such conditions are enumerated, and algorithms are presented. Refinements added to improve execution are presented. Tiny details of data blocks or processing routines are not included. (A separate section is provided for critical actions in the proposal format of this chapter.)

This section shows the reader that the program has been carefully considered since important or critical problems are indicated and plans for dealing with them are suggested. It also indicates that the proposer understands the proposed program and has a plan for obtaining it.

3.5.1.6 Evaluation of the Plan

This section estimates space requirements and indicates a walkthrough of processing for a typical input and a worst case input. The processing walkthrough indicates how the overall scheme and the critical actions will perform for various inputs.

3.5.1.7 Proposals in Industry

Test Plans Proposals in industry will contain much of the information above and may also contain the discussion of this section. Large or complex programs may require a carefully planned sequence of tests. If applicable, such a sequence is outlined. Foreseeable problems and testing difficulties are indicated. In certain situations, as, for example, in the validation of a statistical program, the test methods and data should be carefully arranged and pertinent test methods indicated.

Deliverable Items   This section states exactly what items are proposed to be delivered and in what forms. For example, a program might be delivered as a card deck, or on a tape, or on a disk, or as a running component on the customer's own computer. Deliverable items can include documentation, various kinds of manuals, and so on. Sometimes the main deliverable item is programming services rather than a particular program—in this case, the proposer indicates that a certain quantity of effort will be expended, without assurance of any other result.

Schedules   This section gives time estimates for the phases of program development. For small projects, total personnel and total time estimates may be given for each of the development phases. For larger projects, schedules may be given for each major subsystem, and the effort within each phase may be given in finer detail.

3.5.2 Ongoing Documentation

3.5.2.1 Documentation Concepts

As a design is developed, it exists in the designers' heads and/or in written form (i.e., documentation). In the absence of the designers, the documentation is the only form in which the existing design can be precisely communicated. If the designers happen to be working on many projects at the same time, they tend to forget design details, and a written statement of the design can be helpful to them.

Thus everyone agrees that documentation is important. Unfortunately, designers often neglect to document; they visualize documenting as the preparation of a long, formal, document, which will keep them from their work for many hours.

Documenting can aid rather than hinder the work of design. Ogdin [Ogd 78] describes a helpful documenting technique called the *working design manual*. A working design manual is an organized collection of (usually short) memoranda or working papers pertaining to a project. The manual is intended to be *informal* and *incremental*.

The term *informal* means that the working design manual and each paper or memorandum in it are intended as working papers whose purpose is to aid the design. They are not intended to be formal documents distributed outside the project group. A typical memorandum may outline design objectives, or list reference manuals, or clarify a design point, or point out questions or problems that remain to be dealt with. At later stages of the design, tables, charts, data formats, and initial program versions may be added. The organization is changed and rechanged during the project as the designers feel it is appropriate to do so.

The term *incremental* means that everything is documented as soon as it happens. If the design group decides on a list of design objectives or a list of major design questions to be investigated, a memorandum is immediately written and filed in the working design manual. The same thing happens if an important design decision is made. Previously filed memoranda are updated as desired. Several people, or several groups of people, can be continually contributing to the working design manual.

This method allows easy documentation of points usually left undocumented, namely, aspects or questions that are unclear, unknown, or not yet decided. For example, at the beginning of a project, after noting the overall objectives and design, a designer can write a memorandum indicating questions to be investigated, points that are unclear, information known, and information as yet unknown. Such documents aid in formulating problems and solutions, help focus investigations, and draw attention to difficulties.

The papers in the manual constitute an ongoing, continually updated reference manual, which can also be used in training new project personnel. At the end of the design effort, a formal design document can be written from it.

This style of documenting can be continued throughout all of the phases of system development, including the beginning versions and successive improved versions of the programs and summaries of test results. The manual is then an indicator of progress to date as well as a reference manual. It also usually includes scheduling and other management information.

When the project is over, the working design manual remains as a history of all the data, problems, decisions, and people involved in the project. This is a valuable resource that can be used to suggest problems and solutions for similar projects.

3.5.2.2 Organization of the Working Design Manual

3.5.2.2.1 General   A working design manual is kept in a looseleaf notebook so that pages can easily be added or removed. Ogdin suggests that most one-person software projects can be documented in a one-inch notebook, while complex hardware/software projects may require a two-inch notebook. Projects involving many people may require a separate manual for each subproject and one master manual for the entire system, as well as a special manual to document standards and practices. The master manual would contain specifications and requirements for the whole project, as well as a design specification for each subproject.

The notebook is divided into named sections. The number of sections and the name of each section are chosen for their appropriateness and relevance to the project. Thus designers have freedom to arrange the most useful organization. The manual may be reorganized one or more times during the project, as more useful organizations are perceived.

```
                                    BILLING SYSTEM/---
                                    821015/PG/PROB
                                    (820920/PG/TENT)
                                    ADMIN
                                    Page 9 of


              APPENDIX 3—SECTIONS OF THE MANUAL

    ADMIN        Administration of this manual and project
    OVERALL      Overall objectives and design
    DATA         Reference manuals and data sheets
    CONFIG       Hardware configuration
    FEATURES     Features seen by the user

      .
      .
      .
    DOC          Documentation standards for deliverable manuals
    SCHEDULE     Scheduling of development activities
    STAFFING     Personnel assignments
    REPORTS      Progress reports to management and customer
```

Figure 3.30   A page from a working design manual, showing
revision of the sections of the manual.

Figure 3.30 shows a page from the administrative section of a working design manual. Each page in the manual carries an identification in the upper right-hand corner with the following information:

· Project title
· Subproject title
· Date written
· Writer's initials
· Status of the page
· Revision information if appropriate
· Section name
· Page number

The page in Figure 3.30 is for a billing system: The dash line following the project title indicates that the page pertains to the whole system rather than to a subsystem.

An unambiguous form for the date is a sequence of six digits in which the first two digits give the year, the second two (01 through 12) give the month, and the last two give the day. Thus October 15, 1982, is written as 821015.

Page status indicates how tentative or final the information is. Ogdin suggests that the following five status categories are usually sufficient:

COMM (for communiqué)
TENT (for tentative)
PROB (for probable)
FIRM
FINAL

A communiqué usually gives information other than specifications or decisions. For example, a communiqué might report on a meeting with a vendor or on a commercially available software package, or it might raise issues or questions that require resolution.

The date, the writer's initials, and page status are usually written on one line. If the page is a revision, then the date, writer's initials, and status of the previous page are shown on the next line, in parentheses. The revised page should also indicate which lines are changed from the previous page. In Figure 3.30 the lines differing from the previous page are marked with a vertical bar.

3.5.2.2.2 Administrative Section　　Every working design manual has an administrative first section (usually named ADMIN), which describes the purpose and content of the manual and how the manual is to be maintained. This information acts as an introduction to the manual for new project personnel.

The administrative section has several appendixes:

1. Appendix 1: *Distribution*. This is a list of the names and addresses of the holders of the master manual and of each copy, for the secretarial staff to use when sending out updates.

2. Appendix 2: *Design Team*. This is a list of all project participants (giving initials, full name, and other appropriate information for each participant) that identifies each project number and the initials that that member will be using in writing memoranda to the manual.

3. Appendix 3: *Sections of the Manual*. This is a list of all sections, giving for each section a name (e.g., ADMIN) and a short (one or two line) definition of its contents.

Any of the appendixes may be revised during the project.

3.5.2.2.3 Other Sections　　The OVERALL section usually contains objectives given by management and a nontechnical discussion of the desired software and its design. The DATA section contains data sheets and background information. The SCHEDULE and STAFFING sections give day-to-day management information such as schedules of activities, resource estimates, and records of resource consumption.

The SCHEDULE section can also contain an agreed-upon schedule of project (or subproject) milestones. Figure 3.31 shows a form that could be used for such a schedule [Willi 75, Ingr 78]. The form indicates the particular routines included in the schedule and the project personnel responsible for the project or subproject. The responsible project personnel agree with their supervisor or customer as to when they will receive requirements and a design specification (line 1 in Figure 3.31) and start work, when they will provide test results confirming successful operation (line 6), and when they will provide documentation for the project as built (line 7).

```
                                    BILLING SYSTEM/INPUT EDIT
                                    820720/PG/FINAL
                                    SCHEDULE
                                    Page 1 of ____

        PROJECT   BILLING SYSTEM
        SUBPROJECT   INPUT EDIT
        RESPONSIBLE   Jane Smith, Mary Doe
        ROUTINES INCLUDED   EDITCHECK, EDITERROR
```

Line	Description	Due date	Date complete	Originator	Reviewer
1	Receive requirements				
2	Preliminary design				
3	"Code-to" design				
4	Test plan				
5	Code				
6	Test results				
7	Documentation				
8	Problem reports				
9	Notes				
10	Reviewer's comments				

Figure 3.31 Project schedule form.

The intermediate due dates for lines 2, 3, 4 and 5 are then scheduled by the project personnel. As each milestone is completed, one of the project personnel (designated as responsible for the schedule) enters the date and initials the schedule. A reviewer assigned by the supervisor or customer then reviews the work done and initials the schedule if the work is satisfactory. A separate binder with a section for each line in the form can be maintained to hold the project results. If assigning responsibility for due dates is important, one-person subprojects can be arranged.

REFERENCES

[Ingr 78] Ingrassia, F. S. "Combating the 90% Syndrome," *Datamation*, January 1978.

[Kat 71] Katznelson, J. "Documentation and the Management of a Software Project—A Case Study," *Software—Practice and Experience*, April–June 1971.

[Lec 67] Lecht, C. P. *The Management of Computer Programming Projects.* New York: American Management Associations, 1967.

[Ogd 78] Ogdin, C. A. *Software Design for Microcomputers.* Englewood Cliffs, NJ: Prentice-Hall, 1978.

[Weinb 71] Weinberg, G. M. *The Psychology of Computer Programming.* New York: Van Nostrand Reinhold, 1971.

[Weinw 70] Weinwurm, G. F. (ed.). *On the Management of Computer Programming.* Philadelphia: Auerbach, 1970.

[Willi 75] Williams, R. D. "Managing the Development of Reliable Software," *Proceedings of International Conference on Reliable Software*, Los Angeles. (IEEE Catalog No. 75CH094-7CSR.) New York: IEEE Computer Society, 1975.

PROBLEMS

1. Describe the differences between design documentation and maintenance documentation. What kinds of information should each document contain?

2. Describe the differences between a design proposal and a final design document. For whom is each document intended? What kinds of information should each document contain?

3. Your employer is a publisher of games and puzzles. In order to speed up the development of new puzzles, your employer has asked three software developers to propose solutions for a crosstics program, as given in Problem 13 of Appendix D.

(a) Are there any unclear points in Problem 13? If so, list them and state why they are unclear. Has important information been left out of the problem statement? If so, what is it?

(b) You will have to evaluate the three proposals that your employer has received. State what points a proposal must cover (or what information it must contain) to be:
(1) barely acceptable.
(2) a good proposal.
(3) an excellent proposal.

4. Your employer (still a publisher of games and puzzles) has now asked for proposals on the map coloring program, Problem 14 in Appendix D.

(a) State any unclear points in Problem 14. Why are they unclear? Has any important information been left out of the problem statement. If so, what is it?

(b) You will now have to evaluate the proposals. State what points a proposal must cover (or what information it must contain) to be:
(1) barely acceptable.
(2) a good proposal.
(3) an excellent proposal.

5. Describe how you keep track of ideas and problems as you develop a design. Compare your method with the working design manual.

6. Your project, which has been maintaining a working design manual, has just hired a new person. Because everybody else is very busy at the moment, you wish to start training the new person by using the working design manual. What instructions should you give about reading the manual?

7. Your software development team has been writing PASCAL compilers for several years. You have just been assigned a new compiler to write, and a new person has just been hired. Describe how you will train the new employee in your methods if:

(a) You have not been maintaining working design manuals for each project.

(b) You have been maintaining working design manuals for each project.

8. Each page of a working design manual carries an identification in its upper right-hand corner. Is all this identification really necessary? For each piece of data in the identification, state why it is or is not necessary.

PROJECT OUTLINE: Design Proposal   Propose a design solution for a problem in Appendix D. Your proposal should, as a minimum, include answers to the following questions. (Questions labeled *Optional* may be omitted if not applicable to your proposal.)

Imagine that you are proposing a solution to a technical manager in your company, or that your proposal is an attempt to win a contract from a customer company to program this problem. In either case, you may assume that the reader is technically competent to evaluate your proposal. Your aim is to convince the reader that you understand the problem and its various difficulties, and that you have a correct solution in mind. Keep your discussions clear and to the point.

It is a good idea, after you are finished, to read through your proposal to ensure that your answers all agree and that the walkthroughs of questions 13 and 14 really do reflect the operation of your proposed solution. An even better idea is to think of several worst case inputs (see question 14) before beginning work on the design solution, and then to build the proposed solution so that it can handle these worst case inputs. Last, but not least, try for a solution that at least anticipates enhancements in the required processing.

A. Scope of Solution

1. State any assumptions or restrictions about inputs and outputs that are important to your design formulation. (If there are none, just answer, "None.")

2. (*Optional.*) State any improvements or enhancements of the given problem that your solution provides.

3. (*Optional.*) State any critical or important design objectives that your proposal is intended to meet, in addition to the prime objective of providing a correct solution. (Examples of such objectives are minimal execution time, portability, table-driven algorithms, etc.)

B. Overall Approach

4. Briefly discuss each major data block (object), describing its form (array, table, etc), number of dimensions, maximum size of each dimension, how an element is subscripted, and what information an element holds.

5. Briefly define each major processing routine (action).

6. Provide a data flow diagram of your solution.

7. Provide an overall flowchart containing all the major processes of your solution. The processes in your data flow diagram should also appear in the flowchart.

Note: Answers 4 through 7 should all agree. If questions 6 and 7 are answered first, these answers will provide the data blocks and processes to be described in questions 4 and 5.

8. (*Optional*.) If there are implementation details you consider critical or important, or any programming difficulties you foresee, discuss them briefly. Explain the data flow diagram or flow chart as necessary.

C. Analysis of Critical Actions

9. Identify the critical actions of your solution.

10. For each critical action identified, discuss the important conditions and problems that the action must consider, and propose a solution.

11. If applicable, indicate refinements that have been added to improve execution speed.

D. Evaluation of the Plan

12. Estimate the space required in core memory for the major data blocks.

Note: Solutions requiring more than 128K words are *not* acceptable.

13. Walkthrough the processing of a typical input by your solution.

14. Give a worst case input that poses the greatest possible difficulty for your solution. Why does this input cause difficulty? Walkthrough the processing of such an input by your solution.

15. Does your solution work for the inputs of your answers to 13 and 14? Does it work for all worst case inputs?

16. Discuss how your solution would be affected by enhancements in the required processing.

3.6 EVALUATING THE DESIGN

3.6.1 Overview

Completing a design is the developer's first step in obtaining a software system that meets the functional and quality specifications discussed in Chapter 2.

Since the purpose of a design is to preview the workings and characteristics of the final system, the design should be judged against both kinds of specifications as soon as it is done. In this way, any deficiency can be found at the earliest stage, before the development proceeds to greater detail.

As a development moves from phase to phase, into greater and greater detail, deficiencies and errors become harder and more expensive to fix. Ideally, the development results should be evaluated at the end of each phase for errors and deficiencies, so that each phase involves a cycle of creation followed by evaluation.

The correctness of a design is always of paramount concern. Correctness can be evaluated by the designer or by a review group (see Section 10.3). In either case, the design concept is examined to see whether it properly handles each input situation. At least two inputs are walked through the design, as in the project outline following Section 3.5. During the examination, the designer or review group plays devil's advocate, trying to think of conditions that will cause the design to fail. The evaluation tries to find deficiencies so that they can be remedied during the design phase.

In addition to a data flow diagram, a design concept includes techniques, standards, and practices chosen to meet the various quality specifications. Section 3.6.2 discusses the development of such techniques. Section 3.6.3 presents review methods developed by Gilb [Gilb 79] to systematically evaluate whether the chosen collection of techniques meets a quality specification. The collections of techniques and evaluations can, of course, be kept in a QUALITY section of the working design manual discussed in Section 3.5.

A key aspect of a design is its *suitability* to the desired task, that is, the extent to which the characteristics of the designed system match desired characteristics. Section 3.6.4 presents criteria that can be used to evaluate the suitability of any system. These criteria can be combined into any quality specification.

In addition to the evaluation methods of Section 3.6, the user's reactions to the design can be obtained if a draft of the user's manual is written at the end of overall design and reviewed by the user. This review can reveal assumptions, restrictions, or design features that are unacceptable to the user.

Finally, when the design concept has been completed and evaluated, it is time to devise a *test plan*, that is, a plan for testing and evaluating the software as it is completed. Testing is the most expensive and most time-consuming development phase, but it is less burdensome if plans are made in advance. Test planning can be done concurrently with detailed design and coding, and, in fact, the test plans may influence the sequence in which portions of the software are developed. For example, if a decision table specification is available and the relative frequency of each column is known, it will usually be desirable to schedule the development and test so that the most frequent input cases are tested first. Section 5.4 discusses test strategies involving many modules, while Chapter 9 discusses testing single modules.

3.6.2 Auxiliary Techniques and Practices

Sections 3.2, 3.3, and 3.4 describe methods for obtaining an overall layout of data blocks and processes as a first step in developing a desired software system. If it is carefully done, the initial design also includes techniques, standards, and practices chosen to meet various quality specifications. Examples are:

- To meet a user input quality requirement, a particular input technique is specified;
- To meet a portability requirement, the use of PASCAL is specified;
- To meet a maintainability requirement, logical records are to be arranged in a certain way.

Section 2.4 shows that a quality specification can be obtained by first outlining broad objectives and then successively refining and quantifying these objectives. The auxiliary techniques are developed by a continuation of this procedure. A first question is whether a quality attribute is really a class of attributes. For example, if there is a requirement that "99.9 percent of potential input errors are detected," and if there are two classes of users (e.g., clerks and executives), then there are really two error detection quality requirements—which may require different techniques.

Every quality attribute has an impact on many different aspects of the resulting software/hardware/people system. Typically, a given quality attribute has an impact on

- Programs or processes
- Data blocks or data base
- People and organization
- Hardware
- Documentation

The designer determines for each aspect of each quality attribute, techniques that will help to satisfy that aspect of the quality requirement. Thus a given quality attribute may result in hardware techniques, documentation techniques, and so on. A particular aspect may be divided into subaspects if it is helpful to do so (e.g., subaspects "application programs" and "utility programs" might be used instead of "programs").

For each quality attribute, a *technique list* is developed. Table 3.2 [Gilb 79] shows a partial technique list developed by Gilb for the maintainability

Table 3.2 Partial technique list for maintainability specification.
(First published in the *Pergamon Infotech State of the Art Report on Structured Software Development*, Pergamon Infotech Ltd., 1979. Reprinted by permission.)

Description / Reference Code	Text Specification / Further Details
M.DBA	Full data base audit program shall be built to selectively test all codes, records, relations.
M.RLH	All logical records shall have a record level hash total check.
M.RC	Error recovery programs shall be selectively correcting and initiated by simple operator action command.
M.LST	Program logical structure shall be forward flow, no backward go tos. Maximum module size 50 statements (non comment code).
M.TXT	Program text shall be logically grouped by indentation. Comments shall be made for at least 30% of source lines on average.
M.2PG	All record update logic modules shall exist in distinct logic versions for comparison and for spare parts maintenance use.
M.AST	'Assertion' statement logic comments shall be included for at least each 10 program statements, and checked for all changes.
M.INS	Formal inspection of all proposed changes shall be carried out before approval given Fagan/IBM method).
M.MPG	Maintenance programmers shall be considered qualified only when they can pass artificial bug finding tests at 90% in 5 minutes level.
M.TEL	Shift operators shall have home telephones and duty roster for qualified maintenance programmers and rules for when to call.
M.LIB	All programs and all text documentation shall be available on a central machine library.

specification of Table 2.11.[5] Each technique is given a mnemonic reference code that uniquely identifies it. For example, the data base audit program technique is given the code M.DBA, M for maintenance and DBA for data base audit. Similarly, the record level hash technique is named M.RLH, and so on. A given technique may help more than one quality attribute.

A technique may be refined into subtechniques, and a technique tree given, just as quality attributes may be refined into subattributes.

3.6.3 Evaluation of Techniques

A technique list such as Table 3.2 describes each technique and shows to which qualities it contributes. It is important to review the techniques with respect to every combination of quality and aspect, to determine:

· Which techniques contribute to each combination of quality and aspect
· Whether some combinations have not been provided for

A *quality review* chart can be used for this purpose. Table 3.3 shows a maintainability review, that is, a quality review chart for the maintainability specification of Table 2.11. Each row of Table 3.3 names a quality attribute of Table 2.11, and each column names an aspect. Thus each square represents a particular aspect of a particular attribute. In each square are placed the reference codes (from Table 3.2) of the techniques that contribute to that aspect of that attribute. Thus the chart summarizes on one page every combination of quality attribute and aspect, and the techniques that contribute to that aspect.

A quality review chart indicates whether a list of techniques covers all aspects of a set of quality specifications. If a square is blank, that combination of aspect and attribute has not been explicitly provided for. The designer must then determine whether for that combination, the design has a potential weakness which might result in the software not meeting the quality specification. A 0 in a square indicates the determination that no technique is necessary for that combination.

---

[5]The partial technique list of Table 3.2 is shown using the same format as Table 2.11, even though the information could be shown in a simpler format. Gilb advocates the use of a single all-purpose form (boxed-in leftmost column, top ruled so as to delineate columns and permit long text headings, and dots that demarcate the "squares" due to intersecting rows and columns). Depending on the intended purpose, the columns may be ignored (as they are here), or (as in Tables 2.11, 3.2, and 3.3), the open part of the form may be regarded as squares (each formed by an intersection of a row and a column) which are filled in. Column headings are included or omitted as appropriate. Although it appears complex at first, the all-purpose form is easy to work with and serves for all of the quality specifications and summaries that Gilb advocates.

Table 3.3 Quality review chart for maintainability specification.
(First published in the *Pergamon Infotech State of the Art Report on Structured Software Development*, Pergamon Infotech Ltd., 1979. Reprinted by permission.)

Aspect / Attribute	Application Programs	Utility Programs	Data Base	People and Organization	Hardware
Problem Recognition			M.DBA M.RLH M.RC	M.MPG	
Administrative Delay				M.TEL	0
Tool and Document Collect	M.TXT. M.2PG M.LIB	M.LIB	M.LIB	M.LIB	M.LIB
Problem Analysis		M.AST		M.MPG M.AST	
Change Specification	M.2PG			M.MPG	
Active Correction	M.2PG		M.2PG	M.MPG	
Local Correctness Test	M.AST	M.AST			
Global Side-Effect Test	M.AST M.DBA M.RLH	M.AST M.DBA M.RLH	M.INS	M.INS	M.AST M.RC M.RLH M.DBA
Independent Change Audit	M.INS	M.INS		M.INS	0
Recovery from Effect of Problem					

An entirely blank row in a quality review chart indicates that no techniques at all have been specified for that quality attribute and suggests a potential major design weakness. Thus Table 3.3 indicates that no techniques have been provided for the quality Recovery from Effect of Problem and, consequently, further design is required. In sum, a quality review chart clearly indicates areas of potential design weakness.

Evaluation of the design cannot be complete without an estimate of the quality levels actually achieved by the design. Such an *estimate of achieved quality levels* indicates, based on the techniques chosen,

· Which quality levels are expected to fall far short of planned levels
· Which quality levels are expected to just meet planned levels
· Which quality levels are expected to far exceed planned levels

In other words, the estimate indicates how strongly the chosen techniques guarantee that planned quality levels will be met. If the achieved level of any quality is far below the planned level, then further design is needed for that quality. The overall design is not complete—and development should not proceed to the next phase—until the estimate of achieved quality levels indicates that all the planned quality levels will be met. Remember that any system deficiency is most easily fixed in the design phase.

An estimate of achieved quality levels can be indicated in two ways. One way is to quantize the quality review chart, adding to each technique reference code a numeric estimate of the contribution of that technique to the planned quality level. Gilb [Gilb 79] suggests that the estimate be made as a percentage contribution toward the planned level. Thus, in the second row, fourth column of Table 3.3, we might write M.TEL(50%), thereby indicating that the technique M.TEL contributes 50 percent toward the planned level of administrative delay. The sum of contributions in a row would then indicate the extent to which the planned level is expected to be achieved:

· A total of 50 percent would indicate that the planned level is not expected to be achieved because the chosen techniques go only 50 percent of the way toward guaranteeing the planned level
· A total of 100 percent would indicate that the planned level is expected to be just barely achieved because the chosen techniques go exactly 100 percent of the way guaranteeing the planned level
· A total of 200 percent would indicate that the planned level will be comfortably achieved or exceeded because the chosen techniques provide a safety factor of 2 in guaranteeing that the planned level will be met

As shown in the third row of Table 3.3, one technique may contribute in many ways toward a quality level. Also, some techniques make major contributions while others make minor contributions. Accordingly, Gilb [Gilb 79] suggests an *estimated-quality-level chart* as in Table 3.4. In this chart, each

Table 3.4 Estimated-quality-level chart.(First published in the *Pergamon Infotech State of the Art Report on Structured Software Development*, Pergamon Infotech Ltd., 1979. Reprinted by permission.)

Technique Reference Code / Attribute and Planned Level	Full Data Base Audit Program	Distinct Software Logic Module Copies		Assertion Logic per 10 Statements			
				Maintenance Programmer Qualification			
					All Other Minor Specific		
	M.DBA	M.2PG	M.AST	M.MPG	RLP, RC LST, TXT TEL, LIB	Inspection M.INS	Sum, %
Problem Recognition (60 min)	80%	10%	5%	0%	?	0%	95%
Administrative Delay (60 min)	0	95% (BUGS) IF ONLINE REPLACE-MENT	0	0	0	0	DESIGN NEEDED
Tool and Document Collection (10 min)					50%(TEL) 90%(M.LIB)		90%
Problem Analysis (5 to 10 min)	30%	30%	20%	15%	5%	5%	105%
Change Specification (5 min?)	0	0	0	50%	10%	20%	80%
Active Correction (15 to 30 min)	0	95% IF ONLINE BUG CORRECTION	−10%	80%	10–30%	−20%	ABOUT 100%
Local Correctness Test (5 min)	10%	30%	30%	20%	5%	30%	ABOUT 100%
Global Side-Effect Test (100× act. corr.)	80%	5%?	15%	5%	0%	15–25%	ABOUT 100%
Independent Change Audit (same day)	50%	4%	5%	0%	1%	40%	100%
Recovery from Effect of Problem (2 hr.)	0	0	0	0	0	0	DESIGN NEEDED

row names a quality attribute and each column names a technique or collection of techniques. In each square is placed the percentage contribution of the technique(s) to the planned level of the named quality. Table 3.4 is an estimated-quality-level chart showing the contributions of the techniques of Table 3.3 to the planned quality levels shown in Table 2.11.

The percentage contributions in Tables 3.3 and 3.4 are the designer's subjective estimates since there is currently no objective way to estimate such contributions. However, several simple practices can help the designer obtain reasonable estimates. First, any uncertainty in an estimate can be explicitly expressed as, for example, 80% ± 20%, to explicitly express an estimation range. Second, the designer can document previous experience with the technique(s) or papers about the technique(s) that lead to the estimate. Estimates can be reviewed by the designer's peers (see the discussion of peer reviews in Section 10.3). Last but not least, the designer can build in a *safety factor*, designing to estimated quality levels of 200 percent, 300 percent, or even 1000 percent for critical qualities.

Even though the percentages in an estimated-quality-level chart are subjective and may include uncertainty, the chart does provide a systematic evaluation of a design with respect to all planned quality levels. And this evaluation highlights deficiencies and allows for remedy during the design stage.

An estimated-quality-level chart can also be used to estimate the cost effectiveness of each technique, that is, the effectiveness per unit cost. Each technique yields a set of percentage contributions to each quality, as in Table 3.4. If we assign weights to the qualities, as in the MECCA model of Section 2.4, then an overall percentage contribution can be calculated for each technique. If cost estimates are available for each technique, then cost effectiveness can be calculated by the formula

Cost effectiveness=overall percentage contribution / cost for each technique

For example, in Table 3.2, the overall percentage contribution/cost of each technique toward maintainability could be calculated, as could the cost effectiveness of each technique toward achieving maintainability.

Since the most cost effective technique should be given the highest priority for implementation, the cost effectiveness calculations rank the techniques in a priority order for implementation. If a tight budget were given for maintainability, then the priority ranking would allow the designer to choose a set of techniques from among those in Table 3.4 that would stay within the budget and also get the most "maintainability for the money."

Recall that the maintainability specification of Table 2.11 is an "exploded" specification giving subsidiary quality factors for maintainability. Other qualities will require other sets of techniques, and each set of techniques can be ranked in order of cost effectiveness. Moreover, if each major quality is assigned a weight as in the MECCA model, then an overall percentage contribution to the entire system quality level can be calculated for each technique.

Thus system cost effectiveness can be calculated by the formula

$$\text{System cost effectiveness} = \frac{\text{overall percentage contribution to entire system}}{\text{cost}}$$

for each technique, and all techniques proposed for the system can be ranked in order of cost effectiveness. (Those techniques that contribute to two or more qualities can be expected to have high system effectiveness.) These calculations can allow a system to be built within a given budget and yet have the "most quality for the money."

3.6.4 Criteria for Suitability

In evaluating a design, it is important to determine whether the proposed system is *suitable* for its intended task, that is, whether its characteristics match those of the intended task. Roughly speaking, a design is suitable for a task if the user is better off with the system than without it. Put more sharply: a design is suitable only if the user is not worse off with the system than without it.

Mehlmann [Meh 81] has proposed four criteria of design suitability:

1. Doing assigned tasks should not take longer with the system than without it.

Although this criterion seems obvious, it is not easy to meet because the user, having to deal with a computer system as well as the assigned tasks, may actually have more to do than before.

2. Information to which the user has access should not be less accurate with the system than without it.

3. The user should have access to as much needed information with the system as without it.

In evaluating with respect to this criterion, it is important to distinguish between needed information and extraneous information. A different amount of information will be needed in each specific situation. Thus the system may be expected to offer fast response when little information is required as well as full details in exceptional conditions. A problem may arise when a user wants information that is not actually needed. Then the designer must convince the user that less information is sufficient, or must satisfy the user in some other way, perhaps by providing reports not available without the system.

4. The user should not have a more boring task when using the system, than he previously had without the system.

In other words, the system should not take over the most enjoyable parts of the user's task, leaving the user with the boring parts. Such a situation leads to poor employee morale. On the other hand, if the system does the boring, repetitive work and the user does the nonroutine work, higher productivity and better employee morale result.

These criteria can be formulated as qualities, namely:

· Time to perform assigned tasks
· Accuracy of user information
· Amount of information accessed by user
· Enjoyability of tasks

and the existing (presumably manual) system can be studied to determine the quality levels. The existing quality levels should become the worst case levels for design purposes, if these criteria are to be met.

REFERENCES

[Gilb 79] Gilb, T. "Structured Design Methods for Maintainability," *Infotech State of the Art Report on Structured Software Development*, Infotech. Maidenhead, England, 1979.

[Gilb 81] ———. "Design by Objectives: A Structured Systems Architecture Approach." Unpublished manuscript, 1981.

[Meh 81] Mehlmann, M. *When People Use Computers*. Englewood Cliffs, NJ: Prentice-Hall, 1981.

PROBLEMS

1. Describe how evaluation information can be incorporated in the working design manual of Section 3.5.

2. How do you or your software group keep track of techniques to be used, and their purpose, as you develop a design? Compare your method with the technique list.

3. Why is each technique in a technique list assigned a unique reference code?

4. How do you or your software group evaluate the impact of techniques on planned quality levels? Compare this method to the use of technique lists, quality review charts, and estimated-quality-level charts.

5. In the estimated-quality-level chart, the estimates of percentage contributions are subjective. Does this make the estimates invalid? Why or why not? How would review of the estimates by a peer group achieve more valid estimates?

6. Why would a designer include enough techniques to achieve an estimated quality level of 200 percent or more?

7. After working a while at your new job, you have discovered that the project leader is very informal about design and tries to get programs coded as soon as possible. As unofficial historian, you have been keeping track of design decisions. You have just reminded the leader that the specification calls for 99 percent portability and noted that no techniques have been adopted to ensure the portability.

   "That's OK," is the answer. "Let's code the programs first, get them working, then go back and fix them for portability."

   What are the problems with your leader's approach? What outcomes can most likely be expected? What should you say?

PROJECT OUTLINE: Quality Specification and Technique Evaluation Consider a problem in Appendix C or D.

1. Derive a quality specification for the problem.

2. Provide a list of techniques in the form of Table 3.2 that should ensure the planned quality levels.

3. Provide a quality review chart for the list of techniques.

4. Provide an estimated-quality-level chart. Be sure to explicitly indicate any uncertainties in your estimates. Give a reason for each estimate.

Note: This project can be integrated with the design proposal of Section 3.5: The quality specification (1 here) answers question 3 of the design proposal; the technique list (2) answers question 8 of the design proposal; and answers to 3 and 4 of this project can become answers 17 and 18, respectively, of the design proposal.

Part Three
SYSTEM DESIGN
AND DEVELOPMENT

Introduction to module organization: Organizing a system into modules . . . diagramming organizations of modules . . . variations in organization

Design and development of module organization: Principles of organization . . . organizing via top-down design . . . organizing by isolation of design factors . . . strategies for testing

chapter four
Introduction to
Module Organization

4.1 ORGANIZATION AND ITS ANNOTATION

4.1.1 What Is Organization?

Careful program structuring eases the difficulties of testing and allows better understanding of the program's complexity. This fact becomes more important for programs larger than one person can accomplish, and it is crucial for those enormous programs that lie beyond the intellectual grasp of any one person [Par 75a, Bela 77].

Programs are commonly arranged as collections of subroutines. This chapter discusses the use of subroutine mechanisms specifically for organizing programs into collections of independent subprograms. In Section 4.1 we define system organization and show how to diagram it. In Section 4.2 we discuss characteristics of different organizations.

Conforming to industry usage, we say that a program system is a collection of independent pieces called *modules*. We refer to the program piece comprising the main program as a module, and we also refer to subprogram pieces as modules. In concept, every module of a program system, except for the main program module, is a subroutine (in PASCAL terminology, a procedure) or a function subprogram. Accordingly, in concept, every module (except for the main program module) is called (or invoked) via a subroutine call, is given zero or more input parameters (i.e., subroutine arguments), performs some task, and returns zero or more output parameters (i.e., results).

In practice, modules are implemented in various forms. Examples are subroutines and functions in FORTRAN, procedures and functions in PASCAL, or macros in a macro-assembly language. Our discussion will not consider the differences among these implementations.

Examination of a large number of programs would reveal certain recurring characteristics. We would find that a program always contains a collection of data elements; that it typically has several program segments; and that it typically uses devices such as readers, printers, and disks. Larger programs are usually composed of subroutines, and, typically, some of these subroutines in turn make use of other subroutines. Information is transferred between modules in the following ways:

· Arguments are passed through subroutine call and return mechanisms
· One module accesses or sets data contained in another module
· Data is available to several modules, via use of common data areas

The collection of programs, subroutines, data sets, and devices, together with the arrangements for information transfer between parts of a program system, is called the *organization* of the program system.

The organization of a program system determines how it can be maintained or modified. For example, modifying the structure of a common data area may require modifying every program that references that data area, while a module accessed only via subroutine calls may be modified independently of other parts of the program, except possibly for modification of the subroutine calls. Thus examining the organization of a program is essential in evaluating the program.

4.1.2 Organization Diagrams

An *organization diagram*, in conjunction with two data usage tables, summarizes the organization of a program system. The entire collection of subroutines, their control relations, and their data communications are captured

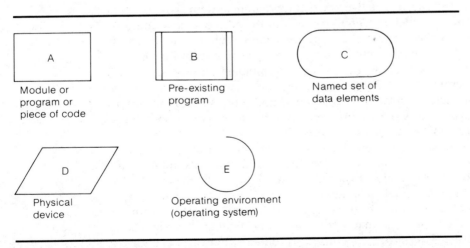

Figure 4.1   System components used in organization diagrams.

in a single diagram. Of course, no single diagram can capture all of the information about a program system. The organization diagram, in order to concisely capture the system's organization, omits some information about the sequence in which subprograms execute. (Our notation is derived from the organization diagrams of Stevens et al. [Ste 74] and Yourdon and Constantine [You 75b].) Figure 4.1 shows the kinds of system components considered in organization diagrams.

Rectangle A in Figure 4.1 designates either an entire program (or module) or a portion of a program (i.e., a piece of code). Rectangle B designates a library routine, or a facilities program, or any other program furnished to the system in a completed form. Figure C designates a named collection of data, such as a variable, a table, or a common data set. Figure D designates a device such as a printer or card reader, while Figure E designates an operating system subprogram.

In all following discussions, the term *program* may also be taken to mean "piece of code," and may refer to a preexisting program such as the one labeled B in Figure 4.1 or to a program such as the one labeled A in the same figure.

System components may be connected via the four types of links shown in Table 4.1. In the definitions of Table 4.1, C_1 and C_2 are any two system components.

The restrictions on C_1 and C_2 in Table 4.1 define all physically possible links. A link "D calls P," where D is a physical device and P is a program, is disallowed only because it is physically impossible for a device to call a program. Some examples of links are shown in Figure 4.2. (Call links are discussed further in Section 4.1.4.)

Table 4.1 Links between system components

Type of Link	Definition	Restrictions on C_1, C_2
Reference	$C_1 \longrightarrow\!\square\ C_2$ C_1 references data in C_2	C_1 not a physical device C_2 not a physical device
Call	$C_1 \longrightarrow\!\bullet\ C_2$ C_1 calls C_2 (a subroutine or function or physical device call)	C_1 not a physical device
Go to	$C_1 \longrightarrow\ C_2$ the text of C_1 has a transfer of control to somewhere in the text of C_2	C_1 not a physical device C_2 not a physical device
Include	$C_1 \longrightarrow\!\triangleleft\ C_2$ the text of C_1 includes the text of C_2	C_1 not a physical device C_2 not a physical device

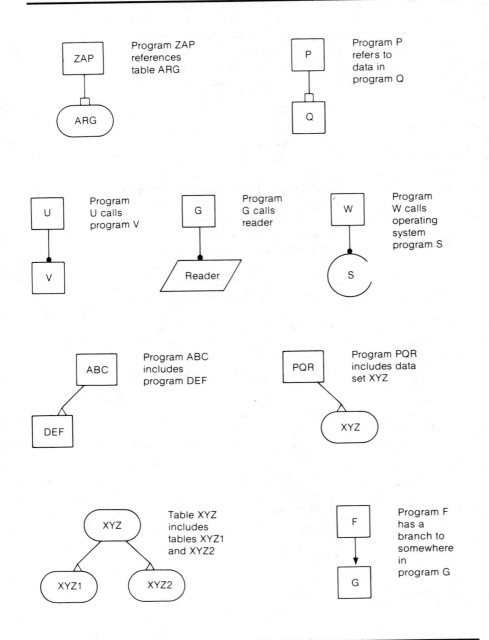

Figure 4.2 Examples of links between system components.

Within the definitions of Table 4.1, many logically improper kinds of links are possible. For example, a link "X calls P," where X is a data table and P is a program, is logically improper since a data table cannot logically call a program. That action is appropriate only for a program or an operating system subprogram. Accordingly, we will say that a link "X calls P" is pathological.[1]

The definitions of Table 4.1 also allow links in which a system strongly interacts with a portion of the operating system. An example is "P references S," where P is a program and S is an operating system subprogram. Such interaction is undesirable except for systems designed to support an operating system, and, accordingly, we will say that a link "P references S" is anomalous.[2]

Table 4.2 classifies links as either ordinary, anomalous, or pathological. The use of anomalous or pathological links in a system indicates poor organization; in designing a system, one should use only ordinary links.

Table 4.2   Ordinary, anomalous, and pathological links

Type of Link	Ordinary Usage	Anomalous Usage	Pathological Usage
Reference	$P \,—\!\square\, X$ $P_1 \,—\!\square\, P_2$	$P \,—\!\square\, S$ $S \,—\!\square\, X$ $S \,—\!\square\, P$ $S_1 \,—\!\square\, S_2$	$X \,—\!\square\, P$ $X_1 \,—\!\square\, X_2$ $X \,—\!\square\, S$
Call	$P_1 \,—\!\bullet\, P_2$ $P \,—\!\bullet\, D$ $P \,—\!\bullet\, S$ $S \,—\!\bullet\, D$	$S \,—\!\bullet\, P$ $S_1 \,—\!\bullet\, S_2$	$P \,—\!\bullet\, X$ $X \,—\!\bullet\, P$ $X_1 \,—\!\bullet\, X_2$ $X \,—\!\bullet\, D$ $X \,—\!\bullet\, S$ $S \,—\!\bullet\, X$
Go to	$P_1 \,—\!\!\to\, P_2$	$S \,—\!\!\to\, P$ $S_1 \,—\!\!\to\, S_2$ $P \,—\!\!\to\, S$	$P_2 \,—\!\!\to\, X$ $X_1 \,—\!\!\to\, X_2$ $X \,—\!\!\to\, P$ $X \,—\!\!\to\, S$ $S \,—\!\!\to\, X$
Include	$P_1 \,—\!\triangleleft\, P_2$ $P \,—\!\triangleleft\, X$ $X_1 \,—\!\triangleleft\, X_2$	$S_1 \,—\!\triangleleft\, S_2$	$P \,—\!\triangleleft\, S$ $X \,—\!\triangleleft\, P$ $X \,—\!\triangleleft\, S$ $S \,—\!\triangleleft\, P$ $S \,—\!\triangleleft\, X$

[1]Systems for which concealment of code is of the utmost importance may embed portions of programs within data tables, thereby creating pathological links.
[2]Obviously such links will not be anomalous for a system designed to support an operating system.

In Table 4.2, P, P_1, and P_2 are programs; X, X_1, and X_2 are named sets of data elements; S, S_1, and S_2 are operating system subprograms; and D is a physical device.

The use of only ordinary links does not guarantee a good organization. Figure 4.3(*a*) shows a portion of a typical organization in early micro-computer-based systems, which had very little memory. In this system, program V calls program U and program P calls program Q. When called by P, Q usually returns via the call/return mechanism, but sometimes Q transfers control to program R. On the basis of further tests, R either transfers back to Q, or R transfers control to program U, which "returns" to program V via the call/return mechanism—even though U was not called this time by V! In other words, U improperly uses the existing call/return mechanism between V and U. This complex and error-prone organization was used instead of the alternate organization of Figure 4.3(*b*) in order to save about a dozen bytes of memory.

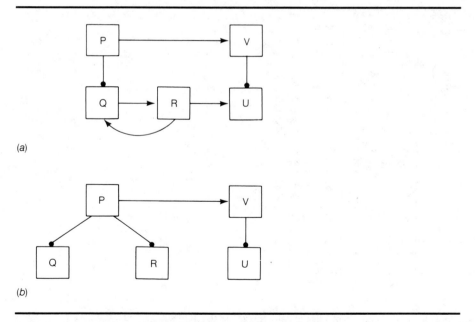

(*a*)

(*b*)

Figure 4.3 Two alternative organizations. (*a*) A poor organization. (*b*) A better alternative.

4.1.3 Characteristics of Diagrams

In an organization diagram, each system component is considered a physical entity, and is shown only once in the diagram. A system component may have more than one link to another system component, and may have links to many other components.

The go to link (⟶), as used in organization diagrams, means only that a transfer of control is possible between two programs. For example, in Figure 4.3(a), a transfer of control is possible from program R to program Q and transfer is also possible from R to U. Accordingly, in Figure 4.3(a), there is a go to link from R to Q and also a go to link from R to U.

The sequence in which programs execute and the sequence of calls from a program to its subroutines are not shown in these diagrams. For example, in Figure 4.4, the text of program ABC includes the texts of programs DEF and GHI—but the diagram does not imply that DEF precedes GHI in the text of ABC. Also, in this example, declaration of the array XXX is included in the text of DEF, and the array is referenced by both DEF and GHI.

The include (⟶◁) link is a relation between the texts, or listings, of system components. That is, "C_1 includes C_2" means that the listing of C_1 includes the listing of C_2. It is sometimes necessary that several conceptually distinct modules be packaged together as one physical module, and the include link allows this relation to be shown. Alternatively, this link can be used to show the organizations of segments of a program text.

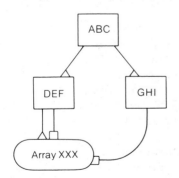

Figure 4.4   A program with two subprograms.

Table 4.3 Summary of properties of the include (——◁) link

Situation	Implication
1. A ——◁ B and B ——◁ C	A ——◁ C
2. A ——◁ B and B ——□ C	A ——□ C
3. A ——◁ B and A not ——◁ C and B ——● C	A ——● C
4. A ——◁ B and A not ——◁ C and B ——▶ C	A ——▶ C
5. A ——◁ B and C ——◁ B	C ——□ A
6. A ——◁ B and C ——● B	C ——● A
7. A ——◁ B and A not ——◁ C and C ——▶ B	C ——▶ A

"C_1 includes C_2" means that C_2 is actually part of C_1, and thus this link has some unusual properties. Table 4.3 summarizes the implications of situations involving system components A, B, and C.

Figure 4.4 shows examples of situations 1 and 4 of Table 4.3. Since in Figure 4.4, "ABC includes GHI" and "GHI references XXX," it is implied that "ABC references XXX." The situation "ABC includes DEF" and "DEF references XXX" yields the same implication. Also, since "ABC includes DEF" and "DEF includes XXX," it is implied that "ABC includes XXX."

4.1.4 Call Links between Modules

4.1.4.1 Input and Output Parameters

Probably the most important information in an organization diagram is contained in the call links between modules. The pattern of such links graphically illustrates the pattern of module usage. For example, a module used by many others will be seen to have many call links to it, while a module that makes many calls will be shown with that many call links from it.

It is assumed that for every link "A calls B," module B returns to A at a location in A immediately following the call to B. Given this assumption, A can regard the operation of B (including the operation of any modules called by B) as a single irreducible operation. All sensible strategies for organizing program systems share this assumption. Organizations containing modules that violate this assumption can be expected to behave chaotically rather than in a predictable fashion, and can be expected to be difficult to maintain and modify.

Every call link is in concept a subroutine call, in which certain quantities (called *input parameters*) are sent to the called routine, and quantities (called *output parameters*) are produced by and returned by the called routine.

As an example, suppose that abc is an m × n array and invert is a procedure that inverts arrays. The statement invert(abc,m,n)

uses input parameters abc, m, and n. Since abc is modified by invert, abc is also an output parameter.

Next, suppose that abc and yxz are both m × n arrays and invcopy is a procedure that inverts an array and also copies the inverted array into a second array. The statement

invcopy(abc,m,n,xyz)

has input parameters abc, m, and n (assuming that abc will be inverted) and output parameters abc and xyz. Note that xyz is not used in the calculation of invcopy and thus is not an input parameter. In sum, a given parameter may be either an input parameter, or an output parameter, or both, though coding conventions or language restrictions may prohibit some of these possibilities.

Also, the statement

y:=z+sin(x)

contains a call to a function module sin. The quantity x is sent to the module sin and thus is an input parameter. The result of the function's calculation is returned to the calling statement via the name sin, and thus sin is an output parameter. In fact, for every function module f, the name f itself is an output parameter.

Finally, a module need not use input or output parameters. A function get that brings to the calling routine one input character at a time, uses the output parameter get, but no input parameter. Indeed, no input parameter is necessary. Suppose job is a procedure divided into subprograms process1 and process2, and each subprogram is contained in its own module. The sequence

```
procedure job;
    begin
    process1;
    process2
    end
```

calls process1 to perform the first subprogram and process2 to perform the second program. No parameters are used.

4.1.4.2 Interface Description: Description of Formal Parameters

The connection between a calling module and a called module can be described either in terms of the formal parameters of the called module or in terms of the actual parameters. Speaking loosely, we may say that the description in terms of formal parameters takes the viewpoint of the called module,

Table 4.4   An interface table

Module and Calling Sequence	Formal Parameter	Input	Output	Use	Significance of Parameter
f(x)	x	✔		P	
	f		✔	M	
. . .					

while the description in terms of actual parameters takes the viewpoint of the calling module.

Both types of description are useful. The description in terms of formal parameters, which we call an *interface description*, states in a canonical form the relation of a called module to the calling modules. We suggest for this purpose an interface table arranged as in Table 4.4. (Interface descriptions are not given for physical devices such as readers or printers.) As shown in the sample interface description in Table 4.4, one row of the table is used for each parameter of a module.

The interface table lists for each (called) module:

1. The module calling sequence
2. Each formal parameter
3. Whether each parameter is an input parameter (if so, a check is made in the input column)
4. Whether each parameter is an output parameter (if so, a check is made in the output column)
5. The use of each parameter (explained below)
6. The significance of each parameter

The meaning and use of the formal parameters are constant for every call of the module.

In diagramming an existing program, we wish to indicate the actual use of subroutine parameters. It is important to check that each input parameter is not used in a trivial way. That is, such an examination might reveal that the parameter serves no real purpose.

The use column of an interface description contains mnemonics that indicate roughly how the parameter is used in the module. A list of mnemonics and their significance is given in Table 4.5. The usages shown in the table are not precise and are intended only to give a rough idea of the parameter usage. A parameter may have more than one use.

Table 4.5   Types of parameter usage

Mnemonic	Significance
P	The parameter is "processed"; i.e., it appears on the right-hand side of an assignment statement and thus is used directly to compute the value of some other variable.
M	The parameter is modified; i.e., it appears on the left side of an assignment statement.
T	The parameter is transferred with its value unchanged by the called module to another module via a subroutine or function call in the called module.
C	The parameter is used as a control variable, perhaps by acting as a switch index or as a flag value, or by specifying a function to be used by the called module.
I	The parameter is transferred to another module (see t above) and is modified by that other module.

4.1.4.3 Interface Description: Access to Other Data

A module receives data through its input parameters, and may also have direct access to data in other programs. Our diagramming convention is that data received as an input parameter is shown using the call link (——•), while data accessed directly (i.e., not received as a parameter) is shown using the reference link (——□).

Figure 4.5 shows two ways in which a procedure zip could reference an array abc declared in the main program and global to zip. In Figure 4.5(a), zip contains a statement that directly accesses abc. Accordingly, the organization diagram of Figure 4.5(b) shows zip with a reference link (——□) to abc. In Figure 4.5(c), abc is transferred to zip as an input parameter, and the organization diagram in (d) shows zip without a reference link. Through carelessness, the procedure zip could be written so that abc is transferred to zip as an input parameter, but zip also contains a statement x:=abc[x] which directly references abc. In this case, the organization diagram of Figure 4.5(b) is appropriate since zip actually has access to abc in two different ways.

The interface of a called module with the rest of the system includes directly accessed data as well as the data accessed through its call parameters. A *data access table* arranged as in Table 4.6 may be used to list for a module each data object directly accessed and the location of the data. The sample description in Table 4.6 is for the program segment of Figure 4.5(a).

The module's access to such data is constant for every call of the module since the data is explicitly named in the module.

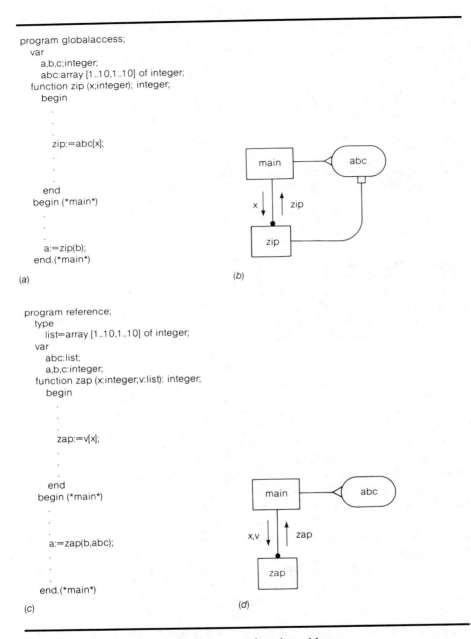

```
program globalaccess;
  var
    a,b,c;integer;
    abc:array [1..10,1..10] of integer;
  function zip (x;integer); integer;
    begin
        .
        .
        .
        zip:=abc[x];
        .
        .
    end
  begin (*main*)
        .
        .
        .
        a:=zip(b);
  end.(*main*)
```

(a)

(b)

```
program reference;
  type
    list=array [1..10,1..10] of integer;
  var
    abc:list;
    a,b,c:integer;
  function zap (x:integer;v:list): integer;
    begin
        .
        .
        zap:=v[x];
        .
        .
    end
  begin (*main*)
        .
        .
        a:=zap(b,abc);
        .
        .
  end.(*main*)
```

(c)

(d)

Figure 4.5 Modes of access to data. (*a*) A function with access to global data. (*b*) Organization diagram for program in *a*. (*c*) A function with access only through its input parameters. (*d*) Organization diagram for program in *c*.

Table 4.6   A data access table

Called Module	Data Accessed	Module Containing Data
zip	array abc	main
.		
.		
.		

4.1.4.4   Usage Description: Usage in Terms of Actual Parameters

A calling module may ascribe, from one usage to the next, very different meanings to the actual parameters of a call.

In complex systems, and especially when arguments are passed from module to module for several levels, understanding the system process requires a description in terms of actual parameters, which we call a *usage description*. We suggest for this purpose a usage table arranged as in Table 4.7.

In the column labeled actual parameter sequence, the calling sequence is recorded exactly as it appears in the program. A separate entry is made for each usage. For example, there would be another entry if R calls F, and yet another if S calls F. However, if a calling module makes several identical calls (e.g., Q calls F(x) in three different places), only one entry need be made.

Examples of call links are diagrammed in Figure 4.6. In each diagram, the actual parameters passed are shown along each link. In other words, these diagrams give a usage description of the calls.

Table 4.7   Format of usage description table

Calling Module	Called Module	Actual Parameter Sequence	Other Effects and Comments
Q	F	x	
.			
.			
.			

4.1.4.5 Patterns of Module Calls

The diagram of Figure 4.6(*a*) does not indicate whether the module AA of that figure calls BB just once or whether it calls BB a number of times. The diagram of Figure 4.6(*b*) leaves unspecified whether

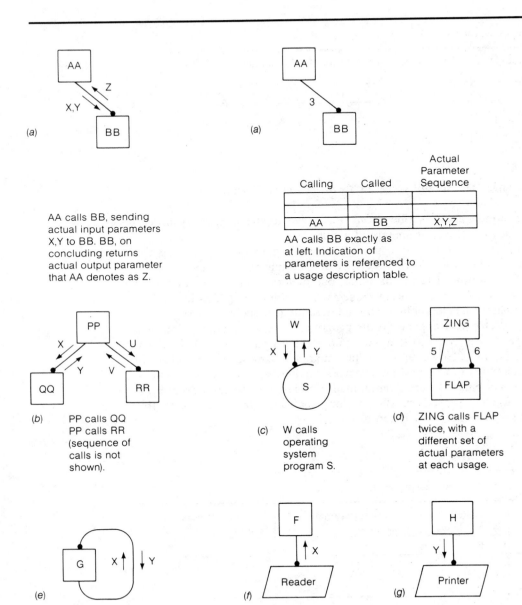

(a)

AA calls BB, sending actual input parameters X,Y to BB. BB, on concluding returns actual output parameter that AA denotes as Z.

(a)

Calling	Called	Actual Parameter Sequence
AA	BB	X,Y,Z

AA calls BB exactly as at left. Indication of parameters is referenced to a usage description table.

(b)   PP calls QQ
PP calls RR
(sequence of calls is not shown).

(c)   W calls operating system program S.

(d)   ZING calls FLAP twice, with a different set of actual parameters at each usage.

(e)   G calls itself (recursive call).

(f)   F calls reader to input X.

(g)   H calls printer to output Y.

Figure 4.6   Examples of call links.

Table 4.8   Notations for expression of call patterns

	Notation	Meaning
(a) Simple expressions	N {N} N·Q Q|R	The module N is called once The module N is called repeatedly N is called, then Q is called Either Q or R is called, but not both ("exclusive or" operation)
(b) General expressions	{E} $E_1 \cdot E_2$ $E_1 \| E_2$	The pattern of calls denoted by E is repeated an indefinite number of times The pattern E_1 is followed by the pattern E_2 Either the pattern E_1 or the pattern E_2 occurs, but not both

PP calls first QQ, then RR
PP calls first RR, then QQ
PP calls either QQ or RR or both
PP calls either QQ or RR but not both

It is sometimes useful to diagram or tabulate this information.

For any module M, we may use the data composition notation of Chapter 2 to express the pattern of module calls made by M. Let us assume modules N, Q, and R. Some simple expressions for these modules are shown in Table 4.8(a). In Table 4.8(b), each E, E_1 or E_2 is an arbitrary expression formed using module names and the operations shown in (a).

4.1.5 Construction of Organization Diagrams

The organization of a system can be captured by an organization diagram together with a set of tables (namely, an interface table, a data access table, a usage table) and the set of calling-pattern expressions. The purpose of these notations is to clarify important details or organization. Thus, though the situation shown in Figure 4.7(a) might also be properly diagrammed as in (b), Figure 4.7 (a) is preferred because the explicit indication of the table is clearer.

Organization details imposed by a given language may be omitted if such details are commonly understood. For example, the situation shown in Figure 4.8(a) for a FORTRAN program might also be diagrammed as in (b) since FORTRAN always requires that COMMON C be declared in each of PQR and XYZ. Obviously, the declarations of COMMON C in each module must be identical.

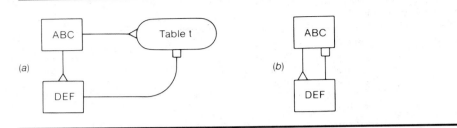

Figure 4.7 The best diagram is the one that clarifies essential details.

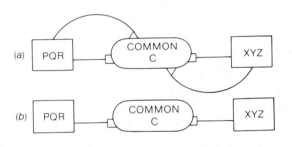

Figure 4.8 Equivalent diagrams of a FORTRAN program.

The call links between modules may depend on conventions in the programming language. For example, in PASCAL, the main program might contain the call

zip(zap(b))

requesting the execution of module zip with one parameter having the value zap(b). In this situation, because zip's parameter is a call by value parameter, it is the main program that calls zap, and zip receives only a value. However, in ALGOL zip's parameter may be an ALGOL call by name parameter, in which case zip calls zap, because zip receives the expression "zap(b)" and evaluates this expression whenever it is needed.

REFERENCES

[Bela 77] Belady, L. A., and Lehman, M. M. *The Characteristics of Large Systems*. IBM Report RC6785, 1977. (Also in [Ram 78] and [Weg 79].)*

[Hug 77] Hughes, J. K., and Michtom, J. I. *A Structured Approach to Programming*. Englewood Cliffs, NJ: Prentice-Hall, 1977.

[Mye 75] Myers, G. J. *Reliable Software through Composite Design*. New York: Petrocelli/Charter, 1975.

[Par 71] Parnas, D. L. "Information Distribution Aspects of Design Methodology." Technical Report, Dept. of Computer Science, Carnegie-Mellon University, Pittsburgh, PA, 1971. (Also in *Proceedings of IFIP Congress, 1971*.)*

[Par 75] ———. "Software Engineering or Methods for the Multi-Person Construction of Multi-Version Programs," *Proceedings of 4th Informatik Symposium; Lecture Notes in Computer Science, No. 23; Program Methodology*. New York: Springer-Verlag, 1975.

[Par 76a] ———. "On the Design and Development of Program Families," *IEEE Transactions on Software Engineering*, Vol. SE-2, No. 1, March 1976.

[Ste 74] Stevens, W. P.; Meyers, G. J.; and Constantine, L. L. "Structured Design," *IBM Systems Journal*, 1974. (Also in [Ram 78], [Berg 79], and [Fre 80b].)*

[You 75b] Yourdon, E., and Constantine, L. L. *Structured Design*. New York: Yourdon, 1975. (Republished in 1979 by Prentice-Hall.)

PROBLEMS

Give an organization diagram, interface table, data access table, and usage table for each of the following situations. Recall that subroutine parameters in FORTRAN are always call by reference. In PASCAL, subroutine parameters may be either call by value or call by reference, and are assumed to be call by value if the parameter type is not given as var (signifying variable or call by reference).

1. CALL ZIP(X,Y,J)   in MAIN program
   .
   .
   .

```
SUBROUTINE ZIP(R,S,K)
INTEGER K
REAL R,S
S = 0.0
```

---

*See Appendix B: Bibliography.

```
      IF (K.NE.0) S = R**2
      RETURN
      END
```

2. CALL ZAP(A,B,C,I)   in MAIN program
```
      .
      .
      .
      SUBROUTINE ZAP(X,Y,Z,J)
      INTEGER J
      REAL X,Y,Z
      IF (X.LE.Y) THEN
        J = 1
      ELSE
        Z = SQRT(X−Y)
        J = 2
      END IF
      RETURN
      END
```

3.
```
      SUBROUTINE ZING
      INTEGER A,B,C
      A = 1
      B = 7
      CALL FIRST(A,B)
      C = 10
      CALL SECOND(C)
      RETURN
      END


      SUBROUTINE FIRST(X,Y)
      INTEGER X,Y,C,K
      COMMON C,K
      C = X+5
      CALL THIRD(C)
      Y = C
      RETURN
      END


      SUBROUTINE SECOND(D)
      INTEGER C,D,K
      COMMON C,K
      CALL FOURTH(D)
      K = 4
      CALL FIRST(D,K)
      CALL FIFTH(D,K)
      RETURN
      END
```

```
      SUBROUTINE THIRD(C)
      INTEGER C
      C = C+9
      RETURN
      END


      SUBROUTINE FOURTH(E)
      INTEGER C,E,K
      COMMON C,K
      IF (C.GT.20) E = C*K+4
      IF ((C−K).LT.3) E = C+K−1
      RETURN
      END


      SUBROUTINE FIFTH(X,M)
      INTEGER M,X
      M = M/2
      IF (M**2.LE.5) THEN
        X = 5
      ELSE
        X = 7
      END IF
      RETURN
      END
```

Discuss the naming conventions of variables and subroutines in this example. Which practices are good, and which are poor?

4.
```
      DIMENSION VECT(1000)
      INTEGER OLDLOC
      COMMON/A/OLDLOC, NEWLOC, VECT
      READ (*,10) IFLAG, OLDLOC, NEWLOC, NBR
   10 FORMAT (418)
      IF (IFLAG.NE.1) THEN
        IF (NEWLOC.LT.OLDLOC) NBR = -NBR
        CALL SHIFT(NBR, LAST)
      ELSE
        CALL SET(VALUE)
      END IF
      STOP
      END

      SUBROUTINE SET(VAL)
      DIMENSION ARY(1000)
      COMMON/A/LSTOLD, LSTNEW, ARY
      DO 10 I = LSTOLD, LSTNEW
   10 ARY(I) = VAL
      RETURN
      END

      SUBROUTINE SHIFT (KOUNT, NEWEND)
      IF (KOUNT.LT.O) THEN
        CALL MOVEDN(-KOUNT, NEWEND)
      ELSE IF (KOUNT.GT.O) THEN
        CALL MOVEUP (KOUNT, NEWEND)
      END IF
      RETURN
      END

      SUBROUTINE MOVEDN(K, LAST)
      DIMENSION VECT(1000)
      COMMON/A/LSTOLD, LSTNEW, VECT
      DO 10 I = 1,K
      IFROM = I-1+LSTOLD
      LAST = I-1+LSTNEW
   10 VECT(LAST) = VECT(IFROM)
      RETURN
      END

      SUBROUTINE MOVEUP(K, LAST)
      COMMON/A/LA, LB, ARY
      DIMENSION ARY(1000)
      LAST = LB+K-1
```

```
      LTO = LST+1
      LFR = LA+K
      DO 10 I = 1,K
      LTO = LTO-1
      LFR = LFR-1
 10 ARY(LTO) = ARY(LFR)
      RETURN
      END
```

5. ```
   program calcarrays;
      type
         list1:array [1..10] of real;
         list2:array [1..2] of real;
      var
         x,y,z,t:real;
         i:integer;
         check:boolean;
         abc,def:list1;
         normal:list2;
      procedure set (var a: list1;s1,s2:integer;z:real);
         var
            i:integer;
         begin (*set*)
            for i:=s1 to s2 do a[i]:=z
         end (*set*);
      procedure fix (var aa:list1;ss1,ss2:integer);
         var
            i:integer;
            temp:real;
         procedure add (u:real);
            var
               j:integer;
            begin (*add*)
               for j:=ss1 to ss2 do aa[j]:=aa[j]+u
            end (*add*);
            begin (*fix*)
               if check=true then temp:=x+normal[1]
                             else temp:=y+normal[2];
            add(temp)
         end (*fix*)
      function ff (w:real):real;
         var
            temp:real;
         begin (*ff*)
            if w<3.0 then ff:=w
                     else begin
                          temp:=w/3.0;
                          ff:=w*ff (temp)
                       end
         end (*ff*);
```
```

```
begin (*main*)
  x:3.0;y:=7.0,z:=2.0;
  set (abc,1,10,0.0);
  set (def,1,10,5.0);
  normal[1]:=1.0;normal[2]:=4.0;
  check:=false;
  fix (abc,1,10);
  check:=true;
  fix (def,1,10);
  for i:=1 to 5 do begin
                  t:=abc[i]+ def[i+2];
                  abc[i]:=ff(t)
                end
end (*main*)
```

6. Contrast the diagrams of the FORTRAN and PASCAL programs. What effect does the language used have on the patterns of data reference that can be arranged? Can measures be taken in FORTRAN programs to achieve the isolation given by the call by value mechanism of PASCAL? If so, what are they, and can they be implemented via a preprocessor to the FORTRAN compiler?

4.2 VARIATIONS IN SYSTEM ORGANIZATION

4.2.1 The Effect of Data Placement

A program system can be organized as a collection of subroutines in many different ways. There may be more than a dozen ways to organize even the simplest system, while the number of variations of a complex system is bewildering. And some of the possible organizations may be intricate, even for simple systems.

To properly understand how system organizations can be developed, a designer should be familiar with all of the possible organizations and know how each one works. If you have dealt with many system organizations, you can safely skip this section; if not, you are advised to read this section carefully.

Almost every design involves one or more blocks of data; in the division of the program into modules, each data block must have a place of residence. In other words, each data block must be assigned a module in which to reside. These data assignments strongly affect the functioning of the system.

Three kinds of assignments are possible for a data block:

1. The data block may be assigned as *global* or *common* data, available to an entire group of modules of the system. In this case, the data block is, in effect, assigned to the module M such that, for each module G in the group having access to the data block, either $G=M$; or M calls G; or M calls M_1, M_1 calls M_2, . . . , M_{K-1} calls M_K, M_K calls G.

2. The data block may be assigned its own module, which will also contain code to place individual data values in the block or to get individual data values from the block, as appropriate. A data block such as a dictionary, which is required to maintain its status in between executions of the module, can be achieved in ALGOL by the use of **own** variables, or in FORTRAN by the use of a labeled COMMON variable available only to the dictionary module.

3. The data block may be assigned to a process module, with no other modules having direct access to the data.

To show the effects of different placements of data, we now develop all organizations of modules for PRIME, a program that computes and prints the first 1000 primes. This program can be written using the basic design of Figure 4.9, in which a subprogram fill table computes the primes and puts them in a table p, while a program print table prints the primes.

The arc shown in Figure 4.9 from table p to fill table indicates the possibility that fill table will use the contents of table p in computing each next prime. (In the sieve of Eratosthenes, each potential prime is divided by all previous primes, not including 1; the candidate is prime if not evenly divisible by any of these previous primes.) We now assume that fill table will definitely use table p in this way, so that there is maximum interaction between fill table and table p. We also assume that the data block print lines is always included with the action print table.

Table p is the major data block of this program. Placement of this table determines which organizations of modules are possible, and how well each organization will work. We will exhaustively develop the organizations possible with each placement of table p, and we will examine how each of these

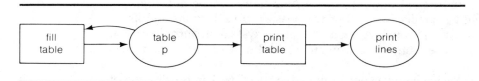

Figure 4.9 Basic design of program PRIME.

organizations works. We wish to show the large number of organizations that can be used to implement even a simple program such as PRIME and to show in detail the interfaces between modules required by each organization.

In the following discussions, variations of the parent module PRIME are named PRIME1, PRIME2, and so on. Variations of the module F containing the fill table action are named F1, F2, and so on; and variations of the module P containing the print table action are named P1, P2, and so on. The basic schemes are designated:

PLAN 1:   Table p global to F and P.
PLAN 2:   Table p assigned to its own module TABLE (variations are
          TABLE1, TABLE2, and so on).
PLAN 3:   Table p assigned to PRIME, or F, or P, and only that module has
          direct access to table p.

Subschemes are designated PLAN 1.1, PLAN 1.2, and so on, and each organization name (e.g., ORG 1.1, ORG 1.3.2) indicates the variation it implements.

4.2.2 A Digression: Diagramming Conventions

In discussing the detailed workings of each organization, we wish to discuss for the benefit of the beginner the sequence of execution of the modules, and the sequence of execution of major actions within each module. Since organization diagrams omit some of this information, we will use an additional type of diagram.

An organization diagram determines the sequence of execution of the modules but does not determine the sequence of major actions. Instead, the sequence of execution of major actions is determined by the code inside each module. Consider, for example, modules AA, BB, and CC such that AA calls BB and BB calls CC. Suppose also that, in addition to calling BB, AA performs the major action actAA, and likewise BB performs actBB and CC performs actCC.

Table 4.9 shows three different sets of pseudocode for AA, BB, and CC. In each case, AA calls BB and BB must return, in order that AA complete its execution. In this technical sense, the execution of BB must be comleted before the execution of AA. Likewise, CC completes its execution before BB does. However, for the code in (*a*) in Table 4.9, actAA is performed before BB is called, and actBB is performed before CC is called, so that the sequence of major actions is actAA, then actBB, then actCC. The code in (*b*) results in the sequence actCC, then actBB, and then actAA; while the code in (*c*) results in actAA, then actCC, and then actBB.

Notice that an organization diagram shows the interconnection of modules, but does not precisely determine the sequence of major actions, while an

Table 4.9 Module coding determines the sequence of actions actAA, actBB, and actCC

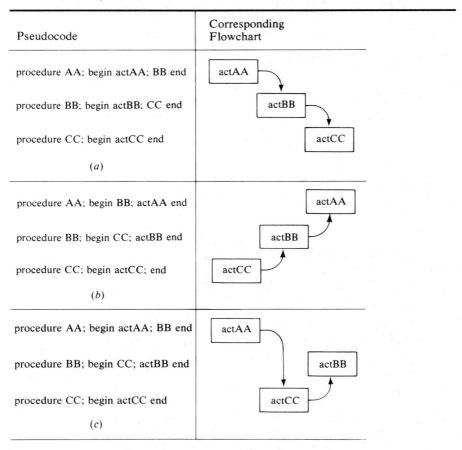

Pseudocode	Corresponding Flowchart
procedure AA; begin actAA; BB end	
procedure BB; begin actBB; CC end	
procedure CC; begin actCC end	
(a)	
procedure AA; begin BB; actAA end	
procedure BB; begin CC; actBB end	
procedure CC; begin actCC; end	
(b)	
procedure AA; begin actAA; BB end	
procedure BB; begin CC; actBB end	
procedure CC; begin actCC end	
(c)	

ordinary flowchart captures the sequence of major actions but loses the organizational information.

To capture both the organization and the sequence of major actions, a *tiered flowchart* such as in Figures 4.10 and 4.11 may be used. In a tiered flowchart, the sequence of major actions in a module is drawn from left to right, as in an ordinary flowchart, but the sequence is enclosed in a rectangle labeled with the module name. A circle in the middle of the left boundary of the rectangle denotes the beginning of the action in the module, and a circle in the right boundary denotes the end of the action. A call to another module is shown as an action box with the name of the called module in the action box, and a call

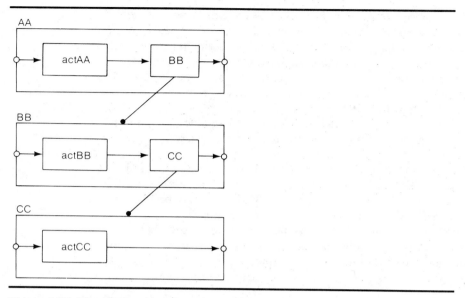

Figure 4.10   Tiered flowchart for code in Table 4.9(*a*).

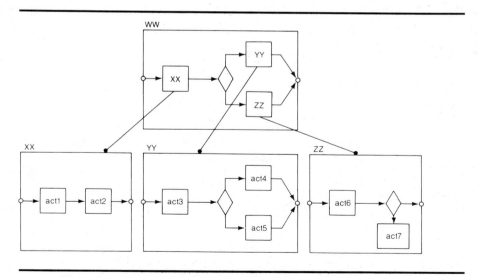

Figure 4.11   Sequential and conditional calls in a tiered flow-chart.

link is drawn from that box to a copy of the chart of the called module, shown at a lower level. (The chart of a module is drawn for each distinct usage of the module, showing the actions pertinent to that usage.) As an example, Figure 4.10 shows the tiered flowchart for the code of Table 4.9(*a*). Sequential and conditional calls can also be indicated in such charts, as shown in Figure 4.11.

The information level of a tiered flowchart is intermediate between that of the organization diagram and that of detailed flowcharts of each module. While tiered flowcharts may contain too much detail to be able to summarize the organization of a large system, they are useful in understanding portions of a large system.

Another aid in understanding the operation of an organization of modules is to trace the sequence of actions that occurs for a specific input. For this purpose, a *time-line chart* as shown in Tables 4.10 and 4.11 may be used. On each line of the chart, a level number, an action, and comments are entered. The action entered on the first line is the first action of the highest level module, and has level 1. An action may be a call to another module; in this case, on the next line the level number is incremented by 1 and the action is indented to the right. On the line at which control returns to the calling

Table 4.10   Time-line chart for code in Table 4.9(*a*)

Level	Action	Comments
1	actAA	
1	BB	
2	actBB	
2	CC	
3	actCC	
3	END	
2	END	
1	END	

Table 4.11   Time-line chart for code in Figure 4.11

Level	Action	Comments
1	XX	
2	act1	
2	act2	
1	YY	
2	act3	
2	act4	
2	END	
1	END	

module, the level is decremented by 1 and the indentation to the right is removed. The action END signifies termination of the called module whenever the calling module has no further actions. This tracing technique assumes that a module always returns to its caller, at the location in the calling module immediately following the call.

4.2.3 PLAN 1: Table p Global to F and P

PLAN 1 is the first kind of assignment noted in Section 4.2.1, namely, place-ment of table p so that it is global to F and P. The possible variations in this scheme are all shown in Table 4.12.

The table shows three different arrangements of call relations between PRIME, F, and P, all of which allow table p to be global to F and P. The basic scheme is that of PLAN 1.1 and ORG 1.1.1. Because (as noted in Section 4.2.2) the sequence of major actions can be preserved no matter whether F calls P or P calls F, PLAN 1.2 and PLAN 1.3 are also possible. In PLAN 1.2, since PRIME calls F and F calls P, table p may be placed either in PRIME or in F, and will in either case be global to F and P. Thus ORG 1.2.1 and ORG 1.2.2 arise, and a similar situation yields ORG 1.3.1 and ORG 1.3.2.

In PLAN 1.1, the most straightforward arrangement, table p is contained in the main program module PRIME1 and is accessible to the subsidiary modules

Table 4.12 Variations in PLAN 1: Table p global to P and F

```
PLAN 1.1: PRIME ———● F, PRIME ———● P

      ORG 1.1.1
         ⎧ PRIME ———● F
         ⎨ PRIME ———● P
         ⎩ PRIME ———◁ table p

PLAN 1.2: PRIME ———● F, F ———● P

      ORG 1.2.1                      ORG 1.2.2
         ⎧ PRIME ———● F                 ⎧ PRIME ———● F
         ⎨ F ———● P                     ⎨ F ———● P
         ⎩ PRIME ———◁ table p           ⎩ F ———◁ table p

PLAN 1.3: PRIME ———● P, P ———● F

      ORG 1.3.1                      ORG 1.3.2
         ⎧ PRIME ———● P                 ⎧ PRIME ———● P
         ⎨ P ———● F                     ⎨ P ———● F
         ⎩ PRIME ———◁ table p           ⎩ P ———◁ table p
```

F1 and P1. The organization diagram of ORG 1.1.1 is shown in Figure 4.12(*a*), and the tiered flowchart is shown in (*b*).

The calls by PRIME1 to modules F1 and P1 have no parameters. With this placement of data, table p acts as a buffer between the two processes fill table and print table.

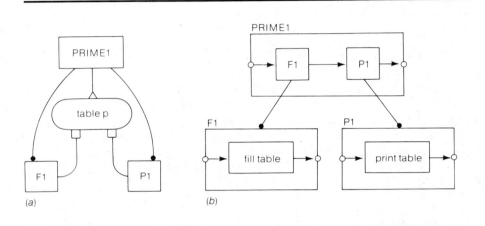

Figure 4.12 The organization ORG 1.1.1. (*a*) Organization diagram. (*b*) Tiered flowchart.

Figure 4.13 shows organizations and tiered flowcharts for PLAN 1.2 and PLAN 1.3. Comparison of Figure 4.12(*b*) with Figure 4.13(*c*) and (*f*) shows that all of these organizations yield the same sequence of major actions.

The calls shown in Figure 4.13 have no parameters. In ORG 1.2.1 and 1.2.2, the modules P2 and F2 have equal accessibility to table p, and the module PRIME2 does not itself access table p. Hence these organizations are equivalent with respect to access to the table, and ORG 1.3.1 and 1.3.2 are similarly equivalent.

A variation of ORG 1.1.1, which is possible in FORTRAN implementations, is the use of a labeled COMMON block containing table p and available only to the modules F and P. In this variation, the table has its own communications block, but it does not have its own module, and it is not embedded in one of the modules. This organization is shown in Figure 4.14.

In FORTRAN implementations involving many modules, each group of modules requiring common access to data can have a labeled COMMON block available only to modules of that group.

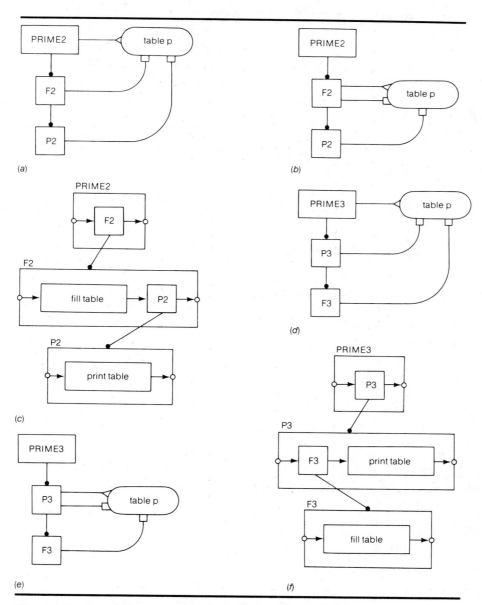

Figure 4.13 Organizations and tiered flowcharts for PLAN 1.2 and 1.3. (*a*) The organization ORG 1.2.1. (*b*) The organization ORG 1.2.2. (*c*) Tiered flowchart for ORG 1.2.1 and 1.2.2. (*d*) The organization ORG 1.3.1. (*e*) The organization ORG 1.3.2. (*f*) Tiered flowchart for ORG 1.3.1 and 1.3.2.

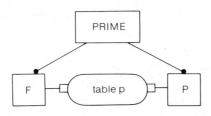

Figure 4.14   A variation of ORG 1.1.1.

4.2.4 PLAN 2: Table p Assigned to Its Own Module TABLE

The second type of data placement is to assign table p its own module TABLE and to have all access to table p—either putting primes into the table or getting primes from the table—done via calls to TABLE by the other modules. The variations possible in PLAN 2 are all shown in Table 4.13.

Table 4.13   Variations in PLAN 2: Table p assigned to its own
module TABLE(TABLE ——◁ Table p,
TABLE ——□ Table p)

```
PLAN 2.1: F ——● TABLE, P ——● TABLE
    ORG 2.1.1                    ORG 2.1.2                    ORG 2.1.3
    ┌ F ——● TABLE               ┌ F ——● TABLE               ┌ F ——● TABLE
    │ P ——● TABLE               │ P ——● TABLE               │ P ——● TABLE
    │ PRIME ——● F               │ PRIME ——● F               │ PRIME ——● P
    └ PRIME ——● P               └ F ——● P                   └ P ——● F

PLAN 2.2: TABLE Calls One of {F,P}, Is Called by the Other
    ORG 2.2.1                    ORG 2.2.2
    ┌ PRIME ——● F               ┌ PRIME ——● P
    │ F ——● TABLE               │ P ——● TABLE
    └ TABLE ——● P               └ TABLE ——● F

PLAN 2.3: TABLE Called Only by PRIME
    ORG 2.3.1                    ORG 2.3.2
    ┌ PRIME ——● TABLE           ┌ PRIME ——● TABLE
    │ TABLE ——● F               │ TABLE ——● F
    └ TABLE ——● P               └ F ——● P
    ORG 2.3.3                    ORG 2.3.4
    ┌ PRIME ——● TABLE           ┌ PRIME ——● TABLE
    │ TABLE ——● P               │ PRIME ——● F
    └ P ——● F                   └ PRIME ——● P
```

As this table indicates, the module TABLE can be called by other modules and also can call other modules. Since there are now four modules rather than three, PLAN 2 has more variations than PLAN 1. Although all of these organizations can be realized, the more bizarre ones require elaborate collaboration between modules.

PLAN 2.1 is the simplest variation of PLAN 2. The organization diagram of ORG 2.1.1 is shown in Figure 4.15(*a*), and the tiered flowchart is shown in (*b*). Figure 4.16 shows organization diagrams for ORG 2.1.2 and 2.1.3. These organizations preserve the sequence of actions of ORG 2.1.1 (recall the comparison between Figures 4.12 and 4.13), and the actions fill table (within F5 and F6)

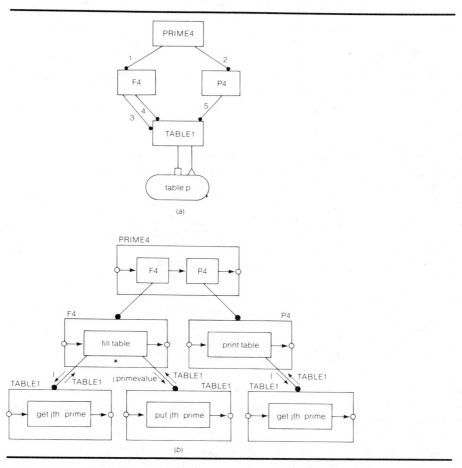

Figure 4.15 The organization ORG 2.1.1 (see Table 4.14 for a description of parameters). (*a*) Organization diagram. (*b*) Tiered flowchart.

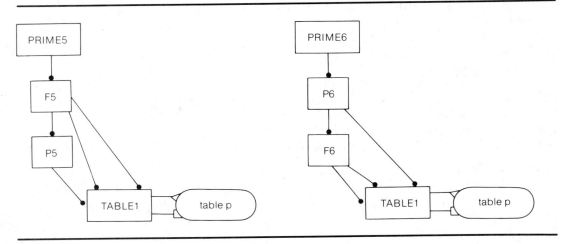

Figure 4.16 Organizations ORG 2.1.2 and 2.1.3.

and print table (within P5 or P6) make the same calls to TABLE as their counterparts in Figure 4.15. Thus ORG 2.1.2 and 2.1.3 are effectively identical to ORG 2.1.1 and need not be separately analyzed in detail.

In Figure 4.15, the calls by PRIME4 to F4 and P4 use no parameters. For calls to get the jth prime from TABLE1, an input parameter j is required and TABLE1 is the output parameter. (In order to use the values in table p for its calculations, fill table makes repeated calls to get primes.) For a call placing a prime in the table, two input parameters are needed: the value PRIME and the place j in the table.

What is the internal structure of the TABLE1 module? The tiered flowchart of Figure 4.15(*b*) shows that a get action is required to get the jth prime from the table, and a put action is required to put a prime into the table. Since the module is a subroutine, parameters will be sent to TABLE1 and returned from TABLE1 via a parameter table. A data flow diagram of TABLE1 is shown in Figure 4.17.

In order for the module to know which action (get or put) to take, there must be a control parameter c, and the module must contain a small control program that inspects the control parameter and activates get or put as appropriate. The wavy arrows from control to get and put signify that control activates get or put as appropriate (see [Phi 67, Phi 71]). The interface table and usage table for Figure 4.15 are given in Table 4.14.

In the organization ORG 2.1.1 of Figure 4.15, the module TABLE1 acts as a buffer between F4 and P4, as in Figure 4.9. However, table p is now isolated in a separate module; and F4 and P4 have access to individual values via subroutine calls, but do not have access to the entire table. The costs of this

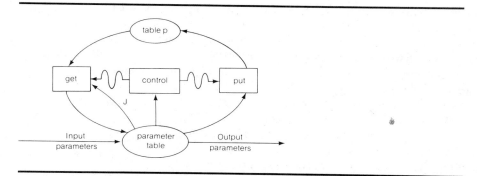

Figure 4.17   Data flow diagram of TABLE1 module.

Table 4.14   Interface and usage tables for ORG 2.1.1 in Figure 4.15

Module and Calling Sequence	Formal Parameter	Input	Output	Use	Significance of Parameter
F4					No parameters used
P4					No parameters used
TABLE1(c,j,primevalue)	c	✔		C	c=1=>get c=2=>put
	j	✔		P	jth place in table
	primevalue	✔		P	Value to be put into jth place
	TABLE1		✔	M	Returned value of jth prime

(*a*) Interface Table.

Line	Calling Module	Called Module	Actual Parameter Sequence	Comments
1	PRIME4	F4	---	No parameters used
2	PRIME4	P4	---	No parameters used
3	F4	TABLE1	1,j,0	Third parameter unused
4	F4	TABLE1	2,j,primevalue	primevalue is value to be placed in table at position j
5	P4	TABLE1	1,j,0	Third parameter unused

(*b*) Usage Table.

isolation are the extra actions get, put, and control required in the TABLE1 module, and, of course, the space and time required for the subroutine calls. The advantage of isolating table p is that the internal structure of the table can now be changed without in any way affecting the operation of F4 and P4. Although such an advantage is trivial for this example, in the case of a more complex table (e.g., a dictionary in a compiler) it might be very important.

You have no doubt observed that in lines 3 and 5 in Table 4.14(b) we have $c=1$, primevalue$=0$, and an unused third parameter, while in line 4 we have $c=2$ and primevalue$\neq0$. Thus it would be possible to use only the parameters j and primevalue, with the convention that primevalue$=0$ implies get and primevalue$\neq0$ implies put. But using primevalue for both data and control is a poor choice. It would obscure the meaning of the various parameters, and it would hinder the addition to the module of further actions. For example, we might wish to add an initialize action to TABLE1, so that TABLE1 could be directed to zero the table at the beginning of the calculation. If the control parameter c is used, we need only specify another control value, say, $c=0$ means initialize. Without the explicit control parameter, a new special value of primevalue would have to signify initialize.

An organization can be devised that allows F4 and P4 to be unaware of the control parameter required by TABLE1. Such an organization is shown in Figure 4.18(b), and the code for the new modules GETPRIME and PUT-PRIME is shown in Figure 4.18(a).

The modules GETPRIME and PUTPRIME compose calls to TABLE1 by adding appropriate control parameter values.

We now examine the organizations which implement PLAN 2.2. The organization ORG 2.2.1 is shown in Figure 4.19, and interface and usage tables for ORG 2.2.1 are given in Table 4.15.

The intention of ORG 2.2.1 in Figure 4.19(a) is that F5 fills table p by repeated calls to TABLE2 [see lines 2 and 3 in Table 4.15(b)]. When the table is full, F5 causes the print to occur by calling TABLE2 [see line 4 in Table 4.15(b)], which in turn calls P5. TABLE2 is made to call P5 by the use of an additional control code $c=3$. But now a problem occurs because the print table action needs values from table p. In the organizations thus far discussed, print table has obtained these values via a call from the module containing print table to the module containing table p, indicating which (jth) value was wanted. However, here TABLE2 is calling P5, and obviously TABLE2 cannot know in advance which value(s) P5 needs. Recall that P5 may be printing the primes sequentially in columns, the first column being

1
2
3
5
.
.
.

and the number of columns is, of course, unknown to TABLE2.

There are two ways in which ORG 2.2.1 can be made to work. The arrangement shown in Table 4.15 is that TABLE2 calls P5 repeatedly; at each call, P5 returns a value to TABLE2; and TABLE2 and P5 share a convention regarding

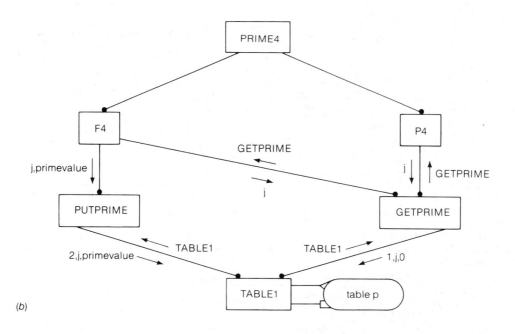

(a)
```
procedure PUTPRIME(j,primevalue:integer);
   var
      dummy:integer;
   begin
      dummy:=TABLE1(2,j,primevalue)
   end

function GETPRIME(j:integer): integer;
   begin
      GETPRIME:=TABLE1(1,j,0)
   end
```

(b)

Figure 4.18 Isolating the control parameter from F4 and P4. (*a*) Code for new modules. (*b*) Organization diagram.

the meaning of that returned value. To implement this arrangement, TABLE2 contains the following code:

```
j:=P5(1,1);
while j<>0 do
  begin
    nextwanted:=p[j];
    j:=P5(j,nextwanted)
  end
```

Table 4.15   Interface and usage tables for ORG 2.2.1 in Figure 4.19

Module and Calling Sequence	Formal Parameter	Input	Output	Use	Significance of Parameter
F5					No parameters used
TABLE2 (c,j,primevalue)	c	✔		C	c=1=>get c=2=>put c=3=>cause table to be printed
	j	✔		P	jth place in table (significant only for c=1, c=2)
	primevalue	✔		P	Value to be put into jth place (significant only for c=2)
	TABLE2		✔	M	Returned value of jth prime
P5(j,value)	j	✔		P	jth place in table
	value	✔		P	Value of jth prime
	P5		✔	M	Index of next prime needed by P5 (P5=0 signifies no more primes needed)

(a) Interface Table.

Line	Calling Module	Called Module	Actual Parameter Sequence	Comments
1	PRIME5	F5	---	No parameters used
2	P5	TABLE2	1,j,0	Third parameter unused
3	F5	TABLE2	2,j,primevalue	Value to be put into table at position j
4	F5	TABLE2	3,0,0	Second parameter unused
5	TABLE2	P5	j,nextwanted	nextwanted is value of jth prime (a) First call by TABLE2 is P5(1,1) (b) At each call, P5 returns index of next prime wanted (c) If P5 returns 0, TABLE2 ceases to call

(b) Usage Table.

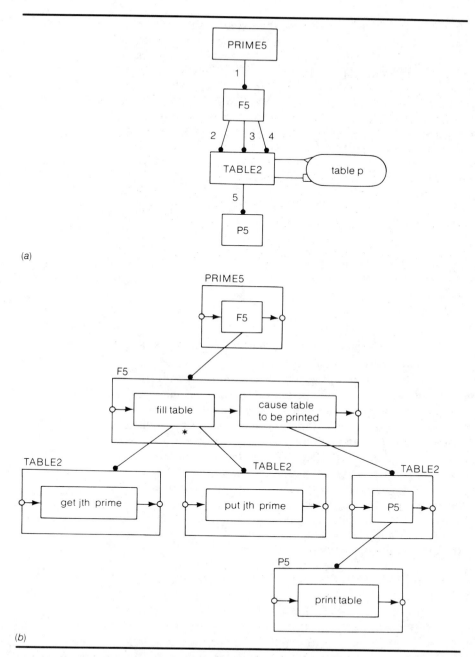

Figure 4.19 The organization ORG 2.2.1 (see Table 4.15 for a description of parameters). (*a*) Organization diagram. (*b*) Tiered flowchart.

Thus, at each call of P5 by TABLE2, P5 returns the index of the next prime needed by P5. Then TABLE2 in its next call gives the value of the prime just requested as an input parameter. The cycle of calls stops when P5 returns 0. This elaborate convention shared by TABLE2 and P5 effectively allows P5 to call TABLE2, even though the organization specifies that TABLE2 calls P5.

Alternatively, ORG 2.2.1 can work if P5 has its own table and can maintain that table unchanged between calls on P5. In this case, P5 need not return a value. This solution can be implemented in ALGOL but not in PASCAL. TABLE2 contains the statement (in ALGOL code):

```
for j:=1 step 1 until 1000 do P5(j,p[j]);
```

while P5 has the following form (in ALGOL-based pseudocode):

```
procedure P5(j,value);
   begin
   integer j,value;
   integer array copy-of-table-p[1:1000];
   own copy-of-table-p;
   copy-of-table-p[j]:=value;
   if j=1000 then print table
   end
```

In other words, TABLE2 calls P5 1000 times, at each (jth) call giving P5 the jth prime as an input parameter. At each call, P5 copies the given value into its table, and at the last call (j=1000), P5 performs the action print table.

Either arrangement of ORG 2.2.1 (1) depends on special meanings being given to input or output parameters; (2) requires a special kind of communication in which each module participates in (and thus must have knowledge of) the control of the other module's function; and (3) may require extra storage. In contrast to ORG 2.1.1, the modules in ORG 2.2.1 are highly interdependent. Thus ORG 2.2.1 is a poor organization in comparison to ORG 2.1.1.

ORG 2.2.2 is shown in Figure 4.20(*a*). In this organization, TABLE3 calls F6, requesting that F6 supply the jth prime for table p. However, in similar fashion to ORG 2.2.1, the action fill table needs values from table p that resides in module TABLE3. If F6 is supplied with its own table, as shown in (*b*), then fill table can use the table in F6 as a copy of table p. In this case, F6 does not require the values from table p, and P5 can return at each call the requested jth prime for table p. [Development of interface and usage tables for the organization of Figure 4.20(*b*) is left as an exercise in Problem 1 at the end of this section.]

If F6 does not have its own table, then the call of F6 by TABLE3 can be made to work only by an even more elaborate convention, which in effect allows F6 to call TABLE3. This also is a poor organization in comparison to ORG 2.1.1.

The final variation of PLAN 2 is PLAN 2.3, in which TABLE is called only by PRIME. Figure 4.21 shows all the organizations which implement PLAN

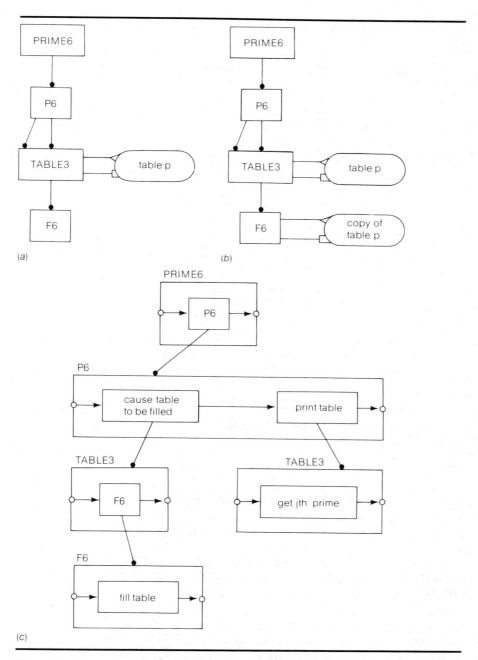

Figure 4.20   The organization ORG 2.2.2. (*a*) Organization diagram. (*b*) Alternative with F6 having extra storage. (*c*) Tiered flowchart for organization (*a*).

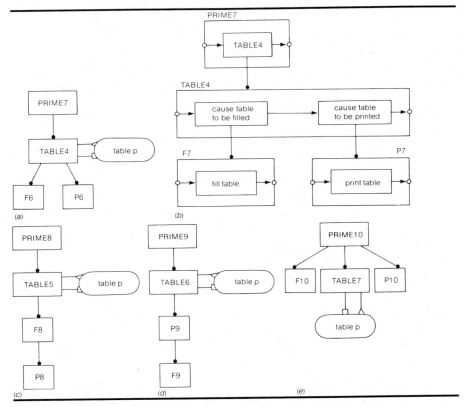

Figure 4.21 Organizations that implement PLAN 2.3. (*a*) and (*b*) ORG 2.3.1. (*c*) ORG 2.3.2. (*d*) ORG 2.3.3. (*e*) ORG 2.3.4.

2.3. The organizations ORG 2.3.2 and 2.3.3 need not be discussed since they are effectively identical to ORG 2.3.1.

In the organization ORG 2.3.1 shown in Figure 4.21(*a*), TABLE4 calls P6 exactly the way that TABLE2 calls P5 in ORG 2.2.1 in Figure 4.19. Also, TABLE4 calls F6 in exactly the way that TABLE3 calls F6 in ORG 2.2.2 in Figure 4.20. Thus ORG 2.3.1 has the difficulties both of ORG 2.2.1 and of ORG 2.2.2. Hence, ORG 2.3.1, 2.3.2, and 2.3.3 are all poorer organizations than either ORG 2.2.1 or 2.2.2.

Finally, the organization ORG 2.3.4 in Figure 4.21(*e*) has all of the difficulties of ORG 2.3.1 in Figure 4.21(*a*), and also involves the module PRIME10 in transfer of data. Thus ORG 2.3.4 is a poorer organization than ORG 2.3.1.

By contrasting the various organizations, we have achieved relative rankings of the organizations which implement PLAN 2. These rankings may be expressed in the following way:

$$
\begin{bmatrix} \text{ORG 2.1.1} \\ \text{ORG 2.1.2} \\ \text{ORG 2.1.3} \end{bmatrix}
\quad \begin{matrix} \text{preferable} \\ \text{to} \end{matrix} \quad
\begin{bmatrix} \text{ORG 2.2.1} \\ \text{ORG 2.2.2} \end{bmatrix}
\quad \begin{matrix} \text{preferable} \\ \text{to} \end{matrix}
$$

$$
\begin{bmatrix} \text{ORG 2.3.1} \\ \text{ORG 2.3.2} \\ \text{ORG 2.3.3} \end{bmatrix}
\quad \begin{matrix} \text{preferable} \\ \text{to} \end{matrix} \quad
\begin{bmatrix} \text{ORG 2.3.4} \end{bmatrix}
$$

PLAN 2.1 yields the most preferred organization implementing PLAN 2.

4.2.5 PLAN 3: Table p Assigned to One of F, P, or PRIME

The third scheme (PLAN 3) of data placement is the isolation of table p in one of the process modules or in PRIME itself, with the other modules having access only to individual values via subroutine calls. All the possible variations in PLAN 3 are shown in Table 4.16.

We first consider organizations implementing PLAN 3.1, in which table p is placed in module F containing the fill table action. ORG 3.1.1 is shown in Figure 4.22.

The interface and usage tables for ORG 3.1.1 above are shown in Table 4.17. F11 performs two kinds of actions, and thus, in concept, a control parameter is

Table 4.16   Variations in PLAN 3: Table p assigned to one of F, P, or
PRIME

PLAN 3.1: Table p Assigned to F

ORG 3.1.1	ORG 3.1.2	ORG 3.1.3
PRIME ⟶ F PRIME ⟶ P P ⟶ F	PRIME ⟶ P P ⟶ F	PRIME ⟶ F F ⟶ P

PLAN 3.2: Table p Assigned to P

ORG 3.2.1	ORG 3.2.2	ORG 3.2.3
PRIME ⟶ F PRIME ⟶ P F ⟶ P	PRIME ⟶ F F ⟶ P	PRIME ⟶ P P ⟶ F

PLAN 3.3: Table p Assigned to PRIME

ORG 3.3.1	ORG 3.3.2	ORG 3.3.3
PRIME ⟶ F PRIME ⟶ P	PRIME ⟶ F F ⟶ P	PRIME ⟶ P P ⟶ F

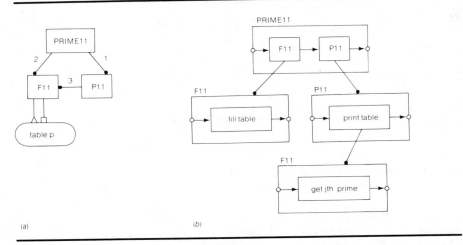

Figure 4.22 The organization ORG 3.1.1 [see Table 4.17 (*b*)].
(*a*) Organizational diagram. (*b*) Tiered flowchart.

Table 4.17   Interface and usage tables for ORG 3.1.1 in Figure 4.22

Module and Calling Sequence	Formal Parameter	Input	Output	Use	Significance of Parameter
P11					No parameters
F11(c,j)	c	✔		C	c=0=>fill table c=1=>get jth prime
	j	✔		P	jth place in table
	F11		✔	M	Returned value of jth prime

(*a*) Interface Table.

Line	Calling Module	Called Module	Actual Parameter Sequence	Comments
1	PRIME11	P11		No parameters required
2	PRIME11	F11	0,0	Second parameter unused
3	P11	F11	1,j	Get jth prime

(*b*) Usage Table.

required. (It would be possible, though dubious practice, to have j=0 activate the fill table action, and j≠0 activate the get jth prime action.)

The organization ORG 3.1.2 is shown in figure 4.23(*a*). This organization may be implemented in two somewhat different ways, as shown by the tiered

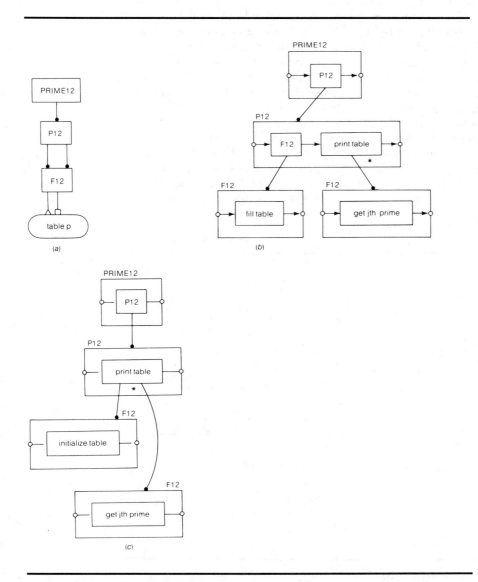

Figure 4.23 The organization ORG 3.1.2.

flowcharts of Figure 4.23(*b*) and (*c*). The implementation of Figure 4.23(*b*) differs from that of Figure 4.22 in that F8 is called only from the P8 module, rather than from both P8 and PRIME8. The module F12 in Figure 4.23(*b*) is identical to the module F11 in Figure 4.22. Thus ORG 3.1.2, if implemented as in Figure 4.23(*b*), is equivalent to ORG 3.1.1.

The implementation of Figure 4.23(*c*) shows the module F12 with an action initialize table, which zeroes the values in the table, and an action get jth prime, which returns the jth prime to P12. F12 can be implemented so as to entirely fill table p immediately following the initialize table action, or F12 can be implemented so as to calculate each jth prime as it is called for by P12.

ORG 3.1.3 is shown in Figure 4.24. In this alternative, the module F13 first performs the action fill table and then calls P13 to have the table printed. This situation, in which F13 calls P13 without knowing which values P13 needs, is almost identical to the situation of Figure 4.19 where TABLE2 calls P5. The organization can be made to work only if P13 has its own table into which the contents of table p can be copied, or if F13 and P13 collaborate as was described for Figure 4.19. The organization of Figure 4.24 is thus a poor one.

PLAN 3.2 calls for placement of table p in module P containing the print table action. There are basically two variations on this theme, the first of

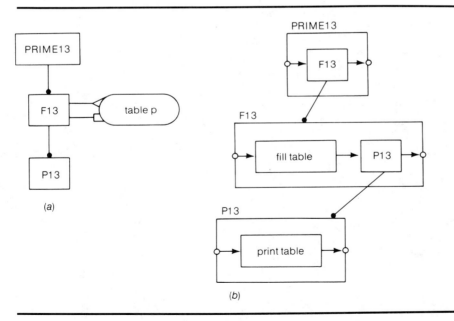

Figure 4.24   The organization ORG 3.1.3.

which is shown in Figure 4.25. ORG 3.2.1 and 3.3.2 differ only trivially. The modules P14 and P15 perform the identical actions get jth prime, put jth prime, and print table. A control parameter is required for both P14 and P15. The interface and usage tables for ORG 3.2.1 in Figure 4.25(a) are shown in Table 4.18. (ORG 3.2.2 is not treated in detail since it differs only trivially from ORG 3.2.1.)

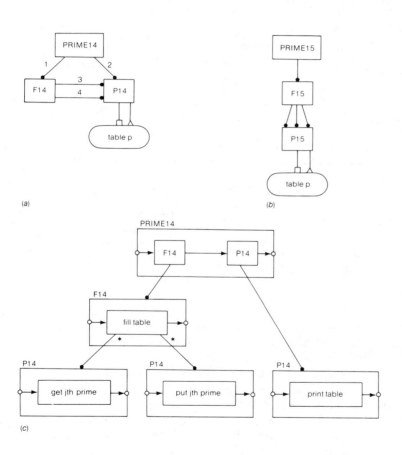

(a)

(b)

(c)

Figure 4.25   The organizations ORG 3.2.1 and 3.2.2 (see Table 4.18). (a) ORG 3.2.1. (b) ORG 3.2.2. (c) Tiered flowchart for ORG 3.2.1.

Table 4.18   Interface and usage tables for ORG 3.2.1 in Figure
4.25(*a*).

Module and Calling Sequence	Formal Parameter	Input	Output	Use	Significance of Parameter
F14					No parameters required
P14(c,j,primevalue)	c	✔		C	c=0=>print table c=1=>get jth prime c=2=>put jth prime
	j	✔		P	jth place in table
	primevalue	✔		P	Value to be put in table
	P14		✔	M	Returned value of jth prime

(*a*) Interface Table.

Line	Calling Module	Called Module	Actual Parameter Sequence	Comments
1	PRIME14	F14		No parameters required
2	PRIME14	P14	0,0,0	To print table
3	F14	P14	1,j,0	Get jth prime
4	F14	P14	2,j,primevalue	Put jth prime

(*b*) Usage Table.

The second variation of PLAN 3.2 is ORG 3.2.3, which is shown in Figure
4.26. As in Figure 4.20, the arrangement of Figure 4.26 can work only if F16
has its own copy of table p, or if F16 and P16 have an elaborate convention that
in effect allows F16 to call P16, even though formally P16 calls F16. Hence
ORG 3.2.3 is a poor organization in comparison to ORG 3.2.1.

A final variation of PLAN 3 is PLAN 3.3, placement of table p in the
PRIME module. Figure 4.27 shows all the organizations which implement
PLAN 3.3. ORG 3.3.1 in Figure 4.27(*a*) has the same difficulties as ORG 2.3.1
in Figure 4.21, and hence is poor in comparison with ORG 3.2.3. ORG 3.3.2
and 3.3.3 in Figure 4.27(*c*) and (*d*) show two even more awful variations.
These organizations share the same difficulties as ORG 3.3.1 and also force the
middle module to act as a conduit for the data flowing between the top and
bottom modules. Thus ORG 3.3.2. and 3.3.3 are poor in comparison to ORG
3.3.1. In sum, all of the organizations yielded by PLAN 3 are poor in comparison to organizations yielded by PLAN 1 or 2.

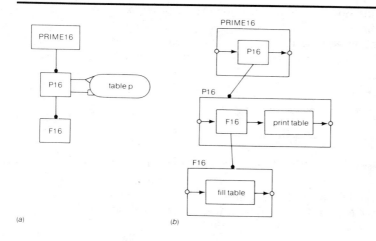

(a)   (b)

Figure 4.26   The organization ORG 3.2.3.

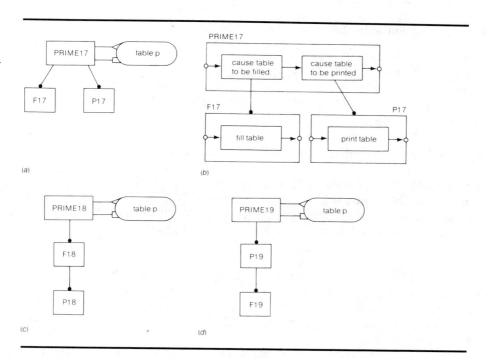

(a)   (b)

(c)   (d)

Figure 4.27   Organizations that implement PLAN 3.3. (*a*) ORG
3.3.1. (*b*) Tiered flowchart for ORG 3.3.1. (*c*) ORG
3.3.2. (*d*) ORG 3.3.3.

Complicated interfaces between modules must be avoided if the program is to be easy to maintain and modify. Accordingly, each proposed organization should be analyzed as in this section, to determine the interfaces required. To further determine the operation of a proposed organization, time-line charts can be drawn for several inputs.

REFERENCES

[Phi 67] Phillips, C. S. E. "Networks for Real Time Programming," *Computer Journal*, May 1967.

[Phi 71] ———. "Software Engineering, The Key to Expansion of Real Time Systems," in *Infotech State of the Art Report 3: Real Time*. Maidenhead, England: Infotech, pp. 252–256, 1971.

PROBLEMS

1. Complete the interface and usage tables for the organizations of:

   (a) Figure 4.20(*a*)   **(g)** Figure 4.24
   (b) Figure 4.20(*b*)   **(h)** Figure 4.26
   (c) Figure 4.21(*a*)   **(i)** Figure 4.27(*a*)
   (d) Figure 4.21(*c*)   **(j)** Figure 4.27(*c*)
   (e) Figure 4.23(*b*)   **(k)** Figure 4.27(*d*)
   (f) Figure 4.23(*c*)

2. Give a tiered flowchart for the organization of Figure 4.21(*c*).

3. The organization ORG 3.1.2 in Figure 4.23(*a*) and (*c*) can fill table p incrementally, as the print table action requests primes. Discuss ORG 2.2.2 in Figure 4.20(*a*) with respect to this capability. If ORG 2.2.2 can fill table p incrementally, provide a tiered flowchart, interface table, and usage table achieving this feature.

4. Suppose that in ORG 2.2.2 in Figure 4.20(*a*), TABLE3 tests whether the jth prime has been placed in table p and calls F6 only if the jth prime has not already been placed in the table. Give a tiered flowchart, interface table, and usage table that accomplish this feature. Does TABLE always require two different kinds of calls?

PROJECT OUTLINE: Organization Diagrams   Derive the organization diagram, interface tables, and usage tables for the program system of Problem C in Appendix E.

chapter five
Design and Development
of Module Organization

5.1 PRINCIPLES OF ORGANIZATION

5.1.1 Introduction

It is now well understood that a program can be too big for one person to do and that a complex program may even lie beyond the intellectual grasp of just one person. Such programs require the efforts of many people. The developers of these programs must devise ways to chop a big job into manageable pieces, divide the pieces among many people, and get all of these pieces of work done.

Chapter 5 presents methods for dividing a system into manageable pieces and for implementing and testing the collection of pieces. Although it is generally agreed that a large program should be divided into modules if it is to be manageable, this division is no guarantee of a well-organized program. (As we saw, some of the organizations in Section 4.2 would be very difficult to develop and maintain.) Section 5.1 presents principles of module organization; Section 5.2 describes module organization via top-down design; Section 5.3 discusses the use of isolation of design factors and data abstraction to achieve a module organization; and Section 5.4 presents strategies for coding and testing and for achieving the best sequence of module implementation and testing.

The organization methods of this chapter share the objective of achieving a rational organization by reducing dependencies between modules. In other words, it is desired to isolate the effects of each different design decision so as to allow easy program modification and thereby provide in advance for possible change. All of these methods use three important principles, which are outlined below [Ros 75].

1. *Principle of localization.* All code affected by a particular design decision should be localized within one specific program segment.

    When this principle is followed, a change in a particular design decision is equated with a change in the effect of the corresponding program segment, and the necessary code modifications are isolated within that segment. Since modification of a design decision is accomplished by revision of the associated program segment, the cost of program maintenance is minimized.

2. *Principle of information hiding.* Details pertinent only to one design decision are "hidden" in the associated program segment. These details are made inaccessible to other program segments since such details should not affect the other program segments.

   As an example, suppose that it is decided to use a particular list structure for a certain data table, and this decision is associated with program segment A. If a segment B, external to A, is allowed to reference the table using knowledge of the structure, then B will be sensitive to any changes in the structure and may have to be modified if the structure is changed. This would violate the principle of localization. To enforce the principle of localization, segment B is not allowed to have knowledge of data structures in A.

3. *Principle of abstraction.* Each program segment is defined at a given level of refinement, and is defined solely in terms of its relation as a unit to other segments of the program.

   A program segment is defined so that it may be understood as a unit, without knowledge of its details and without knowledge of how it is used at higher levels. The essential properties of the segment are clarified, while details are omitted so that alternate implementations are possible.

Lastly, all of the methods require that modules be constructed to satisfy the following three conditions.

1. Each module has a single entry point and a single exit point (a multiple-entry-point module is, in concept, several distinct modules, packaged together).

2. Each module always returns to its caller, at the location in the calling routine immediately following the call.

3. There are no pathological or anomalous links between modules (see Section 4.1).

If these conditions are met, then a module A may regard the action of any called module B (including the actions of any modules B calls) as a primitive, irreducible action. Care must also be taken to avoid or to provide especially for cycles of calls such as A calls B, B calls C, and C calls A.

Satisfaction of conditions 1 through 3 is a prerequisite for a good organization rather than a guarantee that a good organization has already been achieved.

5.1.2 Isolation of Common Functions

Isolation of common functions in separate modules is one of the oldest methods for program organization [Dij 72b]. In particular, mathematical and input/output routines are commonly modularized [Tur 80]. As was shown in Section 3.1, common functions suitable for isolation in a module can be deduced from a data flow diagram. Each set of identical or almost-identical actions in the diagram can be replaced by a single routine that appropriately generalizes the actions, using parameters as necessary.

Common function isolation may be used in conjunction with any of the other organization methods.

5.1.3 Deriving Organization by Using Data Flow Diagrams

A top-down organization, an organization based on isolation of design factors, or an organization based on data abstraction may be derived by a series of operations on a data flow diagram.

In each case, the derivation process is begun with a data flow diagram in which common functions have already been isolated. Each desired grouping of objects and actions within a module is shown by a dashed-line boundary drawn on the data flow diagram, as in Figure 5.1. Any combination of objects and actions may be grouped in a module.

Each arc passing into a module signifies information needed by the module, and each arrow passing out of a module signifies information the module must

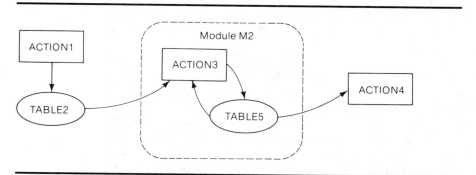

Figure 5.1   Grouping of ACTION3 and TABLE5 in module M2.

supply. Since the most desirable means of transferring information is via subroutine calls, each arrow in or out of the module signifies a call to or from the module.

For example, module M2 in Figure 5.1 requires information from TABLE2 and gives information to ACTION4. In the final organization, M2 must call the module containing TABLE2 to obtain the information, or that module must call M2 to give the information.[1] Similarly, M2 must call the module containing ACTION4 to give the required information, or M2 must be called by that module. As we have seen in Section 4.2, it may be possible to arrange for M2 to call both of the other modules, or for M2 to be called by both, or for M2 to call one and be called by the other.

Although the data flow diagram does not determine the direction of each call, the simplest possible interface is achieved when the call is made by the module requiring information. Using this guideline, module M2 would call the module containing TABLE2 and would be called by the module containing ACTION4.

Next, further boundaries are drawn:

1. Within the now-existing module boundaries, to delineate further isolation of objects and/or actions,
2. To group existing modules, objects, and actions,
3. To enclose the entire data flow diagram in a boundary signifying the parent module.

In Figure 5.2, the outer boundary signifies the parent module P. Module M2 has now been grouped with ACTION1 and TABLE2 in module M1; within M2, module T has been designated for TABLE5. With this set of boundaries, there is information transfer between M1 and P (which contains M1) and between M2 and M1 (which contains M2).

Since M1 is within the boundaries of P, we require that P (or a module within P but exterior to M1) calls M1, and, since M2 is within the boundaries of M1, we require that M1 (or a module within M1 but exterior to M2) calls M2. If ACTION1 and TABLE2 had been grouped in module M3, then either M1 could call M2, or M3 could call M2.

Also, because M2 is in M1, it can be called *only* by M1 or modules in M1 exterior to M2. If ACTION4 wishes to call for the information in TABLE5, it must call M1, which will call M2, which will call T. The information will be transferred from T to M2 to ACTION4.

In Figure 5.3, module U contains modules V and W, which are exterior to each other (i.e., V does not contain W, and W does not contain V). Also, there is no module X such that U contains X and X contains V; and there is no module Y such that U contains Y and Y contains W. In this situation, V may

---

[1] An exception occurs if TABLE2 is global or common data, in which case module M2 can access it directly, without any calls.

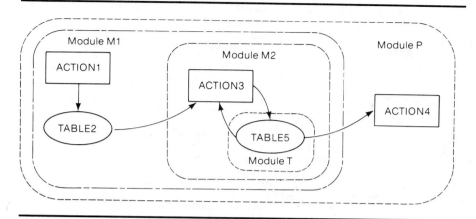

Figure 5.2 Further module boundaries.

be called only by U, or by W, or by another module meeting the same conditions as W.

If information is desired from V by the arc leading outside U, there must be a call to U, which then calls V for the information. If W contains a module Z that requires information from V, then Z must call W, which then calls V for the information.

Every module boundary isolates some group of objects and actions within a module. Figure 5.2 has several levels of isolation (T within M2, M2 within M1, M1 within P) and a corresponding hierarchy of modules. We may arrange as many levels of isolation as are useful in the design.

For any two boundaries, the areas enclosed are disjoint, or one area is confined in the other. Thus sets of module boundaries can be drawn to partition the data flow diagram so as to form disjoint sets of modules.

The principles of partitioning data flow diagrams are given in Table 5.1, and the basic steps in deriving an organization (common to the strategies of top-down design, design factor isolation, and data abstraction) are given in Table 5.2.

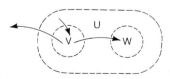

Figure 5.3 Module U contains module V.

Keep the information of Tables 5.1 and 5.2 in mind, and review the organizations developed in Section 4.2. You will then see that some of these organizations are based on the diagrams shown in Figure 5.4.

Table 5.1   Principles of partitioning data flow diagrams

Boundaries

1. Each dashed-line boundary signifies desired isolation of a group of objects, actions, and/or modules in a module.
2. Module boundaries may be nested within other module boundaries, so that levels of isolation are achieved.
3. Every module boundary partitions the data flow diagram into disjoint sets of modules; namely, the set within the boundary and the set outside the boundary.
4. The outermost boundary enclosing the entire data flow diagram signifies the parent module.

Calls

5. Let U be the module whose boundary most immediately contains the modules V and W, where V and W are exterior to each other.
   (a) Then V may be called only by U or by W.
   (b) V is not called by any module exterior to or containing U, or by any module contained in W.

Data Access and Transfer

6. A module can directly access data common or global to it.
7. Except for situation 6 above, every transfer of data requires a set of one or more calls.
8. Suppose data transfer is required from module X to module Z. Suppose also that $U \supset W_1 \supset W_2 \supset \cdots \supset W_k \supset X$ and $U \supset Y_1 \supset \ldots \supset Y_m \supset Z$. Then the data must be transferred either via the set of calls X calls Y_1, Y_1 calls Y_2, . . . , Y_{m-1} calls Y_m, Y_m calls Z or via the set of calls Z calls W_1, W_1 calls W_2, . . . , W_{k-1} calls W_k, W_k calls X.

Table 5.2   Basic steps in deriving organization

1. Identify basic groupings of objects and actions.
2. Isolate each basic grouping with a module boundary.
3. Draw further boundaries as appropriate, to include modules within other modules.
4. Develop program organization in accordance with rules 5, 6, 7, and 8 of Table 5.1.

REFERENCES

[Bela 77] Belady, L. A., and Lehman, M. M. *The Characteristics of Large Systems*. IBM Report RC6785, 1977. (Also in [Ram 78] and [Weg 79].)*

---

*See Appendix B: Bibliography.

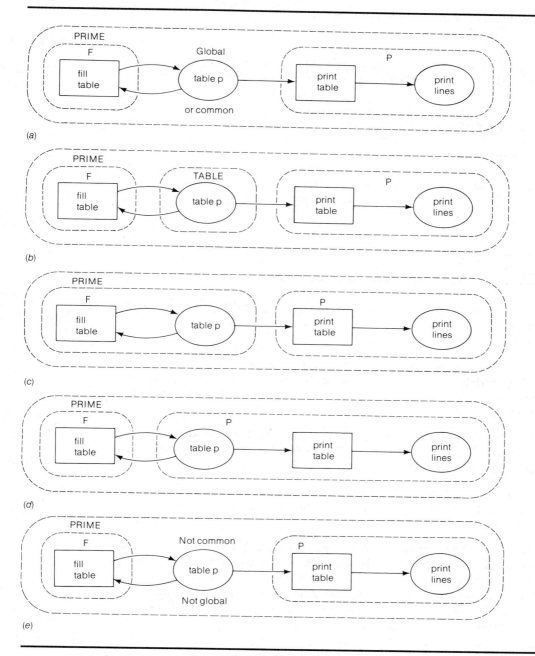

Figure 5.4 Data flow diagrams from which some of the organizations in Section 4.2 were derived. (*a*) PLAN 1: table p is global or common. (*b*) PLAN 2: table p is in its own module TABLE. (*c*) PLAN 3.1: table p is in module F. (*d*) PLAN 3.2: table p is in module P. (*e*) PLAN 3.3: table p is in module PRIME.

[Dij 72b] Dijkstra, E. W. "Notes on Structured Programming," in O.-J. Dahl, E. W. Dijkstra, and Hoare (eds.), *Structured Programming*. New York: Academic Press, 1972.

[Par 75a] Parnas, D. L. "Software Engineering or Methods for the Multi-Person Construction of Multi-Version Programs," *Proceedings of 4th Informatik Symposium; Lecture Notes in Computer Science, No. 23: Program Methodology*. New York: Springer-Verlag, 1975.

[Ros 75] Ross, D. A.; Goodenough, J. B.; and Irvine, C. A. "Software Engineering; Process, Principles, and Goals," *Computer*, May 1975. (Also in [Fre 80b].)*

[Tur 80] Turner, J. "The Structure of Module Programs," *Communications of the ACM*, May 1980.

PROBLEMS

1. Why is it important that each module have a single entry point and a single exit point? Show how a system problem could result if this condition is violated.

2. Why is it important that a called module always returns control to the calling module, at the location in the calling module immediately following the call? Show how a system problem could result if this condition is violated.

3. The discussion accompanying Figure 5.1 states that a module receiving information may be either the calling module or the called module. Give three examples of each situation.

4. Assume that in Figure 5.2, module P calls module M1, and that ACTION4 is a part of module P. Give an organization diagram (see Section 4.1) corresponding to Figure 5.2.

5. Suppose that the module boundaries of Figure 5.2 are altered so that module T enclosing TABLE5 is no longer isolated within module M2 or M1. In other words, module T is isolated only within module P. Draw the altered module boundaries. What mechanisms are now necessary to transfer information between ACTION3 and TABLE5? Provide an organization diagram reflecting the altered boundaries.

6. Give organization diagrams for:
   - (a) Figure 5.4(*a*)
   - (b) Figure 5.4(*b*)
   - (c) Figure 5.4(*c*)
   - (d) Figure 5.4(*d*)
   - (e) Figure 5.4(*e*)

---

*See Appendix B: Bibliography.

5.2 ORGANIZING VIA TOP-DOWN DESIGN

5.2.1 Principles of Top-Down Design

The organizing principle of top-down design is that subsidiary modules are assigned so as to "decompose" a module's function. In other words, the modules subsidiary to a given module M divide among themselves the responsibility for performing module M's function.

Top-down design assumes that the design decisions to be embodied in the desired program are all known. These decisions can be ranked in importance, the most important ones being those that

1. Affect the largest possible portion of the total design
2. Cause complex problems to be segmented into collections of simpler sub-problems
3. Restrict further decisions as little as possible

The philosophy of top-down design is that the highest level decisions should be the most important ones and that detailed decisions should be deferred to the lowest levels possible. Thus the most important decisions determine overall structure, while detailed decisions determine the structure of small program segments [Fre 80a]. From this viewpoint, the strategy consists of the following steps:

1. Determine what the design decisions are.
2. Rank the design decisions in importance.
3. Design the structure by making important decisions first. Defer detail decisions as long as possible. At each level, choose the structure that preserves the most options for later decisions.

In deriving an organization of modules, each successive level is obtained by considering the various design decisions that must be made. The most important of these decisions is then expressed by choosing a set of boundaries that partition a portion P of the data flow diagram into major subportions P1, . . . , Pn. Since each of the newly created boundaries defines a module, the partitioning determines a decomposition of the corresponding module P into modules P1, . . . , Pn. In accordance with top-down design philosophy, the partitioning of the entire data flow diagram into major subdiagrams is associated with one or more broad design decisions, while the partitioning of each subdiagram is associated with more detailed decisions.

5.2.2 Steps in Organizing via Top-Down Design

Typically, a highest level (0th level) module is given functional responsibility for an entire process. As shown in Figure 5.5, this corresponds to the boundary enclosing the entire data flow diagram.

The overall functional responsibility is divided at the next (1st) level among a set of subsidiary modules. As shown in Figure 5.6, subfunctions are assigned to subsidiary modules P1, . . . , Pn, corresponding to the partition of the data flow diagram into n major subdiagrams. The subfunctions may be assigned on the basis of sequence of execution, so that P1 is the first subprocess performed, P2 is the second, and so on. An alternative is that each module performs a different *kind* of function. For example, if P has the responsibility for processing all transactions to a file, then P1, . . . , Pn may each have responsibility for one particular kind of transaction. Figure 5.7 shows a portion of a data flow diagram containing a module TRAN which has the responsibility of processing all of the contents of a transaction file into a data file. The diagram indicates that three different transaction types TRAN1, TRAN2, and TRAN3 are processed. At the next level, the subfunctions TRAN1, TRAN2, and TRAN3 are assigned, respectively, to modules T1, T2, and T3.

The assignment of subsidiary modules on the basis of transaction type is called a transaction-based or transaction-driven assignment [Jac 75, You 75b].

The two bases for assignment of subsidiary modules, namely, *execution sequence* and *kind of function*, may be intermixed throughout the organization. For example, the modules P1, . . . , Pn of Figure 5.8 may each perform a different kind of transaction, but the modules subsidiary to any one of these might be assigned on the basis of execution sequence.

We intend that each subsidiary module have the responsibility for exactly one subfunction, and that it have responsibility for all of that subfunction. Thus the responsibility for each subfunction is isolated in precisely one module, in conformance with the principles of localization and information hiding. This practice fosters independence of modules. Conversely, if a function is spread out among many modules, these modules must cooperate, and

Figure 5.5 Level 0 module has overall responsibility.

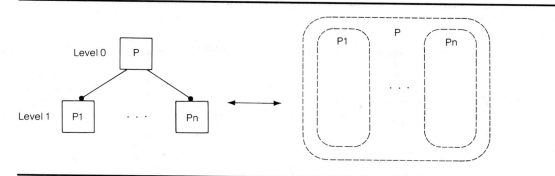

Figure 5.6 Subfunctions assigned to n subsidiary level 1 modules.

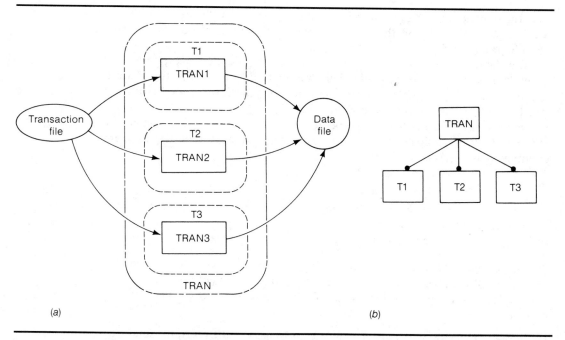

(a)   (b)

Figure 5.7 Assignment of subsidiary modules on the basis of type of transaction. (*a*) Partition of data flow diagram. (*b*) Refinement step assigning subsidiary modules.

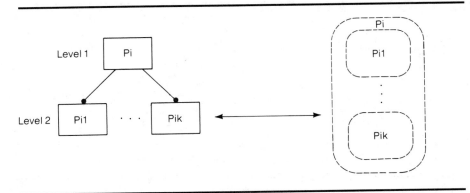

Figure 5.8   Subfunctions of a level 1 module assigned to level 2
modules.

thus the dependencies between modules are increased. As in stepwise refinement, it is important that the input, function, and ouput of each subsidiary module at each level are precisely defined.

After the first level of modules has been completely defined, subfunctions of each Pi may be assigned to subsidiary modules Pil, . . . , Pik to create a second level of modules. This is accomplished by a partition of the Pi diagram into k subdiagrams, as shown in Figure 5.8.

Similarly, after all modules have been assigned at the ith level, subsidiary modules may be assigned at the (i + 1)st level by partitioning the diagram defining each ith-level module.

5.2.3 Treatment of Data Blocks

The partitioning of a diagram into subdiagrams must take into account the placement of data blocks. As was noted in the discussions of Section 4.2, this can be done in many ways. One style of partitioning is to adopt the following convention:

Convention 1: Every data block required to be accessed by several subsidiary modules will be common or global to these modules.

Figure 5.9 shows the diagram defining a module Q, which is partitioned in accordance with convention 1 into subdiagrams Q1, Q2, Q3, and Q4. The data blocks DATA1 and DATA2, each of which is accessed by several modules, are

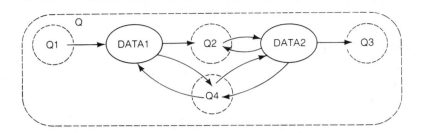

Figure 5.9 Partitioning using global data blocks.

assumed to be global or common to these modules. For example, DATA1 is global or common to Q1, Q2, and Q4. [Figure 5.4(*a*) shows a partitioning of the PRIME program diagram in accordance with convention 1.]

Chapter 7 discusses the technique of *stepwise refinement*, the application of top-down design within a module or program segment. The concern of stepwise refinement is to subdivide a segment of program text into subsegments so that each design decision is localized within one subsegment. (In contrast, the concern of this section is to derive an organization of modules for a given task.) Stepwise refinement does not explicitly consider the use of subroutines, and thus is not specifically concerned with the use of subroutine parameters to accomplish transfer of data. Usually stepwise refinement requires that program segments share access to data blocks. Top-down partitioning in accordance with convention 1 yields shared access of data blocks, and thus the organization of program modules obtained using convention 1 corresponds exactly to the structure of program segments obtained via stepwise refinement (see Chapter 7).

An equivalent convention is:

Convention 2: Every data block required to be accessed by several subsidiary modules will be assigned its own module.

Figure 5.10 shows partitioning of the module Q in accordance with convention 2 into subdiagrams Q1, Q2, Q3, Q4, and also D1 (containing DATA1) and D2 (containing DATA2).

[Figure 5.4(*b*) also shows the partitioning of the PRIME program in accordance with convention 2.] Convention 2 also achieves shared access of data blocks (though by a slightly different mechanism), and thus the organization of modules obtained using convention 2 also corresponds exactly to the structure of program segments achieved by stepwise refinement.

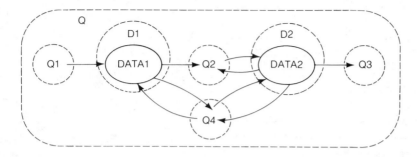

Figure 5.10   Partitioning in accordance with convention 2.

5.2.4 Organization and Hierarchy

The organization diagram resulting from top-down design is, in concept, a tree as in Figure 5.11.

In such organizations, the functional responsibilities are strictly organized. For example, the functional responsibility of P1 is independent of the functional responsibilities of P2 and P3, and the modules P11 and P12, which have responsibility for subfunctions of P1, are invoked only by P1. In other words, the functional responsibility of each module is precisely indicated by its position in the organization chart.

The analogy is often drawn between this kind of organization diagram and the organization chart of a business corporation, in which lines of authority and subordination are also clearly drawn.

5.2.5 Elimination of Duplicate Modules

In a diagram such as Figure 5.11, it might happen that the function of P23 is identical to the function of P31, so that the same module can serve in both places. The designer may elect to have duplicate copies of the same module, to preserve the functional independence between P2 and P3 in case future changes in requirements force a change between the desired functions of P23 and P31. Alternatively, the designer may elect to eliminate one module and have a single module called both by P2 and P3.

Similarly, if it is found that P11 and P121 have identical functions, the designer may elect to eliminate one of them. The result of eliminating P31 and P11 is shown in Figure 5.12.

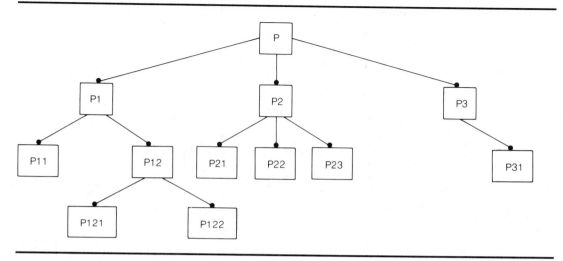

Figure 5.11 A typical organization diagram designed top-down.

If later it is found that P23 and P122 have identical functions, then P23 might be eliminated and the diagram of Figure 5.13 obtained.

An important principle of the top-down organization is that a module may call only those modules that are subordinate to it in the hierarchy. To retain the essence of this principle in situations such as in Figures 5.12 and 5.13, we adopt the rule that a module may call only those modules at levels lower than its own (except, of course, for recursive modules that call themselves). This rule prevents the possibility of a cycle of calling relations (e.g., A calls B, B calls C, and C calls A) that might result in a nonterminating program. In accordance with this rule, whenever one of two identical modules is to be eliminated, we eliminate the module at the higher level and retain the module at the lower level. This procedure was followed in obtaining Figures 5.12 and 5.13.

5.2.6 Transform Analysis

An important style of top-down design is *transform analysis*, which was originally presented in Stevens, Meyers, and Constantine [Ste 74] and later described fully in Yourdon and Constantine [You 75b]. This technique uses the concept of a *highest level input*, that is, a data element that is an input but is "furthest removed from physical input." Transform analysis assumes that a set of highest level inputs can be identified by "starting along the physical inputs

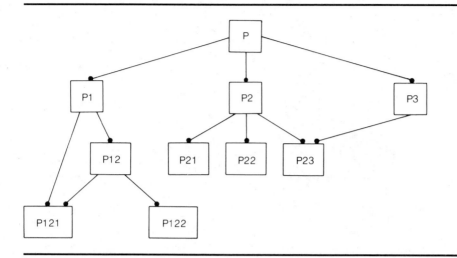

Figure 5.12 Organization obtained when P23 and P31 have identical functions, P11 and P121 have identical functions, and P31 and P11 are eliminated.

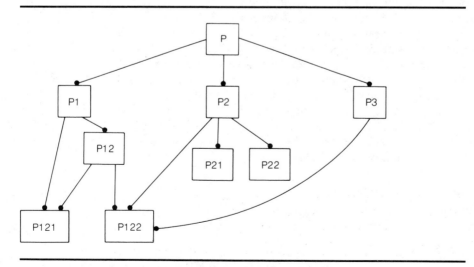

Figure 5.13 Organization obtained when P31, P11, and P23 all have functions identical to the functions of other modules and are thus eliminated.

and moving inward . . . until we identify a stream that can no longer be considered as incoming" [You 75b, p. 192]. This identification must be subjective, but "the aim is to go as far from the physical inputs as possible," and "experienced designers will not differ by more than one or two actions in the judgment" of where the input actions end [p. 194].

It is also assumed that a set of *highest level outputs* can be identified in the same way. Once the sets of highest level inputs and outputs have been identified, the data flow diagram is partitioned into three major sections:

1. An *input plan*, which produces the highest level inputs from the physical inputs
2. An *output plan*, which produces the physical outputs from the highest level outputs
3. A *transform plan*, which produces the highest level outputs from the highest level inputs

Figure 5.14 shows a simple example with physical inputs I1, I2, and I3; highest level inputs I*1, I*2, and I*3; physical outputs O1 and O2; and highest level outputs O*1 and O*2.

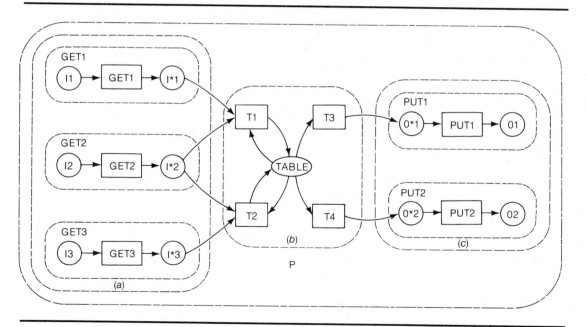

Figure 5.14   Partition of data flow diagram of program P into (*a*) input plan, (*b*) transform plan, and (*c*) output plan.

An input plan is further partitioned into diagrams GET1 (which obtains the first highest level input), GET2, . . . , GETk (which obtains the kth highest level input). Likewise, an output plan is further partitioned into diagrams PUT1 (which processes the first highest level output to physical outputs), PUT2, . . . , PUTn (which processes the nth highest level output to physical outputs). All data flow between the input plan and the transform plan, or between the transform and the output plan is routed through the parent module P. The 0th level and 1st level modules obtained by transform analysis for a typical problem are shown in Figure 5.15. Each module GET1, . . . , GETk is responsible for obtaining a given high-level input; each module PUT1, . . . , PUTn is responsible for processing a given high-level output; and the modules T1, . . . , Tm collectively perform the functions of the transform plan.

Each module GETj obtains a high-level input Ij from one physical input or from a collection of physical inputs whose processing merges. In terms of the data flow diagram, each GETj is a module boundary that isolates the processing of Ij from the rest of the data flow diagram. The technique assumes that no information will flow across the boundaries from any $GETj_1$ to any $GETj_2$ (e.g., that there is no data flow between the GET1 subplan and the GET5 subplan).

Transform analysis also has the convention that information transfer between modules either consists only of individual values or that the values transferred are contained in a buffer available only to the modules involved. This is a variation of convention 1. With the adoption of this convention, data blocks involved in information transfer can be ignored, and each data flow arc can be assumed to transfer a stream of individual values (Figures 5.15 through 5.19 use this assumption).

Subsidiary modules of each GETj are obtained in a standard fashion. Assume that the GETj portion of the data flow diagrams produces the highest level input Ij as the output of an action A which merges and processes several

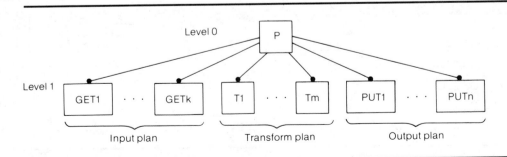

Figure 5.15 Major input, transform, and output modules.

next-highest-level inputs Ij1, . . . , IjM. This situation is shown in Figure 5.16(*a*).

The GETj portion of the data flow diagram is now partitioned into subdiagrams A (containing the action A), GETj1 (which produces Ij1), . . . , GETjM [which produces IjM, as in Figure 5.16(*b*)]. Again, all data transfers are routed through the parent module, so that GETj and its subsidiary modules appear as in Figure 5.16(*c*). Each of GETj1, . . . , GETjM is assigned subsidiary modules in exactly the same fashion, and the same pattern is followed for their subsidiary modules also.

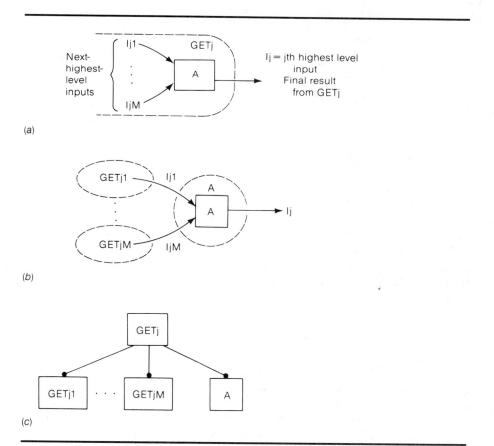

(*a*)

(*b*)

(*c*)

Figure 5.16 Derivation of subsidiary modules of GETj. (*a*) The jth highest level input is produced by merging and processing of the next-highest-level inputs. (*b*) Partitioning of GETj diagram. (*c*) Organization of input plan modules corresponding to (*a*) and (*b*).

Figures 5.17 through 5.19 show an example of this technique. Figure 5.17 shows the processing of physical inputs I1, I2, and I3 to achieve the highest level input I. The entities I1a, I1b, I2a, I3a, and I23 are all intermediate-level inputs. Figure 5.18 shows this diagram with all module boundaries imposed, and Figure 5.19 shows the corresponding module organization.

Notice that the actual physical inputs are most deeply isolated and that the level of isolation decreases as the plan moves farther from actual physical input. (The modules PUT of the output plan are treated in a symmetric way, so that a similar tree structure of PUT modules and action modules is obtained.) Information flows upward through the GET modules and downward through the PUT modules.

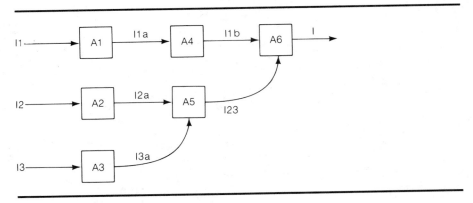

Figure 5.17   Processing of physical inputs I1, I2, and I3 to achieve the highest level input I.

REFERENCES

[BrownR 76] Brown, R. "Technique and Practice of Structured Design a la Constantine," in *Infotech State of the Art Report: Survey of Structured Programming Practice*, Part II, Vol. II. Maidenhead, England: Infotech, 1976.

[Fre 80a] Freeman, P. "The Nature of Design," in P. Freeman and A. I. Wasserman (eds.), *Tutorial on Software Design Techniques*, 3rd ed. (IEEE Catalog No. EHO 161-0.) New York: IEEE Computer Society, 1980.

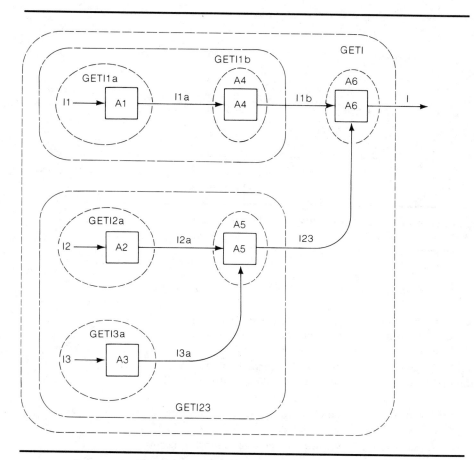

Figure 5.18   Input data flow of Figure 5.17, with module boundaries imposed.

[Hug 77] Hughes, J. K., and Michtom, J. I. *A Structured Approach to Programming*. Englewood Cliffs, NJ: Prentice-Hall, 1977.

[Jac 75] Jackson, M. A. *Principles of Program Design*. New York: Academic Press,
1975.

[Mye 75] Myers, G. J. *Reliable Software through Composite Design*. New York:
Petrocelli/Charter, 1975.

[Mye 76b] ————. *Software Reliability: Principles and Practices*. New York: Wiley-
Interscience, 1976.

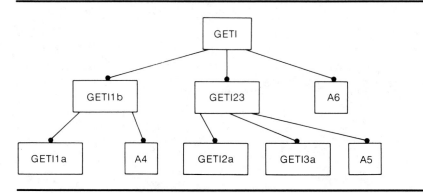

Figure 5.19   Organization of input plan modules for the data flow of Figure 5.17.

[Mye 78] ———. *Composite/Structural Design*. New York: Van Nostrand Reinhold, 1978.

[Par 72c] Parnas, D. L. "On the Response to Detected Errors in Hierarchically Structured Systems." Technical Report, Dept. of Computer Science, Carnegie-Mellon University, Pittsburgh, PA, 1972.

[Par 75b] ———, and Siewiorek, D. P. "Use of the Concept of Transparency in the Design of Hierarchically Structured Systems," *Communications of the ACM*, July 1975.

[Ste 74] Stevens, W. P.; Meyers, G. J.; and Constantine, L. L. "Structured Design," *IBM Systems Journal*, 1974. (Also in [Ram 78], [Berg 79], and [Fre 80b].)*

[Ste 75] ———; ———; and ———. *Structural Design*, New York: Yourdon, 1975.

[You 75a] Yourdon, E. *Techniques of Program Structure and Design*. Englewood Cliffs, NJ: Prentice-Hall, 1975.

[You 75b] ———, and Constantine, L. L. *Structured Design*. New York: Yourdon, 1975. (Republished 1979 by Prentice-Hall.)

PROBLEMS

1. In a banking system, each transaction is held in a transaction buffer, while the customer account is held in a customer file. Transactions may either

*See Appendix B: Bibliography.

update an account via a deposit or withdrawal, or may change the status of an account by creating the account or deleting the account.

(a) Draw the data flow diagram of this arrangement. Assign module boundaries on the basis of transaction type. Provide an organization diagram reflecting the data flow and boundaries, assuming a parent module named MAIN.

(b) If there is more than one way to assign boundaries on the basis of transaction type, try the assignment each different way. Contrast the resulting organization diagrams.

2. The program that produces the ABC Corporation's yearly financial report uses a two-step process. An INITIAL PROCESS subprogram processes the input data (held in an input file) into an intermediate file. The FINAL PROCESS subprogram then finishes the calculation, placing its results in an output file.

(a) Draw the data flow diagram of this arrangement.

(b) Assign module boundaries on the basis of sequence of execution, assuming that all files are global. Draw the corresponding organization diagram.

(c) Assign module boundaries on the basis of sequence of execution, assuming that each file is assigned its own module. Draw the corresponding organization diagram.

(d) Contrast the organization diagrams obtained in (b) and (c). Which do you prefer? Why?

3. Derive top-down module boundaries for the student grading program of Figure 3.6. Give the corresponding organization diagram.

4. Derive top-down module boundaries and an organization diagram for the secret sums program of Figure 3.24.

5. Assign module boundaries on the basis of transform analysis and derive the organization diagram for:

(a) The situation of Problem 1.

(b) The situation of Problem 2.

6. Derive module boundaries based on transform analysis for the student grading program of Figure 3.6. Provide the corresponding organization diagram.

7. Derive module boundaries based on transform analysis for the secret sums problem of Figure 3.24. Provide the corresponding organization diagram.

5.3 ORGANIZING BY ISOLATION OF DESIGN FACTORS

5.3.1 Some Design Problems

A system of modules can be organized using the principle of factor isolation enunciated by Parnas [Par 72b, Par 76a]. It is worth repeating that the objectives of factor isolation are exactly the same as those of top-down design: to allow easy program change, modification, and enhancement, thereby providing in advance for possible changes in problem requirements. Section 5.3.1 describes the considerations on which the factor isolation method is based.

The data usage shown in Figure 5.20, where a data object interacts with several processes, is found in many programs. For example, every compiler has a data object SYMBOL TABLE that contains permissible identifiers and characteristics associated with each identifier. In Figure 5.20, P1 enters information into SYMBOL TABLE; P2 reads from SYMBOL TABLE; and P3 both reads and enters information.

The data flow diagram may be implemented so that SYMBOL TABLE becomes directly accessible to all three processes by its placement in a common data area. The organization diagram of Figure 5.21 shows this data usage, and the structure of the table can possibly be arranged for maximum efficiency of the processes.

However, since SYMBOL TABLE is accessed by all three processes, its internal structure is known to them. Each process, in accessing the table, depends on this knowledge of internal structure. In this sense, all three processes are dependent on the structure of the table. Any future change (correction, modification, or enhancement) in the structure of SYMBOL TABLE potentially requires changes in each of the three processes, so that any such

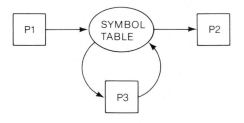

Figure 5.20 A typical data usage situation.

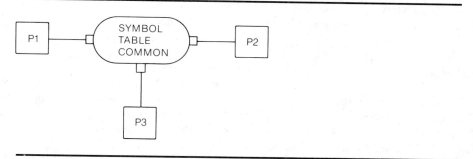

Figure 5.21   Placement of SYMBOL TABLE in a common data
area.

changes must include examining P1, P2, and P3 to determine the necessary
changes in these processes. Naturally, if a required change in P1, P2, or P3 is
accidentally overlooked, program errors will arise.

In sum, such an implementation has the advantages of simplicity, directness,
and (possibly) efficiency, and the disadvantage of sensitivity to changes in the
structure of the table. Thus the arrangement is highly desirable if the structure
of the table never changes, but it becomes more undesirable with each change
in the table since any change potentially requires changes in all three processes. The cost and effort of maintaining such an arrangement might easily
become excessive.

On balance, the problem of sensitivity to change is perceived by designers
as far outweighing other problems, and a major concern of good design (especially in large systems) is minimizing such sensitivity. How can this be done?

Sensitivity to change arises because each process, in accessing the table,
knows and *depends on* the structure of the table. Therefore, removing these
dependencies will remove the sensitivity. If we isolate the table within a
module, allowing the three processes to access the table only via calls to the
module, we can expect that the processes will no longer be sensitive to
changes in the table since the structure of the table will be unknown to them.
In the data flow diagram of Figure 5.22(*a*), the table is isolated within a module
boundary to define a module ST.

In accordance with the principles of partitioning, the arrows in and out of
the module now designate transfers of information via calls. The corresponding organization diagram is shown in Figure 5.22(*b*). Only module ST directly
accesses SYMBOL TABLE, while P1, P2, and P3 communicate with SYM-
BOL TABLE via calls to module ST. Loosely speaking, all communication
between the table and each of the three processes now occurs with module ST
as an intermediary.

The reason why a data object should be placed in its own module is to isolate details of the object's structure, hiding those details from other modules.

Data base management systems isolate the details of data elements in exactly the manner of Figure 5.22. A collection of data objects (data tables, files, etc.) is isolated within the data base module exactly as SYMBOL TABLE is isolated in module ST. Other modules then access this data only via subroutine calls to the data base management module, in the same fashion that P1, P2, and P3 access SYMBOL TABLE via subroutine calls to ST. The technique of Figure 4.18 is used to isolate other modules from control parameters.

The capability of hiding details of data elements from other modules is a principal reason for the popularity of data base management systems. Once the data elements have been isolated, details of the structure of files and tables can be changed as necessary without affecting the collection of programs. The data base management module can also change the format of requested data items to meet the needs of the requesting program. Thus isolation of data in the data base promotes system flexibility.

In principle, SYMBOL TABLE is now isolated from P1, P2, and P3. However, the input and output parameters of ST could possibly indicate details of the structure of SYMBOL TABLE and thus cause P1, P2, and P3 to be dependent on the table structure. For example, suppose that SYMBOL TABLE is originally a linked list whose elements are accessed via pointers and that P1, P2, and P3 obtain elements by first calculating appropriate pointer

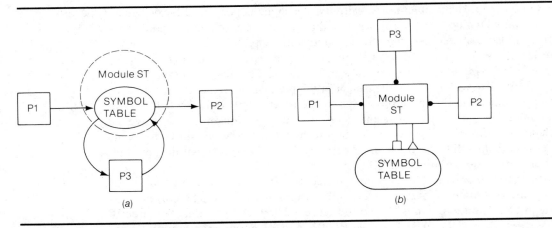

Figure 5.22   Isolation of SYMBOL TABLE in module ST. (*a*)
Partition of data flow diagram. (*b*) Corresponding
portion of organization diagram.

values. Now suppose that, after creation of the module ST, P2 still calculates a pointer value and then passes this value as the input parameter to ST, while ST still gives a pointer value as output to P3. Obviously, the pointer value still indicates the structure of the table, and thus P2 and P3 have not really been isolated from the table. Design of the calls to the module is needed in addition to isolation of the design features in the module, to ensure that these calls do not reveal the design features.

Recall that P1 enters information into the table; P2 reads from the table; and P3 does both, and these programs can no longer directly access the table. Module ST must now provide appropriate programs ENTER, READ, and SEARCH, as well as a control program to activate the appropriate program. The internal details of module ST shown in Figure 5.23 are similar to the internal details shown for the TABLE1 module in Figure 4.17.

When SYMBOL TABLE is isolated in module ST, P1 must be modified to call ST instead of directly accessing the table, and so must P2 and P3. Obviously, modifications such as these are always required when isolation is introduced, and with this understanding we will omit mentioning such modifications.

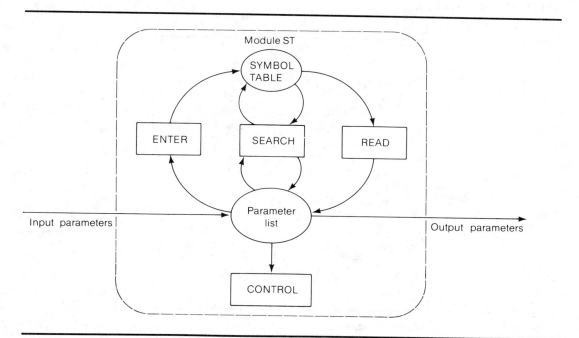

Figure 5.23 Details of module ST. (Note: CONTROL activates ENTER, SEARCH, or READ as appropriate.)

In contrast to the organization in Figure 5.21, isolation requires a separate module for the data structure, extra calling sequences (with both space and time costs), and extra accessing and control programs within the separate module. On the other hand, P1, P2, and P3 are no longer affected by changes in the structure of SYMBOL TABLE, or by most other changes in ST. The contents of the module may be independently coded, checked out, modified, or enhanced. For these reasons, isolation is a much preferred technique.

Any group of objects and actions may be isolated in a module, and there are many situations in which such isolation removes dependencies between modules. One such situation is the use of an input CHARACTER BUFFER accessed by several processes, as in Figure 5.24(a). Here CHARACTER BUFFER may be isolated, together with the mechanisms PUT CHAR IN and TAKE CHAR OUT for direct access to the buffer at the character level, in a module CB1. This isolation is diagrammed as the dashed-line boundary in Figure 5.24(a).

Module CB1 may be easily implemented as a function that returns to P1 or P2 either the next character or an "empty buffer" indication. (The "empty buffer" indication may be either a separate parameter or a special character value.) Thus P1 and P2 become independent of the detailed structure of CHARACTER BUFFER.

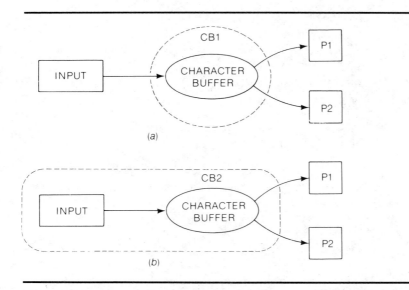

Figure 5.24 Alternative method of isolating a character buffer. (a) Isolation of CHARACTER BUFFER in module CB1. (b) INPUT program and CHARACTER BUFFER isolated in module CB2.

Figure 5.24(*a*) does not require that all input precede the operations P1 and P2. The process may proceed incrementally—a little input, a little P1 or P2, again a little input, and so on.

An alternative technique is isolation of the INPUT program together with the buffer, as in Figure 5.24(*b*), so that the rest of the program can regard bringing data to the buffer and storing the data in the buffer as one indivisible unit. In this variation, CB2 can be implemented as a function that either returns a character or an "end of input" indication. If the buffer happens to be empty, the module itself uses the INPUT program to fill the buffer again, unless the end of input is encountered. As far as P1 or P2 is concerned, the entire character input process occurs automatically, allowing either of these processes to receive a character on demand. That is, P1 demands a character by calling CB2, and (if there is one) immediately receives it.

In either variation, the program INPUT may also be isolated within a module so that INPUT can read either cards or tape or disk and the rest of the program need not know about the input medium. If INPUT and CHARAC-TER BUFFER are isolated within CB3, and INPUT is further isolated in module IN, two levels of isolation are achieved, as shown in Figure 5.25. The isolation technique may be carried to as many levels as appropriate.

5.3.2 Steps in the Isolation Method

The system organization is derived in four steps:

1. Identify design factors subject to change, modification, or enhancement. Determine which factors (that is, groupings of actions and/or objects) might change as the system evolves.

2. Isolate each factor within a module.

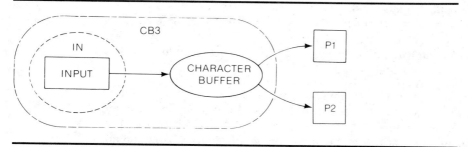

Figure 5.25 Two levels of isolation.

3. Include modules in other modules as appropriate.

4. Develop program organization in accordance with principles 5, 6, 7, and 8 of Table 5.1.

Isolation is used to obtain independent chunks of program, namely, the modules. If properly done, isolation allows independent understanding and development of the modules, and it minimizes sensitivity to change.

Notice that the organizaton is derived by isolating portions of the data flow diagram. Modules are not assigned according to the steps in a flowchart, or according to the sequence of processes; they are not assigned on the basis of "each major step is a module." The overriding consideration is isolation of each design factor, to minimize the sensitivity of the design to changes in any factor.

The isolation method embodies the principle of information hiding [Par 71, Par 76a] since its intent is to hide details of the design factor from other parts of the program. Such information hiding is complete only when the module interfaces also do not reveal information about the design factor. To reveal as little information as possible, these interfaces should be as simple as possible.

5.3.3 Key Design Points

When design factors are isolated, the most important question to keep in mind is: *What factors should be isolated?* In other words, which design decisions are subject to change, modification, or enhancement? Each solution should be analyzed with respect to this question.

Parnas [Par 72b] offers the following suggestions for isolation:

· A data structure and its internal linkings, accessing procedures, and modifying procedures are all in the same module.
· A routine and the sequence of instructions calling it are in the same module (for assembly language systems).
· Control blocks are hidden in a "control block" module since the formats of these control blocks change frequently.
· Character codes, alphabetic orderings, and similar data are hidden in a module for greatest flexibility.

A second important question is: *What is the best organization of modules?* We have seen in Section 4.2 that a data flow diagram may be implemented using many different patterns of modules. We should ask which isolation pattern best isolates the various factors and how many levels of isolation are required. An associated question is whether workable calling sequences can be devised for a given structure.

Associated with the problem of workable calling sequences is a third question: *What are the best interfaces?* For any isolation pattern, alternative interface schemes may be arranged. As noted previously, the most desirable scheme is the one in which input and output parameters are most simple, abstract, and least revealing of information about the module. We should develop each alternative to a level of detail sufficient to allow a choice of the best interface.

5.3.4 Data Abstraction

Data abstraction is a type of factor isolation that seeks to isolate each data object and its associated actions. The isolation of SYMBOL TABLE in module ST, as shown in Figure 5.23, is an example of data abstraction. Another example, shown in Figure 5.26, is the isolation of a pushdown stack. Some of the isolation suggestions of Section 5.3.3 refer specifically to data abstraction problems.

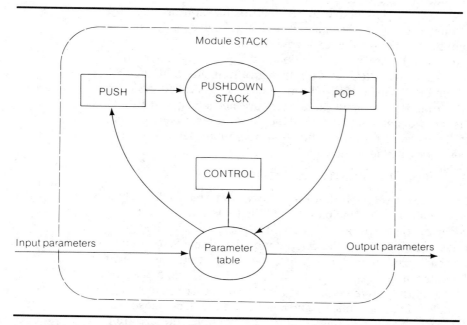

Figure 5.26   Data flow diagram of module STACK. (Note: CONTROL activates PUSH or POP as appropriate.)

When the data object and its associated actions are isolated as a group, any other module in the system can refer to the object only by a subroutine call that applies one of these actions to the data object. Thus the object and its actions become a closed system, the details of which are hidden from other modules. The data object is said to be *abstracted* because it is available to other modules only via a selected set of operations that have defined results. For example, PUSHDOWN STACK in Figure 5.26 can be accessed only via the PUSH operation, which places a value on the top of the stack, or via the POP operation, which retrieves the value at the top of the stack. A key problem in the data abstraction strategy is the choice of an appropriate set of actions for the data block.

5.3.5 An Example: Modularization of Secret Sums Design

We now derive a module organization for the secret sums problem discussed in Section 3.3. The entire data flow diagram of Figure 3.24 is designated as module SS and shown in Figure 5.27. Ordinarily a program of this size (the problem can be coded in 200 to 300 lines) would not be extensively modularized; however, it is instructive to see the organization obtained by using factor isolation. Be aware that many alternative and equally correct organizations may be derived for this data flow diagram.

The first step shown in Figure 5.27 is isolation of the puzzle-solving portion within a module designated PROC. With this arrangement, SOLUTION FLAG is kept within PROC and initialized each time PROC is called. SS calls PROC to process a puzzle; no input parameters are necessary, and PROC returns the value (true or false) of SOLUTION FLAG after processing the puzzle. If PROC is declared a Boolean function, the entire "end program" may be accomplished by a statement such as

if not PROC then writeln ('NO SOLUTIONS EXIST').

The data flow arc from SOLUTION FLAG to AT END determines the call SS calls PROC in accordance with principles 5 and 7 in Table 5.1.

Table 5.3 summarizes the steps taken in deriving the organization and gives interface and usage descriptions for the derived modules. Table 5.3(*a*) shows the step at which each module is derived, lists the design factor associated with each module, and notes calls to or from the module. Table 5.3(*b*) describes the interfaces of the derived modules. Table 5.3(*c*) describes the usage of the derived modules. The line numbers given in Table 5.3(*c*) label those arcs in the data flow diagram that determine calls. For example, the arc from SOLUTION FLAG to AT END determines the call SS calls PROC, and in Figure 5.27 this arc is marked by a 1. All of the labeled arcs of Table 5.3(*c*) are shown in Figure 5.31.

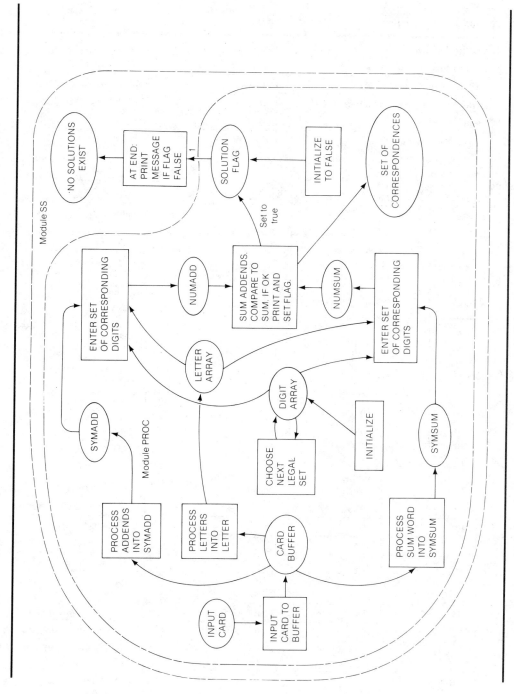

Figure 5.27 Data flow diagram of secret sums problem, with puzzle-solving portion isolated in module PROC.

Table 5.3 Summary of derived module organization

Step	Design Factor	Module	Comments
1	Entire program	SS	SS calls PROC
1	Puzzle-solving portion	PROC	SS calls PROC
2	INPUT CARD, input program, and buffer	A	P1, P2, and P3 call A
3	Input program	B	A calls B
4	DIGIT ARRAY and actions	C	P4, P5 calls C

(*a*) Table of Modules.

Module and Calling Sequence	Formal Parameter	Input	Output	Use	Significance of Parameter
PROC	PROC		✔	M	Value of SOLUTION FLAG
A	A		✔	M	Next character/end of text marker
B	B		✔	M	B=true on return signifies buffer has been filled; B=false signifies no more input
C(task,char)	task	✔		C	Task=0=>INITIALIZE Task=1=>CHOOSE NEXT LEGAL SET Task=2=>GET CORRESPONDING DIGIT
	char	✔		P	Puzzle character
	C		✔	M	Value of corresponding digit

(*b*) Interface Table.

Line	Calling Module	Called Module	Actual Parameter Sequence	Comments
1	SS	PROC	---	One call to solve puzzle
2	P1	A	---	Get next character
3	P2	A	---	Get next character
4	P3	A	---	Get next character
5	A	B	---	Fill buffer with contents of next card
6	P4	C	2,puzzlechar	Get corresponding digit
7	P5	C	2,puzzlechar	Get corresponding digit
8	P6	C	1,0	CHOOSE NEXT LEGAL SET
	PROC	C	0,0	Initialize DIGIT ARRAY

(*c*) Usage Table.

As a next step, we isolate the entire input mechanism and card buffer in module A. This isolation allows the rest of PROC to proceed independently of buffer characteristics and input mechanisms. The relevant portion of the data flow diagram is shown in Figure 5.28. To avoid confusion, the different process boxes are denoted P1, P2, and P3; later these actions will also be isolated within modules. Step 2 of Table 5.3(*a*) describes this isolation step, and lines 2, 3, and 4 of Table 5.3(*c*) show how processes P1, P2, and P3 use module A.

Note again that the arcs 2, 3, and 4 determine, respectively, the calls P1 calls A, P2 calls A, and P3 calls A. A convention that provides a natural organization is that the called module always transfers information to the calling

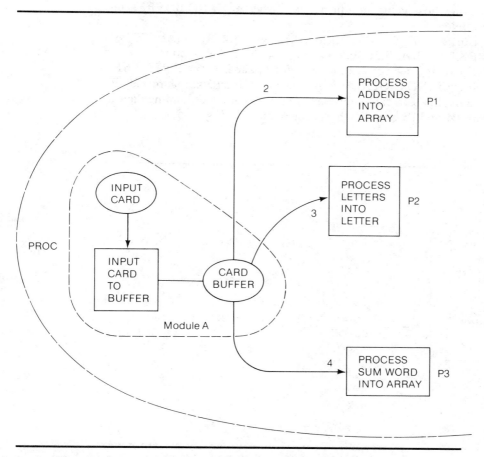

Figure 5.28 Isolation of input mechanism and CARD BUF-FER in module A.

module. In other words, the calling module always requests information and the called module delivers it. We have been following this convention, and we will continue to do so.

INPUT CARD and the input program may be further isolated in a module B. This might be done to increase the program's portability since the system- or machine-dependent input program is now isolated in a separate module. The isolation step is shown in Figure 5.29; it is summarized by step 3 in Table 5.3(a) and line 5 in Table 5.3(c).

We have arranged that CARD BUFFER is global to module B. At each call, module B is required to fill CARD BUFFER with the contents of the next card. Since, at each call, B must return to A an indication of whether the buffer has been filled or whether there is no more input, B has been made a Boolean function whose value on return tells A whether CARD BUFFER has in fact been refilled.

We now isolate DIGIT ARRAY, together with the INITIALIZE and CHOOSE NEXT LEGAL SET actions, in a module C. This step is shown in Figure 5.30. Following our convention, C will be called by the ENTER SET OF CORRESPONDING DIGITS actions, labeled P4 and P5 in Figure 5.30. P4 or P5 can give module C a character c and C returns a corresponding digit d. The calls from P4 and P5 are shown as arcs 6 and 7 in Figure 5.30.

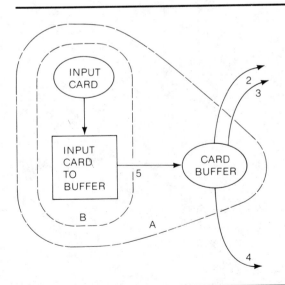

Figure 5.29 Isolation of INPUT CARD and the input program in module B.

The CHOOSE NEXT LEGAL SET action determines each new combination of digit values in the DIGIT ARRAY. This action is most appropriately called by the SUM ADDENDS, COMPARE TO SUM action, which is labeled P6 in Figure 5.30. (P6 will later be assigned to a module.) The call from P6 to C is shown as arc 8.

The INITIALIZE action of module C can be activated by a call from PROC. No arc is shown for this call.

Because module C performs three different actions, it requires a control parameter. Table 5.3(*b*) and (*c*) describes the control parameter and its use.

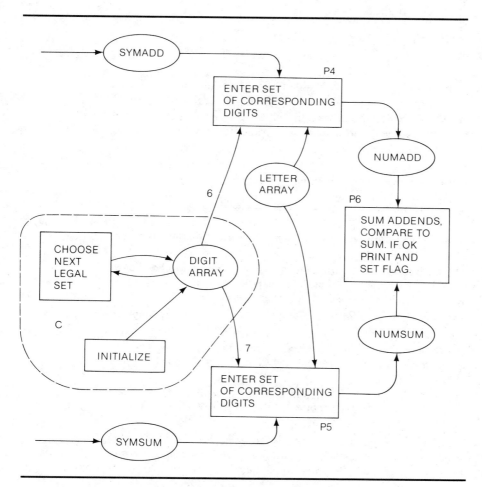

Figure 5.30 Isolation of DIGIT ARRAY, INITIALIZE, and CHOOSE NEXT LEGAL SET in module C.

[The technique of Figure 4.18 can be used to hide knowledge of the control parameters from the other modules.]

Since module C isolates a data object together with all of its associated actions, this module is an example of the data abstraction strategy discussed in Section 5.3.4.

The derivation may be continued to obtain the modules

D: containing NUMADD, NUMSUM, and SUM ADDENDS and COMPARE (P6)
E: containing SYMADD and P4
F: containing SYMSUM and P5
G: containing P1
H: containing P2 and LETTER ARRAY
I: containing P3

The data flow diagram of PROC with all of these module boundaries is shown in Figure 5.31. Completion of Table 5.3 is left as an exercise (Problem 4) at the end of this section. Since the entries in Table 5.3(*c*) explicitly show all call relations between modules, the organization diagram can be drawn directly from this table.

REFERENCES

[Mye 76a] Myers, G. J. "Comparative Design Facilities of Six Programming Languages," *IBM Systems Journal*, 1976.

[Par 71] Parnas, D. L. "Information Distribution Aspects of Design Methodology." Technical Report, Dept. of Computer Science, Carnegie-Mellon University, Pittsburgh, PA, 1971. (Also in *Proceedings of IFIP Congress 1971*.)

[Par 72a] ———. "A Technique for Software Module Specification with Examples," *Communications of the ACM*, May 1972.

[Par 72b] ———. "On the Criteria to Be Used in Decomposing Systems into Modules," *Communications of the ACM*, December 1972. (Also in [Ram 78] and [Fre 80b].)*

[Par 73] ———, and Price, W. R. "The Design of the Virtual Memory Aspects of a Virtual Machine," *Proceedings of ACM SIGARCH-SIGOPS Workshop on Virtual Computer Systems*, March 1973.

[Par 75a] ———. "Software Engineering or Methods for the Multi-Person Construction of Multi-Version Programs," *Proceedings of 4th Informatik Symposium*; *Lecture Notes in Computer Science, No. 23: Program Methodology*. New York: Springer-Verlag, 1975.

---

*See Appendix B: Bibliography.

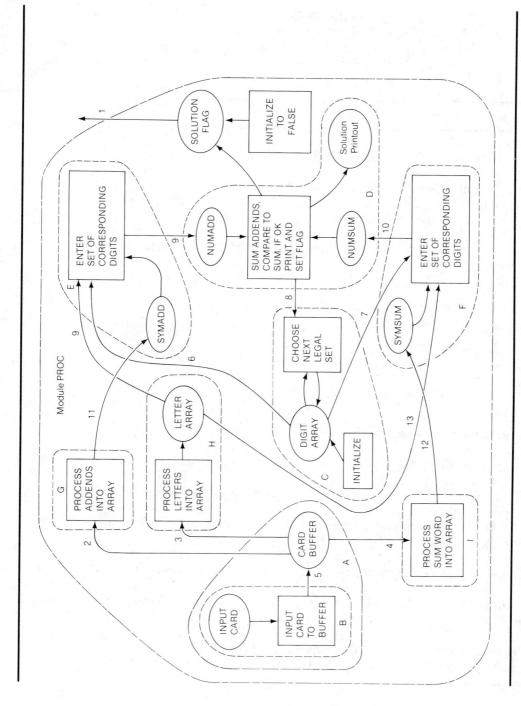

Figure 5.31 Data flow diagram of PROC, with all module boundaries.

[Par 76a] ———. "On the Design and Development of Program Families," *IEEE Transactions on Software Engineering*, Vol. SE-2, No. 1, March 1976.

[Par 77] ———. "The Use of Precise Specifications in the Development of Software," *Proceedings of the 1977 IFIP Congress*, 1977.

PROBLEMS

Problems 1 through 3 refer to the PRIME program of Section 4.2.

1. Which organizations described in Section 4.2 correspond to the data flow diagram in PLAN 3.2 of Figure 5.4? Discuss the input and output parameters required for each interface.

2. Diagram the organizations that correspond to the following data flow diagram:

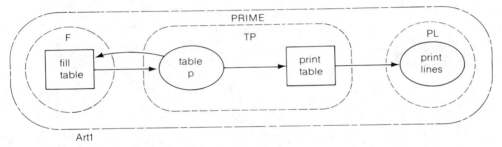

Give interface and usage tables for each organization.

3. (a) Compare the isolation patterns of Problems 1 and 2. What reasons can you give for each pattern?
   (b) Compare the interfaces necessary to implement each pattern. Which pattern allows simpler interfaces?
   (c) What are the advantages and disadvantages of each pattern? Which pattern is best? Why?

Problems 4 through 11 refer to the secret sums problem of Section 5.3.5.

4. Complete the table of modules, interface table, and usage table (Table 5.3) for Figure 5.31.

5. The module PROC contains the variable SOLUTION FLAG. Describe the arrangements necessary if SOLUTION FLAG is kept as part of module SS.

6. Describe the arrangements necessary if module END is created to contain the code for the end program; module PROC always calls END to finish the processing of a puzzle; and END prints the message 'NO SOLUTIONS EXIST' if it is appropriate to do so.

7. In the given solution, no provision is made for the case where PROC discovers format errors in a puzzle. Describe how this situation can be accommodated. What changes in input or output parameters are required?

8. In the given solution, no provision is made for processing more than one puzzle per program execution. If two or more puzzles are to be processed during each program execution, the module arrangements need to provide for an end of input situation in which PROC is called but there is no more input. Describe how this can be accomplished. What changes in input or output parameters are required?

9. Module A, contained within PROC, has the input mechanism and card buffer. Redesign PROC to contain two principal modules: module A and module AA consisting of everything else in PROC. A must call AA. What interfaces are now required? What other changes are necessary?

10. Module C contains DIGIT ARRAY, an INITIALIZATION action, and a CHOOSE NEXT LEGAL SET action. What changes are necessary if:
    (a) CHOOSE NEXT LEGAL SET is isolated within a module CN?
    (b) Module C is redesigned to contain just DIGIT ARRAY and CHOOSE NEXT LEGAL SET, but not the INITIALIZE action?
    (c) You want to allow the numeric radix of the puzzle to vary from one puzzle to the next?

11. What changes are required if modules D, E, and F are redesigned so that:
    (a) Module E contains NUMADD and module F contains NUMSUM?
    (b) NUMADD is isolated in its own module NA, and NUMSUM is isolated in its own module NS?

12. In a desired banking system, each transaction is to be held in a transaction buffer, while the customer account is to be held in a customer file. Transactions may either update the account via a deposit or withdrawal, or may change the status of an account by creating the account or deleting the account. Plans are now being made to reorganize the existing customer file. Unfortunately, the reorganization plan will not be finished until after the system has been written.
    (a) Draw the data flow diagram of this situation. Derive module boundaries, in particular providing for the isolation of the customer file. Provide the corresponding organization diagram.

(b) Assume also that the transaction buffer must be isolated. Derive appropriate module boundaries and provide the corresponding flow diagram.

13. The program desired to produce ABC Corporation's yearly financial report is to use a two-step process. An INITIAL PROCESS subprogram processes the input data (held in an input file) into an intermediate file. The FINAL PROCESS subprogram finishes the calculation, placing its results in an output file. Assign module boundaries in the data flow diagram, provide the organization diagram, and discuss the calling mechanisms for each situation below:
    (a) The intermediate file must be isolated.
    (b) The INITIAL PROCESS subprogram must be isolated.
    (c) Both the intermediate file and the INITIAL PROCESS subprogram must be isolated, but they can be combined in a module.
    (d) Both the intermediate file and the INITIAL PROCESS subprogram must be isolated, but the intermediate file module must be isolated within the INITIAL PROCESS module.

14. Each part of Figure 5.4 has the same data flow diagram but a different assignment of module boundaries. Which objects and actions are isolated in each part? What are the probable reasons for such isolation?

15. Consider the student grading program of Figure 3.6. Which actions or objects are most likely to change and therefore require isolation? Assign module boundaries based on your conclusions, and provide the corresponding organization diagram.

16. Your company has acquired the contract, and you have been assigned the task, to develop a software system that accomplishes map coloring (see Problem 14 in Appendix D).

    The system is to be implemented initially with batch I/O (card input and printer output). However, the customer will be installing a new computer next year and will then require interactive I/O (terminals with CRT display). Obviously, the system should be as portable as possible. When the new computer comes in, the customer also wants to upgrade the coloring algorithm to have fewer inputs that cannot be colored.

    The customer has been told that the system will be complete in three months. However, because of contract commitments, the customer insists on demonstration in two months. It is understood that, for this demonstration, some of the modules may be only partially working or dummy and that the data may be specially selected. The customer insists, however, that the data must actually move through and be processed by the system.

Provide an organization diagram that anticipates the proposed changes and also can be implemented in a preliminary demonstration form as well as the final production form.

PROJECT OUTLINE: Design of System Organization Consider any problem in Appendix D.

1. State any improvements or enhancements to the problem statement that your solution considers. Also state any important design objectives, not otherwise required, which your solution attempts to satisfy.
   (a) Briefly discuss each major data block in your solution.
   (b) Briefly discuss each major action of your solution.
   (c) Provide a data flow diagram of your solution.

   Note: Responses to (a), (b), and (c) should all agree. If the data flow diagram is carefully developed first, it should provide the data blocks and actions for (a) and (b).

2. Develop a module organization.
   (a) Provide a data flow diagram showing all module boundaries.
   (b) Provide a table showing each major data block and the module in which it is isolated.
   (c) Provide an organization diagram and interface, data access, and usage tables. Indicate the significance of each formal parameter.

3. Discuss the organizaton strategy or strategies you have used. Indicate which design factors were chosen for isolation, and why; which data objects have been abstracted, and why; and the basis for each top-down refinement step.

5.4 DEVELOPMENT OF MODULE ORGANIZATION: STRATEGIES FOR CODING, TESTING AND DELIVERY

5.4.1 Testing Strategies

5.4.1.1 Traditional Testing Strategies

When a module organization has been properly designed, the modules are manageable pieces that can be coded and tested by different people.

Testing is the most expensive development activity. Experience shows that successful development (i.e., development on time and within budget) of a collection of modules depends greatly on the sequence in which individual modules are coded and tested. A given organization of modules may require coding and testing of certain modules first, certain others next, and so on. This section presents strategies leading to the best sequences for such coding and testing.

The testing of a collection of modules involves the following kinds of testing activities:

1. *Unit test:* Testing an individual module to determine whether it meets its specifications
2. *Integration test:* Testing two modules together to ensure that interfaces such as calling sequences and common data areas are all arranged correctly so the modules function properly together
3. *System test:* Testing whether a whole system (or subsystem) works according to its specifications
4. *Field test:* Controlled use of a system in its operational environment

Traditionally, these activities have been performed in the sequence shown above [Good 79], which is called the *bottom-up testing strategy*. For the organization of Figure 5.32, bottom-up testing involves the sequence of activities shown in Figure 5.33. First, bottom-level individual modules are unit-

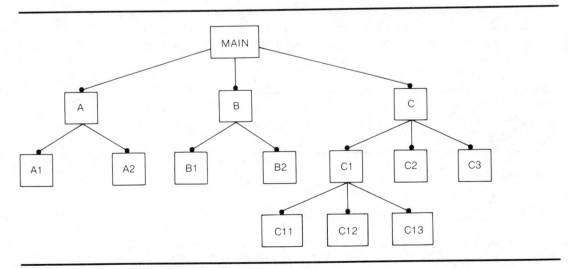

Figure 5.32 Typical module organization.

tested in a stand-alone fashion. Next, integration and subsystem tests are performed for the lowest level subsystems. Subsystems are then each built up to the next higher level, and the testing is iterated. This process continues until the system is complete.

Experience has shown that the traditional testing strategy is usually unsatisfactory because three different kinds of errors commonly occur in collections

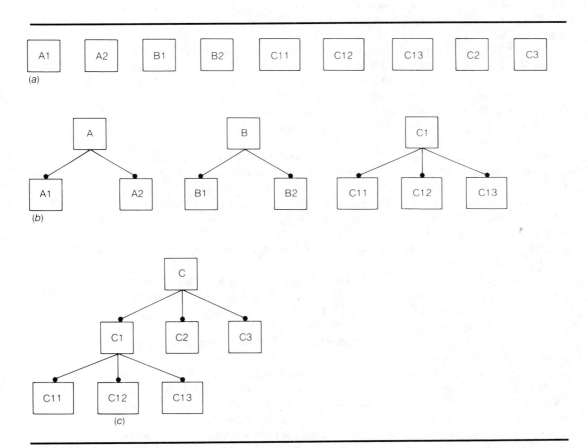

Figure 5.33   Basic sequence of activities in bottom-up testing. (*a*) First, bottom-level modules are unit tested in a stand-alone fashion. (*b*) Next, integration and subsystem tests are performed for the lowest level subsystems. (*c*) Integration and subsystem tests are repeated for the next-higher-level subsystems. Subsystems are built up and the tests are repeated until the system is complete.

of modules. For example, errors in the functioning of individual modules, which are the most easily detected and fixed type of errors, are usually encountered in step (*a*) of Figure 5.33

Systems also commonly contain interaction errors (i.e., errors caused by the interaction of several slightly incorrect modules). This type of error is more subtle than an error in an individual module, and it requires much more time and effort to detect and fix. Because successive steps involve larger and larger numbers of modules, the potential for interaction errors grows as the system is put together. Interaction errors are usually encountered in steps (*b*) and (*c*) of Figure 5.33.

The most important and most time-consuming system errors are interface errors (i.e., errors in communication between modules). Such errors, usually occurring in steps (*b*) and (*c*) of Figure 5.33, arise when the programmers of different modules perceive slightly differently the calling sequences between the modules, or the information to be passed from one module to another. A common occurrence is that the documents specifying these interfaces are incorrect or incomplete.

Problems may arise in even the simplest interfaces. Many years ago, our programming group had built a compiler generation system (a tricky program for those bygone days) and was about to test the complete process for the first time. Data would be input to define a language to the system; a compiler would be produced; a program in the language would be compiled to assembly language; the assembly language program would be assembled by the computer's assembler to object code; and finally the object code would be loaded by the computer's loader and then executed.

The run was started and the compiler was produced; the program in the language was compiled; and then the assembler would not run—even though the assembly language program appeared to be absolutely correct. It took three weeks to learn that in our slightly unusual circumstances (and only those) the assembler required one blank record at the beginning of the assembly language program.

Our system was modified to produce the blank record, and the final run was started again. This time the assembler ran perfectly—but the loader would not load the object program! Another two weeks later, the difficulty was found, a trivial adjustment was made, and the final run went to completion. But five weeks had been spent in finding and eliminating two simple interface problems, and during this time the programming group could accomplish very little else. The time was almost completely wasted.

More complicated interface errors can occur at the interfaces between program and hardware, between program and the computer's operating system, and between the program and other application programs. Yourdon [You 79b], for example, discusses an online system that involved interfaces with the computer's operating system, a new CRT terminal, a new modem, newly installed telephone lines, a telecommunications monitor from one software firm, a data base management system from another software firm, and several major application subsystems. Here is Yourdon's [You 79b] description of what happened.

> The programming manual for the terminal left out some key details that would have caused major problems if their absence had not been detected at the outset. The modem had the nasty habit of dropping bits of data at random intervals. The telephone lines actually worked, but the telecommunications monitor gobbled up all available memory in the computer, fragmented the memory into small pieces, and then shut down the system because it could not obtain enough big chunks of memory. The database management system worked fine, but could only carry out one disk access at a time, a fact which would have caused major throughput problems if it had not been discovered at an early stage. All of the application subsystems had a variety of bugs.

Obviously the proper adjustment of these interfaces required a great deal of time.

As the stories above suggest, interface errors typically require a long time to correct because they involve subtle differences in communication or interpretation. Using the bottom-up testing strategy, interfaces between larger and larger subsystems are tested in successively later and later steps. Thus the most major interfaces—where errors might require recoding of several modules—are not tested until the very last steps. For example, the very last steps in bottom-up testing of the system of Figure 5.32 are the integration of the A, B, and C subsystems with the MAIN program and the test of the whole system.

A system cannot be made to function properly (and often cannot be made to function at all) until all the highest level interface errors have been found and eliminated. A common result of bottom-up testing is that—at the very last moments of the project (usually at the project deadline)—the system is not working properly (or at all) even though all lower-level modules have been thoroughly tested. In such situations, nobody knows what the trouble is, and a massive effort must be mounted to find the problems (almost always interface errors) and fix them. And, of course, it is impossible to tell how long the fixing process will take.

5.4.1.2 Top-Down Testing Strategy

5.4.1.2.1 Overview   The treatment of interface errors in bottom-up testing is unsatisfactory because the highest level interfaces are tested at the last moment and a last-minute crisis inevitably occurs. Such situations cause many software project failures.

Elimination of this problem requires that modules be tested in a different sequence. The *top-down testing strategy*, in concept, calls for the testing of highest level modules first, continuing with testing of lower and lower levels until finally the lowest level modules are tested. The basic top-down sequence of module tests is shown in Figure 5.34 (for the module organization of Figure 5.32).

The sequence of events shown in Figure 5.34 is not precisely correct. Since the module MAIN calls modules A, B, and C, it cannot be completely tested by itself. The modules A, B, and C are required in some form. Standard procedure is to code a *stub* (i.e., a dummy version) of each required module, solely for the purpose of allowing a complete test. The stub contains only

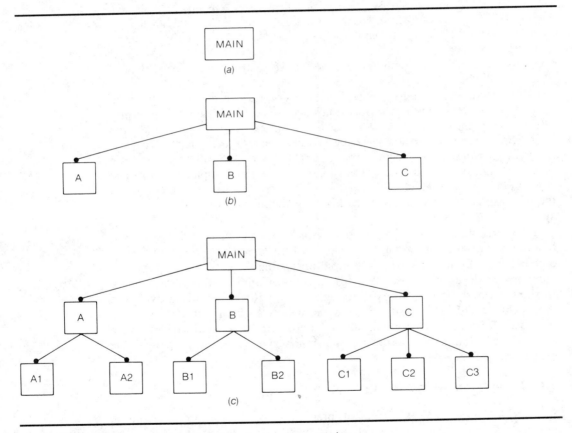

Figure 5.34 Basic sequence of activities in top-down testing. (*a*) Highest level module is tested first. (*b*) Second-highest-level module is tested next, together with highest level. (*c*) Third-highest-level module is now tested together with the two highest levels.

enough code to allow communication between the stub and the module being tested. For example, if module A is called by MAIN and returns a parameter X whose value is a real number, the stub for A might contain only the definitions of module arguments and a statement such as X:=5.5. In the test of MAIN, whenever A is called it will return 5.5 for the parameter X, but it will not at all calculate X.

This procedure does not test the function of module A, but it does test the interface between module A and MAIN, that is, the manner in which information is passed from A to MAIN. Later, module A will be coded using the stub as a nucleus and adding the appropriate calculation of X. If the coding is properly done, it will add the appropriate module function (i.e., the calculation of X) and preserve the already-tested interface between A and MAIN.

Stubs are usually built to do one of the following things [You 79b]:

· Immediately exit with no processing
· Return a constant value (e.g., X:=5.5)
· Return a random number within some range
· Print an output message to signify that the module has executed
· Execute a timing loop that consumes a specified amount of time
· Calculate a rough approximation of the module's function
· Ask an operator for help, and accept the answers from the operator.

Table 5.4 shows the next-lower-level stubs required in the testing of each module of Figure 5.32. The test of a module includes testing the interfaces between that module and any higher level modules with which it communicates, as well as testing the interfaces between the module and the next-lower-level stubs. Top-down testing basically examines the highest level interfaces first and then the next-highest-level interfaces, continuing to the lowest level interfaces. Tests of the functioning of the lowest level modules are done last, while these lowest level modules are in place in the system.

Top-down testing finds interface errors between the largest subsystems at the earliest testing steps, when plenty of time is available to resolve the errors and other activities can continue at the same time. As the project moves

Table 5.4   Stubs required to test each module

Module under Test	Stubs Required
MAIN	A, B, and C
A	A1 and A2
B	B1 and B2
C	C1, C2, and C3
C1	C11, C12, and C13
Any other	None

toward its deadline, the testing process continues to find and resolve interface errors at lower and lower levels—errors confined to interfaces between smaller and smaller subsystems. In other words, the errors are isolated to within successively smaller and smaller portions of the system. Top-down testing thus almost always eliminates a last-minute crisis at project deadline.

The use of stubs is crucial in top-down testing. However, top-down testing does not thereby require a great deal more effort than bottom-up testing. When a lowest level individual module is tested first in bottom-up testing, it is necessary to deliver a sequence of inputs to the module and then accept and check the outputs. For this purpose, a *test monitor* program (equivalently, a *test driver*) is required. The test driver can be a program specially built for the test, or it can be an "outline" (comparable to a stub) of the next-higher-level module that communicates with the module under test. In contrast, when individual lowest level modules are tested last in top-down testing, no drivers are needed because everything is in place. Thus the two testing strategies involve about the same amount of effort.

5.4.1.2.2 *Incremental Testing*

Any testing strategy must deal with the problem of interaction errors, which are caused by the interaction of several slightly incorrect modules. As the number of modules grows, so, too, does the potential for interaction errors, and their detection becomes more difficult.

The detection of interaction errors is easier when modules are added to the system one at a time. For example, for the module organization of Figure 5.32, the module MAIN is first tested as in Figure 5.34. Next, however, only one of the modules A, B, or C is added, and this new combination is tested. When that test is complete, another of A, B, or C is added, and the new combination is tested; finally, the third module is added, and all four modules are tested together.

With this variation, called *incremental* testing, step (*b*) in Figure 5.34 is actually done in three smaller steps, and step (*c*) is actually done in six smaller steps. Detection of interaction errors is easier since if one new module is added to a system that then works incorrectly, the problem is most probably within the new module or its interfaces.

5.4.1.2.3 *Split-Level Testing*

The basic strategy of top-down testing, as seen in Figure 5.34, is to begin testing at the highest level and proceed to lower and lower levels. This basic strategy can be respected while, at the same time, testing is done at lower levels in some parts of the system and at higher levels in other parts of the system.

In other words, for the system of Figure 5.32, it is not necessary to complete step (*b*) in Figure 5.34 (the entire second level) before testing some third-level modules. For example, it might be desirable to test the modules in the sequence MAIN,C,C1,A,C13, so that the tested partial configuration of Figure 5.35 is obtained.

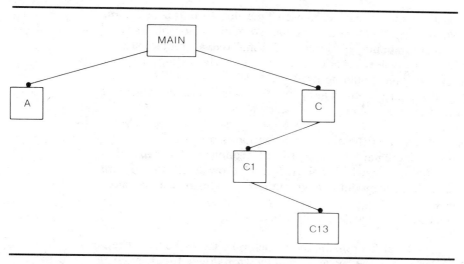

Figure 5.35   Tested partial configuration.

Split-level testing is desirable when some modules are finished ahead of schedule, or when certain modules (e.g., C13 in Figure 5.35) are critical to the system and must be tested very early. In pure top-down testing, the interfaces and functions of the lowest level modules are tested last. However, just as high-level problems may require recoding of low-level modules, problems with the interfaces or functions of lower-level modules may require redesign of upper-level modules. In particular, an interface or function problem in a critical lowest level module may require radical redesign of upper levels. When interfaces have not been well thought out in advance, or when new equipment or systems create unforeseen problems, top-down integration proceeding to lower and lower levels in successive testing steps could necessitate continual redesign of upper-level interfaces. Split-level testing can be used to accomplish both the desired early testing of high-level interfaces and the desired early testing of critical low-level interfaces.

5.4.2 Delivery Strategies: Incremental Development and Delivery

5.4.2.1 Balanced Testing Strategy

Section 5.4.1 has made four major points. First, excessive elapsed time spent in testing is a major problem, and interface errors are responsible for most of this elapsed time. To avoid excessive elapsed time due to interface errors, testing strategy should be top-down in concept. To minimize problems from interaction errors, testing should be incremental. Finally, to accommodate the early testing of crucial low-level modules as well as early testing of major interfaces, split-level testing should be used.

Assuming that there are both major interfaces and crucial low-level modules, a balanced testing strategy can proceed as follows:

1. Stub in all modules, so that the entire organization is present.
2. Construct and test (incrementally) a split-level "young tree" organization (see explanation below), in which only the crucial low-level modules are coded and the high-level modules have sufficient code to test the most major interfaces.
3. Continue the testing in a succession of further steps.

At each step, add and test (incrementally) some branches to the tree, keeping the modules already in the system, building top-down to lower-level modules to test less important interfaces, and adding further lower-level modules to test less critical actions. Thus testing begins with an organization that looks like a young tree, having very few branches. Each successive testing step adds some branches to the tree, and at the end of testing the full tree has been attained.

At each testing step a version of the system is obtained. Version 1 is the result of the first step; version 2 is the result of the second test step; version 3, and so on are successively more complete versions of the system. Many shrewd developers have observed that version 1, version 2, version 3, and so on could be thought of as successively more refined systems delivered to the customer one by one. In fact, many systems have been delivered in successively more refined versions.

5.4.2.2 Delivery Strategy

The choice of the modules for version 1, version 2, and so on is called a *delivery strategy*. Section 5.4.2 describes the delivery strategy called *incremental development and delivery*, in which the successive versions are developed and tested so that they could be delivered to the customer if desired. That is, version 1 is completely developed and tested, then version 2 is completely developed and tested, and so on.

Version 1 contains highest level stubs that can check out the most major interfaces. For example, Yourdon [You 79b] discusses an online system having interfaces with the computer's operating system, a new CRT terminal, a new modem, newly installed telephone lines, a telecommunications monitor, a data base management system, and several major application packages. In this case, his version 1 contained stubs to check all of these interfaces. Each interface had problems that would have caused a crisis, if they had occurred at the end of the project. Since the problems were found early in the probject, there was plenty of time to deal with them. In many cases, work can start on version 2 while the interface problems of version 1 are being dealt with.

A key feature of incremental development and delivery is that the first version actually executes and performs some minimal form of the specified function. In other words, the first version delivers a minimum function, and each further version delivers a further increment of function. Hence the name "incremental development and delivery."

The minimal function of version 1 and the increments of functions of further versions can be chosen based on either of two considerations:

· Amount of processing performed for each input
· Frequencies of different classes of input

Gilb [Gilb 81] tells the story of a system to compute air fares, which involved hundreds of different fare plans such as special weekend rates and special seven-day rates. It appeared that the system would require hundreds of modules and a long time to implement. However, it was found that 60 percent of the air fare transactions were simple round-trip full fare, coach, or first class. Accordingly, version 1 was designed to be operationally used to calculate just these simple fares. Version 1 required relatively few modules and was completed in two months. Version 2 added the capability to compute fares for the second most frequent kind of transaction.

It commonly happens that a few classes of transactions account for most of the volume of transactions. This fact (known in some circles as the *big bang effect*) suggests that initial versions can be operationally useful to the customer much of the time.

Yourdon [You 79b] also discusses the incremental development of a payroll system. About six weeks after the project was begun, a version 1 system had been developed which would accept input transactions and a master file, and produce paychecks. Although version 1 would execute and produce paychecks, it had the following limitations: transactions were not validated (inputs had to be error-free); transactions were not sorted into order (the user of the program had to sort the inputs); transactions changing an employee's status (salary increases or decreases, hiring or firing) were not processed at all; every employee was paid $100 per week, with $15 in taxes withheld; and all payments were by check, with the checks printed in octal code.

This version contained all of the top-level modules, with stubs for the next lower level of modules. The salary calculation module always returned a salary of $100; the tax calculation module always returned a tax of $15; and the transaction validation module always indicated a valid transaction (without actually validating the transaction). The important point about version 1 is that is did accept a master file and transactions, and it did produce paychecks.

Arbitrary numbers were printed on the paychecks just to check the interfaces between modules, and to ensure that the data flowed correctly from module to module.

Each successive version of the system removed some of the limitations. For example, version 2 sorted the input transactions into order, processed some changes in employee status, and computed gross salary in a few simple cases.

Developing the versions in this way has many advantages. Interface problems are caught at an early stage. Each successive version can serve as a more refined prototype, the user reactions helping in the design of further versions. Since the system is built up a little bit at a time, the detailed design of later increments can be delayed so as to have the benefit of experience and user reaction to previous versions.

Even a not-too-useful partial version can be pressed into service on an interim basis (while a better version is readied) if the project deadline has arrived and the software is urgently needed. When the partial versions are operationally useful to the customer, they can be delivered, put in place, and used. This is the best of worlds—the user receives successively greater returns on the software investment, the user gains operational experience (with the possibility of changing future versions), and the developer actually delivers successively more complete parts of the desired system.

REFERENCES

[Bas 75] Basili, V., and Turner, A. "Iterative Enhancement: A Practical Technique for Software Engineering," *IEEE Transactions on Software Engineering*, December 1975.

[Fagan 76] Fagan, M. E. "Design and Code Inspections to Reduce Errors in Program Development," *IBM Systems Journal*, Vol. 15, No. 3, 1976. (Also in [Mil 78].)*

[Gilb 81] Gilb, T. "Design by Objectives: A Structured Systems Architecture Approach." Unpublished manuscript, 1981.

[Good 79] Goodenough, J. B. "A Survey of Program Testing Issues," in P. Wegner (ed.), *Research Directions in Software Technology*. Cambridge, MA: M.I.T. Press, 1979.

[Par 76b] Parnas, D. L.; Handel, G.; and Wurges, H. "Design and Specification of the Minimal Subset of an Operating System Family," *IEEE Transactions on Software Engineering*, December 1976. (An alternate version of this paper was presented at Eurocomp 76.)

[Par 79] ———. "Designing Software for Ease of Extension and Contraction," *IEEE Transactions on Software Engineering*, March 1979. (Also in [Ram 78] and in [Fre 80b].)*

---

*See Appendix B: Bibliography.

[You 79b] Yourdon, E. "Top-Down Design and Testing," in G. D. Bergland and R. D. Gordon (eds.), *Tutorial: Software Design Strategies*. Long Beach, CA: IEEE Computer Society, 1979.

PROJECT OUTLINE: Incremental Development and Delivery Strategy
Consider any problem in Appendix D.

1. Develop a system organization following the Project Outline of Section 5.3 (p. 289).

2. Use the strategy of incremental development and delivery to determine the sequence for coding and testing of modules. Recall that the first version of the system is to consist of some fully coded modules and some stubs and be able to accept inputs and produce an output. The function performed by this partial system will usually be a partial one, and the data may be specially selected to meet stated restrictions. Thereafter, version 2, version 3, and so on are to be developed, each successive version having a larger function or diminished restrictions placed on the data.

    List the sequence in which your modules are to be coded and tested. For each version (e.g., version 1, version 2, etc.) state the fully coded module required, dummy modules required, functions performed by the partial system, and restrictions imposed on the data by the partial system.

Part Four
MODULE DEVELOPMENT

Module design: algorithms for critical actions . . . data-structure-based design . . . the finite state model . . . table-directed processes

Module implementation: components of structured programs . . . stepwise refinement . . . top-down design . . . retrofitting old programs

Program construction: characteristics of commonly used programming languages . . . programming style . . . efficiency considerations . . . evaluation of program code . . . program maintenance documentation

Verifying program correctness: basic issues . . . specification-based testing . . . program-based testing . . . debugging

chapter six
Design of Modules

6.1 ALGORITHMS FOR CRITICAL ACTIONS

6.1.1 Introduction to Module Design

Part Two (Chapters 2 and 3) has focused on understanding a given problem and formulating an overall approach. Chapter 3 noted the importance of critical actions and necessary algorithms while concentrating on a "big picture" approach in which data flow and essential transformations were blocked out.

The "big picture" is necessary for medium-scale and large-scale systems. Because such systems grow too large for one person to implement, a major problem is how to divide the work among many people. This concern has motivated Part Three (Chapters 4 and 5), which deals with methods for organizing a system as a collection of modules and with strategies for best implementing and testing a system that consists of many modules. In other words, the concerns of Part Three are how to chop a large job into manageable pieces and how to get the collection of pieces done.

Part Four (Chapters 6 through 9) now focuses on the development of a single module: its design, construction, and testing.

Chapter 6 discusses the design of a single module or a small system. Section 6.1 gives general hints for determining and evaluating algorithms for critical actions. In its discussions, this section continues the secret sums example of Section 3.2, showing the development of an algorithm for the critical action of the example in Section 3.2 and also pointing out possible refinements for greater efficiency.

Section 6.2 describes how the design of a module may be based on the compositions of the data flows handled by the module. Variations of this technique have been used successfully in business data processing, especially in Europe.

A module design can also be based on the use of a formal model. Section 6.3 outlines how the finite state machine model can be used to design modules. The finite state machine embodies a view, which should be understood by program designers, of the essential nature of a program.

Finally, Section 6.4 describes the technique of table direction in which a program is arranged as sets of tables in conjunction with a general table-handler. The tables contain specific processing details and, in effect, direct the processing of the program, while the table-handler embodies a pattern or archetype of the desired algorithm.

The methods of Sections 6.2, 6.3, and 6.4 are not mutually exclusive. Indeed, they are often combined. For example, the technique of Section 6.2 implicitly uses the finite state machine as an underlying model, and the finite state machine may be implemented as a table-directed process. (See Section 6.3 for discussions of both these points.) Furthermore, the techniques of this chapter may also be used to organize a larger system into modules. The principles embodied in the techniques can be applied at any level.

There are many design techniques in addition to those discussed in this chapter. For example, algorithms may be based on dynamic programming models, on methods of simulation and modeling, or on artificial intelligence methods. You are encouraged to seek these out. Floyd [Flo 79], for instance, provides an important discussion of design paradigms, mentioning in particular divide-and-conquer [Gre 78] and branch-and-bound [Law 66, Nil 71]. Collections of algorithms may be found in [Aho 74, Horo 76, Horo 78].

6.1.2 Examination of Critical Actions

Many of the actions of a data flow diagram are either obvious or are standard processes such as sorting. Actions that are neither standard nor obvious are called *critical actions*. A design proposal should consider such actions, indicating difficult points and proposing algorithms. Accordingly, the second step in design is to examine the completed data flow diagram to find critical actions and then analyze them.

An algorithm for a critical action is often the key to the solution of a problem. Also, it may sometimes happen that portions of the algorithm can be spread through the system, so that one complex action is replaced by a set of simpler actions throughout the system.

If analysis of a critical action does not yield a solution, the designer should investigate the technical literature, where the solution to the given problem may already exist. Or, the literature may reveal that the desired action cannot be implemented, either for theoretical reasons (in extremely rare cases) or because certain required computing techniques are not yet available.

It is important to know that some algorithms are not possible. For example, there cannot exist a function T whose input is any program R and whose output is the boolean value T(R) given by

$$T(R) = \begin{cases} \text{true if R terminates when run} \\ \text{false if R does not terminate when run} \end{cases}$$

We can demonstrate this informally by assuming that T does exist and terminates for every input program R. Now we construct program P whose pseudocode is as follows:

```
Program P; (*uses T as a function*)
  var x:integer;
  function T(R:text):boolean;
    begin (*Place the definition of T here*)end;
begin
  while T(P) do x:=1
end.
```

Now if T(P)=true, then program P loops forever. If T(P)=false, then P terminates. In both cases, T(P)=true should correspond to P terminating. This contradiction shows that T cannot exist.

We should be very cautious when a required algorithm appears too powerful or too all-encompassing. It may be very difficult to determine that a particular algorithm cannot exist, but once this fact is known much effort can be saved. Total solutions need not be considered any longer, and partial solutions may be useful.

Methods of implementing actions may be classified either as algorithms or as heuristics. An *algorithm* is a procedure that has been proved to work in all cases. In contrast, a *heuristic* is a method that may not always be correct but that works in most cases, or it is a method that gives an answer close to the desired one rather than giving precisely the desired answer. It is important to understand the distinction between these two types of solutions.

A common failing in programming is to use a heuristic when an algorithm is both necessary and achievable. Unfortunately, it often seems easier to cook up a heuristic that almost always works rather than invest the effort to develop and prove an algorithm. The problem lies in the "almost": sooner or later the system fails and must then be fixed. And, if the heuristic is not replaced by an algorithm, the system will continue to fail. In contrast, a correct and properly debugged algorithm will not fail at all.

Although some problems require a heuristic solution because no algorithm is known or because the required algorithm is not computable, such problems are rare. Thus the designer should strive to devise algorithms rather than heuristics. This section discusses ways of devising algorithms and also suggests how heuristics can be added to a solution to give better efficiency. Of course, the devising of algorithms is an art, and we can only give some small hints here. See the references at the end of this section for more detailed discussions.

6.1.3 Rules of the Game

To implement an action, we must understand clearly what the action is required to do. In other words, we must ask: What is the problem? The solution can be undertaken only when the problem is understood.

To get at the problem's essence, it is helpful to view the problem as a game. When this view is taken, details of the situation are seen to be either rules of the game and intrinsic to the situation or extraneous clutter that can be ignored. In problems involving chess, or tic-tac-toe, or poker, this view is obvious since certain details (especially rules of procedure) are explicitly stated to be game rules. In the secret sums problem in Section 3.2, there are rules for corresponding digits to letters and for performing the required additions. Understanding these rules can lead to an efficient algorithm. The dean's disciple problem (Problem 11 in Appendix D) involves switching of classrooms. Here one should ask: What are the rules for switching rooms?

In addition to rules of procedure, every game has criteria for winning situations. In tic-tac-toe or in chess, there are situations in which one player wins and the game stops, while in poker there are criteria for ranking the players' hands after a set sequence of play. In the secret sums problem, the criterion for winning is that the addition is successful; in the dean's disciple problem, the criterion is that all classes have rooms.

6.1.4 Assumptions

Beware of assumptions that allow a simpler solution but are not justified by available data or facts. In the dean's disciple problem, for example, there is a great temptation to assume that all classes meet either on Monday–Wednesday–Friday or on Tuesday–Thursday. This assumption, which greatly simplifies the problem, is unjustified.

A much better approach is to generalize the conditions of the problem to allow a more uniform approach. For example, in the dean's disciple problem, it is best to assume that classes might meet on *any* combination of days and hours. Do not be afraid to generalize; it often happens that the solution to a general problem is simpler and more efficient than a solution to a restricted problem.

Every important assumption should be validated by checking it against known facts to see if it is justified.

6.1.5 Analysis

Given the rules of procedure and the criteria for winning, the next question is: What sequence of moves or set of conditions forces a win? In discovering these sequences or conditions, we are discovering the key to the desired algorithm. For some problems, though, it is more fruitful to consider the questions: Under what conditions is the win *not* attained? Are there conditions that force failure?

As examples, in the secret sums problem, we should ask the questions:

· What conditions result in the addition being successful?
· What conditions result in the addition being unsuccessful?

and in the dean's disciple problem, we should ask:

· Under what conditions can all classes be assigned rooms?
· Under what conditions can all classes not be assigned rooms?

In this analysis, we should always be prepared to pursue several alternate solutions. The analysis, if properly done, should result in at least an informal proof that the solution does work.

Equivalently, a problem may be regarded as an abstract mathematical system, the rules of procedure being axioms and the criteria for winning being desirable properties. In this analogy, our analysis should result in theorems stating conditions for which the desirable properties are or are not attained.

In some situations, it is useful to consider the question: Are there conditions that force bounds on the solution? This question is important when there are many cases or when execution speed is an important factor.

In some situations, patterns of conditions may be found. If such patterns exist, the solution may be simplified by *encoding* them. Encoding may also be used to achieve efficiency while preserving generality. Suppose that it is desired to sort class listings, where classes are given Monday through Friday. For the sake of a simple discussion, assume that classes meet at 1 P.M., 2 P.M., . . . , 8 P.M. and that each class meets at most once a day.

Since classes can meet from one to five times a week, several sort passes might be required. However, the meeting times of a class can be encoded as a five-digit decimal number $N_1N_2N_3N_4N_5$ defined as follows:

N_1=time of meeting on Monday, 9 if no Monday meeting
·
·
·
N_5=time of meeting on Friday, 9 if no Friday meeting

However, after the last day of a class's meeting, each of the succeeding digits is set to 0. Thus a class meeting only Monday at 3 has the encoding 30000, a class meeting Monday and Wednesday at 3 has the encoding 39300, a class meeting Monday at 3 and Wednesday at 2 has the encoding 39200, and a class meeting Monday, Wednesday, and Friday at 3 has the encoding 39393.

When these numbers are sorted into ascending order, the corresponding classes are arranged in proper scheduling order. A succession of sort passes may be replaced by a simple encoding and one sort pass. Equally important, the encoding assigns a unique integer to each pattern of meetings, and the integers assigned to two different patterns can be easily compared. Also the encoding embodies the desired sorting sequence and assigns each pattern a unique ranking. Thus it can easily be seen whether the encoding scheme leads to a correct sorting order.

Encoding techniques can be used when there are a large number of patterns or combinations, to unify the entire scheme and assign unique rankings.

6.1.6 Using Experience

The visualization and analysis techniques can be based on your own experience. Try to solve a sample of the problem by hand. Work at it, get into it. Then ask yourself: What am I doing? What are the rules for what I am doing? What conditions am I finding?

For the secret sums problem, successful solutions are usually found by those who attempt to solve the puzzle

$$\begin{array}{r} \text{SEND} \\ +\text{MORE} \\ \hline \text{MONEY} \end{array}$$

by hand. By assuming that M does not correspond to 0, some are led to a set of restrictions on the correspondences and then to a set of heuristics that can quickly determine in certain cases that solutions are impossible. Others become aware of the rules for addition: The rightmost column is added first, then the next to rightmost, and so on. This rule of procedure forces a sequence of conditions to be met if the addition is to be successful, namely:

D+E=Y must be successful, then
N+R=E must be successful, and so on

In other words, success is possible only if

Addition of the rightmost column is successful, then
Addition of the next-to-rightmost column is successful, and so on

Conversely:

If addition of the rightmost column is not successful for $D \longleftrightarrow d_1$, $E \longleftrightarrow d_2$, $Y \longleftrightarrow d_3$, then the addition will not be successful, no matter what digits correspond to the other letters.
If addition of the rightmost column is successful, but addition of the next-to-rightmost column is not successful for $N \longleftrightarrow d_4$, $R \longleftrightarrow d_5$, $E \longleftrightarrow d_2$, then the

addition will not be successful no matter what digits correspond to the other letters.

By working the problem, and paying attention to how we are working the problem, we discover an iterative set of conditions that yields success or an alternative that does not yield success.

6.1.7 Evaluation

Once a solution has been developed, it must be evaluated. The evaluation seeks to determine whether the solution is *always* correct or to determine the *conditions under which* the basic solution is correct. This step is crucial if we are to develop good algorithms. Failure to evaluate, in the belief that we do not make mistakes, is foolhardy.

For a program that plays tic-tac-toe, we might ask:

· Will the program always win if it is possible to win?
· Under what conditions will the program win?
· If the program loses, is this because the *solution is imperfect* or because *no win is possible*?

These questions may be phrased in a general way, as follows:

· Does the solution *always* work?
· Under what conditions is the solution sure to work?
· If the solution fails, is it because the strategy is imperfect or because no solution is possible (i.e., even a perfect strategy must fail)?

To evaluate a solution, find test inputs that the solution must handle and then process these inputs using the solution. Try to think of difficult or pathological cases that the solution may not handle. In effect, the program is being tested before it is written. Think of the solution as a proof and try to discover counterexamples. It is important to have the mental attitude that some else's solution is being tested.

6.1.8 Refinements for Efficiency

Some theoretically correct algorithms are not feasible in practice because they cannot be performed in a reasonable time. Calculation of the order of magnitude of the number of operations required can detect such situations. In the secret sums problem, for example, if there are 10 letters, then testing for every value of the "DIGIT number"—from 0 . . . 0 to 9 . . . 9—requires 10^{10} tests. Testing every "DIGIT number" value in which all digits are distinct requires 10! tests, or a little more than 3×10^6 tests.

Experience has shown that 10! is a rough practical limit on the number of operations; beyond this number, algorithms become infeasible. Thus the algorithm suggested in Section 3.2 is barely feasible for 10 letters, and it would not be feasible for 20 letters (assuming a radix ≥20). Sorting 100,000 numbers by brute force is not feasible since the number of operations required is about $(10^5)^2 = 10^{10}$.

A rough estimate of the number of operations required should be made for each algorithm. If the algorithm requires an excessive number of operations, improvement may be possible by using one of the methods outlined below. Later, in Section 8.3, we discuss the improvement of speed through the use of measurement techniques.

6.1.8.1 Refinement of the Algorithm

Improvement in execution speed is usually best obtained through examination and refinement of the algorithm. For example, in the secret sums problem, it was observed that CHOOSE NEXT LEGAL SET is the critical action of the program. Since this action must cycle through a sequence of numbers from 0 . . . 0 to 9 . . . 9, its operation will determine the speed of the program. Indeed, execution times of student programs for the secret sums problem have varied by a factor of 2000, due to differences in the handling of this action.

One possible refinement stems from the requirement that each letter corresponds to a different digit. We may design the CHOOSE NEXT LEGAL SET action to choose successive permutations of a set of digits. However, if there are K<10 distinct letters in the puzzle, the action must also choose different combinations of K digits to permute. The analysis of execution speed of this method is complex.

Another refinement follows directly from the conditions inherent in the problem. We have noted previously that in the solution of

```
  SEND
+ MORE
 MONEY
```

if the addition D+E=Y is not successful, then no solution exists (for the digit values assigned to D, E, and Y) no matter what values are assigned to the remaining digits. Stated more generally: there is a solution only if the least significant (rightmost) column adds correctly; other digits need be assigned values only when that column adds correctly. If the least significant column adds correctly, then there is a solution only if the next-least-significant column adds correctly; and so on. Thus we may improve speed by proceeding column by column.

Creation of the array LETTER from SYMADD and SYMSUM, column by column, was mentioned in Section 3.2 with this variation is mind. Figure 6.1 shows the contents of the arrays LETTER and DIGIT, written from left to right. In the figure, the letter D is assigned the digit 2, the letter E is assigned the digit 4, and so on. We think of DIGIT as the decimal number 24738951.

The conditions just mentioned imply that if DIGIT=247 . . . does not work, then the next higher value of DIGIT that *could* work is 24800000. Thus if DIGIT=247 . . . does not work, we may (still with the assurance that all solutions will be found) increase DIGIT[3] to 8. Incrementing DIGIT[3] in this way effectively increases the "DIGIT number" by 10^6. For any two values assigned to D and E, at most one value assigned to Y will work, and thus, in effect, 9×10^6 values of DIGIT are considered by nine tests of the rightmost column. The improvement given by this refinement depends on the puzzle.

6.1.8.2 Bounds on the Problem

For many problems, bounds inherent in the situation allow reduction of the number of operations. For example, in the secret sums problem, the requirement of distinct digits implies that that 987 . . . ≥DIGIT≥0123. . . . Using these bounds instead of 999 . . . ≥DIGIT≥000 . . . yields a 2.5 percent reduction in the number of operations.

A bound given in the problem can be used to terminate a partially complete calculation when it can be seen that the bound will be exceeded. In Problem 6 in Appendix D, for example, a knight must make M captures within N moves. Although in theory all sequences of N moves must be checked, each partial sequence of moves may be tested against the condition:

(moves made)+(moves required to complete captures)≤N

If this condition is false, then capture within N moves is not possible, and a new partial sequence can be investigated.

Many problems suggest a measure of goodness for the output, such as elapsed time in Problem 5 in Appendix D or number of moves in Problem 6 in Appendix D. A rough bound on this measure can be used to terminate the

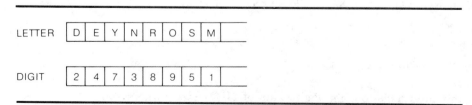

Figure 6.1   Contents of the LETTER and DIGIT arrays.

calculation of outputs whose measure is predicted to exceed this bound. When an output is obtained whose measure does not exceed the bound, then the value for that output serves as a bound on further calculations.

6.1.8.3 Precalculations

Precalculation is the technique of explicitly calculating once, and then saving for further use, values that would otherwise be calculated many times during the operation of the algorithm. This technique can be used at all levels of the design.

An example is the action CHOOSE NEXT LEGAL SET, which, as discussed in Section 3.2, has a subaction

if any two positions in the array have the same value, repeat step 1

This subaction appears to require two nested loops. However, an array USE may be maintained, such that

$$USE[I] = \begin{cases} 1 \text{ if the digit I is in use} \\ 0 \text{ if the digit I is not in use} \end{cases}$$

By this means, checking whether the digit I is used by some other digit is accomplished by testing whether USE[I]=1.

At another level, the action ENTER CORRESPONDING DIGITS INTO NUMADD has subactions

find LETTER[K] such that LETTER[K]=SYMADD[I,J]

and

enter DIGIT[K] into NUMADD[I,J]

The first subaction appears to require a search of the LETTER array each time that digits are entered into NUMADD. However, since the contents of SYMADD do not change during the entire processing of the puzzle, for each SYMADD[I,J] the same search (yielding the same result) would be done many times. Immediately after the SYMADD and LETTER arrays are filled, this search can be precalculated. More precisely, for each SYMADD[I,J],

1. LETTER[K] is found such that LETTER[K]=SYMADD[I,J]

and then

2. SYMADD[I,J] is set to the value K

As a result of this precalculation, the digit value of NUMADD[I,J], corresponding to the letter that was originally in SYMADD[I,J], is the value

DIGIT [SYMADD[I,J]].

Thus the repeated search is eliminated. If the same precalculation is done for SYMSUM, the digit value of NUMSUM [I,J] is the value

DIGIT [SYMSUM[I,J]].

Given the precalculation, the actions SUM ADDENDS and ENTER CORRESPONDING DIGITS INTO NUMADD can be combined to sum the Ith column as follows:

```
sum[I]:=0;
for J:=1 to number of addends do
   sum [I]:=sum[I]+DIGIT[SYMADD[I,J]].
```

Thus the arrays NUMADD and NUMSUM can be eliminated during coding, though they are necessary in concept.

6.1.8.4 Heuristics

Heuristics, or "rules of thumb," can be used to enhance algorithms in many problems. In the secret sums problem, for example, a solution exists only when the sum word has at least as many letters as the largest addend word. If n addends have letters in the most significant addend column, then the highest carry from that column is $n-1$, which implies for

SEND
+MORE
MONEY

that $M \longleftrightarrow d_M \leqslant 1$.

Rules like these can be used to bound the values that digits corresponding to various letters can take or to rule out impossible cases. In the same way, rough calculations can be made in many problems to predispose the algorithm to a certain direction, while at the same time the use of the algorithm ensures that all cases are examined.

REFERENCES

[Aho 74] Aho, A. V.; Hopcroft, J. E.; and Ullman, J. D. *The Design and Analysis of Computer Algorithms*. Reading, MA: Addison-Wesley, 1974.

[deB 70] de Bono, E. *Lateral Thinking: Creativity Step by Step*. New York: Harper Colophon Books, 1970.

[Flo 79] Floyd, R. W. "The Paradigms of Programming," *Communications of the ACM*, August 1979.

[Gre 78] Green, C. C., and Barstuo, D. "On Program Synthesis Knowledge," *Artificial Intelligence*, June 1978.

[Horo 76] Horowitz, E., and Sahni, S. *Fundamentals of Data Structures*. Rockville, MD: Computer Science Press, 1976.

[Horo 78] ———, and ———. *Fundamentals of Data Computer Algorithms*. Rockville, MD: Computer Science Press, 1978.

[Kob 74] Koberg, D., and Bagnall, J. *The Universal Traveler*. New York: Harmony Books, 1974.

[Law 66] Lawler, E., and Wood, D. "Branch and Bound Methods: A Survey," *Operations Research*, July–August 1966.

[Nil 71] Nilsson, N. J. *Problem Solving Methods in Artificial Intelligence*. New York: McGraw-Hill, 1971.

[Polya 54a] Polya, G. *Induction and Analogy in Mathematics*. Princeton, NJ: Princeton University Press, 1954.

[Polya 54b] ———. *Patterns of Plausible Inference*. Princeton, NJ: Princeton University Press, 1954.

[Polya 57] ———. *How to Solve It*. Garden City, NY: Doubleday Anchor Books, 1957.

PROBLEMS

1. A program is desired that, given a set of 100 integers: (a) computes the sum of these integers and (b) prints out 50 of the given integers, so that the sum of these 50 integers is half the sum of part (a). Can the 50 integers of part (b) always be found? Why or why not?

Problems 2 through 6 concern problems in Appendix D.

2. Consider Problem 1 of Appendix D.
   (a) What are the rules for choosing a maximum element?
   (b) Can there be more than one such element in a row? In a column?
   (c) Discuss the correctness of the following assumptions.
       (1) There can be only one maximum element in an array.
       (2) There can be more than one maximum element in a row, but in that case all elements of the row are equal.
   (d) Give five test inputs that embody difficult situations.
   (e) A proposed algorithm for computing the maximum value in row i sets rowmax to 0 and then compares each (jth) element of the row in turn to rowmax. If rowmax<name[i,j], then name[i,j] becomes the new value of rowmax. Is this correct?

(f) Give an algorithm for this problem, and calculate the order of magnitude of the number of operations required.

3. Consider Problem 5 of Appendix D.
   (a) What are the rules for choosing a schedule of train connections?
   (b) What condition does the chosen schedule satisfy?
   (c) Can more than one schedule satisfy the condition?
   (d) Can a schedule always be found? Why or why not?
   (e) Discuss the reasonableness of the following assumptions.
      (1) All trains are local trains.
      (2) All trains run at the same speed.
      (3) At each station, a train from each route leaves once every hour of the day, at the same time past the hour.
      (4) The schedule of trains is the same for each day of the week.
      (5) The schedule of trains for holidays is the same as for ordinary days.
   (f) Give five test inputs that embody difficult conditions.
   (g) The following algorithms have been proposed for choosing schedules of trains. Are they correct?
      (1) Maintain a table of distances of each station from the destination station. In calculating a route, each (next) station chosen must have a smaller distance to the destination.
      (2) Reject any train that goes past the destination station and does not stop there.
   (h) Give an algorithm for this problem, and calculate the order of magnitude of the number of operations required.
   (i) State three refinements that your algorithm incorporates, or that can be added to your algorithm, to decrease the operations required.

4. Consider Problem 6 of Appendix D.
   (a) What are the rules for a legal knight move?
   (b) What is the criterion for a successful sequence of moves?
   (c) What conditions are satisfied by a successful sequence?
   (d) Give five test inputs that embody difficult situations.
   (e) A proposed algorithm avoids placing the knight on any square where it has been previously positioned. Is this correct?

5. Consider Problem 8 of Appendix D.
   (a) What is the condition for an unsuccessful marriage?
   (b) What is the condition for a successful marriage?
   (c) "No man can prefer two different women equally, and vice versa." Is this assumption correct?
   (d) Give five test inputs that embody difficult situations.
   (e) The following algorithm has been proposed: Take the first name on the list of men, pair him with his first choice, and delete their names from the lists of men and women. Then take the first name on the list of women, pair her with her first choice, and delete their names from the

lists. Choose all the marriages in this way, giving first a man his choice, then a woman her choice, then a man, . . . , and so on until all the marriages are completed. Is this correct?

6. Consider Problem 11 of Appendix D.
   (a) Under what conditions should a class be assigned to a new room?
   (b) Under what conditions should a class not be assigned to a new room?
   (c) Under what conditions can all classes be assigned rooms?
   (d) Under what conditions can all classes not be assigned rooms?
   (e) Discuss the reasonableness of the following assumptions.
      (1) All classes meet either on Monday–Wednesday–Friday or on Tuesday–Thursday.
      (2) All classes are one hour long.
      (3) The scheduled hours for any two classes are either identical or do not overlap.
   (f) Give five test inputs that embody difficult situations.

7. A test file is to be output on a typewriter, and it is desired to hyphenate the output words if possible. Give three different algorithms for hyphenating the text.

8. The disks at a computer center, which are filled mainly with text files in ASCII character codes, have become too full. It is desired to compress these files, to relieve the congestion.
   (a) Give three different algorithms for compressing the text.
   (b) How does each work?
   (c) What is the worst case for each?
   (d) What is the expansion algorithm for each?
   (e) Discuss the effect of each algorithm on a file containing English prose and on files containing card images of programs.

6.2 DATA-STRUCTURE-BASED DESIGN

6.2.1 Introduction to Serial File Processing

The design and construction of a program can be based on the structures[1] of its input data flows and output data flows. Stated more precisely, the data flow

---

[1]The term *data structure* as used in Section 6.2 refers to the structure of the sequences of symbols that comprise a data flow. In Section 2.2, the term *composition* was used to refer to this kind of structure.

As used here, the terms *data structure* and *data-structure-based design* do not refer to the type or structure of any data objects in memory (e.g., trees, lists, arrays, or records) that might be used to store data.

definitions of Chapter 2, which express the composition of each data flow (i.e., the structure of the sequences of symbols that comprise the data flow), can be used in a systematic manner to derive a program. Jackson [Jac 75, Jac 76] and Warnier [War 76, War 78] have both suggested variations of such a derivation procedure, and each of the variations has achieved consistent and successful results in implementing business data processing programs.

This method can be illustrated by a simple example. Consider a program for printing invoices for sales of auto parts from an input file consisting of groups of records, one group for each invoice. The first record in each group is an identifier record containing the invoice number, the character 'I,' and then the customer's name, customer's address, and a discount percentage. Each succeeding record in the group contains the invoice number, the character 'P,' and a part name, quantity, and price.

Each invoice begins with the invoice number and the customer's name and address. For each part record input, an invoice line is printed showing part name, quantity, price, and total value, where total value=quantity×price.

The last few lines of the invoice depend on the discount percentage in the identifier record. If this discount percentage is 0, a total amount, equal to the sum of the total values of the parts, is printed with the words 'FINAL AMOUNT.' If the identifier record has a nonzero discount percentage, the last three lines of the invoice are

TOTAL AMOUNT	total amount
LESS DISCOUNT	discount
FINAL AMOUNT	final amount

where discount=total amount×percentage discount, and final amount=total amount−discount. Figure 6.2 shows PASCAL-based pseudocode for producing the invoices.[2] In all the programs in this section, a boolean variable more-data (signifying that a file is not empty) is used in conjunction with a boolean function readin, defined as

```
function readin(var textfile:text):boolean;
    var temp:boolean;
    begin
    temp:=not(eof(textfile));
    if temp then read(textfile);
```

---

[2]Recall that PASCAL allows the use of arbitrary files for input or output and also provides standard files called "input" and "output." A *rewrite* operation causes an arbitrary file to be an empty file and then makes it ready for output. A *reset* operation makes an arbitrary file ready for input, either by moving the first record to a buffer or by setting eof (the end of file indicator) if the file is empty. Each subsequent read operation (1) moves information from the buffer to desired variables and then (2) either moves the next record to the buffer or sets eof if the file is empty. The reset and rewrite operations are automatically done for the standard files "input" and "output."

Reset and rewrite are analogous to the OPEN operation in COBOL. However, all PASCAL files are closed automatically when the program terminates; a reset or rewrite operation on an open file closes that file and rewinds or adjusts it appropriately before opening it again.

```
    readin:=temp
  end
```

This arrangement allows the design method of Section 6.2 to function properly.

This example (a typical business data processing problem) primarily involves moving data from one file to another. Likewise, the techniques of Figure 6.2 are prototypic of business data processing methods:

· All desired processing is accomplished in one pass through the file
· Each record is read in turn and is processed immediately
· Data elements from an input record are output immediately if possible and otherwise are saved in memory for the shortest possible time
· Additional variables are used only as necessary

This processing style, called *serial file processing,* allows a file of unlimited length to be processed using a small amount of core memory, independent of the length of the file. Thus, the program of Figure 6.2 can process equally well an input file of 100 records or one of 100,000 records.

The ability to process variable-length files with a small program, whose size is independent of the lengths of the files processed, allows the use of inexpensive microcomputers. Moreover, the sizes of business files continually change as inventories change, employees go on vacation, and so on.

Serial file processing is most useful when the output for each input record or group can be independently calculated, as in the calculation of each invoice from an input group in our example. But a variable-length file cannot be sorted in one serial pass because the first output record cannot be determined until the last input record has been read. However, many schemes exist for sorting via a sequence of serial passes, where the first pass splits the initial input file into two or more output files, further serial passes process from two or more input files to two or more output files, and a final serial pass merges two or more input files into one sorted output file.

6.2.2 Composition Diagrams

6.2.2.1 Data Flow Definitions

The program of Figure 6.2 has another very important characteristic, namely, that the structure of the program mirrors the composition of the input data flow. The input consists of groups of records, and, accordingly, the program contains a while loop that is executed once for each group. Each group of records consists of one identifier record followed by an indefinite number of

```
          program invoice (recordfile, invoicefile);
              (*file, variable and readin function declarations omitted*)
          begin
              reset(recordfile);
              rewrite(invoicefile);
              moredata:=readin(recordfile);
              while moredata do
                  begin (*each group*)
(*identifier record*) groupnumber:=number;
                    totalamount:=0;
                    writeln(invoicefile, groupnumber, name, address);
                    moredata:=readin(recordfile);
                    while (moredata) and
                            (groupnumber=number) do
                        begin (*each part record*)
                          totalvalue:=quantity*price;
                          writeln(invoicefile, partname, quantity, price, totalvalue);
                          totalamount:=totalamount+totalvalue;
                          moredata:=readin(recordfile)
                        end (*each part record*);
(*final lines*) if percent=0 then writeln(invoicefile, 'FINAL AMOUNT', totalamount)
                            else begin
                                writeln(invoicefile, 'TOTAL AMOUNT', totalamount);
                                discount:=totalamount*percent;
                                writeln(invoicefile, 'LESS DISCOUNT OF', discount);
                                finalamount:=totalamount-discount;
                                writeln(invoicefile, 'FINAL AMOUNT', finalamount)
                                end
              end (*each group*)
          end.
```

Figure 6.2 Pseudocode for producing invoices.

part records, and, accordingly, the program contains a sequence of lines to process the first record, followed by a while loop executed once for each part record. The program also mirrors the structure of its output data flow.

The method of Section 6.2 shows how to derive a serial file processing program so that its structure always corresponds to the compositions of its input data flows and output data flows. This method assumes that:

· Inputs and outputs are serial files, which may be considered to be held on magnetic tapes
· The structure of each input and each output is explicitly defined via data flow definitions
· Each data file is passed through only once

The derivation method depends on the composition of each data flow, as expressed by the data flow definitions of Chapter 2. The sequence or logic flow of the finished program is determined by this composition and the correct allocation of operations.

Recall that, in Chapter 2, a notation was introduced to describe the composition of data flows. The operation $\cdot$ means "followed by," and thus the definition

$X=Y\cdot Z$

means that the data flow X consists of Y followed by Z. The operation $|$ is used to separate alternatives, and thus the definition

$A=B\,|\,C\,|\,D$

is read "A consists of one (and only one) of the alternatives B, C, or D." Brackets [ ] are used to surround an optional component, so that the definition

$E=[F]\cdot G$

means that E consists optionally of F, followed by G. In other words, E will consist of F followed by G if the optional component F is present, or it will consist only of G if the optional component F is not present.

Braces { } are used to enclose a repeated component. If there is a lower limit to the number of repetitions, it is written as a subscript just to the right of the expression. For example, the definition

$Integer=\{Digit\}_1$

states that an integer is a sequence of one or more digits. If no lower limit is stated, then the lower limit is understood to be 0, that is, the component may not occur at all. If an upper limit is given, it is written as a superscript just to the right of the expression. For example, the definition

$Label=\{Digit\}_1^5$

states that a label consists of from one to five digits.

Finally, any expression enclosed in parentheses ( ) is understood as a single entity with respect to the rest of the expression. Thus either of the expressions

$(E\cdot F\cdot G)$
$(H\,|\,J)$

would be understood as a single entity in the context of a larger expression. When the operators $\cdot$ and $|$ are used in the same expression, the operator $\cdot$ has higher precedence than $|$. Thus the expression

$P\cdot Q\,|\,R\cdot S$

is understood to mean

$(P\cdot Q)\,|\,(R\cdot S)$

in the same way that multiplications take effect before additions in arithmetic expressions.

6.2.2.2 Describing Data Flow with Composition Diagrams

All of the definitions that collectively describe a data flow may be combined to obtain a *composition diagram* showing the entire composition of the data flow [War 76]. A composition diagram uses left brackets [of varying sizes. When a named data flow D appears to the left of such a bracket, as, for example,

D[

the diagram to the right of the bracket defines the entire composition of D. A defining expression for D, in terms of the highest level components of D, is written from top to bottom immediately to the right of the bracket, in accordance with the data flow definition of D. The expression must be either a single component name, or a sequence of component names, or an alternation of component names. A component name may be optional (in which case it is enclosed in square brackets []) or it may be repeated (in which case it is enclosed in braces { }). Operators ● for sequence and ▮ for alternation are used. (These are the operators used in Chapter 2, except that they are now written larger.)

Some definitions and corresponding diagrams are shown in Figure 6.3. A data flow definition may be more complex than a strict sequence or alternation of terms, as shown in the last three examples of Figure 6.3. In this case, new symbols (e.g., Q, V, AA and BB in Figure 6.3) are used and additional levels are added to the diagram as necessary, forming a diagram in which each defining expression consists of a strict sequence or alternation of components names.

A bracket and defining expression are now given for each highest level component (e.g., Q or V or AA of Figure 6.3) in accordance with its data flow definition. This process is continued for as many levels as there are definitions, and the resulting diagram shows the total composition of the data flow D.

In the last example of Figure 6.3, the component A can be defined by using one, two, or three data flow definitions. The rules used in forming composition diagrams yield the same diagram for A, no matter whether one, two, or three definitions are used.

As a further example, consider the input data flow of the example of Section 6.2.1. This data flow is described by the definitions of Figure 6.4(*a*) and by the diagram in (*b*).

6.2.2.3 Program Diagrams

A fundamental tenet of data-structure-based design is that the structure of the program (or module) should mirror the structure of the inputs and outputs.

Definition	Diagram
$X = Y \cdot Z$	$X \begin{bmatrix} Y \\ \bullet \\ Z \end{bmatrix}$
$A = B \mid C \mid D$	$A \begin{bmatrix} B \\ \blacksquare \\ C \\ \blacksquare \\ D \end{bmatrix}$
$E = F \cdot \{G\}$	$E \begin{bmatrix} F \\ \bullet \\ \{G\} \end{bmatrix}$
$H = I \mid \{J\}$	$H \begin{bmatrix} I \\ \blacksquare \\ \{J\} \end{bmatrix}$
$K = L \cdot (M \mid N) \cdot P$	$K \begin{bmatrix} L \\ \bullet \\ Q \quad \begin{bmatrix} M \\ \blacksquare \\ N \end{bmatrix} \\ \bullet \\ P \end{bmatrix}$
$R = S \mid T \cdot U$	$R \begin{bmatrix} S \\ \blacksquare \\ V \quad \begin{bmatrix} T \\ \bullet \\ U \end{bmatrix} \end{bmatrix}$
$A = B \mid C \cdot (D \mid E) \cdot F \mid G$	$A \quad AA \begin{bmatrix} B \\ \blacksquare \\ BB \begin{bmatrix} C \\ \bullet \\ \begin{bmatrix} D \\ \blacksquare \\ E \end{bmatrix} \\ \bullet \\ F \end{bmatrix} \\ \blacksquare \\ G \end{bmatrix}$

Figure 6.3 Data flow definitions and corresponding composition diagrams.

Thus a program whose input is defined as in Figure 6.4 has, in principle, the form of Figure 6.5. (The program of Figure 6.2 has this form.)

A sequence of data flow components in Figure 6.4 is mirrored by a sequence of program components in Figure 6.5, and an iterated component in Figure 6.4 is mirrored by a while loop in Figure 6.5. Similarly, an alternation of data flow

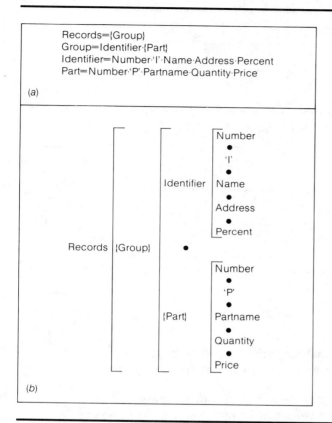

```
Records={Group}
Group=Identifier·{Part}
Identifier=Number·'I'·Name·Address·Percent
Part=Number·'P'·Partname·Quantity·Price
```

(a)

(b)

Figure 6.4 Composition of input data flow. (*a*) Data flow definitions. (*b*) Composition diagram.

components would be mirrored by if-then-else statements or case statements. An optional component would be mirrored by an if statement. Assuming these correspondences, the program processrecords can itself be diagrammed as in Figure 6.6.

A rule put forth by Warnier [War 76] is that every repeated program must include a beginning subprogram, which is executed once, and an ending subprogram, which is executed once. According to this rule, the programs processgroup and processpart should each have beginning and ending subprograms. The rule may sensibly be extended to specify that every program must have a beginning subprogram and an ending subprogram, each of which is executed once. Assuming this extended rule, the program processrecords has the structure of Figure 6.7.

```
(*processrecords*) while another group do
(*processgroup*)       begin
                          processidentifier;
                          while another part do
                              processpart
                       end
```

Figure 6.5 Program to process the composition of Figure 6.4.

```
processrecords │ {processgroup} │ processidentifier
               │                │        •
               │                │ {processpart}
```

Figure 6.6 Composition diagram of the program process-records.

The beginning subprogram usually initializes variables or files, prints titles, and the like. The ending program usually prepares for the next iteration, prints totals, and the like.

The beginning subprogram has another important function. Since each group in Figure 6.4 is distinguished by a particular invoice number, the subprogram begingroup in Figure 6.7 must set the variable groupnumber to that particular value, if processidentifier does not do so. All succeeding components of the group are required to satisfy the condition groupnumber=number, as in Figure 6.2.

Stated more generally, each while loop processes a set of elements. Usually an explicit condition is specified for membership in the set, such as a given number or a given type code (e.g., 'I' or 'P'). The membership condition is included in the condition of the while loop. This membership condition may have to be set by the beginning subprogram.

6.2.3 The Design Procedure

6.2.3.1 Overview

Section 6.2.3 presents a formal procedure for obtaining programs such as Figure 6.2, whose structure mirrors the structures of its input data flows and

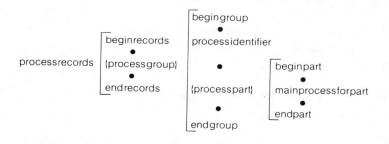

Figure 6.7 Extended form of the program processrecords.

its output data flows. The procedure requires that:

· A composition diagram can be given for each input data flow and each output data flow.
· The structures of the input data flows and output data flows can be combined to yield a program structure.

Further requirements are given in Section 6.3.4.2. A program derived in this way has the following characteristics:

· The program remembers nothing from one execution to the next.
· The program's initial state is fixed.
· Everything in the program text is associated with the input data flows and output data flows, as defined by the composition diagrams.
· The program structure derived from the composition diagrams is sufficient for a workable program. Operations are allocated to program components without the use of additional program logic.
· All desired processing is accomplished with only one pass through each data file.

The design procedure itself consists of six steps:

1. Find the composition of each input data flow and each output data flow.
2. If there are two or more inputs, derive a composite input diagram combining all of the input data flows.
3. Identify each output data flow component with an input data flow component for which that output is given.
4. Combine all input structures and all output structures using the identifications of step 3 to determine a program structure diagram.

5. List the executable operations required for each data flow component of an input or output.

6. Determine an appropriate place in the program structure for each operation and derive a program code diagram showing the operations placed in the program structure diagram.

The required program can be written directly from the code diagram. The six steps are explained below.

6.2.3.2 Steps in the Procedure

Step 1   We now show details of this procedure using the example of Section 6.2.1.

The composition of the input was given in Figure 6.4. The output is described by the definitions of Figure 6.8(*a*) and the diagram of (*b*).

Because this design procedure derives the program directly from the composition diagrams, it is crucial to correctly diagram each input and output. Even seemingly superfluous data flow components should be included in the diagram, to provide a correct program structure into which later program modifications can be fitted. For example, for the program now being derived, the input record groups defining invoices might themselves have been grouped according to customer. An additional structural level, say Customergroup, would then be defined, and the highest three levels of Figure 6.4(*b*) would be

Records[{Customergroup}[{Group}

Although superfluous for the present program, the Customergroup component provides a structure which can accommodate future modifications based on customer groupings. For example, printing for each customer, the sum of all invoice final amounts for that customer, is a Customergroup process.

Step 2   Since the example has only one input, we omit discussing step 2 for the moment. Section 6.2.3.4 discusses methods to be used when there are two or more inputs.

Step 3   In step 3, we identify each output component with an input component for which that output is given. Obviously, the program must in fact output each output component and, accordingly, such an identification must be found for each output component. Each problem statement dictates the identifications for that particular problem.

More precisely, the identification process is done for each output component that itself has components, to eliminate unnecessary work. An output component Y is identified with an input component X if, on an occurrence of the component X, exactly one occurrence of the component Y (no more and no less) can immediately be output.

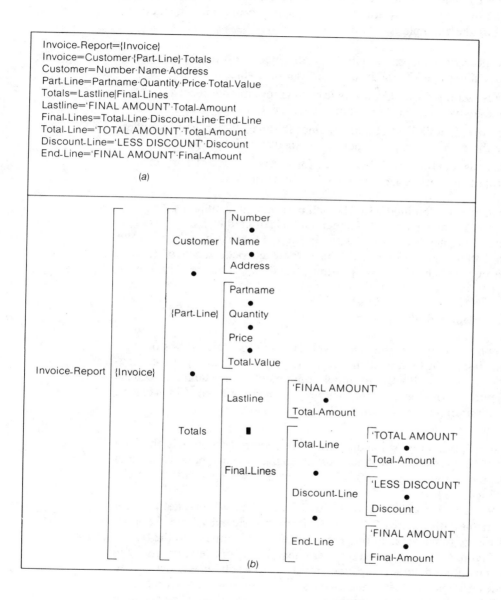

Invoice-Report={Invoice}
Invoice=Customer·{Part-Line}·Totals
Customer=Number·Name·Address
Part-Line=Partname·Quantity·Price·Total-Value
Totals=Lastline|Final-Lines
Lastline='FINAL AMOUNT'·Total-Amount
Final-Lines=Total-Line·Discount-Line·End-Line
Total-Line='TOTAL AMOUNT'·Total-Amount
Discount-Line='LESS DISCOUNT'·Discount
End-Line='FINAL AMOUNT'·Final-Amount

(a)

Figure 6.8 Composition of output. (*a*) Data flow definitions.
(*b*) Composition diagram.

In determining identifications, we proceed from left to right (from highest to lowest levels) in each composition diagram, hoping to find identifications at each level. For the example, we find:

(A) Invoice_Report is identified with Records since the total set of records can immediately yield exactly one total set of invoices.

(B) Invoice is identified with Group since each group of input records (having the same invoice number) can immediately yield exactly one invoice.

(C) Customer is identified with Identifier since for an occurrence of Identifier, exactly the component Customer can immediately be output.

(D) Part_Line is identified with Part since for an occurrence of Part, exactly the component Part_Line can immediately be output.

Usually when Y is identified with X, each part of Y is identified with a part of X. However, Y may have a part that cannot be identified with any part of X. In the example, Invoice is identified with Group, but there is no part of Group with which Totals can be identified. Since for each occurrence of Group, exactly one occurrence of Totals is output, Totals is identified with Group even though Invoice is also identified with Group.

(E) Totals is identified with Group.

This exception situation arises whenever an output contains totals or summaries of the input. Further, in such a case the parts of the exception component cannot be identified with any input component. For example, because Totals is identified with Group here, neither Lastline nor Final_Lines can be identified with an input component.

Step 4   In step 4, the composition diagram of the required program is obtained by merging the input diagram with the output diagrams, while preserving all of the identifications found in step 3. For the example, step 4 results in the diagram of Figure 6.9.

Figure 6.9 has been specially drawn with different kinds of bracket lines for easy comparison with Figures 6.4 and 6.8. Portions originally from the input diagram of Figure 6.4 have solid bracket lines, while portions from the output diagram of Figure 6.8 have dashed bracket lines. Some brackets, originally in both input and output diagrams, are shown with both a solid line and a dashed line. In some circumstances, it is necessary to add a component and bracket to the program diagram, and these additional brackets are shown as lines of slash marks.

The merged diagram of Figure 6.9 is derived from left to right, or, equivalently, from highest to lowest levels. In (A), Invoice_Report (the highest level output component) is identified with Records (the highest level input compo-

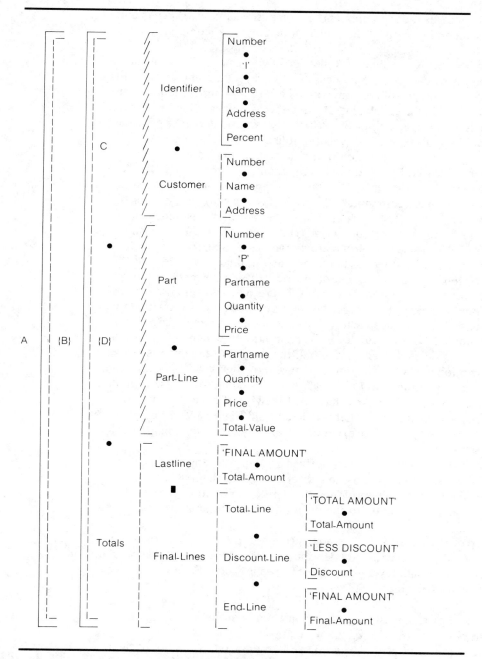

Figure 6.9 Composition diagram of required program.

nent). Figure 6.9 merges these components and uses the name A. Likewise, in (B), Invoice is identified with Group. In Figure 6.9 these components are merged as B.

The merging process is continued for as many levels as possible. But there are two exceptions to the merging process. One exception, common to both (C) and (D), arises when one of the components is an actual input record or an actual output record. For example, in (C), Identifier is a physical input record and Customer is a physical output line. Similarly, in (D), Part is a physical input record and Part_Line is a physical output line. In this circumstance, the identification is preserved by creation of a new component consisting of the input component followed by the output component.

The second exception arises as in (E) above, when an output component Y is identified with an input component X, but Y has a part y that cannot be identified with any part of X. In this circumstance, the part y is added in its entirety to the defining diagram for the merged X and Y, in an appropriate place. In Figure 6.9, Invoice and Group are merged as B, and Totals (which is identified with Invoice) is added in its entirety as the final component of B.

As a result of step 4, each component of the input diagram is merged with an output component or appears on its own in Figure 6.9, and, likewise, each output component appears either merged or on its own. Conversely, with only trivial exceptions, the program structure can consist only of input components or output components. For example, if every input component with only a solid-line bracket is deleted from Figure 6.9, the diagram remaining is (with two trivial exceptions) exactly the output diagram of Figure 6.8. The exceptions are components C and D in Figure 6.9, which become trivial if the input components Identifier and Part are removed. Likewise, if every output component with only a dashed-line bracket is deleted from Figure 6.9, the diagram remaining is (with the same two exceptions) exactly the input diagram of Figure 6.4.

Always check the program diagram derived in step 4 to ensure that it includes as subdiagrams the composition diagram of every input and every output. Also make sure that the program diagram does not contain any other (nontrivial) diagrams, in addition to the diagrams of inputs and outputs.

Step 5 In step 5, the executable operations required for each component of the program composition diagram are determined and listed. Executable operations are written in a high-level language or in pseudocode. Several types of operations commonly occur:

· Each file read or written may have to be made ready at the beginning of the program and closed at the end of the program.
· If an iterated component of the diagram uses a membership condition, then an operation is required to initialize the membership condition.
· A common operation is the output of totals of various sorts. If this is done,

then operations are required to initialize the totals and to accumulate the totals.

· A read operation (always performed by our readin function) is required to obtain each input record and a write operation is required to send out each output record.

For the example, we obtain the following operations:

1. reset (recordfile) ⎫
2. readin (recordfile) ⎬ obtain input records
3. rewrite (invoicefile)
4. writeln (invoicefile, groupnumber, name, address)
5. writeln (invoicefile, quantity, partname, price, totalvalue)
6. writeln (invoicefile, 'FINAL AMOUNT', totalamount) ⎬ produce output lines
7. writeln (invoicefile, 'TOTAL AMOUNT', totalamount)
8. writeln (invoicefile, 'LESS DISCOUNT OF', discount)
9. writeln (invoicefile, 'FINAL AMOUNT', finalamount)
10. groupnumber:=number   initialize while loop condition
11. totalvalue=quantity*price   calculate totalvalue for partline
12. totalamount:=0 ⎫ initialize and accumulate
13. totalamount:=totalamount+totalvalue ⎬ total amount
14. discount:=totalamount*percent ⎫ calculate discount and
15. finalamount:=totalamount − discount ⎬ final amount

Step 6 Next, each operation is assigned a place (or places) in the program structure to obtain a *program code diagram*. If the program composition diagram has been correctly derived from the data flows, allocation of these operations to places in the program is a trivial task. If the allocation is, indeed, trivial, then the first five steps were successful; if not trivial, the first five steps should be reexamined. The program code diagram of Figure 6.10 shows clearly how the operations of our example fit into the structure.

With the exception of the read operation, which occurs in several places in the program, each operation is linked with a specific program component. The pattern of read operations follows a simple rule. The first read operation for any component occurs just before the program for that component. If the component is repeated, then a read operation is the last operation of the component program. In Figure 6.10, the recordfile is read just before the B program, just before the D program, and as the last operation of the D program. In other words, the file is positioned so that at the first (next) execution of any component, the record required by that component is already in memory. Note also that the last read operation in D serves for the next execution of D or the next execution of B.

The required program, which can be written directly from the program code diagram, is shown in Figure 6.2.

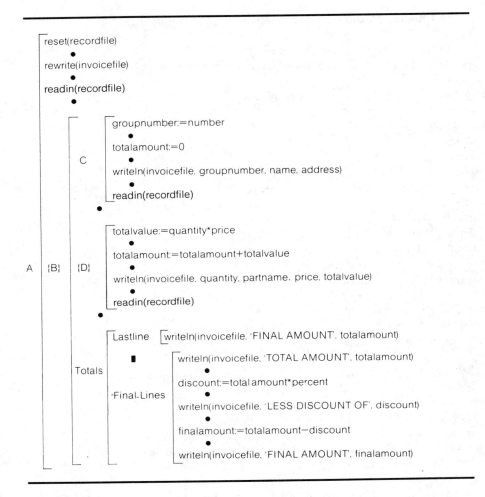

Figure 6.10 Program code diagram.

6.2.3.3 Checking the Procedure

At each step of this procedure, there are criteria for the correctness of the step itself and also implicit checks on the correctness of previous steps [Jac 76]. In step 1, for example, we check to ensure that the data definitions and composition diagrams represent all known facts about the compositions of the inputs and outputs. The diagrams are deemed to be right only if they do in fact represent all known facts. Suppose that, for the example just finished, the

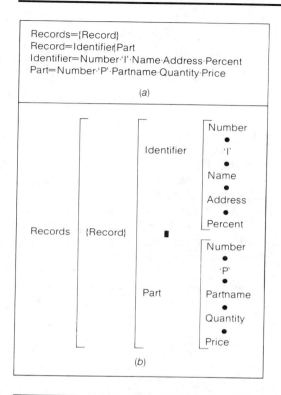

Records={Record}
Record=Identifier|Part
Identifier=Number·'I'·Name·Address·Percent
Part=Number·'P'·Partname·Quantity·Price

(a)

(b)

Figure 6.11   Incorrect composition of input. (*a*) Definitions. (*b*) Diagram.

input was incorrectly described using the definitions and diagram of Figure 6.11.

At step 1, our check should reveal that the definitions of Figure 6.11 do not represent everything known about the Records data. If these incorrect definitions are kept, then at step 3, the output component Totals cannot be identified with any input component, even though Totals represents a summary of a group of input records.

At this point the error should be clear since there is an output component that cannot be identified with any input component. However, a careless person might go on to step 4, attempting to develop a composite diagram from the diagrams of Figures 6.8(*b*) and 6.11(*b*). At the third level (counting from the left), this attempt should break down, since Figure 6.8(*b*) requires a sequence of elements while Figure 6.11(*b*) requires an alternation of elements.

After step 4, we check to ensure that:

1. With only trivial exceptions, every component of the program composition diagram corresponds exactly to a component of an input or an output, and
2. Each input or output diagram is fully included within the program diagram.

6.2.3.4 Using Multiple Inputs

Many business applications require two or more inputs. In *file merging*, two similar files are combined to yield a single file. In *file updating*, a transaction file is processed against a master file to update the master file. For example, employee weekly time records can be processed against an employee master file containing year-to-date salary and taxes paid for each employee, to produce salary checks and also a new employee master file reflecting the latest week's earnings.

When multiple inputs are used, the input files must be synchronized to effectively form one composite input. Step 2 determines a composite diagram that combines the different data flows.

Suppose that input files A and B are to be combined to form a composite input file I, where

$$\begin{cases} A = \{a\} \\ B = \{b\} \\ I = \{i\} \end{cases}$$

The precise method of combining records a and b will depend on the application. Some common patterns are:

1. $i = a \cdot b$ $I \left[\{i\} \left[\begin{array}{c} a \\ \bullet \\ b \end{array} \right. \right.$

2. $i = a \cdot [b]$ $I \left[\{i\} \left[\begin{array}{c} a \\ \bullet \\ [b] \end{array} \right. \right.$

3. $i = a \cdot \{b\}$ $I \left[\{i\} \left[\begin{array}{c} a \\ \bullet \\ \{b\} \end{array} \right. \right.$

4. $i = a \mid b$ $I \left[\{i\} \left[\begin{array}{c} a \\ \blacksquare \\ b \end{array} \right. \right.$

Pattern 1 could occur when two different files are precisely synchronized for a calculation. An example is the use of two different files of employee information, where each file is in order by employee number, and each file has the same set of employee numbers.

Pattern 2, where i contains an optional component b, arises in updating applications, where A is the master file and B is the transaction file. The b records are optional because there need not be a transaction for each master record (for example, there may not be a weekly time record for each employee).

Pattern 3 arises in updating applications where there can be more than one transaction for each master record, as in banking applications. This pattern also arises when one file contains identifier records and the other contains groups of transactions pertaining to the identifier record.

Pattern 4 arises when the next input is to be chosen from either a or b, but not in a rigid rotation as in pattern 1. An example is the use of two employee master files, each in order by employee number and each file containing a different set of employees, where each next input is the record (from either A or B) having the lowest number.

A standard program technique for keeping multiple files in synchronization is to initially read the first record of each input file, so that the first record of each input file is in memory. Then, any subprogram wishing to process a record of an input file uses the record already in memory and then reads the next record of that file into memory. For example, a subprogram that processes a record of file B will use the record of B already in memory and then perform the function readin (B). Thus, as any subprogram ends (and the next subprogram begins), the appropriate records of the input files are already in memory.

As an illustration, suppose that the invoice program does not have a single input file, but instead has one input file (Ifile) containing Identifier records and a second input file (Pfile) containing Part records. Let us use the name Set to denote a group of Part records corresponding to a single invoice. There is of course one such group for each Identifier record.

Assume that Ifile is the master file and is always read first, and assume that there are Part records for every Identifier record in Ifile. The two files can be considered to be combined according to pattern 3, the composite input group i having the diagram

$$
i \quad \left[\begin{array}{l} \text{Identifier} \\ \bullet \\ \{\text{Part}\} \end{array} \right.
$$

Alternatively, since there is exactly one Set for each Identifier, the files can be considered to be combined according to pattern 1, yielding the diagram

$$
i \quad \left[\begin{array}{l} \text{Identifier} \\ \bullet \\ \text{Set} \, [\{\text{Part}\} \end{array} \right.
$$

where (as shown) Set is a group of Part records. Set can be eliminated from the composite diagram because it serves only to name a group of Part records, and thus the two ways of combining the files yield the same diagram.

If the composite input is named Records, and the name Group denotes a composite input group, then the composite input for the two files Ifile and Pfile is identical to the single-input composition diagram of Figure 6.4(b). Thus, the composition diagram of the required program is identical to Figure 6.9. A slightly different program code diagram is required because two input files must now be synchronized.

The merging and synchronizing of multiple input files is combined with the required calculation. Thus, the required processing is accomplished with only one pass through each file, as required by this design technique.

Multiple outputs can be handled in the same way as multiple inputs, by forming a composite output diagram which combines all required output. However, the handling of multiple outputs is simpler, because the output files do not have to be synchronized. The program composition diagram, program code diagram and pseudocode can now be derived as for a single output.

6.2.3.5 Separation into Smaller Subprograms

The required program structure depends on the number of inputs and outputs and on their complexity. However, it may be possible to separate the required program into simpler independent subprograms by using intermediate data objects. To illustrate this point, Figure 6.12(a) shows a program P with four inputs and four outputs. Obviously the structure of P must reflect the structures of all eight inputs and outputs, and thus we may expect P to be rather complex. However, we may separate P into either the form of Figure 6.12(b) or of (c). In either case, the subprogram P_A is required to mirror only the structures of the inputs, while P_B mirrors only the structures of the outputs. Finally, (d) shows that P_A may be further subdivided into a set of simpler transformations.

Intermediate data objects may also be used to achieve compatibility among the various data flow structures, as discussed in Section 3.3.1.

6.2.4 Error Processing

Inputs to a program can never be expected to be perfect. Error checking of all sorts is required, and this processing accounts for much code in business data processing systems. It is desirable to process errors according to specifications and in such a way that erroneous inputs interfere as little as possible with the processing of nonerroneous inputs.

The design technique of Section 6.2.3 provides a program structured as an arrangement of nested components, corresponding precisely to the composition of input and output data flows. Error processing can easily be built into this processing scheme. To incorporate error processing into a lowest level process P, which directly performs input, we elaborate the diagram of P, to obtain

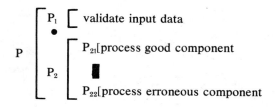

For a higher-level process P, which does not directly perform input, we elaborate the diagram of P to obtain

$$P \begin{bmatrix} P_1[\text{process good component} \\ \bullet \\ [P_2][\text{process erroneous component} \end{bmatrix}$$

In other words, P_1 (which should contain input and validation processes) is performed until a severe error is found. If such an error is found, then the optional error process P_2 is performed. This elaboration can be carried out at all levels, giving rise to a system of error processes.

If error processing is elaborated in this way for the diagram of Figure 6.10, the result is the diagram of Figure 6.13. The component A_2 is introduced to allow for the processing of an entirely erroneous input file. Totals is not elaborated since it does not read input and is executed only after a group has conclusively been determined to be a good group.

For each group of data having the same invoice number, there is now a component B_1, which processes the data if it is a good group, and a component B_2, which processes the data if it is an erroneous group. The decision whether a group is erroneous is made by C_1 and D_1, the processes that validate input. A group will first be processed by B_1. If a sufficiently severe error is encountered, C_1 or D_1 sets a flag that causes B_1 to terminate and B_2 to be executed. Similarly, C_1 and D_1 can set a flag that causes $\{B\}$ to terminate and A_2 to be executed.

Every process of Figure 6.10 is included in Figure 6.13. The processes B, C, and D of Figure 6.8 become the processes B_1, C_{21}, and D_{21} of Figure 6.13. The error elaboration also preserves the structure of Figure 6.10. Thus, if all of the error elaborations are removed from Figure 6.13, the result is (with some trivial exceptions) the diagram of Figure 6.10.

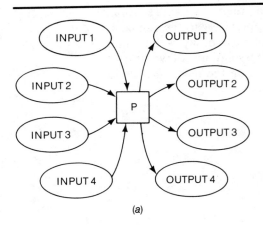

(a)

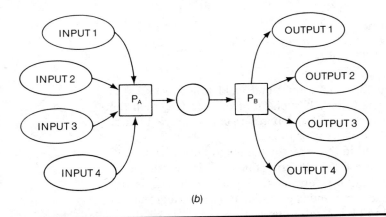

(b)

Figure 6.12 Separation of a program into simpler subprograms using intermediate data objects. (*a*) Process P with four inputs and four outputs. (*b*) Division of P into simpler processes P_A and P_B by using an intermediate data object. (*c*) Alternate division of P into simpler processes P_A, P_B, and P_C. (*d*) Division of P_A into simpler processes P_{A1}, P_{A2}, and P_{A3}.

An error process such as B_2 usually lists each record of the erroneous group in an error report. Since an error may occur anywhere in a group, process P_1, which validates a component, will not in general recognize an erroneous group until some processing has already occurred under the assumption that a good

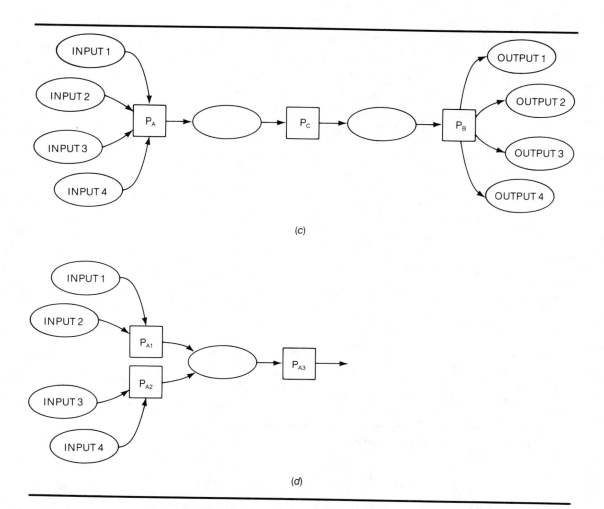

(c)

(d)

group is being processed. In this case, certain partial computations may have to be undone (Jackson [Jac 75] calls this a "backtracking" problem).

In our example, the process D_1 may decide that a Part record has an error severe enough to cause the whole group to be erroneous. In principle, B_2 should write each record of the erroneous group to an error report, flagging those records that cause the group to be erroneous, while B_1 should give no output. However, when the error happens, an initial portion of the invoice has already been written to the invoicefile. B_1 has already given a spurious output and B_2 has lost some records it should output. These are the partial computations that must be undone.

When you elaborate a program diagram to include error processing, always check whether there are partial computations that have to be undone in case of

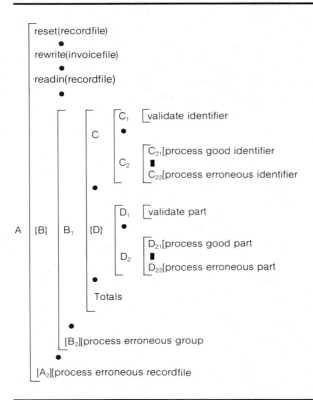

Figure 6.13 Processing structure elaborated to include error processing.

error. In many instances it is not necessary to undo any computations. When calculations must be undone, the next question is how to undo them.

In general, the only troublesome partial computations are the unwanted reading and writing of serial files, as just noted. Some systems provide input and output procedures capable of *noting* and later *restoring* the state of a file and its buffers [Jac 76]. When such procedures are available, a *note* operation can be made the very first operation in B_1, prior to C, and a *restore* operation can be the very first operation in B_2. If these procedures are not available, then B_1 can be modified so as to write each record to a temporary file as it is read, while B_2 can be modified to retrieve the records from the temporary file.

Figure 6.14 shows the program code diagram of Figure 6.10, elaborated to include use of an errorfile, a temporary record file, a temporary invoice file, functions checkidentifier and checkpart for validating records, and an error print procedure for printing error messages. Figure 6.15 shows the corresponding program code. As can be seen from comparing Figures 6.14 and 6.15, the program code follows immediately from the code diagram.

Checkidentifier and checkpart can each be written to find as many errors as desired. Each error type can be assigned an index number n and a specific message stored as MESSAGE[n], the nth element of a message array. As each error is found by checkindentifier or checkpart, its index number can be placed in an array ERROR. The procedure errorprint, by using simple code such as

```
for i:=1 to ERRORCAP do
  if ERROR[i]>0
    then writeln(errorfile, MESSAGE[ERROR[i]]);
```

can then print a message for each error found.

Each validation function returns a value 0, 1, 2, or 3, either signifying that no error is present or indicating the maximum severity of errors. These values are used to set flags that determine the levels at which error processing is done. A record error, depending on its severity, may result in an error process for that record alone, for the group of records defining an invoice, or for the entire file. Construction of the functions checkidentifier and checkpart for this example are left as an exercise (see Problem 6 at the end of Section 6.2).

The method of Figures 6.14 and 6.15 is not too inefficient if disk can be used for the temporary files. Alternatively, if the input and output files are both on disk and specific records of each file can be accessed, then in the event of an error, records can be deleted from the output file and other records transferred from the input file to the error file. (This is equivalent to the *note* and *restore* procedures discussed above.) A final possibility for our example is that the input records and the computed output records are stored in arrays in memory, and the output records are written to the invoice file when the record group is found to be entirely good, or the input records are written to the error file in case of a severe error. Unfortunately, the use of such arrays puts a bound on the maximum number of records in an invoice, and the consequences of this bound must be dealt with.

6.2.5 Some Final Comments

Section 6.2 has shown how a program can be derived from the compositions of its input data flows and output data flows. A diagramming technique [War 76] was used first for the composition of input and output data flows, then for the structure of a program, and then for the program code diagram—an outline of a program complete with code.

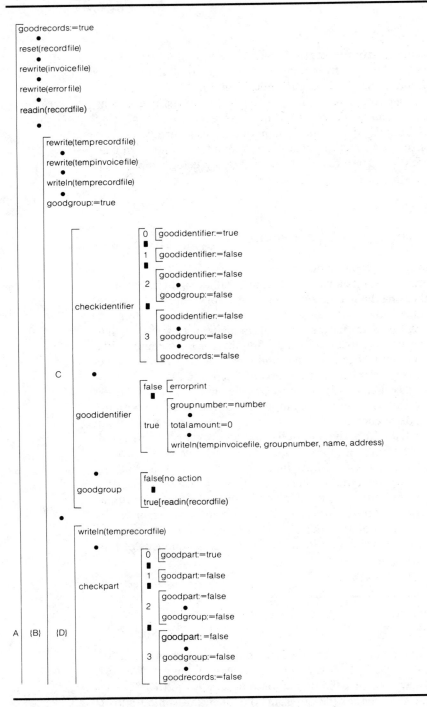

Figure 6.14 Program code diagram including error processing and backtracking.

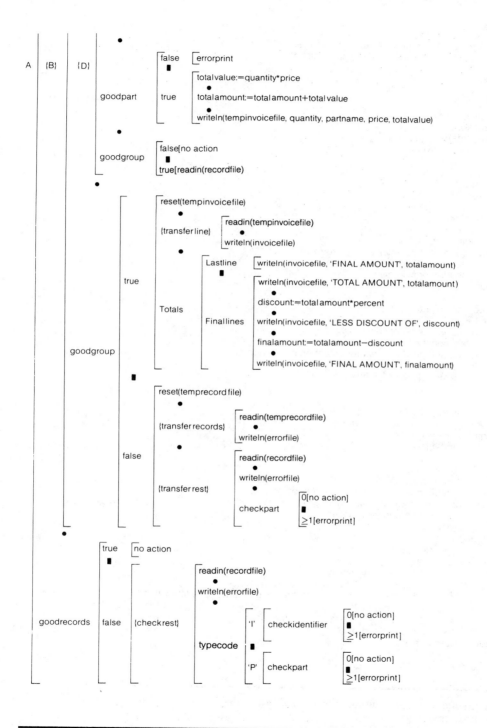

```
program invoice2(recordfile, invoicefile, errorfile, temprecordfile, tempinvoicefile);
  (*file, variable and readin function declarations omitted*)
  begin(*main*)
    goodrecords:=true;
    reset(recordfile);
    rewrite(invoicefile);
    rewrite(error file);
    moredata:=readin(recordfile);
    while(goodrecords) and (moredata)do
      begin(*process records*)
        rewrite(temprecordfile);
        rewrite(tempinvoicefile);
        write(temprecordfile);
        goodgroup:=true;
        (*begin process identifier*)
        case checkidentifier of
          0:goodidentifier:=true;
          1:goodidentifier:=false;
          2:begin goodidentifier:=false;goodgroup:=false end;
          3:begin goodidentifier:=false;goodgroup:=false;
                  goodrecords:=false
            end
        end;
        if not goodidentifier thenerrorprint
          else begin
                groupnumber:=number;
                totalamount:=0;
                writeln(tempinvoicefile, groupnumber, name, address);
                if goodgroup
                  then moredata:=readin(recordfile)
                end;
        (*end process identifier*)
        while(goodgroup) and (moredata)
              and (groupnumber=number) do
            begin(*process part*)
                writeln(temprecordfile);
                case checkpart of
                    0:goodpart:=true;
                    1:goodpart:=false;
                    2:begin goodpart:=false;goodgroup:=false end;
                    3:begin goodpart:=false;goodgroup:=false;
                            goodrecords:=false
                      end
                end;
                if not goodpart then errorprint
                else begin(*process good part*)
                        total value:=quantity*price;
                        totalamount:=totalamount+totalvalue;
                        writeln(tempinvoicefile, partname, quantity, price, totalvalue);
                        if goodgroup
                          then moredata:=readin(recordfile)
                      end(*process good part*)
            end(*process part*);
```

Figure 6.15 Pseudocode including error processing and backtracking.

```
        if goodgroup then begin(*totals for good group*)
                            reset(tempinvoicefile);
                            while readin(tempinvoicefile) do
                                writeln(invoicefile);
                            if percent=0 then writeln(invoicefile, 'FINAL AMOUNT', totalamount)
                              else begin
                                   writeln(invoicefile, 'TOTAL AMOUNT', totalamount);
                                   discount:=totalamount*percent;
                                   writeln(invoicefile, 'LESS DISCOUNT OF', discount);
                                   finalamount:=totalamount−discount;
                                   writeln(invoicefile, 'FINAL AMOUNT', finalamount)
                                   end
                         end(*totals for good group*)
              else begin(*process bad group*)
                            reset(temprecordfile);
                            while readin(temprecordfile) do
                                writeln(error file);
                            while (moredata) and
                               (groupnumber=number) do
                               begin
                                   moredata:=readin(recordfile);
                                   writeln(errorfile);
                                   if checkpart>0 then errorprint
                               end
                         end(*process bad group*)
        end(*process records*);
    if not goodrecords then
        while readin(recordfile) do
           begin(*checkrest*)
              writeln(errorfile);
              if (typecode='I') and (checkidentifier>0)
                   then errorprint;
              if (typecode='P') and (checkpart>0)
                   then errorprint
           end(*checkrest*)
end(*main*).
```

Program code diagrams are shown in Figures 6.10 and 6.14. Each of these diagrams contains all the three forms (sequence, alternation, repetition) found in structured programs. Not surprisingly, the program code diagram can represent any structured program.

This diagram can also annotate record structures. For example, Figure 6.16 shows the declaration in PASCAL of the structure of the input records used in our example, and Figure 6.17 shows an equivalent diagram. Compare

```
type
    digit:0..9
    code=(I,P);
    alfa=packed array[1..30]of char;
    numeral=array[1..6]of digit;

    inrec=record
            number:numeral;
            case typecode:code of
                I:(name:alfa; address:alfa; percent:real);
                P:(partname:alfa; quantity:integer; price:real)
            end(*inrec*)
```

Figure 6.16   Declaration of record format.

Figures 6.4 and 6.17. Figure 6.4 diagrams the sequence of components as they flow into the program: one group after another, each group consisting of an Identifier record followed by a repeated indefinite sequence of Part records. In contrast, Figure 6.17 shows a static structure that accommodates the alternate formats of the Identifier and Part records. Figure 6.17 is truly a diagram of data *structure*, and it is so labeled.

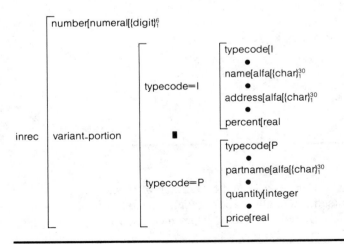

Figure 6.17   Structure diagram of record format.

In programs where input data is to be stored in memory or data is to be output from memory, diagrams such as Figure 6.17 can be used to ensure that the data structures used in memory are compatible with the input or output data flows. For many systems, only the required output is specified, and the designer is free to specify the rest. In such cases, the diagram of the output flow will determine appropriate input flow compositions and/or memory data structures [Orr 77].

REFERENCES

[Col 81] Coleman, D.; Hughes, J. W.; and Powell, M. S. "A Method for the Syntax Directed Design of Multiprograms," *IEEE Transactions on Software Engineering*, March 1981.

[Hugh 79] Hughes, J. W. "A Formalization and Explication of the Michael Jackson Method of Program Design," *Software—Practice and Experience*, March 1979.

[Jac 75] Jackson, M. A. *Principles of Program Design*. New York: Academic Press, 1975.

[Jac 76] ———. "Constructive Methods of Program Design," in K. Samuelson (ed.), *Proceedings of First Conference of the European Cooperation in Informatics; Lecture Notes in Computer Science, Vol. 44*. New York: Springer-Verlag, 1976. (Also in [Berg 79] and [Fre 80b].)*

[Orr 77] Orr, K. T. *Structured Systems Development*. New York: Yourdon, 1977.

[War 76] Warnier, J. D. *Logical Construction of Programs*. New York: Van Nostrand Reinhold, 1976.

[War 78] ———. *Program Modification*. Leiden and London: Martinus Nijhoff, 1978.

PROBLEMS

1. Provide a composition diagram for:
   (a) The report of Problem 1 of Section 2.2.2.
   (b) The report of Problem 2 of Section 2.2.2.
   (c) The report of Problem 3 of Section 2.2.2.
   (d) The input of Problem 2 of Appendix D.
   (e) The input of Problem 4 of Appendix D.
   (f) The outputs of Problem 11 of Appendix D.

---

*See Appendix B: Bibliography.

2. The input to a bank's transaction processing program is structured according to the following data flow definitions:

input=date·{customer_transaction}·'END'
date=year·month·day
customer_transaction=account_number·(deposit|withdrawal)
deposit='D'·amount
withdrawal=['W']·amount

The symbols D and W in the last two definitions are transaction codes, and END is a reserved sequence of characters signifying end-of-input.

(a) Provide a composition diagram corresponding to the data flow definitions.

(b) Provide a composition diagram of the program process-input.

3. The input stream to a program is a file of records, each record containing an order number, a product number, and a quantity. An order can contain several products. The records are already sorted in ascending order by product number.

The output of the program is a report, one line for each record, in the same order as the input records. Each output line contains an order number, product number, quantity (all from the input record) product price, and product total. The final line of the report is a grand total equal to the sum of all product totals.

The program contains a table PRODPRICE, each entry of which contains a product number and corresponding product price. On each output line the product total equals product price times quantity.

(a) Provide a composition diagram of the input stream.

(b) Provide a composition diagram of the output stream.

(c) Identify an input component for each output component.

(d) Provide a composition diagram for the program.

(e) List the executable operations of the required program.

(f) Provide a program code diagram and pseudocode for the required program.

4. A file of records is arranged into groups. The first record in each group is a header record containing, among other information, the value of a key. Each succeeding record in the same group is a detail record containing the same key value and also an integer amount. The groups are arranged in ascending order on the basis of their key value. It is desired to produce a report showing for each key value the totals of the amounts on the detail records.

(a) Provide a composition diagram of the input stream.

(b) Provide a composition diagram of the output stream.

(c) Identify an input component for each output component.

(d) Provide a composition diagram for the program.

(e) List the executable operations of the program.

(f) Provide a program code diagram and pseudocode for the required program.

5. A program is desired for Problem 4 but the input has been incorrectly diagrammed as follows:

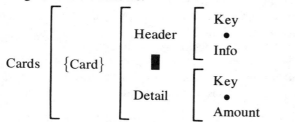

(a) Derive the program composition diagram that results from using this incorrect input.

(b) State why the diagram just derived can (or cannot) achieve the desired processing.

6. Consider the example of Section 6.2.4.

(a) List the errors of format or sequence that can occur in Identifier records.

(b) List the errors of format or sequence that can occur in Part records.

(c) Give the program code for the functions checkidentifier and checkpart and the procedure errorprint.

7. The president of Super Airlines receives a daily report on the operations of her airplanes. Super Airlines flies only back and forth between San Francisco and Los Angeles (a trip taking 50 minutes), and the flights leave every hour on the hour from 10 A.M. to 10 P.M. Every evening, from reports filed by the pilots, a set of punched cards is prepared for each airplane. Each punched card contains the airplane number, an hour of day using the 24-hour clock (e.g., 10 for 10 A.M., 12 for 12 noon, 13 for 1 P.M., etc.) and one of the codes OUT or FLY. The code OUT signifies that the plane was out for repairs, and in this case the card contains a reason for the outage. The code FLY indicates that the plane flew beginning that hour, and in this case the card contains a destination (SFO or LAX), a sales amount (total of tickets sold), and a costs amount (fuel costs, etc.). Within the set for each airplane, the cards are in order by time (earliest time first), and the sets are arranged in order by airplane number (lowest number first). The report given to the president the next morning lists each input card and has a final totals line showing (for the flights taken) the total of all sales, the total of all costs, and the profit=total sales − total costs.

(a) Provide composition diagrams of the input and output streams.

(b) Identify an input component for each output component.

(c) List the executable operations of the required program.

(d) Provide a composition diagram, program code diagram, and pseudocode for the required program.

(e) The president has decided that she would also like a totals line for each airplane, showing (for the flights taken) the total of sales, costs and profit for that airplane. Provide an extended program code diagram and pseudocode including this modification.

(f) The program obtained in (e) is to be extended to allow for input errors. An error card will be ignored in preparation of the president's report, but an error report will be printed containing one line for each erroneous card. Provide an extended program code diagram allowing for errors.

(g) Provide pseudocode for the extended program that allows for errors.

8. The president of Super Airlines has decided that the report of Problem 7 does not give her the information she needs. She wants to find out which hours of the day are most heavily traveled, and also which airplanes are costing the most for repairs. She has asked for a new report to be produced from the input cards of Problem 7. The new report will contain a line for each airplane, showing

> Airplane number
> Total daily sales=total of sales for all flights actually flown by that airplane
> Total daily costs=total of costs for all flights actually flown by that airplane
> Daily gross profit=total daily sales − total daily costs
> Total daily outage=total of repair costs for all OUT cards+ $1000\times$(number of flights for which airplane was out)
> Daily net profit=daily gross profit − total daily outage

Each OUT card will now have a repair costs field. The new report will also contain a line for each hour of the day, showing

> Hour of the day
> Total hourly sales=total of sales for all flights actually flown that hour
> Total hourly costs=total of costs for all flights actually flown that hour
> Hourly gross profit=total hourly sales − total hourly costs
> Total hourly outage=total of repair costs for that hour+ $1000\times$(number of flights out that hour)
> Daily net profit=hourly gross profit − total hourly outage

Finally, the new report will have a final totals line showing

Final sales=total of all sales for flights actually flown
Final costs=total of all costs for flights actually flown
Final gross profit=final sales − final costs
Final outage=total of outage and repair costs for all flights not flown
Final net profit=final gross profit − final outage

(a) Provide composition diagrams of the input and output streams.
(b) Identify an input component for each output component.
(c) List the executable operations of the required program.
(d) Provide a composition diagram, program code diagram, and pseudocode for the required program.
(e) State the errors that can occur. Provide an extended composition diagram of the program, allowing for errors.
(f) It has been decided that erroneous cards will not be used in the calculation. However, the word ERROR will appear at the extreme right of the line for any airplane for which an erroneous card is found. Provide a program code diagram and pseudocode for the extended program that processes errors in this fashion.

9. Real Rock Records, a wholesale record dealer, uses a file of punched cards to keep track of its inventory of record titles. When a new title is put into inventory, a punched card with the word NEW, the record's number, title, artist, company, and the quantity of records is put into the file in order by record number. During each month, every time records are sent out, a punched card with the word OUT, the record number, title, artist, company, and quantity of records sent out is added to the file as the last of the set of cards for that record. Every time replacement records come into the inventory, a punched card with IN, the record number, title, artist, company, and quantity of records is added to the file as the last of the set of cards for that record.

   At the end of every month, the punched card file is processed by a program INVEN to produce a new punched card file giving the inventory status at the end of the month. All of the cards produced begin with the word STOCK.

(a) Provide composition diagrams of the output and input. Identify an input component for each output component.
(b) Provide a composition diagram and a pseudocode version of program INVEN.
(c) An extended version of INVEN, called INVEN1, is now desired. INVEN1 will produce the new punched card file and also a report summarizing the activity for each record. This report will have the title SUMMARY ACTIVITY, and for each record will have a line containing the record number, title, artist, company, stock on hand at

beginning of month, total records placed in inventory, total records taken from inventory, and stock on hand at end of month. Provide the composition diagram of the summary report, and identify an input component for each summary report component.

(d) Provide a program code diagram and a pseudocode version of IN-VEN1.

(e) An alternative extended program called INVEN2 is desired, which will allow for input errors. INVEN2 produces an error report entitled INPUT ERRORS, each line of which lists an erroneous input card and states the processing action taken for that error. The last line of the report reads END OF INPUT ERROR CARDS. INVEN2 is intended to produce the new punched card file in the same way as INVEN, ignoring the contents of erroneous input cards as necessary. State the errors that could occur in the input. Give an extended program code diagram which includes listing each error card but ignoring the error card in the calculations. Give the pseudocode for INVEN2.

(f) You have just had the brilliant idea of writing an extended program INVEN3, which combines the functions of INVEN1 and INVEN2. Specifically, INVEN3 will also produce the summary report in exactly the same way as INVEN1, except that if any card for a given record title is found to be erroneous, the word ERROR will appear after the stock on hand at end of month for that record title. Thus the summary report will also indicate the presence or absence of input errors, though it will not indicate the specific errors. Give the pseudocode for INVEN3. You may assume that the two report files can be produced concurrently.

10. An employee master file has a record for each employee, containing employee number, last name, first name, hourly rate, year-to-date gross salary, year-to-date federal taxes withheld, and year-to-date state taxes withheld. The records are in ascending order by employee number.

A weekly time file, also in ascending order by employee number, contains a record for each employee who worked during that week. The record has the employee's number and total hours worked for the week.

A program is desired to print each employee's paycheck and update the master file. Employees are to be paid their hourly rate for total hours ≤40, 1.5×hourly rate for all hours in excess of 40. Federal tax withheld is 10 percent of gross salary, and state tax withheld is 3 percent of gross salary.

(a) Provide composition diagrams for each input and output.

(b) Provide a program code diagram.

(c) Provide a pseudocode version of the program.

11. International Computer Products keeps close watch on both the domestic and foreign sales of its microcomputers. Each month the company ac-

cumulates a file, kept in order by product number, of domestic sales. Each record in the file represents one sale and contains a product number and a quantity. An identical file is accumulated for foreign sales. At the end of the month, these files are processed against a product description file (also in order by product number), each record of which contains a product number, text description, a domestic price, and a foreign price. (Companies often have different domestic and foreign prices for their products.) Two reports are produced for the vice-president in charge of sales. The inactive products report has a line giving product number and description for each product that has had no sales during the month. The active products report has, for each product sold during the month, a line giving product number, description, total quantity sold, value of domestic sales, and value of foreign sales. These are defined as follows:

Total quantity=sum of quantities from all sales (both foreign and domestic)
Value of domestic sales=domestic price×(sum of quantities of domestic sales)
Value of foreign sales=foreign price×(sum of quantities of foreign sales)

The active products report also has a final line showing total domestic sales (=sum of domestic sales for all products) and total foreign sales (=sum of foreign sales for all products).

(a) Provide composition diagrams of each input and each output. Also give the diagrams of the composite input, obtained by merging the different input streams. Identify an input component for each output component.

(b) Provide a program code diagram and a pseudocode version of the required program.

(c) What errors could occur in the input streams? Give an extended program code diagram allowing for input errors.

(d) Give a pseudocode version of the extended program, allowing for input errors, which also produces an error report with a line for each error.

12. A sales company maintains a customer master file, an invoice file, and a payment file. The customer master file contains a record for each customer. The customer record has a customer number, name, address, telephone number and balance due. The invoice file has a record for each item purchased. Each item record has a customer number, invoice number, date, part name, quantity, and price. An invoice may have one or many items. There may be no invoices, one invoice, or many invoices for a given customer. The payment file has a record for each payment made by a customer. The payment record has customer number, date, and amount paid. These files are all in ascending order by customer number, within customer number by date (if applicable), and within date by invoice number.

A program is run once a month using all three files. An invoice is printed for each group of item records with the same invoice number. A monthly bill is produced for each customer who has made a purchase or payment, showing the previous monthly balance, the transactions during the month in order by date, and the ending balance. The customer master file is updated to show the new balance.

(a) Provide composition diagrams of each input and output. Give the diagram of the composite input.

(b) Provide a program code diagram and a pseudocode version of the desired program.

6.3 THE FINITE STATE MACHINE

6.3.1 Initial Concepts

The *finite state machine* is a model familiar to hardware designers, discussed in many texts [Min 67, Hop 69] and useful in software design, especially in compilers. (See the references at the end of this section.)

For the purpose of illustrating the model, let us consider example 1: a program whose input is a stream of 1s and 0s, and which must indicate whether, in the stream of 1s and 0s, there has been at least one occurrence of the sequence 101. We wish to trace the basic structure of this program.

We begin with an assertion: Regardless of the language in which the program is written, regardless of the way in which the 1s and 0s appear—in a file, as characters on a card, via a 1-bit hardware buffer—and regardless of the way in which 1s and 0s are tested, there are places or locations within the program that have certain special meanings. First and most obvious, there is a location at which the program starts, which is labeled START in Figure 6.18. Next (we assert) there is a location (labeled SEEN1 in the figure) at which the program has seen the first symbol of the sequence 101. By the same token, there must also be locations at which two symbols and then three symbols have been seen

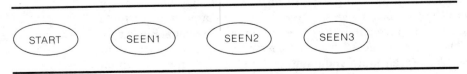

Figure 6.18 The four significant locations of the program.

by the program. These locations are labeled SEEN2 and SEEN3 in the figure. If the program arrives at the location SEEN3, then an occurrence of the sequence 101 has been detected. Thus the program intrinsically has four distinct locations.

How does the program get from one such location to another? Again, regardless of the program's language, input/output methods, or testing mechanisms, it can only get from START to SEEN1 by detecting a 1. This is diagrammed in Figure 6.19 by using an arrow from START to SEEN1, labeled with the symbol detected (i.e., 1). Similarly, the program can get from SEEN1 to SEEN2 only by detecting 0; from SEEN2 to SEEN3 only by detecting 1. All of these transactions are summarized in Figure 6.19. Of course, if the program in location START detects a 0, it stays at START; if in location SEEN1 it detects a 1, the program stays at SEEN1 (the sequence might be . . . 1101 . . .); and so on. We summarize all of the important transitions of the program in Figure 6.20, which is left to you to analyze.

Now consider example 2, a program with the same input as example 1, but which detects *every occurrence* of the sequence 101. Specifically, for every input symbol, the example 2 program

Outputs a 1 if the input symbol is the third symbol of a sequence 101
Outputs a 0 otherwise

Figure 6.19 Transitions from START to SEEN3.

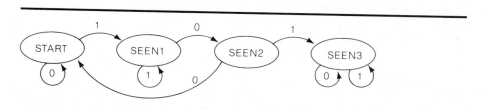

Figure 6.20 Summary of transitions of the desired program.

We now use a label x/y for each arrow, where x is the input symbol detected by the program and y is the output symbol. The complete diagram of the example 2 program in this notation is given in Figure 6.21.

Figures 6.20 and 6.21 are "abstract programs" that contain only the program details that are absolutely required regardless of implementation. Those details are the significant program locations, which we now call *states*, and the transfers of control from one state to another, which we now call *transitions* or *arcs*. Each diagram contains a finite number of states, together with the transitions between these states, and thus is said to define a *finite state machine* (FSM).

Each arc is labeled with a *condition* that must be satisfied if the program transfers from one state to another via that arc. Each condition above is the presence of a particular character (1 or 0) in the input; but, generally, an arc might have any condition or set of conditions (e.g., u<v≤w, or NAME NOT FOUND IN TABLE).

The sequence in which the program will test conditions is not considered in this model. For example, a set of arcs such as in Figure 6.22(*a*) might be implemented in either of the ways shown in (*b*).[3]

In example 2, each arc's label also includes an *action* performed when the program traverses that arc. In the example, each action is the output of a single character, but, generally, an arc might be labeled with any action (or subroutine) or set of actions, such as SORT TABLE or PRINT ERROR MESSAGE [Oli 76]. We may also adopt the convention that each state includes an appropriate action or set of actions, which the program is to perform immediately on arriving in that state.

In sum, an FSM diagram shows the essence of a program's method. The finite state machine is considered to have a finite set $S=\{s\}$ of states, a finite

---

[3]In this discussion, we assume that a finite state machine is *deterministic*, that is, for any given state and any given input symbol or condition, the output and next state are uniquely determined. In other words, a deterministic FSM can transfer control via at most one arc. Thus, in Figure 6.22(*a*) the conditions C_1 and C_2 are required to be disjoint.

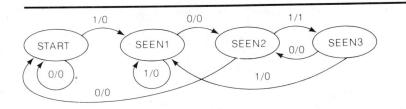

Figure 6.21 Diagram of example 2.

set $X=\{x\}$ of input symbols, and a finite set $Z=\{z\}$ of output symbols. At a sequence of time instants $t=1,2,3,\ldots$, the machine receives inputs x_1, x_2, x_3, and so on. The machine responds instantaneously to each x_t, producing a unique output z_t and a unique next state s_{t+1}, which are completely described by two functions

$$s_{t+1}=f(x_t,s_t)$$
$$z_t=g(x_t,s_t)$$

where s_1 is the initial state (or start state) of the machine. At every instant, the entire status of the FSM is captured by the value of the state variable, and the entire reaction of the FSM is prescribed by the state variable and the input symbol.

An FSM diagram can be derived from any existing program, and (as we show in the next section) a program can easily be constructed from an FSM diagram.

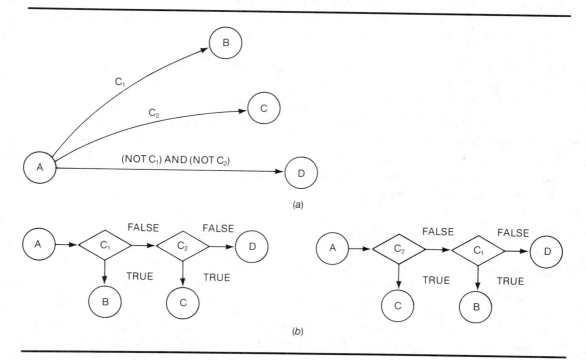

(a)

(b)

Figure 6.22 Program arcs and their implementations. (a) A set of program arcs in a finite state machine. (b) Possible implementations of the tests in (a).

The FSM diagram has two important virtues, which can easily be seen in the examples. Each diagram is *complete*, in that

· *All* transitions between states are shown
· At each state s, the conditions for transfer to any state (including transfer back to s itself) are *exhaustively enumerated*

Such a diagram shows an exhaustive analysis of the program's method. Even if it is not implemented directly, such an analysis provides the programmer with a sharply defined version of the proposed program method. For this reason, finite state models are always used by hardware designers.

Furthermore, the FSM diagram is straightforward to verify, and in many cases its correctness can be proved. In character processing such as in our example, the proof is particularly simple. The correctness of an FSM with n states is established when the model's operation is proved for all inputs of length ≤n. In other words, for either example, proof of correct operation for all input sequences of length ≤ 4 implies correct operation for input sequences of any length whatsoever. The sequences of length ≤4 are:

```
0   00   000   0000
1   01   001   0001
    10   010   0010
    11    .     .
          .     .
          .     .
```

Thus proof of correctness for 30 input sequences suffices to prove correct operation for all input sequences.

6.3.2 From Finite State Machine to Program

A program can be constructed from an FSM in a straightforward manner. (A similar technique is used in Section 7.3 for putting "unstructured" programs into "structured" format.) An integer state variable STATE with values in the set $\{1,2,3, \ldots, N\}$ is used, where STATE=1 is the initial state and STATE=N is the terminal or "exit" state. The general form of the program obtained is shown as a flowchart in Figure 6.23(a) and as pseudocode in (b). The program cycles using a while loop until the exit state value is encountered. The while condition may be adjusted for the use of two or more exit state values.

For the FSM of example 2, construction of the program is begun with assignment of the integers 1, 2, 3, and 4 to the states START, SEEN1, SEEN2, and SEEN3, as pictured in Figure 6.24. START is now represented by STATE=1, SEEN1 by STATE=2, and so on.

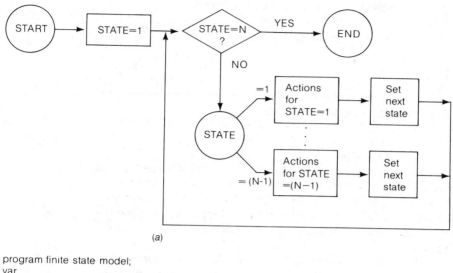

(a)

```
program finite state model;
var
   STATE:integer;
begin
   STATE:=1;
   while STATE<>N do
     begin
       case STATE of
         1:begin
             Actions for state 1;
             Set next state
           end;
         2:begin
             Actions for state 2;
             Set next state
           end;


     (N-1):begin
             Actions for state (N-1);
             Set next state
           end
     end
end.
```

Figure 6.23 General form of program implementing a finite
state machine. (a) Flowchart. (b) Pseudocode.

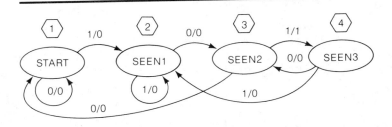

Figure 6.24 Assignment of integer labels to the states.

Example 2 does not have an explicit exit state. However, we assume that the program receives characters from the standard input file, and accordingly, the while loop condition is "not eof(input)." The program uses a one-digit variable c, and read (c) is placed at the beginning of the loop to accomplish the digit input at each cycle. Figure 6.25 shows a program for example 2, which we call program FS1.

The condition for the entire while loop of program FS1 is the presence of a further character to be processed. Each next character is placed in the variable c by a read function.[4] All other actions in the loop are based on tests of c and STATE.

Assuming this processing style, the translation from the FSM diagram of Figure 6.24 to program FS1 is completely mechanical. The diagram is translated into a sequence of program segments, each of the form:

1. Test for a particular value of STATE.
2. Perform appropriate tests and actions for that value of STATE.

Within each segment corresponding to a value of STATE, there are further tests on c and appropriate actions for each value of c. This technique follows the form of Figure 6.23 and obtains a structured program for any arbitrary FSM diagram.

An alternate technique, which is especially convenient when the sets of states and conditions are reasonably small, is the use of tables or arrays to specify actions and next states. For example 2, a 4×2 array NEXT may be arranged so that NEXT[STATE,c] contains the next state for that combination of STATE and c values. Similarly, a 4×2 array SYMBOL may be arranged so

---

[4] In real life, there is always the possibility of an erroneous input symbol, $s \neq 0$ and also $s \neq 1$. Although in example 2 no provision is made for this possibility, the example could easily be modified to explicitly deal with symbols that are neither 0 or 1.

```
program FS1;
var
  STATE:integer;
  c:0..1;
begin
  STATE:=1;
  while not eof(input) do
    begin
    read(c);
    case STATE of
      1:if c=1 then
                 begin write(0); STATE:=2 end
               else write(0);
      2:if c=0 then
                 begin write(0); STATE:=3 end
               else write(0);
      3:if c=1 then
                 begin write(1); STATE:=4 end
               else begin write(0); STATE:=1 end;
      4:if c=0 then
                 begin write(0); STATE:=3 end
               else begin write(0); STATE:=2 end
    end
end.
```

Figure 6.25   Program FS1 for implementation of example 2.

that SYMBOL[STATE,c] contains the appropriate output character. For example 2, the arrays NEXT and SYMBOL appear as in Figure 6.26(a), and program FS2 in (b) operates by using these arrays. Notice that the arrays NEXT and SYMBOL in Figure 6.26(a) are filled in mechanically based on the FSM diagram, while program FS2 is compact and simple. If desired, the arrays NEXT and SYMBOL could be combined as a 4×2 array of records, each record containing one value of NEXT and one value of SYMBOL.

For any FSM, we may construct a data table, arranged as an array of records, where each record indicates the conditions and actions pertinent to a given arc. For example 2, each record could have the structure shown in Figure 6.27. Denote the table as FSM and let each record have the fields currentstate, inchar, outchar, and nextstate. Thus, for the Ith record:

- FSM[I].currentstate specifies a value of the current state
- FSM[I].inchar specifies a value of the current input character
- FSM[I].outchar specifies an output character
- FSM[I].nextstate specifies a next state

The number N of records will be equal to the number of arcs in the diagram.

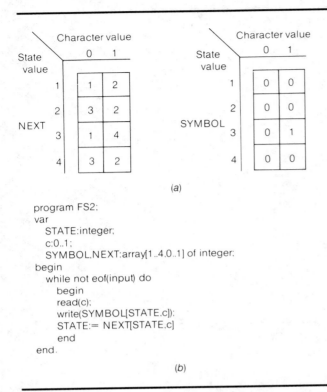

(a)

```
program FS2;
var
    STATE:integer;
    c:0..1;
    SYMBOL,NEXT:array[1..4,0..1] of integer;
begin
    while not eof(input) do
        begin
        read(c);
        write(SYMBOL[STATE,c]);
        STATE:= NEXT[STATE,c]
        end
end.
```

(b)

Figure 6.26 Alternative implementation using arrays. (*a*) The arrays NEXT and SYMBOL. (*b*) Program FS2, which uses the arrays NEXT and SYMBOL.

For example 2, the data table FSM could appear as in Figure 6.28, where each row is a record. (In the figure, the rows are deliberately arranged in arbitrary order.)

Program FS3 in Figure 6.29 shows the definition and use of the data table FSM. An error check is included in program FS3 in case a combination of state and

State	Input character	Output character	Next state

Figure 6.27 Row of a data table for a finite state machine.

2	1	0	2
1	0	0	1
3	0	0	1
4	0	0	3
3	1	1	4
1	1	0	2
4	1	0	2
2	0	0	3

Figure 6.28   The array FSM for example 2.

character that is not accounted for in the data table FSM should occur. (Of course, error checks can also be included in programs FS1 and FS2.)

Provided that program FS3 is correct and the number of rows N is sufficient, the values of FSM may be read in as data, for any finite state machine of this type. In other words, once program FS3 is checked out, say, in conjunction with tables for example 2, it can be used as a vehicle to test further models of the same type. Data for a further model would be prepared on an input file, the file would be read by program FS3, and the model would be tested. If variations of such a model are desired on a routine basis, a software system can be built to mechanize verification of the model and production of the desired programs (see Section 6.4).

Often a problem is best solved by using a separate model for each independent aspect and then combining these separate models into a single solution. For example, a solution to Problem 2 in Appendix D may be formulated by using one model for end-of-line checking and another model for accumulation of characters in a word buffer as well as for word-size checking. Each of these models can be verified separately and then combined into a single solution.

A general method may be stated for combining N independent models. Suppose models A, B, C, . . . are used. In implementing model A, use a state variable STATEA; for model B, use a state variable STATEB; and so on.

For a character processing program these models can be combined in a while loop containing the following segments:

· Segment 1: Input a character.

```
program FS3;
type
  arc=record
         currentstate:integer;
         inchar:0..1;
         outchar:0..1;
         nextstate:integer
       end
var
  STATE,I:integer;
  c:0..1;
  FSM:array[1..N] of arc;
  FOUND:boolean;
begin
  STATE:=1;
  FOUND:=true;
  while (not eof(input)) and (FOUND) do
    begin
    read(c);
    I:=1;
    FOUND:=false;
    while (not FOUND) and (I<=N) do
      begin
      if (STATE=FSM[I].currentstate) and (c=FSM[I].inchar)
        then begin
             write(FSM[I].outchar);
             STATE:=FSM[I].nextstate;
             FOUND:=true
             end
        else I:=I+1
      end;
    if not FOUND then
      write('configuration not in table')
    end.
end
```

Figure 6.29   Program FS3 for example 2, using the data table
FSM.

- Segments 2 to (N+1): These implement each of the N models and may appear in any sequence at all. An implementation may have any of the forms given in the previous section.
- Segment (N+2): There may be actions that depend on more than one model. In this case, we provide for each model to set flags or indicate its condition via a state variable. This segment contains tests for such compound conditions, together with appropriate actions.

In sum, the models are formulated and implemented independently, and a special program segment provides all necessary interactions.

6.3.3 Derivation of Optimized Programs

6.3.3.1 Elimination of Redundant Tests

The array FSM can be arranged to show, in careful order, each situation of the desired process and the consequences of that situation. This form, shown in Table 6.1, is known as a *state table*. All conditions pertaining at each state are enumerated, and thus all situations possible in the process are enumerated. Although this table uses a character as a condition, a state table may contain quite general conditions or sets of conditions; and though the table shows only an output action, in other tables complex actions or sets of actions may be appropriate [Oli 76, Wilk 77, Land 79].

Program FS1 in Figure 6.25 and Table 6.1 were both derived mechanically from the FSM diagram. Yet program FS1 has a dynamic aspect, being arranged entirely as sequences of tests and actions, while Table 6.1 has a static aspect, being arranged entirely as an assemblage of situations and consequences. In the program the sense of situation is lost, while in the table the sense of sequence is lost.

Situation and sequence are equally important aspects of a process. It is characteristic of programmers to be comfortable with sequence and uncomfortable with situations, and the reverse is true of hardware designers. We suggest that all computer professionals should master both of these aspects.

The static formulation of the state table allows the process to be stated in different ways while the exact nature of the process is formally preserved. We may ask, for example, Which groups of situations give rise to the same next

Table 6.1 State table showing all situations and consequences for example 2

Situation		Consequence	
State	Input	Next State	Output
1	0	1	0
1	1	2	0
2	0	3	0
2	1	2	0
3	0	1	0
3	1	4	1
4	0	3	0
4	1	2	0

state? More generally, we may ask, Is there a group of situations, all of which give rise to the same consequence? Are there several such groups? To answer these questions, the table may be redrawn with the rows ordered to focus on the desired consequences. For example 2, Table 6.1 may be redrawn according to the next state column, as in Table 6.2.

Table 6.2 expresses the identical process as does Table 6.1, since it differs only in the arrangement of rows; and we have seen from the discussion of program 3 that the sequence of rows doesn't matter. However, Table 6.2 has a different appearance, suggesting alternative ways of translating the FSM diagram into active code similar to program FS1.

In arranging groups of situations that give rise to the same next state, we discover that the situations within each group also cause the same output. In other words, Table 6.2 shows groups of conditions such that all situations within each group have the same entire consequence. This is a fortunate happening, and normally will not occur.

Table 6.2 may be used to achieve a program similar to program FS1 but "optimized" in the sense that it contains fewer tests and fewer redundant actions. (Certainly the code of program FS1 is straightforward and mechanical rather than elegant.) We hope to discover, within Table 6.2, tests that isolate groups of situations having the same consequence. If this can be done, one test will serve for the group of situations, so that the consequence (in our example, the next state and output) need be written only once.

Table 6.3 shows a division into groups of rows, with respect only to the output symbol. We find (as we intuitively expect) that the output 1 is given only for STATE$=3$ and $c=1$; in every other situation, an output 0 is given.

Table 6.2 State table for example 2. Rows ordered according to next state

Situation		Consequence	
State	Input	Next State	Output
1	0	1	0
3	0	1	0
1	1	2	0
2	1	2	0
4	1	2	0
2	0	3	0
4	0	3	0
3	1	4	1

Table 6.3   Division with respect to output only

Situation		Consequence	
State	Input	Next State	Output
1	0	1	0
3	0	1	0
1	1	2	0
2	1	2	0
4	1	2	0
2	0	3	0
4	0	3	0
3	1	4	1

Table 6.4 shows a division into groups of rows, with respect only to the next state, each division including all aspects of the situation that are *common to all rows in the group*. Thus we find that

c=0 ⟵⟶ group A or group C

while, to distinguish between group A and group C,

STATE=1   or   STATE=3 ⟵⟶ group A
STATE=2   or   STATE=4 ⟵⟶ group C

Table 6.4   Division with respect to next state only

Situation		Consequence		
State	Input	Next State	Output	
1	0	1	0	Group A
3	0	1	0	
1	1	2	0	
2	1	2	0	Group B
4	1	2	0	
2	0	3	0	Group C
4	0	3	0	
3	1	4	1	Group D

and, similarly,

c=1 ⟷ group B or group D

while, to distinguish between group B and group D,

STATE=3 ⟷ group D
STATE=any other value ⟷ group B

By a stroke of luck, the same set of conditions (STATE=3 and c=1) isolates both group D (next state=4) and the output 1. By using this information, we may now (again mechanically) derive another active program, called program FS4, as follows:

```
program FS4;
var
  STATE:integer;
  c:0..1;
begin
  STATE:=1;
  while not eof(input) do
    begin
    read(c);
    if c=1 then
          begin
          if STATE=3 then          Major division
                    begin
                    write(1);
                    STATE:=4            Group D
                    end
                  else
                    begin
                    write(0);
                    STATE:=2            Group B
                    end
          end
        else begin
              write(0);
              if (STATE:=2) or (STATE:=3)
                then
                  STATE:=1      } Group A
                else
                  STATE:=3      } Group C
            end
    end
end
```

Figure 6.30 Program FS4 for example 2.

Program FS4 is the kind of clever code we might instantly have written, without any analysis. However, not only is program FS4 clever, but *we know it is correct* because:

1. It has been obtained from a (presumably verified) FSM diagram.
2. The clever sequence of tests was derived by a formal process from the state table.

Thus the use of this technique can obtain both correctness and clever sequencing.

6.3.3.2 State Reduction

We may also ask, Are there groups of situations that, without changing any outcome of the given FSM solution, can be eliminated entirely from the table? Has the (presumed correct) FSM solution been formulated as compactly as it might be?

A technique known as *state reduction* (which is discussed in texts on sequential machines) eliminates entire states by merging them with other states. That is, the states $s_1, s_2, \ldots, s_N$ might be coalesced if each state table row for s_1 is, except for the situation state number, identical with a row for s_2, identical with a row for $s_3, \ldots,$ identical with a row for s_N. In other words, if every state in the set has identical consequences for all situations, then the states can be coalesced into one state.[5]

If we now reexamine Table 6.1, we find that the sets of rows for STATE=2 and STATE=4 are identical (except, of course, for the 2 and 4 in the STATE column). Thus states 2 and 4 may be coalesced, with no change in the functioning of the solution. The merging is done by eliminating one of the states (we choose to eliminate state 4), and, wherever that state number (i.e., 4) occurs in the next state column, substituting the other number (i.e., 2). The reduced table is shown as Table 6.5.

In general, though not in this example, coalescing a set of states creates the possibility that a further set of states can be coalesced. Thus, after each set of states is coalesced, the reduced table should be examined to see if it can be reduced further. So, once again ordering the rows according to the next state, we obtain Table 6.6.

---

[5]This condition can be extended slightly. Suppose that $s_1, s_2, \ldots, s_N$ have identical consequences except that, in some rows, the next state for s_1 is one of $\{s_1, s_2\}$ while the next state for s_2 is the other state in this set. In this circumstance, s_1 and s_2 may be coalesced, whereupon the difference in next state will disappear.

Table 6.5 Reduced state table for example 2

Situation		Consequence	
State	Input	Next State	Output
1	0	1	0
1	1	2	0
2	0	3	0
2	1	2	0
3	0	1	0
3	1	2	1

Table 6.6 Reduced state table, with rows ordered according to next state

Situation		Consequence		
State	Input	Next State	Output	
1	0	1	0	Group E
3	0	1	0	
1	1	2	0	
2	1	2	0	Group F
3	1	2	1	
2	0	3	0	Group G

With respect to next state only, we may distinguish three groups of rows, namely,

Group E $\longleftrightarrow$ next state=1
Group F $\longleftrightarrow$ next state=2
Group G $\longleftrightarrow$ next state=3

Observe that

$c=1 \longleftrightarrow$ group F
$c=0 \longleftrightarrow$ group E or group G

while to distinguish between group E and group G,

STATE=2 $\longleftrightarrow$ group G
STATE=any other value $\longleftrightarrow$ group E

and also

STATE=3 $\quad$ and $\quad$ c=1 $\longleftrightarrow$ output(1)
Otherwise $\longleftrightarrow$ output(0)

A reduced version of program FS4, called program FS5, is now derived as follows:

```
program FS5;
var
  STATE:integer;
  c:0..1;
begin
  STATE:=1;
  while not eof(input) do
    begin
    read(c);
    if c=1 then                         Major division
          begin
          if STATE=3 then write(1)
              else write(0);                      Group F
          STATE:=2
          end
        else
          begin
          write(0);
          if STATE=2 then STATE:=3 }  Group G
                    else STATE:=1 }  Group E
          end
    end
end.
```

Figure 6.31 Program FS5 for example 2.

By applying some formal techniques to a theoretical solution, we have arrived at a quite respectable program.

6.3.4 Applications of the Model

6.3.4.1 General Remarks

The status of a finite state machine at time t is captured by a state variable s_t. The machine's response to an input symbol x_t at time t is to give an output z_t

and change to a new status s_{t+1}, as determined by the functions

$s_{t+1} = f(x_t, s_t)$

$z_t = g(x_t, s_t)$

These reactions are completely determined by x_t and s_t.

Some problem situations (e.g., program control) are naturally characterized in this way [Sal 76]. An obvious structure for an interactive program is a set of states such that the user's input causes the program to give a set response and to change state. For a game-playing program, for example, different game situations could be defined analogous to states and an FSM model used to cause the program to make comments to the opponent, indicating the program's view of how the game is going. Deliberately modeling the control structure as an FSM makes testing easy [Cho 78].

The finite state model can be used to examine the behavior of a group of cooperating programs, where each program controls its own behavior by examining some common data and some privately held data. Since each program's control structure may be modeled as a finite state machine, the entire system can be modeled as a nondeterministic composite machine [Gilbe 72].

As shown in examples 1 and 2 of Section 6.3.1, an FSM can be used to detect specific symbol sequences within an input stream. Any symbol sequence detectable by an FSM may be annotated by a *regular expression*. Figure 6.32 shows the notations used in regular expressions and the basic method of forming an FSM for each notation.

Let $a, \ldots z, A, \ldots Z, 0, \ldots, 9$ and so on be a finite collection of symbols. A regular expression E is a finite composition of these symbols, using only the operators $\cdot$, $|$, and the braces $\{\}$ of Figure 6.32, as well as parentheses () to delineate expressions. Some regular expressions are

a

$b \cdot b \cdot b$ or b^3 (an abbreviation for $b \cdot b \cdot b$)

$\{a\} \cdot b \cdot b$

Regular expressions delineated by parentheses, for example, $E_1 = (\{a\} \cdot b \cdot b)$ and $E_2 = (a^5 | b^3)$, may also be combined using these operators. Thus we may write

$E_1 \cdot E_2 = (\{a\} \cdot b \cdot b) \cdot (a^5 | b^3)$

or

$E_1 | \{E_2\} = (\{a\} \cdot b \cdot b) | \{a^5 | b^3\}$

Lexical analyzers in compilers are almost always modeled as finite state machines. Weinberg [Weinb 73], for example, discusses an FSM model for spelling correction.

The FSM has some important limitations. The choice $z_t = g(x_t, s_t)$ cannot be delayed; z_t must be output when x_t is received. Suppose we wished to have a

Notation	Meaning	FSM to Detect
a	a symbol	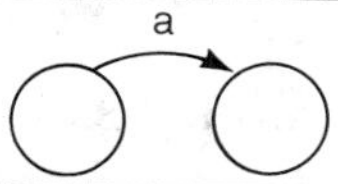
a·b	The symbol a followed by the symbol b	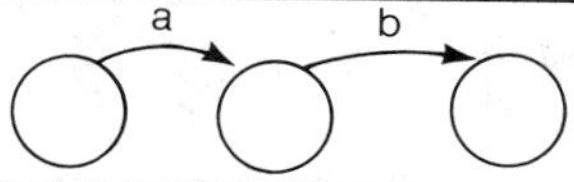
a^N	Sequence of N occurrences of the symbol a. An abbreviation for $\underbrace{a \cdot a \cdots a}_{N \text{ times}}$	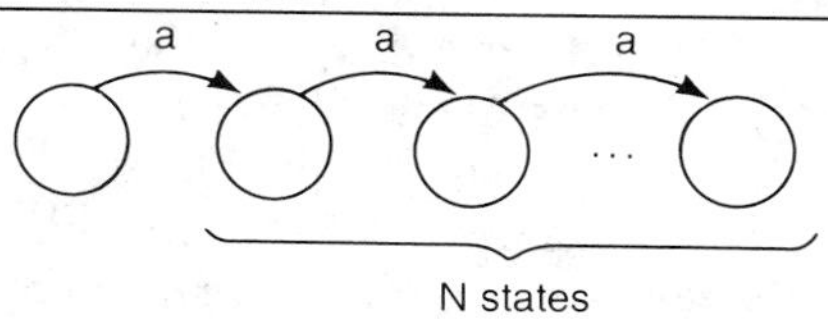
{a}	An indefinite number (0 or more) of occurrences of the symbol a	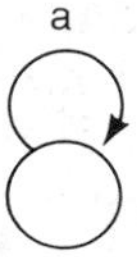
a|b	Symbol may be either a or b	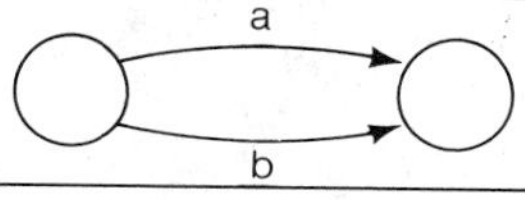
E	A regular expression. M is machine that detects it. The initial and final states of M are specifically distinguished	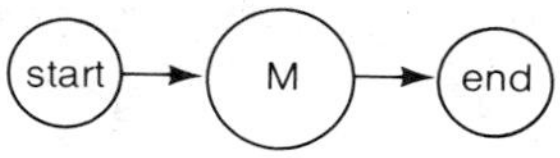
$E_1 \cdot E_2$	The expression E_1 followed by the expression E_2	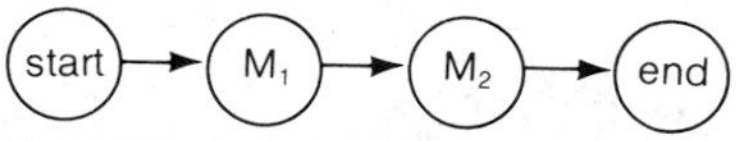
E^N	Sequence of N occurrences of E. An abbreviation for $\underbrace{E \cdot E \cdots E}_{N \text{ times}}$	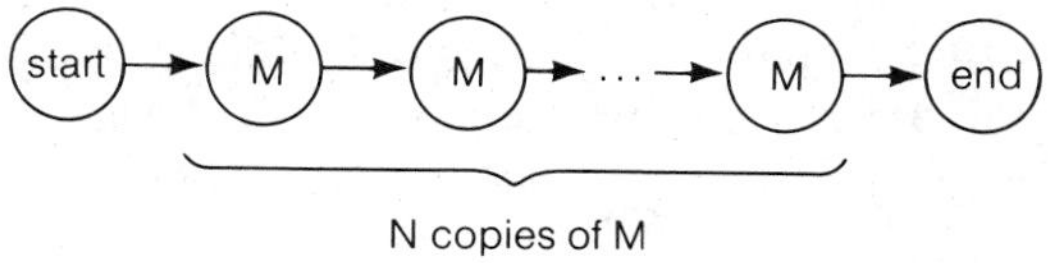
{E}	An indefinite number (0 or more) of occurrences of E	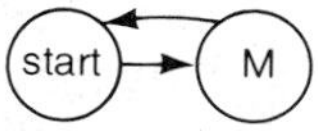
$E_1\|E_2$	Expression may be either E_1 (detected by M_1) or E_2 (detected by M_2)	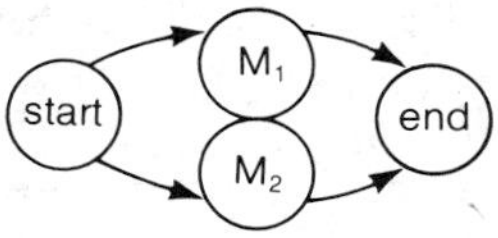

Figure 6.32 Regular expressions and their detection by finite state machines.

program that would detect one of two input sequences, abc or abd, and which would

Output 123 for the input abc
Output 345 for the input abd

Since the first symbol is not determined until the c or d appears, but must be chosen by an FSM when the first symbol appears, in principle this job cannot be done by an FSM. By extending the model to allow z_t to be a finite string of symbols instead of just a single symbol, this difficulty can be avoided.

Also, the machine's new status s_{t+1} is determined by s_t and the single input symbol x_t. Since $s_t = f(x_{t-1}, s_{t-1})$, the state s_{t+1} can be made dependent on two successive symbols $x_{t-1} x_t$. In the same way, s_t can be made to depend on a sequence of $3, 4, \ldots, N-1$ symbols if the FSM has N states. However, a machine with N states cannot "remember" a sequence of more than $N-1$ symbols. Thus there are very simple problems for which no FSM exists. An example is the processing of an input sequence $x_1 \ldots x_{2k}$ to detect whether the sequence is a palindrome, that is, whether the conditions

$x_1 = x_{2k}$
$x_2 = x_{2k-1}$
.
.
.
$x_k = x_{k+1}$

are all simultaneously satisfied.

6.3.4.2 Data-Structure-Based Design Revisited

The data-structure-based design method of Section 6.2 derives program structure from the structure of input and output files. Data-structure-based design is done in four steps:

1. Find the composition of each input and output.
2. Find correspondences between components of the inputs and outputs.
3. Determine a program structure by combining the input and output structures and using the correspondences of step 2.
4. List the executable operations and find a place in the program structure for each operation.

Any program that can be derived by this procedure is equivalent to a generalized sequential machine (GSM), an extension of the FSM [Hugh 79]. You have undoubtedly noticed that the notations of regular expressions (see Figure 6.32) are all also used in data flow definitions. In fact, when a data flow component can be expressed in terms of the basic symbols (e.g., letters, digits) or basic components (e.g., name, age) by using a single data definition, no matter how complicated, that definition is a regular expression and is detectable by an FSM. (The brackets [ ] used in data flow definitions are not really necessary since an expression such as A·[B]·C can always be written as A·C|A·B·C.) That same condition (expression by a single definition) is also necessary to obtain a composition diagram. Thus every data-structure-derived program processes input streams described by regular expressions and produces output streams described by regular expressions.

The transformation from input stream to output stream is done in a uniform way, subject to precise rules. Thus, if R,Q are regular expressions and ϵ is the null string (containing no symbols), then the following identities are satisfied:

$$R \cdot \epsilon = \epsilon \cdot R = R$$
$$R|Q = Q|R$$
$$R|R = R$$
$$\{\{R\}\} = \{R\}$$
$$\{\epsilon\} = \epsilon$$

Furthermore, the data-structure-based rules for producing output are:

$$\text{output}(R \cdot Q) = \text{output}(R) \cdot \text{output}(Q)$$
$$\text{output}(R|Q) = \text{output}(R)|\text{output}(Q)$$
$$\text{output}(\{R\}) = \{\text{output}(R)\}$$

In comparison, according to Hughes [Hugh 79], a function f is computable by a GSM if and only if

- f preserves initial subsequences; that is, for any w,u,v, if w=u·v, then f(w)= f(u)·f(v)
- f has bounded outputs; that is, there is an integer bound B such that, for any sequence of symbols w and single symbol a, length(f(w·a))−length(f(w))≤B
- $f\{\epsilon\} = \epsilon$ i.e., null input produces null output
- If the output is described by a regular expression, then the input is also described by a regular expression

The data-structure-based rules for processing input streams to output streams meet these conditions. Thus every data-structure-derived program is equivalent to a generalized sequential machine. The input and output structures are determined in a notation that is equivalent to regular expressions, and the transformation from input to output obeys precise, uniform rules. These features provide the consistency, assurance of correctness, and teachability that have made the method successful.

On the other hand, the data-structure-based design can be successfully applied only to a limited class of problems. For example, a sorting problem cannot be solved by data-structure-based design since a sort is not GSM-computable [Hugh 79].

REFERENCES

[Cho 78] Chow, T. S. "Testing Software Design Modelled by Finite-State Machines," *IEEE Transactions on Software Engineering*, May 1978.

[Chu 78] Chung, P., and Galman, B. "Use of State Diagrams to Engineer Communications Software," *Proceedings of 3rd International Conference on Software Engineering*, 1978.

[Con 63] Conway, M. E. "Design of a Separable Transition-Diagram Compiler," *Communications of the ACM*, July 1963.

[Gilbe 72] Gilbert, P., and Chandler, W. J. "Interference Between Communicating Parallel Processes," *Communications of the ACM*, June 1972.

[Hei 64] Heistand, R. E. "An Executive System Implemented as a Finite-State Automaton," *Communications of the ACM*, November 1964.

[Hen 75] Henderson, P. "Finite State Modelling in Program Development," *Proceedings of International Conference on Reliable Software*, Los Angeles. (IEEE Catalog No. 75CH0940-7CSR.) New York: IEEE Computer Society, 1975.

[Hop 69] Hopcroft, J., and Ullman, J. *Formal Languages and Their Relation to Automata*. Reading, MA: Addison-Wesley, 1969.

[Hore 79] Horejs, J. "Finite Semantics: A Technique for Program Testing," *Proceedings of 4th International Conference on Software Engineering*, 1979.

[Hugh 79] Hughes, J. W. "A Formalization and Explication of the Michael Jackson Method of Program Design," *Software—Practice and Experience*, March 1979.

[Joh 68] Johnson, W. L., et al. "Automatic Generation of Efficient Lexical Processors Using Finite State Techniques," *Communications of the ACM*, December 1968.

[Land 79] Landau, J. V. "State Description Techniques Applied to Industrial Machine Control," *Computer*, February 1979.

[Min 67] Minsky, J. *Computation: Finite and Infinite Machines*. Englewood Cliffs, NJ: Prentice-Hall, 1967.

[Oli 76] Oliver, S. R., and Jones, N. D. "Program Control via Transition Matrices—A Novel Application of Microprogramming," *SIGPLAN Notices*, April 1976.

[Par 76b] Parnas, D. L. "State Table Analysis of Programs in an Algol-like Language," *Proceedings of ACM National Conference*, 1976.

[Sal 76] Salter, K. G. "A Methodology for Decomposing System Requirements into Data Processing Requirements," *Proceedings of 2nd International Conference on Software Engineering*, 1976. (Also in [Fre 80b].)*

[Weinb 73] Weinberg, G. M.; Yasukawa, N.; and Marcus, R. *Structured Programming in PL/C; An Abecedarian*. New York: Wiley, 1973.

[Wilk 77] Wilkens, E. J. "Finite State Techniques in Software Engineering," *Proceedings of COMPSAC*, November 1977.

*See Appendix B: Bibliography.

PROBLEMS

1. Each part of this problem specifies an input sequence and an output of a 1 or a 0 for each input symbol. In each of the descriptions below, the symbol s signifies the current input symbol. Provide a finite state model for each description below.

   (a) Input is a sequence of 1s and 0s,

   $$\text{Output} = \begin{cases} 1 \text{ if s ends a sequence 11 or a sequence 00} \\ 0 \text{ otherwise} \end{cases}$$

   (b) Input is a sequence of A's and B's,

   $$\text{Output} = \begin{cases} 1 \text{ if s ends a sequence of an even number of A's followed} \\ \text{by an even number of B's} \\ 0 \text{ otherwise} \end{cases}$$

   (c) Input is a sequence of decimal digits and blanks (so that the sequences of digits between blanks form unsigned decimal numbers),

   $$\text{Output} = \begin{cases} 1 \text{ if s is a blank and the preceding number is} \\ \text{divisible by 20 or divisible by 25} \\ 0 \text{ otherwise} \end{cases}$$

   (d) Input is a sequence of A's and B's,

   $$\text{Output} = \begin{cases} 1 \text{ if s ends a sequence of m A's and n B's such} \\ \text{that } m+n=5q \text{ for some } q \geqslant 1 \\ 0 \text{ otherwise} \end{cases}$$

   (e) Input is a FORTRAN program,

   $$\text{Output} = \begin{cases} 1 \text{ if s is a blank and the preceding symbols are a} \\ \text{FORTRAN reserved word (e.g., READ, WRITE,} \\ \text{IF, GOTO, DO, etc.)} \\ 0 \text{ otherwise} \end{cases}$$

2. Design a program, based on a finite state model, which determines if an input puzzle card for project 4 contains a "proper" puzzle.

3. Each action of a program that, in state m and detecting the current input symbol A, outputs a B and enters the next state n, can be specified by a "statement" of the form

   D(m,A)=(B,n)

   Design a program, based on a finite state model, which can process such statements, entering the values from the card into appropriate places in the array FSM. (In other words, this program is given a set of statements of the form above and from these loads the array FSM.)

4. Extend programs 1, 2, 3, and 4 so that, in case a situation arises that was not provided for, an error output is given indicating precisely the error condition.

5. Extend program 3 so that, when an input sequence is processed, a sequence of lines of the form

   is output, where the x's are input characters, the arrow points to the current input symbol, and n is the current state.

6. The input to a bank's transaction processing program is structured according to the following data flow definitions:

   Input=date·{customer-transaction}·'END'
   Date=year·month·day
   Customer-transaction=account-number·(deposit|withdrawal)
   Deposit='D'·amount
   Withdrawal=['W']·amount

   The symbols D and W in the last two definitions are transaction codes, and END is a reserved sequence of characters signifying end of input.
   (a) Provide a finite state model that processes this input stream, giving the following output:

   The letter B at completion of input of the date
   The letter T at completion of input of each transaction
   The letter E at input of the sequence END

   Extend the data flow definitions as necessary so that all components (e.g., account-number, amount) are completely specified. (Hint: The model is simplified if each component has a unique first symbol. For example, each account-number might begin with the character #, and each amount might begin with the character $.)

(b) Extend the finite state model for errors in the input stream. The extended model outputs the letter X, if no date is given, and the letter I at completion of each incorrect transaction.

(c) Compare the solution of (b) above with the solution of Problem 1 of Section 6.2.

Each of the next two problems requires a finite state model that performs some action for each input symbol. The action may be output of a symbol, or addition of a symbol to the buffer, or output of a buffer, or some other action. Accordingly, the set of actions to be performed must first be determined and then used in the processing of the input symbols.

7. Input is a Roman numeral ≤MMM (as in Problem 3 of Section 2.3.2) followed by a period. Output is the equivalent number in Arabic notation. (Hint: Make sure you understand the rules for forming Roman numerals.)

8. Input consists of strings of text, which have been prepared for some printing device. In addition to alphanumeric characters, the text contains the characters: N, which signifies the start of a new line; B, which signifies a blank; and E, which signifies end of the text and appears only as the last character.

You may assume that all "words" in the text are composed of the characters {a,b} and that there are no punctuation or numeric characters. Each input string begins with N, consists of "words" separated by sequences of B and/or N characters, and ends with E. B and/or N characters may (or may not) appear before the first "word" or after the last "word."

(a) Provide a finite state model whose output is the sequence of words, one at a time. Assume that the output device will handle any output word.

(b) Can this model be applied to Problem 2 of Appendix D?

(c) Give data flow definitions and a composition diagram for the text input. Also give a data-structure-based program whose output is the sequence of words, using the method of Section 6.2.

(d) Compare the solutions of (a) and (c).

9. Consider the lending library system shown in Figure 3.13.

(a) List each possible state of each customer process, each book process, each loan process, and the library process.

(b) Provide a finite state model showing how each process progresses from state to state, the input that causes each transition, and the output given during each transition or state.

(c) Devise a set of tables for each process to use to determine its output and next state, based on its current state and current input.

6.4 TABLE-DIRECTED PROCESSES

6.4.1 Basic Concepts

Most programmers have seen the use of a program variable (or in PASCAL the use of a constant declaration) to "hide" a specific constant from the program. For example, a variable TCAP initialized to 25 (or in PASCAL declared as const TCAP=25) may represent a table capacity of 25. Since the name TCAP appears everywhere in the program in place of the specific constant 25, the table capacity may be changed everywhere throughout the program by initializing TCAP to a different value (say, 30). By using the variable name TCAP and hiding the constant in TCAP, the program text has been made into a function of the TCAP value. In a sense, this technique produces a class of programs, one program for each possible value of TCAP.

Values such as TCAP are parameters of the program, comparable to subroutine parameters, and are isolated because they might vary from time to time. In arranging the program to use the variable TCAP instead of using a constant, the programmer analyzes the pattern of use of the table capacity and changes the program to work with a variable rather than a constant.

A technique found in most business data processing is the use of numeric codes to direct the processing. In a banking system, the first data in the record containing a deposit transaction might be a numeric code of 1 (called a *transaction code*) while a withdrawal transaction might have a numeric code of 2. The appropriate subprogram for processing each transaction is always chosen by examination of the transaction code. A program that operates in this way is called *transaction-driven*. The transaction code acts as a parameter to the program, and the value in the transaction code directs the process.

Table-direction is an extension of these ideas. In a table-directed program P, for example, constants are hidden in data tables $T_1, T_2, \ldots, T_k$. As shown in Figure 6.33, these tables are combined with an interpreter program P* so that P consists of the tables $T_1, \ldots, T_k$ together with P*. Again, the effect is a class of programs, one program for each particular set of constants in the tables $T_1, \ldots, T_k$.

More formally, a *table function* is a function defined for a finite number of values that may be summarized in a table. A process P that calculates the function by means of such a table is a *table-directed process*.

The purpose of table-direction is to allow easy variation of a process by using the data values in the tables as parameters to the process. To understand the origins of this method, consider a commercial application such as a program to bill customers. Each company wants its billing program to reflect its desired options and choices. Suppose now that a service bureau contracts with the companies A, B, C, D, and E to do their billing. Naturally, the five

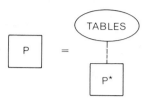

Figure 6.33   Components of a table-directed process.

companies have different processing options in mind, but the service bureau wishes to write only one program. If there are 20 different YES/NO options, the billing program can be parameterized by the use of 20 flags.

The parameterization can be done in two different ways. One is to arrange the billing program as a procedure whose arguments are the flags, while each call passes the appropriate set of values. A second way is that each company's set of flag values resides on a file that is read by the program into a one-dimensional array VALUE, after which the program can test the Jth flag by examining VALUE[J].

The second method is table-direction. There are many variations of this idea. Obviously, the parameters of a table-directed process can be more than just binary flags. For example, each company may specify a different time span (e.g., 30 days, 60 days, 90 days) after which an account is to be sent to a collection agency. The desired value (e.g., 30, 60, 90) would then be given in the VALUE array.

The parameter values need not be read in each time. Instead, a two-dimensional array VALUE can be used, in which the Ith row corresponds to the Ith customer. Thus, when the parameter I is given, signifying the Ith customer, the program uses the values VALUE[I,1], . . . , VALUE[I,J], . . . , VALUE[I,20], still assuming that there are 20 parameters for each customer. Alternatively, an array of records can be used, one record for each customer, and different types of parameters used.

An interactive program could request a user to input the company name and then look up the name in a table to determine the record index I. Figure 6.34 shows the use of a customer name table to yield a record index.

Many tables of parameters can be used for each customer, and, accordingly, each row of the customer name table in Figure 6.34 can contain many indexes, pointers, or offsets. Alternatively, the tables for each customer can be read from files, and the rows of the customer name table can give the locations of appropriate tables.

Key words or codes in transaction inputs to the program can be used to directly drive the execution of subprograms or subroutines. For example,

Name	Index		Value
ABC	1		Values for ABC
PQR	2		Values for XYZ
XYZ	3		Values for PQR
.			.
.			.
			.

Figure 6.34 Customer name and value tables.

suppose that each customer payment transaction begins with the key word PAY. An action table can be used, in which each row explicitly specifies a sequence of subprograms to be executed. Figure 6.35(a) shows a typical row of such a table, which specifies that for the transaction key word PAY, actions 7, 15, 12, 11, and 1 are to be performed in sequence. (Action 1 is the input of the next record.) Figure 6.35(b) shows the control structure of the program.

A different word-action table can be given for each customer, so that each customer can have a different set of key words, and the sequence of actions for a given key word can be varied. A system constructed in this way is easily extended. To add a new action, simply write the action, put it in place according to its number, and modify the rows of the action table as desired. A variation of this method has been used for a generalized user interface for applications programs [Bas 81].

In many FORTRAN systems, format interpretation is done in a table-directed manner. Each format code (e.g., I,F) causes execution of an appropriate subroutine (e.g., integer conversion, floating-point conversion), and the numeric values in the format specification further direct the subroutines. Business data processing systems commonly use table-direction in editing and validating input data [Pad 73, Coa 74].

This book contains several examples of table-direction. One of the models of Section 3.4, for example, embodies table-direction. In Section 6.3, two table-directed implementations of a finite state machine are shown in Figures 6.26, 6.27, 6.28, and 6.29. Lastly, Section 8.2.1.3 discusses the use of table-directed algorithms in checking key words and in testing for permissible combinations.

In each case, a model of the process is derived, in which each type of variation is isolated. The particular values specifying a desired variation are hidden in tables or "variation variables." The interpreter program P* is then constructed as an archetype or pattern of the desired algorithm, using table

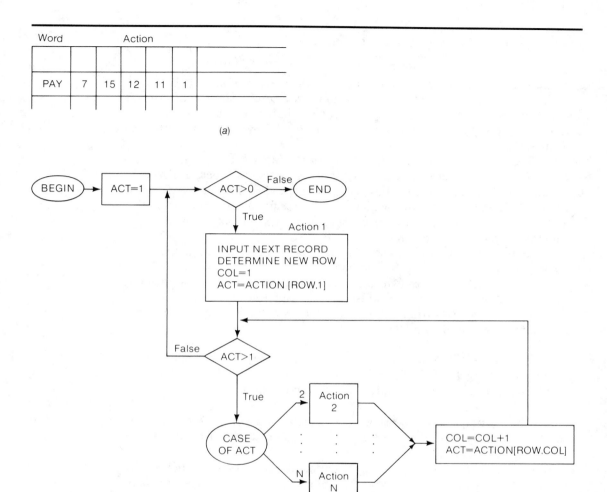

Word		Action					
PAY	7	15	12	11	1		

(a)

Figure 6.35 Key-word-driven subprogram execution. (*a*) Word-action tables. (*b*) Control structure of program.

elements or variation variables instead of constants. Consequently, the interpreter P* embodies the pattern of usage of the variation values. The mechanisms of P* are concerned with cycling or searching through the tables and with general conditions in the tables. P* is ignorant of specific values, since these are hidden. Consequently, once P* has been completely verified, it is guaranteed to perform correctly with any proper table.

6.4.2 Important Problems in Table-Direction

To illustrate some of the concepts and difficulties inherent in table-direction, let us consider a program that takes as an input a source string S of symbols and gives as output a target string T of symbols. The function f, which translates from S to T, is defined over substrings of S by a function table such as in Table 6.7.

Table 6.7 is interpreted as follows. When the input substring ABC is detected within the string S, the output symbol X is output to appear as part of T; when PQ is detected in the input, RST is output; and so on. Thus f(ABC)=X, f(PQ)=RST, and so on. In this way, Table 6.7 specifies a conversion from S to T. An interpreter program that detects substrings of S and outputs appropriate substrings of T is now required.

It is important to ask (as we should about any proposed technique), how we could get into trouble using this method.

The source substrings shown in Table 6.8 suggest difficulties in detecting source substrings. The program must have specific rules for detecting a substring in the source substring column. But which string (or strings) of Table 6.8 should be detected for, say, S=XABCX?

1. Should it be ABC? And, if so, should it be the first or last entry of the table?
2. Should it be AB? Or BC? Or C?
3. Should it be some set or sequence of the above substrings?

And, which string (or strings) should be detected for, say, S=XABCAX? In this case, we have all of the possibilities just mentioned, and also CBA, which "overlaps" ABC in the source string.

To resolve such questions, the specification of a process using such a table must state a *detection procedure* that indicates how substrings are to be detected. There are many possible procedures, among them

· Choose the longest substring

Table 6.7 Table of string substitutions

Source Substring	Target Substring
ABC	X
PQ	RST
•	
•	
•	

- Choose the shortest substring
- Choose *all* substrings

No one procedure is "best," or "required"; but the given procedure must be able to resolve conflicts among possible choices, such as those in Table 6.8. The interpretation procedure may allow different substrings to be chosen in some sequence; for example, for S=XABCX, a particular interpretation may allow choice of AB, then BC, then C, then ABC.

Another question to be resolved is: What are the rules for forming the target string? Also, What target string should be given for a substring that does not appear in the table? For the input S=XABCX, assuming X is not in the source substring column:

1. Should it be ignored, and no output given?
2. Should it be transmitted to the target string (so that the target substring is X)?

Again, it does not matter which interpretation is chosen, if the chosen interpretation can resolve potential conflicts of output.

The problem of detecting substrings and giving output for them can be handled in another way. The detection procedure may be arranged so that one substring at a time is chosen, and the process is allowed also to transform the detected substring, producing a new input substring. The processing function may now be shown as in Table 6.9.

Table 6.9 is interpreted as follows. If S=. . .ABCBA. . . and ABC is detected, then X is output as part of the target string, and also C replaces ABC in the source (i.e., ABC is transformed to C), so that after the replacement or transformation, S=. . .CBA. . . and CBA can now be detected.

However, this technique allows some dangerous possibilities, as shown in Table 6.10. For example, if S=. . .X. . ., and X is detected using Table 6.10, then S=. . .Y. . . after transformation of X. According to Table 6.10, it is possible that Y is now detected. Thus we may have an infinite sequence of detections: first X, then Y, then X, then Y, and so on.

Table 6.8   Table illustrating difficulties in interpretation

Source Substring	Target Substring
ABC	
AB	
BC	
C	
CBA	
ABC	

Table 6.9   Enhanced table of string substitutions

Source Substring	Source Transform	Target Substring
•		
•		
•		
ABC	C	X
•		
•		
•		
CBA	D	Y

Table 6.10   Table specifying an infinite processing loop

Source Substring	Source Transform	Target Substring
•		
•		
•		
X	Y	Z
•		
•		
•		
Y	X	Z

6.4.3 Overview of Principles

It is worth repeating that an interpreter P* does not know the specific values in a calculation; it knows only how to use or interpret the table. In the example just discussed, an interpreter does not have "built into it" particular substrings ABC, or X, or PQR; all of these specifics are data in the table.

Some arrangements of data, such as those in Table 6.10, can disrupt a table-directed process. In other words, combining a given interpreter and a given table may result in errors. If an interpreter has been chosen, the intended data tables should be analyzed for consistency with that interpreter.

A properly constructed interpreter P* contains an explicit procedure for each possible consistent condition of its tables. Such conditions are defined in a general way since the interpreter does not deal with data details. For the previous example, the following conditions may be defined:

- Two substrings in the table are identical
- Two substrings are in the table, and one contains the other (e.g., ABC contains AB, or ABC contains BC)
- Two substrings in the table "overlap" (e.g., ABC and CBA "overlap" in the symbol C)
- Two substrings in the table have none of the above relations (i.e., there is no "conflict" between the two substrings)
- A substring is not in the table

Thus, though P* must contain a procedure for each possible condition, there are only five such conditions and so P* needs only five distinct procedures. Since the conditions are disjoint (i.e., with respect to any one or two given substrings, only one of the conditions can hold), these procedures can be independent, and hence they can be independently verified. P* can be verified or tested with any data, provided that all of the general conditions above are checked. If P* is found to operate correctly, *its operation has been proven; and P* is now guaranteed to operate correctly with any consistent data tables*. Checkout of P* for only five distinct conditions is sufficient to guarantee correct operation of P* with any consistent data.

A program arranged as a table-driven process can be developed in a careful sequence of steps:

1. Tables that can be used to direct the process are visualized. The pattern of processing is determined in terms of parameters, so that constants, substrings, or special data words can be arranged as data in tables. In a sense, a model of the process is defined with abstract situations and actions. Then, each concrete situation or action of the intended processing becomes a specific instance that can be arranged in a table.

2. An interpreter (or set of interpreters) is developed and thoroughly tested for all possible distinct conditions of the tables. If the tables are well designed and the conditions are well thought out, this step should proceed quite rapidly.

3. Specific data are now inserted in the tables, and the entire program is tested. At this point, the interpreter has been verified, so that all adjustments, corrections, modifications, and so on can be made by changing data in the tables.

A program developed in this way is very general, flexible, and easy to modify and extend.

Each row in Table 6.9 or 6.10 is a specific instance of the abstract action: detect a source substring x, transform it to the source substring y, and add the target substring z to the output. The entire transformation from S to T is given by the set of specific instances, together with appropriate sequencing and interpretation.

These actions, together with their sequencing and interpretation, constitute a model of the process. A notation x // y // z may be used to represent the action of a given row of a table such as Table 6.9. Written in this way, the action may be considered as a statement in a model language (having only one statement type) in which any such transformation can be expressed. A set of such transformation statements may be thought of as a program. A model language may have as many statement types as there are abstract situations and actions in the model. As in every programming language, the interpretation and sequencing we have assumed become the implicit sequencing and interpretation in the model language.

These ideas lead to the notation of a *generator system*, as shown in Figure 6.36. By using such a system, a desired process is expressed as a program in a model language. This program is subjected to a consistency analysis and then is transformed by a table-builder program into process tables. The desired process consists of the process tables in conjunction with an interpreter program P*.

Optionally, the generator system may include programs to optimize and then transform the process tables into an active process P. In this case, the desired process is obtained as the active process $\mathcal{P}$. These techniques are now commonly used to produce compilers and specialized sort routines.

With the use of a generator system, an active detector can be produced via a two-step sequence: First, a table-directed detector is written, and then the tables are mechanically transformed into active code. This roundabout procedure has some advantages. A table-directed program is usually simple, dealing with a limited number of independent cases, and is accordingly easy to program and checkout. Once the interpreter is checked out, the specific details of the process can be devised, checked out, and easily corrected and/or modified, since these details are only data in tables. Optimization information such as frequency counts can be kept as the program is run in table-directed form.

As a last step, the tables can be transformed into the most efficient arrangement as dictated by the optimization information, and active code can then be produced. The resulting program is known to be both correct and finely tuned; and if modifications are required, a next version of the program may be obtained by revision of the data tables, checkout, and reoptimization. This procedure is not at all efficient if only a "one-shot" program is desired, but it may be very efficient for the continual maintenance and modification of often-used programs.

On the other hand, a process can be left in table-directed form, as in Figure 6.36(a), and the process and the generator system can be combined into a single system that provides its users with the capability to easily change system behavior. For example, a table-directed billing system and its generator might be combined so that a company could specify or change its processing options via the generator portion of the system.

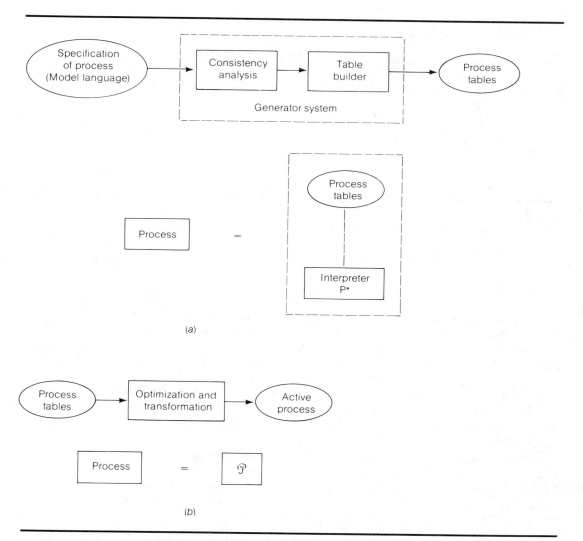

Figure 6.36   A generator system. (*a*) Basic generator system.
(*b*) An optional step.

6.4.4 Efficiency Questions

The discussion of the previous string transformation example implicitly assumed the source substring table to be a two-dimensional character array as in Figure 6.37.

A	B			• • •
B	C			
A	D			
B	E			
•				
•				
•				

Figure 6.37   Source substrings arranged as a two-dimensional array.

The searching of such an array is inefficient since no advantage is taken of the fact that AB and AD begin with the same letter as do BC and BE.

However, once a detection procedure has been chosen, the source substring table can be transformed so that the greater computing efficiency is achieved. The sequences in Figure 6.37 can be arranged as a tree of alternatives, as in Figure 6.38(a). The first symbol of a detected sequence may only be an A or a B. If an A, the second symbol must be either a B or D; if a B, the second symbol must be C or E. The tree of alternatives may be implemented as a threaded table (or linked table), as in Figure 6.38(b).

A main table (with entries labeled as 100 and 101) contains the possible alternative first symbols of a detected sequence, namely, A and B. The entry for A has a link to a subtable (with entries labeled 200, 201) containing possible second symbols in the case where A is the first symbol. And so on. (Certain detection procedures may restrict the order of symbols appearing in such tables.)

The use of a different data structure will cause the appearance of the detection program to change, even though the rules of interpretation have not changed.

The execution time of the detection program depends on the order in which symbols appear in the tables. Provided that rearrangement of this order is permissible for the given detection procedure, the tables may be rearranged in accordance with frequency count information to minimize execution time. Suppose that the detection program for our example is run for some suitable time (perhaps a month), that statistics are kept on the relative frequence of each sequence, and that relative frequencies are obtained as follows:

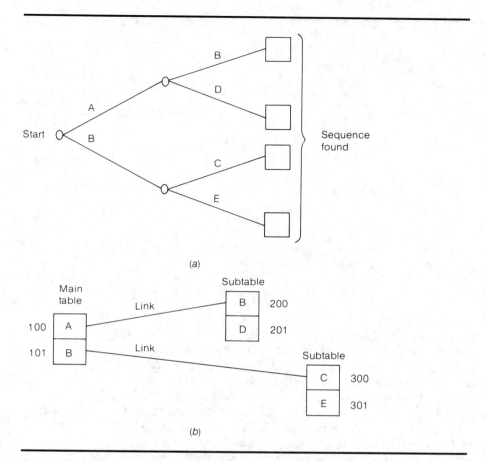

Figure 6.38   Tree of alternatives (a) and its implementation (b).

Sequence	Relative Frequency
AB	20
AD	15
BC	10
BE	55

In this case, the execution time of the detection program may be minimized with a table rearranged as in Figure 6.39.

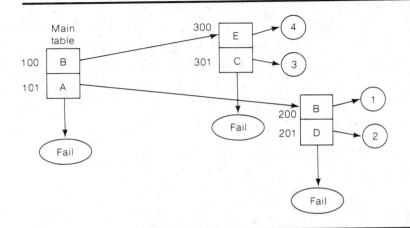

Figure 6.39 Implementation table rearranged to minimize execution time.

Figure 6.39 has been arranged so as to completely delineate the action taken for any specific sequence of characters. If first an A and next a B are detected, the detector program concludes that sequence 1 has been detected. Similarly, if B and then E are detected, the program concludes that sequence 4 has been detected. On the other hand, if A is detected but the next character is neither B nor D, the program concludes that the search fails, that is, that the sequence beginning with A is not in the table. Similarly, if a character examined with respect to the main table is neither A nor B, the search fails.

If the action of the detector program is kept in mind for each specific sequence, and each circled number or label in the diagram is interpreted as the label of a program location, active code that emulates the table-driven detector can be written as in Figure 6.40.[6]

The code above makes exactly the same sequence of tests as does the table-driven detector. The transformation from tables to active code can be mechanized if each entry of the linked tables is written as a sequence of four entities:

(100,B,300,l01)
(101,A,200,FAIL)
(200,B,1,201)
(300,E,4,301)
(310,C,3,FAIL)

---

[6]We do not advocate ever writing code in such a form; this code form is shown in Figures 6.40 and 6.41 only to illustrate the case with which active code can be mechanically generated.

and the text macro

CODE(L,C,X,Y)=[L':if symbol='C' then go to 'X' else go to 'Y']

is applied to each entry in turn. Of course, this code is crude, but the mechanical transformation into active code can be made more sophisticated. By adding an "unconditional fail" table entry at the end of each subtable, and by allowing the program flow to "fall through" on inequality, we can mechanically obtain the active code shown in Figure 6.41. Equivalent structured programs could also be mechanically produced.

```
100:   if symbol='B' then go to 300 else go to 101;
101:   if symbol='A' then go to 200 else go to 9999 (*fail*);
200:   if symbol='B' then go to 1 else go to 201;
201:   if symbol='D' then go to 2 else go to 9999 (*fail*);
300:   if symbol='E' then go to 4 else go to 301;
301:   if symbol='C' then go to 3 else go to 9999 (*fail*);
```

Figure 6.40   Program steps that emulate a table-driven detector.

```
100:   if symbol='B' then go to 300;
101:   if symbol='A' then go to 200;
102:   go to 9999 (*fail*);
200:   if symbol='B' then go to 1;
201:   if symbol='D' then go to 2;
202:   go to 9999 (*fail*);
300    if symbol='E' then go to 4;
301:   if symbol='C' then go to 3;
302:   go to fail;
```

Figure 6.41   Alternative program steps to emulate a table-driven detctor.

6.4.5 Table-Directed Design for a Tic-Tac-Toe Program

We now develop a design deliberately using table-direction rather than a "head-on" approach. Suppose that a program is desired to play tic-tac-toe so that the program never loses a game and always wins if a win is possible.

Recall that the game is played on a grid of squares; a player moves by placing an X or 0 in one of these squares. A typical position is shown in Figure 6.42(a). A player wins when three of that player's marks are in a "winning line." In Figure 6.42(b), a slashed line is shown for each possible winning line.

Specifically, we have to design the strategy of the desired program. An intuitive "best strategy" for a player about to move can be stated as follows:

1. If possible, make a winning move, which completes a winning line.
2. If a winning move is not possible, then block an opponent's winning move if necessary.
3. Otherwise, make the "best possible" move.

The best possible move of rule 3 will later be defined more precisely.

To begin, number the squares of the tic-tac-toe board as in Figure 6.42(c). Assume a one-dimensional array BOARD of size 9, and represent the ith tic-tac-toe square by BOARD[i].

How can the program's strategy be implemented? (You may find it worthwhile to stop reading and to return to the discussion after thinking about this question.)

The program might be designed to explicitly test for each specific board position and then give a move for that board position. Since there are $3^9 = 19{,}683$ different board positions, such explicit tests would require a great deal of code. Taking advantage of board symmetries could reduce the number of required distinct positions by many factors (say, 20). However, if the program considers only a subset of the board positions, then subroutines are required to transform an arbitrary board position to a program-considered board position, to keep track of the required transformation, and to transform the computed move back to the original arbitrary position to communicate with the opponent.

We insist on using the table-direction philosophy; the program is to know nothing, and the specific details are to be stated explicitly as data. The set of

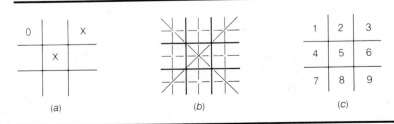

(a) (b) (c)

Figure 6.42 Diagrams pertaining to tic-tac-toe.

winning positions can be explicitly given as data in an 8×3 array called WIN, as in Figure 6.43.

There are eight possible winning lines, each involving three squares, and, accordingly, each row of WIN lists three squares that constitute a winning line. (The rows may appear in any order, and within a row the squares may appear in any order.)

Given the array WIN, conditions for a winning move or a blocking move may be stated precisely and compactly, as follows:

A. A winning move exists if, for some row of WIN, the player's marks occupy any two of the squares named in the row and the remaining square named is empty.
B. A blocking move exists if, for some row of WIN, the opponent's marks occupy any two of the squares named in the row and the remaining square named is empty.

To implement strategy rules 1 and 2, we need only a small program that evaluates BOARD with respect to conditions A and B. An array WIN of appropriate numbers of rows and columns can be used for any variant of tic-tac-toe (such as a 4×4, or 5×5, or a three-dimensional game), or for any game for which winning combinations can be tabulated.

To simplify the programming, numeric codes can be used for marks so that

1	2	3
4	5	6
7	8	9
1	4	7
2	5	8
3	6	9
1	5	9
3	5	7

Figure 6.43 The array WIN.

the sum of codes in the squares named by a row of WIN uniquely represent the board situation. Choose the codes

Empty	0
Program	+10
Opponent	−1

so that an empty square is represented as a value of 0, a program mark by a value of +10, and an opponent's mark by a value of −1. Situations of interest then have the numeric representations shown in Table 6.11.

Figure 6.44 shows program checkwin, which evaluates a position for winning or blocking moves.

Some simple code can evaluate whether the program has won or has lost, can win or block. Because the constants have been isolated, this evaluation code can be used unchanged for other variants of the game, if the values of PWON, OPWON, PWINS, BLOCK are changed appropriately.

If a win is not possible, and a block is not necessary, step 3 of the intuitive strategy calls for the "best possible" move. In this circumstance, the best possible move is one that gives the program a win in two moves. The original strategy may now be extended:

3. Make a move that gives the program a two-move win.
4. If necessary, block the opponent's two-move win.
5. Otherwise, make the "most strategic" move.

One way of implementing step 3 is to compare the array BOARD with the array WIN, searching for two rows in WIN that meet all of the following conditions:

(a) The two rows have a square in common, which is empty on the board.
(b) For each row, placing two program marks in the squares named in the row will form a winning line.

Table 6.11 Situations and corresponding numeric representations

Situation	Sum of Codes in Squares Named in a Row of WIN
Program has won	+30
Opponent has won	−3
Program has winning move	+20
Program needs blocking move	−2

```
program checkwin;

const
    PWON=30;
    OPWON=-3;
    PWINS=20;
    BLOCK=-2;

type
    gamestatus=(lost, won, canwin, canblock, undecided);

var
    BOARD:array [1..9] of integer;
    WIN:array [1..8,1..3] of integer;
    winrow, blockrow:array [1..8] of integer;
    i,j, sum, numberwins, numberblocks:integer;
    thisgame:gamestatus;

begin
    thisgame:=undecided;
    numberwins:=0;
    numberblocks:=0;
    for i:=1 to 8 do
      begin
      winrow[i]:=0;
      blockrow[i]:=0
      end;

(*evaluation using WIN array*)
i:=1;
while (i<=8) and (thisgame<>lost) and (thisgame<>won) do
  begin
  sum:=0;
  for j:=1 to 3 do sum:=sum +BOARD[WIN[i,j]];

  if sum=PWON then thisgame:=won;
  if sum=OPWON then thisgame:=lost;
  if sum=PWINS then
    begin
    thisgame:=canwin;
    numberwins:=numberwins+1;
    winrow[numberwins]:=i
    end;
  if(sum=BLOCK) and (thisgame<>canwin) then
    begin
    thisgame:=canblock;
    numberblocks:=numberblocks+1;
    blockrow[numberblocks]:=i
    end.
  i:=i+1
  end
end.
```

Figure 6.44 Program to evaluate position for a winning or
                 blocking move.

Since it is the program's turn, the opponent cannot block the placement of a program mark in the common square, and the program will win in two moves. An identical search, examining the board for two-move wins of the opponent, will determine whether a block of an opponent's two-move win is necessary and where such a block must be made. If an opponent has more than one two-move win, then the opponent will win.

Another way of finding two-move wins involves changing the code of Figure 6.44 into a subroutine EVAL whose formal argument is a board B. Two-move wins could be found by code that copies BOARD into a new array BOARD1 and then cycles through all possible program moves. For each possible program move, the code would make the move on BOARD1 and call EVAL(BOARD1). A move for which EVAL(BOARD1) yielded NPWIN$\geq$2 would be a move allowing the program to win in a two-move sequence. Variants of this technique have been used in more general "look-ahead" problems, such as chess-playing programs.

For step 5, the move can be made in the square that appears in the greatest number of still-possible winning combinations. For each still-empty square, count the number of rows in WIN such that (1) the still-empty square is named in the row and (2) the opponent does not have a mark in any of the named squares of that row. This strategy chooses square 5 if the board is entirely empty—a move that is always a "no-lose" move. The code required to implement this strategy is left as an exercise (see Problem 1).

The entire strategy just derived embodies some sophisticated criteria that can be used for other variants of the game and that should not require much more than 100 lines of code. A general but short program has been achieved, using a three-part philosophy:

1. The program knows nothing about specific details.
2. Details are given explicitly *as data in tables*.
3. The program is an evaluator of possibilities, cycling through them and using prescribed evaluation criteria.

This approach is useful in many programming situations.

The technique just shown may be said to compute, by evaluating possible board positions, an "index of desirability" for each possible move and then choose the move whose index is highest. Programs that play more complex games may evaluate board positions in several different ways, thereby computing several indexes of desirability. A composite index is then computed by a formula such as $I=k_1i_1+k_2i_2+\cdots+k_Ni_N$, where i_1 is the first index, k_1 is a multiplicative coefficient, and so on. Such a program may also be given the means to evaluate final outcomes (i.e., win or lose) and (based on these outcomes) to adjust the constants $k_1, \ldots, k_N$. This technique obtains a program that can learn from past experience and adjust its future behavior.

REFERENCES

[Bas 81] Bass, L. J., and Bunker, R. E. "A Generalized User Interface for Applications Programs," *Communications of the ACM,* December 1981.

[Coa 74] Coaker, F. W. "Table-Directed Editing for a Data Storage System," *Information Storage and Retrieval*, 1974.

[Nau 77] Naur, P. "Control-Record-Driven Processing," in R. Yeh (ed.), *Current Trends in Programming Methodology*, Vol. 1. Englewood Cliffs, NJ: Prentice-Hall, 1977.

[Pad 73] Padgett, M. I. "Tree Driven Data Input and Validation," *Computer Journal*, November 1973.

PROBLEMS

1. Write code that implements the entire strategy of the tic-tac-toe program.

2. Find the Tax Rate Schedules in the latest Federal Income Tax Forms booklet. Produce a table-directed program that computes the tax due for a given income I and tax status (single, head of household, etc.).

3. Whizzer Autos has been having trouble feeding parts into its production lines. The set of parts required for a given car depends on the options chosen by the purchaser. For example, the upholstery required for the rear seat may depend on the body color, the body style, the quality of upholstery, and whether or not the car is air conditioned. (The air-conditioning option might require extra space for air ducts.) In general, each option influences the choice of parts. The engineering department has specifications showing exactly how the parts are chosen for each combination of options. A program is desired that produces a parts list for the car from a punched card containing the options specified by a purchaser.
   (a) Provide a design for the required program. State any assumptions on which your design is based.
   (b) How are the engineering department's specifications reflected in your design?
   (c) How can the program be changed to reflect a change in specifications? Who makes the change?

4. Consider the lending library system shown in Figure 3.29.
   (a) List the types of messages that would be sent from one process to another [see part (a) of Problem 2 in Section 3.4].

(b) For each type of message given in part (a), list the information required in the message.

(c) For each type of message, devise a table structure and (if necessary) a set of encodings via which the message can be transmitted and received.

chapter seven
Module Implementation
Using Top-Down Design

7.1 COMPONENTS OF STRUCTURED PROGRAMS

7.1.1 Introduction

This chapter presents methods for developing the program text of a single module or a very small program. Because a typical program may be corrected or modified many times (and by many different programmers unfamiliar with it), the most important qualities of a program text are that it is easily

- Understood
- Demonstrated to be correct
- Maintained or modified

This chapter shows how to derive the program text in order to attain these qualities.

As a first step in achieving these desirable qualities, we require a program text to be composed according to carefully defined rules. Section 7.1 describes the *structured program* introduced by Dijkstra [Dij 70, Dij 72b], which, in principle, uses only the three forms shown in Figure 7.1. (A greater variety of forms is permissible in practice and these are described later.) Any programmable calculation can be programmed using only these forms. And when only these forms are used, the resulting program is easily understandable to programmers seeing it for the first time. There are fewer intricacies and "clevernesses" to be puzzled through. Thus maintenance personnel can discover quickly which portions of the program require maintenance or modification. In contrast, program structures that have many blocks intricately interconnected are difficult (or impossible) to comprehend fully.

Section 7.2 describes *stepwise refinement*, a technique for partitioning the program text using the structured program forms. The programmer uses the control forms to break a portion of the program text into several smaller independent programs that can be coded by different programmers. In the same way, each of the smaller independent portions is itself broken down into

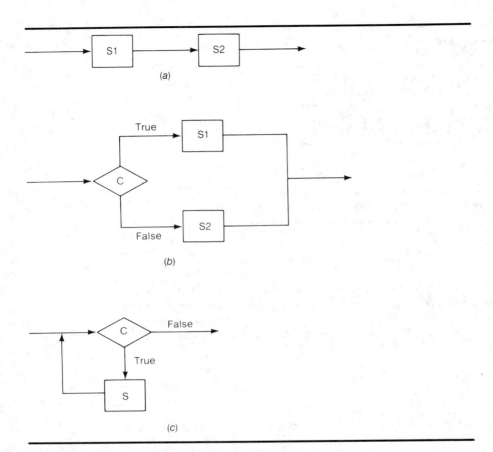

Figure 7.1 Basic forms of flow of control in structured programs. (*a*) *Sequence:* execute S1, then execute S2. (*b*) *Choice:* if condition C is true, execute S1; if condition C is false, execute S2. (*c*) *Iteration:* test condition C; if false, calculation proceeds to next step along arrow labeled false. If C is true, then S is executed and C is tested again. Thus S is repeatedly executed while C continues to be true.

further independent subportions. Stepwise refinement is a variant (intended for single modules or very small programs) of the top-down design strategy already discussed in Section 5.2.

Section 7.3 describes a method for converting any program so that it uses only structured program forms.

The requirement of carefully defined structure helps in demonstrating correctness; its help in testing can be seen clearly in a hardware testing situation. Suppose we are to test a binary adder whose inputs are two 36-bit numbers A and B and whose output is the 36-bit sum S.

If the structure of the adder is not known, then, to establish correctness, all combinations of the inputs A and B must be tried. Unfortunately, A can have any one of 2^{36} different values, as can B. Trying all combinations of these values requires 2^{72} different tests, which at the rate of a million tests per second would need more than 100 lifetimes, assuming 100 years per lifetime. In short, the device cannot be completely tested by trying all combinations of input values.

On the other hand, if the adder is known to have a carefully defined structure, then the testing situation is much different. For example, the adder of Figure 7.2 is composed of 36 identical and independent subadders named unit 0, unit 1, . . . , unit 35. The inputs are $A=a_{35}a_{34} \ldots a_2a_1a_0$ (base 2) and $B=b_{35} \ldots b_0$ (base 2). Unit i has inputs a_i, b_i, and c_{i-1} (the "carry" from the next-lower-order digit—we define $c_{-1}=0$); unit i computes s_i (the ith bit of S) and c_i, the ith carry bit. Since unit i is independent of all other units, establishing its correctness requires only the eight tests in which all combinations of a_i, b_i and c_{i-1} are tried while the outputs s_i and c_i are observed. Thus the adder can be completely tested using only $8 \times 36 = 288$ tests.

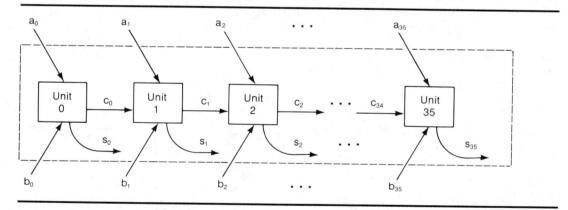

Figure 7.2 A binary adder consisting of 36 identical but independent subadders.

7.1.2 Forms Permissible in Structured Programs

Table 7.1 shows forms that may be used in structured programs. In Table 7.1, C denotes a condition to be tested. Each notation S (or S1, or S2, etc.) denotes the text of a program segment, which may be either a single statement or a group of statements using the forms of Table 7.1. Each form is shown as it appears in PASCAL and in FORTRAN 77.

Table 7.1 Structured control forms and their annotation

Form	Pascal	Fortran 77	Comments
→ S1 → ⋯ → SN →	begin S1;...;SN end	S1 S2 . . SN	Sequence or concatenation of statements

C True → S / False	if C then S	IF(C)
		S
		ENDIF
			S is executed if C is true; otherwise S is skipped

C True → S1 / False S2	if C then S1 else S2	IF(C)
		S1
		ELSE
		S2
		ENDIF
			S1 or S2 is executed, depending on C

S1 =1 ⋮ i ⋮ =N SN	case i of
	1:S1;
	2:S2;
	.
	.
	N:SN
	end
		IF(I=1)
		S1
		ORIF(I=2)
		S2
		.
		.
		ORIF(I=N)
		SN
		ENDIF
			Generalization of above. i is a condition that may have any of the values 1,...,N. If i=K, then SK is performed. Undefined for i<1 or i>N.

C False → True S	while C do S	WHILE(C)
		S
		END WHILE
			C is tested. If false, calculation proceeds to the next step along the arrow labeled false. If true, then S is executed and C is tested again. S is thus repeatedly executed until C is false

S → C True / False	repeat S until C	REPEAT S UNTIL(C)	S is executed, then C is tested. If true, calculation proceeds to the next step along the arrow labeled true. If false, S is executed and C is tested again

Use of the forms of Table 7.1 imposes a strict structure on the program text. Figure 7.3 shows the forms in a typical small program. Each form defines a localized segment of text, in which all the components of the form appear in strict sequence. Furthermore, the components are executed in precisely the sequence in which they appear in the program text, except that only one alternative in a conditional statement (an if statement or case statement) is executed. With this exception, if the components of a form appear in the text as step 1, step 2, step 3 in sequence, then the execution sequence is step 1, then step 2, then step 3. If step 1 appears in the text with component steps 1.1 and 1.2, then the execution sequence of step 1 is step 1.1 and then 1.2. The strict correspondence between the text placement of segments and their sequence of execution greatly improves the understandability of programs.

```
Sequence                  begin
                          found:=false;
    Iteration             i:=1;
                          while i<n and not found do
                              begin
        Choice            if abc[i]>x then begin
            Sequence                      found:=true;
                                          answer:=abc[i]
                                      end
                                  else i:=i+1
                              end
                          end
```

Figure 7.3   Control forms in a typical small program in PAS-
CAL.

As shown in Figure 7.3, the forms of structured programs require the use of compound statements in which a sequence of simpler statements is grouped and regarded as one statement. As an example, in PASCAL the statements

    found:=true
    answer:=abc[i]

can be grouped with the symbols begin and end to form a single compound statement

    begin found:=true; answer:=abc[i] end

which may then be used as a component of another form, as, for example,

    if abc[i]>x then begin found:=true; answer:=abc[i] end

The if statement thus formed is again regarded as a single statement, which may be a component of another form.

Table 7.1 is not an exhaustive list of permissible forms. Any form that may be represented by a structured program using only the forms of Table 7.1 may itself be regarded as a permissible form.

In particular, we may regard as permissible the DO statement of FORTRAN 77:

DO(I=1,N)
    S
END DO

where S is one or more statements. The structured program corresponding to the DO statement is shown in Figure 7.4(a). However, Figure 7.4(a) does not take into account any peculiariies of loop-index handling in FORTRAN. For example, if S includes a statement I=I+5, this statement might have no effect at all on I since in many variants of FORTRAN statements inside the loop are not allowed to alter the loop-index value. We also regard as permissible the for statement of PASCAL:

for i:=1 to n do S

which corresponds to the structured program of Figure 7.4(b).

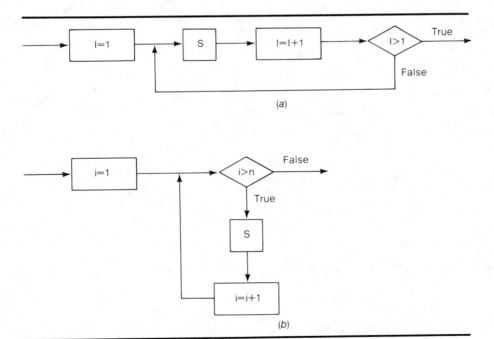

Figure 7.4   Other forms that may be used in structured programs. (a) DO statement in FORTRAN. (b) For statement in PASCAL.

7.1.3 A Formal View of Structured Programs

A structured program contains only *helpful structures*, that is, structures that foster the independence of program segments. A helpful structure has *one entry point and one exit point*. As in Figure 7.5, a dashed-line boundary can be drawn around a helpful structure (i.e., a portion of a program) so that only one arrow enters in through this boundary and only one arrow leaves through it.

Unfortunately, not every structure having this property is helpful. The concept of a helpful structure can be made more precise with the aid of several definitions, giving in terms of program flowcharts.

Definition 1: A program is *proper* if: (a) its flowchart has exactly one input and exactly one output arc, and (b) for each condition or action box in the flowchart, there is a path from the input arc to that box to the output arc.

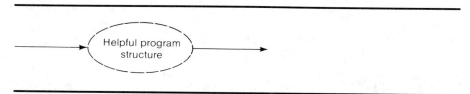

Figure 7.5 A helpful program structure has one entry point and one exit point.

All of the programs of Table 7.1 are proper, as are the programs of Figure 7.6. The programs of Figure 7.7 are not proper. Program (*a*) of Figure 7.7 has two entry arcs, program (*b*) has two exit arcs, and programs (*c*) and (*d*) do not meet condition b of definition 1.

We use the term *subprogram* to mean a portion of the flowchart around which a dashed-line boundary is drawn, as in Figure 7.8. A subprogram is proper if it meets the conditions of definition 1.

Definition 2: A *prime* program is a proper program that does not contain any proper subprogram having more than one box.

The programs of Table 7.1 are all prime, as are the programs of Figure 7.6. The programs of Figure 7.8(*a*) and (*c*) are nonprime.

Prime programs with more than three boxes have complex flows of control, so that errors in one box may affect many other boxes in the program. Accordingly, a prime program must be tested or verified as an interconnected unit. Such a program must be considered unhelpful.

Definition 3: A *reduction* of a nonprime program P is a program P' obtained by substituting an action box for a prime subprogram of P.

Figure 7.8(*b*) is a reduction of (*a*), and (*d*) is a reduction of (*c*). In each case, a single action box is substituted for the subprogram shown within the dashed-line boundaries in (*a*) and (*c*).

Definition 4: A program is *structured* if either: (a) it is a sequence, choice, or iteration form of Figure 7.1; or (b) it is nonprime and every prime subprogram is a sequence, choice, or iteration form, and (c) each successive reduction of the program satisfies either (a) or (b).

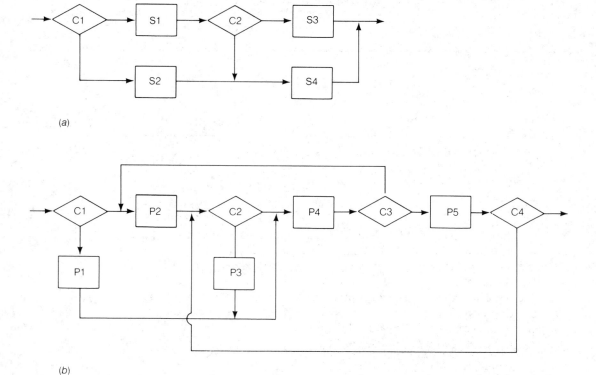

(a)

(b)

Figure 7.6 Proper programs.

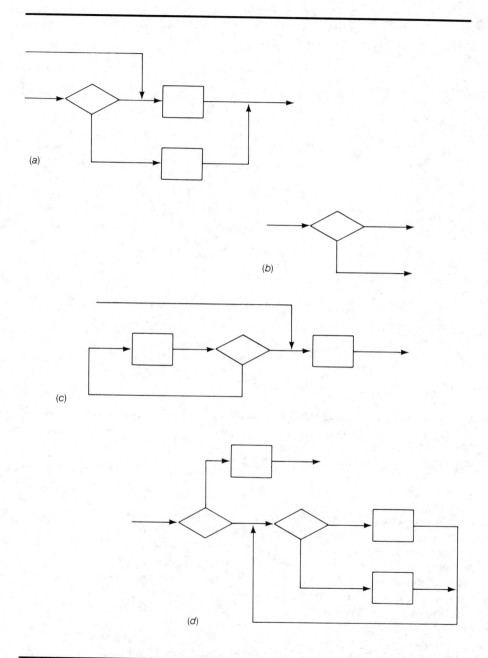

Figure 7.7   Nonproper programs.

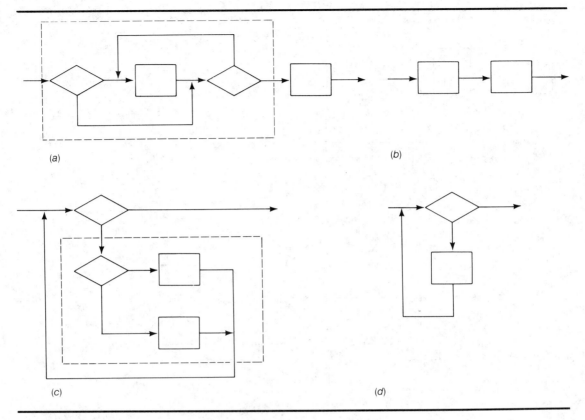

Figure 7.8 Nonprime programs and their reductions. (*a*) Nonprime program. (*b*) Reduction of program (*a*). (*c*)
Nonprime program. (*d*) Reduction of program (*c*).

Figure 7.9 shows a structured program. The smaller areas are reduced first,
and later the larger areas are reduced. The testing or verification process
follows exactly the same pattern. Due to the simplified flow of control, each
subprogram can be tested or verified independently of the others and, once
verified, can thereafter be assumed to be correct. Making an analogy, the
verification of a structured program is the sum of the verifications of its parts,
while the verification of a prime program is much more complex than the sum
of verifications of its parts.

Structured programs can be annotated neatly by conventional flowcharts, if
each control form has its own area of the flowchart and this area is allowed
only one entry and one exit arc. Each action within this area then has its own
subarea. This is the method that was used in Figure 7.9.

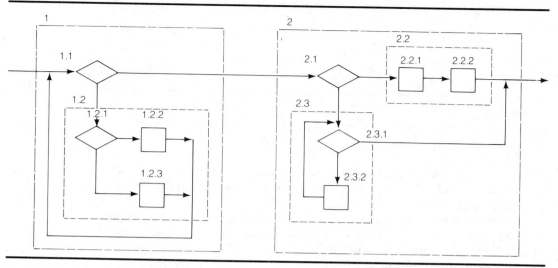

Figure 7.9   A structured program.

Also, in Figure 7.9, the components are numbered to indicate the exact composition of the flowchart. The major actions are numbered 1 and 2, the components of 1 are 1.1 and 1.2; the components of 1.2 are 1.2.1, 1.2.2, and 1.2.3, and so on.

Within the structured program's text, there is a strict correspondence between the positions of program segments and their sequence of execution (recall Figure 7.3). For this reason, a structured program can be diagrammed using flowblocks [Nas 73], tree diagrams, or (if the program uses only the forms of Figure 7.1) the program structure diagrams of Section 6.2.

7.1.4 Methods of Information Transfer

In structured programs, information is transferred between different parts of a program by the use of explicit flags or data variables. A careful style of programming is required. For example, consider a PASCAL program that finds, for a given value x and a one-dimensional array abc of size n, the value of the element of abc with the smallest subscript i such that abc[i]$\geqslant$x. Solution 1 in Figure 7.10 is an attempt at such a program

Solution 1 has a grave difficulty. Since the range of values in abc is not known, it is possible that the first value in abc that is $\geqslant$x is, in fact, 0. Thus, if answer=0 after the program segment executes, there is no information as to

```
answer:=0;
for i:=1 to n do
   begin
   if abc[i]≥x then answer:=abc[i]
   end
```

Figure 7.10 Solution 1.

whether a value ≥x was ever found. To interpret the value of answer, we need a separate piece of information that indicates whether the condition abc[1]≥x was ever satisfied.

Now consider solution 2 in Figure 7.11. In solution 2, the result found=true indicates that abc[i]≥x is true for some i, and answer is an appropriate value of abc. If found=false after execution of the for statement, the value of answer is ignored. Accordingly, the initializing of answer is no longer necessary.

```
found:=false;
for i:=1 to n do
   begin
   if abc[i]≥x then begin
                    found:=true;
                    answer:=abc[i]
                    end
   end
```

Figure 7.11 Solution 2.

Unfortunately, solution 2 also does not work. If there are several values of abc that are ≥x, then answer will be set several times and will contain the value of the *last* element of abc that is ≥x. We may ensure that answer is set only once, in solution 3 in Figure 7.12.

The condition not found is satisfied only when found=false. Thus the first time that abc[i]≥x for some i, found will be set to true and answer will be set. Thereafter, if abc[i]≥x, the condition not found will not be satisfied and thus answer is set only once.

Solution 3, though correct, requires every element of abc to be considered, even though the condition abc[i]≥x might be met at the first or second element of abc. Alternatively, solution 4 in Figure 7.13 uses the value of found to control execution as follows.

```
found:=false;
for i:=1 to n do
   begin
   if abc[i]≥x then begin
                     if not found then
                         begin
                         found:=true;
                         answer:=abc[i]
                         end
                  end
   end
```

Figure 7.12   Solution 3.

```
found:=false; i:=1;
while i≤n and not found do
   begin
   if abc[i]≥x then begin
                     found:=true;
                     answer:=abc[i]
                     end
               else i:=i+1
   end
```

Figure 7.13   Solution 4.

In solution 4, the index is increased until either $i>n$ or $abc[i]≥x$ and found is set to true. In either case, the next iteration of the loop, the condition $i≤n$ and not found, is not met, so that execution of the loop ends.

REFERENCES

[Boh 66] Bohm, C., and Jacopini, G. "Flow Diagrams, Turing Machines, and Languages with Only Two Formation Rules," *Communications of the ACM,* May 1966.

[Dij 70] Dijkstra, E. W. *EWD249: Notes on Structured Programming*, Report 70-Wsk-03, 2nd ed., Technical University of Eindhoven, Netherlands, April 1970.

[Dij 72b] ———. "Notes on Structured Programming," in O.-J. Dahl, E. W. Dijkstra, and Hoare (eds.), *Structured Programming*. New York: Academic Press, 1972.

[Nas 73] Nassi, I., and Schneiderman, B. "Flowchart Techniques for Structured Programming," *SIGPLAN Notices*, Vol. 8, No. 8, August 1973.

PROBLEMS

1. Devise a structured program, using only the forms of Figure 7.1, which implements
   (a) The case statement of Table 7.1.
   (b) The repeat-until statement of Table 7.1.

2. As in Figure 7.3, show the forms in the programs of
   (a) Figure 7.10.   **(c)** Figure 7.12.
   (b) Figure 7.11.   **(d)** Figure 7.13.

3. As in Figure 7.9, draw a flowchart and number the actions of the programs of
   (a) Figure 7.3.   **(c)** Figure 7.11.
   (b) Figure 7.10.   **(d)** Figure 7.12.

4. Draw program structure diagrams (as in Section 6.2) of the programs of
   (a) Figure 7.3.
   (b) Figure 7.13.

5. The program of Figure E.1 is written in FORTRAN 77. Write an equivalent structured program, using the forms of Table 7.1 and the DO statement if desired, but not the GO TO statement. The equivalent program should do *exactly* the process done by the program of Figure E.1. (Do not rework the program's process to make it "nicer.")

7.2 STEPWISE REFINEMENT: A TOP-DOWN DESIGN STRATEGY

7.2.1 Introduction to Stepwise Refinement

7.2.1.1 Problems in Understanding and Maintaining Programs

The use of structured program forms does not of itself guarantee that a program will be correct, or easily understood, or easily maintained and modified. Unfortunately, it is easy to write poor programs in any notation. Ease of understanding and ease of maintenance and modification have to be deliberately designed into the program text. Section 7.2 describes *stepwise refinement* [Dij 70, Wir 71, Dij 72b], a design strategy that seeks to implant these qualities into the program text. Stepwise refinement is a careful statement of the good techniques long practiced by the best programmers. It is a variant (intended for single modules or very small programs) of the top-down design strategy already discussed in Section 5.2. Stepwise refinement develops a program via successive *refinement steps*, each of which partitions a portion of the potential program text into several parts, using the structured program forms. In accordance with the top-down design philosophy, enunciated in Section 5.2.1 and in Section 7.2.3.1, initial steps deal with large program segments and broad design decisions, while later steps deal with small program segments and detail design decisions.

What makes a program easy to understand, maintain, and modify? Very simply put, if lines of code that work together in a program also appear together in a local segment of the program, that code will be easily understood. In that case, any change to the working of these lines of code can be accomplished entirely within the local program segment. Thus maintenance and modification are made easier.

Jackson [Jac 75] clearly shows this principle. Suppose that it is desired to calculate a multiplication table and print it on a line printer in the following format:

```
1
2    4
3    6    9
     . . .
9   18   27   36   45   54   63   72   81
10  20   30   40   50   60   70   80   90   100
```

The program in Figure 7.14 does this job.

Figure 7.14 is a structured program that correctly produces the multiplication table. However, lines of code that work with each other are not adjacent to each other. For example, the first output line is calculated by the segment firstline, but is printed by the segment w1 which is inside a for loop; at each execution of the do-cols segment, the previously calculated output line is printed; and the last output line (calculated by the ninth execution of the do-cols segment) is printed by the w2 segment.

This arrangement of code could be difficult for an unfamiliar programmer to understand, even through the program is trivial. A considerable improvement in understanding is obtained when adjacent segments calculate an output line and print that line, as in Figure 7.15.

In Figure 7.15, the first output line is calculated by firstline and then printed by the adjacent segment w1; within the otherlines segment, each line is calculated by do-cols and printed by the adjacent segment w2. This program is more straightforward and easier to understand.

Now consider some possible modifications of the problem. We might wish to output in a different format, as follows:

```
1   2   3   4    5   6   7   8   9   10
    4   6   8   10  12  14  16  18   20
                 . . .
                             81   90
                                 100
```

As before, multiples of 1 are on the first line, multiples of 2 are on the second line, and so on. The only change is that a different set of values is to be printed on each line. To accommodate this simple change, Figure 7.15 must be almost completely rewritten. Notice that firstline must be recoded for the new calculation of the first output line, while do-cols must be recoded for the new calculation of the rest of the output lines. In other words, the code for calculation of an output line appears in two nonadjacent places in the program.

```
              program mult1;
                 var
                   row, col:integer;
                   line:array [1..10] of integer;
                 begin
                   for i:=1 to 10 do line [i]:=0;
(*firstline*)      line[1]:=1;
(*otherlines*)   for row:=2 to 10 do
                     begin
               (*w1*) for j:=1 to 10 do
                         if line [j]=0 then write('      ') else write(line[j]:5);
                       writeln;
            (*do-cols*) for col:=1 to row do line[col]:=row*col
                       end;
               (*w2*) for j:=1 to 10 do
                         if line[j]=0 then write ('      ') else write line([j]:5);
                       writeln
                     end
```

Figure 7.14   Program to produce a multiplication table (adapted
                   from [Jac 75, p. 3]).

Last but not least, in the new format the first column of the second output line is blank, whereas the first column of the first output line is not blank. However, the program of Figure 7.15 assumes that each succeeding output line calculation will write over the values of the preceding line.

Another possible modified format is the following:

```
10  20  30  40  50  60  70  80  90  100
 9  18  27  36  45  54  63  72  81
 . . .
 3   6   9
 2   4
 1
```

```
        program mult2;
            var
                row, col:integer;
                line:array [1..10] of integer;
            begin
                for i:=1 to 10 do line [i]:=0;
(*firstline*)   line[1]:=1;
    (*w1*) for j:=1 to 10 do
                    if line[j]=0 then write ('        ') else write(line[j]:5);
                writeln;
(*otherlines*) for row:=2 to 10 do
                begin
        (*do-cols*) for col:=1 to row do line[col]:=row*col;
            (*w2*) for j:=1 to 10 do
                        if line[j]=0 then write ('        ') else write (line[j]:5);
                    writeln
                end
            end
```

Figure 7.15 An improved multiplication table program.

Here the only change is that the output lines are printed in exactly the reverse order. Once again, firstline must be recoded or, alternatively, firstline and w1 must both be moved to the end of the program; and, of course, otherlines must be recoded. In other words, code that establishes the sequence of ouput lines also appears in two nonadjacent places in the program. Again, though Figure 7.15 assumes that the values in each output line will be written over, the changed format requires successively more blanks in each line.

7.2.1.2 Principles of Design for Easy Modification

How could the original program be written so that either of the desired format changes could be easily accommodated? The precise sequence in which lines are printed is a design decision embedded in the program; the precise set of values to be printed in an output line is another design decision. In each case, the code that embodies the decision—the code that works together to effect the decision—appears in several nonadjacent places in the program.

Ross [Ros 75] suggests three important principles which allow easy program modification. The first of these is the

Principle of localization: All code that embodies a particular design decision should be localized within one specific program segment.

According to this principle, for our example, all of the code that determines the precise set of values to be printed in an output line should be localized within one specific segment; and, similarly, all code that determines the sequence in which lines are printed should be localized in one specific segment.

If this is done, a change in a given decision can be accomplished by revision of the program segment associated with that decision.

A second important principle is the

Principle of information hiding: Details pertinent only to one design decision are "hidden" in the associated program segment. These details are made inaccessible to other program segments since such details should not affect the other program segments.

For our example, the details that determine the precise values to be printed in an output line should not be accessible to the code that determines the sequence of lines, and vice versa.

Finally, top-down design uses the

Principle of abstraction: Each program segment is defined at a given level of abstraction, and is defined solely in terms of its relation as a unit to other segments of the program.

In our example, the output structure is a sequence of lines, each line consisting of a sequence of numbers. Thus it is appropriate to have a program segment outline that performs the entire calculation and printing of one output line. Similarly, it is appropriate to have a program segment outtab that performs the entire table calculation and output, by repeated executions of outline. The segment outline is understood by outtab as a unit, without knowledge of its details. On the other hand, outline is understood by segments interior to it without knowledge of how it is used at higher levels. Of course, outline should be arranged so that each calculation and printing of an output line is independent of the calculations of other output lines.

```
      program mult3;
         var
            row, col: integer;
            line:array [1..10] of integer;
         begin
(*outtab*) for row:=1 to 10 do
    (*outline*) begin
                for i:=1 to 10 do line [i]:=0;
    (*do-cols*) for col:=1 to row do line[col]:=row*col;
                for j:=1 to 10 do
                   if line[j]=0 then write ('      ') else write(line[j]:5);
                writeln
                end
         end
```

Figure 7.16 A program that easily accommodates changes (adapted from [Jac 75, p. 5]).

The program of Figure 7.16 is constructed according to these principles. For this program, designing the sequence in which lines are printed is accomplished simply by changing the constants in outtab for statement; changing the values printed in each line is accomplished by simply changing the do-cols segment. Either of these changes may be made independently of the other.

Recall the data-structure-based design technique of Section 6.2, in which the program structure is derived from input structures and output structures. In this example, the output structure and the program structure both have the diagram

table[{line}[{number}

In other words, the output component line corresponds to the program segment outline, and the output component table corresponds to the program segment outtab. The technique of Section 6.2 derives program segments in an almost identical manner. Indeed, all good design methods use the three principles we have just enunciated.

7.2.2 Mechanics of Stepwise Refinement

7.2.2.1 The Basic Steps

Stepwise refinement is a design strategy for systematically developing a program text. The development proceeds via successive *refinement steps*, each of which partitions a portion of the potential program text into several parts, using the structured program forms. Each part is then refined via a further step, the process being iterated for smaller and smaller portions of text until actual code is obtained.

Stated more precisely, the strategy begins by viewing the intended program as a single whole entity—a single action that performs the entire process correctly. As in Figure 7.17(a), we assume the intended program P, an initial data environment E_I, and a final data environment E_F. We also assume that the transformation from E_I to E_F is precisely defined.

The first refinement step serves to refine this view of the program by redefining the single action P as a *structure of actions*, using only structured forms. (We discuss later the criteria used in choosing an appropriate structure.) The structure is said to be the *refinement* of P. As an example, we may redefine P to consist of a sequence of two actions, P1 and P2, as in Figure 7.17(b).

When P is redefined in this way, precise specifications must be given for P1, for P2, and also for the interim data environment E_{12} calculated by P1 and used as the initial data environment of P2.

An important goal of this strategy is to obtain an informal assurance that the program's operation will be correct. Accordingly, we now verify that the just-obtained structure of actions (namely, the sequence P1,P2) will accomplish the process P if performed according to our specifications. If the sequence of transformations $E_I \rightarrow E_{12}, E_{12} \rightarrow E_F$ accomplishes the transformation $E_I \rightarrow E_F$, P1 and P2 may hereafter be presumed to be correct. The refinement of P into the sequence P_1, P_2 and the verification of this refinement together constitute a level of the design. The design has now progressed from the beginning (level 0) to a first refinement (level 1).

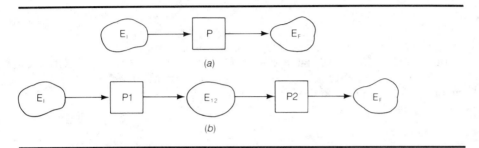

Figure 7.17 The first refinement step. (*a*) Beginning view of a program: level 0. (*b*) The first refinement: level 1.

The next design level is obtained in a similar way, by refinement of each of P1 and P2 and verification of each refinement as before. This cycle of obtaining each new level by (1) refinement of an action and (2) verification of correctness of the refinement continues for as many levels as required to obtain a level of detail sufficiently low that program coding can begin. If the verifications are careful, they will ensure that at each level the refinement is correct and therefore that every action of the design should be correct. If each piece is carefully implemented, the program should operate correctly.

Finally, the completed design is examined for the occurrence of identical or very similar actions that occur at different places in the design. These actions become the subroutines of the program.

7.2.2.2 Illustration of the Basic Steps

To illustrate the mechanics of stepwise refinement, we now develop a procedure sort(table,size), where table is the name of a one-dimensional array to be sorted, and size is the number of elements in the array [Cai 75]. The sort is required to be done via a sequence of sort passes. Within each sort pass, pairs of elements are compared (element 1 is compared to element 2, element 2 is compared to element 3, etc.), and if element i and element i+1 are not in correct order, they are interchanged. The sequence of sort passes ends when, during an entire sort pass, no two elements are interchanged.

The algorithm outlined above may be proved to be correct for arrays with two or more elements, and, accordingly, we proceed with code development. The first view of the intended program is as a single action sort, assumed to be correct, as in level 0 of Figure 7.18.

Our first decision is to divide the program into error and nonerror portions,[1] depending on whether size<0. Figure 7.18 shows in pseudocode form this refinement of the sort action.

Level 0   *Level 1*

sort ——————— if size<0 then errorprocess
                          else sortok

Figure 7.18   Refinement of the sort action.

For errorprocess, we assume that only an error printout is required. Accordingly, at the next level, errorprocess is redefined as a write statement, as shown in the pseudocode of Figure 7.19. Further development deals only with sortok.

Level 1   *Level 2*
  .
  .
  .
errorprocess ——————— write('SIZE ERROR IN SORT CALL')

Figure 7.19   Refinement of errorprocess.

The next design decision must concern size=0 and size=1 because the required basic strategy does not work for these values. Assuming that these values are not errors, for size<2, the table must be considered already sorted. The refinement of sortok in Figure 7.20 reflects this decision since if size<2, sortok actually does nothing.

---

[1] As given, the specification does not state how to interpret size=0 or size=1. The proof of the algorithm requires two or more elements. This is an imperfection in the specification that in a more complex situation would require clarification from the customer. We assume in this discussion that size=0 and size=1 are not error conditions.

Level 1   *Level 2*
.
.
.
sortok——————if size>1 then sortitems

Figure 7.20   Refinement of sortok.

Sortitems is to be done via the required sequence of sort passes that terminates when no items are interchanged during a sort pass, as in Figure 7.21.

Figures 7.22 and 7.23 show the refinements of sortpass and compare/interchange, which continue to follow the required basic strategy.

Level 2   *Level 3*
.
.
.
sortitems ——————— repeat sortpass until no items interchanged

Figure 7.21   Refinement of sortitems.

Level 3   *Level 4*
.
.
.
sortpass——————— for i:=1 to size-1 do
                                compare/interchange

Figure 7.22   Refinement of sortpass.

Level 4   *Level 5*
.
.
.
compare/interchange ——————— if table[i]>table[i+1] then
                                interchange table[i] and
                                table[i+1]

Figure 7.23   Refinement of compare/interchange.

The design at level 5 has sufficient detail to be coded directly. The required program is obtained by first substituting code for the statement "interchange table[i] and table[i+1]," thereby obtaining actual code at level 5, the lowest level of detail. All of this actual code is now substituted for compare/interchange at level 4, so that actual code is obtained at level 4. The actual code of level 4 is now substituted at level 3, and so on successively through all of the levels. In sum, a complete program is obtained from stepwise refinement design by substituting actual code at the lowest levels of detail and then moving this code upward through the design levels.

This process obtains the PASCAL code of Figure 7.24. The higher-level action names are retained in Figure 7.24 as comments. For example, compare/interchange now appears as a comment immediately preceding the code that compares elements and interchanges them if necessary. Also, dashed lines now outline the code corresponding to each higher-level action.

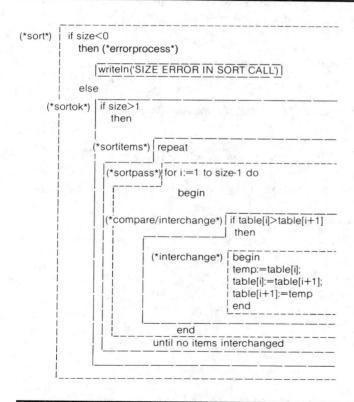

Figure 7.24 The sort program.

Note that the design uses a condition "no items interchanged," but has no mechanism for determining this condition. The development of designs by stepwise refinement commonly requires the use of as-yet-undetermined conditions. In the sort program, it is easily seen that the condition for ending the algorithm is no items interchanged; but since the design is to be further refined, we do not yet know how the condition will be computed.

In such situations, it is usual to assume the existence of the condition (as we have done) and later—when the algorithm has been developed—to go back and provide appropriate computations for the condition. This will always be possible, if the following precautions are taken:

· The condition is well defined and has a straightforward computation. A common mistake is the use of a condition that implicitly requires the entire algorithm, as, for example, the condition is N prime? within a program that computes whether an integer N is a prime.

· The condition is implemented as a Boolean variable with the values true or false or as an integer variable having for this example the values 0 and 1. For an integer variable, the condition might appear in the code as

until items_interchanged=0

while for a Boolean variable, the condition might appear in the code as

until no_items_interchanged

· Provision is made for setting and resetting the variable that represents the condition.

We may use a Boolean variable no_items_interchanged, which is set true as the very first action of sortpass and is reset false within the interchange action. With these inclusions, the sortpass action of Figure 7.25 is obtained.

```
(*sortpass*) begin
             no_items_interchanged:=true;
             for i:=1 to size -1 do
               begin
(*compare/interchange*) if table[i]>table[i+1]
                    then
          (*interchange*) begin
                         no_items_interchanged:=false;
                         temp:=table[i];
                         table[i]:=table[i+1];
                         table[i+1]:=temp
                         end
               end
             end
```

Figure 7.25 Revised sortpass action.

You should confirm that if no interchanges occur during a pass, then further passes are not performed; while if an interchange occurs then a further pass is performed.

7.2.3 Application of Stepwise Refinement

7.2.3.1 The Overall (Top-Down) Philosophy

As the stepwise refinement strategy progresses, each successive level of refinement deals with a smaller segment of the program. Thus the initial levels deal with broad structure (i.e., large program segments) while the later levels deal with detail structure (i.e., small program segments). The intention is that the initial levels dealing with broad structure should be determined by the most important design decisions, while more detailed decisions should be deferred as many levels as possible. In this way, the code implementing each design decision is squeezed into the smallest possible portion of the program text.

Stepwise refinement assumes that all design decisions to be embodied in the desired program are already known. These decisions can be ranked in importance, the most important ones being those that

- Affect the largest possible portion of the total design
- Cause complex problems to be segmented into collections of simpler subproblems
- Restrict further decisions as little as possible

The entire stepwise refinement strategy thus consists of the following steps:

0. Determine what the design decisions are.
1. Rank the design decisions in importance.
2. Design the structure:
  (a) Make important decisions first. Defer detail decisions as long as possible.
  (b) Divide and rule. Each refinement should separate a problem into independent subproblems, each subproblem being isolated in one program segment [Dij 70].
  (c) At each level, choose the structure that decides as little as possible and thus preserves the most options for later decisions [Dij 70].

In other words, at each level the various design decisions are considered and the most important of these decisions is expressed by choice of a control form.

Step 2(c) proposes that each refinement should embody one simple decision. Thus any complex decision is broken up into simpler decisions that are ranked and become the basis for a succession of refinements. In this way, detail decisions are deferred and provision is made for future partial changes of the complex decision.

7.2.3.2 An Example: Computing Primes

To see how stepwise refinement is applied, consider a program to compute and print the first 1000 prime numbers [Dij 70, Dij 72b, Par 76a]. Module organizations for this problem were discussed in Section 4.2. We will develop the first few levels of refinement of this program, beginning by listing the design decisions that must be made. Our purpose is to determine all possible variations of the desired program and to develop the program so as to preserve the most options for change, in case it is desired to modify the program after it is written.

Table 7.2   Possible design variations of the PRIME program

Design Aspect	Possible Variations
Basic sequence	1. Compute all primes at once, then print all primes 2. Compute each output page of primes, then print each output page 3. Compute and print each prime

Print format	1. Print one prime per line
	2. Print more than one prime per line
	   2.1. Print primes row by row
	   2.2. Print primes column by column

Method of computing primes	1. Divide N by every odd number $\leq \sqrt{N}$ 2. Sieve of Eratosthenes
Type of data array used	1. None 2. One dimensional 3. Two dimensional
Page format	1. Do not allow explicitly for output pages 2. Allow explicitly for output pages

Table 7.2 lists some of the possible variations of the desired program. The user will be aware of page format and print format, while the method of computing primes may heavily influence program speed. Accordingly, our refinement choices should allow easy change to page format, print format, or the method of computing primes.

As before, the design is begun with a single action, called PRIME. We assume that PRIME correctly performs the intended process. We wish to make a first refinement choice that

· Preserves the most options with respect to variations in page format, print format, and method of computing primes

- Affects the largest possible portion of the total design
- Separates a problem into independent subproblems, each isolated in one program segment
- Decides as little as possible (thereby deferring detail decisions and leaving most options for lower-level decisions)

Is there such a choice?

We choose to refine PRIME into a table p, a process fill table that fills table p with the first 1000 primes, and a process print table that prints the contents of table p, as in Figure 7.26.

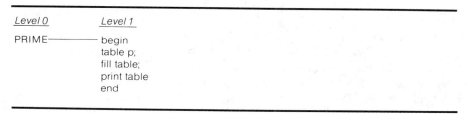

Level 0   Level 1

PRIME─────────── begin
                 table p;
                 fill table;
                 print table
                 end

Figure 7.26   Refinement of PRIME.

We ensure the correctness of this refinement as follows: PRIME is redefined as the sequence fill table, print table. The action fill table is required to place the first 1000 primes in table p, and print table is required to print the contents of table p. It appears that if fill table places the first 1000 primes in table p, and print table prints the contents of table p, then the first 1000 primes are computed and printed. Thus the refinement may be assumed correct.

Why is this the first refinement, and how well does it fulfill the requirements just listed? Note first that this refinement separates the desired program into two independent subprograms. All questions regarding the method of computing primes are now isolated in fill table, while all questions regarding page format and print format are now isolated in print table. The refinement affects the total design since it structures the design into three main portions (counting the table as a portion). The refinement makes no decision whatever about the details of the print format or the details of computing primes. The refinement makes a choice of basic sequence, but *any* refinement is required to choose a basic sequence. We may conclude that this refinement decides as little as possible and thus fulfills all of our requirements.

The refined design embodies the data flow shown in Figure 7.27. In drawing a data flow arrow from table p to fill table, we assume that fill table will obtain each new prime via use of previously obtained primes. Note that we have used a data object as a buffer to isolate the two subprograms, exactly as would be done with the data flow techniques of Section 3.3. The use of an intermediate data object to separate a task into two independent subtasks is a fundamental technique.

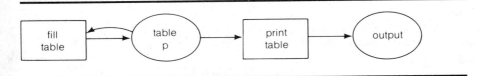

Figure 7.27   Data flow diagram of PRIME program.

The next level involves refinements of the actions fill table and print table and of the data object table p. Since table p interacts with both of the actions, the table structure must be matched to both of them. Thus the actions fill table and print table may be independently refined and programmed only after the table structure has been decided. Further refinement can proceed in either of two ways:

· First choose a table structure and then refine the actions independently
· Partially refine each of the actions, examine the calculations in each, and choose a table structure appropriate for those calculations

If the second choice is taken, the table structure is better fitted to both fill table and print table because the design of the table then reflects design decisions in both subprograms. However, the principles of localization and information hiding are then violated since nonadjacent code segments correspond to the same design decision and since fill table and print table do not hide their internal details from the table. If table p were well fitted to the two subprograms and we wished to modify print table, we might then be forced to modify table p and then to modify fill table as a result of modifying table p.

A less sensitive choice is to immediately determine a table structure that is as simple as possible. Again, our choice should fulfill the requirements previously listed. We refine table p as a one-dimensional array, as in Figure 7.28, such that p[1] contains the first prime, p[2] contains the second prime, and so on. The refinement of Figure 7.28 preserves the most options and decides as little as possible.

It is instructive to consider an alternative refinement of table p. If the image of the desired printout is first determined (e.g., 8 primes per line printed column by column), then table p can be refined to embody that choice (e.g., 125 rows × 8 columns). Such a choice simplifies the required program by expressing a detail of print format at a high level of design. In other words, this

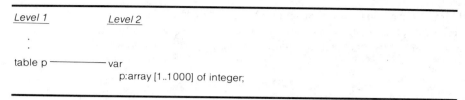

Level 1   Level 2

table p ——————— var
                       p:array [1..1000] of integer;

Figure 7.28   Refinement of table p.

choice does not decide as little as possible. Since fill table is required to place primes in table p, the code of fill table must now reflect the choice of print format (perhaps by the use of two for statements). Thus, instead of isolating subproblems, this choice causes a detail of one subproblem to be reflected in the code for another subproblem. Any change in the print format would now require a change in the fill table segment. In sum, this "simplification" eliminates many options for variations in the program.

We now consider some refinements of print table. Recall the print format variations of Table 7.2. If more than one prime is to appear on each output line, then each output line must be formatted. This is especially important if the number of character positions per line is not known prior to program execution, or if the number of primes per line is not known. If there is to be only one prime per line, the formatting is trivial.

We choose to allow one or more primes per line. Recall that print format choice 2.1 of Table 7.2 has the primes printed in order, row by row, for example:

     1   2   3   5   7
    11   13   17   19   23

Print format choice 2.2 has the primes printed column by column, as, for example:

    1   x   x   x
    2   x   x   x
    3   x   x   x
    .   .   .   .
    .   .   .   .
    .   .   .   .

If the primes are to be listed in columns, then the number of lines must be calculated in advance, so that the primes appearing on the same line as 1 may be determined. We choose to calculate the number of ouput lines in advance, but defer the decision of printing row by row or column by column.

Finally, we must decide whether page formatting is to be explicitly provided for. We choose to provide a program segment for formatting pages, and, consequently, the number of lines per page must also be calculated. Thus the first refinement of print table ensures that one or more primes may appear on each line, the number of output lines will be calculated before the printout, and that page formatting will be provided. The design thus far is shown in Figure 7.29.

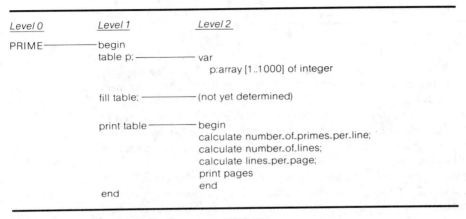

Figure 7.29 Partial design of program PRIME.

Although this refinement may appear to have decided many details, in reality the refinement merely preserves options. The number of primes per line can be set to 1 at a lower level; also, the calculation of the number of lines can be a null action at a lower level, as can the calculation of lines per page if page formatting is not really needed. On the other hand, if the program formatting is written without explicit page formatting and page formatting is later desired, the program structure is ready to accommodate it.

A refinement of print pages is shown in Figure 7.30. Once the quantity lines_per_page has been calculated, the action print lines may be defined to

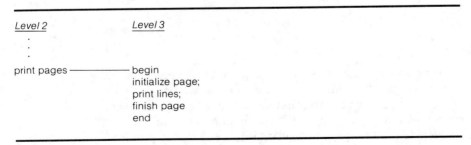

Figure 7.30 Refinement of print pages.

output precisely that many lines. An appropriate refinement of print lines is shown in Figure 7.31. In the figure, the action outputline formats and prints one line as necessary.

Level 3   *Level 4*
  .
  .
  .

print lines ——————— for i:=1 to lines_per_page
                         do outputline
  .
  .
  .

Figure 7.31   Refinement of print lines.

The entire design may be developed in this way down to actual program text. As the design levels become more detailed, the refinements involve more actual code, until finally an entire structured program has been developed. Dijkstra [Dij 72b] discusses the design of this example in great detail, while Wirth [Wir 71] develops detailed designs of other problems.

When the entire program text has been obtained in this way, it will consist of three main segments, as shown in Figure 7.32. As a result of the stepwise refinement strategy, all the code pertaining to filling the table will be contained in the fill table segment, while all code pertaining to output will be in the print table segment. Accordingly, modifying the output process of the program will require changing only the code in the print table segment.

declaration of table p

fill table

print table

Figure 7.32   Main program segments of PRIME program.

The print table segment will consist of subsegments, as shown in Figure 7.33. All code pertaining to actual output of lines is localized in the subsegment print lines, so that modifying details of output of individual lines requires only changing code in the print lines segment. Thus stepwise refinement localizes the code pertaining to each design decision, and deferring detailed decisions causes details to be localized in smaller segments of the program.

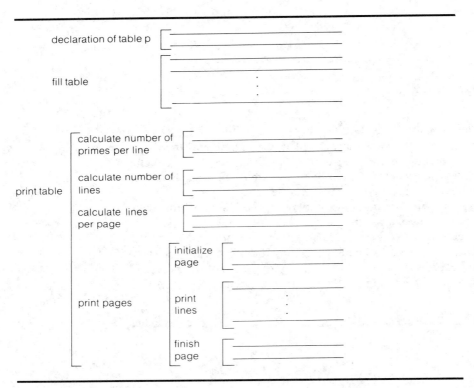

Figure 7.33 Subsegments of print table code segment.

7.2.4 Relation to Data Flow Diagrams—Continuation of Secret Sums Example

In Chapter 3 we saw how data flow methods can be used to determine an overall approach to a program. Data flow methods yield a data flow diagram and an object-action table, which together indicate the key objects and actions necessary in the program, as well as the data flow between objects and actions. Stepwise refinement can then be used as the second step, to develop the final program text.

When this two-step development is done, the stepwise refinement proceeds as usual (i.e., as presented in Section 7.2.3), except that the data flow diagram and object-action table are used as a guide. Since the data flow diagram indicates a concept rather than a concrete implementation, the final program text need not agree with it in complete detail.

To illustrate such a two-step development, this section presents the stepwise refinement of the secret sums example begun in Section 3.3. Figure 7.34 shows the data flow diagram developed in Section 3.3, and Table 7.3 shows the associated object-action table.

This problem embodies the following design aspects:

· The method of representing the puzzle on an input card
· The method of printing the solution

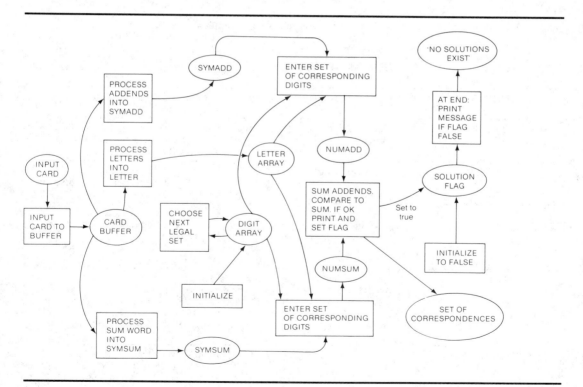

Figure 7.34 Complete flow diagram of secret sums solution.

· The method of choosing the next legal set
· The method of entering corresponding digits into the NUMADD and NUM-SUM arrays
· The methods of processing letters into the SYMADD, SYMSUM, and LETTER arrays

Table 7.3 Objects and associated actions for the secret sums example

Step	Object	Significance	Associated Actions
0	INPUT CARD	Holds contents of puzzle card	Input Card to CARD BUFFER
0	SET OF CORRESPONDENCES	Printout of a solution consisting of letters and corresponding digits	Sum Addends and compare
0	'NO SOLUTION EXISTS'	Message indicating puzzle has no solution	At End Print Message if SOLUTION FLAG False
1	SOLUTION FLAG	Indicates whether a solution has been found	Initialize to False Sum Addends and Compare Check FLAG at end
2	NUMADD	Holds addend words in numeric form	Enter Set of Corresponding Digits Sum Addends and Compare
2	NUMSUM	Holds sum word in numeric form	Enter Set of Corresponding Digits Sum Addends and Compare
3	SYMADD	Holds addend words in symbolic form	Process Addends into SYMADD Enter Set of Corresponding Digits into NUMADD
3	SYMSUM	Holds sum word in symbolic form	Process Sum Word into SYMSUM Enter Set of Corresponding Digits into NUMSUM
4	LETTER	Array of distinct letters (each letter in the puzzle appears exactly once in this array)	Process Letters into LETTER Enter Set of Corresponding Digits into NUMADD Enter Set of Corresponding Digits into NUMSUM
4	DIGIT	Array of corresponding digits (DIGIT[I] is the value corresponding to LETTER[I])	Initialize Choose Next Legal Set Enter Set of Corresponding Digits into NUMADD Enter Set of Corresponding Digits into NUMSUM
5	CARD BUFFER	Holds contents of puzzle card	Input Card to CARD BUFFER Process Addends into SYMADD Process Sum Word into SYMSUM Process Letters into ARRAY

To preserve the most options, each of the above methods should be achieved by a localized code section. Note that in the data flow diagram, the data objects are buffers that isolate the actions from each other, as in the PRIME program example of Section 7.2.3.2. If the data objects of Figure 7.34 are assigned as the stepwise refinement proceeds, then, as a result, each action of Figure 7.34 will be assigned its own local code segment. In other words, the pattern of objects and actions in Figure 7.34 leads to the localization desired in stepwise refinement.

As before, the refinement strategy begins by assuming a single action, secret_sums, as in Figure 7.35. The program is required to process an indefinite sequence of 80 character records, each record holding the contents of one punched card. Thus the basic sequence is a while loop using the condition eof (input) and executed once for each card. Figure 7.35 shows the refinement obtained, assuming the use of PASCAL.[2] (The refinement shown as level 1 actually embodies several successive refinement steps.)

---

[2]The initial refinement is particularly simple in PASCAL because the reset operation sets eof if the file is empty, and each read operation sets eof if the last record is being read. Thus the first (next) execution of the while loop can test eof before the first (next) execution of the read operation.

In most programming languages, each read operation must set eof for itself. In this situation, a program (in order to be correct) must execute so as to test eof immediately after each read. Two refinement patterns are commonly used.

.
.
.
begin
read;
while not eof do
   begin
     .
     .
     .
   read
   end
	var
	  more_data:boolean;
	  .
	  .
	  .
	begin
	more_data:=true;
	while more_data do
	  begin
	  read;
	  if eof then more_data:=false
	     else begin
	       .
	       .
	       .
	      end
	  end

The first pattern has an initial read whose eof setting is tested by the first execution of the while loop; and the last operation of the while loop is a read whose eof is tested at the next execution of the while loop.

The second pattern uses a flag (more_data) as the while loop condition. Although it is slightly more complex, the second pattern has only one read statement, as opposed to the two widely separated read statements in the first pattern. Also, the eof test for the read occurs in the very next line of the program text, so that the intended sequence of events is unmistakable. In sum, the second pattern is preferable if the features of PASCAL reset and read are not available.

The refinement of Figure 7.35 explicitly uses the object CARD_BUFFER and the action input_card_to_buffer of Figure 7.34 and groups all the other actions and objects of Figure 7.34 within the code segment process_one_card. Figure 7.36 shows the refinement of process_one_card with the actions of Figure 7.34 divided into three groups: processing letters into arrays, trying all solutions, and finally checking the solution flag at the end.[3] The rest of the objects of Figure 7.34 must be defined in the refinement of process_one_card since these objects are used throughout process_one_card.

Figure 7.36 also shows refinements of the code segments put_letters_into _arrays and check_flag. Note that the action of check_flag is exactly as suggested by Figure 7.34. The actions put_sum_word_into_SYMSUM, put_addends_into_SYMADD, and put_letters_into_LETTER are also shown in level 3 of Figure 7.36. We intend a tiny variation from Figure 7.36, namely, that put_letters_into_LETTER will take its inputs from SYMSUM and SYMADD rather than from CARD_BUFFER. (This variation is also discussed in Section 3.3.)

Figure 7.37 shows the refinement of try-all-solutions. The boolean variable DONE must be set true by choose_next_legal_set when the set of all possibilities has been exhausted. The integer variable BASE has been added so that the code dealing with the DIGIT array is independent of the number base 10; a different base can be used simply by setting BASE to the appropriate value.

Note that at level 3 the refinement of secret_sums consists almost entirely of the actions and objects of Figure 7.34.

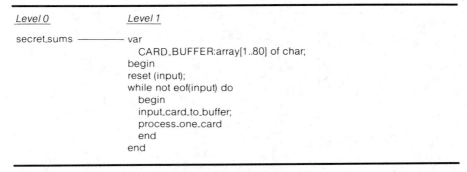

Level 0	Level 1
secret_sums ————	var
	CARD_BUFFER:array[1..80] of char;
	begin
	reset (input);
	while not eof(input) do
	begin
	input_card_to_buffer;
	process_one_card
	end
	end

Figure 7.35 First refinement of secret_sums.

---

[3]An alternative in refining process_one_card would be to group all the initializing code into a first code segment. In the interest of following the principle of localization, we place the code initializing an object just before the code that first accesses the object (except in the case of SOLUTION_FLAG).

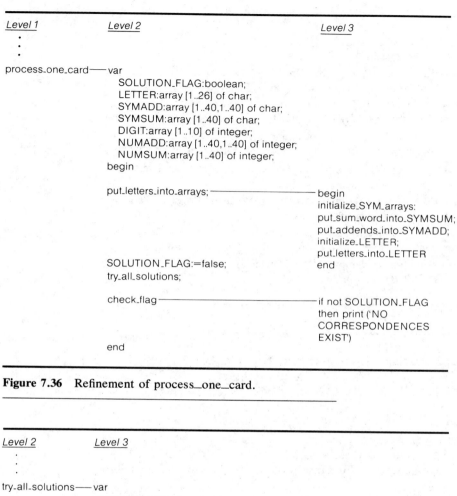

```
Level 1                Level 2                            Level 3
    .                     .
    .                     .
    .                     .
process_one_card——var
                       SOLUTION_FLAG:boolean;
                       LETTER:array [1..26] of char;
                       SYMADD:array [1..40,1..40] of char;
                       SYMSUM:array [1..40] of char;
                       DIGIT:array [1..10] of integer;
                       NUMADD:array [1..40,1..40] of integer;
                       NUMSUM:array [1..40] of integer;
                    begin

                    put_letters_into_arrays;——————————————begin
                                                          initialize_SYM_arrays:
                                                          put_sum_word_into_SYMSUM;
                                                          put_addends_into_SYMADD;
                                                          initialize_LETTER;
                                                          put_letters_into_LETTER
                    SOLUTION_FLAG:=false;                 end
                    try_all_solutions;

                    check_flag————————————————————————————if not SOLUTION_FLAG
                                                          then print ('NO
                                                          CORRESPONDENCES
                                                          EXIST')

                    end
```

Figure 7.36 Refinement of process_one_card.

```
Level 2                Level 3
    .
    .
    .
try-all-solutions——var
                       DONE:boolean
                       BASE:integer
                    begin
                    DONE:=false;
                    BASE:=10;
                    initialize_DIGIT;
                    while not DONE do
                       begin
                       enter_digits_into_NUMADD;
                       enter_digits_into_NUMSUM;
                       sum_compare_print;
                       choose_next_legal_set
                       end
                    end
```

Figure 7.37 Refinement of try_all_solutions.

REFERENCES

[Cai 75] Caine, S. H., and Gordon, E. K. "PDL—A Tool for Software Design," *Proceedings of National Computer Conference*, 1975. (Also in [Fre 80b].)*

[Dij 70] Dijkstra, E. W. *EWD249: Notes on Structured Programming*, Report 70-Wsk-03, 2nd ed., Technical University of Eindhoven, Netherlands, April 1970.

[Dij 72b] ———. "Notes on Structured Programming," in O.-J. Dahl, E. W. Dijkstra, and Hoare (eds.), *Structured Programming*. New York: Academic Press, 1972.

[Jac 75] Jackson, M. A. *Principles of Program Design*. New York: Academic Press, 1975.

[Par 76a] Parnas, D. L. "On the Design and Development of Program Families," *IEEE Transactions on Software Engineering*, Vol. SE-2, No. 1, March 1976.

[Ros 75] Ross, D. A.; Goodenough, J. B.; and Irvine, C. A. "Software Engineering; Process, Principles, and Goals," *Computer*, May 1975. (Also in [Fre 80b].)*

[Wir 71] Wirth, N. "Program Development by Stepwise Refinement," *Communications of the ACM*, April 1971. (Also in [Fre 80b].)*

PROBLEMS

1. Consider one of the following problems in Appendix D:
   - (a) Problem 5
   - (b) Problem 7
   - (c) Problem 11
   - (d) Problem 13
   - (e) Problem 14
   - (f) Problem 16
   - (g) Problem 17

   Describe the design decisions that must be made for this program, and show the variations of each decision. Use top-down design to derive a pseudocode refinement that allows most options for these design decisions.

2. The following problem is adapted from a discussion in [Jac 75]. An automobile parts supply company is writing a program to print invoices from a customer master file and a transaction file. The customer master file contains customer number, name, and address and is in ascending sequence by customer number. The transaction file contains one record for each item billed (the record contains customer number, invoice number, date, item description, amount, and price) and these records are in ascending order by date within invoice number within customer number.

   As is usual, there will be no invoices for some customers and many invoices for others. Also, because of data entry errors, there may be transaction records for which no customer record exists. Such transaction records are to be listed in an error report.

---

*See Appendix B: Bibliography.

A programmer has begun a top-down design of this program, and has thus far arrived at the refinement shown below in pseudocode form (individual refinement steps have been omitted):

```
begin
reset (transactionfile);
reset (masterfile);
read (transactionfile);
read (masterfile);
while not eof (transactionfile) do
   begin
   if transaction_cust_num>master_cust_num
      then read (masterfile)
      else if transaction_cust_num<master_cust_num
            then begin
                 diagnose_error;
                 print_error_record_diagnosis;
                 read (transactionfile)
                 end
            else begin
                 key:=transaction_invoice_num;
                 while (key=transaction_invoice_num) and
                   (not eof (transactionfile)) do
                   begin
                   produce_invoice_line;
                   read (transactionfile)
                   end;
                 finish_invoice
                 end
   end
end
```

(a) Determine if this solution will work in all situations.
(b) Are code segments that work together placed adjacent to each other? Show which segments are well placed in this respect and which are not. Give reasons for your classifications.
(c) Describe the design decisions that must be made for this program and the variations of each decision. Does this solution allow the decisions to be made independently?
(d) (*1*) Revise the given solution to obtain solution 2, which also lists on an error report the customer numbers of those customers for whom at least one invoice was produced.
   (*2*) Revise solution 2 to obtain solution 3, which also lists on the error report, together with an asterisk, the customer numbers of customers for whom no invoice was produced.
   (*3*) Revise solution 3 to obtain solution 4, which includes with each customer number printed in (*1*), the total amount invoiced to that customer.

(4)   Revise solution 4 to obtain solution 5, which instead of printing each erroneous transaction record, instead prints the customer number together with an E for each customer for whom at least one erroneous transaction record has occurred.

(5)   Discuss the difficulties encountered in these changes.

(e) Redesign the initial solution using the method of Section 6.2. Make the changes to the redesigned solution as required in (d). Discuss the relative difficulty of changing the original solution and the redesigned solutions.

7.3 RETROFITTING OLD PROGRAMS

7.3.1 A Preliminary Conversion

This section presents a technique for converting a program written with go to statements into an equivalent program using only the structures of Table 7.1 [Coop 67]. This conversion does not alter the logic (or possible poor structure) of the original program, it merely rearranges the program into a structured format. Such conversions are useful if it is desired to have all programs of an installation in structured format and reprogramming is not desired.

Consider a program having M start points (entry points) $S_1, S_2, \ldots, S_M$, and N end points (exit points) $E_1, \ldots, E_N$. The program may have an arbitrary structure, and the start or end points may be anywhere in the structure. The conversion obtains an equivalent program having an entry section containing all the entry points, an exit section containing all the exit points, and a main section.

If the conversion is applied to an already structured section of a program, the conversion only adds complexity to that section. Accordingly, we first group portions of the program in such a way that each structured format section of the original program will be treated as a single unit. Specifically, if any structure of Table 7.1 is found within the program, then the operations and/or conditions comprising that structure will be grouped into one unit, which will then be considered one operation. This grouping process will be continued until it is no longer possible.

As an example, the program of Figure 7.38(a) is in this way transformed to the program of (b), which is, in turn, transformed to the program of (c). However, the program of Figure 7.39(a), because of the additional entry arc, can be transformed only to the program of (b).

7.3.2 The Cooper Transformation

Each structured format portion of the program is now treated as a single unit. If the preliminary procedure consolidates the entire program into one operation, then the original program was already in structured format. Figure 7.40 shows a sample program to be transformed.

The transformation of a program has three phases: the flow of control is annotated, program segments are "pulled out," and the program segments are reconnected in different format but with the flow of control unchanged. The detailed steps are as follows:

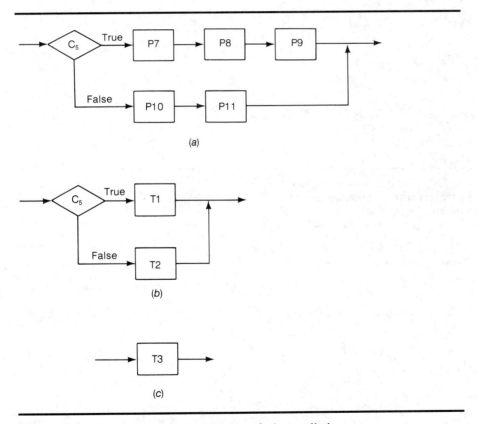

(a)

(b)

(c)

Figure 7.38 Successive transformations of the preliminary procedure. (a) Initial form of program. (b) First transformation of program. (c) Second transformation of program.

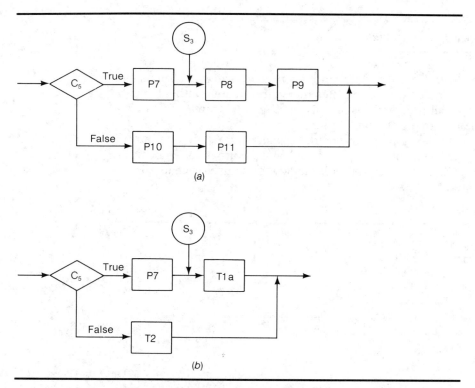

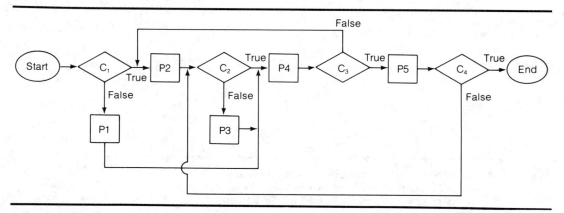

Figure 7.39 Transformation of a program having an entry arc. (*a*) Program with additional entry arc. (*b*) Transformation of program.

Figure 7.40 A sample program to be transformed.

Annotate the Flow of Control

1. Mark with an integer value the entry of each operation and of each condition, such that the operation or condition either has two or more entries or is entered from a start point. These entries may be marked in any arbitrary order. Let the integers $1, \ldots, K$ be used in this way.

2. Mark each end point E_j with the integer value $K+j$. Thus $E_1, \ldots, E_N$ are marked, respectively, with $K+1, \ldots, K+N$.

The example is shown in Figure 7.41 with integer markings added. Note that C_1 (entered from a start point) and C_2 (two entries) have been marked, but not C_3 or C_4. Similarly, P2 and P4 have been marked, but not P1, P3, or P5. Thus, in step 1, the integers $1, \ldots, 4$ are used. Since there is only one end point, in step 2 it is marked with the integer 5.

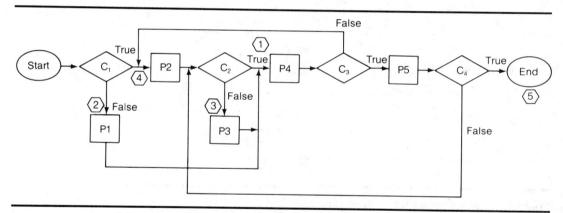

Figure 7.41 Sample program with integer markings added.

Pull Out Program Segments

3. For each entry marked $1, 2, \ldots, K$, draw the program segment $\mathcal{P}$ consisting of the marked entry, all unmarked connections, operations, and conditions in sequence with that entry, and showing the exit points of the segment. If an exit arc terminates at an entry marked with the integer j, then the arc is drawn

For the example, these segments are shown in Figure 7.42.

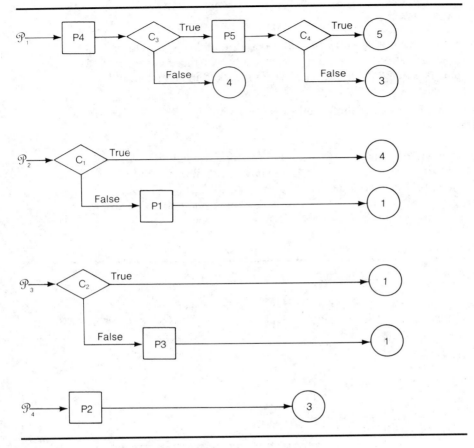

Figure 7.42 Segments of the sample program.

Reconnect Segments

4. Assume an integer variable next, not otherwise used in the program. For each program segment $\mathcal{P}_i$, form a "revised segment" $\mathcal{P}_i'$ as follows: for every arc

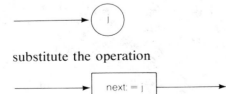

substitute the operation

For the example, we obtain Figure 7.43.

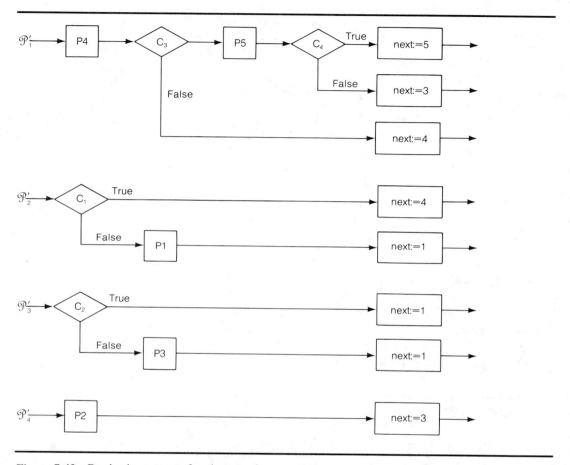

Figure 7.43   Revised segments for the sample program.

5. For each start point S_a entering the diagram at an entry marked with j, form an initializing program segment

For the example we obtain

The desired structured format program will now have the standard form shown in Figure 7.44.

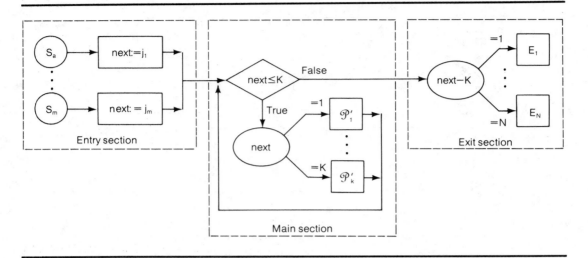

Figure 7.44 Standard form of structured format program.

For the example, the desired program is shown in Figure 7.45.

Compare the original program and this structured format version to see that the actual sequence of execution is unchanged.

REFERENCES

[Boh 66] Bohm, C., and Jacopini, G. "Flow Diagrams, Turing Machines, and Languages with Only Two Formation Rules," *Communications of the ACM*, May 1966.

[Coop 67] Cooper, D. C. "Bohm and Jacopini's Reduction of Flow Charts," *Communications of the ACM*, August 1967.

PROBLEMS

1. Transform the program of Figure 7.6(*a*) into structured format using the Cooper conversion.

2. Transform each of the flowcharts on page 450 into structured format using the Cooper conversion.

3. Flowchart the program of Figure E.1 in Appendix E. Derive an equivalent program in structured format using the Cooper conversion.

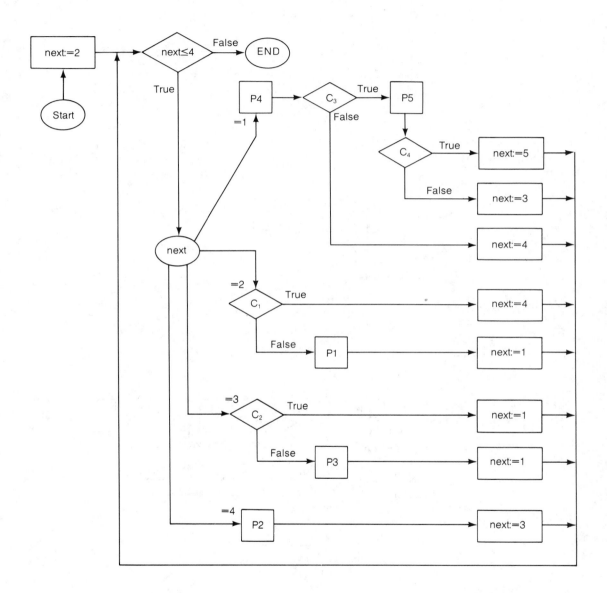

Figure 7.45 Structured format version of sample program.

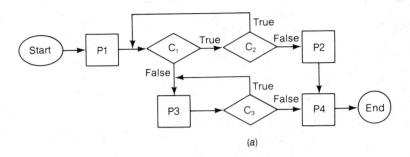

(a)

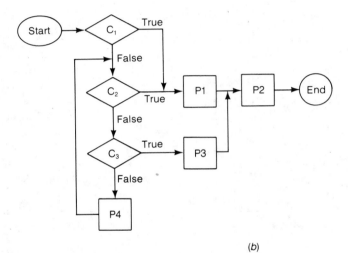

(b)

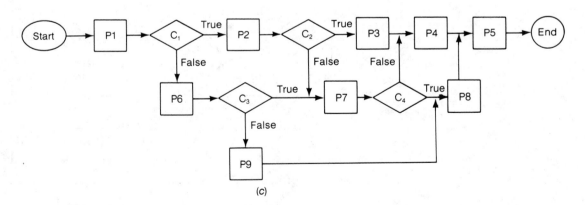

(c)

chapter eight
Issues in
Program Construction

8.1 CHARACTERISTICS OF COMMONLY USED PROGRAMMING LANGUAGES

8.1.1 Contents of This Chapter

When the program code is finally written, many practical issues must be faced. First, we have to choose the programming language best suited to the application. Next, it is important to write the code clearly and to document it well, in order that corrections and modifications can be easily made. After the code has been written, we may wish to evaluate it; or if the program runs a bit slowly, we may wish to improve its efficiency slightly.

Chapter 8 discusses all of these issues. Section 8.1 describes characteristics of popular programming languages, to aid in the choice of a language. Section 8.2 suggests points of programming style. Section 8.3 describes a simple approach for achieving efficiency; Section 8.4 presents techniques for evaluating the final code; and Section 8.5 discusses program maintenance documentation.

8.1.2 Classes of Programming Languages

The use of an appropriate language can greatly simplify a programming problem, while the use of an inappropriate language can introduce unnecessary difficulty. This section outlines some significant features of various popular languages, comparing important points of variation.

An incredible variety of languages has been developed since the advent of the digital computer. Histories of programming languages have been written [Sam 69, Knu 77] and a conference on the history of programming languages was held in Los Angeles in 1978 [Wex 78]. A roster of current languages is published periodically in the *SIGPLAN Notices* [Sam 78].

In the main, languages have been developed in four broad application areas: numeric/scientific calculations (ALGOL, APL, BASIC, FORTRAN, PL/1); business data processing (COBOL, PL/1); military data processing (JOVIAL, PL/1); and computer science research in symbol manipulation and artificial intelligence (LISP, SNOBOL).

Numeric/scientific languages have generally dealt with calculations on single variables and on arrays, and thus have tended toward precise and concise notations, as well as careful provision for procedures and functions. In contrast, COBOL is used for almost all business data processing, and its primary concerns are: (1) processing of files and records having complex structures, and (2) self-documenting notation, so that any program is comprehensible to a nonprogramming supervisor. As a result, COBOL lacks formal notations (e.g., it does not provide functions or procedures with formal arguments), and its notations tend to verbosity.

Military data processing languages have handled numeric/scientific calculation and also complex data structures. These languages have many of COBOL's facilities for processing complex data structures, but use the notational style of the numeric/scientific languages.

In computer science research, LISP is used in artificial intelligence applications that require arbitrarily recursive operations on list structures. Accordingly, LISP provides both recursive list structures and recursive functions and procedures in strict mathematical notation. On the other hand, SNOBOL deals primarily with operations on strings of alphanumeric symbols, and its notation is reminiscent of FORTRAN.

In addition to the application-oriented languages, there has been a continuing development of machine-oriented languages, from early assembly languages to the present macroassembly languages [Fer 66, Met 79] and high-level machine-oriented languages that allow the direct use of machine instructions within an ALGOL-like program text. Macroassembly languages allow machine and efficiency considerations to be directly approached, while the macronotational facility provides high-level notational power.

The suitability of a language for a given problem is determined by its notational characteristics, by its compilation characteristics, and by its operational characteristics. Both the limitations (or lack of limitations) of the language's compiler and the support given by the language's operational system during execution influence the ease of use of the language. For example, the provision in FORTRAN for separate compilation of subroutines greatly aids the development of large systems in FORTRAN, and this feature has begun to appear in some later versions of other languages. The BASIC language has become enormously popular because of its extremely simple notation and (equally as important) its pleasant and friendly interactive operation. APL is also highly prized because of its interactive operation.

Accordingly, this section discusses important compilation and operational features as well as notational features.

8.1.3 ALGOL

ALGOL, which is used for numeric/scientific calculations, was the first language to provide a structured flow of control and a formally defined syntax. Recursive procedures are provided. A deficiency is that there are no standard provisions for input and output; each implementation has its own input/output features. Most systems provide procedures for character-by-character input and output.

ALGOL provides a subprogram unit called a *block*. The structure of blocks within an ALGOL program determines how variable names are interpreted and how subprograms communicate. A block is a program segment preceded by the word **begin**, succeeded by the word **end**, and containing data declarations. In Figure 8.1, block 1 declares integers x,p; block 2 declares integers x,q; and block 3 declares integers a,b,x. Block 3, which completely contains blocks 1 and 2, is said to be global to block 1 and global to block 2. In general, any block may contain any number of other blocks.

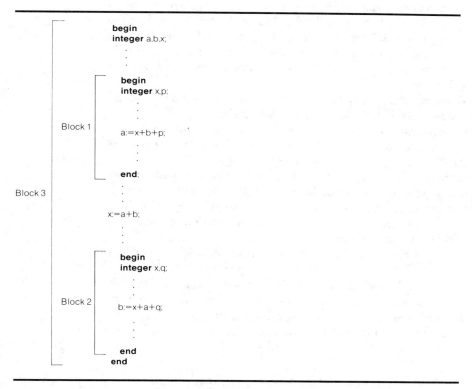

Figure 8.1   Block structure in ALGOL.

There are two conventions for interpretation of variable names and for variable usage:

1. The text within a block may refer to any variable declared in that block, or declared in any block global to that block.
2. When a name has been declared in several blocks, the variable referred to by the name is the "innermost," or most local, declaration.

Convention 1 dictates that the text of block 1 may refer to all variables declared in block 1 and also to all variables declared in block 3. Similarly, the text of block 2 may reference the variables declared in block 2 and also those in block 3. For example, both block 1 and block 2 refer to the variables a,b declared in block 3. However, since block 1 is not global to block 2, block 2 may not refer to the integer p or to any other variable of block 1, and, similarly, block 1 may not refer to q or to any other variable of block 2. Since block 1 is not global to block 3, and block 2 is not global to block 3, block 3 may not refer to any variables declared in block 1 or block 2.

A variable x is declared in each of the blocks. By convention 2, any reference to x in block 1, as, for example, in the statement a:=x+b+p, is a reference to the variable declared in block 1 itself. Similarly, the name x in the statement b:=x+a+q in block 2 refers to the variable declared in block 2. The name x in the statement x:=a+b in block 3 refers to the variable declared in block 3 since, by convention 1, the text of block 3 cannot refer to variables of block 1 or block 2.

The body of a procedure used in a block must be declared within the block.[1] The procedure body is itself regarded as a block and the conventions above apply. (Note that procedures may be declared within procedures.) Thus a procedure may freely reference any variable global to it, while the variables of the procedure itself are inaccessible to the block calling it.

Arrays in a procedure or block may be defined with dimensions of variable size. More precisely, an array may be defined with maximum size N, where N is an argument to the procedure or a variable global to the block. In either case, N is evaluated and storage is assigned at each invocation of the procedure or block during program execution.

Formal parameters of procedures may be either *name* parameters, in which case the address of the actual parameter is passed to the procedure, or may be *value* parameters, in which case only a value derived from the actual parameter is passed to the procedure. Thus the procedure has direct access to name parameters, as in FORTRAN; for value parameters, the procedure has access only to the value derived from the actual parameter. Parameters whose mode is undeclared are assumed to be name parameters.

---

[1]An exception occurs for a block defining the body of a procedure, one of whose parameters is a procedure.

8.1.4 APL

APL, an interactive language with simple syntax and very powerful "built-in" functions, has been used in both numeric and commercial applications. The basic data objects of APL are arrays, which may contain either numeric or literal values. Operations are defined on entire arrays, so that one may write A+B to denote the addition of arrays A and B. Other operators allow catenation of two arrays; one may catenate C=[1   2   3] and D=[4   5   6   7] to obtain the array E=[1   2   3   4   5   6   7]. A primitive operator ρ yields the size of an array. For

$$A = \begin{bmatrix} 1 & 2 & 3 \\ 4 & 5 & 6 \\ 7 & 8 & 9 \end{bmatrix}$$

the expression ρA yields [3   3] since A is of size 3 in each of 2 dimensions, and one may also write $\rho\rho$A, which yields 2, the rank (number of dimensions) of A.

There are three statement types in APL: assignment, branch, and miscellaneous. Functions may have one, two, or no arguments. In APL, expressions are evaluated strictly from right to left without any precedence between operations. For example, the expression

X*Y+Z

is evaluated in APL as X*(Y+Z), whereas in ALGOL or FORTRAN this expression is evaluated as (X*Y)+Z.

APL provides 47 primitive functions, each represented by a single symbol or a single symbol with overstrike. Certain operators modify the behavior of other operators in a systematic way. For example, the operator / modifies a function to apply over all elements of a list, so that we may write +/L to sum the items of L. Due to its concise and powerful notation, APL programs have become famous for their brevity, and especially for intricate one-line programs. However, because of their brevity and intricacy, APL programs are also usually hard to understand.

8.1.5 BASIC

BASIC is a simple interactive language, originally developed to teach programming to naive users. The system emphasizes friendliness to users, and the user has the impression of interacting directly with the programs. User commands for program execution, listing of programs, retrieving old programs from disk, and so on, are fully integrated within the system. Data in BASIC may be numeric (users need not distinguish between real and integer variables) or strings. Arrays of numeric or string values may be used. Default subscript ranges are provided for undeclared arrays; printing is done in a standard format so that users need not learn about formats; and so on.

Not surprisingly, BASIC has become enormously popular, and it is implemented on almost every microcomputer. There are now some business-oriented versions of BASIC for microcomputers. However, in its microcomputer implementations, BASIC does not provide structured flow of control.

Two features of BASIC make it difficult to write large systems. First, every variable is defined throughout the entire program. If a variable X is used in a certain way in one part of the program, care must be taken to ensure that it is used in the same way in other parts of the program. When several smaller programs are combined to form a larger program, name conflicts may arise. There is no way, as in ALGOL, for each subprogram to independently maintain its own set of names.

Second, BASIC does not provide for the definition of procedures with formal arguments. In many of the other languages, one may, for example, define a function TAX(AMOUNT) with the formal parameter AMOUNT. All of the variables defined within the function body are independent of variables in the rest of the program. This function may be invoked in another part of the program by a statement such as DEDUCTION:=TAX(1000.00). When the function is invoked, the actual parameter (e.g., 1000.00) is automatically transferred to the function, and the result of the function's calculation is transferred back as the value of TAX. In BASIC, a function cannot be defined in this way and there is no mechanism for the transfer of values between function and calling program.

8.1.6 COBOL

COBOL (*CO*mmon *B*usiness *O*riented *L*anguage) evolved as a common language for business data processing. A prime concern of this language is efficient handling of large files and records. Sophisticated file and record structures, part-word items, character handling, buffered input/output, and structured flow of control are provided. A program may, by means of a COPY statement, incorporate portions of other COBOL programs that have been archived.

Figure 8.2 shows a typical record structure in COBOL. Each elementary item is defined via a PICTURE clause (PICTURE may be abbreviated as PIC). In the PICTURE clause, X signifies an alphanumeric character and 9 signifies a numeric digit. Thus LAST-NAME consists of 18 alphanumeric characters, MIDDLE-INITIAL is one alphanumeric character, and STATE is two alphanumeric characters, while ZIP consists of five digits and COURSE-NUM consists of three digits. In the PICTURE clause of a numeric item, the letter V indicates the position of a (virtual) decimal point. Accordingly, GPA is stored as a units value, a tenths value, and a hundredths value.

Figure 8.2 also defines a hierarchy of data organization. STUDENT-RECORD (preceded by the integer level number 01) is comprised of the sub-records NAME, ADDRESS, and GRADES (each of which is preceded by the level number 02). ADDRESS is comprised of NUMBER, STREET, and CITY-STATE-ZIP (each at level 03), while CITY-STATE-ZIP consists of CITY, STATE, and ZIP.

```
01 STUDENT-RECORD.
    02 NAME.
        03 LAST-NAME PIC X(18).
        03 MIDDLE-INITIAL PIC X.
        03 FIRST-NAME PIC X(10).

    02 ADDRESS.
        03 NUMBER PIC 9(5).
        03 STREET PIC X(20).
        03 CITY-STATE-ZIP.
            04 CITY PIC X(20).
            04 STATE PIC XX.
            04 ZIP PIC 9(5).

    02 GRADES.
        03 GPA PIC 9V99.
        03 THIS-SEMESTER-INFO.
            04 COURSE-AND-GRADE
                OCCURS 10 TIMES.
                05 DEPT PIC X(4).
                05 COURSE-NUM PIC 999.
                05 GRADE PIC X.
```

Figure 8.2   A typical COBOL record structure.

Arrays of records may also be defined. In Figure 8.2, COURSE-AND-GRADE is declared as occurring 10 times, so that THIS-SEMESTER-INFO is an array of records, each record giving the department, course number, and grade of a specific course.

COBOL was designed so that programs would be self-documenting and readable by nonprogrammers. Accordingly, to accomplish this statement

TAX:=1000.00;

the COBOL programmer writes

MOVE 1000.00 TO TAX.

Variable, record, and file names are chosen to be self-documenting, and thus a simple statement might appear as

MOVE TEMP-CUSTOMER-NAME TO MASTER-CUSTOMER-NAME.

Because of COBOL's syntax and programming style, writing a COBOL program is tedious, and simple programs require hundreds of lines.

In COBOL as in BASIC, each name of a data entity is defined over the entire program text. Thus when small programs are combined to form a larger program, any name appearing in two or more subprograms must be changed if the name is used differently in each subprogram.

8.1.7 FORTRAN 77

FORTRAN 77 is customarily used for numeric/scientific calculations. The first version of FORTRAN, which appeared in the mid-1950s, was the first high-level programming language. Since that time the language has remained popular, has continued to be supported by computer manufacturers, and has evolved steadily.

The language provides structured flow of control, but not block structure or recursive procedures. An important feature is that subprograms are separately compilable. In addition to passing parameters, programs may communicate via common access to certain data areas, appropriately named COMMON data areas. Input or output formats are determined by FORMAT statements, which may appear as program statements or as data in an array, or may be read in at execution time.

In FORTRAN 77, arguments are passed "by reference" to subroutines. In other words, the address of the parameter is passed to the subroutine, which then manipulates the parameter using the given address. Consequently, if the subroutine modifies the value of the parameter for any reason, the modified value remains in the data of the calling program. If, for example, the parameter to be passed to subroutine XYZ is a numeric constant such as 10, the FORTRAN compiler will create a storage location (called, say, TEN) and place the value 10 in it. The subroutine is then passed the address of TEN. If the subroutine were to increase this value to 11, then the next call XYZ(10) again causes XYZ to receive the address of TEN, which now contains the value 11.

8.1.8 JOVIAL

JOVIAL was developed for the programming of a large, real-time system, which needed extensive numeric calculation and also much data in memory.

JOVIAL provides a structured flow of control, but not block structure or recursive procedures. Variables are either main program variables or are local to a procedure or function. Formatted input/output is not a standard feature.

Definition and handling of data is sophisticated in JOVIAL. Single data entities, called *items* in JOVIAL, may be declared as requiring a specified number of bits. In other words, an item may use only part of a word. A sequence of items can be grouped as an entry, similar to a record in COBOL. A table consists of a sequence of entries. Overlays of structure within an entry are permitted. Appropriate object code for extraction of items from whole words, and insertion of items into whole words, is provided by the compiler. The language contains built-in functions for manipulating specific bits or bytes of items.

8.1.9 LISP

LISP is used in artificial intelligence and formal symbol manipulation work. The number of users is small, and there is no standard specification for LISP. The most widely used version is LISP 1.5 [Weis 67].

LISP was developed to process list structures, and as a formal mathematical system for describing computable functions. Its concepts are radically different from those of the other languages discussed. Every data element or constant in LISP is written as a *symbolic expression*, which may be either an *atom* or a *list*. An *atom* is a string of letters, digits, and other characters not having a special use in LISP; examples are A or ONION or JOHNMCCAR-THY. A *list* consists of a left parenthesis, followed by 0 or more atoms or lists separated by spaces, followed by a right parenthesis. Examples of lists are

```
()
(A)
(A ONION A)
(PLUS 3(TIMES X PI))
```

In other words, lists may contain other lists, which in turn may contain further lists, ad infinitum. Every LISP calculation is a manipulation of some lists. In the process of calculation, new lists may be formed by the concatenation of other lists or the extraction of lists from within other lists. All necessary storage is automatically provided by the LISP run-time system.

Although LISP allows sequential programs containing assignment statements and go to statements, calculations are primarily expressed as functions. LISP provides six primitive list-manipulation functions, and a LISP program is built up by the definition of further functions. Thus a LISP program usually consists of a collection of functions, with no explicit sequence indicated. Each nonprimitive function is defined by a condition expression, which, in concept, has the form:

if p_1 then e_1 else if p_2 then e_2 . . . else if p_n then e_n.

When evaluated, such an expression yields the value e_i (which may be an expression containing further function calls), where p_i is the first of the "p expressions" found to be true. Functions are usually recursively defined, that is, one or more of the expressions e_k may contain a call to the function itself.

Functions are written as symbolic expressions and this tends to be cumbersome due to the many nestings of parentheses. LISP is usually cumbersome for small problems (because some very small details must be precisely dealt with) and very powerful for large problems, because arbitrary amounts of recursion and list manipulation are automatically supported by the run-time system. For example, an interpreter for LISP programs can itself be written in 87 lines of LISP.

8.1.10 PASCAL

PASCAL is a relatively new language that has become popular in academic circles and also among microcomputer users. It combines features of AL-GOL, FORTRAN, and COBOL with additional data declaration and handling capabilities.

PASCAL's syntax is modeled after ALGOL's. PASCAL provides structured control forms and recursive procedures and allows the declaration of procedures within the main program and within other procedures, thereby achieving ALGOL's block structure. (In PASCAL, all blocks must be procedures, whereas in ALGOL any program segment containing data declarations is a block.)

As in FORTRAN, unsigned integers are used as statement labels, and array dimensions must have fixed bounds. PASCAL's for statement corresponds to the DO loop of FORTRAN, having index steps of only 1 or -1, but (as in ALGOL) it is executed only as long as the control variable lies within both of the specified limits. Procedure parameters may be passed by reference (as in FORTRAN) or by value (as in ALGOL).

PASCAL allows easy definition and manipulation of abstract data types, independent of machine representations. A hierarchy of data types is provided, and arbitrary types and structures may be declared.

A scalar data type is one that has a linearly ordered set of distinct values. Every data type and structure is built up from scalar types. The standard scalar types integer, real, boolean, and character are provided, and arbitrary scalar types may be declared. For example, in Figure 8.3, the scalar type day is defined by enumerating identifiers that denote successive integer values beginning with 0. (In other words, sun denotes 0, mon denotes 1, . . . , sat denotes 6.) A variable of type day, such as d in Figure 8.3, can have one of the values sun, mon, . . . , sat. We may write statements such as

```
        hours[tues]:=4;
        for d:=mon to thurs do S;
```

ignoring the underlying set of integer values.

```
type
    day=(sun,mon,tues,wed,thurs,fri,sat);
    workday=mon..fri;
    alpha='A'..'Z';
    week=set of day;

var
    d:day;
    w1,w2,w3:week;
```

Figure 8.3 Declarations of scalar and set variables.

A scalar type may also be defined as a subrange of a standard or previously defined scalar type. Thus workday is a type having the values mon, . . . , fri of day, while the type alpha corresponds to COBOL's alphabetic data type.

A set type is based on a scalar type, and a variable of a set type may have any subset of the set of values in the scalar type. For example, the variable w1 in Figure 8.3 may have any subset (including the empty set) of the set of values {sun,mon,tues,wed,thurs,fri,sat} of the scalar type day. We may write

```
        w1:=[mon,tues,sat];
        w3:=w2+w1;(*set union*)
        w3:=w2*w1;(*set intersection*)
        w3:=w2−w1;(*set difference*)
```

and we may test for set equality (or inequality), set inclusion, and set membership.

A record type defines a structure consisting of a fixed number of components. The components may be of any type, including records. For example, the type student in Figure 8.4 has a structure identical to that of STUDENT-RECORD in Figure 8.2. Files and variables of type student may be declared as in Figure 8.4. Standard read and write operations are provided for files, as is automatic file buffering.

For any type T, a pointer type p_T may be defined, consisting of an unbounded set of values pointing to elements of type T. This is done by a declaration of the form type p= ↑ T. A variable of type p_T can then be used to construct linked lists of elements of type T. For example, typelink= ↑ student

defines link as the set of values pointing to elements of type student. If the declaration of student is extended as follows:

student=record
         ⋮
    next:link;
         ⋮
    end

the variable next can point to the next element in the list.

```
type
  digit=0..9;
  courseandgrade=record
                   dept:array[1..4]of char;
                   coursenum:array[1..3]of digit;
                   grade:char
                 end;
  student=record
            name=record
                   lastname:array[1..18]of char;
                   middleinitial:char;
                   firstname:array[1..10]of char
                 end;
            address=record
                      number:array[1..5]of digit;
                      street:array[1..28] of char;
                      citystatezip=record
                                     city:array[1..20]of char;
                                     state:array[1..2]of digit;
                                     zip;array[1..5]of digit
                                   end;
                    end;
            grades=record
                     gpa:real;
                     semesterinfo:
                         array[1..10]of courseandgrade
                   end
          end;
  stufile=file of student;
var
  newstudent:student;
  studentfile:stufile;
```

Figure 8.4 PASCAL record structure corresponding to Figure 8.2.

The standard procedure new(p) is provided to allocate memory space for a new element, to create the element, and to assign an appropriate value (pointing to the new element) to the pointer variable p.

8.1.11 PL/1

PL/1 is intended to combine in a single language the best features of ALGOL, FORTRAN, COBOL, and JOVIAL. The syntax is modeled after ALGOL, including structured flow of control and block structure. Recursive procedures are provided. However, subroutines may be separately compiled and may share data, as in FORTRAN. Parameters are passed by reference, as in FORTRAN. Data structures of JOVIAL and COBOL are inluded; input/output facilities essentially combine those of FORTRAN and COBOL. Because of the large number of features in PL/1, it is hard to learn to use the language effectively.

8.1.12 SNOBOL4

SNOBOL4 is used for text processing and symbol manipulation. Each variable is a string whose length (i.e., number of characters) is unbounded and may vary during execution. Concatenation (formation of a new string from two strings placed in sequence) is a basic operation in the language. Another basic operation is a "pattern match," in which the contents of a string are examined to see if they match pattern elements. These pattern elements may be literal strings (i.e., constants), may be variables, or may have certain other special values. A pattern match can be used to determine the flow of computation as well as to replace certain portions of the examined string. In short, string handling is completely automatic.

Integer and real data types are also recognized in SNOBOL4. An integer is a string whose characters are all numeric digits (e.g., 976), and a real number consists essentially of two integers separated by a period. The usual arithmetic operations may be performed on integer and real variables; however, in some implementations inappropriate results may be obtained when the program contains arithmetic expressions involving several multiplications and/or divisions. SNOBOL4 should be regarded as excellent at handling strings but poor at arithmetic.

SNOBOL4 programs may contain arrays and tables. An array is a collection of data items (which need not be of uniform type) referenced by numeric subscripts. A table is a collection of data items, where the "subscript" of an item is a string that may have any value. For example, an item in the table AUTHOR might be accessed via the subscript SNOBOL4, using the notation

AUTHOR('SNOBOL4'). Programmer-defined data structures may define new data types.

In SNOBOL4, both input and output are considered to be sequences of lines. Input and output of a line are basic operations; for example, the statements

```
TEXT = INPUT
OUTPUT = TEXT
```

first transfer an input line to the variable TEXT and then transfer the contents of TEXT to an output line. Of course, this transfer could also be accomplished by the statement

```
OUTPUT = INPUT
```

A program is considered to be a sequence of statements, with usually one statement per line. Continuation lines, as in FORTRAN, are required for statements requiring more than one line. A statement may contain four parts, all of which are optional: a label, a condition, an action, and a flow-of-control portion. A condition or an action can either succeed (if the condition is met or the action can be completed) or can fail. The flow-of-control portion may unconditionally specify the label of the next statement to be executed, or may specify (in any order) the next statements in case of success or failure, or may be null. If the flow-of-control portion is null, execution continues with the next statement in sequence. Since flow of control is specified entirely by these means, SNOBOL4 programs are badly nonstructured.

As in BASIC and COBOL, all names are defined over the entire program text. Although procedures and functions are provided, each procedure must be declared via a special DEFINE statement which must be "executed" before the function is called. The procedure body is not delineated from the rest of the program. Thus it is possible to go to a function, and the program must be arranged carefully to avoid procedures being executed when inappropriate.

REFERENCES

[Fer 66] Ferguson, D. E. "Evolution of the Meta-Assembly Program," *Communications of the ACM*, March 1966.

[Gri 72] Griswold, R. E.; Poage, J. F.; and Polonsky, I. P. *The SNOBOL4 Programming Language*. Englewood Cliffs, NJ: Prentice-Hall, 1972.

[Ive 62] Iverson, K. E. *A Programming Language*. New York: Wiley, 1962.

[Jen 74] Jensen, K., and Wirth, N. *PASCAL User Manual and Report*, 2nd ed., New York: Springer-Verlag, 1974.

[Knu 77] Knuth, D. E., and Pardo, L. T. "Early Development of Programming Languages," in *Encyclopedia of Computer Science and Technology*, Vol. 7, pp. 419–493. New York: Marcel Dekker, 1977.

[Met 79] Metzner, J. R. "A Graded Bibliography on Macro Systems and Extensible Languages," *SIGPLAN Notices*, February 1979.

[Mye 76a] Myers, G. J. "Comparative Design Facilities of Six Programming Languages," *IBM Systems Journal*, 1976.

[Pol 75] Polivka, R., and Pakin, S. *APL: The Language and Its Usage*. Englewood Cliffs, NJ: Prentice-Hall, 1975.

[Sam 69] Sammett, J. *Programming Languages: History and Fundamentals*. Englewood Cliffs, NJ: Prentice-Hall, 1969.

[Sam 78] ———. "Roster of Programming Languages for 1976–1977," *SIGPLAN Notices*, November 1978.

[Weis 67] Weissman, C., *LISP 1.5 Primer*. Encino, CA: Dickenson, 1967.

[Wex 78] Wexelblat, R. L., ed. "Preprints of ACM SIGPLN History of Programming Languages Conference, Los Angeles, 1978," *SIGPLAN Notices*, August 1978.

PROBLEMS

1. What are the favorite languages of programmers at your computing center? Why are these languages favored?

2. What languages are taught to beginners at your university? Why are these particular languages taught?

3. What features should a language have to be most easily taught to beginners? Based on these features, make up a model for evaluating languages using the MECCA method of Section 2.4. Use this model to evaluate three languages.

4. Which languages lend themselves most easily to top-down design? To table-directed processing? To modularizing by isolation of design factors? Which language features are most suitable for each method?

5. For an application area of which you have knowledge (e.g., business data processing, operating systems construction, or compiler construction), make up a model for evaluating languages using the MECCA method of Section 2.4. Use this model to evaluate three languages.

6. Extend Problem 5 to two different application areas. Compare the models. Do the models require the same features, or does one model emphasize features that make a language unsuitable for the other application area?

7. Section 8.1 does not discuss macroassembly languages (see [Met 78]). Read about two macroassembly languages and outline their features, comparing them to the languages in Section 8.1.

8.2 PROGRAMMING STYLE

A program has a dual function: it directs a computer in the execution of an algorithm, and it also conveys design and techniques to other programmers who may need to change the program. The term *programming style* refers to the manner in which these directions and ideas are expressed in the program text, and to the degree of clarity and readability of that program text. It has been said that readability is the single best criterion of program quality.

The style in which a program text is written determines its effectiveness in communicating with:

· The program user, via its input format design and forgiveness (or nonforgiveness) of minor errors
· The maintenance programmer, via comments, assertions, error detection, and diagnostic techniques
· A possible audience of different compilers and computers, via a programming style that enhances portability

This section sketches some important points of style. (You are also advised to study one of the many manuals of programming style, e.g., [Ker 74].)

8.2.1 Communication between Program and User

8.2.1.1 Self-Documenting Communication

A program's method of communicating with the user is a crucial aspect of style. Inconvenience of use usually results in increased cost, user aggravation, and demands for program change. In fact, changing a program to accept and process new classes of inputs is a common form of modification, and thus extension of the program's communication facilities will inevitably be required. To aid this expected modification, it is important that communication between the user and the program be both general and flexible.

Section 8.2.1 outlines some principles and techniques for achieving flexible and general program/user communications. These suggestions emphasize the convenience of using the program, a concept that is applied in all really successful programming systems.

The concept of self-documenting communication is that the program should explicitly cue to the user its needs for information and its sequence of actions, in addition to its output of reports and calculation results.

For either interactive processing or batch processing, it is useful if a program uses an initial output line such as

    ***BEGIN PROCESSING - PROGRAM XX

or

    ***HELLO - PROGRAM XX NOW EXECUTING

to indicate the beginning of program execution. Similarly, a program can use a final output line such as

    ***END PROCESSING - PROGRAM XX

or

    ***PROGRAM XX TERMINATING NORMALLY

to indicate the end of execution. If the initial line is produced by the program's first executable statement, and the final line is produced by the last executable statement, then the appearance of both of these lines in the output indicates to the user that the program terminated normally instead of aborting. When a program is run interactively but produces output via a batch printer, these output lines can be directed to the user terminal only.

    A program executed in batch mode should use a line such as

PROCESSING FOR INPUT . . . IS

or

INPUT RECORD IS: . . .

or

NEXT CASE PROCESSED IS . . .

to echo each input. A convenient interactive program always explicitly prompts the user to give an appropriate input and states precisely what processing is done via output lines such as

DATA ACCEPTED

or

NAME PLACED IN FILE

    In some applications (e.g., compiling), a program must process an entire input file and can only give correct output if all data records in the file are correct. To aid in searching such an input file for errors, it is useful to have an explicit, consistent, self-contained file structure. This kind of structure can be obtained by using special records (I prefer records filled only with asterisks) to indicate

- Beginning of data
- End of data section
- End of data file

and also the use of explicit title records to indicate the type of data. These practices result in a data file with the following structure:

```
                    *** . . . ****              Begin data record
                    *** DATA TYPE MNEMONIC      Title record
    Section         .
                    .
    of data         .
                    *** . . . ****              End data section record
                    *** DATA TYPE MNEMONIC      Title record
    Section         .
                    .
    of data         .
                    *** . . . ****              End data section record
                      .
                      .
                      .
                    *** . . . ****              End data file
                    *** . . . ****
```

With such a structure, data sections may be arranged in any order and new data elements can easily be created. This file structure is entirely portable from one installation to another. Finally, a user is able to perceive what input data elements are required, and in what order, solely by examination of such an input structure.

8.2.1.2 Input Format Design

Input formats may be designed so that the largest possible set of "correct" inputs is obtained. Obviously, any input format sets a boundary between the class of nonerroneous inputs and that of erroneous inputs. Consider, for example:

Format 1: One data field is separated from the next by exactly one "blank."
Format 2: One data field is separated from the next by one or more "blanks."

Comparing the two formats, we note that there are input cards that under format 2 are nonerroneous inputs, while under format 1 these same cards are erroneous. Clearly, format 2 is more flexible than format 1.

Early assembler programs used fixed fields of columns for the operation code and each operand of an assembly language instruction. As many users learned to their dismay, one card containing one character in a wrong column might destroy the usefulness of an entire program assembly. In later assemblers, fields could have variable length and were delimited by blanks or commas.

A favorite technique of beginning programmers is requiring the first input record to state the number of input records following it. This format is extremely rigid. If the user miscounts the records, errors will occur, and this first record must be changed every time a record is added to or deleted from the input file. For safety's sake, the user must count the input records every time the program runs.

To allow a program to detect format errors without system interference, we suggest that all input data be read as alphanumeric characters. Inputs are read in exactly this fashion by COBOL programs, which moreover can reaccess a given input record many times and can thus process the record in many different ways. In FORTRAN programs, which can have only one access to any given input record, it is common practice to read via FORMAT statements that also edit the input data into floating form, integer form, and so on. If such FORMAT statements are used, and an integer field contains an alphabetic symbol, it is likely that the program will abort.

A better practice is reading all input in alphanumeric format, using error checks to ensure correct data type, and then data formatting by the program's own formatting routines. Such a technique does not require excessive execution time and saves time in using the program. Also, the required formatting subprograms are (if properly written) portable from one program to another and can be reused as desired.

8.2.1.3 Plotter Control Example

The examples of Sections 8.2.1.3 and 8.2.1.4 suggest ways to provide flexible and general communications and also show that these flexible methods can be implemented quite easily.

Let us assume we need to process a card deck containing control information for a plotting device. Since plotters require much control information, such as scale, maximum deflections, etc., and since lack of proper control causes improper operation, this program is crucial to the plotter operation.

The plotter requires control functions to be specified in groups. We may visualize, say, 20 different kinds of control cards; and if card type 10 is used, then types 11, 18, 19 must also be used, whereas if type 8 is used, then types 13, 9, 6, 20 must be used.

A program has been written that requires the control cards to be input in a strict sequence. This program is regarded as not entirely satisfactory because:

1. It is difficult to prepare input for the program.

2. The program logic that checks for correct control-card sequence is a complicated sequence of tests and jumps.

3. It is expected that the plotter will be modified to require slightly different sets of control cards, and perhaps some new types. Accordingly, the logic above will have to be completely redone.

What is the best way to format and process these control cards?

Recalling our philosophy of self-documentation and explicit convention, we first require that each control card begin with an explicit control word (e.g., scale, max, min) signifying the type of card. To allow the user to check the cards previous to input, the input deck will now be "self-indicating."

These control words can be used to direct the processing of the program. We use a two-dimensional array WORDS, each row of which contains one of the control words, as in Figure 8.5. (The symbol ƀ in Figure 8.5 denotes the "blank" character.)

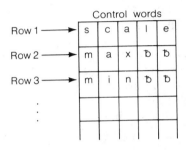

Figure 8.5 The array WORDS.

The words can appear in the array in any order. A simple table lookup program such as in Figure 8.6 can determine that the Ith word is present (i.e., that the letters on the card match the letters of row I). The Ith processing section can be executed for the Ith word. Additional control types would be accommodated by (1) addition of the new control words to the array, (2) addition of the appropriate processing sections, and (3) addition of new "positions" to the case statement that chooses the processing sections.

Testing for the occurrence of specific combinations of control cards can also be accomplished by the use of explicit data. The permissible combinations can be held in, say, a data array COMBI in which each row states a required combination of control cards, as in Figure 8.7. For example, row A in Figure 8.7 would signify that if type 10 occurs, then types 11,18,19 are also required, and row B would signify that if type 8 occurs, then types 18,9,6,20 are required. However, a given type (e.g., 9 or 19) might occur in several different rows. We may (if we desire) also require that card types appear in the order shown, (e.g., 10,11,18,19 for row A). If alternative combinations (e.g., either 5,6,7 or 5,12,13) can occur, we may allow COMBI to contain both sets of combinations.

```
(*partial program showing control word lookup*)

const
   BLANK:=' ';
   WORDSCAP:=20;
var
   CARD:array[1..80]of char;
   WORDS:array[1..WORDSCAP, 1..5]of char;
   I:integer;
   found:boolean;
begin
   .
   .
   .
   (*search for control word*)
   I:=1;
   found:=false;
   (*a blank row in WORDS terminates the search*)
   while (I<=WORDSCAP) and (WORDS[I,1]<>BLANK) and (not found) do
      begin
         found:=true;
         for J:=1 to 5 do
            if (WORDS[I,J]<>BLANK) and (WORDS[I,J]<>CARD[J])
               then found:=false;
         if not found then I:=I+1
      end;
   if not found then errorprocess (*procedure to diagnose errors*)
            else case I of
                     1:S1;
                      .
                      .
                      .
                end.
   .
   .
   .
end
```

Figure 8.6 Table lookup of control words.

COMBI

	.	⋮				
Row A	10	11	18	19	0	0
		⋮				
Row B	8	13	9	6	20	0

Figure 8.7 The array COMBI.

Next, a one-dimensional array OCCURS can be used to hold a history of the control-card types that occur in the input. This array is initialized to all 0s and then the occurrence of control word I is used to set OCCURS[I] to a nonzero value, as well as to perform the appropriate processing.

If the sequence of cards is not important, then control word I is used to set OCCURS[I]=1. The cards occur in any order, and the condition of the OCCURS array, for example,

0	1	1	0	0	0	1	0	1	1	0

always indicates which types have occurred at some time in the sequence.

If the sequence of cards is important, then the elements of OCCURS can be set to 1,2,3, and so on, indicating the exact sequence in which types have occurred.

Finally, at the end of processing, OCCURS is examined to see if the conditions of the rows of COMBI have been met. Thus the checking program of Figure 8.8 tests for OCCURS[COMBI[A,1]]≠0; and, if so, the program requires that the elements of OCCURS specified by COMBI[A,2],COMBI[A,3], and so on, be present. If sequence is important, the program can check whether the elements of the row of COMBI have occurred in the order specified.

Figure 8.9 shows a variation of the combination-checking program that provides for alternative combinations. The program of Figure 8.9 checks all combinations given in the table for a specific "master type." All combinations found are accepted by the program; and if no combinations at all are found, error messages are given for each possible combination.

Thus, by the use of explicit conventions, a program has been obtained that

· Can allow input cards to occur in any order
· Allows the types of input cards to be easily extended
· Allows the required combinations of inputs to be easily modified and/or extended

The original program assumed that the sequences and combinations of input cards were all predetermined and known to the program, while the new program assumes that no explicit details are known to the program, that these details are all data values. Also, instead of complex control logic to determine required processing and combinations, the new program contains

· A table lookup program that finds WORD[I]
· A one-line history program that records the occurrence of WORD[I] via the statement OCCURS[I]:=1
· A case statement to direct the processing to section I
· A checking program that, after all inputs have been processed, examines the OCCURS array as directed by the entries of the COMBI array

```
(*partial program showing checking of combinations*)

const
   CONTROLCAP:=25;
   COMBICAP:=50;
var
   OCCURS,typeOK:array[1..CONTROLCAP]of integer;
   COMBI:array[1..COMBICAP]of integer;
   combination,complete,required:boolean;
   i,j,k:integer;
begin
   for i:=1 to CONTROLCAP do
      begin
         OCCURS[i]:=0;
         typeOK[i]:=0
      end;
   .
   .
   .

   (*statement SI of Figure 8.6 includes OCCURS[I]:=1*)
   .
   .
   .

   (*check that required combinations have occurred*)
   required:=true;
   for i:=1 to COMBICAP do
      begin (*no check necessary if COMBI[i,1]=0*)
         if COMBI[i,1]>0
            then begin (*check this row*)
                  combination:=true;
                  for j:=2 to 6 do
                     if (COMBI[i,j]>0) and (OCCURS[COMBI[i,j]]=0)
                        then begin (*give error message*)
                           combination:=false;
                           writeln('type';COMBI[i,j],'required
                                 when type',COMBI[i,1],'is used')
                           end;
                  required:=required and combination;
                  if combination
                     then (*accept complete combination*)
                        for j:=2 to 6 do
                           if COMBI[i,j]>0 then typeOK[COMBI[i,j]]:=1
            end
      end;
   (*check types not in complete combinations*)
   complete:=true;
   for k:=1 to CONTROLCAP do
      if (OCCURS[k]>0) and (typeOK[k]=0)
         then begin
               complete:=false;
               writeln('type',k,'is not used in any complete combination')
         (*note that a combination may consist of only one type*)
   .
   .
end;
```

Figure 8.8   Checking that proper combinations have occurred.

```
(*check for combinations - alternative combinations allowed*)
required:=true;
while (i<=COMBICAP) and (COMBI[i,1]>0) do
  begin
    (*find the rows for this master type*)
    first:=i;
    j:=first;
    while (j+1<=COMBICAP) and (COMBI[j+1,1]=COMBI[i,1]) do j:=j+1;
    last:=j;

    (*check all combinations for this master type*)
    anycombination:=false;
    for m:=first to last do
      begin
        thiscombination[m]:=true;
        for n:=2 to 6 do
          if (COMBI[m,n]>0) and (OCCURS[COMBI[m,n]]=0)
            then thiscombination[m]:=false;
        anycombination:=anycombination or thiscombination[m]
      end;

    if anycombination
      then (*accept all complete combinations, ignore incomplete combinations*)
          for m:=first to last do
            if thiscombination [m]
              then for n:=2 to 6 do
                  if COMBI[m,n]>0 then typeOK[COMBI[m,n]]:=1
      else (*give error messages*)
          begin
            required:=false;
            writeln('no complete combinations found for type', COMBI[m,1]);
            writeln('possible combinations are:');
            for m:=first to last do
                write(COMBI[m,1]..COMBI[m,6]);
          end
              begin
                for k:=1 to 6 do write(COMBI[m,k]);
                writeln
              end;
        i:=last+1
      end;

    (*check types not in complete combinations*)
    complete:=true;
    for k:=1 to CONTROLCAP do
      if (OCCURS[k]>0) and (typeOK[k]=0)
        then begin
            complete:=false;
            writeln('type',k, 'is not used in any complete combination')
          end;
      (*note that a combination may consist of one type*)
```

Figure 8.9 Checking when alternative combinations are allowed.

Because the actual details (e.g., the word SCALE, or the fact that type 10 requires also types 11,18,19) are not embedded in the program (e.g., as conditions in if statements) but instead occur explicitly as data, the control processing can be arranged as a set of subprograms, each performing one specific, precisely defined action on this data. Such subprograms can be easily written, and easily checked out. If they are properly written, then their operation does not depend on the actual contents of the tables, so that the contents can be varied as desired.

8.2.1.4 Sorting Bibliographic Titles

We now desire to have a program that, given a file of fixed-length records containing bibliographic titles, sorts these records in order of author, then (within author) title, then (within title) journal, then year. Two questions of importance are:

· What are useful extensions of this specification?
· What is the "best" input format?

The discussion below suggests the reasoning involved in attacking these questions. (We do not insist that the particular formats arrived at are "the best.") Obviously, the elements (e.g., author) within each title are of variable length, and a title (or even one of the elements) may require more than one record. Accordingly, a free-format input may be used as follows:

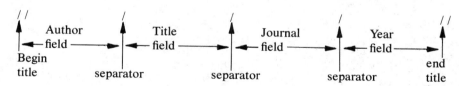

The use of // as a "begin" or "end" marker allows any title to span several records if necessary.

Consider how the scope of the desired program might be usefully extended. One possible extension is that the user specifies the sort order of titles. Possibly a user may wish to know all titles published within a given journal, in order to search the journals most efficiently. To provide for variable sort order, an input record of the form:

    SORT   J,Y,T,A

can be used to specify the order of sorting. (Here we assume J=journal, Y=year, T=title, and A=author.) Then, in case the sort record is omitted, or the originally specified order is desired, there should be a sort default condition: If no sort record is included in the input, the sort order is to be A,T,J,Y.

Variable sort order can be implemented within the program by the use of a table called SORTORDER. For the sort record above, the SORTORDER table would contain the values shown in Figure 8.10(*a*), while if no sort card were used, the SORTORDER table would contain the values shown in (*b*). The sort algorithm can then use the sort order specified by the table. The cost of this extension is a slight modification of the sort algorithm (i.e., the use of a table to determine sort order) plus small routines to process a sort card and to put in the default sort order.

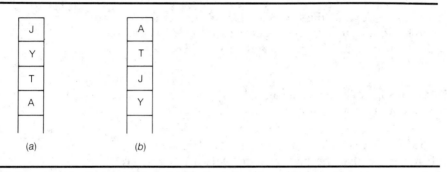

(a)   (b)

Figure 8.10   Variable sort order using a SORTORDER table. (*a*) Values corresponding to a sort card. (*b*) Default values.

Another possible extension is that input fields are given in any arbitrary order, each field type being indicated by a mnemonic. For example, an input having fields in the order J,Y,T,A might appear as

/ /J/ . . . journal . . . /Y/ . . . year . . . /T/ . . . title . . . /A/ . . . author . . . / /

This extension could be implemented by

1. The input program placing the fields in some standard order, or by
2. The program using a table (based on the appearance of these indicators) to tell the sort algorithm where the fields are, or by
3. The sort algorithm searching each input for the field indicators.

There should also be a field order default condition: If field indicators are not used, then fields are assumed to be in the order A,T,J,Y.

A final possibility is the use of arbitrary field mnemonics, the different possible fields being indicated by a record such as

FIELDS X,P,Q

and, in this case, there should be a mnemonic default condition: If no fields record is provided, then the fields are to be A,T,J,Y. This extension also may be implemented by the use of a table in which the mnemonics are stored.

If all of these extensions are adopted, the resulting program appears enormously more flexible than the original program. Input fields may be arbitrary and may occur within the inputs in arbitrary sequence. The user may specify an arbitrary sort order.

The cost of these extensions is minimal—a few tables and a few small routines. The required sort algorithm is basically unaffected. Thus the suggested extensions are easy as well as useful, requiring only the use of self-indicating input together with a very modest amount of table-driven control.

8.2.2 Self-Documenting Conventions in the Program Text

It is important that a program be easily understandable by someone other than the author, even in the absence of auxiliary documentation such as maintenance manuals. Comments in the program can be used to document important functions and algorithms. Techniques such as block indentation can be used to emphasize the program structure, and program variables can be carefully annotated.

A program consisting of several major sections can make this division apparent to the reader by using separators between sections. Each section can be preceded by a comment line consisting only of asterisks, followed by a comment line stating the section name and function, for example:

```
*****************************************************************
WRAPUP -- CLOSE FILES AND END PROGRAM
```

Statement labels within each section can follow the name of the section. For example, the section WRAPUP might use only labels WRAP1,WRAP2, and so on. In FORTRAN, a range of statement numbers can be adopted for each section and indicated in the section's header, as, for example:

```
C*****************************************************************
C WRAPUP -- CLOSE FILES AND END PROGRAM --
C              LABELS 5000 - 5999
```

Standard naming conventions can be used for data, such as standard suffixes ARY for array, TAB for table, and FLG for flag. For example, a personnel table might be named PERTAB and items within the table named PERNAM (name), PERADD (address), and so on. A data dictionary can be included, indicating the meaning of each data item, and this inclusion should greatly help anyone understand the program.

A practice that contributes both to readability and to maintainability is the use of an explicit variable name for each important constant. For example, a program whose calculations involve the number of bits in the computer word might declare a variable NUMBITS, indicate its meaning in the data dictionary, and then initialize it appropriately. With this practice, the significance of the constant is clearly understood at each use (since the name NUMBITS appears, rather than just a constant such as 32 or 48), and the entire program may be made appropriate for a different computer merely by changing the initialization of NUMBITS. This practice is made easy by the DATA statement of FORTRAN and the constant declaration feature of PASCAL.

8.2.3 Error Avoidance, Defensive Programming, and Diagnostics

One aspect of style is the way in which a program deals with error situations. It is worth repeating that input formats should be made as flexible as possible so that potential errors are avoided. Also, of course, a program embodies restrictions on inputs and should give a diagnostic message whenever any restriction of an input, such as maximum array size, is violated.

The term *defensive programming* signifies a program style that realizes that error situations will arise both from improper input and from errors in the program. A defensive program makes no assumptions about a situation, but instead tests all possibilities and provides diagnostic messages and alternative processing if appropriate. Kernighan and Plauger say that

> We test explicitly for the last possible condition and print 'can't happen' when the impossible occurs . . . the first time we ran this code, it said 'can't happen' . . . we got that message often in the process of adding the rest of the code and shaking it down . . . we finally decided to leave the messages in for all time, instead of pretending to be perfect [Ker 81, pp. 153–154].

A careful design includes a specific test and a specific action for each possible condition.

The program action in response to an error can consist of diagnosis and printout of an error message, or it can include attempted partial processing and/or attempted error correction.

Programs usually require diagnostic tracing during debugging, and such diagnostic messages should be incorporated in the program. They can be excised later if desired. The production of diagnostic messages can be made conditional on a control card or message from the terminal. As an example, a batch program might normally require a blank card at the beginning of each data deck. Replacing the blank card with a card having a nonblank character in, say, column 15 could then direct the output of diagnostic message 15 if the appropriate error occurs.

8.2.4 Programming for Portability

Portability is a measure of the ease with which a program can be transferred from one operating system to a different one, or from one computer to a different one. A fully portable program is one that can be transferred without any rewriting at all, while a nonportable program is one which cannot be transferred without complete rewriting. Since computers become obsolescent in three to five years, and since operating systems are constantly being modified, portability is a very desirable characteristic. This section points out some problems in achieving portability and offers some solutions.

Language Portability can be effectively blocked by an inappropriate language or by an inappropriate style of programming. If the language chosen is available only at the programmer's installation, or only for one computer, then the program cannot easily be transferred. An obvious example is the use of assembly language. However, if a macroassembly language is used, and if the system is arranged to have a reasonably small number of primitive macros (i.e., macros defined only in terms of assembly language instructions), then the system can be transferred to another macroassembly language by rewriting the primitive macros and perhaps changing some syntax. Exactly this technique was used in implementing SNOBOL.

If a high-level language is used, the program should avoid language features or eccentricities peculiar to one installation or one computer. Such features almost always fail at another installation; at best the program will abort, necessitating rewriting, while at worst (for subtle errors) the program will run improperly until the error is detected. If a standard exists for the language, the best practice is to write within the standard.

Word Size and Number Representation Every computer has its own word size (e.g., 8 bits, 16 bits, etc.) and its own method of representing numbers (e.g., sign and magnitude, 1's complement, 2's complement, etc.), which obviously cannot be changed. To the extent that it deals directly with these characteristics, a program loses portability. For example, a program involving numerical analysis techniques cannot be transferred without examining the effect of the new computer's precision, truncation, and roundoff properties on the calculations.

Any reference to a specific characteristic, such as word size, should be accompanied by a program comment warning that the usage is machine-dependent. If possible, the characteristic should be made explicit, for example, by use of a variable NUMBITS or WRDSIZ to signify word size. Use of information based on knowledge of the numeric representation method (e.g., testing the sign bit) should be avoided.

Character Handling and Character Codes Portability is also enhanced if the character-handling technique of a program is independent of the computer used. For example, a standard internal format of one character per word can easily be transferred from one computer to another. Of course, the program's input/output routines must be arranged to transform data to and from this internal format.

Although every computer may have different character codes, a program can be made independent of specific numeric codes for characters. If only a few codes are dealt with, say, perhaps those for 0 and 1, explicit variables zero and one containing the appropriate constants can be used. Alternatively, the code values might be placed in an array CODES, where, say, CODES[0] is the code for 0, CODES[1] is the code for 1, and so on. If program calculations are written in terms of CODES[0] and so on, then transfer to a new computer may be accomplished by placing a new set of appropriate numeric values in CODES.

Programs such as compilers, which perform calculations using the codes of input characters, usually require that the codes of certain characters have specific values. For example, it is usually required that the code for 0 be the numeric value 0, that the code for 1 be the numeric value 1, and so on. One portable way of fulfilling this requirement is the use of an internal code set that has the desired values together with a table array CODES containing each pair of computer and internal codes side by side. In other words, CODES[I,1] contains a character's computer code, and CODES[I,2] contains the corresponding internal code. On input, each character is found as CODES[J,1] for some J and replaced for internal use by CODES[J,2]. On output, each character is found as CODES[J,2] for some J and replaced by CODES[J,1]. Thus the internal processing is independent of the computer's numeric codes.

REFERENCES

[Ker 74] Kernighan, B. W., and Plauger, P. J. *The Elements of Programming Style.* New York: McGraw-Hill, 1974.

[Ker 81] ———. *Software Tools in PASCAL.* New York: Addison-Wesley, 1981.

PROBLEMS

1. List the points of type mentioned in Section 8.2. With respect to these points, evaluate
   (a) Problem B of Appendix E.

(b) Problem C of Appendix E.

(c) A program in a popular computing magazine.

2. Read Kernighan and Plauger [Ker 81] and examine their use of defensive coding and check for "impossible" conditions. Is defensive coding a sensible procedure? State your reasons.

3. Examine a program in a popular computing magazine. What percentage of the code must be changed to move the program to a new computer? What is the basis for your estimate?

8.3 EFFICIENCY CONSIDERATIONS

8.3.1 What Is Efficiency?

The phrase *execution efficiency* refers to a program's requirements for memory and for time. A program that is faster than another is said to be more efficient in its use of time, and a program that uses less memory space than another is said to be more efficient in its use of space. However, it is well known that space can be traded for speed or vice versa. For example, an algorithm can always be made to run faster by the use of straight-line code in place of loops. Greater speed is obtained because maintaining the loop index is no longer required; but the straight-line code incurs extra memory costs. Conversely, an algorithm can be squeezed into a smaller memory by the use of pseudocode packed into tables; however, then the pseudocode must be interpreted, requiring extra time.

Let $C(s,t)$, where s,t are space and time usages in convenient units, be a cost function expressing the total cost of a program for space and time. Because users have widely differing needs and costs, $C(s,t)$ must be measured according to the application at hand. Depending on the actual costs for space and time, the user and software developer can agree on the relative emphasis between space and time, and on the form of the function. As an example, constants k_1, k_2 might be agreed upon and used in a cost function such as

$C_1(s,t) = k_1 s + k_2 t$

or

$C_2(s,t) = (k_1 s) \cdot (k_2 t)$

Such a cost function can be expanded to include response times, communication costs, and so on. The most efficient program with respect to $C(s,t)$ is the one that minimizes the value of $C(s,t)$.

8.3.2 Efficiency versus Completeness

One way to obtain efficiency is to restrict the program's function. For example, the set of allowable inputs might be restricted, or processing of some errors might be omitted or abbreviated, or some manipulation of the inputs might be deleted from the program and done manually. In other words, efficiency is obtained at the cost of a less complete, or less robust, or less comprehensive program.

Obtaining efficiency in this way is a poor idea. When the total cost of use of a program is calculated, including the cost of the personnel who run the program, the more comprehensive and robust program almost always has the lowest cost of use. For example, a compiler that quits after one error in a source program will always execute more quickly and use less space than a compiler (otherwise identical) that responds to every error. However, finding *all* the errors with the "more efficient" compiler will require at least one run per error, as contrasted to simply one run for the compiler that detects every error. Thus the cost of finding *all* errors in a source program will be higher for the less comprehensive compiler.

8.3.3 Efficiency versus Adaptability

Efficiency may also be obtained by exploiting the peculiarities of the program's environment, application, or method. Some examples are:

· Using special machine instructions
· Basing the algorithm on the number of bits in the machine word
· Allowing the operating system to initialize values
· Using a special feature of the programming language dialect
· Using a special algorithm that happens to work for the data values currently being processed

Unfortunately, the greater use that a program makes of the peculiarities of its circumstances, the harder it will be to change that program when the circumstances change. Stated more generally, the better adapted a system is to the peculiar features of a particular environment, the less adaptable it is to new environments. Using a special feature of the language dialect makes it harder to change to a new dialect; relying on a peculiar feature of the operating system makes it harder to change to a new operating system.

Weinberg [Weinb 71] describes an algorithm in an assembler program that translated symbolic operation codes (e.g., add) to the corresponding machine-code bit patterns. The bit pattern of the symbolic operation code (treated as a numeric value) was multiplied by a special numeric constant to obtain the address of the required machine-code bit pattern. The algorithm was possible only because the special numeric constant happened to work for the particular operation codes used.

Unfortunately, an algorithm that relies on particular data values may have to be scrapped when other values are used. When a dozen more symbolic operation codes were added to the assembly language, the special numeric constant would no longer yield a compact set of unique addresses. In fact, no such constant could be found that would work for the new codes. Finally, after much effort had been spent in trying to find a new constant, the algorithm was abandoned and a more general algorithm was used.

In sum, the specialized algorithm shaved a few microseconds off each program execution for a few months time—and then caused much wasted effort. In contrast, the use of a more general algorithm from the start would have cost a few more microseconds at each program execution, but the modification would have been trivial. From the viewpoint of total cost (including the cost of program maintenance), the use of the specialized algorithm was a mistake.

8.3.4 Impact of the Algorithm

We hereafter consider only the minimization of execution time, which has continually been the main concern of programmers. Execution time is primarily determined by the program's algorithm. As an example, students have written programs for the secret sums problem described in Chapter 3. The execution times of these student programs have varied by a factor of 2000 to 1. Some student programs written in BASIC on a time-sharing system, and with paticularly inefficient algorithms, were unable to solve two-letter puzzles in several hours of interactive terminal time. Other student programs, with efficient algorithms, were able to solve SEND+MORE=MONEY in five seconds of CPU time.

If minimum execution time is an important requirement for a program, effort should be spent in analyzing the algorithm. Kernighan and Plauger [Ker 74] examined a supposedly efficient bubble-sort program and found it to run more slowly than a simple bubble-sort program. Next, a simple shell-sort program was examined and found to run even faster, when more than 50 items were to be sorted. Their discussion concludes with the motto: "Don't diddle code to make it faster—find a new algorithm."

8.3.5 Impact of the Programming Language

A recurring controversy among programmers is whether programs require less execution time when written in an assembly language or in a high-level language. It has been argued that the assembly code produced by high-level-language compilers is always 15 to 25 percent slower than directly pro-grammed assembly code, so that programs should be written directly in as-sembly code to achieve the least execution time. However, programming directly in assembly language is almost always less advantageous than pro-gramming in a high-level language.

Remember that the program's algorithm is much more crucial to efficiency than the programming language. While execution time may vary by 25 percent due to a poor language, it may vary by huge factors due to a poor choice of algorithm. (Recall the discussion of Section 8.3.4.)

For some high-level languages, optimizing compilers exist that can yield much improved assembly code. Programs written in high-level languages and optimized in this way can sometimes be *more* efficient than programs origi-nally written in assembly language.

Concern with program speed often arises in problems where memory must be conserved by packing data items into parts of computer words. But lan-guages such as PL/1, JOVIAL, and COBOL allow procedures and data to be defined independently of each other. After the program's algorithm has been checked out, its speed can often be increased by adjusting the data definitions and allowing the optimizing compiler to take advantage of computer instruc-tions on subwords. In contrast, it is quite difficult to change data definitions in assembly language.

In exceptional cases, portions of a high-level-language program may be rewritten directly in assembly language, for greater speed. Section 8.3.6 dis-cusses the circumstances under which this might be done.

8.3.6 Efficiency via Program Measurement

The execution times of program segments can be measured or carefully esti-mated to detect segments with excessive time costs, and those segments can be rewritten to improve program speed. This simple procedure has had some spectacular successes [Knu 71, Nem 71, Book 72] in improving performance.

Estimation of program execution times can be based on statement fre-quency counts [Knu 71, Sti 75], that is, the number of times each statement is executed when the program is run. The program to be examined is input to a preprocessor program that, by assigning costs to the various computer opera-tions (e.g., load, add, store) in the object code of each program statement, estimates the total time cost of one execution of that statement. The prepro-cessor also inserts code into the program to cause counts to be incremented as each statement is executed. Then, when the program under examination is executed, frequency counts and time cost estimates for each statement are obtained as in Figure 8.11.

Table 8.1 summarizes the time cost for each routine based on the cost estimates of Figure 8.11. It is immediately apparent that the routine FUN uses over half the time of the program and therefore that execution time could be markedly improved by rewriting FUN. Some systems produce bar graphs showing the percentage of total execution time cost associated with each routine [Nem 71].

Table 8.1   Time costs summarized by routine

Routine	Time Costs	Total Time Costs, %
MAIN	1762	3
RK2	24,782	41
FUN	33,600	56

	EXECUTABLE STATEMENTS	EXECUTIONS	COST
10	READ (5,1) XO,YO,H,JNT,IENT	2	100
	IF (IENT) 20,40,20	2	4
20	WRITE (6,2) H,XO,YO	1	50
	CALL RK2 (FUN,H,XO,YO,JNT,IENT,A)	1	2
	STEP=FLCAT(JNT)*H	1	11
	X=XO	1	1
	DO 30 I=1,IENT	1	2
	X=X+STEP	30	60
30	WRITE (6,3) X,A(I)	30	1530
	GO TO 10	1	1
40	STOP	1	1
	END		
	FUNCTION FUN(X,Y)	1200	18000
	FUN=1./X	1200	9600
	RETURN	1200	6000
	END		
	SUBROUTINE RK2(FUN,H,XI,YI,K,N,VEC)	1	15
	H2=H/2.	1	8
	X=XI	1	1
	Y=YI	1	1
	DO 2 I=1,N	1	2
	DO 1 J=1,K	30	60
	T1=H*FUN(X,Y)	300	2700
	T2=H*FUN(X÷H2,Y+T1/2.)	300	5400
	T3=H*FUN(X÷H2,Y+T2/2.)	300	5400
	T4=H*FUN(X÷H,Y+T3)	300	3300
	Y=Y+(T1+2.*T2+2.*T3+T4)/6.	300	6900
1	X=X+H	300	900
2	VEC(I)=Y	30	90
	RETURN	1	5
	END		

Figure 8.11   Estimate of time costs for a sample program. (From *An Empirical Study of FORTRAN Programs* by D. E. Knuth. Copyright 1971. Reprinted by permission of John Wiley & Sons, Ltd.)

As an alternative, execution time can be measured by program status sampling. A system program periodically interrupts the program being measured and notes the location of the current instruction. Sampling may be done by a hardware monitor system or by a hardware/software monitor [Knu 71, Nem 71, Book 72].

Using both techniques, a study of execution times of FORTRAN programs [Knu 71] arrived at two findings:

1. Less than 4 percent of a program text generally accounts for more than half its running time.

2. Input/output editing seems to use up more than 25 percent of the running time of FORTRAN programs, in spite of the extremely infrequent occurrence of actual input/output statements.

The first finding has been roughly corroborated by other studies. We might thus expect that 3 to 6 percent of the program text (most probably a few inner loops) will use 50 percent of the execution time. Therefore, execution time may easily be improved by measuring execution time, detecting the crucial text lines, and optimizing these lines. In a 1000-line program, for example, about 40 lines would be crucial, and improving the execution time of these lines by 50 percent would improve the entire program's execution time by 25 percent.

Thus dramatic improvement may be obtained at very little cost. Amusingly, this cost estimate technique was used on the frequency count preprocessor discussed by Knuth [Knu 71], and the cost estimate showed that the preprocessor spent half its time in two inefficient loops. These loops were simplified in less than an hour's work, and the execution time of the preprocessor was reduced by 50 percent.

A similar incident is reported by Nemeth and Rovner [Nem 71]. A flowchart interpreter program which had been running more slowly than expected was found to spend excessive time in calculating a distance function $SQRT(X**2+Y**2)$. The report continues:

We therefore changed the distance function to $ABS(X)+ABS(Y)$. While these distance functions are not mathematically equivalent, they perform identical functions in the interpreter. This trivial modification of the program produced an improvement of 43 percent and took about two man-hours to discover and implement [Nem 71, p. 664].

The second finding implies that the execution time of FORTRAN programs can be improved substantially either by reducing the amount of input/output editing or by linking the program to more efficient input/output routines. One way to reduce input/output editing is to perform all read/write actions using an alphanumeric, one character per word format and to perform editing in the program itself. This technique improves error detection and error tolerance (recall the discussion of Section 8.2.1.2) as well as improving efficiency.

The performance of large systems can be improved by iteration of the following four steps [Book 72]:

1. Obtain a system profile.
2. Identify areas for potential improvement.
3. Effect specific changes.
4. Obtain a system profile (to check supposed improvements and also to iterate).

When attempting to improve performance in this way, remember [Book 72]:

· Look for the obvious.
· Don't waste time measuring things that don't affect performance.
· More effort is required to achieve each successive increment of improvement.

These techniques provided striking results in one case study [Book 72]. A data center system configuration, initially a linked IBM 360/50 and 360/40, was reduced to a 360/50 alone, which performed work better than the initial configuration had done and also had sufficient capacity for new work. Total annual recurring savings to the data center were $275,000 [Book 72].

REFERENCES

[Book 72] Bookman, P. G.; Brotman, B. A.; and Schmitt, K. L. "Use Measurement Engineering for Better System Performance," *Computer Decisions*, April 1972.

[Ker 74] Kernighan, B. W., and Plauger, P. J. *The Elements of Programming Style*. New York: McGraw-Hill, 1974.

[Knu 71] Knuth, D. E. "An Empirical Study of FORTRAN Programs," *Journal of Software Practice and Experience*, Vol. 1, 1971.

[Nem 71] Nemeth, A. G., and Rovner, P. D. "User Program Measurement in a Time-Shared Environment," *Communications of the ACM*, Vol. 14, No. 10, October 1971.

[Sti 75] Stillman, R. B. "FORTRAN Analysis by Simple Transforms," *Proceedings of the Computer Science and Statistics 8th Annual Conference on the Interface*, University of California at Los Angeles, 1975.

[Weinb 71] Weinberg, G. M. *The Psychology of Computer Programming*. New York: Van Nostrand Reinhold, 1971.

PROBLEMS

1. Are space and time efficiencies of a program always important, only important in certain circumstances, or never important? Explain your position, giving examples.

2. It has been said that the costs of computers are continually decreasing while the hourly costs of programming are continually increasing. If this is true, what impact does it have on the relative importance of efficiency and completeness? On the relative importance of efficiency and adaptability?

3. Consider the special algorithm described in Section 8.3.3. Assume that the specialized algorithm saves 100 microseconds at each execution, that computer cost is $100 per hour, and that the assembler is used 5000 times a year for a period of 5 years.
   (a) Calculate the total dollar savings over the five-year period due to use of the algorithm.
   (b) Assume that a programmer costs $300 per week and takes a week to try to salvage the algorithm. Calculate the total cost of trying to modify the algorithm. Compare this cost with the total potential savings given by the algorithm over a five-year period. Consider the expenditure of time in the algorithm as an investment to be recouped in execution time savings. How much effort should the programmer have spent in trying to salvage the algorithm?

4. Assume that in improving performance, a greater effort is required to achieve each successive increment of performance, and also that successive increments are smaller and smaller. By analogy to Problem 3, describe how you would determine the appropriate time to stop trying to improve the system.

8.4 EVALUATION OF PROGRAM CODE

8.4.1 Code Examination to Determine Program Quality

Many aspects of program quality can be checked by examining the program text. Quality checklists (see [Fagan 76, Boe 78]) can be used in code inspections and structured walkthroughs.

In a study of software quality, Boehm and others [Boe 78] concluded that software utility depends on seven intuitive, overlapping quality components:

1. *Portability:* The ease with which a program can be transferred to a new environment, while continuing to operate easily and well.
2. *Reliability:* The extent to which a program can be expected to perform satisfactorily. Components of reliability are:
   (a) the extent to which the program performs correctly for legal inputs;
   (b) the number of bugs that surface when the program is made operational;
   (c) the probability of an incorrect result persisting undetected; and
   (d) the extent to which the program performs satisfactorily for unplanned inputs (robustness).
3. *Efficiency:* The extent to which full use is made of resources.
4. *Human engineering:* The extent to which use of the program is made easy, quick, and pleasant for users.
5. *Testability:* The extent to which a program helps in the establishment of test criteria and the evaluation of program performance.
6. *Understandability:* The extent to which the program makes its purpose clear to the evaluator.
7. *Modifiability:* The extent to which a program anticipates the incorporation of changes.

These intuitive quality components cannot be directly measured by examining a program text. However, they depend on such text attributes as:

1. *Device-independence:* The extent to which the program is executable without change on new computer configurations.
2. *Completeness:* The extent to which the program can stand alone, without other programs or systems.
3. *Accuracy:* The extent to which outputs are sufficiently precise for their intended use.
4. *Consistency:*
   (a) Internal consistency is the use of uniform notation, terminology, and symbology within the program;
   (b) External consistency is the extent to which the program content is traceable to requirements.
5. *Device-efficiency:* The extent to which full use is made of devices.
6. *Accessibility:* The ease with which components of a program can be selectively used.
7. *Communicativeness:* The extent to which the program helps the specification of inputs and provides useful and informative outputs.
8. *Structuredness:* The extent to which the parts of a program are organized into a definite pattern.
9. *Self-descriptiveness:* The extent to which a program clearly indicates its objectives, assumptions, constraints, inputs, outputs, components, and status.
10. *Conciseness:* The omission of excessive information.

11. *Legibility:* The extent to which a program delineates its function and the functions of those of its component statements.
12. *Augmentability:* The extent to which a program easily accommodates expansions in data storage requirements or computations of component functions.

These text attributes can be directly measured by examination. Examples of preferred and undesired usages for both intuitive and text attributes are given in Boehm et al. [Boe 78, Chapter 3].[2]

A dependency structure can be shown as in Figure 8.12 relating the intuitive attributes, the text attributes, and metrics for the text attributes. Each of the single horizontal lines shown under metrics in Figure 8.12 denotes a specific test that detects an anomaly for that text attribute. (See [Boe 78] for tables of such tests.) With the automation of such metrics, the author of a program could receive a report showing where anomalies occurred in the software and why they are considered anomalies.

Figure 8.12 shows that software utility has three components, corresponding to the possible uses of a program:

· Usability "as is" denotes how well (easily, reliably, efficiently) the program can be used as is
· Maintainability denotes how easy the program is to maintain (understand, modify, and retest)
· Usability in a changed environment denotes the extent to which the program can still be used in a new environment

In Figure 8.12 a line from box A to box B on A's right means that A requires B, or, equivalently, A depends on B. Thus usability as is requires that a program have reliability, efficiency, and human engineering,[3] but does not require that the user test the program, modify it, understand its internal workings, or try to use it elsewhere. Maintainability requires the user to understand, modify, and test the program, but does not require the other attributes (except that if the user's computer system is changing, portability may be required).

Dependence between intuitive and text attributes is shown in the same way. For example, portability requires both completeness and device-independence. Note that [Boe 78]:

· A program that does not initialize its own storage is not complete and thus is not portable even though it may be device-independent

---

[2]A somewhat different set of quality components, also developed for predicting quality by code analysis [McCal 77], is described in McCall [McCal 79].
[3]There are special applications for which further attributes, such as security, are required.

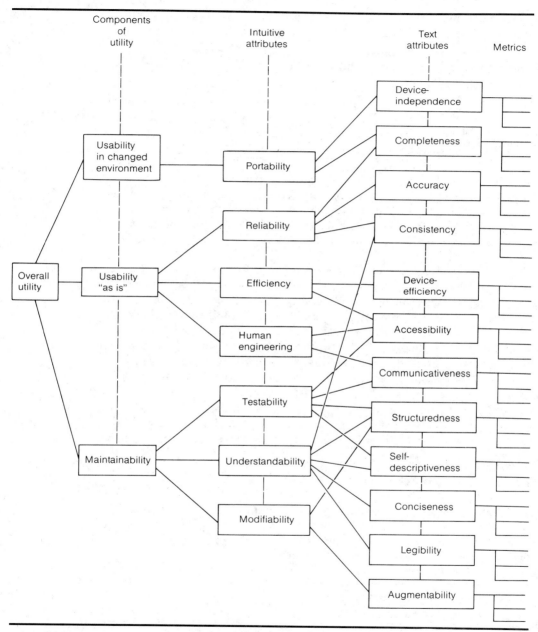

Figure 8.12 Dependency structure relating intuitive attributes, test attributes, and metrics. (Copyright 1978 by North-Holland. Reprinted by permission.)

- A program whose input or output formats implicitly depend on computer word size is not device-independent and thus is not portable even though it may be complete
- A program that is device-independent and complete is portable even though it may not have any other text attribute

8.4.2 An Example: Evaluation of Constant, Variable, and Subroutine Usage

In industry as well as in classrooms, programs often use constants, variables, and subroutines in inappropriate, or inefficient, or "just plain stupid" ways. This section shows how to find these defective usages by using checklists and a simple procedure, and discusses how to remedy the defects. The evaluation techniques of this section are intended for readers without experience in program evaluation.

The following tables contain categories of usage for constants, variables, and subroutines. Each category has a numeric rating. In each table, the categories are arranged with poorest usage (rating 0) first, next poorest usage (1) next, and so on. A constant (or variable or subroutine) is evaluated by comparing its usage with each usage in turn of the appropriate table. In other words, the constant is compared first with the usage category of rating 0; next with the category of rating 1; and so on through all the categories. The *measure* or *goodness rating* of the constant is the rating of the first usage category that accurately describes its usage.

Tables 8.2, 8.3, and 8.4 are intended as guides. Their categories of usage are not exhaustive, and the assigned measures are not absolute. It is hoped that you will soon develop additional categories as well as a personal way of using the tables.

8.4.2.1 Evaluation of Constants

The categories in Table 8.2 are interpreted as follows:

Table 8.2   Evaluation of constants within a single program or subroutine

Measure	Category of Usage
0	Machine-dependent
1	System-dependent
2	Table or array capacity
3	One of a set of values that should be placed in an array
4	Otherwise

• *Measure 0:* A value based on machine characteristics, as, for example a constant denoting the number of bits per word (i.e., using, say, the constant 32 to indicate 32 bits per word). Use of machine-dependent parameters decreases the portability of a program and increases the difficulty of maintenance.

Remedy: If such parameters must be used, the following steps are suggested:

1. Isolate the parameter in a variable (e.g., BITS).
2. Wherever the variable name is mentioned, insert a warning message (e.g., 'BITS IS MACHINE DEPENDENT -- NUMBER OF BITS PER WORD').

• *Measure 1:* A value based on system characteristics, as, for example, a constant denoting the total number of disk units or indicating a specific unit.
Remedy: If possible, follow the steps suggested for measure 0.

• *Measure 2:* A constant signifying a table or array capacity is used within the program code, as, for example, in a test to determine whether the array has been filled.
Remedy: The best practice is:

1. Isolate the parameter in a variable, say, XCAP for an array X.
2. Insert a warning message at the array declaration (e.g., 'CHANGE OF CAPACITY REQUIRES CHANGE OF XCAP').

A special problem occurs when, because of small word size (e.g., 8 bits in a microcomputer), the constant is close to the maximum value possible to contain in a word (e.g., the constant 250 in an 8-bit word). If double-word constants are not available, insert a warning message (e.g., 'CAPACITY LIMITED BY WORD SIZE').

• *Measure 3:* Programs often contain sets of constants, as, for example, capacities, or time durations, or boundary values.
Remedy: Isolate the set of constants as elements of an array (instead of embedding them in the program code). In this way the intent of the constants is documented, and the values of the constants can be easily modified.

• *Measure 4:* A constant that is not in one of the other three categories is properly used.
Remedy: None required.

A measure of less than 4 indicates a defective usage that should be remedied (the constant should then be reevaluated also). When all constants have a measure of 4, all defective usages have been eliminated.

Note that a preferred way of dealing with a constant is to isolate it as the value of a variable. For example, the constant 3.1416 might be isolated as the value of a variable PI.

8.4.2.2 Evaluation of Variables

Table 8.3 states categories of usage appropriate for evaluating variables within the confines of one program of one subroutine, but not for evaluating the transfer of information *between* programs or routines. Different categories of usage are appropriate for evaluating parameters transferred between subroutines.

Table 8.3   Evaluation of variables within a single program or subroutine

Measure	Category of Usage
0	Never referenced or set
1	Set but never referenced
2	Requires initial value, but never initialized
3	Initial value sometimes not set when required
4	Redundant at time of use
5	Redundant settings to the same value
6	Set by side effect
7	Implicitly used as an element of an array or record
8	Acts as a loop index but not declared as a loop index
9	Incomprehensible or misleading name
10	Otherwise

Below are the interpretations and remedies for each category of usage of Table 8.3. Note, however, that these measures do not apply to variables that merely name constants. As indicated in Section 8.4.2.1, the use of an identifier to isolate the value of an important constant (e.g., PI=3.1416) is preferred usage.

- *Measure 0:* The variable is declared in a type declaration, but its value is not set by any program statement,[4,5] and its value is not used by any program statement.

---

[4]In the evaluation of a formal argument of a subroutine, it is assumed that the calling of the subroutine initializes (i.e., sets) the value of the argument at the moment of the call. Accordingly, initializing statements or other statements setting the value are not required.
[5]Values may be set or initialized by input statements or by data statements.

Remedy: Eliminate the variable from the program.

- *Measure 1:* The variable is declared in a type declaration, or (in the case of a subroutine) as a formal argument. Its value is not used by any program statement.[4]

  Remedy: Eliminate the variable from the program.

- *Measure 2:* The variable's value is not set by a program statement.[4,5] Or, a program statement using the value is always executed prior to execution of any statement that sets the value.[5]

  Remedy: Provide appropriate initialization statements.

- *Measure 3:* There is at least one execution sequence in which a program statement using the variable's value is executed prior to the execution of a statement that sets the value.[6] This situation may occur when different circumstances require different initial values; or when a special usage of the variable is intended to initialize it, but does not in fact do so.

  Remedy: Provide appropriate initialization statements for each execution sequence.

- *Measure 4:* The variable's value, each time the value is used, differs from the value of another variable in the same program by the same additive constant (e.g., $+5.3$ or -2) or the same multiplicative constant (e.g., 3 or $1/5$). Examples are the use of the variables I and J, where each time J is used, its value is $J = I - 2$; or the use of variables X and Y, where each time Y is used, its value is $Y = 1/5 * X$.

  Remedy: Eliminate a redundant variable, such as J, from the program and replace each reference to J by the arithmetic expression (e.g., $I - 2$) giving the desired value.

- *Measure 5:* The variable is repeatedly set to the same value. This situation commonly occurs when a variable in a DO or for loop is set prior to any use of its value, and the value is not changed within the loop. After the first execution of the loop, the continued settings of the variable to the same value are unnecessary.

  Remedy: Remove the statement that sets the variable from the loop.

  Note: This category does not apply to formal argument variables or to input variables that, during execution, repeatedly receive the same values. Although a program may be called repeatedly with the same actual parameter value, or may repeatedly receive the same actual input value, the called or receiving program cannot anticipate that the value will repeatedly be the same. Such a program must assume that the actual value received will be different each time.

- *Measure 6:* In many languages, a subroutine or procedure is allowed to set the values of variables that are not explicitly called out as input or output parameters but that are global to the procedure. The setting by a procedure of such a global variable is called a *side effect*. Such usage inevitably leads to

---

[6]Remember that values may be set or initialized by either input or data statements.

problems in maintenance and modification because a programmer unfamiliar with the side effect may not realize when the variable is set.

Remedy: At the least, a warning comment should be given with every call of the subroutine. The best technique, though, is to construct the procedure so as to eliminate the side effect.

- *Measure 7:* A similar process is performed on each of a sequence of variables; or a sequence of variables is produced by a similar calculation; or a collection of variables is used in concert.

Remedy: Organize variables into arrays and organize related data values into records if this can be achieved with simple code changes.

That is, usage can be improved if the code can be easily rearranged so that the sequence of values used or produced can be coalesced into an array or if related values can be organized into records or table entries. For example, a program with the calculations

y1:=f1(x1);y2=f2(x2); . . . ;yk:=fk(xk);

can be improved by coalescing the variables y1,y2, . . . ,yk into an array and coalescing x1, . . . , xk into an array to obtain the code

y[1]:=f1(x[1]);y2:=f2(x[2]); . . . ;yk:=fk(x[k]);

Even greater improvement is obtained if we can easily rewrite the program as

for i:=1 to k do y[i]:=g(x[i],i);

where g(x[1],1)=f1(x[1]),g(x[2],2)=f2(x[2]), and so on.

- *Measure 8:* The variable occurs within a loop but is not formally the loop index, though its value is used in place of the value of the loop index. (This situation may also give rise to measure 4.)

Remedy: Rewrite the loop so that only one of the variables is used.

- Measure 9: The variable has an incomprehensible or misleading name.

Remedy: Change the name so that the significance of the variable is easily understood.

- *Measure 10:* The variable, which is not in any of the other nine categories, is properly used.

Remedy: None required.

8.4.2.3 Evaluation of Subroutines

The categories in Table 8.4 are interpreted as follows:

- *Measure 0:* Within the system of programs containing the subroutine, there is no program that calls the subroutine.

Remedy: Eliminate the subroutine from the system.

- *Measure 1:* The subroutine sets the value of a global variable that is not in its argument list.

  Remedy: Rewrite the subroutine, either eliminating setting the variable or placing the variable name in the argument list.

- *Measure 2:* Values needed in the calculation are not passed to the subroutine; or values are passed through COMMON; or global values are used.

  Remedy: Pass all values through the argument list.

- *Measure 3:* Some arguments are not referenced.

  Remedy: Eliminate these arguments, unless they are reserved for future expansion of the system.

- *Measure 4:* Several subroutines perform variations of the same process. This situation typically arises when the programmer does not observe that a process can be parameterized.

  Remedy: Coalesce the subroutines if the length of the coalesced subroutine (not counting procedure headings and declarations) is equal to or less than 75 percent of the sum of the lengths of the individual subroutines.[7]

- *Measure 5:* A subroutine contains several unrelated processes.

  Remedy: Split the subroutine if the sum of the lengths of the split subroutine bodies (not counting procedure headings and declarations) is equal to or less than the length of the original subroutine body.

- *Measure 6:* The subroutine has an incomprehensible or misleading name.

  Remedy: Change the name.

- *Measure 7:* A subroutine, which is not in any of the other six categories, is properly used.

  Remedy: None required.

Table 8.4 Evaluation of subroutines

Measure	Category of Usage
0	Never called
1	Produces side effects
2	Too few arguments passed
3	Too many arguments passed
4	Can be coalesced with other subroutines into one subroutine
5	Can be split into several independent subroutines
6	Incomprehensible or misleading name
7	Otherwise

---

[7]The 75 percent rule of thumb is based on the expectation that if unrelated functions are coalesced into one routine, the length of the program text will not be reduced; however, if related functions can be parameterized, then substantial reduction in the program text should be achievable.

REFERENCES

[Boe 78] Boehm, B. W., et al. *Characteristics of Software Quality.* Amsterdam: North-Holland Publishing Company, 1978.

[Fagan 76] Fagan, M. E. "Design and Code Inspections to Reduce Errors in Program Development." *IBM Systems Journal*, Vol. 15, No. 3, 1976. (Also in [Mil 78]).*

[McCal 77] McCall, J.; Richards, P.; and Walters, G. *Factors in Software Quality*, 3 vols., NTIS AD-A049-014, 015, 055, November 1977.

[McCal 79] McCall, J. A. "An Introduction to Software Quality Metrics," in J. D. Cooper and M. J. Fisher (eds.), *Software Quality Management.* New York: Petrocelli, 1979.

PROBLEMS

Evaluate the variables in each of the following programs.

1.
```
var
      a:array a[1 . . 10]of real;
      q:real;
      i:integer;
begin
for i:=1 to 10 do
      begin
          q:=6.7;
          a[i]:=q*i*i
      end
end
```

2.
```
     READ(5,10)COST1,COST2,COST3,COST4,COST5
     READ(5,10)PROFT1,PROFT2,PROFT3,PROFT4,PROFT5
  10 FORMAT(5F5.2)
     PRICE4=COST4+PROFT4
     PRICE1=PROFT1+COST1
     PRICE5=PROFT5+COST5
     PRICE2=COST2+PROFT2
     PRICE3=PROFT3+COST3
     END
```

---

*See Appendix B: Bibliography.

3.
```
      SUBROUTINE ZIP(A,B)
      DATA E/5.2/
      IF (A.LT.O) GO TO 10
      F=A+E*B
      GO TO 20
   10 F=A+E*F
   20 B=B*(F**2)
      RETURN
      END
```

4.
```
    var
         x,y,z:real;
    begin
         x:=3.7;
         y:=2.4;
         z:=x+y+z
    end
```

5.
```
    var
         a,b,c:integer;
    begin
         b:=1;
         a:=5*b
    end
```

6.
```
    procedure ff(x,y:integer);
    var
         g,h,i:integer;
    begin
         g:=5*x*y;
         h:=7*g*i;
         i:=i*i
    end
```

7.
```
      COMMON FST,SEC,THRD
      DATA FST/1.0/,SEC/2.2/,THRD/3.7/
      THRD=SEC*THRD+SEC**2
      END
```

8.
```
      DIMENSION VECT1(10),VECT2(10)
      DATA VECT1/0,0,0,0,0,0,0,0,0,0/
      DATA VECT2/0,1,2,3,4,5,6,7,8,9/
      DO 100 I=4,8
      J=I−1
      K=10−I
      VECT1(J)=VECT2(K)
  100 CONTINUE
      END
```

9.
```
      READ(5,10) PAR1,PAR2,PAR3
      PI=3.14
      PAR2=PAR3+PI*(PAR2**2)
   10 FORMAT(3F6.3)
      END
```

10.
```
      procedure move (array1:list);(*list declared as a type in main*)
      var
          i,j:integer;
      begin
          j:=5;
          for i:=1 to 80 do
              begin
                  array1[j−1]:=array1[j];
                  j:=j+1
              end
      end
```

11.
```
      procedure pqr(x:integer; var y:real);
      var
          g,h:real;
      begin
          h:=1.7;
          if x>=5 then begin
                          g:=2.4;
                          y:=(h+y)*g
                       end
                     else y:=(h−y)*g
      end
```

12.
```
      procedure change(var x:list; r:list);
      var
          pi:real;
          i:integer;
```

```
      begin
          for i:=1 to 10 do
              begin
                  pi:=4.0*atan(1.0);
                  x[i]:=2.0*r[i]*r[i]
              end
      end
```

13.   FUNCTION TOTAL(XIN,ZCHECK)
        DIMENSION XIN(8,8),ZCHECK(8)
        READ(SYSIN,10)(ZCHECK(I),I=1,8)
        READ(SYSIN,10)((XIN(I,J),I=1,8),J=1,8)
     10 FORMAT(8F12.4)
        TOTAL=0.0
        DO 100 I=1,8
        SUM=0.0
        DO 200 J=1,8
        SUM=SUM+XDATA(I,J)
    200 CONTINUE
        ZCHECK(I)=SUM
        TOTAL=TOTAL+SUM
    100 CONTINUE
        RETURN
        END

8.5 PROGRAM MAINTENANCE DOCUMENTATION

8.5.1 General

The maintainers of a program need, in addition to the program itself, descriptions of various aspects of the program. This information is given in a program maintenance document. Cross-checking between design and program descriptions is made easier when design documents and program descriptions follow exactly the same format [Goos 73]. If a careful classification scheme is created very early in the project, it will act as a documentation standard to enforce the completeness of documentation of details [Goos 73].

To allow easy modification and maintenance, the maintenance document should describe clearly the places in the program where insertion can be made, and should also distinguish between the goals of a particular portion and the algorithm actually used. If this is not done, the maintainer must experiment with the program to determine the essential features of an algorithm or data structure. For the same reasons, all error handling should be extensively described.

As much as possible, discussions should be cross-referenced to the source program listing. Conversely, when source program comments provide sufficient information about particular points in the code, reference back to the maintenance manual is unnecessary.

The following sections describe the major portions of a program maintenance manual.

8.5.2 System Description

A basic description is given of what the system does and how it works, including a brief discussion of interfaces with other systems. A diagram showing system boundaries may be appropriate.

8.5.3 System Specification

An overall specification is stated, indicating the general objectives of the program and any important restrictions or limitations that have been imposed on these objectives. If possible, an abstract statement is given of the problem to be solved; and if the program uses a small set of standard solutions to the abstract problem, these solutions are also stated.

Also included, if appropriate, are the relation of the program to other programs or program systems (e.g., that other programs require specific input or output formats, or file structures), or the relation of the program to its hardware environment (e.g., that a certain minimum memory is required, or a special character set is required).

8.5.4 System Structure

The major data entities (input files, output files, data blocks, etc.) and their significance and use are described. The major processing routines are outlined briefly. The sequence of major processing routines is given, as is an overall data flow diagram. If the pattern of use of major routines is based on an important algorithm, that algorithm is discussed.

Both permanent files and scratch files need to be described. For each file, details of record structure and means of access are given. The uses of permanent file data are also stated. If permanent file data is used by several programs, there is a possibility that two or more programs may need to access the file at the same time. In this case, the programs needing access must synchronize their activities, and provisions for such synchronization need to be discussed.

Files and data blocks accessed by many modules in the fashion of COMMON blocks in FORTRAN systems need to be carefully described, and the patterns of access by different modules should also be precisely stated.

For programs organized into modules, organization diagrams are needed to indicate the organization, the subroutine calls, and the parameters passed.

Some programs may require special descriptions or diagrams. Programs that use absolute addressing require memory maps or overlay diagrams, as in Figure 8.13. Some real-time programs require cyclic patterns of overlays, which can be diagrammed as in Figure 8.14.

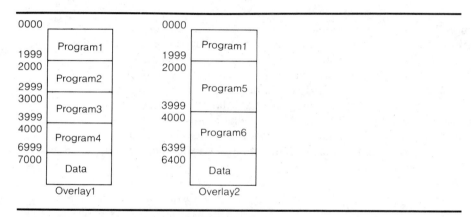

Figure 8.13   Two arrangements of programs in the computer memory.

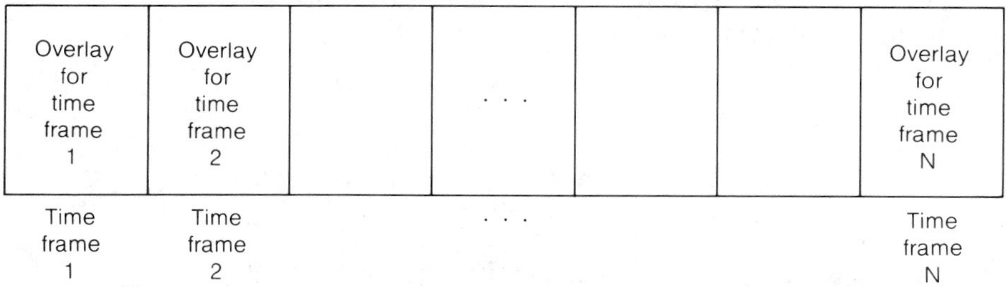

Figure 8.14   Overlay pattern for real-time programs.

The program maintenance manual describes in detail all module interfaces, data, data formats, and algorithms.

In large cyclic real-time systems, the reading of required routines into core at each time frame may itself become very costly in time. But it is possible to design an arrangement of the overlays and the sequence of read operations to minimize the time required for the sequence of read operations. Also, in some real-time systems, the actual timing of routines may be crucial, and in these situations timing diagrams should be given.

8.5.5 Description of Processing Routines

A separate section describing each module is included. Each section first gives a basic description of how the module works, including interface descriptions, and then provides details of internal structure, data, and algorithms.

The input and output parameters of each module are carefully described. The overall function of the routine is stated, and important algorithms are fully discussed. When a structured programming language has been used, it is preferable to describe algorithms using pseudocode, which preserves the program structure and has English explanations in place of program statements [Goos 73]. The names and meaning of significant data items are given, as well as any crucial implementation details.

8.5.6 Sample Execution

Sample data inputs are given and discussed, and the results of a program execution using this data are provided. Any important restrictions or error problems pertaining to this data are discussed. Any unusual ways in which the program relies on the operating system are also indicated.

8.5.7 Test Procedures

The sequence of tests used to verify the program, and the important aspects of the program behavior tested, are indicated. Important segments of test data are given. If test data in machine processable form are also supplied, the tests can be used for regression testing when changes are made to the program.

REFERENCES

[Goos 73] Goos, G. "Chapter 4.B Documentation," in F. L. Bauer (ed.), *Advanced Course in Software Engineering*. (Lecture Notes in Economics and Mathematical Systems No. 81.) New York: Springer-Verlag, 1973.

[Har 73] Harper, W. L. *Data Processing Documentation: Standards, Procedures and Applications*. Englewood Cliffs, NJ: Prentice-Hall, 1973.

[Hay 78] Hayes, J. A. "User-Accessible Publications: Help Your RSTS/E User Help Himself," *Proceedings of Digital Equipment Computer Users Society (DECUS) Symposium*, Spring 1978.

[Hay 79] ———. "Program Maintenance: A Common-Sense Approach," *Proceedings of Digital Equipment Computer Users Society (DECUS) Symposium*, December 1979.

[Nau 76] Naur, P.; Randell, B.; and Buxton, J. N. (eds.). *Software Engineering Concepts and Techniques, Proceedings of the NATO Conference*. New York: Petrocelli/Charter, 1976.

[Wals 69] Walsh, D. *A Guide for Software Documentation*. Boston: Inter-Act, 1969.

PROBLEMS

1. Read an article that presents a program in one of the computer magazines. Examine the article for the items of information mentioned in Section 8.5.1. Is the program properly documented? State your reasons.

2. Write a maintenance document for:
   (a) Problem B of Appendix E.
   (b) Problem C of Appendix E.

3. Find at least six references on documentation. Summarize the points made in each. Write an overview of the problems and principles of documentation.

chapter nine
Verifying Program
Correctness

9.1 BASIC ISSUES

9.1.1 Proof and Testing

Despite our best intentions, errors tend to arise in formulating program specifications, in designing the required system, and in coding the programs. Since a system is suitable for operational use only when the effects of such errors are reduced to an acceptable level, it is important to verify that the system does in fact operate according to specifications. Errors found during verification can be eliminated, or, in special circumstances, the system might be redesigned to make the effect of the errors unimportant.

Verification is an important activity. Testing, the usual form of final system verification, commonly requires 40 to 50 percent of the total elapsed time and resources of the development effort, especially for larger systems [Boe 73b, Mye 79].

This chapter deals primarily with verifying correctness, specifically with testing and methods for developing test cases.[1] Section 9.1 classifies testing methods, discusses the psychology of testing, and suggests ways to prepare a program for proof or testing. Section 9.2 discusses test-case development for testing against specifications. Section 9.3 presents methods for program-based test-case development, and Section 9.4 deals with debugging methods.

Proving and testing are the two basic ways of verifying that a program performs its intended function. In verification by proof, characteristics of program operation are formally deduced from the program text. In verification by testing, the program is executed with selected inputs, and the outputs of these executions are observed.

Proof proceeds from "inside" the program. All details of the specification, the program, and its subprograms are assumed to be known. First, it is neces-

---

[1]Correctness does not guarantee operational suitability since a correct program may be unusable if it is not sufficiently robust or does not have sufficient utility or performance, while a robust program with minor errors may be usable. Generally, a program will be unsuitable if it fails to meet the required quality level for one or more critical qualities. Thus, it is necessary, as noted in Chapter 1, to plan for and verify quality levels for all desired qualities.

sary to show that each subprogram, due to the precise nature of the algorithm used, provides for certain cases of input and, for these cases, gives desired output. Next, it must be shown that collections of subprograms appropriately process their inputs. Larger and larger collections of subprograms are considered until the performance of the entire program is proved. In this way, the proper performance of the program is deduced from the program text.

In contrast, testing proceeds from "outside" the program. The properties of the program are determined by subjecting it to sequences of experiments. In each experiment, a selected input point (called a *test case* or *test point*) is presented to the program, the program is executed, and the resulting output point is observed. These executions of the program are performed in an environment whose characteristics are known or controlled. Finally, the test results serve as a basis for inferring the behavior of the program.

Each of these methods has important strengths and weaknesses [Ger 79]:

- Testing can provide concrete evidence that at least a partial solution has been obtained; but testing cannot show that the program does not have some major error that has been bypassed by the set of test cases. This is the genesis of Dijkstra's famous saying [Dij 72b, p. 6], "One can verify the presence of a bug by testing, but never the absence of a bug."
- Proving can show that a plausible overall solution has been found, but it cannot show that the implementation does not have trivial errors that will cause incorrect results. Moreover, proofs for even small programs are usually long, intricate, and prone to error, so that a proof might be wrong.
- Proof techniques currently ignore the program's language and environment (its operating system, hardware, and users), which may cause errors in program operation, whereas testing usually incorporates these factors.

Proving and testing deal with different kinds of information. Proofs yield conclusions about a program's overall behavior in a postulated environment, while testing yields accurate information about the program's actual behavior in an actual environment [Good 75]. Some properties can be shown only by proof, some can be shown only by testing, and some can be shown either way [Good 79]. There are also programs whose correctness cannot be shown at all [How 76, Good 79].

Thus neither method is entirely sufficient. Several authors [Ger 76, Tan 76, DeMi 79] have noted the difficulties of proof methods, while others [Good 75, Ger 76, How 78d] have noted difficulties inherent in testing methods.

The serious programmer must use a combination of proving and testing. In principle, verification will include both a demonstration that the program should work, due to its construction, and (since proofs can themselves contain errors) a sequence of tests as well.

9.1.2 Categories of Test Methods

Testing methods may be classified according to the amount of program information assumed in the test. In *black box testing* (also called *specification-based testing*), the program is viewed as a black box whose internal structure is unknown. Test cases are chosen for each input subclass determined in Chapter 2, and each test output point is checked to see if it conforms to the decision tables in Chapter 2. Such tests are almost always extended to include error classes, to ensure that the system recognizes erroneous inputs and produces appropriate outputs for such inputs.

Black box testing commonly uses a small amount of knowledge about the program's internal structure to simplify testing. For example, if a system does not remember information from one execution to the next, and if all variables of the program are properly initialized for every execution, then each execution is independent of all others and the outcome for a given test case is independent of previous test cases. On the other hand, systems such as operating systems and airlines reservation systems remember information from one execution to the next, and the result for a given test may depend on all previous test cases *and* on the sequence in which they occurred. Thus characteristics of such a system must be ascertained via *sequences* of test cases.

Even the single bit of knowledge that the system does (or does not) remember data from one execution to the next allows simplified testing. If this fact were not known, the testing would have to proceed very cautiously. A series of hypotheses about characteristics of the program would have to be made, and each hypothesis would then have to be verified by testing. Of course, the first characteristic to be determined would be whether the system is one that remembers data from one execution to the next.

However, the tester first has to consider how long a sequence of test cases is needed to determine whether the system remembers. This preliminary question is answered by a preliminary series of test cases. In this situation, knowledge of the number of variables in the program or the number of bits of storage allows a limit on the length of the required sequences of experiments to be derived.

In *white box testing* (also called *program-based testing*), the internal structure of the program is known to the tester. Test cases are determined by examining the program listing, and the test goal is to cause execution of a specified group of execution paths within the program.

Design-based testing seeks to verify the design of the program and important subprograms. Test cases are constructed based on the properties of the design element in question. For example, if the response of a subprogram is based on a finite-state model (see Chapter 6), test cases are devised to cycle the model through all possible sequences of states. If the design involves data abstraction techniques, such as use of a stack module as in Figure 5.26, test cases are arranged to cause the stack module to perform desired sequences of push and pop operations. Design-based testing might also require the output of intermediate values within the program.

In summary, test points for black box testing are derived from the specification, and the program structure is ignored. In white box testing, test points are derived from examining the logic shown in the program listing, and the possibility of other significant test cases is ignored. Design-based testing derives test points from properties of the design element being tested. Thus in black box and white box testing, test cases can be derived in a systematic way, while in design-based testing, the test points depend on the properties of the design element under test.

When correctness with respect to specifications is evaluated without knowledge of the program structure or design, it is difficult or impossible to determine whether the program under test exactly preserves the subclasses of the specifications. Since even the smallest program can allow vast numbers of possible inputs, and since a feasible test can include only a tiny fraction of these inputs, a test showing all correct results is statistically inconclusive. Thus, in general, a black box test cannot guarantee correctness.

On the other hand, though white box testing can be expected to reveal more errors than ad hoc testing methods, studies [Hetz 76, How 78c] have shown that the principal white box technique (branch testing, discussed in Section 9.3) is relatively ineffective when it is not supported and complemented by the use of other methods. The effectiveness of more general white box methods has not been widely studied. It has been suggested [How 78b] that path testing can only be successfully applied to top-down designed programs, since otherwise the number of paths become too large.

White box testing cannot ensure that all errors are detected, even if all paths of the program are executed. One situation that might not be detected is missing control paths. For example, a program might contain an assignment statement $x:=a/b$, not preceded by a test for $b=0$. In this situation, all paths containing the statement can be successfully exercised with $b \neq 0$, even though execution of the statement with $b=0$ will cause the program to fail. All paths might be exercised without detection of an incorrect or inadequate test. For example, the incorrect statement "if $(x+y+z)/3=x$" might be used in place of the correct statement "if $(x=y)$ and $(y=z)$." Also an inappropriate calculation such as $x:=w*w$ instead of $x:=w+w$ may not be detected when the path is exercised.

Thus specification-based and program-based testing should be regarded as complementary techniques. The use of specification-based tests, supplemented by program-based tests, is in many cases the most effective error discovery method [How 80]. Section 9.2 will discuss the development of black box tests and Section 9.3 will outline white box testing methods.

9.1.3 Psychology of Testing

Perhaps the most important aspect of testing is its psychological orientation and impact. It is an interesting fact that

> Surprisingly often, software testing and reliability activities are not considered until the code has been run the first time and found not to work . . . cost of testing is still 40–50 percent of the development effort . . . [there is] lack of an advance test plan to efficiently guide testing activities [Boe 79b, p. 58].

Why does such a state of affairs continue to occur?

One reason is that a mental "programming attitude" tends to develop during the construction of a program. In placing together a solution, the programmer almost always becomes convinced that the solution works for all cases, and since the solution is obviously correct, extensive testing is obviously unnecessary. This attitude results from optimism, from pride of authorship, and from admiration of the constructed edifice. Quite naturally, the discovery of an error would be painful to the proud author, and would involve extra work. Thus the process of developing a program inclines its author to believe that it is error free and needs no further examination.

Moreover, the creation of a program is perceived as a constructive, challenging, and creative activity, and as an opportunity for innovation. The creator of a program often views it as an extension of him- or herself [Weinb 71]; the program is both a powerful slave and a symbol of the programmer's having conquered the mighty computer (see Weizenbaum's discussion of "The Compulsive Programmer" [Weiz 76]). The discovery of an error in the program may then be felt to be a negative reflection on the programmer.

In contrast to such glories of creation, testing is perceived to be dull and uninteresting and, consequently, the testing activity is slighted (as are all verification activities).

Nevertheless, testing and other verification processes are at least as important as program construction and can be equally as challenging and exciting. It is not sufficient to just have faith in a program. Verification seeks to gain an *objective confidence* in a program's performance by putting stress on that performance. In the same way, a designer plays devil's advocate with a solution, trying to invalidate it (see Section 1.3), and a proof is checked by repeated consideration of potential counterexamples.

Confidence in a program's performance is gained through an effective sequence of tests that assumes that the program has errors that the test will uncover. In other words, a mental "testing attitude" is needed, which actively seeks to destroy a solution and assumes that it will be successful in doing so. The importance of a proper testing attitude is argued eloquently in *The Art of Software Testing* [Mye 79, Chap. 2], which suggests the following definition:

Testing is the process of executing a program with the intent of finding errors.

We are led immediately to a corresponding notion of success in testing [Mye 79]:

A test case is successful if it detects a previously undiscovered error.

Clarifying the psychological goal of testing increases the chances of testing success [Mye 79]. That is, if we are given the goal of finding errors and the understanding that a test case that finds an error is successful, then we tend subconsciously to select test cases that have a high probability of finding errors.

Conversely, if the given goal is to "demonstrate that no errors are present," we tend to select test cases that have a low probability of finding errors. Moreover, this goal is a much more difficult one, and the knowledge of its difficulty discourages efficient performance.

These definitions suggest that the testing attitude is exactly the opposite of the programming attitude, since testing is devoted to tearing down the edifice the programmer has built. Many programmers find it difficult to adopt the testing attitude after having built the program, and thus are not fully capable of performing adequate testing. Using independent teams for testing or other verification of large systems is now commonly urged [Fagan 76, Fuj 77, Mye 79]. The idea that a programmer is ill prepared to verify his or her own work leads also to the concepts of team efforts such as egoless programming, and to design reviews, walk-throughs and code inspections. These are discussed in Chapter 10.

For a large system, developing a comprehensive sequence of tests requires extensive effort and time. It is unreasonable to expect a programming team to expend such an effort, especially in the midst of trying to create the program. For this reason also, it makes sense to give a copy of the specifications to an independent test team and have them devise a test plan and test cases.

For small systems, a programmer can achieve a good solution and avoid the psychological pain of trying to destroy the solution by *first* designing a comprehensive sequence of tests (the sequence of tests thus sharply defines the specification) and *then* designing the solution to meet the sequence of tests. In developing the tests, every complicated situation the program will confront can be foreseen and an appropriate input point can be included in the tests. As the program develops, it can be tested to see whether it can handle these situations.

Below is a list of testing principles intended to evoke correct testing attitudes [Mye 79, Chap. 2]:

1. The purpose of testing is to find errors.
2. Assume that errors will be found.

3. A test case is successful if it detects a previously undiscovered error.
4. The probability that more errors exist is proportional to the number of errors already found.
5. Avoid testing your own work.
6. An organization should not test its own work.
7. A test case should define the expected result.
8. Input points in error classes should be tested, as well as input points in the planned input class.
9. Thoroughly inspect the results of each test case; otherwise errors may be overlooked.
10. Make sure there are no spurious outputs.
11. Do not throw away test cases; you may need to use them again.

9.1.4 Designing for Verification

Proving and testing can both be made easier if the design and programming anticipate these activities [Pool 73, Pai 78]. For example, proof and testing are aided when design decisions are localized and when structured programming is used. Stepwise refinement (see Chapter 7) develops an informal proof as the program is written. Designs based on finite-state models or table-driven processes (see Chapter 6) are especially convenient for testing. It may even be possible, for a finite-state model with a small number of states or a table-driven process with small number of independent subsections, to devise a complete test which ensures correct operation for all possible inputs.

The design of the RC4000 multiprogramming system [Bri 73] is an excellent example of designing for verification. This design directly addressed the problem of systematically testing the program by the simplest possible techniques. The RC4000 is a system of utility and monitor programs intended to allow concurrent execution of many processes. It was foreseen that because of the simultaneous handling of many programs, testing could be very difficult, and there might even be situations that could not be reproduced. Accordingly, the designers specifically considered questions such as:

1. How can a test event be well defined and reproducible?
2. How can interference between concurrent events be avoided?
3. What minimal set of monitor events gives sufficient information about handling of concurrent processes?
4. What form should test output have?
5. What form should a test mechanism have?

The answers to these questions led to incorporating in the design a simple test mechanism, consisting essentially of 2 procedures requiring 50 machine instructions. By using this mechanism together with a series of carefully selected test cases, the system was made virtually error free within a few weeks.

Thus pertinent questions to ask about testing are:

· What is a test event? How is it defined?
· What form should test output have?

And those to ask about design include:

· What are the fundamental processes?
· How do they interact?
· How is the interaction recorded?

Such questions aid design as much as they aid testing.

9.1.5 Devising a Test Plan

Since testing commonly requires 40 to 50 percent of a development effort, it is worthwhile to carefully organize the testing activity. The current high cost of testing is due in part to the lack of an advance test plan. Testing can be organized with respect to three key factors:

1. Levels of system performance
2. Levels of correctness
3. Levels of system integration

For any system, levels of performance can be defined to range from a lowest level (say, merely cycling) to a highest level. These performance levels will obviously vary from program to program. As an example, we give below a partial list of performance levels for an ALGOL compiler:

0. System cycles (i.e., terminates normally for all reasonable inputs)
1. Accepts inputs, rejects gross errors
2. Basic syntax features working (correct processing of identifiers, real numbers, etc.)
3. Complex syntax features working (blocks, compound statements, etc.)
4. Semantics working

A thorough sequence of tests will first check all aspects of level 0 operation, then (after correct level 0 operation has been attained) level 1 operation, and so on. In other words, each lower level of operation is confirmed before the test proceeds to the next higher level. In this way, testing at any level can assume correct operation at all lower levels. Thorough level 0 testing is especially important since normal termination for reasonable inputs is always necessary, and it is easy for programmers, who are preoccupied with the processing of correct inputs, to overlook special situations that might cause looping.

It is important for the tests to ensure, at each successive level, that the program preserves equivalence classes. Such procedures are routinely followed in verifying compilers. For example, in the processing of identifiers, a compiler ought to treat all letters A through Z in the same manner. Accordingly, a first set of tests should ensure that A through Z are, in fact, treated identically. If they are, only A need be used in further testing. Next, the compiler ought to treat identifiers of one, two, three (or more) symbols in an identical manner, and a second set of tests should ensure this equivalency. And so on, in the same manner. Once correct processing is established at a given level, it can be assumed when testing at higher levels.

Levels of correctness can also be defined [Conw 78]:

1. No syntactic errors in the program
2. No compilation errors, and the program cycles to completion for valid inputs
3. Correct output is obtained for at least one test case
4. Correct output is obtained for typical test cases
5. Correct output is obtained for difficult test cases
6. Correct output is obtained for all nonerroneous inputs (i.e., inputs in the planned input class)
7. Correct output is obtained for all nonerroneous inputs and for likely errors
8. Correct output is obtained for all possible inputs

The first three levels are, of course, very primitive, while level 8 may not be achievable. Most systems are tested to a level in the range of 5 to 7, possibly covering difficult cases and likely errors, but not all nonerroneous inputs.

Finally, testing can be done at the unit (subprogram or module) level, or while the modules are integrated into a system, or at the system level. Each level of correctness applies at each performance level and at each system integration level. A test plan can detail a sequence of test phases to be accomplished, each phase consisting of a performance level, an integration level, and the level of correctness to be achieved. The plan thus precisely defines testing goals and effort.

REFERENCES

[Boe 73b] Boehm, B. W. "Software and Its Impact: A Quantitative Assessment," *Datamation*, May 1973. (Also in [Fre 80b].)*

---

*See Appendix B: Bibliography.

[Boe 79b] ———. "Software Engineering: R&D Trends and Defense Needs," in P. Wegner (ed.), *Research Directions in Software Technology*. Cambridge, MA: M.I.T. Press, 1979.

[Bri 73] Brinch Hansen, P. "Testing a Multiprogramming System," *Software—Practice and Experience*, April-June 1973. (Also in [Mil 78].)*

[Conw 78] Conway, R. *A Primer on Disciplined Programming*. Cambridge, MA: Winthrop, 1978.

[DeMi 79] DeMillo, R. A.; Lipton, R. J.; and Perlis, A. J. "Social Processes and Proofs of Theorems and Programs," *Communications of the ACM*, May 1979.

[Dij 72b] Dijkstra, E. W. "Notes on Structured Programming," in O.-J. Dahl, E. W. Dijkstra, and Hoare (eds.), *Structured Programming*. New York: Academic Press, 1972.

[Fagan 76] Fagan, M. E. "Design and Code Inspections to Reduce Errors in Program Development," *IBM System Journal*, Vol. 15, No. 3, 1976. (Also in [Mil 78].)*

[Fuj 77] Fujii, M. S. "Independent Verification of Highly Reliable Programs," *Proceedings of COMPSAC 77*. New York: IEEE Computer Society, 1977.

[Ger 76] Gerhart, S. L., and Yelowitz, L. "Observations of Fallibility in Applications of Modern Programming Methodologies," *IEEE Transactions on Software Engineering*, September 1976. (Also in [Mil 78] and [Ram 78].)*

[Ger 79] ———. "A Discussion of a Survey of Program Testing Issues," in P. Wegner (ed.), *Research Directions in Software Technology*. Cambridge, MA: M.I.T. Press, 1979.

[Good 75] Goodenough, J. B., and Gerhart, S. L. "Toward a Theory of Test Data Selection," *Proceedings of International Conference on Software Reliability*, 1975. (Also in *IEEE Transactions on Software Engineering*, June 1975. And in [Mil 78].)*

[Good 79] ———. "A Survey of Program Testing Issues," in P. Wegner (ed.). *Research Directions in Software Technology*. Cambridge, MA: M.I.T. Press, 1979.

[Hetz 76] Hetzel, W. C. "An Experimental Analysis of Program Verification Methods." Ph.D. dissertation, University of North Carolina, 1976.

[How 76] Howden, W. E. "Reliability of the Path Analysis Testing Strategy," *IEEE Transactions on Software Engineering*, September 1976.

[How 78a] ———. "An Evaluation of the Effectiveness of Symbolic Testing," *Software—Practice and Experience*, 1978.

[How 78c] ———. "A Survey of Dynamic Analysis Methods," in E. Miller and W. E. Howden (eds.), *Tutorial: Software Testing and Validation Techniques*. New York: IEEE Computer Society, 1978.

[How 78d] ———. "Theoretical and Empirical Studies of Program Testing," *Proceedings of 3rd International Conference on Software Engineering*. (IEEE Catalog No. 78CH1317-7C.) New York: IEEE Computer Society, 1978. (Also in *IEEE Transactions on Software Engineering*, July 1978.)

[How 80] ———. "Functional Program Testing," *IEEE Transactions on Software Engineering*, March 1980.

---

*See Appendix B: Bibliography.

[Inf 73] Infotech. *Infotech State of the Art Report on Real-Time Systems*. Maidenhead, England: Infotech, 1973.

[Inf 78] ———. *Infotech State of the Art Report on Program Testing*. Maidenhead, England: Infotech, 1978.

[Mil 78] Miller, E. F., and Howden, W. E. (eds.). *Tutorial: Software Testing and Validation Techniques*. (IEEE Catalog No. EHO 138-8.) New York: IEEE Computer Society, 1978.

[Mills 75] Mills, H. D. "How to Write Correct Programs and Know It," *Proceedings of International Conference on Reliable Software*, Los Angeles, 1975. (Also in [Ram 78]).*

[Mye 79] Myers, G. J. *The Art of Software Testing*. New York: Wiley, 1979.

[Nau 63] Naur, P., "The Design of the GEIR Algol Compiler," *BIT*, 1963.

[Pai 78] Paige, M. R. "Software Design for Testability," *Proceedings of the 11th Hawaii Conference on System Sciences*, 1978.

[Pool 73] Poole, P. C. "Debugging and Testing," in F. L. Bauer (ed.), *Advanced Course on Software Engineering*. (Lecture Notes in Economics and Mathematical Systems, Vol. 81.) New York: Springer-Verlag, 1973.

[Tan 76] Tanenbaum, A. S. "In Defense of Program Testing, or Correctness Proofs Considered Harmful," *SIGPLAN Notices*, May 1976.

[Weinb 71] Weinberg, G. M. *The Psychology of Computer Programming*. New York: Van Nostrand Reinhold, 1971.

[Weiz 76] Weizenbaum, J. *Computer Power and Human Reason*. San Francisco: Freeman, 1976.

PROBLEMS

1. Dijkstra once said, "One can verify the presence of a bug by testing, but never the absence of a bug" [Dij 72b, p. 6]. Is this always true? If so, why? Or are there situations where testing does verify the absence of bugs? If so, what are they and how probable are they?

2. DeMillo, Lipton, and Perlis [DeMi 79] have argued that there are no objective criteria as yet for correctness of a mathematical proof, and that we rely solely on peer review. In other words, proofs may contain errors. We have no way to formally check them for errors, so we accept as valid those proofs that have withstood review for a substantial period of time. For this reason, and also because proofs take large logical jumps and are long and complex, it is difficult or impossible to use proof techniques to verify large programs. What is the current status of proof verification techniques? How useful do you think proof techniques are for large programs?

---

*See Appendix B: Bibliography.

3. The function ZINGO(X), which yields for each positive integer X a value 0 or 1, uses three COMMON integer variables that are never initialized and are "remembered" from execution to execution. ZINGO is coded as follows:

```
        FUNCTION ZINGO(X)
        INTEGER X,A,B,C
        COMMON A,B,C
C   MOD2 COMPUTES THE RESIDUE MODULO 2 OF AN INTEGER
        C=MOD2(A+B+C+1)
        B=A
        A=X
        IF(C.EQ.1)
          ZINGO=MOD2(A*B)
        ELSE
          ZINGO=MOD2((A+1)*(B+1))
        END IF
        RETURN
        END
```

(a) For A,B,C all initially 0, calculate the results produced by ZINGO
   (*1*) for the sequence of inputs X=0,0,0,0.
   (*2*) for the sequence of inputs X−1,1,1,1.
(b) Repeat the calculations above assuming A,B,C all initially 1.
(c) Suppose you were asked to determine ZINGO's calculation without seeing either its specification or its code. How would you go about finding out ZINGO's calculation?

9.2 TEST-CASE DERIVATION IN SPECIFICATION-BASED TESTING

9.2.1 The Test's Purpose

Section 9.2 discusses deriving test cases to determine the correctness of a program with respect to its specifications, without knowledge of the program's internal structure. We assume, however, that the programs under test do not remember information from one execution to another, and that all variables are properly initialized at each execution.[2] Under this assumption, the out-

---

[2]If all variables are not properly initialized at each execution, it is possible that a program will give differing results for the same input. If initialization of variables is left to the operating system, then changes in the operating system may change these initial values, causing program behavior to change. Programs can and should be inspected before testing to ensure that this assumption is met.

come of each execution is independent of the data used in previous executions, and independent of the order in which previous executions have occurred. Therefore, each input point selected for testing can be considered independently of other selected input points.

An input point selected for testing a program is called a *test point* (equivalently, a *test case*). A *test* is a finite collection of test points.

A specification-based (black box) test is derived by considering a decision table derived in Chapter 2. Recall that each column of the decision table represents an input subclass that has a distinct processing function and that every input point in the subclass receives that processing function. Also, all points in the subclass are equivalent in the sense that they receive identical mappings. Thus the input subclasses may be considered as a set of equivalence classes, each having a distinct mapping.

A black box test determines

· Whether the program preserves each subclass as an equivalence class
· Whether correct outputs are given for each subclass

The test must ensure that the program has not, by using inappropriate conditions or improper program paths, split an equivalence class into new and smaller subclasses. A number of test points in each input subclass are required for this purpose. At the same time, the outputs for these test points must be correct.

A comprehensive black box test always tests for error classes (whether or not error classes are explicitly mentioned in the specification) to ensure that the program recognizes erroneous inputs and provides appropriate outputs for such inputs.

Obviously a black box test is possible only when the program specifications are given in a precise manner. In particular, the type and range of each input variable are required to clearly delineate error classes, and, preferably, the specification should indicate action when the variable is out of range and when it is the wrong type.

The steps in specification-based testing are summarized at the end of Section 9.2, as are some rules for choosing test-point values.

9.2.2 Developing a Test: Derivation of Decision Table

9.2.2.1 Initial Derivation of Subclasses

A program is desired that classifies triangles. It takes as input three integer values a,b,c, representing the sides of a triangle. The program determines whether the triangle is equilateral (output is E), isosceles (output is I), or scalene (output is S), and whether it is a right triangle (output is R). For an equilateral triangle, only E is output. (Variations of this program appear in [Ram 76, DeMi 78, Mye 79, and Wey 80].)

The first step is deriving the decision table as in Section 2.3. Each input point has the form $x=(a,b,c)$, where a,b,c are the input values. In the following discussion we define $p=\max(a,b,c)$; q,r are the other two values. Boundaries on the planned input class are:

Exactly three values a,b,c are input
a,b,c are integers
a,b,c are all >0
$p<q+r$

so that possible errors are

Fewer than three values are input, or more than three values are input
One or more of a,b,c not an integer
One or more of a,b,c not >0
$p\geq q+r$

The specification explicitly mentions the outputs E, I, S, R. Since the test is also required to check erroneous inputs, we add the output N signifying not a triangle. Then the possible outputs y are

$y=N$ or
$y=E$ or
$y=I$ or
$y=S$ or
$y=(I,R)$ or
$y=(S,R)$

No boundaries are explicitly imposed on the output class.

There are seven conditions that cause variations in the processing, and these are summarized in Table 9.1.

Table 9.1 Conditions of the example specification

Condition	Possible Values
C_1:exactly three values are input	{T,F}
C_2:a,b,c all integers	{T,F}
C_3:values of a,b,c	{all>0, one or more$=0$, one or more<0}
C_4:p:(q+r)	{$<,=,>$}
C_5:a=b	{T,F}
C_6:b=c	{T,F}
C_7:a=c	{T,F}
C_8:$p^2=q^2+r^2$	{T,F}

The conditions C_1, C_2, C_3, C_4 all deal with boundary conditions on the planned input class. The condition C_4 [p:(q+r), where p is compared to (q+r)] has outcomes in the set $\{<,=,>\}$. The condition C_3 (values of a,b,c) involves three numeric comparisons: a:0,b:0, and c:0, so that there are nine possible outcomes. We abbreviate the possible outcomes of C_3 as follows:

Abbreviation	Meaning
>	all of a,b,c>0
=	one or more of a,b,c=0
<	one or more of a,b,c<0

The analysis of the example specification based on these conditions is given in Table 9.2. The table suggests 15 different subclasses for which test points must be given. For column 16, the result impossible case is shown because a=b=c implies $a^2=b^2=c^2$, so that the condition $p^2=q^2+r^2$ must be false.

Table 9.2   Analysis of example specification

Condition	Condition Values															
	1	2	3	4	5	6	7	8	9	10	11	12	13	14	15	16
Exactly three values input	F	T	T	T	T	T	T	T	T	T	T	T	T	T	T	T
a,b,c all integers	–	F	T	T	T	T	T	T	T	T	T	T	T	T	T	T
Values of a,b,c	–	–	<	=	–	–	>	>	>	>	>	>	>	>	>	>
p:(q+r)	–	–	–	–	>	=	<	<	<	<	<	<	<	<	<	<
a=b	–	–	–	–	–	–	–	F	F	T	T	F	F	F	T	T
a=c	–	–	–	–	–	–	–	F	F	F	F	T	T	F	F	T
b=c	–	–	–	–	–	–	–	F	F	F	F	F	F	T	T	T
$p^2=q^2+r^2$	–	–	–	–	–	–	–	F	T	F	T	F	T	F	T	T
Results ⟶	N	N	N	N	N	N	S	S R	I	I R	I	I R	I	I R	E	Impossible Case

9.2.2.2 Restatement Taking Numeric Conditions into Account

The conditions C_1 and C_5 through C_8 of Table 9.1 are comparisons of numeric values and can be restated to have outcomes in the set $\{<,=,>\}$ as in Table 9.3.

Table 9.3   Restatement of numeric conditions

Condition	Possible Values
C_1': number of values:3	$\{<,=,>\}$
C_5':a:b	$\{<,=,>\}$
C_6':b:c	$\{<,=,>\}$
C_7':a:c	$\{<,=,>\}$
C_8':p^2:(q^2+r^2)	$\{<,=,>\}$

A good rule for numeric relations is to provide explicitly for each of the outcomes $\{<,=,>\}$, as in Table 9.3. In this way a larger number of more precise cases is obtained. Table 9.4 shows the results obtained for each possible combination of the conditions C_5' to C_8', assuming exactly three values are input, a,b,c all integers, values of a,b,c all >0, and $p<q+r$.

Table 9.4   Analysis with restated conditions

Condition	Condition Values																	
	1	2	3	4	5	6	7	8	9	10	11	12	13	14	15	16	17	18
a:b	<	<	<	<	<	<	<	<	<	<	<	<	<	<	<	=	=	=
b:c	<	<	<	=	=	=	>	>	>	>	>	>	>	>	>	<	<	<
a:c	<	<	<	<	<	<	<	<	<	=	=	=	>	>	>	<	<	<
p^2:(q^2+r^2)	<	=	>	<	=	>	<	=	>	<	=	>	<	=	>	<	=	>
Results →	S	S	S R	I	I R	I	S	S R	S	I	I R	I	S	S R	S	I	I R	I

Condition	Condition Values															
	17	18	19	20	21	22	23	24	25	26	27	28	29	30	31	32
a:b	=	>	>	>	>	>	>	>	>	>	>	>	>	>	>	>
b:c	=	<	<	<	<	<	<	<	<	<	=	=	=	>	>	>
a:c	=	<	<	<	=	=	=	>	>	>	>	>	>	>	>	>
p^2:(q^2+r^2)	<	<	=	>	<	=	>	<	=	>	<	=	>	<	=	>
Results →	E	S	S R	S	I	I R	I	S	S R	S	I	I R	I	S	S R	S

Table 9.4 omits all self-contradictory combinations of conditions, as, for example,

a<b   b<c   a>c

Nevertheless, the conditions C_5' through C_8' delineate 32 different subclasses in Table 9.4, in contrast to the 9 different subclasses delineated by C_5 through C_8 in columns 7 through 15 of Table 9.2. Also the conditions C_5', C_6', C_7', and C_8' provide greater refinement in testing whether the program preserves the specification subclasses. A common type of error in programs is substituting one numeric relation for another, as, for example, mistaken use of $\geq$ instead of $>$, or mistaken interchange of $<$ and $\leq$.[3] This type of error shifts the boundaries of subclasses and may coalesce or split subclasses. (See also the discussion of off-by-one errors in [Ker 74, "Common Blunders"].) A test based on Table 9.4 will detect such errors, but a test based on Table 9.2 may not. In particular, Table 9.4 distinguishes between the situations $p^2 < q^2 + r^2$ and $p^2 > q^2 + r^2$, whereas Table 9.2 distinguishes only the case $p^2 \neq q^2 + r^2$.

9.2.2.3 Restatement Taking Symmetry into Account

Table 9.4 has a large number of cases because it does not reflect the intention of the problem statement that the values a,b,c should be processed symmetrically.[4] Table 9.4 is correct, though, in this respect. Even though a program is intended to process these values symmetrically, it may not, in fact, do so. Accidental nonsymmetric processing is also a common error. Intended symmetry in processing has to be established by test.

The following convention allows processing symmetry to be carefully tested while the number of subclasses is sharply reduced.

Symmetry convention: Choose the subclass conditions so that intended symmetries are fully taken into account. Then use all permutations of the values in each test point chosen.

Table 9.5 Conditions reflecting intended symmetry

Condition	Possible Values
$C_8':p^2:(q^2+r^2)$	$\{<,=,>\}$
$C_9:a<b<c$	$\{T,F\}$
$C_{10}:a<b=c$	$\{T,F\}$
$C_{11}:a=b=c$	$\{T,F\}$
$C_{12}:a>b=c$	$\{T,F\}$

To illustrate, Table 9.5 distinguishes five conditions for the example. The first, C_8', which appears also in Tables 9.3 and 9.4, was already formulated to reflect symmetry. By definition, p is the largest of the sides, and q,r are the other two sides.

[3]A white box testing method known as mutation testing [DeMi 78] attempts to detect this kind of error by testing combined with variations of the program text.
[4]Table 9.3 also does not take symmetry into account. Columns 8, 10, and 12 are symmetric situations as are columns 9, 11, and 13.

C_9 represents the condition that all sides are unequal. We first formulate C_9 by assuming a is the smallest side, b the next smallest, and c the largest side. A test point x=(a,b,c) is chosen to satisfy this condition and has all sides unequal, say, x=(3,4,5). Then, following the second part of the convention, all permutations of each chosen test point are used. Thus our choice of x=(3,4,5) implies choice of the set of test points

(3,4,5)	(4,3,5)	(5,3,4)
(3,5,4)	(4,5,3)	(5,4,3)

Using these permutations defines a test point satisfying each of the conditions

a<b<c	b<a<c	b<c<a
a<c<b	c<a<b	c<b<a

Similarly, C_{10} represents the condition that two sides are equal and that the third side is smaller than these. C_{11} is the condition that all sides are equal. And C_{12} is the condition that two sides are equal while the third is larger. Again, the use of all permutations ensures that all intended processing symmetries will be tested. The conditions C_9 through C_{12} are mutually exclusive. That is, exactly one of these conditions will be true for any valid input.

The analysis of the example specification using the conditions of Table 9.5 is shown in Table 9.6, which will be used to develop test points. The results labeled X in Table 9.6, signifying impossible case, are for situations where the relation among the sides contradicts the value for the relation $p^2:(q^2+r^2)$.

Table 9.6 Example analysis reflecting intended symmetry

Condition	Condition Values																	
	1	2	3	4	5	6	7	8	9	10	11	12	13	14	15	16	17	18
Values input:3	<	≥	≥	≥	≥	≥	≥	≥	≥	≥	≥	≥	≥	≥	≥	≥	≥	≥
a,b,c all integers	−	F	T	T	T	T	T	T	T	T	T	T	T	T	T	T	T	T
Values of a,b,c	−	−	<	=	−	−	>	>	>	>	>	>	>	>	>	>	>	>
p:(q+r)	−	−	−	−	>	=	<	<	<	<	<	<	<	<	<	<	<	<
a<b<c	−	−	−	−	−	−	−	T	T	T	F	F	F	F	F	F	F	F
a<b=c	−	−	−	−	−	−	−	F	F	F	T	T	T	F	F	F	F	F
a=b=c	−	−	−	−	−	−	−	F	F	F	F	F	F	T	T	T	F	F	F
a>b=c	−	−	−	−	−	−	−	F	F	F	F	F	F	F	F	F	T	T	T
$p^2:(q^2+r^2)$	−	−	−	−	−	−	−	<	=	>	<	=	>	<	=	>	<	=	>
Results →	N	N	N	N	N	N	S	S R	S	I	X	X	E	X	X	I	I	I R

Note: X=impossible case.

Since $C_9, \ldots, C_{12}$ are mutually exclusive and C_7' has three values, the conditions of Table 9.5 combine to determine 12 possible subcases, shown in columns 6 through 17 of Table 9.6. In contrast, columns 7 through 15 of Table 9.2 show 9 subcases, not taking numeric conditions into account, while Table 9.4 has 32 subcases. Even though Table 9.6 has fewer cases than Table 9.4, the use of permutations ensures that each distinct case of Table 9.4 will be tested.

Table 9.6 also modifies the handling of fewer or more than three input values. Input of less than three values is an error yielding an N output, as before. However, ordinary outputs are indicated for more than three input values. Our intention is to use only the first three values and ignore the rest.

9.2.3 Developing Test Points

We can now develop the test points using Table 9.6. Column 1 deals with the number of values input. Testing this column completely requires input of no, one, and two values. Choose the test points

( )	null input
(3)	one value
(3,4)	
(4,3)	two values

Columns 2 through 18 all assume three or more values are input. Test points will be determined for these columns assuming that exactly three values are input. To ensure that the input of more than three values yields the desired results, each test point determined for these columns can be expanded to include an extra value. Processing of the expanded test point should yield the same result as processing the three-value test point. For example, processing $x'=(3,4,5,6)$ should yield the same result as processing $x=(3,4,5)$.

According to column 2, the output N is yielded when not all a,b,c are integers. Obviously, this condition is intended to be symmetric with respect to a,b,c. Choose the following three test points for subclass 2:

(1,1,A)
(1,A,1)
(A,1,1)

Several further test points could be used to ensure that the program is capable of detecting letters embedded in the middle of strings, for example:

(100,100,1Z1)
(100,1Z1,100)
(1Z1,100,100)

For all the subclasses of columns 3 through 18, a,b,c always have integer values.

Each of the subclasses of columns 3 through 6 yields the output N, and each subclass is determined by a single condition value (in addition to the condition that a,b,c are all integers). For example, column 5 shows that p>q+r causes the output N, no matter what values other conditions have. Thus, according to columns 3 through 6, N is obtained if one or more of a,b,c is less than 0, or if one or more of a,b,c is equal to 0, or if p>q+r. In developing test points for situations where the same output is yielded by any one of several conditions, a principle is: *choose the test points to isolate each condition in turn.* In other words, to isolate the condition of subclass 3, choose a set of test points for which

one or more of a,b,c<0   and   p<q+r

so that the output N is obtained only if the program is sensitive to one or more of a,b,c<0. For subclass 4, choose test points such that

one or more of a,b,c is equal to 0   and   p<q+r

and so on.

Each condition is isolated in turn to detect the situation in which the program under test properly detects all but one of the conditions. If the test point were to simultaneously satisfy two or more conditions, the program's failure to detect one of them could be masked by its detection of the other conditions.

When isolation of each condition is attempted, some conditions may be found to be dependent on others. For example, the condition that three integers are interpretable as the sides of a triangle was formulated as p<q+r, where p=max(a,b,c) and q,r are the other two sides. But, if r<0, then p<q+r can never be satisfied. Thus the condition of subclass 3 may induce the condition of subclass 5 or 6. Luckily, there are several different ways to define the condition that three integers are interpretable as the sides of a triangle:

1. $p<q+r$, where $p=\max(a,b,c)$ and q,r are the other two sides
2. $|p|<|q|+|r|$, where $|p|=\max(|a|,|b|,|c|)$ and $|q|,|r|$ are the other two magnitudes
3. Satisfying all of the following three equations: $a<b+c$, $b<a+c$, and $c<a+b$
4. And, satisfying all of the following three equations: $|a|<|b|+|c|$, $|b|<|a|+|c|$, and $|c|<|a|+|b|$

Definitions 1 and 3 are equivalent (one of the equations of 3 is the equation of 1) and likewise definitions 2 and 4 are equivalent. As noted, definition 1 is satisfied only when a,b,c are greater than 0, but definition 2 can be satisfied when one or more of a,b,c are less than 0 or when one or more are equal to 0. Thus the test points for subclass 3 should be formulated to meet definition 2 since definition 1 cannot be satisfied when one or more of a,b,c are <0 as required by subclass 3. This is the best that can be done, and if the program under test actually uses definition 2, then the test will isolate the conditions for the different subclasses.

In setting out the test points for subclass 3, we also follow the principle: *test the interior and all boundaries of each subclass*. Errors are especially prevalent at boundaries [Boe 79b, Mye 79]. For a numeric-value boundary, choose some test points with numeric values as close as possible to the boundary value. If possible, choose some points exactly on the boundary. This principle and the symmetry convention yield the following test points:

(−1,1,1)	(3,−4,5)	(−4,5,3)
(1,−1,1)	(3,5,−4)	(5,3,−4)
(1,1,−1)	(−4,3,5)	(5,−4,3)

In the test points above, the values −1,1 are the closest negative and positive integer values not equal to 0. (If the input values were real numbers, we might have chosen −0.0001,+0.0001 as the closest negative and positive numbers not equal to 0.) To complete the test for subclass 3, test points such as (1,1,1), which lie just outside the boundary of subclass 3, are also chosen. All such test points lie within subclasses 7 through 18, and will be chosen later. The test point (0,0,0) will also be chosen later. We also choose some test points with more than one negative value:

(5,−5,−5)	(−3,−4,5)	(−4,5,−3)	(−7,−7,−7)
(−5,5,−5)	(−3,5,−4)	(5,−3,−4)	
(−5,−5,5)	(−4,−3,5)	(5,−4,−3)	(−1,−1,−1)

For subclass 4, we choose test points with one or more values equal to 0. Note that, in this case, definition 2 cannot be satisfied. We choose the following points:

(1,1,0)	(3,4,0)	(4,0,3)	(5,0,0)	(0,0,0)
(1,0,1)	(3,0,4)	(0,3,4)	(0,5,0)	
(0,1,1)	(4,3,0)	(0,4,3)	(0,0,5)	

To isolate the condition of subclass 5, test points are chosen so that a,b,c are greater than 0. Let $d=p-(q+r)$. The condition determining subclass 5 is $d>0$, and the limiting numeric value $d=0$ is a boundary. Accordingly, we choose some test points with the smallest values of a,b,c (recall the numeric boundaries a=0, b=0, c=0) that achieve the smallest integer difference $d>0$, namely, d=1. (If real input values were used, we might have chosen d=0.0001.) The following points can be chosen:

Boundary points	(1,1,3)	(7,4,2)	(7,2,4)
	(1,3,1)	(4,7,2)	(2,7,4)
	(3,1,1)	(4,2,7)	(2,4,7)
Interior points	(100,20,21)	(100,21,20)	
	(20,21,100)	(21,20,100)	
	(20,100,21)	(21,100,20)	

To isolate the condition of subclass 6, test points are chosen so that a,b,c are all greater than 0, and d=0. We choose the following points:

(1,1,2)	(10,7,3)	(3,10,7)
(1,2,1)	(10,3,7)	(7,3,10)
(2,1,1)	(3,7,10)	(7,10,3)
(100,51,49)	(51,49,100)	
(100,49,51)	(49,51,100)	
(51,100,49)	(49,100,51)	

For subclasses 7 through 18, the values a,b,c are all integers greater than 0, and the triangle inequality is satisfied (i.e., $p<q+r$). These subclasses are all similar.

The boundaries of subclass 6 are

b_1:numeric values of a,b,c   (e.g., a=0 is a limiting value)
b_2:difference $d=p-(q+r)$ (d=0 is a limiting value)
b_3:difference $|a-b|$ ($|a-b|=0$ is a limiting value)
b_4:difference $|b-c|$ ($|b-c|=0$ is a limiting value)
b_5:difference $p^2-(q^2+r^2)$ ($p^2-(q^2+r^2)=0$ is a limiting value)

To test the boundary b_1, test points with small values of a,b,c are required; to test b_2, test points with a small difference d are required; to test b_3 and b_4, inputs with small differences $|a-b|$ and $|b-c|$, respectively, are required; and finally, to test b_5, test points with small values $|p^2-(q^2+r^2)|$ are required. If possible, some test points need to be chosen close to b_1 but far from b_2, . . . , b_5; then close to b_2 but far from b_1, b_3, . . . , b_5; and so on. The consideration of these points is left as an exercise (see Problem 1 at the end of this section).

The boundaries of subclass 8 differ from those of subclass 7 only in that for subclass 8 the limiting value $p^2-(q^2+r^2)=0$ is required. Thus, if the program under test mistakenly identifies a small difference $p^2-(q^2+r^2)>0$ as $p^2-(q^2+r^2)=0$, the program will give the output for subclass 8 rather than that for 7, and vice versa. In the same way, each of the boundaries b_3 and b_4 separates subclass 7 from one of the subclasses 10 through 18, and all of the subclasses 7 through 18 have the same boundaries b_1 and b_2.

Some test points for subclass 8 are

(3,4,5)	(4,5,3)	(8,15,17)	(15,17,8)
(3,5,4)	(5,3,4)	(8,17,15)	(17,15,8)
(4,3,5)	(5,4,3)	(15,8,17)	(17,8,15)

The derivations of test points for subclasses 9, 12, 13, 16, and 18 are left as exercises (see Problem 2 at the end of this section). In attempting to derive test points for subclass 17, we find that subclass 17 is actually an impossible case. The input values must all be positive integers, but if $b=c$ and $a^2=b^2+c^2$, then $a=c\sqrt{2}$, so that a cannot be an integer. Thus there are no inputs in subclass 17. In general, we must check each input subclass to be sure that it is a possible case.

The steps taken in specification-based testing are summarized below:

1. Derive subclasses, including error classes as well as those of the planned input class. Each logically distinct case should be assigned a subclass.
2. The test's objective is to determine whether the program preserves the given subclasses and gives the correct output for each subclass.
3. Include test points from error classes.
4. Check whether each input subclass is actually a possible case.
5. Include test points for the interior and all boundaries of each input subclass. A subclass may have several different *kinds* of boundaries.
6. Include a test for each alternative class of data, if there are alternate classes.
7. Include test points that test for common errors.
8. Test independent boundaries for output subclasses, if they are specified. Include (if possible) test points that yield results outside the boundaries of each output subclass.
9. Test extreme points (i.e., points that lie on input subclass boundaries and cause output on output subclass boundaries).
10. Test all degenerate cases.

The rules for choosing test-point values are summarized below:

1. Test the interior and all boundaries of each subclass. A subclass may have different kinds of boundaries.
2. Include test points that test for common errors.
3. Explicitly test, when testing a numeric relation x:y, for each outcome in the set $\{<,=,>\}$.

4. Do not assume symmetry in the processing of input values. Symmetry in processing must be established by test. When symmetric processing is intended:
   (a) Form conditions with intended symmetry fully reflected.
   (b) Use all permutations of the values in each test point chosen in the analysis.

5. Choose test points that isolate each specific condition in turn when the same output is yielded for any one of several conditions.

6. Choose some test points, having numeric values as close as possible to the boundary value, for numeric-value boundaries. For each subclass, choose some test points just inside the boundary, and some just outside the boundary. If possible, also choose some points exactly on the boundary.

7. Choose test points that are close to each boundary in turn and far from all the other boundaries, if there are several boundaries. Then choose points close to two boundaries but far from the others; and so on, until points are chosen close to all the boundaries.

8. Test extreme points (i.e., points that lie on input subclass boundaries and cause output on output subclass boundaries).

9. Test all degenerate cases, such as a missing input file, a list of values given 0 values, a list of numbers to be sorted that is already in sorted order or where all numbers are equal.

10. Choose test points, for variables whose processing is similar or related, where the variables have identical values and where they all have distinct values.

11. Include test points, if array values are used as indexes, for which these values are negative or out of bounds.

12. Choose test points, when a variable is used for both input and output, for which a different output value is obtained and points for which the same value is obtained.

13. Vary each component of the test points.

14. Use the special numeric values 0,1 and real numbers that are small in absolute value.

15. Ensure that variables in arithmetic expressions have a measurable effect on the sign and magnitude of the result.

9.2.4 Further Rules for Black-Box-Test Development

9.2.4.1 Boundary Analysis

Rules for further testing situations are discussed in this section, based on the steps and rules listed above. (Many of the specific rules in this section were compiled from [How 78a, How 78d, How 80], and some rules were found in [Mye 79, Fos 80]. For further rules, consult these sources.)

Rule 1 above for choosing test-point values calls for choosing all boundaries of each subclass and also notes that a subclass may have different *kinds* of boundaries. For example, an input may be a list of values V in the range $1 \leq V \leq 99$, so that there are maximum and minimum bounds on the value of each V and also maximum and minimum bounds on the number of values in the list. In this situation, the test should include one point with $V=1$, one point with $V=99$, one point with the minimum number of values, and one point with the maximum number of values.

Another example is the use of input variables u,v, where u is a real number in the range [0,v] and v is a real number in the range [0,∞]. Test points should include the situations $u=v=0$, $u=0<v$, $0<u=v$, $0<u<v$, and the erroneous situations $v=0<u$ and $0<v<u$.

Again, arrays have element values and also dimension values. If the dimensions of an array are variable, then the allowable dimensions must be formally defined. If the allowable dimensions are given as intervals of integers, the interior and end points of each such interval should be tested.

A common occurrence is a record containing data of different kinds, such as

(name, sex, age, height, weight, eye color, hair color)

in which each kind of data has an individual set of possible values and, consequently, an individual set of boundaries. In this situation, each individual set of boundaries should be tested.

A final example is the use of alternative classes of input data, perhaps as determined by a transaction code. The test points should include the interior and boundaries for each class. Similarly, if there are alternative classes of output data, test points are needed to check the interior and boundaries for each class of output data.

Howden [How 78a] notes that some errors can be avoided if, for each input variable, the variable and range are given in the specifications and if the specification also indicates actions to be taken when the variable has the wrong type or is out of range.

9.2.4.2 Output Subclasses

In developing a test, we also need to consider output subclasses and, if possible, use test points that yield invalid outputs. When explicit boundaries are given for an output subclass (e.g., a maximum amount of a paycheck), test points are needed to test the boundaries of this output subclass. We should also construct test points that yield results outside the boundaries of the output subclass. Failure to test the boundaries of output subclasses can lead to billing programs that, for example, demand a payment of $0.00, or to report-printing programs that print a final page having header information but no text lines (see [Ker 74, pp. 83–86] and [How 78c, p. 189]).

In some problems, it is possible to have an *extreme* point that lies on an input subclass boundary. Obviously, a representative set of such points should be tested.

9.2.4.3 Degenerate Cases

In most problems, it is possible to identify degenerate cases, such as no input file given. For a list of input values to be sorted, the list might have no elements, or might have one element, or might have all elements with the same value, or might already be in sorted order. Every such case should be tested. For arrays, degenerate cases are all elements 0, or all elements 1, or all elements with the same value.

9.2.4.4 Choice of Values for Input and Output Variables

If an input or output variable has a small set of discrete values, we need to test all of these values; otherwise, we should test the interior and end point of each numeric interval.

If the processing of variables is similar or specially related, then the test should include test points in which these variables have identical values and test points in which they have distinct values. When all elements of an array are to be processed similarly, we need to choose the element values in accordance with this rule. When two arrays store data from the same set, array elements in corresponding positions should have distinct values.

If array values are used as indexes, we should include in our test cases in which array values are negative, or are repeated, or are outside the size of the array.

If a variable is used both for input and for output, we should choose test points such that the output value of the variable is different from the input value, as well as test points where the output value is the same as the input value.

We need to vary each component of the test point. When M test points have been chosen:

· There should be no ith component that is identical in each test point. For example, if one component is an array, the element values of the array should not be identical from one test point to the next. If the ith component is a numeric value, its sign should not be the same in all the test points.

· There should not be ith and jth components that are the same in each test point. For example, if the first and second components are arrays A and B, we should not have $A_1 = B_1$ (the arrays are equal for the first test point), $A_2 = B_2$ (the arrays are equal for the second test point), . . . , $A_M = B_M$.

9.2.4.5 Special Numeric Values

For a scientific program, test values having special mathematical properties should be included [How 78b, How 80]. The most important such values are 0,1, and real numbers whose absolute values are small. Special array values are arrays with all elements 0, arrays with all elements 1, and arrays with all elements identical.

We also need to ensure that variables in arithmetic expressions have a measurable effect on the sign and magnitude of the result. The following procedure [Fos 80, pp. 260–261] gives test points in which the components vary properly and in which each variable has a measurable effect, for integer arithmetic computations.

Step 1: Let N be the number of variables in the arithmetic expression. Choose the set of N integers $\{i_1, \ldots, i_N\}$ with smallest values such that: $1 < i_1 < i_2 < \ldots < i_{N-1} < i_N$, and if c is a constant in the expression, then c is not chosen.

In other words, the consecutive integers 2, 3, . . . , N+1 are chosen, except that if one of these is a constant in the expression, it is skipped and a further consecutive integer is taken. According to Foster [Fos 80], the values 0 and 1 are not used "because they usually will not produce different results when there are either symbol or operation errors." (However, recall the recent suggestion of using the values 0 and 1 [How 80]. It would be particularly important to assign values that caused a divisor to be 0.)

Step 2: Test case 1, consisting of the first set of values intended for substitution in the expression, is obtained by assigning the lowest odd values from the set of integers to exponent variables, the lowest even values to exponentiated variables, and the next higher values to divisors. The remaining values are assigned to the other variables.

Step 3: If the variables are constrained as absolute (the signs cannot be changed), then we add 1 to each value in test point 1 to obtain test case 2, and omit step 4.

If the variables are not constrained as absolute, then obtain the values of test case 2 by changing the values in test case 1 as follows:

1. Complement the sign of all exponentiated variables.
2. In every sum term and in every difference term, complement the sign of an odd number of variables.

Step 4: Obtain test case 3 from test case 2 by complementing the signs of all values in test case 2. If test case 3 is identical to test case 1, discard test case 3.

Step 5: If any term of the expression is not within an order of magnitude of the result of the expression, rescale the set of integers of step 1 and repeat steps 2 through 4.

As an example, three test cases are shown for the assignment below, assuming $f \neq 0$:

	x:=	a	+	b **	c	+	(d	*	e)	/	f
Test point 1		5		2	3		6		7		4
Test point 2		−5		−2	3		−6		−7		−4
Test point 3		5		2	−3		6		7		4

The results for x, to 2 decimal places, are 23.50, −23.50, and 15.63. If the variables had been constrained as absolute, test points 2 and 3 would have been replaced by (a,b,c,d,e,f)=(6,3,4,7,8,5), with the result 98.20. Since each term is within an order of magnitude of the result, the rescaling of step 5 is not necessary. If the value of the expression is constrained in some way, equal values may be used for some variables provided that each variable has a measurable effect and that components of the input point are properly varied, as suggested in Section 9.2.4.4.

9.2.4.6 Error Guessing

Testers should try to foresee solutions that a program under test might use and test for errors that would occur from such solutions. For example, an "efficient" strategy for Problem 6 of Appendix D might be based on the restriction that the knight never returns to a previously held position. As astute tester should realize that this strategy is incorrect and should include test points that require the knight to return to a previously held position. (Myers [Mye 79] calls the strategy of guessing at probable solutions and their errors *error guessing*.)

In many problems (e.g., Problem 6 in Appendix D), an input is processed with respect to a set of conditions. Based on this processing, the input is assigned either to a class S of inputs for which a solution exists, or a class S′ of inputs for which a solution does not exist. Usually, assignment to S′ is the default situation, signifying that the program has tried to find a solution but has failed.

If the program's algorithm is ad hoc or careless, then the program might assign inputs to S′ that do not properly belong there. To guard against this possibility, the test should include all extreme and unusual input values that might erroneously be assigned to S′. In this way, the test can ensure that the program always finds a solution, if a solution exists.

REFERENCES

[Boe 79b] Boehm, B. W. "Software Engineering: R&D Trends and Defense Needs," in P. Wegner (ed.), *Research Directions in Software Technology*. Cambridge, MA: M.I.T. Press, 1979.

[DeMi 78] DeMillo, R. A.; Lipton, R. J.; and Sayward, F. G. "Hints on Test Data Selection: Help for the Practicing Programmer," *IEEE Computer*, April 1978.

[Fos 80] Foster, K. A. "Error Sensitive Test Cases Analysis," *IEEE Transactions on Software Engineering*, May 1980.

[How 78a] Howden, W. E. "An Evaluation of the Effectiveness of Symbolic Testing," *Software—Practice and Experience*, 1978.

[How 78b] ———. "Functional Program Testing," *Proceedings COMPSAC 78*. New York: IEEE Computer Society, 1978. (Also in [Ram 78]. Revised version in [How 80].)*

[How 78c] ———. "A Survey of Dynamic Analysis Methods," in E. Miller and W. E. Howden (eds.), *Tutorial: Software Testing and Validation Techniques*. New York: IEEE Computer Society, 1978.

[How 78d] ———. "Theoretical and Empirical Studies of Program Testing," *Proceedings of 3rd International Conference on Software Engineering*. (IEEE Catalog No. 78CH1317-7C.) New York: IEEE Computer Society, 1978. (Also in *IEEE Transactions on Software Engineering*, July 1978).

[How 80] ———. "Functional Program Testing," *IEEE Transactions on Software Engineering*, March 1980.

[Ker 74] Kernighan, B. W., and Plauger, P. J. *The Elements of Programming Style*. New York: McGraw-Hill, 1974.

[Mye 79] Myers, G. J. *The Art of Software Testing*. New York: Wiley, 1979.

[Ram 76] Ramamoorthy, C. V.; Ho, S. F.; and Chen, W. T. "On the Automated Generation of Program Test Data," *IEEE Transactions on Software Engineering*, December 1976.

[Wey 80] Weyuker, E. J., and Ostrand, T. J. "Theories of Program Testing and the Application of Revealing Subdomains," *IEEE Transactions on Software Engineering*, May 1980.

PROBLEMS

1. In deriving test points for the example in Section 9.2.2:
   (a) Can test points be chosen close to the boundary b_1 but far from other boundaries of subclass 6? If so, give some test points.
   (b) Give test points that are far from other boundaries but close to:

(*1*) b_2.	(*5*) b_1 and b_2.
(*2*) b_3.	(*6*) b_1 and b_3.
(*3*) b_4.	(*7*) b_1 and b_4.
(*4*) b_5.	(*8*) b_1 and b_5.

   Hint: Determine how close points can be to each boundary.

2. Derive test points for subclass 8 of the example in Section 9.2.2.

---

*See Appendix B: Bibliography.

3. Derive test points for subclasses 10 through 14 of the example in Section 9.2.2.

4. Derive a test for:
- **(a)** Problem 1 of Appendix D.
- **(b)** Problem 2 of Appendix D.
- **(c)** Problem 4 of Appendix D.
- **(d)** Problem 6 of Appendix D.
- **(e)** Problem 8 of Appendix D.
- **(f)** Problem 11 of Appendix D.
- **(g)** Problem 12 of Appendix D.

5. Consider the program of Problem A in Appendix E.
- **(a)** Do part 2 of Problem A in Appendix E.
- **(b)** Determine a specification for the given program.
- **(c)** Derive a specification-based test for the program.

9.3 TEST-CASE DERIVATION IN PROGRAM-BASED TESTING

9.3.1 Introduction to Path-Oriented Testing

A *path-oriented test* is a collection of test points derived from the program structure, with the goal of causing the execution of specific statements, branches, or paths in a program. The basic premise of path-oriented testing is that a collection of test points based on program structure can give significant information about a program's correctness, and that errors can be found through the systematic execution of program paths.

Path-oriented tests have several desirable features. The set of paths in a program can be mechanically determined from the program listing, and the execution of program segments can be monitored. Programs have been written to aid testing by generating appropriate test points, running tests, and keeping track of the statements, branches, and paths executed during tests. Also, the comprehensiveness of a test can be measured by the percentage of executable statements and branch conditions actually exercised by the test. In a report [Mil 79] on a software testing service, the criterion of comprehensive testing was that 85 percent of the nonnull program segments were exercised.

Two path-oriented testing methods are commonly used, each with its own criterion for success. *Statement testing* is successful if, when a program processes the collection of test points, each statement in the program is executed at least once. *Branch testing* is successful if during the test each branch in a program is traversed at least once. To see the difference between these criteria, suppose that the program of Figure 9.1 is to be tested using test points $x = (m,n)$.

```
          begin                                                        a
(*a*)  read(m,n);                                                      ↓
(*b*)  if (m<0 and n≥0) or (n<0 and m>0) then (*c*) s:=−1;  b
(*d*)  m:=abs(m);                                                       ↓   ↘ c
(*e*)  n:=abs(n);                                                      d
(*f*)  z:=0;                                                            ↓
(*g*)  while n>0 do                                                    e
          begin                                                         ↓
             (*h*) z:=z+m;                                             f
             (*i*)n:=n−1                                                ↓
          end;                                                         g
(*j*)  z:=z*s;                                                          ↓
       write (z)                                                      h
       end                                                             ↓
                                                                      i
                                                                       ↓
                                                                      j
```

Figure 9.1   A program and its flowgraph (from [How 78c, p. 194]).

In Figure 9.1, each statement is preceded by a comment that, in effect, labels the statement, using labels a,b,c, . . . , j. The statement labels are used as the nodes of the program's flowgraph, which is a directed graph showing the flows of control from each statement to the next. When the single test point $x=(1,-1)$ is given, all statements of the program are executed via the path a b c d e f g h i g j through the flowgraph.

For this program, the statement-testing criterion is met by using only one test point. However, the paths a b d . . . and . . . f g j are also possible but are untested. The branch-testing criterion requires inclusion of test points that cause one execution of each outcome of each condition. For the program of Figure 9.1, branch testing requires at least one execution of each of the paths b d, b c d, g h, and g j. The test point $x=(0,0)$ causes execution of the path a b d e f g j, and thus the branch-testing criterion requires two test points. In certain special cases (e.g., programs with multiple entry points), a successful branch test may not cause all statements to be executed at least once. The criterion for successful branch testing is usually extended to require that all branches are executed and all statements are executed. With this extended criterion, a successful branch test always causes all statements to be executed at least once.

Programs contain many errors due to executing incorrect sequences of branches. Such an error may not be revealed by branch testing [How 78a] since the error requires a test point that causes the incorrect sequence of branches to be executed. Unfortunately, it is usually impossible to test every possible path through a program since programs with loops commonly allow an unbounded number of paths. For example, the program of Figure 9.1 will execute the while loop exactly $|n|$ times for each integer value of n. In *path testing*, a third path-oriented testing method, the set of paths through a program is grouped into a finite set of classes; a path test is then successful if the test causes execution of at least one path from each class. Unfortunately, path testing has not been extensively studied.

This section discusses deriving test points for branch testing, which is the principal form of path-oriented testing. Section 9.3.2 outlines the general method and problems in branch testing and Section 9.3.3 presents a recently proposed heuristic procedure for deriving test points sensitive to errors [Fos 80].

Branch testing alone is not a sufficient test method, just as specification-based testing alone is not sufficient. However, specification-based testing combined with branch testing is in many situations the best error-detection technique [How 80]. When these methods are combined, each possible branch is tested at least once for each special value of each input or output variable [How 80, p. 165].

9.3.2 Steps in Branch Testing

All execution paths required for branch testing can be determined from the program listing. The key factor in determining test points is calculation of variable values at each condition statement. For example, in determining test points for the program in Figure 9.1, the key questions are the values of m and n at statement b and the value of n at statement g. These values determine the control paths that will be taken.

Thus the first step is to determine, at each condition statement, the sets of values required to cause all branches and all statements to execute. Each set of values is then "backed up" through the program logic to the input, and the values at the input become the test-point values. If the program is substantially correct, then many of the test points derived in this way will be identical to test points derived in specification-based testing. When specification-based and branch testing are combined, the usual procedure is that the specification-based testing is performed first, and records are kept of the branches and statements executed. Branch testing is then used to achieve execution of the remaining branches and statements.

A good principle to follow in branch testing is choosing values that isolate each different combination of conditions. (Myers [Mye 79] calls this principle multiple-condition testing.) For example, statement b in Figure 9.1 contains the test

$$(m<0 \text{ and } n \geqslant 0) \quad \text{ or } \quad (n<0 \text{ and } m>0)$$

and the two values $x=(0,0)$ and $x=(1,-1)$ suffice to cause both true and false results. Table 9.7 shows the outcome, for these two test points, of each condition and combination of conditions. Notice that the condition $m<0$ is false in both cases, so that $(m<0 \text{ and } n \geqslant 0)$ is also false in both cases. In effect, the two test points check only the condition $(n<0 \text{ and } m>0)$. In fact, the program in Figure 9.1 contains two potential errors, namely, that s is not initialized and that m and n are not treated symmetrically in the test. The test points thus far chosen mask these potential errors.

Table 9.7   Condition outcomes caused by test points

m	n	$m<0$	$n \geqslant 0$	$m<0$ and $n \geqslant 0$	$n<0$	$m>0$	$n<0$ and $m>0$
0	0	F	T	F	F	F	F
1	−1	F	F	F	T	T	T

Further test points are needed to achieve the outcome $m<0=$true and $(m<0 \text{ and } n \geqslant 0)=$true. We know from the principle of testing for all of the outcomes $\{<,=,>\}$ in the case of numeric relations, that testing for all combinations of the outcomes $\{m<0, m=0, m>0\}$ and $\{n<0, n=0, n>0\}$ will achieve these results.

Branch testing is sometimes extended to cover all elementary control paths, that is, all distinct paths from entry to exit involving no more than one execution of any loop. For example, the elementary paths of the program in Figure 9.1 are

```
a  b  d  e  f  g  j
a  b  d  e  f  g  h  i  g  j
a  b  c  d  e  f  g  j
a  b  c  d  e  f  g  h  i  g  j
```

Because the test at statement g uses a condition also used at statement b, branch testing conducted according to the multiple-condition principle will exercise all of these paths. However, consider the program and flowgraph in Figure 9.2.

```
begin
(*p*)  if (a>1)and(b=0)then (*q*) z:=z/a;
(* r*)  if(a=4)or(z>1)then (*s*) z:=z+1;
(* t*)  z:=z*a
end
```

Figure 9.2   A second program and flowgraph.

The following combinations of conditions are required for multiple-condition testing:

$$\text{At } p: \begin{cases} a<1,b<0 \\ a<1,b=0 \\ a<1,b>0 \\ a=1,b<0 \\ a=1,b=0 \\ a=1,b>0 \\ a>1,b<0 \\ a>1,b=0 \\ a>1,b>0 \end{cases} \quad \text{At } r: \begin{cases} a<4,z<1 \\ a<4,z=1 \\ a<4,z>1 \\ a=4,z<1 \\ a=4,z=1 \\ a=4,z>1 \\ a>4,z<1 \\ a>4,z=1 \\ a>4,z>1 \end{cases}$$

For the test at p, a can take values from the set $\{0,1,2\}$, and b can take values from the set $\{-1,0,1\}$. For the test at r, a can take values from the set $\{3,4,5\}$ and z can take values from the set $\{0,1,4\}$. Table 9.8(a) shows each combination of a and b values and the resulting path p q r or p r; Table 9.8(b) shows each combination of a and z values and the resulting path r s t or r t.

Table 9.8   Enumeration of possible test values. (a) Conditions at statement p. (b) Conditions at statement r.

a	b	Path	a	z	Path
0	−1	p r	3	0	r t
0	0	p r	3	1	r t
0	1	p r	3	4	r s t
1	−1	p r	4	0	r s t
1	0	p r	4	1	r s t
1	1	p r	4	4	r s t
2	−1	p r	5	0	r t
2	0	p q r	5	1	r t
2	1	p r	5	4	r s t
		(a)			(b)

In this program, the tests at p and at r are partially linked, in that both test the value of a and that statement q modifies the value of z to be used by q. The linkage can be ignored, and test points can be formed by using $z=0$ in conjunction with the values of Table 9.8(a) and $b=1$ in conjunction with the values in (b). The resulting test points and the execution path caused by each point are shown in Table 9.9.

Table 9.9 Some test points for the program in Figure 9.2

Test Point				Test Point			
a	b	z	Path	a	b	z	Path
0	−1	0	p r t	3	1	0	p r t
0	0	0	p r t	3	1	1	p r t
0	1	0	p r t	3	1	4	p r s t
1	−1	0	p r t	4	1	0	p r s t
1	0	0	p r t	4	1	1	p r s t
1	1	0	p r t	4	1	4	p r s t
2	−1	0	p r t	5	1	0	p r t
2	0	0	p q r t	5	1	1	p r t
2	1	0	p r t	5	1	4	p r s t

Note that for $x=(3,0,4)$, the value tested at q is $z=4/3$ since the statement q performs $z:=z/a$. The set of elementary paths in this program is

$$\{p\,r\,t,\,p\,r\,s\,t,\,p\,q\,r\,t,\,p\,q\,r\,s\,t\}$$

The test points enumerated in Table 9.9 do not cause execution of the path p q r s t because the test points for which $a=4$ or $z>1$ do not have $b=0$. Additional test points (3,0,4), (4,0,0), (4,0,4), and (5,0,4) would all cause execution of the path p q r s t.

9.3.3 A Heuristic Method for Deriving Test Points

9.3.3.1 Rules for Error-Sensitive Test Cases

Section 9.3 presents a systematic procedure for deriving test points in accordance with four rules and using the concept of "critical paths" in the program. The following four rules [Fos 80] are said to yield sensitivity to program errors.

Rule 1: When testing a numeric relation x:y in the program, assign values to x and y that achieve each outcome in the set $\{<,=,>\}$.

This rule (which is identical to rule 3 in Section 9.2.3) is intended to detect errors in the relation used, such as the use of $<$ insted of $\leq$ or vice versa.

Rule 2: When a variable is required to be less than (or greater than) a constant, assign the variable value so that it differs from the constant by the smallest decrement (increment) allowed.

If the program contains a condition a$<$c, where a is a variable and c is a constant, then the value c$-$d is assigned to a, where d is the smallest decrement allowed. This rule allows detection of "off by one" errors in increments, decrements, and limits.

Rule 2 precisely defines the term *close to*, which appears in rule 6 of Section 9.2.3. If the constant c is regarded as a boundary, then rule 6 (as made precise by rule 2 above) suggests that a be assigned each value in the set $\{c-d,c,c+d\}$.

Rule 3: Ensure that the variables in arithmetic expressions have a measurable effect on the sign and magnitude of the result.

Rules 1, 2, and 3 are concerned with choosing values at each location in the program, whereas rule 4 is concerned with relations among the test points.

Rule 4: Let the test points chosen be $x_1=(v_{11}, \ldots, v_{1k}), \ldots, x_m=(v_{m1}, \ldots, v_{mk})$. Choose these test points so that

1. There is no ith component such that $v_{1i}=v_{2i}=\cdots=v_{(m-1)i}=v_{mi}$.
2. There is no ith component such that $sign(v_{1i})=\cdots=sign(v_{mi})$.
3. There are no ith or jth components such that $v_{1i}=v_{1j}, v_{2i}=v_{2j}, \ldots, v_{mi}=v_{mj}$.
4. If possible, choose the points so that resulting values within the program are not identical with the values of internal variables.

This rule states that components of an input point should be properly varied, as was suggested in Section 9.2.4.4.

9.3.3.2 Critical Paths in Software

A *critical path* is a program control path from entry point to exit point, counting each loop as having only one iteration, which traverses the largest number of operations and simple conditions [Fos 80].

The critical path concept is intended as a guide when deriving test points. Reasoning by analogy from hardware failure analysis methods, it is plausible that test point values passing through the most conditions and operations will produce a different output from that produced by other paths. If a condition or operation on the critical path has an error, it is highly probable that the output result will be different from the specified output, and thus that the error will be detected. Accordingly, test points are first developed for the most critical path. If possible, the first critical path chosen should be one for which the output result is different from the output yielded by most other paths.

When evaluating the criticality of a path, it is assumed that in a compound condition each simple condition is evaluated in turn, except that these evaluations are discontinued as soon as a condition result is determined. As an example, Figure 9.1 contains the following statements:

(*b*) if (m<0 and n≥0) or (n<0 and m>0) then (*c*) s:=−1;
(*d*) m:=abs(m).

In our evaluation of criticality, the compound condition at b is assumed to be executed as the pattern of simple condition tests shown in the program of Figure 9.3. (The go to statements in Figure 9.3 are used only to show the exact sequence of tests assumed.)

```
    (*b*)  if not(m<0)then goto 10;
           if (n≥0) then goto 20;
    10:  if not(n<0)then goto 30;
           if not(m>0) then goto 30;
(*c*)  20:  s:=−1;
(*d*)  30:  m:=abs(m)
```

Figure 9.3   Program with compound conditions transformed to
                      simple conditions.

For each combination of m and n values, we count the actual number of conditions and operations that would be executed by the program in Figure 9.1. This count determines a critical path—the path for which the number of conditions and operations executed is largest—and also the combination of m and n values that causes that path to be taken.

In this situation, the conditions m>0 and n<0 cause us to evaluate three conditions and statement c, while m<0 and n<0 cause us to evaluate all four conditions but not statement c. There thus appear to be two roughly equal critical paths, either of which might be considered most critical.

In general, critical paths frequently use the false branches from or and inequality conditions, and the true branches from and and equality conditions.

9.3.3.3 Derivation of Test Points

A procedure for systematically developing test points can be based on the rules and the critical-path concept. The procedure is a heuristic one, developed for structured programs in which the calculation of critical paths is reasonably straightforward [Fos 80]. Test points are developed via the following six steps.

Step 1: Use a flowchart or listing of the source code to determine the most critical path. If a critical path has variables that do not receive values in the execution of the path, then first choose some other path(s) that will assign values to these variables. A source listing will be most useful if it is indented and if each simple condition is shown on a separate line.

Step 2: Assign, at the last simple condition on a critical path, variable values in accordance with rule 1 or 2. If there are no branching conditions, assign variables in accordance with rules 3 and 4, or use the procedure of Section 9.2.4.5 for arithmetic expressions.

Step 3: Work assigned values backward from the exit point to the entry point along the critical path by "playing computer" with the flowchart or listing. At each reference to an undefined input variable, assign a value (preferably not 0,1, or a value assigned to another variable) so that the critical path will be taken. Use rule 4 to assign values for arithmetic operations on a branch.

Step 4: Work backward to the immediately preceding simple condition on the path and consider the (numeric or logical) relations between the arguments of the condition. If there is a relation not yielded by the values thus far derived, and if values satisfying this relation would lead to another path, then provide a set of values satisfying the relation.

Step 5: Devise, at each call of a subordinate module or subroutine, additional sets of test values, each set causing extreme values to pass to the subroutine, and additional sets of values that result in returning the extreme values from the subroutine. If the arguments are signed numeric values, provide additional sets of values in which the signs of the argument values are complemented. This step detects interface errors between modules.

Step 6: Repeat steps 1 through 5 for a path, then select the next critical path, until all conditions meet rule 1 or 2 and all operations on every branch meet rules 3 and 4.

REFERENCES

[Fos 80] Foster, K. A. "Error Sensitive Test Cases Analysis," *IEEE Transactions on Software Engineering*, May 1980.

[Gel 78] Geller, M. "Test Data as an Aid in Proving Program Correctness," *Communications of the ACM*, May 1978.

[Hetz 76] Hetzel, W. C. "An Experimental Analysis of Program Verification Methods," Ph.D. dissertation, University of North Carolina, 1976.

[How 78a] Howden, W. E. "An Evaluation of the Effectiveness of Symbolic Testing," *Software——Practice and Experience*, 1978.

[How 78c] ———. "A Survey of Dynamic Analysis Methods," in E. Miller and W. E. Howden (eds.), *Tutorial: Software Testing and Validation Techniques*. New York: IEEE Computer Society, 1978.

[How 80] ———. "Functional Program Testing," *IEEE Transactions on Software Engineering*, March 1980.

[Mil 79] Miller, E. F. "Some Statistics from the Software Testing Service," *Software Engineering Notes*, January 1979.

[Mye 79] Myers, G. J. *The Art of Software Testing*. New York: Wiley, 1979.

PROBLEMS

1. Consider the program of Problem A of Appendix E.
   (a) Draw the flowgraph of this program.
   (b) Give all test points in a statement test of this program.
   (c) Give all test points for a branch test of this program.
   (d) Determine the most critical path in the program.
   (e) Derive a set of test points using the rules of Section 9.3.3.3.

9.4 DEBUGGING: FINDING AND REPAIRING ERRORS

9.4.1 Planning for Debugging

When the processing of a test point gives a different result from the specified one, an error has been found. That is, the test point has been successful in discovering that the program has a fault. The error must now be precisely pinpointed and repaired, a process called *debugging*. The error itself is commonly called a *bug*.

We prepare for debugging by assuming that the program will inevitably contain errors and that the design and programming must be done so as to allow easy detection of the errors. Structuring the system into independent modules will allow quick isolation of an error within a particular module and may also make repair easier. Good design is a good preparation for debugging.

A common preparation is the insertion of diagnostic printouts throughout the program code, so that intermediate results of execution can be monitored if necessary. Placing such diagnostics is easy while the program is being written since the program structure is fresh in the programmer's mind, but it can be very difficult at a later time when the intricacies of the code have been half-forgotten. Diagnostic printouts can be made conditional on special inputs to the program. For example, the program might use an array diagnostic of flags whose elements are set by inputs, and diagnostic printout 30 could be conditional on diagnostic [30] being true.

Yourdon [You 75a] suggests a technique called *antibugging*, inserting numerous error checks into the program to detect erroneous situations as they occur.

9.4.2 Finding the Error: First Principles

Pinpointing the location and nature of a program bug is the most time-consuming task in debugging. Myers [Mye 79] has said that "locating the error is 95 percent of the problem," and Yourdon [You 75a] feels that, in large complex programs, locating a bug might require three to six months.

The advice universally given about debugging is: THINK! Finding a bug is like solving a murder mystery, and the investigator tracing a bug is, indeed, a detective. The classic method for detecting a criminal culprit is meticulously analyzing the clues in the crime to infer a behavior pattern or psychology of the crime and then to infer the culprit from the behavior pattern. Such was the method of Ellery Queen, of Sherlock and Mycroft Holmes, and especially of Hercule Poirot. Also, the detective's analysis must account for *all* of the clues rather than just a few, and that the reconstruction of the crime must explain *why* it happened the way it did and *why* it left the clues it did. The culprit can be caught in only this way.

Like a murderer, a bug also leaves clues that suggest a "psychology" or behavior pattern; and, as in a murder mystery, the investigator uses the clues to infer first the behavior pattern and then the bug's location and nature. The investigator can be sure that the bug has been found only when all of the clues are accounted for, and when the reconstructed sequence of actions explains why the bug causes these particular results. A repair made on the basis of an incomplete reconstruction may fix a symptom rather than the error itself, and such a repair is almost sure to lead to new errors.

We must assume initially that the bug is in our program rather than in other modules, the hardware, the operating system, or the compiler. It is natural to wish that the blame lies elsewhere, but almost always the bug lies in the program being tested rather than in the supporting hardware or software. Although occasionally the fault may lie in the compiler, the operating system, or the machine, we should turn our attention to these possibilities only after we have systematically excluded all possibility of our program being incorrect.

We cannot take anything for granted. We must double check all inputs to make sure that the proper test was made. After all, a fault may lie in the test input data or in the way the test was formulated. For example, we might find upon investigation that a test tape given to us and sworn to be correct is, in fact, in error.

We need to think about all the possible sources of error. If the error is unusual or occurs in a previously working program, we must make sure that the error can be repeated. That is, programs, like cars, sometimes malfunction in a transient, nonrepeatable way; usually the fault cannot be found until the malfunction can be consistently repeated. Also, we should examine the simplest, most obvious clues first, to minimize our effort.

9.4.3 Systematic Detection Procedures

Once an error has been found to be repeatable, the program can be made to repeat the error while inputs are varied. We can experiment with the program, varying the input to pinpoint the circumstances in which the error occurs or systematically excluding or including various portions of the program.

A detection procedure especially suitable for small programs is tracking the error through the program variables at various points in the program. The error can be tracked backward from the point at which the incorrect output is given, or forward from the inputs, by using the program's diagnostic printouts or a debugging aid.

If the error cannot easily be tracked, systematic collection of data, analysis of data, and then devising, refining, and proving of hypotheses are required. The situation is comparable to a game of twenty questions, in which questions (comparable to groups of test data) are used to systematically eliminate the improbable causes.

The first step in systematic error location is collecting data. It is important that all pertinent test data—both data indicating circumstances of incorrect operation and data indicating circumstance of incorrect operation—be collected and considered.

Table 9.10 A form for organizing the clues. (Copyright 1973 by MacDonald and Janes, Publisher. Reprinted by permission.)

?	IS	IS NOT
WHAT		
WHERE		
WHEN		
TO WHAT EXTENT		

Next, the clues or symptoms given by the data are organized so that patterns and unusual circumstances are observable. Table 9.10 shows a form into which this information can be entered. The WHAT boxes concern the general characteristics of the error symptoms; the WHERE boxes, the location(s) of the error in the output; the WHEN boxes deal with the specific times the fault occurs; and the TO WHAT EXTENT boxes are used for any other information about the fault. This information helps to sharply define the fault or symptoms being considered, and the goal of filling all the boxes guides the collection of data.

The IS column of the form contains circumstances and conditions under which a fault occurs, and the IS NOT column contains circumstances and conditions under which the fault does not occur. This organization helps to focus on distinctions between the two sets of circumstances, so that hypotheses about the source of the error can be derived. For example, knowing that the fault occurs when record type A is processed, but not when record type B is processed, leads to the hypothesis that these two types of processing differ in some important way, and that the error lies in the part of the program that carries out the different processing of record type A. If the distinctions between the IS and IS NOT columns are not so sharp, then the likely sources of the error cannot be pinpointed so closely. Therefore, to pinpoint the source of error, we must sharpen the distinctions between the IS and the IS NOT columns.

Another initial step is drawing up a list of potential causes of the fault. The organized clues can now be used to isolate or eliminate each potential fault. Two approaches are possible. In an *inductive step*, we analyze the data to immediately yield a hypothesis of the most probable cause. We then refine this hypothesis (make it as specific as possible), and then verify it. It is crucial to verify that the hypothesized cause of the fault accounts for all of the symptoms; if it does, the cause has been found. If it does not, then the hypothesized cause may be only part of the true cause, or may be only another symptom, and in either case the investigation must continue.

In a *deductive step*, we analyze the data to systematically eliminate possibilities. When all possibilities but one have been excluded, the possibility left is hypothetically the most probable cause. Again, this hypothesis must be refined and verified; and if it cannot be verified, the investigation must continue.

In summary, error detection involves collecting pertinent test data, organizing the data, and then enumerating possible causes. The organization of the data is intended to reveal patterns in the symptoms of the fault and to distinguish (by using Table 9.10) between the circumstances in which the fault occurs and those in which is does not occur. The data-organizing step may necessitate further collection of test data to provide the required information.

After we enumerate the potential causes, we may either pursue an immediate hypothesis or proceed to develop a hypothesis by eliminating potential causes. Typically, we will probably use each of these approaches as the investigation proceeds. For example, we might immediately develop a hypothesis suggested by intuition and when this hypothesis fails, settle down to an elimination procedure, and so on.

The collection of test data can be used as an adjunct to the other activities. For example, we can devise a test case specifically to determine whether a given potential cause can be eliminated, or to refine a hypothesis by sharpening the circumstances, or specifically to verify a hypothesis. Such test cases are like questions asked in the twenty questions game.

In a larger sense, bug detection is an exercise in scientific theorizing about a system. Each test case is an experiment on the system, and the experiments are used in devising and proving a theory about a specific aspect of the system. Accordingly, precision and rigor are needed.

9.4.4 Repairing the Error

An analogy can be made between finding and repairing a program bug and finding and repairing a problem with a car. But, for the analogy to be really precise, the car in question should be a prototype, never-built-before racing car (since most programs are one-of-a-kind devices). If the problem with the car is not a simple construction error such as a disconnected electrical wire (comparable to a simple coding error), it may require major redesign. In the same way, program errors that are not readily identifiable as simple coding errors should be regarded as design errors, and the portion of the program containing the error should be *redesigned*. Experience has shown that when programs are not carefully redesigned, the corrections tend to create new errors.

Corrections should always be made to the source code rather than to the object code. When debugging is done under time pressure, or when the system requires large amounts of recompilation or reassembly, programmers may wish to directly correct system object code in order to save time. However, this procedure should be avoided since it results in an undocumented difference between source and object code. As such changes continue to be made and new programmers replace those with knowledge of the patches, the object code rapidly becomes unfathomable.

Debugging, though usually done under great time pressure, should be done very carefully since failure to properly repair leads inevitably to further bugs.

The list below summarizes the principles of debugging.

Planning

1. Assume that the program will contain errors; design and programming must be done so as to allow easy error detection.

2. Use small, independent modules to help debugging.

3. Insert diagnostic printouts throughout as the code is being written.

Error Finding

4. Think methodically about the bug. You can be sure that you have found it only when your reconstruction accounts for all the clues and shows why each result occurred.

5. Assume initially that the bug lies in *your* program.

6. Don't take anything for granted.

7. See if the error can be repeated.

8. Examine the most obvious clues first.

9. Observe patterns and contradictions in the test data.

10. Enumerate the possible causes of an error.

11. Use analysis of test-data patterns to devise a hypothesis of the most probable cause of the error (inductive step); or use analysis of test-data patterns to systematically eliminate probable causes (deductive step).

12. Refine and prove each hypothesis of the most probable cause.

Error Repair

13. Remember that noncoding errors require redesign.

14. Remember also that error corrections may create new errors.

15. Correct the source code, not the object code.

16. Retest the program after the correction is made.

REFERENCES

[Brow 73] Brown, A. R., and Sampson, W. A., *Program Debugging*. New York: American Elsevier, 1973.

[Mye 79] Myers, G. J., *The Art of Software Testing*. New York: Wiley, 1979.

[Pool 73] Poole, P. C. "Debugging and Testing," in F. L. Bauer (ed.), *Advanced Course on Software Engineering*. (Lecture Notes in Economics and Mathematical Systems, Vol. 81.) New York: Springer-Verlag, 1973.

[You 75a] Yourdon, E. *Techniques of Program Structure and Design*. Englewood Cliffs, NJ: Prentice-Hall, 1975.

PROBLEMS

PROJECT OUTLINE: Comprehensive Test   Problem C in Appendix E contains specifications and code for a set of small program modules. For each module:

1. State the specification.

2. Derive a specification-based test.

3. Derive a branch test.

4. Derive a critical-path-based test.

5. Show the set of test points incorporating the three tests above.

Part Five
OTHER PERSPECTIVES

System management: key points in managing software projects . . . organizing and scheduling . . . resource estimation . . . review procedures . . . constraints on software development

chapter ten
Management Perspectives

10.1 INTRODUCTION TO SOFTWARE PROJECT MANAGEMENT

10.1.1 Steps in Project Management

In almost every kind of endeavor, poor management is the prime reason that enterprises fail. Software development is no exception: Good management is crucial to success, and poor management has often been the cause of failure. This chapter outlines some issues and problems of software management and presents some management techniques that have proved effective. There is a list of books on software management at the end of this section.

Successful management of any project requires four procedures:

1. *Organizing:* Identify the tasks to be performed.
2. *Scheduling:* Develop a schedule of activities for the project, taking into account the time and effort requirements of each task and the necessary sequencing of tasks.
3. *Resource estimation:* Estimate the cost, effort, and other resources that will be needed.
4. *Control:* Monitor the progress of the project, compare progress with the stated plan, and revise the plan as necessary. Also, monitor the quality of the software product.

The first three procedures should, of course, be done at the very beginning of a project since they plan various aspects of the project. For example, the organizing step involves identifying the tasks to be done, dividing them into manageable subtasks, and arranging a project organization defining who is to do each task. It is important that all groups in a project task force have sharply defined responsibilities. Then the scheduling step involves developing a schedule of activities, taking into account the interdependence among tasks (for instance, that certain tasks require others to be done first). And, finally, the resource estimation step forecasts the money, personnel, and other resources that will be needed.

Thus, broadly speaking, it can be said that

- Organizing plans *what* is to be done and *who* is to do it
- Scheduling plans *when* each task is to be done
- Resource estimation plans *how much it will cost*

Each of these plans is important to the success of the project. Not surprisingly, Boehm [Boe 79b] reports that cases of project failure have usually involved:

- Poor organization with groups not having sharply defined responsibilities
- Poor scheduling, leading to wasted effort
- Poor resource estimation, not allowing effective control
- Poor control, failing to monitor the progress or quality of the project

The planning steps determine whether a project is feasible, that is, whether the desired work can be done in the given time and within the given budget. (A project may also be infeasible if its goals are too broad, too vague, or too ambitious [Schw 75].) Problems in scheduling can be identified and dealt with immediately. For example, it may be possible to accelerate the project for an extra cost, or to stretch out the project to save money.

Control is an ongoing activity throughout the course of the project, since both the progress of the project and the quality of the product being turned out must be monitored. Broadly speaking, control seeks to ensure that the quality plan for the product is being met and that the time and money plans for the project are being met.

Section 10.1.2 gives some key points in managing software development projects. These points deal with the procedures just described and also take into account problems peculiar to software development.

Section 10.2 describes methods for organizing and scheduling, while Section 10.3 discusses resource estimation. Section 10.4 deals with procedures for reviewing work done, so as to ensure both the software quality and the progress of the project.

Last, but not least, Section 10.5 discusses constraints that cause software projects to be less timely and more expensive than they might be.

10.1.2 Key Points in Managing Software Development

Use Appropriate Success Criteria   One problem that has caused projects to fail is the use of inappropriate success criteria. That is, the definitions of "success" adopted by management strongly influence programmer behavior [Weinb 71, Boe 79b]. Table 10.1, for example, shows the results of an experiment in which several groups were given the same programming job, but with different major objectives. When the programs were evaluated, it was found that each group had written its programs primarily to satisfy the stated major objective, to the detriment of other program goals.

In the same way, emphasizing "percent coded" tends to cause neglect of preliminary activities such as requirements validation and design validation. Emphasizing minimum time to fix errors encourages concentration on minor errors (rather than on serious errors) and quick fixes that may cause further errors. Emphasizing minimum development cost and time tends to yield software that isn't portable and is hard to maintain.

Table 10.1 Influence of stated objectives on results achieved.*

Major Objective Given to Group	Memory	Output Clarity	Program Clarity	Number of Statements	Programming Hours
Minimize primary memory need	**1**	4	4	2	5
Maximize program output readability	5	**1**	1	5	2–3
Maximize program source text readability	3	2	**2**	3	4
Minimize number of program statements	2	5	3	**1**	2–3
Minimize programming hours	4	3	5	4	**1**

Note: Numbers indicate rank when programs were evaluated: 1=best. 5=worst.
*(Copyright 1974 by The Human Factors Society, Inc. Reprinted by permission. Copyright 1981 by Prentice-Hall, Inc. Reprinted by permission.)

Appropriate success criteria can be reinforced by using quality goals (see Section 2.4), evaluating the design with respect to these goals (see Section 3.6), and inspecting code for quality (see Section 10.4).

Management must act according to the success criteria it espouses. For example, though the necessity for program documentation is universally recognized, many programming establishments still have programmers who are "indispensable" because their programs are undocumented. When crises occur, the "indispensable" programmer is the only one who can correct the situation. If rewarded for this behavior, the "indispensable" programmer becomes a hero or role model for other programmers, who are then motivated to act in the same way. According to Weinberg [Weinb 71], there is only one way of dealing with this situation: "If a programmer is indispensable, get rid of him as soon as possible."

Below are some key points for managing software projects. These points have been collected from all over this book including Sections 10.3 and 10.4, and from Boehm [Boe 79a] and Schwartz [Schw 75]. For other lists of management points, see Schwartz [Schw 75] and Naur et al. [Nau 76].

Understand the Job Successful management will not be possible unless you understand specifically what must be accomplished and the constraints under which you must operate. You should have a written contract or agreement indicating at least the following points [Metz 81]:

1. The scope of the work. This should be a careful statement of what is to be done. A vague scope of work inevitably leads to arguments between customer and developer.
2. The schedule of deliveries. This should include each of the specific programs and documents to be delivered, the form of each item (e.g., cards, tapes, etc.), and where and when they are to be delivered.
3. The names of persons authorized by the customer to approve changes or to accept the final product.
4. Required reviews and progress reports and their dates.
5. The procedures for incorporating customer requests that change the original scope of work.
6. The location at which testing is to be done; the names of person(s) who will control testing; and the priorities for computer time between this project's programmers and others.
7. The specific criteria to be used in judging whether the final product is acceptable.

Estimating Resources and Scheduling Scheduling and resource estimation are usually done together, usually at the beginning of a project, to determine whether the project is feasible. The decision to proceed or not proceed with a project must be made at the very beginning, even though not all the facts may be known.

1. List what is to be done: both the major tasks and the subtasks of each major task.
2. Plan the sequence of required tasks. Don't omit specification and design steps. Remember that: integration and testing require 40 to 50 percent of total effort. And that, for best results, specification and design together should comprise 30 to 40 percent of total effort.
3. Carefully estimate required resources (time, effort, money, computer time), taking into account the program difficulty (see Section 10.3). Be aware of the level of technology required, and the level of expertise of the software team. Beware of optimism (see Section 10.5.3). Determine whether the task is feasible within the given time and cost budgets. Remember that:
   - People cannot be substituted for time—lack of adequate development time is a prime reason for project failure.
   - Shortening development time causes an increase in required total effort, and the project may become a crash project or infeasible.

- Long-term projects can anticipate a turnover of 20 percent per year, and new personnel must be trained and integrated into the project. To maintain this training process, a generous portion of the project staff must be devoted to documentation and education.
- A large project cannot be accomplished in less than 2 years. Also, a large project can sustain a manpower buildup of at most 30 percent per year.
- Additional effort spent in development will minimize total life-cycle costs, including maintenance.
- Iteration of the design may be required, especially for real-time systems.

4. Be sure to make an independent estimate of required resources before talking to superiors or to customers. Do not immediately agree to do a given job with some fixed (perhaps inadequate) resources because "that's all there is." If you undertake to do a project with unreasonably low (more than 20 percent too few) resources, *you have already failed*.

When schedules are drawn up, a project may be pressed into a shorter time schedule than estimated because of politics or outside pressures. It should, of course, be considered unreasonable to penalize a manager for not meeting a schedule that she or he originally regarded as infeasible. However, each manager can maintain an independent set of schedules and estimates, so that the manager's own predictions and own progress can be compared.

Planning and Monitoring Project Phases

1. Monitor progress objectively. Unless tasks and milestones are defined with unusual care, percent-of-completion estimates will be misleading or difficult to determine. Make sure that your staff understands your definitions of required tasks, milestones, and required documentation.

2. Ensure that planning and specification are begun early and are completed. Be sure that the user and the producer of the system understand each other and that the requirements are clear, mutually understood, and agreed upon. Include quality specifications and goals. Make success criteria clear to the software team.

3. Write the introduction to the users manual for designers to use as soon as the specifications are done. Ask the users to comment. After any necessary reworking and review of the specifications, "freeze" them so that further changes can be made only after management review. This process is intended to ensure that the specifications, which serve as the basis for design, will remain relatively stable. Similarly, the overall design document should be frozen to provide a firm basis for detailed design and coding.

4. Begin planning for testing as early as possible. Test planning can be an independent task. Remember that the high cost of testing is due in part to a lack of planning.

5. Use lean staffing in the early phases of the project. Quantity is no substitute for quality—it will only make matters worse. Don't saddle designers with the burden of keeping subordinates occupied.

Standards, Quality Assurance, and Documentation

1. Make up standards (for specifications, for designs, for programs, for documentation) and *enforce* them. Standards will not be followed unless they are enforced.
2. Ensure that program specifications are testable and that specifications for program interfaces are precise.
3. Catch errors as soon as possible by using structured walkthroughs or inspection to review specifications, designs, and code (see Section 10.4). Review specification and design *documents*, not informally stated specifications or designs. Evaluate designs with respect to quality goals (see Section 3.6) as well as for correctness.
4. Don't accept program code without documentation. Review the documentation for correctness, completeness and quality.

Documentation requirements can be used to provide feedback to the designers. If the introduction to the user's manual (containing assumptions and objectives) is written when the specifications are done, it can be used by the designers and users can comment on its appropriateness. If a draft of the entire user's manual is written after overall design (but before detailed design), users' comments can influence the detailed design and can sensitize the designers to problems of ease of use.

The Design Phase Be sure that the design allows for evolution and repair of the system and that it prepares for testing. At the end of overall design, write the draft of the user's manual, for programmers' use. Ask the user to comment. After any necessary reworking and review of the design, "freeze" it so that further changes can be made only after management review.

Choosing the right person for each design task, ensuring design review, and ensuring design documentation are difficult problems. The Multics organization adopted a procedure that dealt simultaneously with all of these issues [Cor 79]. Potential designers were asked to write position papers describing the design problems, their scope, and realistic solutions. Each author of a persuasive position paper was then asked to propose a design. Upon review of this document and agreement by his or her technical peers, the designer would then prepare a set of module designs that he or she was then expected to implement and debug. The designer might be given assistance, but would retain full responsibility.

This design competition allows the best design to establish itself through peer review and at the same time obtain a written design document. In the

Multics organization, the design document was incorporated into the System Programmer's Manual (the definitive description of the system) for use in educating new personnel. Further competitions can be held for the design of major subsystems as the design is successively refined [Mills 79].

Programming

1. Ensure that structured programming is used. Adopt programming standards and enforce them. Programmers should be taught to anticipate possible problems in the input and correct them in their programs.

2. Adopt time and core-storage budgets, and monitor (at least on a monthly basis), how well these budgets are adhered to. For storage budgets, include a safety factor of 25 percent or more.

3. Choose the project programming language carefully.

Testing

1. Implement and test top-down (see Section 5.4). A rigorous program review after coding but before debugging should minimize waste effort in debugging, and should include review of code for logic, algorithmic behavior, and quality by at least one peer [Cor 79].

2. Use a separate test team. An organization should not test its own work, and a programmer should avoid testing her or his own work. Remember that *lost time cannot be made up in the testing phase*.

3. Concentrate testing efforts on modules found to be error prone, that is, modules in which many errors have been found. Rewrite especially error-prone modules (see Section 10.4). Use a small percentage of maintenance time to select and rewrite the most troublesome modules (see Section 10.4).

4. Automate test procedures. Remember that for turnaround times between half an hour and a day, testing costs vary linearly with turnaround time. Also, testing time varies (very roughly) linearly with turnaround time [Cooke 78]. Thus any reduction (say, 10 percent) in turnaround time leads to the same drop (10 percent) in testing costs and time. Since the major reason for large turnaround time is the inclusion of too many manual steps [Cooke 78], the test procedure should be automated via the following steps:

   · Compress test files to manageable size by eliminating redundant cases and using data compression
   · Place all test files online
   · Allow immediate access to the test files
   · Have online composition at the programmer terminal
   · Provide for online test outlay by routing the output back to the programmer terminal

In the experience reported by Cooke, each individual step (performed in the sequence shown above) was found to decrease turnaround time. After 3 years, overall results were an 80 percent decrease in average turnaround time, a 600 percent increase in tests per programmer with resources and operating costs held constant, and no more programmer complaints about test time.

Delivery Develop a system using the strategy of incremental development and delivery (see Section 5.4.2), in which a sequence of successively more refined versions is developed, each succeeding version providing additional increments of function. When necessary, earlier versions can be used as prototypes, or can be used operationally on an interim basis.

BOOKS ON SOFTWARE MANAGEMENT

[Aron 74] Aron, J. D. *The Program Development Process: The Individual Programmer.* Reading, MA: Addison-Wesley, 1974.

[Bro 75] Brooks, F. P. *The Mythical Man-Month.* Reading, MA: Addison-Wesley, 1975.

[Horo 75] Horowitz, E. (ed.). *Practical Strategies for Developing Large-Scale Software.* Reading, MA: Addison-Wesley, 1975.

[Metz 81] Metzger, P. J. *Managing a Programming Project*, 2nd ed. Englewood Cliffs, NJ: Prentice-Hall, 1981.

[Nau 76] Naur, P.; Randell, B.; and Buxton, J. N. (eds.). *Software Engineering Concepts and Techniques, Proceedings of the NATO Conferences.* New York: Petrocelli/Charter, 1976.

[Weinb 71] Weinberg, G. F. *The Psychology of Computer Programming.* New York: Van Nostrand Reinhold, 1971.

[You 79a] Yourdon, E. *Managing the Structured Techniques.* New York: Yourdon, 1979.

REFERENCES

[Boe 79a] Boehm, B. W. "Software Engineering—As It Is," *Proceedings of 4th International Conference on Software Engineering.* New York: IEEE Computer Society, 1979.

[Boe 79b] ———. "Software Engineering: R&D Trends and Defense Needs," in P. Wegner (ed.) *Research Directions in Software Technology.* Cambridge, MA: M.I.T. Press, 1979.

[Bro 74] Brooks, F. P. "The Mythical Man-Month," *Datamation*, 1974. (Also in [Fre 80b].)*

[Bro 75] ———. *The Mythical Man-Month: Essays in Software Engineering*. Reading, MA: Addison-Wesley, 1975.

[Cooke 78] Cooke, L. H. "Express Testing," *Datamation*, September 1978.

[Cor 79] Corbató, F. J., and Clingen, C. T. "A Managerial View of the Multics System Development," in P. Wegner (ed.), *Research Directions in Software Technology*. Cambridge, MA: M.I.T. Press, 1979.

[Hos 61] Hosier, W. A. "Pitfalls and Safeguards in Real Time Digital Systems with Emphasis on Software Management." *IRE Transactions on Engineering Management*, June 1961.

[Metz 81] Metzger, P. J. *Managing a Programming Project*, 2nd ed. Englewood Cliffs, NJ: Prentice-Hall, 1981.

[Mills 79] Mills, H. D. "Software Development," in P. Wegner (ed.), *Research Directions in Software Technology*. Cambridge, MA: M.I.T. Press, 1979.

[Mye 79] Myers, G. J. *The Art of Software Testing*. New York: Wiley, 1979.

[Nau 76] Naur, P.; Randell, B.; and Buxton, J. N. (eds.). *Software Engineering Concepts and Techniques, Proceedings of the NATO Conference*. New York: Petrocelli/Charter, 1976.

[Schw 75] Schwartz, J. I. "Construction of Software: Problems and Practicalities," in E. Horowitz (ed.), *Practical Strategies for Developing Large Software Systems*. Reading, MA: Addison-Wesley, 1975.

[Weinb 71] Weinberg, G. M. *The Psychology of Computer Programming*. New York: Van Nostrand Reinhold, 1971.

[Weinb 74] ———, and Schulman, E. L. "Goals and Performance in Computer Programming," *Human Factors*, Vol. 16, No. 1, 1974.

PROBLEMS

1. It has been said that software people are unsuitable managers because they tend to respond to problem situations as designers rather than as managers. Do you think this is true? Why or why not? If it is true, is this a temporary condition or will it always be a problem?

2. Table 10.1 suggests that program code tends to reflect the major quality objectives emphasized by management. Which quality objectives should management emphasize? Determine a quality goal model (see Section 2.4) for program code. How should management enforce these goals?

---

*See Appendix B: Bibliography.

3. Choose a problem in Appendix C and define the sequence of tasks necessary to obtain the required program. State the milestones that will be used to determine progress. Now reconsider the tasks and milestones you have defined. Is there any way that they could be misunderstood? If so, rework them.

4. This section suggests that when specifications are done, the introduction to the user's manual should be written (including assumptions and objectives), shown to the customer, reworked as necessary, and then used by the designers. Do you agree or disagree? Outline your position.

5. Having just completed the specifications for a complex new system, you have just submitted a two-year, eight-man-year plan for design, development, and testing. Your plan calls for one person to be assigned full-time to testing for the two-year period and another person to work full-time in testing the second year.

   "Ridiculous," says your supervisor. "Who needs all that effort for testing, especially at the beginning of the project? Either assign those people to coding, where they're really needed, or do the project without them."

   What are your justifications? What are your options? What should you do?

6. Comment on the following propositions.
   (a) Standards are a waste of time.
   (b) Documentation is a waste of time.
   (c) Standards for programs and documentation must be defined and enforced.

7. Comment on the suggestion that at the end of overall design, the draft of the entire user's manual should be written, shown to the user, reworked as necessary, and used by the programmers.

8. Comment on the Multics method of combining design review and documentation.

9. Comment on the following propositions.
   (a) A program system should be built to run efficiently so that the smallest possible hardware configuration can be used.
   (b) Hardware is cheap and programming is expensive; buy extra hardware capacity whenever possible.

10. Describe the testing procedures in your organization. What do you think can be done to decrease testing costs?

10.2 ORGANIZING AND SCHEDULING

10.2.1 Organizing

As stated in Section 10.1.1, the three planning steps done at the beginning of a project are organizing, scheduling, and resource estimation. This section discusses organizing and scheduling, while resource estimation is discussed in Section 10.3.

The organizing step identifies all tasks required to satisfy the program specification, divides the tasks into manageable subtasks as necessary, and arranges a project organization to do the tasks. In short, the organizing step determines what subtasks are to be done and who is to do them.

The first step is to identify the kinds of tasks to be done. These normally include:

- The software system itself
- Documentation
- Testing and evaluation
- Reports and reviews
- Management activities

If the project is a large one, the activities usually include:

- Installation
- Training
- Software auditing
- Quality assurance
- Data base administration

and may sometimes include others.

Next, major subsystems of the software are blocked out. If necessary, sub-subsystems are blocked out, and the blocking-out process is continued until the blocks are of reasonable size.[1] This blocking-out of subsystems, subsub-systems and so on, is the top-down decomposition discussed in Chapters 5 and 7, and each block corresponds to a module.

In other words, this blocking-out is in part actually a preliminary design of the organization of modules (see Chapter 5). For example, a payroll system

---

[1]Boehm [Boe 81] suggests the following guidelines for the size of the blocks:
1. For a small (7 man-month) project, a block is at least 7 percent of total effort or 0.5 man-month.
2. For a medium (300 man-month) project, at least 1 percent or 3 man-months.
3. For a very large (7000 man-month) project, at least 0.2 percent or 15 man-months.

might have edit, update, sort, and print subsystems. If the system to be written is very similar to systems already written by the development team, the system block-out can be obtained with very little effort since the team will have developed a solution pattern. If, however, the system to be written is new to the development team, then a preliminary design effort will be necessary to derive the preliminary module organization.

The system block-out is written as a tree-structured chart that managers call a *work-breakdown structure*. Figure 10.1 shows a work-breakdown strucure for a payroll system. Depending on the size of the subsystems, each additional activity (e.g., documentation, test and evaluation) might be done at any subsystem level or at the system level. In Figure 10.1 a separate test and evaluation activity is blocked out for the update system (which presumably is larger and more complex than the others), while a system-wide test and evaluation activity serves the other subsystems.

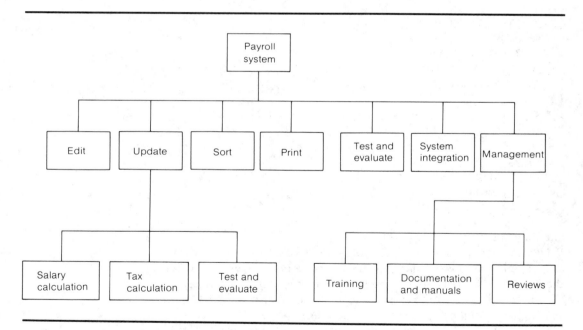

Figure 10.1 Work-breakdown structure of a payroll system.

It is important that the work-breakdown structure include activities to integrate the modules into a complete system (shown as system integration in Figure 10.1) and review activities. Reviews increase productivity, but if they are not specifically budgeted and scheduled they are often not done. For large projects, the use of auxiliary software, such as design language processors or program standards checkers, may greatly increase software productivity. If auxiliary systems are to be developed, they should be added to the work-breakdown structure.

A common result of the resource estimation step is a *costed work-breakdown structure* (a work-breakdown structure with dollar amounts), which allows management review of the cost of each subsystem.

10.2.2 Scheduling: Activity Diagrams

The scheduling step develops a sequence of project activities that will accomplish the tasks of the work breakdown structure. In determining a schedule, dependencies between activities must be considered since not all activities can be overlapped. For example, if design and coding activities are overlapped, much of the coding done before design is finished will usually have to be redone at extra cost.

Dependencies between activities can be explicitly represented. A notation for this is the *activity diagram*,[2] a graph consisting of nodes and directed arcs, in which each node represents an activity and each directed arc represents a dependency. A directed arc from node X to node Y, for example, signifies that activity X must be completed before activity Y can start. In addition, an activity diagram may contain nodes for dummy activities such as start, finish, or other project status points. Figure 10.2 shows an activity diagram for the payroll system blocked out in Figure 10.1. Each node names the activity and also gives the duration of the activity (given as number of weeks in Figure 10.2).

An activity diagram is most easily constructed from the finish node back to the start node. The predecessor nodes of a node Y (i.e., the nodes $X_1, \ldots, X_n$ such that there is an arc from each X_i to Y) are all the activities that must be completed before Y is started. Thus, at each node N in succession (beginning with the finish node and working backward), all activities required by N are identified, a node is drawn for each, and an arc is drawn from the required activity to N. (If the required node has already been drawn, then only the arc is drawn.) When no more predecessor nodes can be found, a start node is drawn, and arcs are drawn from the start node to each node without predecessors.

---

[2]Two types of activity diagrams in common use are the *PERT chart* and the *CPM chart*. PERT is an acronym for *Program Evaluation and Review Technique*, while CPM is an acronym for *Critical Path Method*. The definition used here is that of the PERT chart. In the CPM chart, a directed arc represents an activity and a node represents a partial project status. PERT and CPM charts are equivalent.

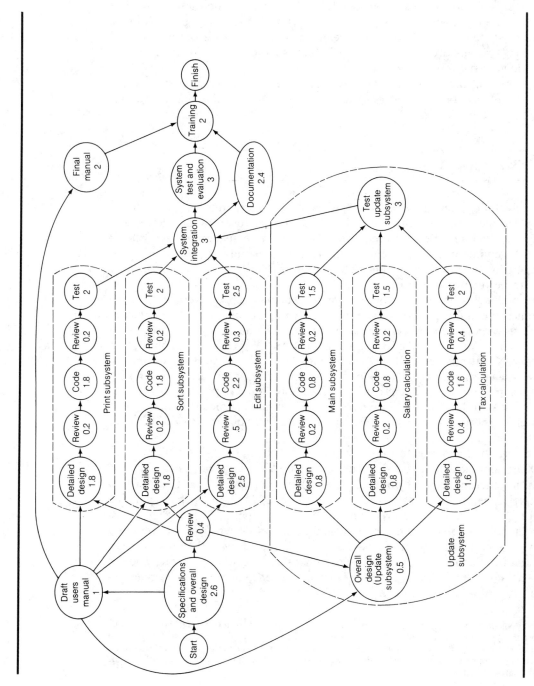

Figure 10.2   Activity diagram for a payroll system.

An activity diagram is complete when it contains sufficient activities to finish every element in the work-breakdown structure. That is, a place in the schedule has been allotted for every task required in the project.

The activity diagram of Figure 10.2 has great detail, including activities for subsystems and subsubsystems. Alternatively, a single node can be given for any subsystem (or subsubsystem, etc.) and a separate, *refinement* diagram can be drawn for the subsystem alone. A refinement diagram can be drawn, if desired, for any activity in an activity diagram.

Recall that a system can be developed by using the strategy of incremental development and delivery, in which successively more complete systems version 1, version 2, and so on are developed and delivered. This development sequence can be diagrammed using dummy activity nodes version 1, version 2, and so on. If done carefully, the activity diagram will show which tasks for later versions can be overlapped with the development of a given version.

10.2.3 Uses of Activity Diagrams

A manager trying to form a coordinated project schedule has four key questions in mind:

1. What is the minimum time necessary to complete the project?
2. Which activities are critical, that is, must be completed on time for the project to be completed in minimum time?
3. What is the latest time that each activity could be started without delaying the entire project's finishing time?
4. How much could each activity's duration be increased without delaying the entire project's finishing time?

Calculating the minimum completion time allows a manager to determine whether a project can actually be done in the allotted time. Calculation of critical activities tells the manager which activities must be watched carefully to ensure successful completion. Because events never go exactly as planned, the manager also needs to know how much leeway there is—how much delay can be tolerated in the startup of each activity and, if the activity takes longer than planned, how much longer a duration can be tolerated. Finally, a manager might like to know how much uncertainty the schedule has, that is, what the most likely deviations from the plans are.

10.2.4 Minimum Time for Project Completion

Activity diagrams can yield all this information. As a start, one can calculate the minimum time necessary to complete the project. For this purpose a number pair (s,f) is computed for each node, where

> s is the *earliest time* at which the activity can *start*
> f is the *earliest time* at which the activity can *finish*

These times are calculated as follows:

1. For the start node, $(s,f)=(0,0)$. Label the start node with $(0,0)$. Hereafter, a node is said to be labeled if it has been assigned a number pair (s,f); otherwise it is said to be unlabeled.

2. For each unlabeled node N, all of whose predecessors are labeled, compute (s_N,f_N) as follows:
   (a) $s_N = \max(f_{X_1}, \ldots, f_{X_p})$, where $X_1, \ldots, X_p$ are the predecessors of N, and f_{X_i} is the earliest finishing time of X_i.

   The activity N can start only after the last predecessor activity has finished. Thus the largest f value for any predecessor determines the start time of N.
   (b) $f_N = s_N + d_N$, where d_N is the duration of N. For the finish node, $f_{finish} = s_{finish}$.
   (c) Label the node N with (s_N,f_N).

3. Repeat step 2 until all nodes are labeled.

Figure 10.3 shows a less detailed activity diagram for the payroll system, labeled with the number pairs (s,f). The label of the finish node gives the minimum time required to complete the project, since $s_{finish} = f_{finish} =$ earliest time at which the project can finish.

The activity diagram must contain one or more paths from start to finish, in which the durations of the nodes in the path sum to exactly f_{finish}. Each such path is called a *critical path*; the arcs of critical paths are drawn using heavier lines as in Figure 10.3. The activities in a critical path are called *critical activities*. If a critical activity actually finishes later than its assigned finished time (either because it does not start on time or because it takes longer than planned), then the minimum time to finish the project is increased beyond the assigned f_{finish}. In short, critical activities must be completed at their assigned times if the project is to be completed in minimum time.

A budget and a duration period are usually allotted for each project. If the calculated minimum completion time is less than the allotted time, then the project as planned has met its time allotment. The extra time can be used as a safety margin, or some activities can be stretched out to reduce costs or reduce personnel needs.

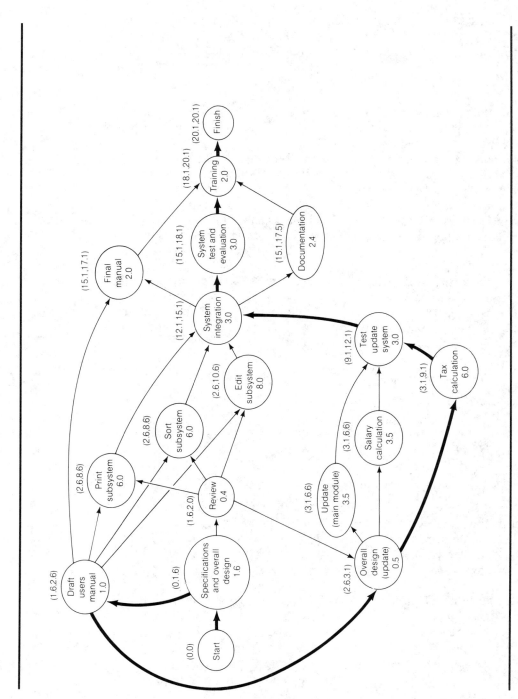

Figure 10.3 Earliest start and finish times of payroll system activities.

If the calculated minimum completion time is greater than the allotted time, then the project as planned cannot be done within the allotted time. It may be possible to shorten the minimum completion time by rescheduling some critical activities to be done in a shorter time. However, if the estimates for individual activities are honest, this becomes dangerous because:

- Reducing the durations of activities on a critical path beyond a certain level causes another path (or paths) to become critical. If additional time reduction is needed, the second path must now be shortened.
- If there are two or more critical paths, then all such paths must be simultaneously shortened to achieve the time reduction. Groups of concurrent activities may have to be shortened.
- *It may not actually be possible to shorten the durations of the activities.* Experience shows that time is the most critical factor in many activities. In general, it is not possible to simply use more people and get the job done in less time.

In sum, shortening a schedule in this way takes all of the leeway out of the plans. There is less margin for errors and delays. The project will usually cost more. The resulting schedule may be only tight, or it may now call for a crash project, or (if some reductions are unrealistic) it may be just plain impossible. (See Section 10.3 for further discussion of these points.)

10.2.5 Slack Time

The leeway in the schedule can be determined by computing for each node a number pair $[s', f']$ where

s′ is the *latest time* an activity can *start*
f′ is the *latest time* an activity can *finish*

Square brackets [ ] are used here only so that the number pairs $[s',f']$ will be distinguishable on an activity diagram from the number pairs (s,f).

This calculation begins at the finish node with the already calculated values $[s_{finish}, f_{finish}]$ and works backward toward the start node. More precisely, the calculation steps are:

1. For the finish node, $s'_{finish} = s_{finish}$, and $f'_{finish} = f_{finish}$. Label the finish node with $[s'_{finish}, f'_{finish}]$.

2. For each unlabeled node N, all of whose successors are labeled, compute $[s'_N, f'_N]$ as follows:
   (a) $f'_N = \min(s'_{Y_1}, \ldots, s'_{Y_q})$ where $Y_1, \ldots, Y_q$ are the successors of N, and s'_{Y_i} is the latest starting time of Y_i. Obviously the activity N must end before its earliest successor begins.

(b) $s'_N = f'_N - d_N$ where d_N is the duration of N.

(c) An exception to steps (a) and (b) is the start node, for which $[s'_{start}, f'_{start}] = [0,0]$.

(d) Label node N with $[s'_N, f'_N]$.

3. Repeat step 2 until all nodes are labeled.

Figure 10.4 shows the diagram of Figure 10.3 labeled with the number pairs $[s',f']$. Now for each node we calculate the value $t_N = f'_N - f_N$. The quantity t is called the *slack time* and is the difference between latest finish time and earliest finish time. For example, in Figure 10.4, the latest finish time of the sort subsystem is 12.1, while its earliest finish time is 8.6. The slack time of the sort system is 3.5, and this activity could finish at any time from 8.6 to 12.1 without delaying the overall project completion. Table 10.2 summarizes the start, finish, and slack times of the activities of Figure 10.4.

Table 10.2 Summary of times for activities

Activity	Start Times		Finish Times		Slack Time
	Earliest	Latest	Earliest	Latest	
Draft user's manual	1.6	1.6	2.6	2.6	0.0
Documentation	15.1	15.7	17.5	18.1	0.6
Edit subsystem	2.6	4.1	10.6	12.1	1.5
Final manuals	15.1	16.1	17.1	18.1	1.0
Overall design (update)	2.6	2.6	3.1	3.1	0.0
Print subsystem	2.6	6.1	8.6	12.1	3.5
Review	1.6	2.2	2.0	2.6	0.6
Salary calculation	3.1	5.6	6.6	9.1	2.5
Sort subsystem	2.6	6.1	8.6	12.1	3.5
Specifications and overall design	0.0	0.0	1.6	1.6	0.0
System integration	12.1	12.1	15.1	15.1	0.0
System test and evaluation	15.1	15.1	18.1	18.1	0.0
Tax calculation	3.1	3.1	9.1	9.1	0.0
Test update system	9.1	9.1	12.1	12.1	0.0
Training	18.1	18.1	20.1	20.1	0.0
Update (main module)	3.1	5.6	6.6	9.1	2.5

Notice that the slack time of every critical activity is 0. This corroborates the previous statement that if any critical activity starts later than planned or takes longer than planned, the entire project will be delayed.

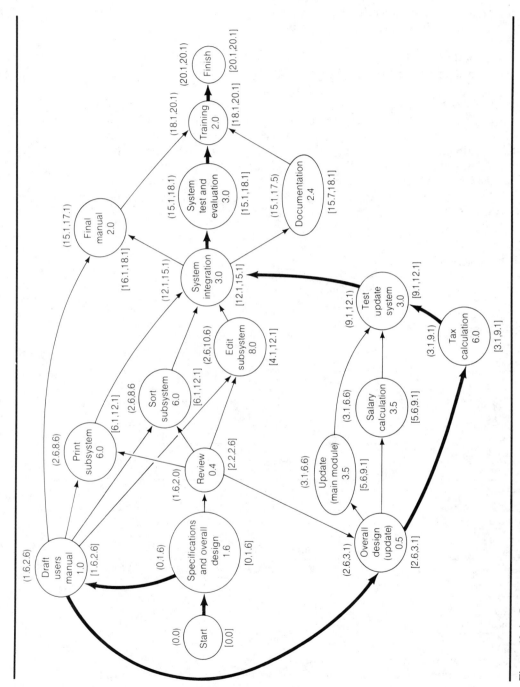

Figure 10.4   Latest start and finish times of payroll system activities.

Slack time can be used to change plans if things go wrong, or it can be utilized to save money. If preceding activities take longer than planned, an activity can be started later than planned. Alternatively, an activity can be allowed to take longer than planned. A wise manager allocates some slack time to as many activities as possible, to provide a margin of safety. In this way the overall plan will not be disrupted if (as usually happens) some activities take longer than planned. The reason for allocating slack time to many activities is that one can never know in advance exactly which activities will take longer than planned.

If sufficient slack is available, an activity might be rescheduled to have a longer duration and reduced level of effort and consequently lower cost. Slack time may also allow two activities to be performed in sequence rather than concurrently, so that the same people can do both jobs.

10.2.6 Activity Summary Using Bar Charts

A schedule of activities can be summarized with the use of a time-oriented bar chart in which time periods are shown from left to right and each activity is shown as a horizontal line. Triangles may be superposed on each activity line to indicate major milestones, and progress may then be indicated by filling in the triangle when the associated milestone has been passed. Figure 10.5 shows a bar chart for the activities of Figure 10.4. Each activity in Figure 10.5 is shown as a solid line from earliest start time to earliest finish time, and as a dashed line from earliest finish time to latest finish time. In other words, slack time is shown as a dashed line.

Although bar charts are easy to understand and easy to change, they do not give a true picture of project status because they cannot reflect dependencies between activities as activity diagrams do. Thus bar charts should not be relied upon in developing a schedule.

10.2.7 Uncertainty in the Schedule

A measure of the uncertainty of a planned schedule and probable deviations from it can be calculated. First, three time estimates t_a, t_b, and t_c are made for each activity.

- t_a is the *most probable duration* of the activity. This is the estimate used in previous discussions.
- t_b is the *optimistic duration* of the activity, that is, a duration that the activity would stay within only 1 percent of the time.
- t_c is the *pessimistic duration* of the activity, that is, a duration that would be exceeded only 1 percent of the time.

An *expected time* T for the activity and a standard deviation σ_T are calculated for the activity, based on a rule of thumb for PERT charts.[3] The PERT rule and uncertainty estimates are based on the characteristics of the normal (Gaussian) probability distribution.

The expected time T is given by the formula

$$T = \frac{4t_a + t_b + t_c}{6}$$

For example, we might estimate for the edit subsystem of Figure 10.3 the times

$$t_a = 8 \qquad t_b = 5 \qquad t_c = 17$$

to obtain T=9. Since a pessimistic estimate is usually at least double the most probable estimate, while the optimistic estimate must be greater than 0, the expected time T is usually biased toward the pessimistic estimate. In other words, T is usually a more conservative estimate than t_a, and has a built-in allowance for delays.

The standard deviation σ_T of the time T is given by

$$\sigma_T = \frac{t_c - t_b}{6}$$

For the expected time of the edit subsystem, $\sigma_T = 2$. Let T* be the *actual duration* of the activity. Then, assuming the characteristics of the Gaussian probability distribution:

· The probability of $|T^* - T| \leq \sigma_T$ is .67.
· The probability of $|T^* - T| \leq 2\sigma_T$ is .95.
· The probability of $|T^* - T| \leq 3\sigma_T$ is .99.

where $|x|$ is the absolute value of x. Thus, for T=9 and $\sigma_T = 2$,

· 67 percent of the time the duration will be ≤ 11.
· 95 percent of the time the duration will be ≤ 13.
· 99 percent of the time the duration will be ≤ 15.

Thus, even though the most probable time t_a is 8, a manager can be reasonably certain of having enough time for the activity only by scheduling a duration of 13. This is why slack time is important. The slack time shown in Figure 10.5 for the edit subsystem may be only enough to allow for the difficulties that will arise.

---

[3]Recall that a PERT chart is an activity diagram.

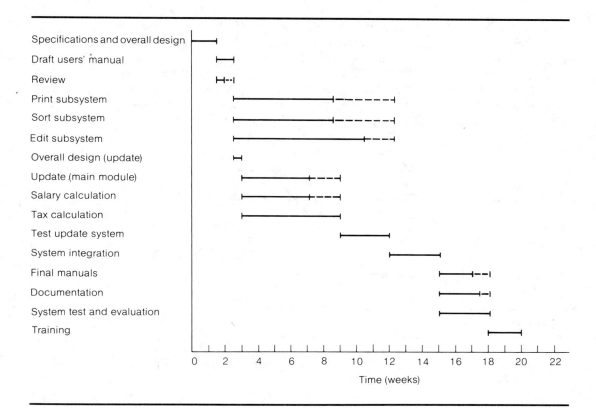

Figure 10.5 Time-oriented bar chart summary of activities.

For a path containing the activities $A_1, \ldots, A_n$, with expected times $T_1, \ldots, T_n$ and associated standard deviations $\sigma_1, \ldots \sigma_n$, an expected time T_{path} for the path and an associated standard deviation σ_{path} are given by

$$T_{path} = T_1 + \cdots + T_n$$
$$\sigma_{path} = \sqrt{\sigma_1^2 + \cdots + \sigma_n^2}$$

Thus an expected time and standard deviation can be calculated for the entire diagram. In this way a manager can calculate the probability of the project being late.

10.2.8 Resource Scheduling

Every activity has resource needs, the most important of which is the number of people required. For a given schedule, a chart of total resource need for each time period can be calculated for the entire project. If, say, the number of people required varies greatly from period to period, or if the number exceeds an allotted number, activities must be rescheduled.

It may be possible to delay the startup of some activities so that the same people can work on a sequence of activities. Alternatively, some activities can be scheduled to take longer and use fewer people. In extreme cases the project time may have to be increased, or more people may have to be allotted to the project.

REFERENCES

[Boe 81] Boehm, B. W. *Software Engineering Economics*. Englewood Cliffs, NJ: Prentice-Hall, 1981.

[Wies 77] Wiest, J. P., and Levy, F. K. *A Management Guide to PERT/CPM*, 2nd ed. Englewood Cliffs, NJ: Prentice-Hall, 1977.

PROBLEMS

1. Name the kinds of activities that appear in a work-breakdown structure in addition to the subsystem blockouts.

2. Your company is in the business of developing data base query systems. You have just been assigned the development of another system, which you estimate will take 6 man-months of effort. You want to allot about a man-month for project management and another man-month for customizing the system for the new customer's needs. (A best estimate is ¼ man-month for work on requirements and ¾ man-month for design.) Your system is to have two subsystems: a query subsystem (for which you estimate 2 man-months: ½ for design and 1½ for programming) and an update subsystem (for which you estimate ¼ man-month for design and ¾ man-months programming). You estimate 1 man-month for testing.

    Draw a work-breakdown structure showing the tasks to be done.

3. Draw an activity diagram showing the courses and prerequisites required for a bachelor's degree in computer science at your university.

4. During their last year at a certain university, geology students must conduct a study of certain minerals. The study involves both a theoretical and an experimental project. The theoretical project consists of a literature review (which usually takes 6 weeks), a theoretical study (10 weeks), and a theoret-

ical report (5 weeks). The experimental project involves selecting and obtaining the minerals (9 weeks), building experimental apparatus (12 weeks) and debugging it (2 weeks), documenting the apparatus design (6 weeks), and using the apparatus to do the experiment (11 weeks). After both projects are complete, a final report is written (1 week).

(a) Draw a work-breakdown structure of the tasks required.

(b) Draw an activity diagram of the tasks.

(c) What is the minimum time required to complete the study? What is the critical path?

(d) Draw a chart showing for each activity in the diagram: the earliest start time, the latest start time, the earliest finish time, the latest finish time, and the slack time.

(e) Draw a bar chart showing each activity in the diagram.

5. The geology students of Problem 4 are finding that the final report usually take two weeks rather than one week. On the other hand, they have found that by grouping together, they can build the apparatus very quickly. Assuming two weeks for the final report, what is the minimum time for completion of the project if building the apparatus is reduced to eight weeks? To six weeks? To four weeks? To three weeks? To two weeks? To one week?

6. Suppose that for each activity in a critical path in Figure 10.3, the time estimates t_a, t_b, and t_c are made as follows:

t_a=duration shown in Figure 10.3
t_b=0.6t_a
t_c=2.2t_a

Calculate $T_{critical}$, the expected minimum time to complete the project, and $\sigma_{critical}$.

7. The developers of the payroll system of Figure 10.3 have decided to shorten the minimum completion time by getting the tax calculation program done faster. What is the minimum completion time if the tax calculation duration is decreased by one week? Two weeks? Three weeks?

10.3 ESTIMATING REQUIRED RESOURCES

10.3.1 Factors Determining System Difficulty

The most important and most difficult task in software management is initially estimating the resources (time, effort, money, and computer time) that will be needed throughout the life of a software development project. If the initial estimate does not provide for sufficient resources, then the project will be in trouble from the very beginning. It will not be possible to complete development with the allotted resources, no matter what anyone says or does, and a project overrun will inevitably result. On the other hand, if the estimated resources are roughly adequate, then the project can be managed so that development can be completed within an acceptable margin of allotted resources.

Improper initial estimates are a major cause of software overruns. Software developers tend to underestimate due to unfounded optimism (see Section 10.5.3). Moreover, customers and supervisors tend to believe that resource requirements have been overestimated. Software developers have often had difficulty in defending cautious estimates to their supervisors and customers. Every programming manager has heard the two classic reactions to resource estimates: "We can't spare that much time and money!" "Why can't it be done for less?"

Section 10.3 presents some facts, guidelines, and theory on which estimations can be based. Section 10.3.1 outlines factors that determine system difficulty, Section 10.3.2 shows relations between time and personnel requirements, and Section 10.3.3 presents a model of resource usage.

Every software development project has a certain inherent level of difficulty determined by its complexity, its size, the experience level of the assigned development team, and the familiarity of the development team with the required level of technology [Put 77, Cor 79].

Although there are no standard measures for complexity, it has become common to classify software projects as easy, medium, or hard, according to the following definitions (derived from [Aron 76]):

- *Easy:* Very few interactions with other system elements. Mathematical and logical routines are usually in this class since they usually interact only with the operating system, file management system, and other supplied programs.
- *Medium:* Some interactions with other system elements. Typically, support programs such as compilers, schedulers, input-output packages, and some data management packages are in this class.
- *Hard:* Many interactions with other system elements. Typically, operating systems, real-time systems, and large applications are in this class.

A rule of thumb is that compilers are three times as difficult as normal batch application programs, while operating systems are three times as difficult as compilers [Bro 74].

Inherent difficulty increases also with the size of the program [Nan 64, Weinw 65, Bro 74], according to the relation

effort is proportional to $N^{1.5}$

where N is the number of instructions and effort is measured in man-months. Thus, if all other factors (complexity, experience of development team, etc.) are equal, and program B is twice the size of program A, then B requires about three times the effort that A requires. If B is three times the size of A, it requires about five times the effort.

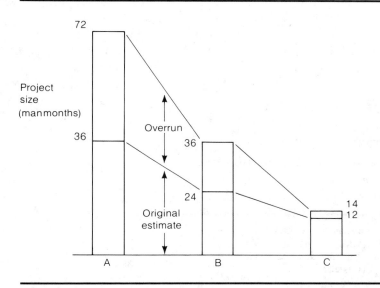

Figure 10.6   History of three FORTRAN compilers. (From *Software Engineering Concepts and Techniques* edited by P. Naur, B. Randell, and J. Buxton. Copyright © 1976 by Mason Charter Publishers. Reprinted by permission of Van Nostrand Reinhold Company.)

The software team's familiarity with the required techniques also strongly determines difficulty. Each team that implements a given design must learn the required techniques for itself, even though the design may have been success-fully implemented elsewhere. Thus a software team's initial experience with a design involves much research and development. As a team has successive experiences with the same design, the implementation becomes a routine effort and the level of difficulty decreases markedly. Figure 10.6 shows the effort expended in implementing FORTRAN compilers A, B, and C succes-sively. Compiler C required less than 25 percent of the effort of compiler A, and the required effort was easier to estimate since compiler C had an overrun of only 16 percent, while compiler A had an overrun of 100 percent.

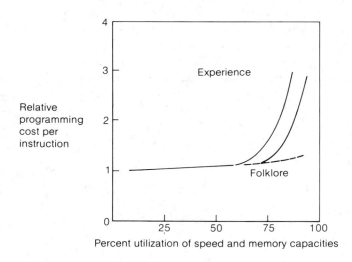

Figure 10.7 Inherent difficulty increases as hardware capacities are approached. (Copyright 1970 by American Institute of Aeronautics and Astronautics. Reprinted by permission.)

Finally, as shown in Figure 10.7, inherent difficulty increases significantly as a system's size and speed requirements approach hardware capacities because there is less and less safety margin. For example, when an initial design indicates that a system requires half of memory, there is a safety margin of 100 percent to take care of errors in the estimate, new requirements, system changes, and unforeseen difficulties. In contrast, when the initial design requires 90 percent of memory for the system, there is a safety margin of only 11 percent. Such a situation might require continual redesign and reprogramming to keep the system size within hardware capacity.

A comfortable safety margin is likewise required for program speed. A program with a 10 percent safety margin in speed will undoubtedly require continual redesign and reprogramming as the system is developed.

To have safety margins of 25 percent, as suggested in Section 10.1, a system should not utilize more than 80 percent of speed or memory capacity. As shown in Figure 10.7, above 80 percent utilization, the inherent difficulty and relative cost begin to skyrocket.

10.3.2 Time and Effort Factors

Two fundamental project costs are the elapsed time from beginning to completion of the project and the total effort measured in man-months or man-years. These costs are not independent.

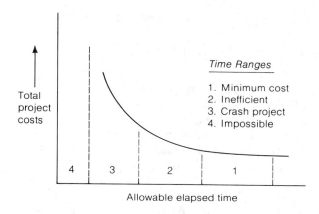

Time Ranges

1. Minimum cost
2. Inefficient
3. Crash project
4. Impossible

Total project costs

4   3   2   1

Allowable elapsed time

Figure 10.8   Variation of total project cost with respect to allowable elapsed time. (From *On the Management of Computer Programming* edited by G. F. Weinwurm. Copyright © 1970 by Auerbach Publishers. Reprinted by permission of Van Nostrand Reinhold Company.)

Figure 10.8 shows that when a long elapsed time (see time range 1) is allowed for a software development project, the required effort is minimum. When a shorter elapsed time (see time range 2) is allowed, a greater effort is required. If the allowed elapsed time is drastically shorter than the minimum cost-time range, the development becomes a "crash project" (time range 3) using extreme amounts of effort, or the project becomes impossible (time range 4). Brooks [Bro 74] claims that more software projects have gone awry for lack of calendar time than for all other causes combined. Figure 10.8 may be summarized by the statement: *Total required effort is lower when project elapsed time is longer.*

When a shorter elapsed time is chosen in preference to a longer one, it is tacitly assumed that the project tasks can be subdivided more finely and therefore that the overall project can be accomplished in a shorter time by using more people. However, certain tasks consist inherently of sequential steps and thus require a certain minimal time, regardless of the number of people used.

A project schedule will not be met if it unreasonably underestimates any of the times required for

- Gathering requirements and defining system functions
- Producing a workable system design
- Testing individual programs
- Integrating programs into the system and completing acceptance tests
- Correcting and retesting program changes
- Restructuring the program due to changes in requirements

or if it splits the job into blocks in advance of system design to try to meet a specified completion date by using more personnel [Nau 76].

The time required by a project depends on the required sequence of steps, while the maximum number of workers depends on the number of independent subtasks. If the number of independent subtasks cannot easily be increased, then adding more people will not allow a shortened schedule. In short: *People cannot be substituted for time.*

Two other factors act to make time more critical than workers. Every project requires some effort in addition to the effort necessary to develop the software. This extra effort is needed for management, for personnel training, and for communication among workers. Obviously, every programmer must be trained in the technology, goals, and plan of work of the project, and thus a training effort varying linearly with the number of workers is required. A long-term project can anticipate a yearly turnover of 20 percent [Bro 74], and, of course, the new workers must also be trained. The time required for such training varies according to system difficulty; for a highly developmental system, training time may be six to nine months [Cor 79].

Communication among workers is obviously necessary for the coordination of the various subtasks. If each of N workers communicates with each of the other $(N-1)$ workers, there are $N(N-1)/2$ communication pairs. Thus doubling the number of workers may quadruple the required communication efforts. (Other organizational structures will have fewer communication pairs but will also have other problems.)

Let $E(W)$ be the total effort put forth by W workers, and let T and C be the efforts for training and communication, respectively. Then

$E(W)=T+C+E_1$

where E_1 is the effort that can be devoted to the project, and T and C are additional efforts that must be expanded. Assuming that training effort varies linearly with W and communication effort varies as W^2, suppose that the allowable elapsed time is halved and the number of workers is doubled. Then

$$E(2W)=2 \cdot E(W)=2T+4C+E_2$$

where E_2 is the new effort that can be devoted to the project. The relation between E_2 and E_1 is

$$E_2=2E_1-2C$$

Thus the usable effort E_2 falls short of $2E_1$. To achieve a usable effort of $2E_1$, further workers must be added, and these workers in turn require training and communication efforts.

Also, as time goes on, the workers will become more familiar with the techniques to be used, and thus become more productive (recall Figure 10.6). Table 10.3, which is based on historical data from the development of large programs at IBM, shows how programmer productivity varies with difficulty and with allowable elapsed time. The table suggests that productivity is highest when a long elapsed time is allowed. My own experience is that productivity varies in the same way for small projects. (See Section 10.3.1 for definitions of easy, medium, and hard programs.)

Table 10.3 Variation of programmer productivity (instructions per man-month) with respect to complexity and elapsed time

Project Complexity	Project Elapsed Time		
	6–12 Months	12–24 Months	More than 24 Months
Easy	440	500	840
Medium	220	250	420
Hard	110	125	125

Table 10.3 can be used to roughly estimate the effort required for a project. The required total effort[4] in man-months is determined by the formula

$$\text{Effort}=\frac{\text{deliverable instructions}}{\text{instructions per man-month}}$$

---

[4]The total effort given by this formula does not include effort required for system design, for system test, or for management and support [Aron 76]. Multiply the result of this formula by 1.25 to obtain total project effort including system design and system test. Then, since management and support usually require as much effort as the project itself, multiply total project effort by 2 to include management and support.

If the number of lines of easy, medium, and hard code can be estimated, then a separate calculation can be made for each category, and total effort can be determined by the formula

$$\text{Effort} = \text{effort}_{easy} + \text{effort}_{medium} + \text{effort}_{hard}$$

As an example, suppose that preliminary design indicates a 50,000-line program, and it is estimated that 10,000 lines are hard, 10,000 are medium, and 30,000 are easy. Suppose also that the project can be accomplished in a minimum of 18 months, but that 30 months may be available.

The total effort required depends on the elapsed time chosen. If the project is done in 18 months, total effort according to Table 10.3 is:

$$\text{Effort} = \frac{30,000}{500} + \frac{10,000}{250} + \frac{10,000}{125} = 180$$

On the other hand, for a 30-month elapsed time, the total effort is:

$$\text{Effort} = \frac{30,000}{840} + \frac{10,000}{420} + \frac{10,000}{125} = 140$$

Choosing an elapsed time of 30 months rather than 18 results in a 22 percent savings in effort,[5] since

$$\frac{\text{Effort}_{30\ mo}}{\text{Effort}_{18\ mo}} = \frac{140}{180} = 0.78$$

Thus there is a tradeoff between time and money costs; shortening the allowable time increases the inherent difficulty of the project. When external constraints (such as the delivery schedule of the overall system containing the software, or user costs incurred by not having the software) force a software manager to accept an inefficient or crash project schedule, the manager should remember that the original schedule was not an optimal one for the software project.

A somewhat different outlook on software costs, based on experience with large military software systems, is shown in Table 10.4. The instruction costs in this table are based on an estimated 15 to 30 high-order language (e.g., COBOL or FORTRAN) instructions per person per day and a typical figure of $35,000 per burdened man-year. Estimates derived from Table 10.4 will usually be higher than estimates derived from Table 10.3.

---

[5]On the other hand, suppose that effort has already been scheduled based on a 30-month elapsed time, and it is suddenly required that the project be done in 18 months. Almost 30 percent more effort will now be required, since $180/140 = 1.285$.

Table 10.4   Factors influencing software cost*

Factor	Relation to Cost
Number of delivered (checked out, documented) source instructions	Cost varies linearly with number of instructions, as modified by other factors
Language	High-order language: $6–$12/source instruction Machine-oriented language: $12–$24/source instruction
Real-time application	Real-time: $30–$60/source instruction
Type of program (utility, application, operating system)	If operating system, multiply cost by 1.5–2.0
Turnaround time	For turnaround times in the range of 30 minutes to 1 day, testing cost varies linearly with turnaround time
Documentation	About 10% of total cost; $35–$150 per nonautomated page
Hardware constraints	Costs rise asymptotically (see Figure 10.7) as full capacity is approached
Schedule realism	If schedule is shortened by N%, add N% to expected cost
Personnel	Expect about 5:1 variability in productivity

When not enough time is allowed for a software project, the inevitable results are schedule slippage or deteriorated performance, or both.

> The problem of project management . . . was to find an acceptable balance among time, cost, and performance. . . . The harried project manager most often uses performance as his last resort escape, if he is really "boxed in" on the other two factors by tight management [Nor 70].

If the software cannot be developed in the allotted time and with the allotted budget, a drop in performance is the only choice.

Software quality, and especially maintainability, is another aspect of performance. Achieving quality requires extra expenditures in time and effort, but later results in decreased maintenance costs. The extra expenditure is best viewed as an investment, the return on which is the decrease in maintenance costs. If not enough time and funds are available, the quality of the final project will be poorer.

Further discussions of factors that influence software costs can be found in Wolverton [Wol 74] and Daly [Daly 77].

---

*Barry W. Boehm, "The High Cost of Software," from Horowitz, *Practical Strategies for Developing Large Software Systems*, © 1975. Addison-Wesley, Reading, MA. Reprinted with permission.

10.3.3 A Model of Resource Usage

10.3.3.1 Introduction

Section 10.3.3 discusses the way in which a project's use of resources (specifically effort) varies from month to month as the development proceeds. A model of project resource use over time [Nor 70, Aron 76] is presented, which can be used in making initial resource estimates for large software projects [Put 77]. More important, the model allows us to understand how development proceeds, how factors such as system complexity and elapsed time influence the effort expended, and how manpower constraints and project slippage can affect a project.

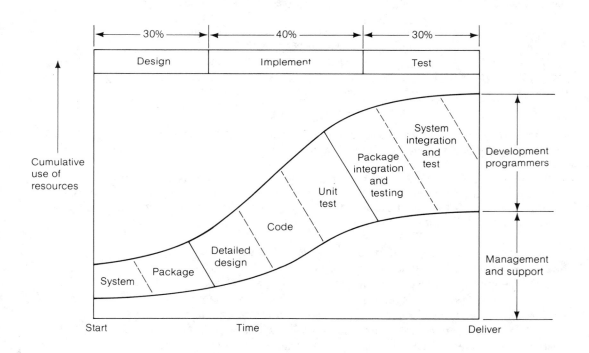

Figure 10.9   Cumulative use of resources in software development. (From *Software Engineering Concepts and Techniques* edited by P. Naur, B. Randell, and J. Buxton. Copyright © 1976 by Mason Charter Publishers. Reprinted by permission of Van Nostrand Reinhold Company.)

Experience has shown that the cumulative use of resources in a software development project ideally follows the pattern of Figure 10.9 [Nor 70, Aron 76]. In the figure, the diagonal-line boundaries between activities indicate that one activity is phased out and another phased in at the same time. Boundaries between portions of a major activity are dashed, while boundaries between major activities are solid lines.[6]

The figure shows management and support resources as well as development resources. Experience has shown that management and support require about 50 percent of the total resources, as much as the development itself.

Figure 10.9 also reflects the fact that development occurs in successive phases: System specification and overall design (system and package in Figure 10.9), programming (detailed design and coding), integration (package integration and system integration), and testing (unit test, package test, and system test). Each phase builds to some peak of effort and then tails off while the next phase begins. For example, the initial design activity inherently requires only a few people but for a long time; it is the gestation period for the fundamental design ideas of the project. As these ideas become sharply focused, and as sections of the project are identified, more and more detailed design and coding can begin, and thus a buildup of personnel naturally occurs. When coding is finished and testing begins, fewer personnel are needed, and the rate of resource usage drops off. Figure 10.10 shows a rough picture of the effort per month required in each phase.

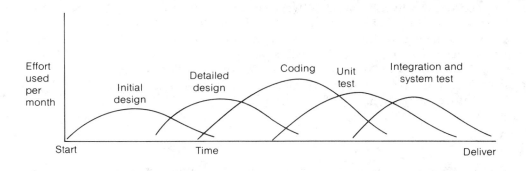

Figure 10.10 Efforts used in each development phase (from [Nor 70]). (Copyright 1963 by John Wiley and Sons, Inc. Reprinted by permission.)

---

[6]Figure 10.9 suggests that 30 percent of the project duration should be allotted to design activities, 40 percent to implementation, and 30 percent to testing. If the activity boundaries are adjusted to show unit testing as a test activity, the time allottments are then 20–30 percent for design, 30 percent for implementation, and 40–50 percent for testing, as suggested earlier [Boe 73b, Bro 74].

10.3.3.2 Project Effort Curves

It has been found that these phases of effort buildup and tailoff have regular patterns. Consequently, the effort per month for the entire project has the general form shown in Figure 10.11(b) [Nor 70, Put 77]. Figure 10.11(b) shows the percent of total project effort used during each month of a project. Figure 10.11(a), which shows the cumulative percent of total effort used at each month, is the integral of the curve in (b) and is identical to Figure 10.10. Figure 10.11(c), which shows the change in current resource usage from month to month, is the derivative of Figure 10.11(b).

Each curve of Figure 10.11 can be described by a comparatively simple equation [Nor 70]. For example, the current (monthly) effort usage [denoted y' in Figure 10.11(b) since it is the derivative of the cumulative usage shown in (a)] is given by

$$y' = 2Kate^{-at^2}$$

where y' = manpower used in each time period
K = total cumulative manpower used by the end of the project
a = shape parameter (governing time to peak manpower)
t = elapsed time from start of cycle

The curve of Figure 10.11(b) is based on $K=1.00$ and $a=0.02$.

In other words, any graph of project monthly effort fits one of the curves of this family. The single parameter a, which governs the shape of the curves, can be regarded as measuring the "push" given to the project. Sharply peaked effort buildups correspond to crash projects, while shallower curves are associated with stretched-out projects. To illustrate this, Figure 10.12(a) shows a family of curves all having $K=1000$ but with varying values of a. Part (b) shows curves all having $a=0.02$ but with varying values of K.

The simple formula for y' allows quick and accurate calculation of the parameters of the curve. The parameter a is related to t_0, the time of greatest resource usage. If we know the month of greatest effort, then the value a can be calculated by the formula

$$a = \left(\frac{1}{2t_0^2}\right)$$

Conversely, if we know the value a, then t_0 can be calculated by the formula

$$t_0 = \left(\frac{1}{2a}\right)^{1/2}$$

The month t_0 of greatest effort, the effort level y_0' of that month, and the total project effort K are related by the formula

$$K = e^{1/2}t_0y_0'$$

Thus, if any two of these are known or can be reasonably estimated, the third value can be immediately calculated.

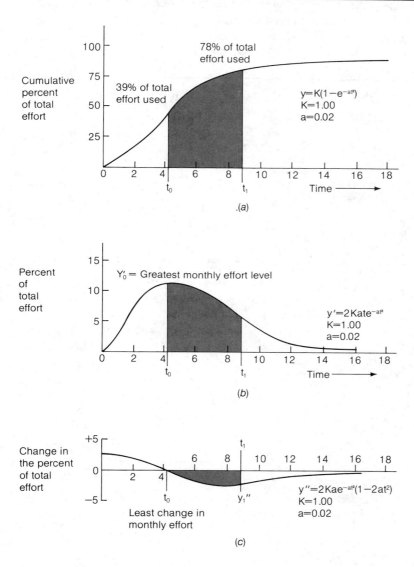

Figure 10.11 Overall project-effort usage from [Nor 70]). (*a*) Cumulative effort usage. (*b*) Current (monthly) usage. (*c*) Change in current effort usage. (Copyright 1963 by John Wiley and Sons, Inc. Reprinted by permission.)

At the time t_1 shown in Figure 10.11, the change y'' in monthly effort level reaches its lowest value y_1''. The value t_1 is given by

$$t_1 = \left(\frac{3}{2a}\right)^{1/2}$$

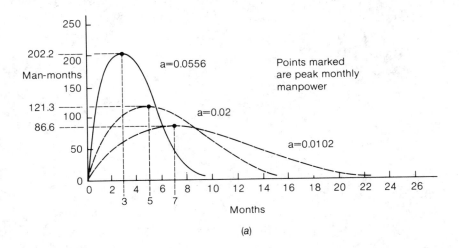

(a)

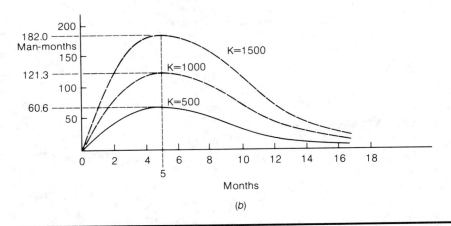

(b)

Figure 10.12 Variations of monthly effort usage, $y' = 2Kate^{-at^2}$ [Nor 70]. (a) Distribution of same total effort, varying the time required (K=1000 for all curves). (b) Shape of distribution for constant time to peak but different total effort (a=0.02 for all curves). (Copyright 1963 by John Wiley and Sons, Inc. Reprinted by permission.)

or, equivalently,

$t_1 = 1.732t_0$

When a project passes the point (t_1, y_1''), 78 percent of the total project effort will have been expended, and the project should be in the cleanup stage.

All project elapsed times can be formulated in terms of t_0. For example, the time t_2, at which 95 percent of total project effort has been expended, can be calculated using the relation between a and t_0 and the formula of Figure 10.11(a) as

$t_2 = 2.45t_0$

At $t_3 = 3t_0$, 99 percent of the total project effort will have been expended. Thus a good approximation is that total project elapsed time is $3t_0$.

10.3.3.3 Deviation from These Effort-Usage Curves

The effort-usage curves of Section 10.3.3.2 result from the natural sequence of development phases and the natural buildup and tailoff of effort in each phase. Experience has shown that projects use minimum resources when effort usage follows these curves.

Whenever project managers have forced different patterns of effort usage, for convenience (in order to have a uniform rate of effort use) or for haste (in order to complete the project earlier), the result has been a higher total effort usage. As an example, Figure 10.13 shows the result of imposing a uniform rate of effort use instead of allowing an effort-use curve as in Figure 10.11(b). With a flat resource rate, some effort is wasted at first, and effort is not available during the intense coding phase, so that, ultimately, the schedule slips and extra effort is required. Recall the guideline in Section 10.1: Use lean staffing in initial phases.

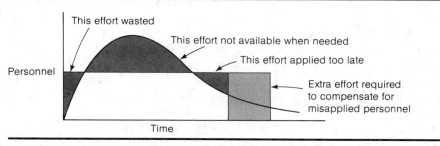

Figure 10.13 Contrast between proper effort usage and uniform effort usage (from [Put 77]). (Copyright 1977 by Institute of Electrical and Electronic Engineers, Inc. Reprinted by permission.)

Software developers often try to obtain uniform effort usage by bypassing the design phase and immediately beginning coding with a large staff. Because this practice omits the careful analysis of specifications and development of overall design, it usually requires massive redesign during the test phase. Thus ultimately a longer completion time as well as higher total costs are incurred. An equally important consequence is that the final product lacks conceptual integrity—a carefully evolved architecture or master plan that integrates all of the features and provides a foundation for improvements. Brooks [Bro 75] relates how, in the development of OS/360, he assigned the analysis of specifications to an implementation group instead of to the architecture group in order to keep 150 programmers employed for the first 6 months of the project. As a result, the specifications were of much lower quality. "The lack of conceptual integrity made the system far more costly to build and change, and I would estimate that it added a year to debugging time" [Bro 75].

Section 10.1 contains the guideline: Don't saddle designers with the burden of keeping subordinates occupied. When a project is forced to take on more people than are actually needed, the extra people must be kept busy somehow. The job of keeping the extra people occupied often distracts the designer from the design—which is the primary task—so that further time and effort are wasted.

10.3.3.4 Inherent Difficulty

Effort usage can be expressed in terms of K and t_0, as

$$y' = (K/t_0^2)te^{(-t^2/2t_0^2)}$$

Data from about 40 systems of varying complexity indicates that the quantity K/t_0^2, where K is measured in man-years and t_0 is measured in years, corresponds to the programming difficulty of a system [Put 77]. It appears that an easy system gives rise to a small value of K/t_0^2, say, $K/t_0^2 = 5$, but as the system becomes more difficult, the value of the quantity increases in a continuous fashion until a very difficult system gives rise to a large value, say, $K/t_0^2 = 125$.

The ratio K/t_0^2 was found to be related to programming rate as shown in Figure 10.14. Additional data points suggest that there may be a set of parallel lines, each line representing a class of software. Figure 10.14 also confirms our intuitive notion that for easy systems more effort can be spent and more program statements written per unit time, while difficult systems require the effort to be stretched out over more time.

Norden [Nor 70] suggests that the effort-usage pattern of engineering and software projects is not amenable to wide tradeoffs of time and effort, but that, instead, the limiting condition is the rate at which problems are identified, or the rate at which ideas or insights can be generated. This rate is not mainly affected by the number of people on the job, but rather by some capability level of the group. This "insight distribution" parameter remains constant over long periods of time, and new people can be added only as more work pieces are identified [Nor 70].

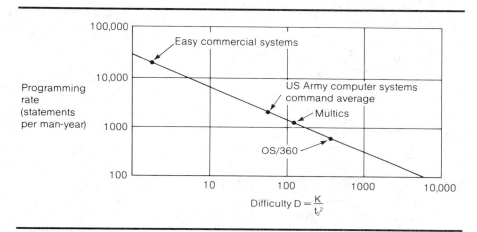

Figure 10.14   Relation between system difficulty and programming rate (from [Put 77]). (Copyright 1977 by Institute of Electrical and Electronic Engineers, Inc. Reprinted by permission.)

Intuition also suggests that an inherently difficult system requires proportionately more ideas or insights per programming statement. Since the rate at which these ideas can be generated is constant for the group, a longer time per statement is required.

Thus the total effort K, the time t_0 to peak usage of effort, and the difficulty $D = K/t_0^2$ are natural parameters of a software development. The time t_0 determines the total project elapsed time. Each software system S has a characteristic difficulty D_S in the form of a minimum required ratio of K to t_0^2. This ratio limits the maximum programming rate P_S for that system in accordance with the graph of Figure 10.14.

We should, though, be cautious in using the graph of Figure 10.14. We can expect that the data points of Figure 10.14 are based on adequately executed projects so that the lowest possible characteristic difficulty D_S was obtained for each system S. However, the actual difficulty D_S^* to be encountered in building S depends not only on the size and complexity of S itself, but also on the allowable elapsed time. For example, suppose that, according to Figure 10.14, $D_S = 5$ and the programming rate is $P_S = 20,000$, based on $t_0 = 24$ months.

If we are now asked to implement the system S with a time to peak manpower of 6 months, the actual difficulty D_S^* will be much greater. In fact, since $t_0^*=t_0/4$, $D=K/t_0^2$, and $D_S^*=K/(t_0^*)^2$, we must have $D_S^*=16D_S=80$ and a corresponding programming rate of $P_S^*=2000$. In other words, doing the job in one-quarter of the base allowable time causes an actual difficulty that is 16 times greater and decreases the programming rate by a factor of 10.

If the system S is to be implemented in 12 months, then $D_S^*=4D=20$ and $P_S^*=6000$.

In sum, the time t_0 is the most sensitive parameter, and cannot be set arbitrarily. Since $D=K/t_0^2$, the sensitivity of D to changes in K is

$$\frac{\partial D}{\partial K} = \frac{\partial}{\partial K}\left(\frac{K}{t_0^2}\right) = \frac{1}{t_0^2}$$

while sensitivity of D to changes in t_0 is

$$\frac{\partial D}{\partial t} = \frac{\partial}{\partial t}\left(\frac{K}{t_0^2}\right) = \frac{-2K}{t_0^3}$$

If the total effort K is increased, the resulting increase in D is large if t_0 is small, while the increase in D is small if t_0 is large. This conforms to our experience that accommodating an additional effort is much harder for a short-term project than for a long-term one.

Since $\partial D/\partial t$ is negative, an increase in t_0 yields a decrease in D, while a decrease in t_0 yields an increase in D, exactly as we would expect. Moreover, $\partial D/\partial t$ is proportional to K and inversely proportional to the third power of t_0. Hence D is much more sensitive to changes in t_0 than to changes in K.

Decreasing the allowed development time below its natural requirement dramatically increases the inherent difficulty of the problem, while allowing extra time decreases the inherent difficulty.

10.3.3.5 Slippage of Project Schedules

This model provides insight into the situation of schedule slippage: What can be done when a software project is found to be behind schedule? Consider, for example, a task estimated at 12 man-months, assigned to 3 people for 4 months, with measurable mileposts A, B, C, which are scheduled to occur at the end of each month. Suppose that milepost A is not reached until two months have passed. The manager's alternatives are, according to Brooks [Bro 74]:

1. Assume that the project must be done on time, and that only the first part was underestimated. In this case, nine man-months of effort must be accomplished in the remaining two months, so that four and a half workers are required. Add two workers to the three already assigned.
2. Assume that the project must be done on time, but that the project effort

should have been estimated at 24 man-months. In this case, 18 man-months of effort must be accomplished in 2 months, requiring a total of 9 workers. Add 6 workers to the 3 already assigned.

3. Reschedule, allowing enough time so that the work can be done properly and further rescheduling will not be necessary.

4. Trim the task. This may be the only feasible action, and it is best done formally.

Choosing either alternative 1 or 2 is disastrous. If alternative 1 is chosen, the two new people will require training by one of the experienced people. If this takes a month, then three man-months will have been devoted to work not in the original estimate. In addition, the task must be rearranged to be performed by five rather than three people, so that some work already done will be lost. At the end of the third month we may expect that milepost B will not be reached and that seven man-months of effort will remain while five people and one month are available. The project is still late, and perhaps it is just as late as if no people had been added.

To compensate for the added training time, four people instead of two could be added at the end of the second month. However, this step would yield a seven-person team, whose organization, task arrangement, and communication problems are much more complex than those of the three-person team. Thus, again, we should expect the project to be late. And adoption of alternative 2 leads to an even worse disaster. This situation has been summarized as Brooks' law [Bro 74]: *Adding workers to a late software project makes it later.*

What does this model suggest about the situation? First, the schedule has a uniform rate of resource usage and thus involves (perhaps inevitably, because it is a small project) some waste of effort. Recall that total project elapsed time is about $3t_0$. For convenience, we choose $t_0 = 2$ months $= 1/6$ year, so that

$$D = \frac{K}{t_0^2} = \frac{1}{(1/6)^2} = 36 \qquad \text{medium difficulty}$$

$$\frac{\partial D}{\partial K} = \frac{1}{t_0^2} = 36$$

$$\frac{\partial D}{\partial t} = \frac{-2K}{t_0^3} = \frac{-2}{(1/6)^3} = -432$$

Although the project is of medium difficulty, the short time duration makes it extraordinarily sensitive to any misestimates of effort or time required. We should expect trouble.

Recall that milepost A is reached at the end of two months. This is shown as the point $(2, E_A)$ in Figure 10.15. Suppose we decide, as in alternative 1, that only the first part was underestimated and that the total effort should have been 15 man-months instead of 12. In other words, effort should have been expended on curve Y of Figure 10.15 rather than on curve X. The effort shown in the shaded area of the figure was required but not expended. To finish the project in 4 months, we require a curve Z beginning at $(2,E_A)$ so that the combined curves X (up to 2 months) and Z (after 2 months) expend as much effort as curve Y. (Curve Z also compensates for the waste caused by the too-late application of effort.) However, the ending tails of curves X and Y are a consequence of the sequential nature of testing. This implies that the desired curve Z cannot in fact be achieved; Z will inevitably have a tail, as do X and Y, and thus we should expect that the project *cannot be achieved on schedule*.

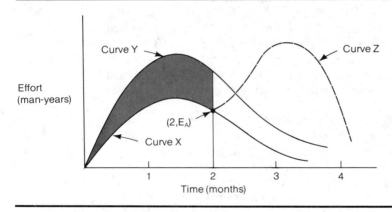

Figure 10.15 An attempt to meet the schedule by expending extra effort.

REFERENCES

[Aron 76] Aron, J. D. "Estimating Resources for Large Programming Systems," in P. Naur, B. Randell, and J. N. Buxton (eds.), *Software Engineering Concepts and Techniques*. New York: Petrocelli/Charter, 1976. (Also in [Put 77].)*

[Boe 73b] Boehm, B. W. "Software and Its Impact: A Quantitative Assessment, *Datamation*, May 1973. (Also in [Fre 80b].)*

[Boe 75a] ———. "The High Cost of Software," in E. Horowitz (ed.), *Practical Strategies for Developing Large-Scale Software Systems*. Reading, MA: Addison-Wesley, 1975.

[Bro 74] Brooks, F. P. "The Mythical Man-Month," *Datamation*, 1974. (Also in [Fre 80b].)*

*See Appendix B: Bibliography.

[Bro 75] ———. *The Mytical Man-Month: Essays in Software Engineering*. Reading, MA: Addison-Wesley, 1975.

[Cor 79] Corbató, F. J., and Clingen, C. T. "A Managerial View of the Multics System Development," in P. Wegner (ed.), *Research Directions in Software Technology*. Cambridge, MA: M.I.T. Press, 1979.

[Daly 77] Daly, E. B. "Management of Software Development," *IEEE Transactions on Software Engineering*, May 1977. (Also in [Put 77] and [Mil 78].)*

[Nan 64] Nanus, B., and Farr, L. "Some Cost Contributions to Large-Scale Programs," *Proceedings of 1964 AFIPS Spring Joint Computer Conference*, 1964.

[Nau 76] Naur, P.; Randell, B.; and Buxton, J. N. (eds.), *Software Engineering Concepts and Techniques, Proceedings of the NATO Conferences*. New York: Petrocelli/Charter, 1976.

[Nor 70] Norden, P. V. "Useful Tools for Project Management," in M. K. Starr (ed.), *Management of Production*. Baltimore, MD: Penguin Books, 1970. (Also in [Put 77].)*

[Pie 70] Pietrasanta, A. M. "Resource Analysis of Computer Program System Development," in G. F. Weinwurm (ed.), *On the Management of Computer Programming*. Philadelphia: Auerbach, 1970.

[Put 77] Putnam, L. H., and Wolverton, R. W. *Quantitative Management: Software Engineering* (tutorial). New York: IEEE Computer Society, 1977.

[Weinw 65] Weinwurm, G. F. "Research in the Management of Computer Programming," Report SP-2059, Santa Monica, CA: System Development Corp., 1965.

[Wol 74] Wolverton, R. W. "The Cost of Developing Large-Scale Software," *IEEE Transactions on Computers*, June 1974. (Also in [Put 77].)*

PROBLEMS

1. You've just been called in as a programming manager to develop a new financial forecasting system for your company. Your development plan calls for an 18-month, 4 man-year effort, based on your analysis of the system's complexity, the fact that specifications are not yet firm, and that one of your key people will be busy on another job for another 4 months.

   "Nonsense," your supervisor says. "That's an unreasonably long development time for such a system. I've already promised the vice-president that she'll have the system a year from now."

   What are your options? What should you do?

2. Your development plan calling for a 12-month, 3 man-year effort to develop a new system has just been approved. However, a new junior programmer has just been hired and has nothing to do. "I don't care if your

---

*See Appendix B: Bibliography.

plan says you won't need him for another six months," your supervisor says. "I want to keep him busy. There must be something he can do, so put him on your project and find something for him."

What are your options? What should you do?

3. Your company has decided that its computer-based operations would be improved by using ZIP language. Your supervisor says, "I've been speaking with Super Compiler Corporation. They tell me that for our specs, they'll deliver a ZIP compiler for 16 man-months effort, in 8 months. Now, your programming crew is just as good as theirs, isn't it?"

"Yes," you say. "On average, our people are about as experienced as theirs, though we don't write any compilers."

"Well, since your people are as good as theirs, I want you to put two good programmers on the job, and I want a ZIP compiler in eight months."

What is your response?

4. You are the leader of a project to develop a microcomputer-based application system that will be marketed by your company. Last month, you submitted a 30 man-month estimate based on total program size (including required data storage, operating system, etc.) of 64K and a main memory of 128K in each microcomputer. Top management is incensed by your estimates. "Don't you know," the president says, "that these 64K memory boards cost $200 each? If we sell 1000 systems, that extra board will have cost us $200,000! It's outrageous and I won't permit it—as of today I am having that second 64K memory board removed from your development computer, and I don't want to see one of those boards back in again. You must build a system that works within the first 64K!"

What is your response?

5. Describe how needed resources can be estimated using Table 10.3. What tradeoffs does this method suggest?

6. A 15,000-instruction program of medium complexity is to be built. Use Table 10.3 to calculate the total effort required (in man-months) if the development time is
   (a) 10 months   (b) 15 months   (c) 25 months

7. A program of easy complexity requires a total effort of 15 man-months and a development time of 15 months. Use Table 10.3 to calculate the total effort if
   (a) The development time is decreased to 10 months.
   (b) The development time is increased to 25 months.

8. A 5000-instruction program of hard complexity is to be built. Use Table 10.3 to calculate the total effort required if the development time is
   (a) 10 months   (b) 14 months

9. Describe how needed resources are estimated by using Table 10.4. What tradeoffs does this method suggest?

10. The dollar amounts in Table 10.4 are based on a typical figure of $35,000 per burdened man-year, as of late 1974. Determine a current typical figure for a burdened man-year, based on
    (a) Inflation since 1974.
    (b) Current salary statistics for the computer industry.

11. The instruction costs in Table 10.4 are based on an estimated 15–30 high-order language instructions per day per person. Assuming 20 working days per month, calculate the monthly productivity rates (in instructions per month) for programs of easy, medium, and hard complexity and for real-time programs. Contrast these productivity ranges with those of Table 10.3.

12. Describe how needed resources are estimated using the method of Section 10.3.3. What tradeoffs does this method suggest?

13. A 15,000-instruction program of medium complexity is to be built. Assume that this complexity is the same as that of the U.S. Army Systems Command Average shown in Figure 10.14, which corresponds to a programming rate of 2000 statements per man-year and difficulty $D=50$.
    (a) At 2000 statements per man-year, how many man-years are required for the 15,000-statement program? In other words, what is the value of K?
    (b) Assuming $K/t_0^2=50$, so that $K/50=t_0^2$, calculate t_0^2 and then t_0.
    (c) What is the expected development time? (Recall that development time $\approx 3t_0$.)
    (d) Compare this estimate with the estimate obtained in Problem 6.
    (e) The development time is now to be changed. A new total effort can be found by calculating the difficulty $D=K/t_0^2$ based on the new value of t_0, reading the new programming rate from Figure 10.14, and calculating the new value of K. Do this for new development times of
        (1) 10 months   (2) 20 months

14. Your 30-month plan for development of an operating system was accepted by your supervisors and by the customer. Now the customer wants the system developed in 15 months and is willing to increase the funding.

Estimate the percentage increase in funding using
(a) Table 10.3.
(b) Table 10.4.
(c) The method of Section 10.3.3.
Compare the results of the different estimates. How closely do they agree? What is the basis for differences among the estimates?

15. Although your 30-month plan for developing an operating system was accepted by the customer and your supervisors, the customer now wants the system developed in nine months and is willing to increase the funding. Estimate the required percentage increase in funding using the method of Section 10.3.3.
(a) Is the project feasible in nine months?
(b) What are your options? What should you do?

PROJECT OUTLINE: Resource Estimation Consider any problem in Appendix C.

1. Block out the design for the given problem.

2. Estimate the size and difficulty of each required module. Estimate the overall difficulty of the entire system.

3. Estimate the resources needed for the system using
(a) Table 10.3.
(b) Table 10.4.
(c) The method of Section 10.3.3.

4. Compare the results of the different estimates. How closely do they agree? What is the basis for differences among the estimates?

10.4 REVIEW PROCEDURES

10.4.1 Introduction to Peer Review

The need of achieving a quality software product, and, in particular, the need to detect and correct errors as soon as possible, has come to be recognized as one of the major problems in the production of software. Not only does the correction of errors become immensely more costly in later stages of development, but the reworking of errors in the test phase tends to cause slippage of the project schedule.

Management procedures based on the idea of *peer review* have been found to be very useful in detecting errors. Although managers had previously used periodic reviews to determine the project's status with respect to its schedule and to identify issues needing special attention, such reviews had not been popular. Reviewees felt that they were being evaluated by management, that errors found would be "used against them," and that they would learn nothing from the review that would help solve their problems.

In a peer review, the work is reviewed by the reviewee's professional colleagues, and management does not participate. The emphasis is on detecting (but not correcting) errors in a nondefensive and open atmosphere. The review is not used as a basis for evaluating the reviewee.

Reviewing of designs or programs by colleagues has continued to grow in popularity among programmers since "egoless programming" was introduced [Weinb 71]. The egoless programmer, not having an ego attachment to the program, seeks critique and evaluation from other programmers and accepts their uncovering in a nondefensive way. DeMillo and his colleagues [DeMi 79] have noted, in a discussion of program proofs, that mathematicians have for hundreds of years verified their proofs entirely by peer review. Although peer review may be a new experience for programmers, it has a long and honorable history.

We will discuss *structured walkthroughs* [IBM 73, Wald 74] and *inspections* [Fagan 76, Koh 75, Koh 76]. Both of these procedures were developed at IBM in the middle 1970s, and both have been found to be beneficial in detecting errors and achieving a higher-quality software product. Although their objectives and style are quite similar, there are five key differences:

1. The roles of participants differ in the two procedures.

2. In the walkthrough review, the design or program under consideration is mentally "walked through" (i.e., executed), while in the inspection review, it is checked against lists of common errors.

3. The structured walkthrough has commonly been more informal and more variable.

4. The inspection procedure more strongly emphasizes follow-up on rework of the errors detected and also insists on reinspection if more than 5 percent of the code or design is to be reworked.

5. The inspection procedure incorporates the use of inspection-derived statistics for project control.

Fagan [Fagan 76] suggests that the inspection review is more effective than the walkthrough review. However, such additional effectiveness may well be due to the incorporation of more forceful follow-up and emphasis on project control (see 4 and 5, above). It seems reasonable to expect that—with additional emphasis on follow-up and with the use of walkthrough-derived statistics for project control—the walkthrough procedure would become more effective.

10.4.2 Common Properties of Walkthroughs and Inspections

Inspections and walkthroughs are both intended to be a regular planned part of the software development cycle. Table 10.5 lists the points at which reviews are planned. Obviously, the completion of a review and rework of errors at each such point may be considered a milestone of the project.

Table 10.5 Reviews planned during software development

Task	Review Points
Program	Specifications complete Detailed design complete Complete source code
Test plan	Test plan complete Test cases complete Completion of execution of unit test plan
Documentation	Program specifications Program design User's guide Operator's guide

In addition, structured walkthroughs can be used to review the results of system planning (namely, project plans, system definition, and task identification) and also to examine work assignments and schedules at major project reviews [IBM 73].

Both review procedures envision that development of a test plan proceeds in parallel with software production. Thus a diagram of the software development cycle, including reviews, has the form of Figure 10.16.

Each of the review triangles in Figure 10.16 represents extra work that has been deliberately added to the development cycle. Extra effort and extra time must be specifically allotted for preparation, for the reviews themselves, and for rework of the errors detected. (If extra effort and time are not allotted, reviews will be ignored.) The time necessary for rework will, of course, vary between installations; Fagan [Fagan 76] suggests 20 hours per 1000 lines of noncommentary source code as nominal rework time for detailed design, and 16 hours per 1000 lines of noncommentary source code as nominal code rework time. The advantage derived from this extra work is that errors are detected close to their point of origin, so that correction is much less expensive (remember that the cost to repair errors rises exponentially with time).

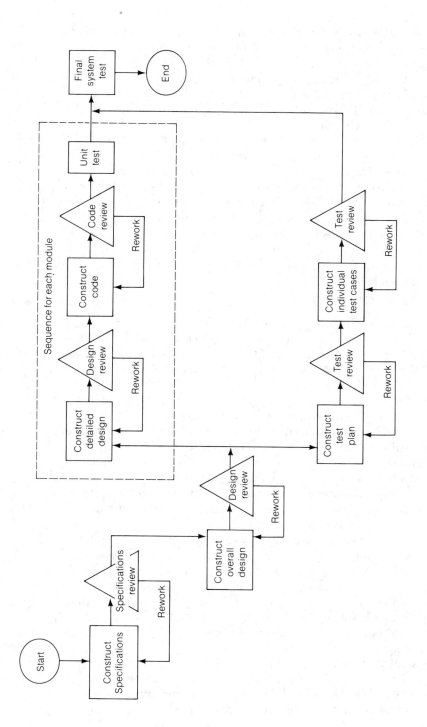

Figure 10.16 The software development cycle including Reviews.

Also, concern with errors begins in the first half of the development schedule instead of in the second half, when recovery from errors may be impossible without adjustments of workers and schedule. Since the reviews extract errors from the software before testing begins, a shorter test phase can be expected. The investment of extra time and effort in reviews yields improvements in programming productivity [Fagan 76].

Each review follows a well-defined and predetermined pattern, in which the roles of the participants are also predetermined. Materials are distributed in advance of the review, and all participants are expected to be familiar with the materials at the review. The review is an uninterrupted meeting of one to two hours, whose objective is to detect (but not correct) errors. A list of errors is accumulated during the review, and this becomes an "action list" for reworking of the design or code. Management does not attend, and the results of the review are not used as a basis for employee evaluation.

10.4.3 Structured Walkthroughs

A walkthrough review is initiated when the developer of a design or program decides that a review is appropriate. The developer (the reviewee) chooses the reviewers and arranges the time and date of the review. A few days before the review, the developer distributes the design or code to the selected reviewers, states the objectives the review will have, and specifies what roles the reviewers should play. The reviewers are expected to examine the given materials and to be familiar with them at the time of the review.

The objective in choosing reviewers is to have reviewers who will have diverse opinions and who can spot errors and inconsistencies in the design or code, or in the way it interacts with its intended environment. Possible reviewers would be a project team member, a member of the test group that will test the product, a potential maintainer of the product, a programming language expert, or the original designer (if code is being reviewed) or a potential coder (if a design is being reviewed).

The review itself consists of a one- to two-hour uninterrupted meeting. If the review has not been completed by that time, an additional meeting is scheduled. Typically, four to six people attend. One member of the group is designated moderator. Another is designated recording secretary and becomes responsible for recording all errors, inconsistencies, and other issues needing attention that are found during the walkthrough. (The resulting list is given to the developer and to each reviewer, and serves as an action list for the developer.) Yet another member is designated the tester.

The focus of the walkthrough is on substantive issues such as basic design flaws or poor logic. Accordingly, minor mistakes such as typographical errors, spelling, and the like are not considered. Instead, lists of such errors are given to the recording secretary or sent to the developer.

After a statement of the review's objectives, the reviewers comment on the general quality, accuracy, and completeness of the design or code. The reviewers express any major concerns they may have and suggest areas to be followed up during the review. Next, the developer gives a brief tutorial about the design or code.

The main part of the review now begins. The developer "plays computer," talking through the execution of the work in a step-by-step fashion, explaining the function of each portion of the design or code, why it is there, and how it will work. This presentation attempts to deal with the major concerns expressed earlier.

Control of the meeting is then passed to the tester who has come prepared with a set of test cases that serve as a focus for questions about the product's logic and assumptions. The developer walks each test input through the logic while the reviewers watch for inconsistencies, errors, interface problems, and deviations from specifications. The tester is responsible for recording and correcting any errors found in the test cases.

Immediately after the meeting, the recording secretary gives copies of the handwritten action list to all the participants. The developer is then responsible for resolving the concerns left on the action list and for notifying the reviewers of actions or corrections made.

Management does not use the action list as a basis for evaluating the developer and does not follow up to see that the items on the action list have been resolved. However, some organizations keep track of the number and severity of errors found after all walkthroughs are completed and evaluate employees on the basis of these records. (Such errors can only be the result of poor walkthroughs or poor resolution of action lists, and the developer is responsible for both of these.) According to the IBM Corporation [IBM 73], it is important to review all technical personnel, from the most junior to the most senior, the same way.

Some organizations accumulate lists of common errors for use by future reviewers and to indicate areas in which the technical staff may need training.

10.4.4 Inspection Reviews

The inspection review is a more formal procedure than the walkthrough and is intended to furnish information for management control of a project (but again, not for management evaluation of employees). Initiation points for program production reviews are

· Specifications complete
· Detailed design complete (each design statement represents 3 to 10 program statements)
· Program unit (or module) complete (first clean compilation has been obtained)

As each situation above is reached, the appropriate review is initiated. Completion of the review and all the required rework is a checkpoint or milestone of the project, indicating that a certain portion of the work has been accomplished and (as much as possible) purged of errors by the review and rework. Rework done as a result of these reviews is 10 to 100 times less expensive than if done in the last half (test phase) of the project [Fagan 76].

Obviously, corrections made in response to a review may themselves contain errors. Although we tend to regard such corrections as error free because they are usually simple, some studies indicate that they are more error prone than the original program [Fagan 76]. Accordingly, it is required that all rework also be inspected by the entire inspection team if the rework is more than 5 percent of the work, and otherwise either by the whole team or by the team member responsible for follow-up on rework.

Every inspection team includes the following four members:

- The *moderator:* a competent programmer, usually (for the sake of objectivity) from an unrelated project, who leads the inspection team. The moderator is responsible for scheduling the review, distributing materials, leading the review, recording the inspection results and reporting them within one day, and following up on rework. For best results, the moderator should be specially trained [Fagan 76] for this role.
- The *designer:* the author of the program design.
- The *coder/implementer:* the programmer responsible for translating the design into code.
- The *tester:* the person responsible for writing test cases or otherwise testing the product.

In a design review, the designer is the reviewee; while in a code review the coder is the reviewee. If the code has many interfaces, coders dealing with these interfaces may be added to the team. In a specifications review, the author of the specifications is a fifth member and the reviewee.

For the design inspection reviews only, there is a preliminary overview session in which the designer describes the overall area being addressed and then describes in detail (logic, paths, dependencies, etc.) the specific area he or she has designed. Design documentation is distributed to the participants at the end of this overview session. For the code inspection review, no overview is necessary since the review team has already participated in the design review and has the design documentation. Accordingly, code listings are distributed. Also, portions of code due to design changes (i.e., made after the design inspection) are examined especially carefully.

The participants then prepare individually for the review, reading the documents and trying to understand the intent and detail of the design or code. The participants are usually also given statistics on error distributions by type (determined from the most recent inspections), so that they can concentrate on finding the most prevalent types of errors. They are also usually given checklists of clues for finding errors.[7]

At the beginning of the review, a "reader" (usually the reviewee) chosen by the moderator narrates the design or code. In a code inspection, the coder discusses the program statement by statement and shows how it paraphrases the design. Every piece of logic is covered at least once, and every branch is taken at least once. As this discussion proceeds, questions are raised and pursued to determine if errors exist. The objective is to detect errors, not to correct them. When the presence of an error is recognized, its type and severity are noted by the moderator, and the inspection is continued to the next point. Obvious solutions are noted but, generally, efforts are not made to pursue solutions in depth. However, R. D. Freeman [Free 75] believes that a few minutes of solution hunting—essentially brainstorming solutions for a particular aspect of design—can reveal major design problems as the inspection team struggles to resolve apparently trivial problems. The moderator can control the discussion of solutions, cutting it off when it becomes nonproductive. The design or code may also be analyzed with respect to an error checklist during the review.[8]

Within a day after the inspection, the moderator produces a report of the inspection findings, using standard forms (discussed in detail in [Fagan 76]). The moderator then follows up on the rework, personally reinspecting the product after rework (at his or her own discretion if less than 5 percent was reworked) or reconvening the inspection team for a full inspection of the reworked product.

The inspection review is an uninterrupted one- to two-hour meeting. (After two hours, inspection teams tire and become less productive.) Since a code inspection proceeds at about 150 statements per hour, the examination of large programs must be accomplished in a series of reviews. It is important that sufficient time for reviews and rework be scheduled and managed with care. If this is not done, immediate work pressures will tend to cause inspections to be postponed or avoided. And the usual result of postponing early inspections is a lengthened overall schedule and increased cost [Fagan 76].

A guide to the required inspection time is shown in Table 10.6. The values given in the table are conservative. Note that inspections of system programs require four to six times the effort of application program inspections. Inspection of a typical systems program, by a team of four people, takes a total of about 90 to 100 man-hours.

Inspection results can be used for project control in several ways. For example, a list of errors (either design or code or combined design and code)

---

[7]Checklists for inspection reviews of specifications and detail design may be found in [Koh 75] and [Asc 76], respectively, while checklists for code inspections may be found in [Asc 76, Mye 79]. A checklist for COBOL programs may be found in [IBM 75] and in [Gilb 77a, Appendix A].
[8]The process of a test inspection review is described in [Lar 75], which is extensively reproduced in [Gilb 77a, Appendix B].

per 1000 code lines for each module immediately shows which modules are most error prone. Such modules can either be tested more stringently or can be entirely rewritten.[9]

Table 10.6   Guide to time required for inspections and rework (adapted from [Fagan 76]). (Copyright 1976 by International Business Machines Corporation. Reprinted by permission.)

Type of Programming	Type of Inspection	Process Operations*			
		Over-view	Prepa-ration	Inspec-tion	Rework
Systems programming	Design	500	100	130	50
	Code	——	125	150	62.5
Applications programming	Design	——	898	652	——
	Code	——	709	539	——

*Numbers indicate the rate of progress: statements per hour. The dashes indicate that no data was available.

If inspections are carried out over a period of time, a consistent error-detection efficiency can be established, where

$$\text{Error-detection efficiency} = \frac{\text{errors found by inspection}}{\begin{array}{c}\text{total errors found in}\\ \text{product by end of testing}\end{array}}$$

Thus the number of errors found in inspection can predict the number of errors remaining in the product. Inspection reports can be summarized to yield statistics on the frequency of occurrence of the different types of errors. These statistics can then be used to prompt reviewers. Also, the frequency distribution of errors for a given module can be compared to the usual distribution, and any large disparities (e.g., an abnormally large number of interconnection errors) can be analyzed.

When testing reveals excessively error-prone code, it may be economical to reinspect such code before continuing the testing [Fagan 76].

---

[9]Weinberg (in [Gilb 77a, p.56]) has observed that a very small part of the program usually requires most of the maintenance effort. He reports that when a small percentage of maintenance time was used to select and rewrite the most troublesome modules, the error rates and maintenance effort were substantially reduced in a short time.

REFERENCES

[Asc 76] Ascoly, J., et al. "Code Inspection Specification," Technical Report TR 21.630. IBM, 1976.

[DeMi 79] DeMillo, R. A.; Lipton, R. J.; and Perlis, A. J. "Social Processes and Proofs of Theorems and Programs," *Communications of the ACM*, May 1979.

[Fagan 74] Fagan, M. E. "Design and Code Inspections and Process Control in the Development of Programs," Technical Report TR21.572. IBM, 1974 (Also extensively quoted in [Gilb 77a].)* (Revised version is Technical Report TR00.2763. IBM, 1976.)

[Fagan 76] Fagan, M. E. "Design and Code Inspections to Reduce Errors in Program Development," *IBM System Journal*, Vol. 15, No. 3, 1976. (Also in [Mil 78].)*

[Free 75] Freeman, R. D. "An Experiment in Software Development," *Bell System Technical Journal, Special Safeguard Supplement*, 1975.

[Gilb 77a] Gilb, T. *Software Metrics*. Cambridge, MA: Winthrop, 1977.

[IBM 73] IBM Corporation. *Structured Walk-Throughs: A Project Management Tool*. IBM, 1973. (Also in [Berg 79].)*

[IBM 75] ———. *COBOL Inspection Checklist*. IBM, 1975. (Also in [Gilb 77a, Appendix A].)*

[Koh 75] Kohli, O. R., and Radice, R. A. "High-Level Design Inspection Specification," Technical Report TR21.601. IBM, 1975.

[Koh 76] ———. "Low-Level Design Inspection Specification," Technical Report TR21.629. IBM, 1976.

[Lar 75] Larson, R. R. "Test Plan and Test Case Inspection Specifications," Technical Report TR21.586. IBM, 1975. (Also extensively reproduced in [Gilb 77a, Appendix B].)*

[Mye 79] Myers, G. J. *The Art of Software Testing*. New York: Wiley, 1979.

[Wald 74] Waldstein, N. S. "The Walk-Thru—A Method of Specification, Design and Review," Technical Report TR00.2536. IBM, 1974.

[Weinb 71] Weinberg, G. M. *The Psychology of Computer Programming*. New York: Van Nostrand Reinhold, 1971.

PROBLEMS

1. Do you agree or disagree that peer review of a person's design or program should not be used to evaluate that person?
   (a) Outline your position.
   (b) How can management ensure that reviews are not used for evaluation purposes?

---

*See Appendix B: Bibliography.

2. Table 10.5 shows the points at which reviews should occur during development.
   (a) Use Fagan's estimates of required effort to find the total effort devoted to reviews in developing a 10,000-line program.
   (b) How much elapsed time would have to be scheduled?
   (c) What impact would this have on the development plan?
   (d) Do you agree or disagree that reviews will not be conducted unless the time and money are specifically allotted for them? State your reasons.
   (e) How can a programming manager justify the extra effort required for reviews? How can the programming manager's supervisor ensure that reviews are actually carried out?

3. Weinberg [Weinb 71] has advocated that programmers be taught "egoless programming," a style of programming in which members of a programming group freely criticize each other's work, and each member takes the criticism in a nondefensive way. Do you think that egoless programming can be taught to the majority of programmers? If it can, will reviews then be unnecessary?

4. Does it make a difference whether a review procedure is more formal (as the inspection is) or less formal (as the walkthrough is)? If you believe it makes a difference, which to you believe is better?

5. Compare the roles of the participants in the inspection and walkthrough reviews. Which would you rather participate in? Why?

6. Develop a single review procedure combining the best features of inspections and walkthroughs.

PROJECT OUTLINE: Software Development, Management, and Review Form a group of three to five people to develop a system via the following steps:

1. Choose a project organization and a leader if appropriate.

2. Determine a project plan and schedule, including carefully defined milestones and a test plan.

3. Determine and write down the system requirements. Collectively review them, reworking them as necessary.

4. Determine and write the program specifications. Collectively review them, reworking them as necessary.

5. Determine and write down the overall design, including assumptions. Collectively review the design document, reworking it as necessary.

6. Write the code and a program summary for each program. Collectively review each program and its summary, reworking them as necessary.

7. Perform necessary testing.

8. Finally, write a paper describing your experiences.

10.5 CONSTRAINTS ON SOFTWARE DEVELOPMENT

10.5.1 The Context of Software Production

It has been said that "software costs too much" and is "unreliable"; that software producers are incapable of meeting time or price budgets; and that "improving software productivity is one of the biggest tasks of the 80s." And the opinion persists that software really is easy to produce and does not require much skill. This section points out some constraints on software development that are often ignored, but that cause great difficulty.

Many special problems and constraints arise in software development because the software system is embedded in an environment. Broad economic or military considerations may dictate the time available for a project [Bro 74, You 79b, Gla 80], regardless of software development considerations. For example, organizations cannot afford to wait more than five years for a system [Put 77, p. 23], even though an optimal development time might be eight years.

Software development is more difficult in projects that also involve hardware development. Hardware is normally unreliable when newly developed. If the hardware is late or the shakedown takes more time than expected, correcting hardware problems may occur simultaneously with program debugging [Cor 79], thus hampering the debugging effort. Unfortunately, the effect of hardware unreliability on software development is often overlooked, and the perception of top system managers is that "software is late." If the system contract involves penalties for lateness, the time pressures on software development become almost unbearable.

In integrated hardware/software systems, and especially in military systems such as avionics systems, all of the complex problems tend to be concentrated in the software:

> If it takes extra work and extra complexity in the software to make the total system function better, then that work and complexity will be assigned to the software. In fact, as systems people come to understand the role of software . . . they begin to see software as a weightless, spaceless sink in which all the system problems can be dissolved . . . the economic and technical reasons for this trend are compelling [Gla 80].

Equally important, because hardware requires a long development time, all changes in specifications and all system corrections tend to be relegated to the software, including corrections for incorrect communications between the hardware designers and the software designers. All last-minute changes are relegated to the software because the hardware can no longer be changed. Thus, at the last minute, the hardware is fixed and the software is still changing, and again the perception is that "software is late."

In many applications, as, for example, in an avionics or an automotive system, the computer should ideally be small, lightweight, and inexpensively replaceable. In such applications, the system design seeks to minimize the cost of hardware and to transfer complexity from hardware to software. This trend is intensified by the fact that multiple copies of software are relatively less expensive than multiple copies of hardware. However, the constraints of the less capable hardware significantly increase the difficulty of software development (see Figure 10.7).

Thus the developers of software systems may be forced into inefficient or crash schedules by external pressures. In systems involving hardware development, the software development usually absorbs complexities that the hardware is unable to handle. In avionics and similar systems, the development is forced onto less and less capable computers. In sum, software developers "are caught in a squeeze not of their own making" [Gla 80].

10.5.2 Software Production Is a New Technology

Software production is a new method of defining and then implementing processes or procedures. Before the advent of automatic data processing, processes were executed by people. Common sense was used to deal with contingencies and difficulties as they arose and to correct obvious mistakes. A process (e.g., for billing or inventory) evolved over a period of years.

In contrast, with the advent of automatic data processing, a process is defined via a program; then, by controlling a computer, the program becomes the embodiment of the process. The program has no common sense but, in principle, foresees every contingency and difficulty of the process. This method has been in use for only 30 years.

The software designer is thus required to invent a set of explicit mechanical procedures that fit the context of the given process and require no common sense for their execution. The rules for these mechanical procedures are extraordinarily complete and precise compared to rules for manual processing (which can presuppose common sense).

In the 30 years of its existence, software production technology has been applied to a greater variety of applications than any other technology. Software systems fly missiles and do bank processing. Some of these applications are of enormous scope and complexity. For example, a 1,000,000-instruction software system has 10,000 component functions (assuming 100 instructions per function), each of which can be specified and developed in at least 2 ways. For such a system, $2^{10,000}$ or about $10^{3,000}$ combinations of function choices, many of which are "correct," must be considered in design [Boe 79a].

Instead of making software production easier, the companion technology of hardware production has hindered the development of software technology. Each new "advance" in hardware (e.g., interrupts, virtual memory) has created a new set of software problems and necessitated the wholesale adoption of new design schemes [Weg 79, Ard 80].

For any given problem, we may regard software production as having a certain level of technology, corresponding to the specific methods available to develop the specifications, general program design, and specific algorithms for that problem.

Whenever new software technologies are incorporated into a system, design iteration is necessary because the impact of the new technologies on other parts of the system is not known. It has been suggested that the development team

> . . . create a perhaps crude and incomplete system, begin to use it and observe the behavior. Then on the basis of the observed difficulties, one simplifies, redesigns and refines the system. In the case of Multics, most areas . . . were redesigned as much as half a dozen times [Cor 79].

In hardware development, it is standard procedure to build a "breadboard" machine and test machines before the final production design is fixed. However, the necessity for design iteration in software development is not usually appreciated. Also, provision for evolution and easy repair of software requires special software production techniques.

For some applications, final specifications cannot be given until a preliminary version of the system has been operated [Inf 73, You 79b]. In this case also, design iteration is required. Large real-time systems are usually implemented in this way [Inf 73].

10.5.3 The Effect of Unfounded Optimism

Users, software developers, and other managers all tend to have expectations that are too high. We all think of software development as easy because it shapes thought-stuff instead of physical materials. We forget that the shaping of ideas is a new technology that can develop only at a finite pace. Unfortunately, this point has generally been ignored. Salespeople and developers have tended to promise too much—systems too far beyond the current state of the art or too difficult for the time allowed—while users and managers have tended to demand too much.

When a system too far beyond the expertise of the development group is attempted, research and development—as well as production—are required within the project effort. If the research is extensive or has not been properly allowed for, the project usually results in slipped schedules, budget overruns, and a poor product. Conversely, as any product becomes standardized (and therefore stable), it becomes more amenable to time and cost controls. Thus difficulties in software development are due in part, according to McClure, to "the refusal of industry to reengineer last year's model" (in [Nau 76]).

The phenomenon of too-high expectations has two other aspects. Unreasonable time and budget limitations are often set due to ignorance or reasons unrelated to the software development [Weg 79, p.179; You 79b, pp.255–256; Gla 80]. Such time and budget limitations ignore the inherent difficulties of software problems and the fact that, in general, people cannot be substituted for time. Specifications are often vague and incomplete ("the banking system of the future"), technically infeasible ("an efficient, optimal network for a total range of problems"), or infeasible within the time and budget constrains set [Schw 75].

It is important to properly estimate the difficulty of a software development, and the amount of research that must go into it. Unfounded optimism can lead to disastrous underestimates. McClure (in [Nau 76, p.45]) gives a procedure for taking into account the influence of optimism on estimates: Before undertaking a project to produce a new software system or component, read the statements below, checking all that apply.

Expressions of Optimism

1. The new system will be substantially superior to its predecessor and to competitive systems.
2. The new system corrects a philosophical defect in the old system.
3. The specification is not yet complete, but it will be finished before any important programming decisions are made.
4. The specification is absolutely firm, unless the X company signs a big order and requests some slight changes.
5. The programming team will be composed of the best programmers from other projects.
6. Because of expansion, a fresh team of programmers with applicable experience will be hired.
7. The new computer is a great machine; the programmers will love it as soon as they get their manuals.
8. The programmers will, of course, have to share the machine with the hardware team checking out the new peripherals and the diagnostic package.
9. Interfacing this system to the rest of the software is trivial and can be easily worked out later.

10. Although the assembler (compiler, loader, file system, etc.) is not completely checked out, it will be readly long before coding is complete.
11. The debug package isn't done but this system can easily be checked out at the console.
12. The budget is only preliminary but it's obviously conservative.
13. The project manager may have missed his budget on his last project, but he's learned his lesson and won't miss this time.

For each statement checked above, add 10 percent to the estimated cost and 1 month to the estimated time. If you checked statement 6, add 30 percent and 6 months. The resulting estimate should be much closer to the final result than the original, assuming the original estimate was honestly made. (Schwartz [Schw 75] suggests that McClure's estimates of the effects of these statements may be low.)

REFERENCES

[Ard 80] Arden, B. W. (ed.). *What Can Be Automated? The Computer Science and Engineering Research Study (COSERS)*. Cambridge, MA: M.I.T. Press, 1980.

[Boe 79a] Boehm, B. W. "Software Engineering—As It Is," *Proceedings of 4th International Conference on Software Engineering*. New York: IEEE Computer Society, 1979.

[Bro 74] Brooks, F. P. "The Mythical Man-Month," *Datamation*, December 1974. (Also in [Fre 80b].)*

[Cor 79] Corbató, F. J., and Clingen, C. T. "A Managerial View of the Multics System Development," in P. Wegner (ed.), *Research Directions in Software Technology*. Cambridge, MA: M.I.T. Press, 1979.

[Gla 80] Glass, R. L. "Real-time: The 'Lost World' of Software Debugging," *Communications of the ACM*, May 1980.

[Inf 73] Infotech. *Infotech State of the Art Report on Real-Time Systems*. Maidenhead, England: Infotech, 1973.

[Mills 79] Mills, H. D. "Software Development," in P. Wegner (ed.), *Research Directions in Software Technology*. Cambridge, MA: M.I.T. Press, 1979.

[Nau 76] Naur, P.; Randell, B.; and Buxton, J. N. (eds.). *Software Engineering Concepts and Techniques, Proceedings of the NATO Conferences*. New York: Petrocelli/Charter, 1976.

[Put 77] Putnam, L. H., and Wolverton, R. W. *Quantitative Management: Software Estimating* (tutorial). New York: IEEE Computer Society, 1977.

---

*See Appendix B: Bibliography.

[Schw 75] Schwartz, J. I. "Construction of Software: Problems and Practicalities," in E. Horowitz (ed.), *Practical Strategies for Developing Large Software Systems*. Reading, MA: Addison-Wesley, 1975.

[Weg 79] Wegner, P. (ed.). *Research Directions in Software Technology*. Cambridge, MA: M.I.T. Press, 1979.

[You 79b] Yourdon, E. "Top-Down Design and Testing," in G. D. Bergland and R. D. Gordon (eds.), *Tutorial: Software Design Strategies*. New York: IEEE Computer Society, 1979.

PROBLEMS

1. What are the major costs in the software life cycle? What can be done to minimize them?

2. Aside from poor management, what are the major problems in software design and development? Are there solutions to those problems? If so, what are they?

3. Have you ever taken part in a software system that failed? If so, do you know why it failed? Was poor management a cause?

4. Do you agree that software failures are due in part to constraints on software production? Write a paper stating your position.

5. Do you agree or disagree with the assertion that advances in hardware technology make software development more difficult? State your reasons.

6. Do you agree that in many software developments there is a need for iteration of the design procedure? Can a project schedule allow for design iteration without an excessive development time? If so, how might this be accomplished?

7. Based on your supervisor's facts, you estimated that a program will require 40 man-months effort and 18 months elapsed time. Your supervisor now says, "I didn't want to concern you, but you will be using a new prototype computer and we will have to hire the programmers for your job. Everything should be fine because the computer will be checked out in a month or two, and we'll be able to hire some really good programmers. I'm counting on you to do the job using your original estimate!" What is your response?

appendix a
Author Index

Aho, A. V., 306
Alberts, D. S., 7, 117
Arden, B. W., 617
Aron, J. D., 574
Ascoly, J., 611

Bagnall, J., 17
Barnes, B. H., 78
Barstuo, D., 306
Bass, L. J., 384
Belady, L. A., 4, 199
Bell, T. E., 34
Bergland, G. D., 28
Bernacchi, R. L., 106
Boehm, B. W., 3, 5, 6, 7, 25, 33, 34, 35, 104, 492, 493, 509, 513, 529, 549, 556, 565, 589
Bookman, P. G., 486, 488, 489
Brinch Hansen, P., 515
Brooks, F. P., 3, 5, 6, 29, 34, 580, 584, 589, 596, 598, 599, 615
Brotman, B. A., 484, 486, 487
Bunker, R. E., 384
Buxton, J. N., 557, 581, 588, 616

Caine, S. H., 422
Chow, T. S., 374
Clingen, C. T., 120, 563, 564, 582, 586, 615
Coaker, F. W., 384
Constantine, L. L., 123, 201, 261, 263
Conway, R., 517
Cooke, L. H., 563, 564
Cooper, D. C., 442
Corbató, F. J., 120, 563, 582, 586, 615

Daly, E. B., 589
DeMarco, T., 38, 55, 60
DeMillo, R. A., 510, 522, 525, 605
Dijkstra, E. W., 249, 403, 416, 427, 428, 435, 508

Fagan, M. E., 514, 604, 606, 610, 611, 612
Farr, L., 580
Ferguson, D. E., 454
Floyd, R. W., 306
Foster, K. A., 532, 533, 535, 540, 543, 544, 549
Franta, W. R., 165
Freeman, P., 28, 255
Freeman, R. D., 611
Fujii, M. S., 514

Gane, C., 38
Gerhart, S. L., 508
Gilb, T., 6, 24, 29, 100, 101, 105, 106, 107, 108, 109, 110, 112, 185, 186, 187, 188, 189, 190, 191, 299, 609, 610
Gilbert, P., 374
Glass, R. L., 615, 616, 618
Goodenough, J. B., 23, 107, 247, 290, 419, 508
Goos, G., 18, 20, 26, 503, 506
Gordon, E. K., 422
Gordon, R. D., 28
Green, C. C., 306

Harper, W. L., 19
Hayes, J. A., 21
Hetzel, W. C., 103, 105, 512
Ho, S. E., 522
Hopcroft, J., 306, 356
Horowitz, E., 29, 306
Howden, W. E., 28, 510, 512, 532, 533, 539, 540
Hughes, J. W., 376, 377

IBM, 605, 606, 609, 611
Infotech, 35, 615
Ingrassia, F. S., 180
Irvine, C. A., 247, 419

Jackson, M. A., 118, 120, 123, 141, 167, 168, 256, 319, 334, 341, 342, 417, 420
Jones, N. D., 367

Katznelson, J., 18, 173
Kernighan, B. W., 28, 468, 480, 485, 523, 531
Knuth, D. E., 453, 486, 487, 488
Koberg, D., 17
Kohli, O. R., 603, 609

Landau, J. V., 367
Larsen, G. H., 106
Larson, R. R., 609
Lawler, E., 306
Lehman, M. M., 4
Lipton, R. J., 510, 522, 525
Lucas, H. C., 120

Marcus, R., 374
McCall, J. A., 490
Mehlmann, M., 193

appendix b
Bibliography

This appendix contains all books and papers cited as references in individual chapters. See also the list of Useful Sources (including lists of periodicals and series) in Section 1.6.

[Aho 74] Aho, A. V.; Hopcroft, J. E.; and Ullman, J. D. *The Design and Analysis of Computer Algorithms*. Reading, MA: Addison-Wesley, 1974.

[Alb 76] Alberts, D. S. "The Economics of Software Quality Assurance," *Proceedings of National Computer Conference*, New York, 1976. (Also in [Mil 78].)

[Alex 64] Alexander, C. *Notes on the Synthesis of Form*. Cambridge, MA: Harvard University Press, 1964.

[Ard 80] Arden, B. W. (ed.). *What Can Be Automated? The Computer Science and Engineering Research Study (COSERS)*. Cambridge, MA: M.I.T. Press, 1980.

[Aron 74] Aron, J. D. *The Program Development Process: The Individual Programmer*. Reading, MA: Addison-Wesley, 1974.

[Aron 76] ———. "Estimating Resources for Large Programming Systems," in P. Naur, B. Randell, and J. N. Buxton (eds.), *Software Engineering Concepts and Techniques, Proceedings of the NATO Conferences*. New York: Petrocelli/Charter, 1976. (Also in [Put 77].)

[Asc 76] Ascoly, J., et al. "Code Inspection Specification," Technical Report TR21.630. IBM, 1976.

[Bas 75] Basili, V., and Turner, A. "Iterative Enhancement: A Practical Technique for Software Engineering," *IEEE Transactions on Software Engineering*, December 1975.

[Bas 81] Bass, L. J., and Bunker, R. E. "A Generalized User Interface for Applications Programs," *Communications of the ACM*, December 1981.

[Bela 77] Belady, L. A., and Lehman, M. M. "The Characteristics of Large Systems," Report RC6785. IBM, 1977. (Also in [Ram 78] and [Weg 79].)

[Bell 76] Bell, T. E., and Thayer, T. A. "Software Requirements: Are They a Problem?" *Proceedings of IEEE/ACM Second International Conference on Software Engineering*, October 1976.

[Berg 79] Bergland, G. D., and Gordon, R. D. *Tutorial: Software Design Strategies*. (IEEE Catalog No. EHO 149-5.) New York: IEEE Computer Society, 1979.

[Bern 74] Bernacchi, R. L., and Larsen, G. H. *Data Processing Contracts and the Law*. Boston: Little, Brown, 1974.

[Boe 73a] Boehm, B. W. "The High Cost of Software," *Proceedings of the Symposium on the High Cost of Software*, Monterey, CA, 1973.

[Boe 73b] ——. "Software and Its Impact: A Quantitative Assessment," *Datamation*, May 1973. (Also in [Fre 80b].)

[Boe 74] ——. "Some Steps toward Formal and Automated Aids to Software Requirements Analysis and Design," *Proceedings of IFIP Congress 74*, 1974.

[Boe 75a] ——. "The High Cost of Software," in E. Horowitz (ed.), *Practical Strategies for Developing Large-Scale Software Systems*. Reading, MA: Addison-Wesley, 1975.

[Boe 75b] ——. "Software Design and Structuring," in E. Horowitz (ed.), *Practical Strategies for Developing Large-Scale Software Systems*. Reading, MA: Addison-Wesley, 1975.

[Boe 75c] ——. "Some Experience with Automated Aids to the Design of Large-Scale Reliable Software," *Proceedings of International Conference on Reliable Software*, Los Angeles. (IEEE Catalog No. 75CHO940-7CSR.) New York: IEEE Computer Society, 1975.

[Boe 78] ——, et al. *Characteristics of Software Quality*. Amsterdam: North-Holland Publishing Company, 1978.

[Boe 79a] ——. "Software Engineering—As It Is," *Proceedings of 4th International Conference on Software Engineering*. New York: IEEE Computer Society, 1979.

[Boe 79b] ——. "Software Engineering: R&D Trends and Defense Needs," in P. Wegner (ed.), *Research Directions in Software Technology*. Cambridge, MA: M.I.T. Press, 1979.

[Boe 81] ——. *Software Engineering Economics*. Englewood Cliffs, NJ: Prentice-Hall, 1981.

[Boh 66] Bohm, C., and Jacopini, G. "Flow Diagrams, Turing Machines, and Languages with Only Two Formation Rules," *Communications of the ACM*, May 1966.

[Book 72] Bookman, P. G.; Brotman, B. A.; and Schmitt, K. L. "Use Measurement Engineering for Better System Performance," *Computer Decisions*, April 1972.

[Bos 71] Bosch, C. A., and Hetrick, W. L. *Software Development Characteristics Study for the CCIP-85 Study Group*. TRW Report 4851.1-003. Cleveland, OH: Thompson Ramo Woolridge Corp., 1971.

[Bri 73] Brinch Hansen, P. "Testing a Multiprogramming System," *Software—Practice and Experience*, April-June 1973. (Also in [Mil 78].)

[Bro 74] Brooks, F. P. "The Mythical Man-Month," *Datamation*, December 1974. (Also in [Fre 80b].)

[Bro 75] ——. *The Mythical Man-Month: Essays in Software Engineering*. Reading, MA: Addison-Wesley, 1975.

[Brow 73] Brown, A. R., and Sampson, W. A. *Program Debugging*. New York: American Elsevier, 1973.

[Brown 75] Brown, J. R., and Lipow, M. "Testing for Software Reliability," *SIGPLAN Notices*, Vol. 10, 1975.

[BrownR 76] Brown, R., "Technique and Practice of Structured Design a la Constantine," *Infotech State of the Art Report: Survey of Structured Programming Practice*, Part II, Vol. II. Maidenhead, England: Infotech, 1976.

[Cai 75] Caine, S. H., and Gordon, E. K. "PDL—A Tool for Software Design," *Proceedings of National Computer Conference*, 1975. (Also in [Fre 80b].)

[Cho 78] Chow, T. S. "Testing Software Design Modelled by Finite-State Machines," *IEEE Transactions on Software Engineering*, May 1978.

[Chu 78] Chung, P., and Galman, B. "Use of State Diagrams to Engineer Communications Software," *Proceedings of 3rd International Conference on Software Engineering*. (IEEE Catalog No. 78CH1317-7C.) New York: IEEE Computer Society, 1978.

[Coa 74] Coaker, F. W. "Table-Directed Editing for a Data Storage System," *Information Storage and Retrieval*, 1974.

[Col 81] Coleman, D.; Hughes, J. W.; and Powell, M. S. "A Method for the Syntax Directed Design of Multiprograms," *IEEE Transactions on Software Engineering*, March 1981.

[Con 63] Conway, M. E. "Design of a Separable Transition-Diagram Compiler," *Communications of the ACM*, July 1963.

[Conw 78] Conway, R. *A Primer on Disciplined Programming*. Cambridge, MA: Winthrop, 1978.

[Cooke 78] Cooke, L. H. "Express Testing," *Datamation*, September 1978.

[Coop 67] Cooper, D.C. "Boehm and Jacopini's Reduction of Flow Charts, *Communications of the ACM*, Vol. 10, No. 8, August 1967.

[Coope 79] Cooper, J. D., and Fisher, M. J. (eds.). *Software Quality Management*. New York: Petrocelli/Charter, 1979.

[Cor 79] Corbató, F. J., and Clingen, C. T. "A Managerial View of the Multics System Development," in P. Wegner (ed.), *Research Directions in Software Technology*. Cambridge, MA: M.I.T. Press, 1979.

[Cou 74] Couger, J. D., and Knapp, R. W. (eds.). *System Analysis Techniques*. New York: Wiley, 1974.

[Daly 77] Daly, E. B. "Management of Software Development," *IEEE Transactions on Software Engineering*, May 1977. (Also in [Put 77] and [Mil 78].)

[Dav 58] Davis, M. *Computability and Unsolvability*. New York: McGraw-Hill, 1958.

[deB 70] de Bono, E. *Lateral Thinking: Creativity Step by Step*. New York: Harper Colophone Books, 1970.

[DeMa 79] DeMarco, T. *Structured Analysis and System Specification*. Englewood Cliffs, NJ: Prentice-Hall, 1979.

[DeMi 78] DeMillo, R. A.; Lipton, R. J.; and Sayward, F. G. "Hints on Test Data Selection: Help for the Practicing Programmer," *IEEE Computer*, April 1978.

[DeMi 79] ———; ———; and Perlis, A. J. "Social Processes and Proofs of Theorems and Programs," *Communications of the ACM*, May 1979.

[Dij 70] Dijkstra, E. W. *EWD249: Notes on Structured Programming*, Report 70-Wsk-03, 2nd ed. Technical University of Eindhoven, April 1970.

[Dij 72a] ———. "The Humble Programmer," *Communications of the ACM*, October 1972.

[Dij 72b] ———. "Notes on Structured Programming," in O.-J. Dahl, E. W. Dijkstra, and Hoare (eds.), *Structured Programming*. New York: Academic Press, 1972.

[Ear 70] Earley, J., and Sturgis, H. "A Formalism for Translator Interactions," *Communications of the ACM*, October 1970.

[Ell 78] Elliot, I. B. "DLP, A Design Language Preprocessor," *SIGPLAN Notices*, 1978.

[Els 76] Elshoff, J. L. "An Analysis of Some Commercial PL/1 Programs," *IEEE Transactions on Software Engineering*, June 1976.

[End 75] Endres, A. "An Analysis of Errors and Their Causes in Systems Programs," *IEEE Transactions on Software Engineering*, Vol. 1, 1975.

[Ewing 79] Ewing, D. W. *Writing for Results*, 2nd ed. New York: Wiley, 1979.

[Fagan 74] Fagan, M. E. "Design and Code Inspections and Process Control in the Development of Programs," Technical Report TR21.572. IBM, 1974. (Also extensively quoted in [Gilb 77a].) Revised version: Technical Report TR00.2763. IBM, 1976.

[Fagan 76] ———. "Design and Code Inspections to Reduce Errors in Program Development," *IBM System Journal*, Vol. 15, No. 3, 1976. (Also in [Mil 78].)

[Fer 66] Ferguson, D. E. "Evolution of the Meta-Assembly Program," *Communications of the ACM*, March 1966.

[Flo 67] Floyd, R. W. "Assigning Meaning to Programs," *Proceedings of a Symposium in Applied Mathematics*, Vol. 19: *Mathematical Aspects of Computer Science*. Providence, RI: American Mathematical Society, 1967.

[Flo 79] ———. "The Paradigms of Programming," *Communications of the ACM*, August 1979.

[Fos 80] Foster, K. A. "Error Sensitive Test Cases Analysis," *IEEE Transactions on Software Engineering*, May 1980.

[Fra 77] Franta, W. R. *The Process View of Simulation*. Amsterdam: North-Holland Publishing Company, 1977.

[Fre 79] Freeman, P. "A Perspective on Requirements Analysis and Specification," *Proceedings of IBM Design '79 Symposium*, 1979. (Also in [Fre 80b].)

[Fre 80a] ———. "The Nature of Design," in P. Freeman and A. I. Wasserman (eds.), *Software Design Techniques*, 3rd ed. (IEEE Catalog No. EHO 161-0.) Long Beach, CA: IEEE Computer Society, 1980.

[Fre 80b] ———, and Wasserman, A. I. (eds.), *Tutorial on Software Design Techniques*, 3rd ed. (IEEE Catalog No. EHO 161-0.) Long Beach, CA: IEEE Computer Society, 1980.

[Free 75] Freeman, R. D. "An Experiment in Software Development," *Bell System Technical Journal, Special Safeguard Supplement*, 1975.

[Fuj 77] Fujii, M. S. "Independent Verification of Highly Reliable Programs," *Proceedings of COMPSAC 77*. New York: IEEE Computer Society, 1977.

[Gan 79] Gane, C., and Sarson, T. *Structured Systems Analysis: Tools and Techniques*. Englewood Cliffs, NJ: Prentice-Hall, 1979.

[Gel 78] Geller, M. "Test Data as an Aid in Proving Program Correctness," *Communications of the ACM*, May 1978.

[Ger 76] Gerhart, S. L., and Yelowitz, L. "Observations of Fallibility in Applications of Modern Programming Methodologies," *IEEE Transactions on Software Engineering*, September 1976. (Also in [Mil 78] and [Ram 78].)

[Ger 79] ———. "A Discussion of a Survey of Program Testing Issues," in P. Wegner (ed.), *Research Directions in Software Technology*. Cambridge, MA: M.I.T. Press, 1979.

[Gilb 77a] Gilb. T., *Software Metrics*. Cambridge, MA: Winthrop, 1977.

[Gilb 77b] ———, and Weinberg, G. M. *Humanized Input: Techniques for Reliable Keyed Input*. Cambridge, MA: Winthrop, 1977.

[Gilb 79] ———. "Structured Design Methods for Maintainability," *Infotech State of the Art Report on Structured Software Development*, Maidenhead, England, Infotech, 1979.

[Gilb 81] ———. "Design by Objectives: A Structured Systems Architecture Approach." Unpublished manuscript, 1981.

[Gilbe 72] Gilbert, P., and Chandler, W. J., "Interference Between Communicating Parallel Processes," *Communications of the ACM*, June 1972.

[Gla 80] Glass, R. L. "Real-Time: The 'Lost World' of Software Debugging," *Communications of the ACM*, May 1980.

[Good 75] Goodenough, J. B., and Gerhart, S. L. "Toward a Theory of Test Data Selection," *Proceedings of International Conference on Software Reliability*, Los Angeles, (IEEE Catalog No. 75CH0940-7CSR.) New York: IEEE Computer Society, 1975. (Also in *IEEE Transactions on Software Engineering*, June 1975. And in [Mil 78].)

[Good 79] ———. "A Survey of Program Testing Issues," in P. Wegner (ed.), *Research Directions in Software Technology*. Cambridge, MA: M.I.T. Press, 1979.

[Goos 73] Goos, G. "Chapter 4.B Documentation," in F. L. Bauer (ed.), *Advanced Course in Software Engineering*. (Lecture Notes in Economics and Mathematical Systems No. 81.) New York: Springer-Verlag, 1973.

[Gre 78] Green, C. C., and Barstuo, D. "On Program Synthesis Knowledge," *Artificial Intelligence*, June 1978.

[Gri 72] Griswold, R. E.; Poage, J. F.; and Polonsky, I. P. *The SNOBOL4 Programming Language*. Englewood Cliffs, NJ: Prentice-Hall, 1972.

[Ham 76] Hamilton, M., and Zeldin, S. "Higher Order Software—A Methodology for Defining Software," *IEEE Transactions on Software Engineering*, Vol. SE-2, No. 1, March 1976.

[Har 73] Harper, W. L. *Data Processing Documentation: Standards, Procedures and Applications*. Englewood Cliffs, NJ: Prentice-Hall, 1973.

[Hay 78] Hayes, J. A. "User-Accessible Publications: Help Your RSTS/E User Help Himself," *Proceedings of Digital Equipment Computer Users Society (DECUS) Symposium*, Spring 1978.

[Hay 79] ———. "Program Maintenance: A Common-Sense Approach," *Proceedings of Digital Equipment Computer Users Society (DECUS) Symposium*, December 1978.

[Hei 64] Heistand, R. E. "An Executive System Implemented as a Finite-State Automaton," *Communications of the ACM*, November 1964.

[Hen 75] Henderson, P. "Finite State Modelling in Program Development, *Proceedings of International Conference on Reliable Software*, Los Angeles. (IEEE Catalog No. 75CH0940-7CSR.) New York: IEEE Computer Society, 1975.

[Het 78] Hetzel, B. "A Perspective on Software Development," *Proceedings of 3rd International Conference on Software Engineering*. (IEEE Catalog No. 78CH1317-7C.) New York: IEEE Computer Society, 1978.

[Hetz 73] Hetzel, W. C. *Program Test Methods*. Englewood Cliffs, NJ: Prentice-Hall, 1973.

[Hetz 76] ———. "An Experimental Analysis of Program Verification Methods." Ph.D. dissertation, University of North Carolina, 1976.

[Hop 69] Hopcroft, J., and Ullman, J. *Formal Languages and Their Relation to Automata*. Reading, MA: Addison-Wesley, 1969.

[Hore 78] Horejs, J. "Finite Semantics: A Technique for Program Testing," *Proceedings of 4th International Conference on Software Engineering*. New York: IEEE Computer Society, 1978.

[Horo 75] Horowitz, E. (ed.). *Practical Strategies for Developing Large Software Systems*. Reading, MA: Addison-Wesley, 1975.

[Horo 76] ———, and Sahni, S. *Fundamentals of Data Structures*. Rockville, MD: Computer Science Press, 1976.

[Horo 78] ———, and ———. *Fundamentals of Data Computer Algorithms*. Rockville, MD: Computer Science Press, 1978.

[Hos 61] Hosier, W. A. "Pitfalls and Safeguards in Real-Time Digital Systems with Emphasis on Software Management," *IRE Transactions on Engineering Management*, June 1961.

[Hosk 73] Hoskyns, John, and Company. *Implications of Using Modular Programming*, Guide No. 1. New York: Hoskyns System Research, 1973.

[How 76] Howden, W. E. "Reliability of the Path Analysis Testing Strategy," *IEEE Transactions on Software Engineering*, September 1976.

[How 78a] ———. "An Evaluation of the Effectiveness of Symbolic Testing," *Software—Practice and Experience*, 1978.

[How 78b] ———. "Functional Program Testing," in *Proceedings COMPSAC 78*. New York: IEEE Computer Society, 1978. (Also in [Ram 78]. Revised version: [How 80].)

[How 78c] ———. "A Survey of Dynamic Analysis Methods," in E. Miller and W. E. Howden (eds.), *Tutorial: Software Testing and Validation Techniques*. New York: IEEE Computer Society, 1978.

[How 78d] ———. "Theoretical and Empirical Studies of Program Testing," *Proceedings of 3rd International Conference on Software Engineering*. (IEEE Catalog No. 78CH1317-7C.) New York: IEEE Computer Society, 1978. (Also in *IEEE Transactions on Software Engineering*, July 1978.)

[How 80] ———. "Functional Program Testing," *IEEE Transactions on Software Engineering*, March 1980.

[Hug 77] Hughes, J. K., and Michtom, J. I. *A Structured Approach to Programming*. Englewood Cliffs, NJ: Prentice-Hall, 1977.

[Hugh 79] Hughes, J. W. "A Formalization and Explication of the Michael Jackson Method of Program Design," *Software—Practice and Experience*, March 1979.

[IBM 73] IBM Corporation. *Structured Walk-Throughs: A Project Management Tool*. IBM, 1973. (Also in [Berg 79].)

[IBM 75] ———. *COBOL Inspection Checklist*. IBM, 1975. (Also in [Gilb 77a, Appendix A].)

[Inf 73] Infotech. *Infotech State of the Art Report on Real-Time Systems*. Maidenhead, England: Infotech, 1973.

[Inf 78] ———. *Infotech State of the Art Report on Program Testing*. Maidenhead, England: Infotech, 1978.

[Ing 76] Inglis, J. "The True History of Unstructured Programming," *IEEE Computer*, February 1976.

[Ingr 78] Ingrassia, F. S. "Combating the 90% Syndrome," *Datamation*, January 1978.

[Int 75] *Proceedings of International Conference on Reliable Software*, Los Angeles. (IEEE Catalog No. 75CH0940-CSR.) New York: IEEE Computer Society, 1975.

[Ive 62] Iverson, K. E. *A Programming Language*. New York: Wiley, 1962.

[Jac 75] Jackson, M. A. *Principles of Program Design*. New York: Academic Press, 1975.

[Jac 76] ———. "Constructive Methods of Program Design," in K. Samuelson (ed.), *Proceedings of First Conference of the European Cooperation in Informatics: Lecture Notes in Computer Science*, Vol. 44. New York: Springer-Verlag, 1976. (Also in [Berg 79] and [Fre 80b].)

[Jac 78] ———. "Information Systems: Modelling, Sequencing and Transformations," *Proceedings of 3rd International Conference on Software Engineering*. (IEEE Catalog No. 78CH1317-7C.) New York: IEEE Computer Society, 1978. (Also in [Ram 78].)

[Jen 74] Jensen, K., and Wirth, N. *PASCAL User Manual and Report*. 2nd ed. New York: Springer-Verlag, 1974.

[Joh 68] Johnson, W. L., et al. "Automatic Generation of Efficient Lexical Processors Using Finite State Techniques," *Communications of the ACM*, December 1968.

[Kat 71] Katznelson, J. "Documentation and the Management of a Software Project—A Case Study," *Software—Practice and Experience*, April–June 1971.

[Ker 74] Kernighan, B. W., and Plauger, P. J. *The Elements of Programming Style*. New York: McGraw-Hill, 1974.

[Ker 81] ———, and ———. *Software Tools in PASCAL*. Reading, MA: Addison-Wesley, 1981.

[Kin 75] King, J. C. "A New Approach to Program Testing," *SIGPLAN Notices*, Vol. 10, 1975.

[Knu 71] Knuth, D. E. "An Empirical Study of FORTRAN Programs," *Software—Practice and Experience*, Vol. 1, 1971.

[Knu 74] ———. "Structured Programming with GOTO Statements," *ACM Computing Surveys*, Vol. 6, No. 4, December 1974.

[Knu 77] ———, and Pardo, L. T. "Early Development of Programming Languages," *Encyclopedia of Computer Science and Technology*, Vol. 7, pp. 419–493. New York: Marcel Dekker, 1977.

[Kob 74] Koberg, D., and Bagnall, J. *The Universal Traveler*. New York: Harmony Books, 1974.

[Koh 75] Kohli, O. R., and Radice, R. A. "High-Level Design Inspection Specification," Technical Report TR21.601. IBM, 1975.

[Koh 76] ———. "Low-Level Design Inspection Specification," Technical Report TR21.629. IBM, 1976.

[Kop 75] Kopetz, H. "On the Connections between Range of Variable and Control Structure Testing," *SIGPLAN Notices*, Vol. 10, 1975.

[Lam 73] Lampson, B. W. "A Note on the Confinement Problem," *Communications of the ACM*, Vol. 16, October 1973.

[Land 79] Landau, J. V. "State Description Techniques Applied to Industrial Machine Control," *Computer*, February 1979.

[Lanh 79] Lanham, R. A. *Revising Prose*. New York: Scribner, 1979.

[Lar 75] Larson, R. R. "Test Plan and Test Case Inspection Specifications," Technical Report TR21.586. IBM, 1975. (Extensively reproduced in [Gilb 77a, Appendix B].)

[Law 66] Lawler, E., and Wood, D. "Branch and Bound Methods: A Survey," *Operations Research*, July-August 1966.

[Lec 67] Lecht, C. P. *The Management of Computer Programming Projects*. New York: American Management Associations, 1967.

[Led 73] Ledgard, H. F. "The Case for Structured Programming," *Bit*, Vol. 13, 1973.

[Led 75a] ———. *Programming Proverbs*. Rochelle Park, NJ: Hayden Book Company, 1975.

[Led 75b] ———, and Marcotty, M. "A Geneology of Control Structures," *Communications of the ACM*, November 1975.

[Lig 76] Light, W. "Software Reliability/Quality Assurance Practices," *Proceedings from the Software Management Conference*. New York: AIAA, 1976.

[Lis 72] Liskov, B. H. "A Design Methodology for Reliable Software Systems," *Proceedings 1972 Fall Joint Computer Conference*, 1972. (Also in [Fre 80b].)

[Lis 75] ———, and Zilles, S. N. "Specification Techniques for Data Abstractions," *IEEE Transactions on Software Engineering*, March 1975. (Also in [Fre 80b].)

[Lon 72] London, K. R. *Decision Tables*. Philadelphia: Auerbach, 1972.

[Lon 74] ———. *Documentation Standards*, Rev. ed. New York: Petrocelli/Charter, 1974.

[Lond 71] London, R. L. "Software Reliability through Proving Programs Correct," *IEEE International Symposium on Fault-Tolerant Computing*, March 1971.

[Luc 81] Lucas, H. C., and Gibson, C. F. *A Casebook for Management Information Systems*, 2nd ed. New York: McGraw-Hill, 1981.

[McCal 77] McCall, J. A.: Richards, P.; and Walters, G. "Factors in Software Quality," 3 vols., AD-A049-014, 015, 055. Springfield, VA: NTIS, 1977.

[McCal 79] ———. "An Introduction to Software Quality Metrics," in J. D. Cooper and M. J. Fisher (eds.), *Software Quality Management*. New York: Petrocelli/ Charter, 1979.

[Meh 81] Mehlmann, M. *When People Use Computers*. Englewood Cliffs, NJ: Prentice-Hall, 1981.

[Met 77] Metzner, J. R., and Barnes, B. H. *Decision Table Languages and Systems*. New York: Academic Press, 1977.

[Met 79] ———. "A Graded Bibliography on Macro Systems and Extensible Languages," *SIGPLAN Notices*, February 1979.

[Metz 81] Metzger, P. J. *Managing a Programming Project*, 2nd ed. Englewood Cliffs, NJ: Prentice-Hall, 1981.

[Mil 78] Miller, E. F., and Howden, W. E. (eds.). *Tutorial: Software Testing and Validation Techniques*. (IEEE Catalog No. EHO 138-8.) New York: IEEE Computer Society, 1978.

[Mil 79] ———. "Some Statistics from the Software Testing Service," *Software Engineering Notes*, January 1979.

[Mill 56] Miller, G. A. "The Magical Number Seven, Plus or Minus Two: Some Limits on Our Capacity to Process Information," *Psychological Review* Vol. 63, No. 2, 1956.

[Mills 75] Mills, H. D. "How to Write Correct Programs and Know It," *Proceedings of International Conference on Reliable Software*, Los Angeles. (IEEE Catalog No. 75CH0940-7CSR.) New York: IEEE Computer Society, 1975. (Also in [Ram 78].)

[Mills 79] ———. "Software Development," in P. Wegner (ed.), *Research Directions in Software Technology*. Cambridge, MA: M.I.T. Press, 1979.

[Min 67] Minsky, M. *Computation: Finite and Infinite Machines*. Englewood Cliffs, NJ: Prentice-Hall, 1967.

[Mon 74] Montalbano, M. *Decision Tables*. Palo Alto, CA: Science Research Associates, 1974.

[Mye 75] Myers, G. J. *Reliable Software through Composite Design*. New York: Petrocelli/Charter, 1975.

[Mye 76a] ———. "Comparative Design Facilities of Six Programming Languages," *IBM Systems Journal*, 1976.

[Mye 76b] ———. *Software Reliability: Principles and Practices*. New York: Wiley-Interscience, 1976.

[Mye 78] ———. *Composite/Structural Design*. New York: Van Nostrand Reinhold, 1978.

[Mye 79] ———. *The Art of Software Testing*. New York: Wiley, 1979.

[Nan 64] Nanus, B., and Farr, L. "Some Cost Contributions to Large-Scale Programs," *Proceedings of 1964 AFIPS Spring Joint Computer Conference*, 1964.

[Nas 73] Nassi, I., and Schneiderman, B. "Flowchart Techniques for Structured Programming," *SIGPLAN Notices*, Vol. 8, No. 8, August 1973.

[Nau 60] Naur, P. (ed.). "Report on the Algorithmic Language ALGOL 60," *Communications of the ACM*, May 1960.

[Nau 63] ———. "The Design of the GEIR Algol Compiler." *BIT*, 1963.

[Nau 77] ———. "Control-Record-Driven Processing," in R. Yeh (ed.), *Current Trends in Programming Methodology*, Vol. 1. Englewood Cliffs, NJ: Prentice-Hall, 1977.

[Nau 76] ———; Randell, B.; and Buxton, J. N. (eds.). *Software Engineering Concepts and Techniques, Proceedings of the NATO Conferences*. New York: Petrocelli/Charter, 1976.

[Nem 71] Nemeth, A. G., and Rovner, P. D. "User Program Measurement in a Time-Shared Environment," *Communications of the ACM*, Vol. 14, No. 10, October 1971.

[New 61] Newell, A. *IPL-V Manual*. Englewood Cliffs, NJ: Prentice-Hall, 1961.

[Nil 71] Nilsson, N. J. *Problem Solving Methods in Artificial Intelligence*. New York: McGraw-Hill, 1971.

[Nor 70] Norden, P. V. "Useful Tools for Project Management," in M. K. Starr (ed.), *Management of Production*. Baltimore, MD: Penguin Books, 1970. (Also in [Put 77].)

[Ogdin 78] Ogdin, C. A. *Software Design for Microcomputers*. Englewood Cliffs, NJ: Prentice-Hall, 1978.

[Oli 76] Oliver, S. R., and Jones, N. D. "Program Control via Transition Matrices—A Novel Application of Microprogramming," *SIGPLAN Notices*, April 1976.

[Orr 77] Orr, K. T. *Structured Systems Development*. New York: Yourdon, 1977.

[Pad 73] Padgett, M. I. "Tree Driven Data Input and Validation," *Computer Journal*, November 1973.

[Pai 78] Paige, M. R. "Software Design for Testability," *Proceedings of the 11th Hawaii Conference on System Sciences*, 1978.

[Par 71] ———. "Information Distribution Aspects of Design Methodology." Technical Report, Dept. of Computer Science, Carnegie-Mellon University, Pittsburgh, PA, 1971. (Also in *Proceedings of IFIP Congress 1971*, Ljubljana, Yugoslavia.)

[Par 72a] ———. "A Technique for Software Module Specification with Examples," *Communications of the ACM*, May 1972.

[Par 72b] ———. "On the Criteria to Be Used in Decomposing Systems into Modules," *Communications of the ACM*, December 1972. (Also in [Ram 78] and [Fre 80b].)

[Par 72c] ———. "On the Response to Detected Errors in Hierarchically Structured Systems." Technical Report, Dept. of Computer Science, Carnegie-Mellon University, Pittsburgh, PA, 1972.

[Par 73] ———, and Price, W. R., "The Design of the Virtual Memory Aspects of a Virtual Machine," *Proceedings of ACM SIGARCH-SIGOPS Workshop on Virtual Computer Systems*, March 1973.

[Par 75a] ———. "Software Engineering or Methods for the Multi-Person Construction of Multi-Version Programs," *Proceedings of 4th Informatik Symposium: Lecture Notes in Computer Science, No. 23: Program Methodology*. New York: Springer-Verlag, 1975.

[Par 75b] ———, and Siewiorek, D. P. "Use of the Concept of Transparency in the Design of Hierarchically Structured Systems," *Communications of the ACM*, July 1975.

[Par 76a] ———. "On the Design and Development of Program Families," *IEEE Transactions on Software Engineering*, Vol. SE-2, No. 1, March 1976.

[Par 76b] ———. "State Table Analysis of Programs in an Algol-like Language," *Proceedings of ACM National Conference*, 1976.

[Par 76c] ———; Handel, G.; and Wurges, H. "Design and Specification of the Minimal Subset of an Operating System Family," *IEEE Transactions on Software Engineering*, December 1976. (An alternate version of this paper was presented at Eurocomp 76.)

[Par 77] ———. "The Use of Precise Specifications in the Development of Software," *Proceedings of the 1977 IFIP Congress*, 1977.

[Par 79] ———. "Designing Software for Ease of Extension and Contraction," *IEEE Transactions on Software Engineering*, March 1979. (Also in [Ram 78] and in [Fre 80b].)

[Pat 80] Patrick, R. L. *Application Design Handbook for Distributed Systems*. Boston: CBI Publishing Co., 1980.

[Pet 76] Peters, L. J., and Tripp, L. L. "Software Design Representation Schemes," *Proceedings of MRI Symposium on Software Engineering*, 1976.

[Pet 77] ———, and ———. "Comparing Software Design Methodologies," *Datamation*, November 1977. (Also in [Berg 79].)

[Phi 67] Phillips, C. S. E. "Networks for Real Time Programming," *Computer Journal*, May 1967.

[Phi 71] ———. "Software Engineering, The Key to Expansion of Real Time Systems," in *Infotech State of the Art Report 3: Real Time*. Maidenhead, England: Infotech, 1971.

[Pie 70] Pietrasanta, A. M. "Resource Analysis of Computer Program System Development," in G. F. Weinwurm (ed.), *On the Management of Computer Programming*. Philadelphia: Auerbach, 1970.

[Pol 75] Polivka, R., and Pakin, S., *APL: The Language and Its Usage*. Englewood Cliffs, NJ: Prentice-Hall, 1975.

[Polya 54a] Polya, G. *Induction and Analogy in Mathematics*. Princeton, NJ: Princeton University Press, 1954.

[Polya 54b] ———. *Patterns of Plausible Inference*. Princeton, NJ: Princeton University Press, 1954.

[Polya 57] ———. *How to Solve It*. Garden City, NY: Doubleday Anchor Books, 1957.

[Pool 73] Poole, P. C. "Debugging and Testing," in F. L. Bauer (ed.), *Advanced Course on Software Engineering; Lecture Notes in Economics and Mathematical Systems*, Vol. 81.) New York: Springer-Verlag, 1973.

[Put 77] Putnam, L. H., and Wolverton, R. W. *Quantitative Management: Software Estimating* (tutorial). New York: IEEE Computer Society, 1977.

[Rai 73] Rain, M. "Two Unusual Methods for Debugging System Software," *Software—Practice and Experience*, Vol. 3, 1973.

[Ram 76] Ramamoorthy, C. V.; Ho, S. F.; and Chen, W. T. "On the Automated Generation of Program Test Data," *IEEE Transactions on Software Engineering*, December 1976.

[Ram 78] ———, and Yeh, R. T. (eds.). *Tutorial: Software Methodology*. (IEEE Catalog No. EHO 142-0.) New York: IEEE Computer Society, 1978.

[Rath 62] Rathbone, R. R., and Stone, J. B. *A Writer's Guide for Engineers and Scientists*. Englewood Cliffs, NJ: Prentice-Hall, 1962.

[Ros 75] Ross, D. T.; Goodenough, J. B.; and Irvine, C. A. "Software Engineering; Process, Principles, and Goals," *Computer*, May 1975. (Also in [Fre 80b].)

[Ros 77a] ———. "Structured Analysis (SA): A Language for Communicating Ideas," *IEEE Transactions on Software Engineering*, January 1977. (Also in [Berg 79] and in [Fre 80b].)

[Ros 77b] ———, and Schoman, K. E. "Structured Analysis for Requirements Definition," *IEEE Transactions on Software Engineering*, January 1977. (Also in [Fre 80b].)

[Sal 76] Salter, K. G. "A Methodology for Decomposing System Requirements into Data Processing Requirements," *Proceedings of 2nd International Conference on Software Engineering*, 1976. (Also in [Fre 80b].)

[Sam 69] Sammett, J. *Programming Languages: History and Fundamentals*. Englewood Cliffs, NJ: Prentice-Hall, 1969.

[Sam 78] ———. "Roster of Programming Languages for 1976–1977," *SIGPLAN Notices*, November 1978.

[Schn 76] Schneiderman, B. "A Review of Design Techniques for Programs and Data," *Software—Practice and Experience*, Vol. 6, 1976.

[Schu 62] Schultz, H., and Webster, R. G. *Technical Report Writing, A Manual and Source Book*. New York: McKay, 1962.

[Schw 75] Schwartz, J. I. "Construction of Software: Problems and Practicalities," in E. Horowitz (ed.), *Practical Strategies for Developing Large Software Systems*. Reading, MA: Addison-Wesley, 1975.

[Sho 75] Shooman, M. L., and Bolsky, M. I. "Types, Distribution, and Test and Correction Times for Programming Errors," *Proceedings of International Conference on Reliable Software*, Los Angeles. (IEEE Catalog No. 75CH0940-7CSR.) New York: IEEE Computer Society, 1975.

[Sim 74] Simon, H. A. "How Big Is a Chunk?" *Science* Vol. 183, No. 8, 1974.

[Smi 81] Smith, P. D., and Steen, S. Y. "A Prototype Crossword Compiler," *Computer Journal*, Vol. 24, No. 2, 1981.

[Som 79] Somerville, I. "S-SNOBOL—Structured SNOBOL," *SIGPLAN Notices*, February 1979.

[Ste 74] Stevens, W. P.; Meyers, G. J.; and Constantine, L. L. "Structured Design," *IBM Systems Journal*, 1974. (Also in [Ram 78], [Berg 79], and [Fre 80b].)

[Ste 75] ———; ———; and ———. *Structural Design*. New York: Yourdon, 1975.

[Sti 75] Stillman, R. B. "FORTRAN Analysis by Simple Transforms," *Proceedings of the Computer Science and Statistics 8th Annual Conference on the Interface*, University of California at Los Angeles, 1975.

[Str 79] Strunk, W., and White, E. B. *The Elements of Style*, 3rd ed. New York: Macmillan, 1979.

[Tan 76] Tanenbaum, A. S. "In Defense of Program Testing, or Correctness Proofs Considered Harmful," *SIGPLAN Notices*, May 1976.

[Tas 74] Tassel, D. Van. *Program Style, Design, Efficiency, Debugging and Testing*. Englewood Cliffs, NJ: Prentice-Hall, 1974.

[Tha 76] Thayer, T. A.; Lipow, M.; and Nelson, E. C. *Software Reliability Study*, TRW Software Series, TRW-SS-76-03, TRW, 1976.

[Tur 80] Turner, J. "The Structure of Modular Programs," *Communications of the ACM*, May 1980.

[Wald 74] Waldstein, N. S. "The Walk-Thru—A Method of Specification, Design and Review," Technical Report TR00.2536. IBM, 1974.

[Wals 69] Walsh, D. *A Guide for Software Documentation*. Boston: Inter-Act, 1969.

[Walt 79] Walters, Gene F. "Application of Metrics to a Software Quality Mangement Program," in J. D. Cooper and M. J. Fisher (eds.), *Software Quality Management*. New York: Petrocelli/Charter: 1979.

[War 76] Warnier, J. D. *Logical Construction of Programs*. New York: Van Nostrand Reinhold, 1976.

[War 78] ———. *Program Modification*. Leiden and London: Martinus Nijhoff, 1978.

[Weg 79] Wegner, P. (ed.). *Research Directions in Software Technology*. Cambridge, MA: M.I.T. Press, 1979.

[Weinb 71] Weinberg, G. M. *The Psychology of Computer Programming*. New York: Van Nostrand Reinhold, 1971.

[Weinb 73] ———; Yasukawa, N.; and Marcus, R. *Structured Programming in PL/C; An Abecedarian*. New York: Wiley, 1973.

[Weinb 74] ———, and Schulman, E. L. "Goals and Performance in Computer Programming," *Human Factors*, Vol. 16, No. 1, 1974.

[Weinw 65] Weinwurm, G. F. "Research in the Management of Computer Programming," Report SP-2059. Santa Monica, CA: System Development Corp., 1965.

[Weinw 70] ——— (ed.). *On the Management of Computer Programming*. Philadelphia: Auerbach, 1970.

[Weis 67] Weissman, C. *LISP 1.5 Primer*. Encino, CA: Dickenson, 1967.

[Weiz 76] Weizenbaum, J. *Computer Power and Human Reason*. San Francisco: Freeman, 1976.

[Wet 78] Wetherell, C. *Etudes for Programmers*. Englewood Cliffs, NJ: Prentice-Hall, 1978.

[Wex 78] Wexelblat, R. L. (ed.). *Preprints of ACM SIGPLN History of Programming Languages Conference*, Los Angeles, 1978, in *SIGPLAN Notices*, August 1978.

[Wey 80] Weyuker, E. J., and Ostrand, T. J. "Theories of Program Testing and the Application of Revealing Subdomains," *IEEE Transactions on Software Engineering*, May 1980.

[Wies 77] Wiest, J. P., and Levy, F. K. *A Management Guide to PERT/CPM*, 2nd ed. Englewood Cliffs, NJ: Prentice-Hall, 1977.

[Wilk 77] Wilkens, E. J. "Finite State Techniques in Software Engineering," *Proceedings of COMPSAC*, November 1977.

[Will 48] Williams, G. E. *Technical Literature*. London: Allen, 1948.

[Willi 75] Williams, R. D. "Managing the Development of Reliable Software," *Proceedings of International Conference on Reliable Software*, Los Angeles. (IEEE Catalog No. 75CH094-7CSR.) New York: IEEE Computer Society, 1975.

[Wir 71] Wirth, N. "Program Development by Stepwise Refinement," *Communications of the ACM*, April 1971. (Also in [Fre 80b].)

[Wol 74] Wolverton, R. W. "The Cost of Developing Large-Scale Software," *IEEE Transactions on Computers*, June 1974. (Also in [Put 77].)

[Wol 75] ———. "The Cost of Developing Large-Scale Software," in E. Horowitz (ed.), *Practical Strategies for Developing Large Software Systems*. Reading, MA: Addison-Wesley, 1975.

[Wul 71] Wulf, W. S.; Russell, D. B.; and Habermann, A. N. "BLISS: A Language for Systems Programming," *Communications of the ACM*, December 1971.

[You 75a] Yourdon, E. *Techniques of Program Structure and Design*. Englewood Cliffs, NJ: Prentice-Hall, 1975.

[You 75b] ———, and Constantine, L. L. *Structured Design*. New York: Yourdon, 1975. (Republished 1979 by Prentice-Hall.)

[You 79a] ———. *Managing the Structured Techniques*. New York: Yourdon, 1979.

[You 79b] ———. "Top-Down Design and Testing," in G. D. Bergland and R. D. Gordon (eds.), *Tutorial: Software Design Strategies*. New York: IEEE Computer Society, 1979.

appendix c
System Problems

C.1 INTRODUCTION

Each problem in this appendix requires you to put together all of the methods in this book. Each problem can be solved by a microcomputer-based system. No program specifications or requirements are specifically stated. Instead, an overall user need is indicated, and pertinent details of the user's quandary are given.

The complete solution of one of these problems requires the following sequence of steps; a project can include as many steps in sequence as desired.

C.1.1 Solution Steps

1. The user's requirement is understood.
   (a) Requirements diagrams are drawn as necessary.
   (b) Necessary data flow components are defined, and a data dictionary is constructed, as necessary.
   (c) Each activity of the requirements diagrams is precisely specified.
   (d) The intended use of the system, both present and future, is carefully considered.
   (e) Where the programming of different subsets of the required activities would entail substantially different costs and benefits, a cost and benefit estimate is made for each alternative.
   (f) A MECCA quality evaluation model is determined to indicate important qualities and their priorities.
   (g) A requirements document is produced, consisting of items a, b, c, and f for the alternative chosen. This document constitutes the agreement between customer and developer about the required activities and data and the customer's scheme for evaluating qualities of proposed solutions.
2. A program specification is determined, which includes:
   (a) User interfaces.
   (b) Inputs and outputs.
   (c) Processes performed.
   (d) Performance boundaries: time, space, money.

(e) A specification document is produced, containing items a, b, c, and d and also the quality evaluation scheme (item 1f). This document constitutes the agreement between customer and developer as to both the functions and the qualities of the desired program.

3. A plan is developed for acceptance testing of the specified system. This includes:
    (a) Overall sequence of tests.
    (b) Specifications for each test.
    (c) Criteria for evaluating the success or failure of each test.
    (d) Measurement of specified qualities of the system.
    (e) Criteria for evaluating the degree of conformance to specifications.
    This step can be done in parallel with steps 4, 5, and 6.

4. A design proposal is derived, containing the following items:
    (a) Major data blocks.
    (b) Major processes.
    (c) Major control flow.
    (d) Critical algorithms.
    (e) Walkthrough of the design.
    (f) Correlation of design features with requirements and specifications.
    (g) Evaluation of the solution using the MECCA quality evaluation model of 1f.

5. A project schedule is developed, which includes:
    (a) Milestones and dates.
    (b) Scheduling of personnel.
    (c) Scheduling of computer resources.

6. The organization of program modules is designed.
    (a) The organization should allow either the development of a minimal system that provides the smallest useful subset of specified functions or the development of a maximal system that provides the largest set of specified functions. Then modules can be dropped to cut the system down or added to provide more capability without redesign of the system.
    (b) A schedule for test and delivery of the modules is determined, based on the incremental development and delivery strategy.

7. Modules are developed.

8. The system is implemented and tested.

C.2 PROBLEMS

---

1. Report Formatter
   Your company's new software system, which is to be sold to small businesses, produces various reports. It would greatly enhance sales if these

reports could be customized for each purchaser. Unfortunately, writing customized output programs for each purchaser would cut deeply into the expected profits, and the purchasers do not employ programmers who could write the programs.

You have been asked to design, build, and document a report formatter program that can be easily used by an nonprogrammer. The nonprogrammer user should be able to compose a report format, including titles and data fields, using a cathode-ray screen, and the formatter program should then automatically be able to output the report with the desired format.

2. Input Editor

Your company's new software system is competing with several systems that have been in the field for several years. Each of the competing systems offers data entry via a terminal using a cathode ray screen with preformatted entries, so that the data-entry person only needs to fill in the form shown by the screen. Market research shows that each customer has grown accustomed to the data-entry format currently in use. Unfortunately, each of the competing systems uses a different format and different terminology.

Although it would like to customize data entry for each customer, your company does not wish to write a separate data-entry program for each customer. You have been asked to design, build, and document an automatic input editor that can be easily used by any nonprogrammer. The nonprogrammer user should be able to compose a data-entry format on the cathode-ray screen, and then the automatic input editor should be able to accept input data in accordance with that format. Your program should include standard kinds of validity checks, as, for example, that there are only 12 months in a year, or that February has only 28 days.

3. Design Language Processing

In documenting or explaining the stepwise refinement of a design, it is most convenient to use free-form text, for example,

print pages
process until no more cards

to initially describe a subprogram and then at further levels of detail to refine the statement of the subprogram. (This is the method used in Section 7.2.)

Several authors have reported on *design languages* that consist of free-form text in conjunction with structured programming reserved words such as if, then, else, while, and so on [Cai 75, Ell 78]. A design written in such a language can be read by a *design-language documenter* to produce a document that contains

· Indentation to indicate nesting
· Underlined key words

· Table of contents
· Index of program segments
· Summary of program segment nesting
· Cross-referencing to indicate where in the document a further refinement
  is located

Caine and Gordon [Cai 75] report that the use of such a design language and processor has been very successful.

Elliot [Ell 78] reports on a processor that produces a program in a standard programming language (e.g., PASCAL) from a design-language program. In Elliot's design language, enclosure of any text within brackets [ ] signifies that the text is a subprogram name. For example, the text

[INTERCHANGE PERM(J) AND PERM(K)]

explains the program process at a high level and also indicates that this text is a subprogram name. Later, the text

```
DEFN [INTERCHANGE PERM(J) AND PERM(K)]
  TEMP=PERM(J); PERM(J)=PERM(K); PERM(K)=TEMP
ENDDEFN
```

refines the subprogram. In general, the text of the refinement of any subprogram may include further bracketed text, indicating further subprograms to be refined. Elliot's system essentially allows specification and expansion of one-line macros with no arguments.

You have been asked to provide a design language and the program production features mentioned above. Specifically:

(a) Provide a design language that allows both documentation and automatic program production.
(b) Design a documenter system.
(c) Design a program producer system.

4. Court Reporters

Ms. Alison Court is head of a group of stenographers who produce transcriptions of court testimony, depositions of witnesses, and the like. She wants to automate their procedure so that the company will remain competitive while coping with inflation and continuing to pay the employees well.

The current procedure is entirely manual. As the testimony proceeds, the stenographer "types" or "keys" it into a small machine called a stenotype machine (see Figure C.1), which produces a long paper type about 2 inches wide with uppercase alphabetic characters across it. The stenographer's method of recording combines phonetic and shorthand principles.

Although all stenographers use basically the same principles in recording, each in time develops his or her own style and set of abbreviations, so

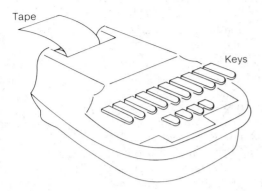

Tape

Keys

Figure C.1 A stenotype machine.

that no stenographer can read another's tape record, even though the characters are printed. Moreover, there have been two schools of stenotyping, one of which distinguishes between long and short vowels while the other does not. Lastly, as the testimony proceeds, the stenographer makes up a set of abbreviations and conventions for the names and terms commonly used in the testimony at hand. For example, in a computer case, the stenographer might devise an abbreviation for microcomputer.

An ordinary day produces five to six hours of testimony. As soon as possible after the session is over, the stenographer reads through the entire stenotype tape and dictates a voice tape, relying on memory to resolve any conflicts or ambiguities in the stenotyped tape. Dictating the voice tape takes about as much time as the original testimony, five to six hours.

A typist then produces the transcript, from the voice tape, according to a prescribed format. For example, there are always 28 lines of text per page (lines deliberately left blank must be specially marked) and certain points in the testimony (such as the beginning of a question or answer) require a new paragraph. Within this format, it is important that the text lines contain as many words as possible. The lawyer clients pay so much per line, and they become angry when they see four lines used where three would have held all the words. The typist usually needs about eight hours to type a six-hour testimony.

When the typing is completed, the stenographer proofreads the transcript, taking two to three hours. The typist then corrects any errors, and the transcript (now finished) is put into a binder.

In all, producing the transcript of a six-hour session requires about eight hours of typing and an extra eight to nine hours of the stenographer's time. Until the final transcript is complete, the stenographer cannot go to another testimony session lest he or she forget details of the previous session. Usually a possible day of work is lost while a transcript is being typed.

Ms. Court thinks that there has to be a better way than transcribing everything three times—stenotyping, then a voice tape, then typing. Since the stenotyping uses a machine with keys, it ought to be easy to attach some other recording device to the stenotype machine to produce a computer-readable transcription. That is, it is desirable to have a system that automatically translates from the stenotyped record directly to a typed record. Of course, such a program would have to take into account each stenographer's personal set of abbreviations, and maybe it could even deal with the abbreviations developed for each specific job. Since the system could not be perfect and since stenographers make mistakes, there would always be conflicts and ambiguities in the translation, but perhaps there could be some easy way to resolve them. What would you suggest?

REFERENCES

[Cai 75] Caine, S. H., and Gordon, E. K. "PDL—A Tool for Software Design," *Proceedings of National Computer Conference*, 1975. (Also in [Fre 80b].)*

[Ell 78] Elliott, I. B. "DLP, A Design Language Preprocessor," *SIGPLAN Notices*, 1978.

---

*See Appendix B: Bibliography.

appendix d
Design Problems

The problems in Appendix D can be used with any chapter of this book and thus provide a design experience that unifies the material. Any of these problems can serve as the subject of a specification analysis (Chapter 2), as the subject of a design proposal (Chapter 3), and as an exercise in structured programming or modularization. Of course, some problems are best used as structured programming examples, some as subjects for specification analysis, some as examples of critical problems and their solutions, and so on.

These problems vary greatly in complexity, though all of them are either larger or more complex than problems in the various chapters. They are sharply defined yet free of large amounts of detail in order to present the essential design issues while avoiding distraction. For this reason many of the problems deal with puzzles or games.

Design problems may be obtained from many other sources. In particular, Yourdon [You 75a] suggests four programming problems that can be used for design proposals, specification analyses, and so on, and also discusses the various design and implementation issues of the problems. (See references at the end of this appendix.)

PROBLEMS

1. Matrix Magic

   The procedure MM (NAME,ROWS,COLUMNS) is used to examine two-dimensional arrays of integer values. In the arguments given to MM, NAME is the name of the array to be examined, ROWS is the number of rows this array has, and COLUMNS is the number of columns. Each time MM is called, it searches the array for array elements whose *values are maximum in their rows but minimum in their columns*.

   More precisely, MM considers arrays of dimension $m \times n$, where $1 \le m \le N$ and $1 \le n \le N$. MM searches NAME for each array value, say, in row I and column J, such that

   NAME[I,J]$\ge$NAME[I,j] for all j=1,2, . . . ,COLUMNS *and*
   NAME[I,J]$\le$NAME[i,J] for all i=1,2, . . . ,ROWS

   For every such value found, MM prints a message

   'ROW' I   'COLUMN' J   'VALUE' NAME[I,J]

However, if no such values are found in the array, MM prints

'NO MAXMIN VALUES FOUND'

2. Text Twiddling
   Given a text consisting of words separated by BLANK characters or by
   NL (new line) characters, convert it to a line-by-line form in accordance
   with the following rules:
   (a) Line breaks must be made only where the given text has BLANK or
   NL.
   (b) Each line is filled as far as possible [see (c)].
   (c) No line will contain more than MAXPOS characters.

3. A Simple Sort
   A procedure SORT (TABLE,SIZE) is desired. TABLE is the name of a
   one-dimensional array that will be sorted by the procedure, and SIZE is
   the number of elements in the array.
   The sort is to be done via a sequence of sort passes. Within each sort
   pass, pairs of elements are compared (element 1 is compared to element 2,
   then element 2 is compared to element 3, etc.); and if element i and
   element (i+1) are not in correct order, they are interchanged. The sequence of sort passes ends when, during an entire sort pass, no two
   elements are interchanged.

4. Secret Sums
   A puzzle

   > SEND
   > +MORE
   > ――――
   > MONEY

   is solved by finding a distinct numeric digit d that corresponds with each
   distinct letter L (i.e., no two distinct letters are assigned the same digit) so
   that when these corresponding digits are substituted throughout the puzzle for their letters, the puzzle becomes a correct arithmetic addition
   problem.
   Write a program that processes a sequence of cards, each card containing a puzzle like the one above, in "free format." For example, some
   possible puzzles are:

   AA=AA
   SEND+MORE=MONEY
   ONE+TWO+FOUR=SEVEN
   HE+CAN+NOT+STAND=NOISE
   ADAM+AND+EVE+ON+A=RAFT

Each card is to be printed out and then checked for errors; if an error exists, an error message is to be given. Otherwise, the program is to find every set of corresponding digits that solves the puzzle. For each set of corresponding digits that solves the puzzle, an output such as

CORRESPONDENCES ARE
LETTER   A   C
DIGIT   5   8 . . .

and so on, is to be given. If no set of corresponding digits solves the puzzle, output

NO SOLUTIONS EXIST

is to be given.

5. Training Tourists
To improve its service to tourists, the Rolling Railway Company is going to automate its customer information service by using computerized information terminals. This is believed to be necessary because there are more than 120 stations spread over the country and travel from one station to another may involve one or more changes of trains. Also, in general, there is more than one way to get from any station to any other station, either by different routes or by different combinations of express and local trains.

At an information terminal, a customer will type in departure (initial) station S_I and destination (final) station S_F, and the terminal should print within 30 seconds the schedule of train connections for which the total elapsed time of the journey from S_I to S_F is minimum.

Your solution should be usable for various transit systems such as Amtrak, or the Los Angeles bus system, or the New York City subway system. Also, it should easily accommodate temporary changes of schedule such as special holiday trains, trains canceled due to breakdowns, and so on.

6. Moscow Mayhem
The Moscow Puzzles, by Boris A. Kordemsky (Gretna, LA: Pelican, 1975), is a famous collection of puzzles. In this collection, Problem 110, Knight's Move, reads as follows: "To solve this problem you need not be a chess player. You need only know the way a knight moves on the chessboard: two squares in one direction and one square at right angles to the first direction. The diagram (Figure D.1) shows 16 black pawns on a board. Can a knight capture all 16 pawns in 16 moves?"

Being lazy, we naturally wish to use a computer to solve such a problem. Accordingly, a program is desired that receives as input
· An initial position P_K of a knight on the chessboard

- Positions $P_1, P_2, \ldots, P_M$ of M pawns on the board
- An integer N

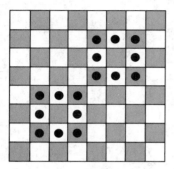

Figure D.1   Chessboard positions of 16 pawns. (Copyright 1972 by Charles Scribner's Sons. Reprinted by permission.)

The program answers the question, Can a knight starting in position P_K capture all M pawns in N or less moves? The program's output is

'NOT POSSIBLE'	if the pawns cannot all be captured
'YES, SEQUENCE IS'	if the M pawns can all be captured by
(followed by any sequence of moves	the knight in N or less moves
of "shortest length" in which all	
pawns are captured)	

Recall that a knight in making one move moves two squares along a row or column, and one square along a column or row.

Ignoring the color of the squares, and assuming the knight is in the center of the board, Figure D.2 shows a * in every square that a knight can move to, from the square marked K, in one move.

Obviously a square may never be initially occupied by two or more pawns, or by a knight and a pawn; thereafter, the knight captures a pawn by moving to the pawn's position.

7. Simple Solitaire

In this simple solitaire card game, played with a 52-card poker deck, the entire card deck is held in the right hand, face up so that the face (showing

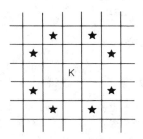

Figure D.2 Possible knight moves from center of chessboard.

rank and suit) of the top card is visible. Next, the cards are successively moved from the right hand to the left hand (keeping their position in the deck) and examined. In other words, the top card is moved and examined, then the card next to the top, then the one beneath that, and so on.

As the cards are being moved from one hand to another, the player is allowed to drop cards to the table, as follows:

(a) If two consecutive cards have the same rank, the two cards may be dropped to the table. For example, if the seven of spades and the seven of clubs occur consecutively, both of these cards may be dropped.

(b) If in a sequence of four consecutive cards, the first and fourth cards have the same suit, then the middle two cards (i.e., the second and third cards) can be dropped. For example, using the notation (rank,suit) to denote a card, if the four cards are

   (3,D)(6,S)(2,H)(7,D)

then the cards (6,S) and (2,H) can be dropped.

(c) After a drop, the cards being moved may be reexamined as if the dropped cards had never been in the sequence. As a result, further drops may be possible in accordance with rules a and b. For example, in the sequence

   (4,H)(6,C)(6,D)(4,S)

the cards (6,C) and (6,D) may be dropped in accordance with rule a. When the cards being moved are reexamined, after this drop, the sequence

   (4,H)(4,S)

now appears, and these cards may now also be dropped.

The game is won if all of the cards being moved can be dropped on the table in accordance with rules a, b, and c, so that no cards remain in the hands.

Notice that the order of the drops may influence the game's outcome. For the sequence

(3,D)(3,C)(7,H)(7,D)

the first two cards could be dropped and then the next two, or, alternatively, the middle two could be dropped. Depending on the surrounding cards, either alternative might be more advantageous.

Write a program that plays this solitaire game and always chooses a sequence of drops that results in the fewest number of cards being left in the hands. In particular, if there is a way that the game can be won, then the program must always find it. The output of the program is to be (assuming an output printer with at least 52 columns):

(1) Two lines showing the initial state of the card deck, top card in column 1, next-to-top card in column 2, . . . , bottom card in column 52. The first line is card rank and the second line is card suit. For example, the line

```
6 7 7 . . . K
S D C     S
```

shows the top card (6,S), next-to-top card (7,D), and so on to the bottom card (K,S).

In addition, the location of the first cards to be dropped is underlined. The line above shows that the cards (7,D) and (7,C) are to be dropped first.

(2) The next two lines show the state of the card deck after the first drop and indicate the loction of the second drop.

(3) In the same way, each further two lines indicates the state of the card deck after a drop and shows the location of the next drop.

(4) The final output line is to be

END OF GAME--n CARDS REMAINING

where n is the number of cards left in the card deck when no more drops can be made.

8. Matchmakers

In a certain village, which still follows its old traditional ways, marriages of young folks are arranged by matchmakers; and each spring there is a mass marriage ceremony. Naturally, the matchmakers receive a fee for each marriage—but if the marriage breaks up in the first year, they must pay a penalty equal to double the fee.

Being very canny, the matchmakers have noticed that all of the marriages that break up within a year do so because one of the partners prefers someone else to his/her spouse—and that "someone else" prefers the partner to her/his spouse. For example, a wife might prefer "another man" to her husband, and, at the same time, the "other man" prefers the wife to his own wife. When that situation occurs, the man and woman preferring each other leave their spouses and go live together—and the matchmakers pay through the nose.

This year, the matchmakers are going to be very scientific. First, they have restricted their attention to a particular group of men and a particular group of women, with equal numbers in each group. Next, they have asked each man to rank the women in the order he prefers them, and they have asked the women to rank the men in the same way. Knowing exactly all the preferences, they want to arrange the largest possible number of marriages, avoiding all breakup penalties by deferring (only as necessary) to the preferences of the young people.

Thus they want a computer program that, given the information about the young people's preferences, will print all of the longest lists of arrangements containing only marriages that are sure not to break up.

9. **The Eight Queens**
A program is desired that places eight queens on a chessboard, in such a way that no queen can capture any other queen.

10. **Shaper**
Write a program that uses the Cooper technique of Section 7.3 to convert any "ordinary" FORTRAN program into structured program form.

11. **The Dean's Disciple**
The Schedule of Classes for each semester is printed long before the semester starts. In the schedule, rooms are assigned to classes on the basis of anticipated enrollment. The actual enrollment almost always differs from the anticipated enrollment, and thus at the close of registration at the beginning of each new semester, several types of situations always occur:

· Some classes, having few or no students, are *canceled* by the dean.

· Some classes have a smaller enrollment than anticipated.

· Some classes have too many students for one instructor to teach. These are *split* by the dean into two concurrent sections, with the new section having a different section number. (Each class section is assigned a unique number, called a *section number*, for identification purposes.) Usually, half the students in the oversize class are transferred to the new section.

· Some classes have a larger enrollment than anticipated, so that the *actual class size exceeds the capacity of the assigned room.*

In the days remaining between registration and the beginning of classes, new rooms must be assigned to classes, subject to the restrictions:

(a) The number of students in a class may not exceed the capacity of the room finally assigned to the class.

(b) Classes may be assigned only to rooms specifically designated for use by the School of Engineering and Computer Science. (Such rooms are called *assignable rooms*.) The set of assignable rooms may change from semester to semester.

(c) The time and day of a class may not be changed.

(d) Lecture classes may not be assigned to laboratory rooms, and vice versa.

The associate dean makes these room adjustments. She has a primary goal:

(e) To maximize the number N of classes that finally have rooms assigned to them;

and a subsidiary goal:

(f) Provided that N is maximized, maximize the number of students in the classes having assigned rooms.

In other words, her goal is to accommodate as many students as possible, subject to the limitations of restrictions a, b, c, and d. If it is at all possible to assign rooms for all classes within these restrictions, she does so, no matter how many room changes are necessary. Notice that a class whose size exceeds the room capacity must be moved. Such a class may be assigned to a "free" room, if one is available; if no free room is available, rooms are switched between classes. Moreover, a class B displaced by an oversize class A may be too large to fit into class A's old room; in this case, class B may be placed in, say, class C's room, and another room has to be found for class C. Class C in turn may be too large to fit into class B's old room; and so on.

One possible way of making the room adjustments is to cancel all room assignments and then reassign rooms for all classes. However, this method results in almost all classes having room changes, and thus causes chaos on the first day of classes, as all the students try to find their new classrooms. Accordingly, the associate dean has adopted a third goal:

(g) Subject to the limitations imposed by goals e and f, as few changes as possible are made to the previous room assignments that appear in the Schedule of Classes.

It is now desired to have a program that, given all the necessary information (including the decisions about split and canceled classes that the dean has already made), will calculate a list of new room assignments, in accordance with goals e, f, and g. Inputs to the program will be:

(1) Old list of class assignments. This includes, for each class in the Schedule of Classes, the schedule print line for that class and the actual enrollment obtained in registration. A special category descriptor may also be given to designate a special class type (e.g., L for lab). (The class is a lecture type if no descriptor is given.)

(2) List of section numbers of canceled classes.

(3) List of pairs of section numbers, each pair indicating the section to be split and the section number of the new section.

(4) List of all rooms to which classes may be assigned. For each room, a seating capacity and possibly a special category descriptor (e.g., L for lab) are given. (The room is the lecture type if no descriptor is given.)

Note: The set of assignable rooms will usually *not* include all rooms in the engineering building and may include rooms in other buildings. Also, this set of rooms might change between runs of the program. Assignable rooms are available to the school at all class hours.

The output of the program will be:

(5) A new list of class assignments, containing a room listing for each class that, in the "adjusted" schedule, has a room.

(6) A set of usage schedules, showing the classes appearing in each assignable room, by day and time period.

(7) A free-room schedule, showing for each day and time period the rooms that are "free" (that have no class at that time).

(8) Either a message 'ALL CLASSES ASSIGNED' or a nonassignable schedule, showing for each day and time period, the classes that cannot be assigned rooms.

Lastly, it is desired that this program be capable of making the room assignments, given the original Schedule of Classes with no rooms assigned.

12. A Postal Problem

A version of this problem was first posed by Lewis Carroll.

Her Majesty's Post Office issues postal money orders, for which the purchaser pays a fee. For example, a fee of 25 pence is paid for a money order of £10. If the person receiving a postal money order does not cash it promptly, the post office imposes a late charge.

According to the *Post Office Guide*, a postal money order becomes overdue after the expiration of three months from the last day of the month of issue. When the money order is overdue, the post office imposes a late charge equal to the original fee. In addition, an additional late charge equal to the original fee is imposed for every three-month period that has elapsed since the postal money order became overdue. Finally, if at least one complete three-month period has elapsed since the money order became overdue, and if a portion of a three-month period has elapsed, then a final late charge equal to the original fee is imposed.

A program is desired that, given the date of purchase of a postal money order, the original fee, and the date on which the money order is cashed, calculates the late charge imposed by the post office.

13. Crosstics

A variant of this problem appears in Wetherell's *Etudes for Programmers* [Wet 78, p.30].

A crosstics puzzle consists of a list of words together with a diagram into which the words are placed. The diagram is a crossword-puzzle diagram without numbers in the squares, and the problem is to find the right placement of the given words. (There is always just one solution that uses all the given words.) As in a crossword puzzle, any two words that intersect must have a letter in common. A sample crosstics puzzle is shown in Figure D.3(a).

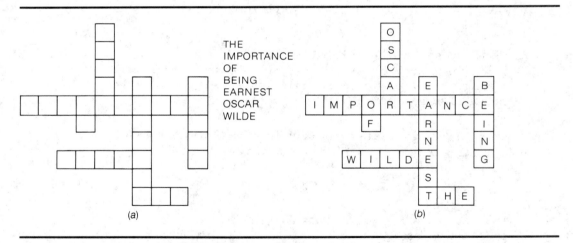

(a)   (b)

Figure D.3 A crosstics puzzle (a) and its solution (b).

As any crossword-puzzle enthusiast knows, all words in a puzzle must have at least two characters. In addition, a crosstics puzzle is *well formed* if:

(a) The diagram forms one connected unit, that is, the words intersect so that there is a "path" from any word to any other word.

(b) The set of words S′ obtained by reading, from the diagram, all sequences of two characters or more (reading from top to bottom or from left to right) is identical to the set of words S given in the input word list.

(c) There is only one way in which the given words can be placed in the given diagram, that is, the placement of the given words in the given diagram is unique.

A program is desired that, given any list of words, constructs a crosstics diagram for that list. The program should output the list of words, the crosstics diagram, and the diagram with the solution filled in. If for the given list there is no crosstics diagram that meets condition a, the program should print 'NO CONNECTED PUZZLE POSSIBLE.' If for the given list, there is no diagram such that condition c is met, the program should print 'NO UNIQUE PUZZLE POSSIBLE'.

Figure D.4 shows two puzzles that can be produced for the same list of input words. In Figure D.4(*a*), squares inside the diagram that cannot be filled are shown in black. Puzzle (*b*) is more interesting than puzzle (*a*) because it is more compact. For example, puzzle (*b*) uses a total of 19 squares while puzzle (*a*) uses 34, including the black squares, and puzzle (*b*) can be enclosed in a rectangle of 6×7=42 squares while puzzle (*a*) requires a surrounding rectangle of 7×10=70 squares.

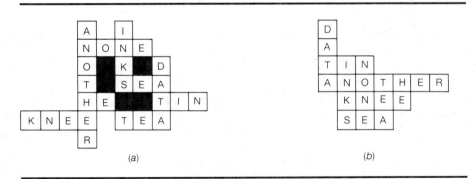

(a) (b)

Figure D.4 Two puzzles for the list {ANOTHER,DATA, HE,INKS,KNEE,NONE,SEA,TEA,TIN}.

The program should construct a puzzle that is as compact as possible and yet is well formed. As suggested above, compactness may be measured in a number of ways, such as the average number of intersections per word (or per character), or the ratio of area of the diagram to the area of the smallest surrounding rectangle.

A similar problem can be found in Smith and Steen [Smi 81].

14. Map Coloring

This problem is by Paul Abrahams [Abr 79]. (Adapted by permission.)

For this problem, a map is formed on an (x,y) grid by a set of line segments. Each line segment is defined by its end points, each end point having integer (x,y) coordinates such that $-999 \leq x \leq +999$ and $-999 \leq y \leq +999$. The line segments form polygons, which in turn define the regions of the map. Islands, or regions within regions, as in Figure D.5, are allowed.

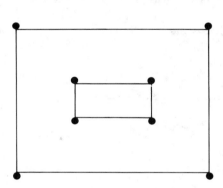

Figure D.5   A region containing another region.

A program is desired that does the following tasks for a sequence of maps.

(a) Reads in up to 300 pairs of points that define the line segments. The line segments may occur in any order, and the two end points of a line segment may be given in any order. The program ensures that the following conditions are met:

(1) If two line segments intersect, the point of intersection is an end point of both segments.

(2) Each line segment has a nonzero length.

(3) If two line segments overlap, they are identical. (A line segment may be entered more than once.)

Any line segments found to violate these conditions are deleted from the input, and error messages are printed naming the offending segments.

(b) Determine the set of vertex points that defines each polygon, and the set of polygons that defines each region. Since islands are allowed, a region may be defined by more than one polygon.

The program also must ensure that every line segment separates two regions. If this condition is not met, the error message 'INVALID MAP' is printed, and a map is not produced.

(c) Uses a set of five colors to determine a color for each region, so that any two regions separated only by a line segment have different colors.

The program should try to distribute the colors evenly, so that each color is used about the same number of times. However, an optimal algorithm is not required, and if a simple coloring algorithm does not work, the map can be rejected. (A naive algorithm will suffice in all but the most pathological cases.)

(d) Prints a list of the regions and their colors, indicating for each region the polygons that define the region and the vertices of these polygons.

15. Radix Conversion

This problem is by Abrahams [Abr 78]. (Reprinted with permission.)

A program is desired that converts numbers written in terms of a radix $r \leqslant 36$ to equivalent decimal numbers. The input numbers appear on cards in the form

$$d_k d_{k-1} \ldots d_0(r)$$

where r is the radix expressed as a decimal integer, and $d_k, \ldots, d_0$ are digits with base r. A radix point may or may not appear; if it does appear, it may appear to the left of, to the right of, or within the sequence of digits. The letters A, . . . ,Z are used as digits with decimal values 10, . . . ,35. A plus or minus sign may precede a number. The decimal value v of an input number is given by the formula

$$v = d_k r^k + d_{k-1} r^{k-1} + \cdots + d_0 r^0 \tag{1}$$

or by the more easily computed formula

$$v = ((\ldots (d_k r + d_{k-1}) r + \cdots) r + d_1) r + d_0 \tag{2}$$

If n digits follow the radix point, then the value given by formula 1 or 2 is divided by r^n.

Examples are

Representation	Decimal Value
−3.7(10)	−3.7
1A(16)	26
−101.1(2)	−5.5
021(3)	7
+41.(22)	106

The input numbers appear on cards with consecutive numbers being separated by one or more blanks. Blanks may or may not appear at the beginning or end of a card, and a single card may contain 0 or more input numbers. Each sequence of nonblank characters surrounded by blanks (or by card boundaries) is considered as a single, possibly illegal, number.

The output is a list of the numbers, each line having one number and its decimal equivalent, arranged in easy-to-read columns. For an input number of incorrect format, the word ILLEGAL appears instead of a value.

Note that a blank always terminates a number; therefore a number with an embedded blank will appear to be two numbers, the first of which will surely be illegal.

16. Poker

A variant of this problem appears in Abrahams [Abr 78].

The game of poker is almost always played with the standard 52-card deck which has 4 suits, each suit having 13 ranks. The suits are spades (S), hearts (H), diamonds (D), and clubs (C). In poker, all suits have equal rank. Within each suit the ranks, from highest to lowest, are A,K,Q,J,10,9,8,7,6,5,4,3,2. Thus the 52 cards of the deck are (A,S),(K,S), . . . , (2,S),(A,H), . . . , (2,H),(A,D), . . . , (2,D),(A,C), . . . , (2,C). In certain categories of poker hands (flushes and straights), the A may also be used as the lowest ranking card, having a lower rank than the 2.

Since the suits have equal rank, a card (r_1, s_1) outranks a card (r_2, s_2) if r_1 is a higher rank than r_2. For example, (6,C) outranks (4,S), and (A,D) has a higher rank than (K,S). If $r_1 = r_2$, then the two cards are tied in rank (i.e., have equal rank); for example, (10,H) and (10,C) have equal ranks.

A *wild card* can "become" any card its holder wishes. Poker may be played without wild cards, or with one or more wild cards. Sometimes a fifty-third card (the joker) is used as a wild card; sometimes all deuces (2s) are wild; somtimes the "one eyes" (cards showing a face in profile) such as (K,S), (J,S), (J,H) are wild.

The many variants of poker share certain essential features. The number of players is not fixed and may vary from 2 to 14 depending on the variant being played. A player is dealt a set number of cards (usually 5 or 7, depending on the variant) and from these chooses a *hand* consisting of 5 cards. Categories of poker hands, from highest to lowest, are as follows:

- *Straight flush:* five consecutive cards of the same suit. The highest straight flush is A-K-Q-J-10 of the same suit, called a royal flush. The A may be used as lowest ranking card, so that 5-4-3-2-A is the lowest straight flush.
- *Four of a kind:* for example, all four 8s with a fifth card.
- *Full house:* three cards of one rank (also called three of a kind) and two cards of another rank (a pair); for example, 10-10-10-3-3.
- *Flush:* five cards of the same suit.
- *Straight:* cards having five consecutive ranks, in two or more suits. The highest straight consists of cards with the ranks A-K-Q-J-10, and (since in straights, A may be used as the lowest ranking card) the lowest straight consists of cards with the ranks 5-4-3-2-A.
- *Three of a kind:* three cards with the same rank, and two other cards, not a pair; for example, J-J-J-A-2.
- *Two pairs:* for example A-A-9-9 and a fifth card.
- *One pair:* for example, 5-5, and three unmatched cards, A-10-2.
- *High card:* none of the above.
- If wild cards are used, the highest category is then five of a kind, which outranks a straight flush.

When two poker hands of different categories are compared, the hand in the highest category wins. For example, any five of a kind beats any straight flush, any straight flush beats any four of a kind, and so on.

When two hands are in the same category, then the most important component of the hand decides the winner; if there is a tie, then the next most important component decides, and so on. In these comparisons, suit does not matter, card rank is important, and A is the highest except when it is used in the lowest straight o straight flush. Thus, for straight flushes, flushes, straights, and high card, the hand with the highest ranking card wins; if these are identical in rank, then the next-highest-ranking card decides, and so on. For four of a kind (five of a kind), full house or three of a kind, the hand with the four (five) or three of a kind of highest rank wins; in case of a tie due to wild cards, the pair (full house) or the highest unmatched card (four or three of a kind) decides. For two pairs, the highest ranking pair decides; if a tie, the next pair decides, if again a tie then the unmatched card decides. For one pair, the rank of the pair decides; if a tie, then the highest unmatched card, and so on.

Note that in many situations, especially when wild cards are used, ties are possible so that neither hand wins. For example, a tie exists between the hand {(Q,H),(Q,C),(7,S),(7,H),(8,S)} and the hand {(Q,S), (Q,D),(7,D),(7,C),(8,D)}.

An encyclopedia or book on games will have more details. In some places, poker is played with additional categories of hands, and there are unusual variants such as lowball (in which the lowest hand wins), high-low (in which the highest and the lowest hand both win), and Chicago [in which the highest hand and the hand holding (A,S) both win].

A program is desired that reads in groups of poker hands, evaluates the hands, and prints out rankings for the hands. Each group consists of a number of records, one record for each hand. Each record designates the name of the player and the cards in the hand. Ranks are designated by 2,3,4,5,6,7,8,9,T,J,Q,K,A; suits by S,H,C,D.

The ranking of hands follows the rules described above for comparing hands. For each group of hands, the program prints out each player's name, his hand, the category of his hand, and the ranking of the hand within the group. The best hand in the group is to have rank=1, and so on. If two or more hands are tied, these hands are to have the same ranking within the group.

Depending on the customer, the program is desired in one of the following versions.

Version 1: Each group has 4 players. Each hand has 5 cards. Wild cards are not to be used. Error checking is not required.

Version 2: Same as Version 1, except that each group of hands is checked to ensure that each card (r,s) is a valid poker card, and that no card is used more than once.

Version 3: Error checking as in Version 2 is required. Each group has a variable number of players. The first record of each group states which wild cards are allowed, or if no wild cards are used, the first record contains the word NONE.

The hands in a group either all have 5 cards or all have 7 cards. The program determines the number of cards (5 or 7) in the game by inspecting the individual hands, as well as ensuring that all hands in a group have the same number of cards.

Version 4: Includes Version 3. In addition, allows 7-card games to be processed in two phases:

(1) The first 5 cards are evaluated and rankings printed. In addition, for each player a possible hand (the best possible category the hand could achieve using the 6th and 7th cards) is calculated and printed.

(2) The 7-card hands are evaluated and printed.

17. Harry's Solitaire

A variant of this problem appears in Wetherell [Wet 78, p. 19].

My old friend Harry used to amuse himself by playing a complicated solitaire card game with a standard 52-card poker deck. In preparation for beginning the game, cards are dealt into seven piles as in Figure D.6(a).

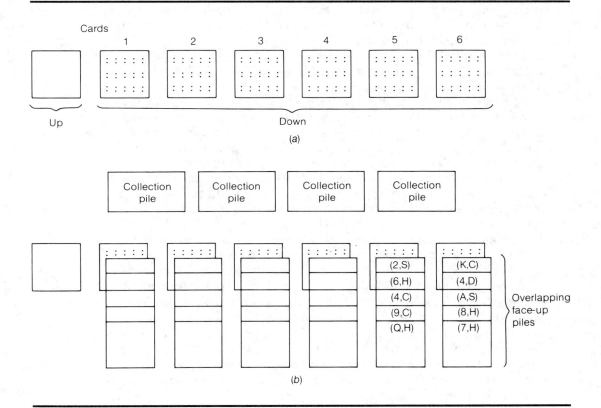

Figure D.6   Arrangement of cards dealt in preparation for the game. (a) Initial arrangement of card piles. (b) Final arrangement of dealt cards.

The leftmost pile in Figure D.6(a) consists of one card face up. Each other pile has 1,2, . . . , 6 cards face down as indicated by the number above the pile. Next, all of the remaining cards are dealt face up, below the face-down piles, as in (b). The face-up cards are all overlapped so that the rank and suit of every face-up card can be seen. The lowest or bottom card of each pile is totally visible.

Space is also left, as shown by the dashed rectangles in (*b*), for special *collection piles*, one collection pile for each suit. The objective of the game is to move cards from the dealt-out piles to the collection piles; the game is won if all of the cards can be placed on the collection piles.

A collection pile for a given suit can be started only when the ace of that suit is the bottom face-up card of one of the seven piles. (In this game, an ace has rank 1 and a king has highest rank.) In general, a card of rank n can be moved to the collection pile for that suit when that card is the bottom face-up card of one of the piles and the collection pile already contains the card of rank (n−1). Thus if the spade collection pile has the ace of spades and the two of spades is a bottom face-up card, the two of spades can be added to the spade collection pile.

Cards can also be moved from one card pile to another. The rule for any such move is that when a card of rank n and suit s is the bottom face-up card of a pile, then the card of rank (n−1) and suit s can be placed immediately below it. In general, the subpile consisting of the face-up card of rank (n−1), suit s, and all cards below it is moved immediately below the card of rank n and suit s. In Figure D.6(*b*), the subpile headed by (6,H) can be moved immediately under the (7,H). Subpiles can be moved underneath the single card on the left, or (preferably) that card can be moved to a collection pile or underneath another pile.

If the move of a subpile exposes a face-down card, that card may be turned face up as part of the move. If the move of a subpile leaves one of the seven piles with no cards at all, then any subpile headed by a king can be placed in that pile. For example, if the single card in the leftmost pile of Figure D.6(*b*) is moved to a collection pile, then the rightmost subpile headed by (K,C) can be moved to become the leftmost pile, and the face-down card thus exposed can be turned face up.

Write a program that plays this solitaire game and always chooses a sequence of moves that results in the maximum number of cards being moved to collection piles. In particular, if there is a way that the game can be won, the program always finds it.

The output of the program is to be a series of pictures of the status of the cards, analogous to Figure D.6(*b*). In each picture, the collection piles are summarized by a line

COLLECTION S: H: D: C:

giving the rank of the highest card in the spade, heart, diamond, and club piles, respectively (0 means no cards in the pile). The next line contains the word DOWN for each pile containing face-down cards and a dash if the pile does not have face-down cards. Initially this line appears as

---   DOWN   DOWN   DOWN   DOWN   DOWN   DOWN

succeeding lines show the face-up cards in each pile. The last line of each picture shows the move that is to be made; either

(a) Movement of one or more cards to collection piles, if that is possible, or

(b) Movement of a subpile to another pile.

The last line of output, when no more moves can be made, is to be

    END OF GAME -- x CARDS COLLECTED

where x is the total number of cards in collection piles.

18. Write a program that implements the lending library system of Figure 3.29 using the static simulation model of Section 3.4.3. For hints, see Problem 1 in Section 3.4, Problem 9 in Section 6.3, and Problem 4 in Section 6.4.

REFERENCES

[Abr 78] Abrahams, P. "Two Programming Problems," *SIGPLAN Notices*, September 1978.

[Abr 79] ———. *SIGPLAN Notices*, April 1979.

[Luc 81] Lucas, H. C., and Gibson, C. F. *A Casebook for Management Information Systems*, 2nd ed. New York: McGraw-Hill, 1981.

[Wet 78] Wetherell, C. *Etudes for Programmers*. Englewood Cliffs, NJ: Prentice-Hall, 1978.

[You 75a] Yourdon, E. *Techniques of Program Structure and Design*. Englewood Cliffs, NJ: Prentice-Hall, 1975.

appendix e
Evaluation Problems

The problems in this appendix concern the evaluation and analysis of given programs. Each problem contains a program listing, perhaps execution results or a brief description of the program's operation, and questions requiring documentation, analysis, and evaluation of the program.

Good design may be learned from the examination of previously written programs. These problems may be used in conjunction with any chapter: the input class, output class and processing function may be inferred from the program; data flow diagrams and organization diagrams may be drawn; or test sequences may be inferred.

A good source for evaluation problems is Kernighan and Plauger [Ker 74].

A. Counting Characters
At your programming job you have been asked to document and test the program in Figure E.1. Analyze the program, answering the following questions.

1. Program Description
   (a) What are the input(s) and output(s) of the program?
   (b) Give a flowchart of the program.
   (c) List all variables of the program, describing for each variable: its significance (or "meaning" or "contents"). Do NOT describe in detail the setting or resetting or testing of variables.
   (d) State briefly the intent of the program.

2. Program Testing
   For each condition discussed in response to the questions below, give an English prose statement of the condition and one test input illustrating the condition.
   (a) List all input conditions that cause this program to abort.
   (b) List all input conditions that cause the program to terminate normally but give incorrect output.
   (c) List all input conditions that cause the program to terminate normally and give correct output.

3. Program Documentation
   Write a paragraph summarizing the process performed by the program and the conditions under which correct performance is obtained. Do NOT restate in words the program flowchart.

661

```
      CHARACTER *72 BUFR
      CHARACTER *1 C,BLANK, COMMA, SCOL, DASH,
     *SLSH, PEROD,
      INTEGER KT, NW, NC, NS
      REAL AWS, ASW
      DATA BLANK,COMMA,SCOL,DASH,SLSH,PEROD
     */' ',',',';','-','/','.'/
     *NW,NC,NS,KT,C/0,0,0,73,' '/
101   FORMAT(1H1,35X,'INPUT TEXT')
102   FORMAT(A)
103   FORMAT(4X,A)
104   FORMAT(////,26X,'NUMBER OF SENTENCES-', I8 / 19X,
     *'AVERAGE NUMBER OF WORDS/SENTENCE-',F8.2,20X,
     *'AVERAGE NUMBER OF SYMBOLS/WORD-',F8.2)
      WRITE(*,101)
10    READ(*,102) BUFR
      WRITE(*,103) BUFR
      KT=KT-72
      IF(C.EQ.PEROD) GO TO 35
20    C=BUFR(KT:KT)
25    IF(C.NE.PEROD) GO TO 40
      NS=NS+1
      NW=NW+1
      KT=KT+3
      IF(KT.GT.72) GO TO 10
35    C=BUFR(KT:KT)
      IF(C.EQ.SLSH) GO TO 75
      GO TO 25
40    IF(C.EQ.BLANK) THEN
         NW=NW+1
         GO TO 70
      END IF
      IF(C.EQ.COMMA) GO TO 70
      IF(C.EQ.SCOL) GO TO 70
      IF(C.EQ.DASH) GO TO 70
      NC=NC+1
70    KT=KT+1
      IF(KT.GT.72) GO TO 10
      GO TO 20
75    AWS=FLOAT(NW)/NS
      ASW=FLOAT(NC)/NW
      WRITE(*,104) NS,AWS,ASW
      STOP
      END
```

Figure E.1 The program for Problem A. (Copyright 1970 by Allyn and Bacon, Inc. Reprinted by permission.)

Further Questions (Optional)

4. Write a structured program without go to statements that performs *exactly the same process* as the given program. (Do not rework the program's process to make it "nicer.")

5. Based on your analysis above, answer the questions in the Project Outline for analysis of an activity specification, at the end of Section 2.3. Pay particular attention to any enhancement of the specification that will improve carrying out the intention of the program (in other words, that will cause the program to be less sensitive to errors).

6. Write a structured program that performs the enhanced process.

B. Number Conversion

Figure E.2 shows a listing and execution results of a program that is claimed to produce, for any decimal number $N \leq 8192$, the number N in binary notation.
Analyze the listing and answer the following questions.

1. Program Description and Analysis
   (a) What are the input and output variables of the program of Figure E.2? What, if any, use does the program make of each input?
   (b) List the variables used by the main program and the variables used by CHANGE1, describing for each variable: its significance (or "meaning") and how it is used. Do NOT describe in detail the setting or resetting or testing of the variables. List all subroutines of the program, describing for each subroutine: its function (or "purpose") and how it is used. Do NOT restate in words the flowchart of each subroutine.
   (c) Provide an organization diagram (see Section 4.1) of the main program and subroutines, including interface description and usage description tables.
   (d) Can the program be given inputs that will cause it to act in an improper fashion or produce an incorrect output? If yes, state all such inputs, the corresponding effects, and how the program can be modified to avoid such inputs. If no, give the analysis that leads to your conclusion.

2. Program Critique and Modification
   (a) Use Table 8.3 in Section 8.4.2 to give the variable name and goodness rating for each variable whose usage could be improved. Do the same with Table 8.4 giving the goodness rating for each subroutine whose usage could be improved.
   (b) Are there ways in which the accompanying program code can be modified to be more concise, or more understandable, or more efficient, or easier to verify, or more error-proof? If so, suggest specific improvements aside from better comments, better variable names, and elimination of unused variables. Your improvements should agree with your previous responses, such as to 2(a).
   (c) Show the code that results if *all* of your suggestions of 2(b) are implemented.

```
PROGRAM CONVERT;
VAR
  X,VAL:INTEGER;
  IFLG:ARRAY[1..4] OF REAL;

  PROCEDURE INITIAL;
    VAR
      I:INTEGER;
      REM:ARRAY[1..20] OF INTEGER;
    BEGIN
      FOR I:=1 TO 10 DO
        REM[I]:=0;
    END;

  PROCEDURE CHANGE1(X1,X2:INTEGER);
    VAR
      IFLG1,I,J,K:INTEGER;
      REM:ARRAY[1..6] OF INTEGER;
    BEGIN
      K:=5;
      I:=K+1;
      IFLG1:=X1 DIV 2;
      WHILE IFLG1>0 DO
        BEGIN
          REM[I]:=X1 MOD 2;
          I:=I−1;
          VAL:=VAL+I;
          X1:=IFLG1;
          IFLG1:=X1 DIV 2;
        END;
      REM[I]:=X1 MOD 2;
      WRITELN;WRITE('THE BINARY EQUIVALENT OF ',X2,' IS:');
      FOR J:=I TO 6 DO
        WRITE(REM[J]);
    END(* CHANGE1 *);

  PROCEDURE CHANGE2(Y1,Y2:INTEGER);
    VAR
      IFLG2,I,J,K:INTEGER;
      REM:ARRAY[1..8] OF INTEGER;
    BEGIN
      K:=7;
      I:=K+1;
      IFLG2:=Y1 DIV 2;
      WHILE IFLG2>0 DO
        BEGIN
          REM[I]:=Y1 MOD 2;
          I:=I−1;
          VAL:=VAL+I;
          Y1:=IFLG2;
          IFLG2:=Y1 DIV 2;
        END;
      REM[I]:=Y1 MOD 2;
      WRITELN;WRITE('THE BINARY EQUIVALENT OF ',Y2,' IS: ');
      FOR J:=I TO 8 DO
        WRITE(REM[J]);
    END(* CHANGE2*);
```

Figure E.2 Program CONVERT.

```
  PROCEDURE CHANGE3(W1,W2:INTEGER);
    VAR
      IFLG3,I,J,K:INTEGER;
      REM:ARRAY[1..10] OF INTEGER;
    BEGIN
      K:=9;
      I:=K+1;
      IFLG3:= W1 DIV 2;
      WHILE IFLG3>0 DO
        BEGIN
          REM[I]:=W1 MOD 2;
          I:=I-1;
          VAL:=VAL+1;
          W1:=IFLG3;
          IFLG3:=W1 DIV 2;
        END;
      REM[I]:=W1 MOD 2;
      WRITELN;WRITELN('THE BINARY EQUIVALENT OF ',W2,' IS:');
      FOR J:=I TO 10 DO
        WRITE(REM[J]);
    END (* CHANGE3 *);

  PROCEDURE CHANGE4(U1,U2:INTEGER);
    VAR
      IFLG4,I,J,K:INTEGER;
      REM:ARRAY[1..13] OF INTEGER;
    BEGIN
      K:=12;
      I:=K+1;
      IFLG4:=U1 DIV 2;
      WHILE IFLG4>0 DO
        BEGIN
          REM[I]:=U1 MOD 2;
          I:=I-1;
          VAL:=VAL+I;
          U1:=IFLG4;
          IFLG4:=U1 DIV 2;
        END;
      REM[I]:=U1 MOD 2;
      WRITELN;WRITELN('THE BINARY EQUIVALENT OF ',U2,' IS:');
      FOR J:=I TO 13 DO
        WRITE(REM[J]);
    END(* CHANGE4 *);

BEGIN(* MAIN *)
  CLOSE(OUTPUT);
  REWRITE(OUTPUT,'PRINTER:');
    WRITELN;
    WRITELN('ENTER A VALUE LESS THAN 8192:');
    READLN(X);
    WRITELN('VALUE ENTERED:',X);
    VAL:=X;
    IF X<=63 THEN CHANGE1(X,VAL)
    ELSE
    IF X<=255 THEN CHANGE2(X,VAL)
    ELSE
    IF X<=1023 THEN CHANGE3(X,VAL)
    ELSE
    CHANGE4(VAL,X);WRITELN;
  CLOSE(OUTPUT);
  REWRITE(OUTPUT,'CONSOLE:');
END.
```

Figure E.2 Program CONVERT (continued).

ENTER A VALUE LESS THAN 8192:
VALUE ENTERED: 8191

THE BINARY EQUIVALENT OF 8191 IS:
1111111111111

ENTER A VALUE LESS THAN 8192:
VALUE ENTERED: 16

THE BINARY EQUIVALENT OF 16 IS:10000

ENTER A VALUE LESS THAN 8192:
VALUE ENTERED: 5389

THE BINARY EQUIVALENT OF 5389 IS:
1010100001101

ENTER A VALUE LESS THAN 8192:
VALUE ENTERED: 333

THE BINARY EQUIVALENT OF 333 IS:
101001101

ENTER A VALUE LESS THAN 8192:
VALUE ENTERED: 8192
Value range error
S#1, P#6, I#57
Type <space> to continue

Figure E.2 Program CONVERT (continued).

---

3. Design of an Alternate Program
Give a program in PASCAL or FORTRAN 77 that accepts as input the

decimal number N and then produces its binary equivalent. Pay attention to style and to error-proofing.

C. Character Transliteration

1. Introduction

The translit program system of Figure E.3, originally shown in Kernighan and Plauger's *Software Tools in PASCAL* [Ker 81] is intended to transliterate character sequences. The translit system is to be used at an interactive terminal; the text to be modified is assumed to be a standard input file, while the modified text is to be output to a standard output file.

The translit system is activated when the user at the terminal types a call to translit. Such a call has the general form

translit <argument 1>   <argument 2>

where <argument 1>,<argument 2> are sequences of m and n characters, respectively, and m≥n≥1. In the sample call

translit abc   pqr

<argument 1> is the sequence abc, and <argument 2> is the sequence pqr. Note that the two arguments are separated by a blank. This call specifies that a——▶p (each a in the input text is to be replaced by a p in the output text), b——▶q, and c——▶r. In general, the first character of <argument 1> is replaced by the first character of <argument 2>, the second character of <argument 1> is replaced by the second character of <argument 2>, and so on. Other characters are simply copied from input to output. We may diagram this set of replacements as follows:

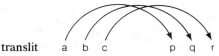

translit   a   b   c   p   q   r

When m>n, that is, when <argument 1> has more characters than <argument 2>, the first, second, . . . , (n−1)st characters of <argument 1> are transliterated as previously described. However, each of the nth, (n+1)st, . . . , mth characters of <argument 1> is processed as follows:

Step (1):   The character is replaced by c_n, the nth character of <argument 2>.
Step (2):   Every sequence of k≥1 occurrences of c_n in the output is replaced by the single character c_n.

As an example, the call

translit   abcs   pq

prescribes that a——▶p, while b——▶q, c——▶q, s——▶q.

Further, every sequence qq. . .q in the output is reduced to the single character q. Thus the input text

arbitrary success

is transliterated to

prqitrpry quqeq

in two steps:

```
arbitrary  success
↓ ↓  ↓   ↓ ↓↓ ↓↓
prqitrpry quqqeqq
↓ ↓  ↓      ↓↓ //
prqitrpry quqeq
```

Various special formats may be used in <argument 1> and <argument 2>. When <argument 2>is omitted in the call, the system assumes that <argument 2> consists of a single blank character and that all characters in <argument 1> are to be deleted. The sequences of <argument 1> or <argument 2> may be enclosed in quotes " and may then include blank characters.

An abbreviation format allows commonly used argument strings to be specified in a shorthand manner. For example,

a-z   signifies abcdefghijklmnopqrstuvwxyz
A-Z   signifies ABCDEFGHIJKLMNOPQRSTUVWXYZ
0-9   signifies 0123456789
a-h   signifies abcdefgh

and so on. Thus the call

translit a-z A-Z

may be written to signify

translit abcdefghijklmnopqrstuvwxyz
ABCDEFGHIJKLMNOPQRSTUVWXYZ

When <argument 2> has one character, all characters in <argument 1> are to be changed to this character as described in steps (1) and (2). When <argument 2> has no characters, all of the characters in <argument 1> are to be deleted. In these two cases only, <argument 1> may be prefixed with the symbol ~, meaning "not." When this is done, the characters in <argument 1> are *not* transliterated according to <argument 2>, but all other characters are transliterated. For example, the notation

translit ~0-9 -

prescribes that all characters except the digits 0 through 9 are to be translated to dashes, while digits 0 through 9 remain unchanged.

Finally, the character @ is used as an *escape character*, signifying that the character following it has a special meaning. In particular, the system recognizes @t as signifying a "tab" character, and it recognizes @n as signifying a "new line" character. Following these conventions, the call

translit " @t@n"   @n

changes each sequence of blanks, tab characters, and new line characters to just one new line character, leaving one word per line.

2. Project Outline

    (a) Give a brief narrative describing clearly how the system operates for someone who will maintain the system.

    (b) Draw an organization diagram of the system and provide interface and usage tables.

    (c) Provide a data flow diagram of the system showing major data blocks and major processes. The diagram should indicate clearly the basic concept underlying the system design; it should not mechanically copy in detail the data flow of the finished system.

    (d) Give specific examples of the use (or lack of use) by this system of the strategies of top-down design and isolation of design factors. If you have a theory about the overall design, make sure you discuss any design features that tend to contradict it.

Keep in mind that these strategies are not the same and may sometimes conflict, even though they use many of the same principles, such as localization and information hiding.

    (e) Assume that the programs have been designed and coded as in the accompanying listings, but that no programs have yet been executed or tested. The programs in the system are to be tested in a strict sequence: some program P_1 is tested first, then another program P_2 is tested second, and so on. When program P_1 is executed and tested, all of the programs P_2, P_3 and so on may be present in dummy form or may be omitted. When P_2 is tested, P_3, P_4 and so on may be present in dummy form or may be omitted. In other words, each module is tested together with all previously tested modules.

The objectives of the execution/test sequence are that (1) the system should cycle (begin and terminate normally) at the earliest possible step; (2) the system should perform some process on the input text (no matter how trivial) at the earliest possible step; and (3) that each further processing capability is added to the system at the earliest possible step.

Describe the sequence of execution test steps. For the ith step, describe

(1) The program to be executed/tested.

(2) Each program included in dummy form and why it is included.

(3) The processing capable of being performed on the input text.

(4) The restrictions imposed on the input text or arguments.

```
(*translit--map characters*)
procedure translit;
const
  NEGATE=CARET;(* ^ *)
var
  arg, fromset, toset:string;
  c:character;
  i, lastto:0..MAXSTR;
  allbut, squash:boolean;
#include "makeset.p"
#include "xindex.p"
begin
  if (not getarg(1, arg, MAXSTR)) then
    error('usage:translit from to');
  allbut:=(arg[1]=NEGATE);
  if (allbut) then
    i:=2
  else
    i:=1;
  if (not makeset(arg, i, fromset, MAXSTR)) then
    error('translit:"from" set too large');
  if (not getarg(2, arg, MAXSTR)) then
    toset[1]:=ENDSTR
  else if (not makeset(arg, 1, toset, MAXSTR)) then
    error('translit:"to" set too large')
  else if (length(fromset)<length(toset)) then
    error('translit:"from" shorter than "to" ');

  lastto:=length(toset);
  squash:=(length(fromset)>lastto) or (allbut);
  repeat
    i:=xindex(fromset, getc(c), allbut, lastto);
    if (squash) and (i>=lastto) and (lastto>0) then begin
      putc(toset[lastto]);
      repeat
        i:=xindex(fromset, getc(c), allbut, lastto)
      until (i<lastto)
    end;
    if (c<>ENDFILE) then begin
      if (i>0) and (lastto>0) then (*translate*)
        putc(toset[i])
      else if (i=0) then (*copy*)
        putc(c)
      (*else delete*)
    end
  until (c=ENDFILE)
end;
```

Figure E.3   The program translit. (Copyright 1981 by Bell Telephone Laboratories, Incorporated and Whitesmiths, Ltd. Reprinted by permission.)

3. Program Listings and Discussion

The program translit is shown in Figure E.3.

Seven functions and procedures are used directly by translit, namely, getc, putc, getarg, error, length, makeset, and xindex. The functions getc and getarg and the procedures putc and error, which are not listed here, are the input/output procedures of the system. A function call getc(c) returns the next character in the standard input file as the value getc. The character is also placed in the variable c. Of course, getc maintains a one-record buffer, reading the next record as necessary.

A procedure call putc(c) puts the character in the variable c onto the standard output file. A one-record buffer is maintained by putc, which writes the buffer as necessary.

The function getarg retrieves the arguments needed by translit from the interactive terminal. Specifically, a call

getarg(n,argstring,MAXSTR)

copies each character of the nth argument (where n is 1 or 2) into a character of the string argstring. The value of MAXSTR indicates the maximum number of characters allotted for the argument. If the nth argument has more characters, then only the number specified by MAXSTR will be entered into the array, and the rest will be lost. The value returned by getarg is the length (number of characters) of the argument if the nth argument exists; if there are less than n arguments, ENDFILE is returned.

A convention of this system is that every character string ends with a special character ENDSTR, signifying "end of string." Accordingly, a string X is represented as X ENDSTR, while an empty or null string is represented as ENDSTR. Thus the function getarg ensures that the string

```
(*length—compute length of string*)
function length (var s:string):integer;
var
  n:integer;
begin
  n:=1;
  while (s[n]<>ENDSTR) do
    n:=n+1;
  length:=n−1
end;
```

Figure E.4   The program length. (Copyright 1981 by Bell Telephone Laboratories, Incorporated and Whitesmiths, Ltd. Reprinted by permission.)

returned ends with ENDSTR and fits within MAXSTR characters including the ENDSTR character.

The procedure error transmits an error message back to the interactive terminal, indicating the error condition found. In this way the user is immediately informed that the desired transliteration cannot be performed.

The function length shown in Figure E.4 is a tiny program that calculates the length of a character string, excluding the ending ENDSTR character.

The Boolean function makeset, shown in Figure E.5, is used by translit to create the strings from inset to outset. Makeset uses a Boolean function addstr and a procedure dodash.

```
(*makeset-make set from inset [k] in outset*)
function makeset (var inset:string; k:integer;
    var outset:string; maxset:integer):boolean;
var
  j:integer;
#include "dodash.p"
begin
  j:=1;
  dodash(ENDSTR, inset, k, outset, j, maxset);
  makeset:=addstr(ENDSTR, outset, j, maxset)
end;
```

Figure E.5   The program makeset. (Copyright 1981 by Bell Telephone Laboratories, Incorporated and Whitesmiths, Ltd. Reprinted by permission.)

The Boolean function addstr used by makeset is shown in Figure E.6. The function addstr tests whether there is room in a string for the next (jth) character. If there is not enough room for the next character, addstr returns

```
(*addstr--put c in outset[j] if it fits, increment j*)
function addstr(c:character; var outset:string;
    var j:integer; maxset:integer):boolean;
begin
  if (j>maxset)then
    addstr:=false
  else begin
    outset[j]:=c;
    j:=j+1;
    addstr:=true
  end
end;
```

Figure E.6   The program addstr. (Copyright 1981 by Bell Telephone Laboratories, Incorporated and Whitesmiths, Ltd. Reprinted by permission.)

false. If there is room, addstr adds the character at the jth position of the string, increments j, and returns true.

The procedure dodash determines whether the character under consideration is part of an abbreviation such as A-Z. If that character is a dash appearing between letters or digits, then there is an abbreviation that must be expanded by dodash, which is shown in Figure E.7. Dodash checks for arbitrary delimiters and returns updated indexes.

```
(*dodash-expand set at src [i] into dest [j], stop at delim*)
procedure dodash(delim:character; var src:string;
        var i:integer; var dest:string;
        var j:integer; maxset:integer);
var
  k:integer;
  junk:boolean;
begin
  while (src[i]<>delim) and (src[i]<>ENDSTR) do begin
    if (src[i]=ESCAPE) then
        junk:=addstr(esc(src, i), dest, j, maxset)
    else if (src[i]<>DASH) then
        junk:=addstr(src[i], dest, j, maxset)
    else if (j<=1) or (src[i+1]=ENDSTR) then
        junk:=addstr(DASH,dest,j,maxset) (*literal -*)
    else if (isalphanum(src[i−1]))
      and (isalphanum(src[i+1]))
      and (src[i−1]<=src[i+1]) then begin
        for k:=src[i−1]+1 to src[i+1] do
            junk:=addstr(k, dest, j, maxset);
        i:=i+1
    end
    else
        junk:=addstr(DASH, dest, j, maxset);
    i:=i+1
  end
end;
```

Figure E.7   The program dodash. (Copyright 1981 by Bell Telephone Laboratories, Incorporated and Whitesmiths, Ltd. Reprinted by permission.)

The function esc shown in Figure E.8 checks for an escape, returns the appropriate character, and sets the index to the proper value.

```
(*esc--map s[i] into escaped character, increment i*)
function esc (var s:string; var i:integer):character;
begin
   if (s[i]<>ESCAPE) then
      esc:=s[i]
   else if (s[i+1]=ENDSTR) then (*@ not special at end*)
      esc:=ESCAPE
   else begin
      i:=i+1;
      if (s[i]=ord('n')) then
         esc:=NEWLINE
      else if (s[i]=ord('t')) then
         esc:=TAB
      else
         esc:=s[i]
   end
end;
```

Figure E.8   The program esc. (Copyright 1981 by Bell Telephone Laboratories, Incorporated and Whitesmiths, Ltd. Reprinted by permission.)

Dodash also uses a Boolean function isalphanum shown in Figure E.9, which returns true if its argument is a letter or a number, and otherwise returns false.

The string fromset in translit holds the set of characters to be translated while the array toset holds the corresponding transliterations. Upon the

```
(*isalphanum--true if c is le er or digit*)
function isalphanum (c:character):boolean;
begin
   isalphanum:=c in
      [ord('a')..ord('z'),
       ord('A')..ord('Z'),
       ord('0')..ord('9')]
end;
```

Figure E.9   The program isalphanum. (Copyright 1981 by Bell Telephone Laboratories, Incorporated and Whitesmiths, Ltd. Reprinted by permission.)

function call index (fromset,c), the function index returns the index of the element of fromset that matches c, or returns 0 if there is no matching element in fromset. The function index is shown in Figure E.10.

```
(*index--find position of character c in string s*)
function index (var s:string; c:character):integer;
var
  i:integer;
begin
  i:=1;
  while (s[i]<>c) and (s[i]<>ENDSTR) do
    i:=i+1;
  if (s[i]=ENDSTR) then
    index:=0
  else
    index:=i
end;
```

Figure E.10 The program index. (Copyright 1981 by Bell Telephone Laboratories, Incorporated and Whitesmiths, Ltd. Reprinted by permission.)

```
(*xindex--conditionally invert value from index*)
function xindex (var inset:string; c:character;
    allbut:boolean;lastto:integer):integer;
begin
  if (c=ENDFILE) then
    xindex:=0
  else if (not allbut) then
    xindex:=index(inset,c)
  else if (index(inset, c)>0) then
    xindex:=0
  else
    xindex:=lastto+1
end;
```

Figure E.11 The program xindex. (Copyright 1981 by Bell Telephone Laboratories, Incorporated and Whitesmiths, Ltd. Reprinted by permission.)

The function xindex uses index and also adjusts for special conditions. For example, when all characters except those in <argument 2> are to be transliterated, the flag allbut is set to true. In this case, xindex inverts the result returned by index.

REFERENCES

[Ker 74] Kernighan, B. W., and Plauger, P. J. *The Elements of Programming Style*. New York: McGraw-Hill, 1974.

[Ker 81] ———, and ———. *Software Tools in PASCAL*. Reading, MA: Addison-Wesley, 1981.

Index